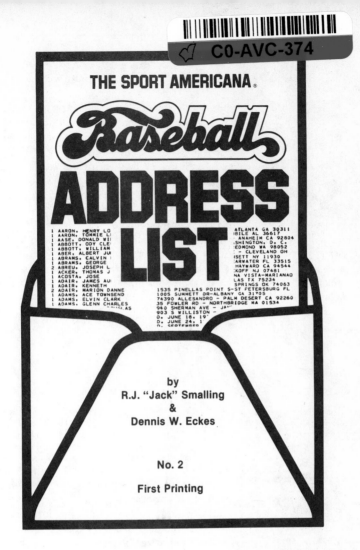

THE SPORT AMERICANA®

Baseball

ADDRESS LIST

by
R.J. "Jack" Smalling
&
Dennis W. Eckes

No. 2

First Printing

ISBN 0-937424-14-5

Printed in U.S.A. 1982

ABOUT THE AUTHORS

Jack Smalling has been an avid autograph collector for eighteen years and a card collector for more than thirty years. His collection of big league autographs is one of the best in the country. Reproductions of many of these signatures appear in this publication. He was educated at Iowa State University, obtaining a B.S. in Modern Languages and an M. Ed. in School Administration. His athletic activities have included officiating for twenty years—football, basketball and baseball. After a successful high school baseball career, he played thirteen years at the semi-pro level. A teaching and coaching career of fifteen years ended in 1979 when he joined the Compass Insurance Agency, Ltd., in Ames, IA, to sell commercial and personal lines of insurance. He and his wife, Marge, have four sons.

Denny Eckes has been an avid trading card collector since the age of eight. He interrupted that hobby temporarily, only long enough to acquire an education, family, and career. He has returned with zest to the hobby over the past seven years, during which time he founded Den's Collectors Den, one of the largest and most reputable sports memorabilia establishments in the country. Mr. Eckes holds a BS in chemistry and an MBA in quantitative methods, both from the University of Maryland. Before the establishment of Den's Collectors Den, he held positions as research chemist, information analyst, scheduling engineer, and program manager for a large engineering firm. Among his other published works are *The Sport Americana Football and Basketball Card Price Guide, The Sport Americana Baseball Card Price Guide* and *The Sport Americana Alphabetical Baseball Card Checklist.*

THE SPORT AMERICANA
BASEBALL ADDRESS LIST
NO. 2

TABLE OF CONTENTS

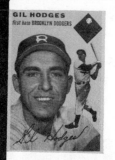

PREFACE

This book concentrates on the personal signatures or autographs of baseball players. We attempt to provide the background, explanations, and wherewithal for a collector to begin or augment his collection. Many illustrations taken from what we believe are authenic signatures are presented for your observation. Some helpful hints are provided so that your autograph hunting pursuits may be simplified and fruitful.

When reading and using this book, please keep in mind, the moral and legal rights of the ballplayers themselves. Some are more cooperative than others, some have more time to comply with your requests than others, but all are entitled to respect, privacy, and the right to affix or not affix his signature based on his own personal thoughts or moods.

There might be nothing more distinctive and personal that a person may do throughout his life than write his own name. This signature, how it changes from childhood to senility, its thin or broad stroke, its clarity, neatness, and readability is a reflexion of the character, mood, and personality of the signer. Perhaps for these reasons, a person's signature has become his universally accepted mark for identification, acknowledgement, and legal and contractual agreement.

As these addresses are under constant update because of the transient nature of the society in which we live, we should appreciate any information you can provide concerning the validity of the information and addresses contained herein. Please send all correspondence concerning address corrections, changes of address or death notices to:

R.J. "Jack" Smalling
2308 Van Buren Avenue
Ames, IA 50010

We hope this edition of the Sport Americana Baseball Address List provides a useful, interesting and enjoyable tool for your autograph and baseball historical pursuits.

Sincerely,

Jack Smalling
Denny Eckes

AUTHENTICITY

One of the enjoyable features of collecting autographs is knowing that one possesses an original mark made by another human being, a human being who for one reason or another has distinguished him or herself in the eyes of the collector. Facsimile autographs, autographs signed by someone other than the one whose name appears on the autograph, or photographs or copies of autographs do not comply with the definition of a true autograph; hence, they are of no value to the collector.

The only way one can be absolutely sure that an autograph is authentic is to personally witness the signer as he affixes his autograph. Practically speaking, were directly obtained autographs the only ones collected, logistic problems would prevent anyone from having but a modest collection. While authenticity can only be assured by directly obtaining autographs, many sources offer a high probability that an autograph is valid.

Knowing how a person's signature is supposed to look is a first step toward ascertaining authenticity. Facsimile autographs to compare with ones you are attempting to validate can be found on baseball cards, in books or magazines, or quite possibly, from the many facsimile autographs found in the text of this book. The reputation of the secondary source (dealer, friend, other collector) from whom you are obtaining the autograph is of utmost importance. Unfortunately, even the most reputable source may be unaware that he possesses a non-legitimate autograph.

Obtaining an autograph from a logical source increases the probability that an autograph is authentic. Other variables being equal, a resident of Boston is much more likely to have a valid autograph of a Red Sox player than is a resident of Butte, MT. A seventy-year old is much more likely to possess an autographed Babe Ruth ball than is a twelve-year old. Autographs obtained from the estate or from personal friends of the autographer are highly likely to be authentic. Autographs from financial or legal documents, such as cancelled checks or contracts, or any notarized communications can be considered authentic.

HOW TO OBTAIN AUTOGRAPHS

Although the text of this book is intended to provide the information necessary to obtain autographs through the mail, there are other ways to obtain autographs of ballplayers. There are basically two general categories by which you can obtain an autograph—first hand or directly, where you actually watch the ballplayer affix his signature, and second hand or indirectly, where you are not present at the time the ballplayer signs the autograph. As autograph collectors place such a high concern on authenticity, obtaining autographs first hand is preferential. Practically speaking, some autographs are impossible to obtain first hand, while many others are near impossible or at best very difficult to obtain first hand; hence, most collectors obtain a considerable portion of their collections via the indirect method.

OBTAINING AUTOGRAPHS FIRST HAND

The most obvious place to obtain a ballplayer's autograph is at the ballpark. The traditional crowd around the clubhouse awaiting the departure of their favorite players after the game, pens and papers in hands, is still perhaps the most viable means to obtain autographs. Many clubs provide special nights at the ballparks where, before the game, fans are encouraged to chat, photograph, and obtain autographs from the local team members who are available for these activities for the time periods specified.

Local merchants sometimes sponsor promotional activities at their establishments and feature a ballplayer as the guest celebrity. The ballplayer is normally available to sign autographs, and the merchants might well provide a medium (photo, postcard, etc.) for obtaining the autograph.

Other opportunities arise at hotels, airports, celebrity dinners or other public places where a ballplayer might chance to be during the course of his normal routine. However, we must emphasize again the necessity for patience and politeness when requesting an autograph in person from a ballplayer. Quite often time may allow only a few or no signatures to be signed before the ballplayer's schedule requires him to halt the autograph activities.

More and more over the past few years, the many sports collectibles conventions and shows held across the country have been featuring guest baseball players. These shows provide excellent opportunities for obtaining autographs from of the most popular ballplayers.

Each year the Baseball Hall of Fame in Cooperstown, NY, holds induction ceremonies for newly elected members. Not only do the newly elected members attend, but also many of the members who have been previously elected are in attendance. There is probably no other time or place that occurs during the year when one can obtain, in person, as many living HOFer autographs as on induction day in Cooperstown.

OBTAINING AUTOGRAPHS INDIRECTLY

Most collectors, by necessity, obtain the bulk of their collections indirectly. Trading with other collectors, purchasing from dealers, purchasing from private parties, or bidding at auction from estate liquidations, hobby paper ads, or at sports collectibles conventions are the most prevelant methods which do not involve the sports personality himself. The most common way to obtain an autograph from the sports personality without the presence of the sports personality is through the mail. It is for this purpose that the SPORT AMERICANA BASEBALL ADDRESS LIST is most useful.

Autograph collecting is a reasonably popular hobby. It is not uncommon to find other collectors with autograph interests similar to yours. It is also not uncommon to find collectors who posses more than one autograph of the same player, a duplicate which they can be convinced to part with in exchange for an autograph which they desire but do not possess— one which you yourself may have in duplicate. These conditions form the basis for trade negotiations from which both parties can obtain satisfaction. Most trading is not quite this simple; however, the underlying motives of all tradings are to obtain something you do not posses and desire to have for something you have but do not place such a high value on as you do the item you desire to obtain.

3

Dealers in autographed material exist just as they do for any collectible. Many specialize in particular types of autographs. In any event, these dealers have acquired autograph material and are willing to sell it at a given price(a price which may or may not be negotiable). These dealers can be found at sports collectibles conventions, at local flea markets, and from advertisements in the hobby papers or autograph oriented periodicals (including this book).

A check of your local newspapers, particular the auction section of the Sunday editions, is an excellent way to become aware of estate and private party autograph sales and auctions. The auction method offers you the opportunity to obtain autographs you desire for amounts less than you might pay to a dealer. In fact, because of the scarcity of certain autographs, the auction method may be the only available way to obtain a particular autograph. In such cases a fair market value might not be known, and the auction offers a means to arrive at a price based on the value of the autograph to the collector.

OBTAINING AUTOGRAPHS THROUGH THE MAIL

A large number of active and retired baseball players honor autograph requests made through the mail. One of the prime purposes of compiling this book is to provide the collector with the wherewithal to obtain autographs he or she desires through the mails. The authors do not profess to know all players who will comply with your autograph requests nor those who will not comply. The authors also do not promote or sanction any harassment or excessive requests on your part of the ballplayers contacted through the addresses found in this Address List. To the contrary, we emphatically suggest a polite, patient and respectful course in obtaining autographs through the mail.

Ballplayers, particularly active players during the baseball season, have schedules much tighter and more regimented than the normal 9 to 5 worker. Mail they receive may not be opened for lengthy periods. Many schedule limited time periods that they devote to autograph requests. Quite possibly, dependent on the number of autograph requests a particular player receives, your autograph request might not be answered for a considerable period of time. Be patient. The authors know of cases where years have elapsed before an autograph request was returned.

Like everyone else, ballplayers are human beings and appreciate politeness. Words such as "please" and "thank you" are as pleasantly received and as revered by ballplayers as they are by parents of teenagers (fortunately, ballplayers hear them much more often). Excessive requests, imperative tones, and impoliteness are justifiably scorned.

Some ballplayers do not honor autograph requests, either in person or through the mail. Some change their autographing philosophies over the years, becoming more liberal or conservative in their autographing habits. Whatever a player's thoughts or ideas are on accepting or rejecting autograph requests, they should be respected.

The mechanics of obtaining autographs through the mail are quite simple. Send the request, postpaid, to the ballplayer, including a politely written request outlining what you are asking of the ballplayer, any material that you wish to have autographed, and a SASE (self-addressed stamped envelope) large enough to contain the material you wish to be autographed and returned to you. Never send an autograph request postage due. To do so is presumptuous, in poor taste and completely uncalled for.

Do not send an unreasonable amount of material for autographing. A limit of three items per request has become the accepted practice of collectors. An exception to this limit is considered permissible if you have duplicates of the item you wish to have autographed, and you would like to give the ballplayer the opportunity to keep one of the duplicates for his own enjoyment. Ballplayers like most of us enjoy seeing and having interesting photos or other material concerning themselves, particularly if the item is novel or the ballplayer has never before seen it. Many collectors use this method, as a gesture of good faith and intent when requesting autographs through the mail. However, the limit of three items you wish to have signed and returned to you, exclusive of the items you wish to present to the ballplayer at his option to keep, is still the accepted standard.

It is not considered unreasonable to request a short personalization with an autograph; for example, "To John from...", or "Best Wishes to Gayle from...", etc. Requesting a two-page letter or an answer to a question that requires a dissertation is unreasonable. Do not do it.

Always include a SASE with sufficient postage to cover the material you expect might be returned to you. The SASE alleviates the need for the ballplayer to package and address your reply himself; it enables you to pay, as you should, for return postage; and it assures that the reply will be sent to the party requesting it (assuming you can competently write your own address on an envelope).

VALUES

The authors have purposely avoided any reference to price in the text of this book. Like other collectibles, there is a definite price structure for the autographs of ballplayers. Until recently, there was no price guide by which the collector could ascertain the value of his or her collection. The SPORT AMERICANA MEMORABILIA & AUTOGRAPH PRICE GUIDE, available at your local bookstore and described on the inside back cover of this book, provides the guidelines for autograph values.

Without printing prices for the autographs of specific ballplayers, we should like to present a discussion of values within a context of scarcity and desirability, which when all results are in, are the prime determinants of value for any collectible.

LIVING OR DECEASED

Like artists and martyrs, the values of whose accomplishments during their lifetimes is magnified and glorified after death, the value of a ballplayer's autograph increases considerable after his death. The deseased ballplayer can no longer, of course, sign autographs; hence, the supply of the autograph of this player ceases at this point in time. All autographs of deceased ball-players must be obtained second hand after his death, making authenticity questionable.

HALL OF FAME MEMBERS

The pinnacle of success for a ballplayer is election to baseball's Hall of Fame. This honor is limited to the most skillful and proficient players and those others who have made the most significant contributions to the game. The autographs of these men are among the most desireable and have, other factors being equal, the highest value to collectors.

POPULARITY AND NOTORIETY

While popularity can generally be measured by ballplaying skill, there are certainly exceptions. Many ballplayers whose skill on the field was limited, have achieved success and notoriety in other walks of life (William A. "Billy" Sunday, Joe Garagiola, Chuck Connors, Jim Thorpe to name but a few). The more popular the ballplayer, whether his popularity was derived by playing skill or by some other means, the higher the value placed on his autograph.

CONDITION AND TYPE OF AUTOGRAPH

Autographs, like other collectibles, exist in various physical conditions— from the weekest, broken pencil autograph to the boldest, unbroken indelable ink signature. The higher value is placed on the better condition autograph of the same person. Many types of media are available on which to obtain autographs. There are the relatively bland cuts and 3 X 5 varieties at one end of the spectrum and the most elaborate pieces of one of a kind items autographed by the player portrayed at the other end. In between there is a muriad of possible forms and designs that the autograph medium may take. The same autograph has a higher value based on the more interesting, enjoyable and attractive medium on which the autograph is written.

see PAGE 149

6

MAJOR LEAGUE TEAM ADDRESSES

BASEBALL COMMISSIONER'S OFFICE

Bowie Kuhn, Commissioner
75 Rockefeller Plaza
New York, NY 10019
(212) 586-7400

AMERICAN LEAGUE OFFICE
Joseph E. Cronin, Chairman
Leland S. MacPhail, Jr., President
280 Park Avenue
New York, NY 10017
(212) 682-7000

BALTIMORE ORIOLES
Edward Bennett Williams, Chairman
Jerold C. Hoffberger, President
Memorial Stadium
Baltimore, MD 21218
(301) 243-9800

BOSTON RED SOX
Jean R. Yawkey, President
24 Yawkey Way
Fenway Park
Boston, MA 02215
(617) 267-9440

CALIFORNIA ANGELS
Gene Autry, Chairman, President
P.O. Box 2000
2000 State College Blvd.
Anaheim Stadium
Anaheim, CA 92806
(714) 937-6700 & (215) 625-1123

CHICAGO WHITE SOX
Jerry M. Reinsdorf, Chairman
Eddie M. Einhorn, President
324 W. 35th Street
Comiskey Park
Chicago, IL 60616
(312) 924-1000

CLEVELAND INDIANS
F. J. O'Neill, Chairman
Gabe Paul, President
Municipal Stadium
Boudreau Blvd.
Cleveland, OH 44114
(216) 241-5555

DETROIT TIGERS
John E. Fetzer, Chairman & Owner
James A. Campbell, President
Tiger Stadium
Detroit, MI 48216
(313) 962-4000

KANSAS CITY ROYALS
Ewing Kauffman, Chairman
Joe Burke, President
P.O. Box 1969
Royals Stadium
Kansas City, MO 64141
(816) 921-2200

MILWAUKEE BREWERS
Allan H. (Bud) Selig, President
201 S. 46th Street
County Stadium
Milwaukee, WI 53214
(414) 933-1818

MINNESOTA TWINS
Calvin R. Griffith, Chairman, President
501 Chicago Avenue, S.
Hubert H. Humphrey Metrodome
Minneapolis, MN 55415
(612) 375-1366

NEW YORK YANKEES
George M. Steinbrenner III, Owner
Lou Saban, President
Yankee Stadium
Bronx, NY 10451
(212) 293-4300

OAKLAND A'S
Roy Eisenhardt, Chairman, President
Oakland Coliseum
Oakland, CA 94621
(415) 638-4900

SEATTLE MARINERS
George L. Argyros, Owner
Daniel F. O'Brien, President
P.O. Box 4100
419 Second Avenue, S.
The Kingdome
Seattle, WA 98104
(206) 628-3555

TEXAS RANGERS
Eddie Chiles, Chairman, President
P.O. Box 1111
Arlington Stadium
Arlington, TX 76010
(817) 273-5222

TORONTO BLUE—JAYS
R. Howard Webster, Chairman
Box 7777
Adelaide St. Post Office
Exhibition Stadium
Toronto, Ontario
Canada M5C 2K7
(416) 595-0077

NATIONAL LEAGUE OFFICE
Charles S. Feeney, President
Suite 1602
One Rockefeller Plaza
New York, NY 10020
(212) 582-4213

ATLANTA BRAVES
William C. Bartholomay, Chairman
R. E. (Ted) Turner, President
P.O. Box 4064
521 Capitol Avenue
Atlanta Stadium
Atlanta, GA 30302
(404) 522-7630

CHICAGO CUBS
Andrew J. McKenna, Chairman, President
1060 West Addison Street
Wrigley Field
Chicago, IL 60613
(312) 281-5050

CINCINNATI REDS
James R. Williams, Chairman
William J. Williams, Chairman
Richard Wagner, President
100 Riverfront Stadium
Cincinnati, OH 45202
(513) 421-4510

HOUSTON ASTROS
Al Rosen, President
P.O. Box 288
8701 Kirby
The Astrodome
Houston, TX 77001
(713) 799-9500

LOS ANGELES DODGERS
Peter O'Malley, President
1000 Elysian Park Avenue
Dodger Stadium
Los Angeles, CA 90012
(213) 224-1500

MONTREAL EXPOS
Charles R. Bronfman, Chairman
John J. McHale, President
P.O. Box 500, Station M
4545 Pierre de Coubertin
Olympic Stadium
Montreal, Quebec
Canada H1V 3P2
(514) 253-3434

NEW YORK METS
Nelson Doubleday, Chairman
Fred Wilpon, President
J. Frank Cashen, Chief Operating Officer
Shea Stadium
New York, NY 11368
(212) 672-3000

PHILADELPHIA PHILLIES
William Y. Giles, President
P.O. Box 7575
Broad St. and Pattison Ave
Veterans Stadium
Philadelphia, PA 19148
(215) 463-6000

PITTSBURGH PIRATES
John W. Galbreath, Chairman
Daniel M. Galbreath, President
Three Rivers Stadium
600 Stadium Circle
Pittsburgh, PA 15212
(412) 323-1150

ST. LOUIS CARDINALS
August A. Busch, Jr., President
250 Stadium Plaza
Busch Memorial Stadium
St. Louis, MO 63122
(314) 421-3060

SAN DIEGO PADRES
Ray A. Kroc, Chairman
Ballard F. Smith, Jr., President
P.O. Box 2000
9449 Friars Road
San Diego Stadium
San Diego, CA 92120
(714) 283-4494

SAN FRANCISCO GIANTS
Robert A. Lurie, President
P.O. Box 24308
Candlestick Park
San Francisco, CA 94124
(415) 467-8000

TRIPLE A LEAGUE TEAM ADDRESSES

AMERICAN ASSOCIATION
Joe Ryan, President
P.O. Box 382
Wichita, KS 67201
(316) 267-0266

DENVER BEARS
James H. Burris, General Manager
P.O. Box 4419
Mile High Stadium
Denver, CO 80204
(303) 433-8645

EVANSVILLE TRIPLETS
Aubrey D. Ryals, Chairman
Alvin V. Dauble, President
P.O. Box 417
1600 N. Main St.
Bosse Field
Evansville, IN 47703
(812) 423-3333

INDIANAPOLIS INDIANS
Henry R. Warren, Jr., Chairman
Max B. Schumacher, President
1501 W. l6th St.
Bush Stadium
Indianapolis, IN 46202
(317) 632-5371

IOWA CUBS
Ken Grandquist, President
2nd & Riverside Dr.
Sec Taylor Stadium
Des Moines, IA 50309
(515) 243-6111

LOUISVILLE REDBIRDS
A. Ray Smith, Chairman, President
P.O. Box 36407
Kentucky State Fairgrounds
Cardinal Stadium
Louisville, KY 40233
(502) 367-9121

OKLAHOMA CITY 89ers
Allie Reynolds, Chairman
Patty Cox, President
P.O. Box 75089
State Fairgrounds
All Sports Stadium,
Oklahoma City, OK 73147
(405) 946-1453

OMAHA ROYALS
Ewing M. Kauffman, Chairman
P.O. Box 3665
1202 Bert Murphy Ave.
Rosenblatt Stadium
Omaha, NE 68103
(402) 734-2550

WICHITA AEROS
Milton Glickman, Chairman
H.B. "Spec" Richardson, President
P.O. Box 82
300 So. Sycamore
Lawrence/Dumont Stadium
Wichita, KS 67201
(316) 267-3372

INTERNATIONAL LEAGUE
Harold M. Cooper, President
P.O. Box 608
3969 First St.
Grove City, OH 43123
(614) 871-1300

CHARLESTON CHARLIES
Cal O. Carlini, Chairman
P.O. Box 4298
35th St. & MacCorkle Ave., SE
Watt Powell Park
Charleston, WV 25304
(304) 346-0734

COLUMBUS CLIPPERS
Donald Borror, President
1155 W. Mound St.
Franklin County Stadium
Columbus, OH 43223
(614) 462-5250

PAWTUCKET RED SOX
Bernard G. Mondor, President
P.O. Box 2365
One Columbus Ave.
McCoy Stadium
Pawtucket, RI 02861
(401) 724-7303

RICHMOND BRAVES
William C. Bartholomay, Chairman
R. E. (Ted) Turner, President
P.O. Box 6667
3001 North Blvd.
Parker Field
Richmond, VA 23230
(804) 359-4444

ROCHESTER RED WINGS
William P. Blackmon, Chairman
Wally Lord, President
Silver Stadium
Rochester, NY 14621
(716) 467-3000

SYRACUSE CHIEFS
Royal L. O'Day, Chairman
Donald R. Waful, President
MacArthur Stadium
Syracuse, NY 13208
(315) 474-7833

TIDEWATER TIDES
Richard J. Davis, President
P.O. Box 12111
Metropolitan Park
Norfolk, VA 23502
(804) 461-5600

TOLEDO MUD HENS
Henry L. Morse, President
2901 Key St.
Lucas County Stadium
Maumee, OH 43537
(419) 893-9483

PACIFIC COAST LEAGUE
William S. Cutler, President
2101 E. Broadway Rd.
Tempe, AZ 85282
(602) 967-7679

ALBUQUERQUE DUKES
Robert & Walter Lozinak, Co-Chairmen
P. Patrick McKernan, President
P.O. Box 26267
Stadium & University Blvd.
Albuquerque Sports Stadium
Albuquerque, NM 87125
(505) 243-1791

EDMONTON TRAPPERS
Peter Pocklington, Owner
Mel Kowalchuk, President
12315 Stony Plain Road, No. 202
Renfrew Park
Edmonton, Alberta
Canada T5N 3Y8
(403) 482-6917

HAWAII ISLANDERS
David B. Elmore, Chairman & President
2222 Kalakaua Ave., No. 1214
Aloha Stadium
Honolulu, HI 96801
(808) 922-9736

PHOENIX GIANTS
Edward B. Vallone II, President
5999 E. Van Buren
Municipal Stadium
Phoenix, AZ 85008
(602) 275-4488

PORTLAND BEAVERS
Ron Tonkin, Chairman & President
1205 S.W.18th Ave.
Civic Stadium
Portland, OR 97205
(503) 223-2837

SALT LAKE CITY GULLS
Larry Schmittou, President
65 West 1300 South
Derks Field
Salt Lake City, UT 84115
(801) 363-7676 or 363-7817

SPOKANE INDIANS
Larry Koentopp, Chairman
Tim Finnerty, President
P.O. Box 4442
N. 602 Havana
Spokane Indiana Baseball Stadium
Spokane, WA 99202
(509) 535-2922

TACOMA TIGERS
E. J. Zarelli, Chairman
P.O. Box 11087
2525 Bantz Blvd.
Cheney Stadium
Tacoma, WA 98411
(206) 752-7707

TUCSON TOROS
William A. Estes, Chairman & President
P.O. Box 27045
Hi Corbett Field
Tucson, AZ 85726
(602) 325-2621

VANCOUVER CANADIANS
Nelson M. Skalbania, Chairman
Jim Pattison, President
4601 Ontario St.
Nat Bailey Stadium
Vancouver, B.C.
Canada V5V 3H4
(604) 872-5232

HOW TO USE THE ADDRESS LIST

The Address List is composed of five sections:

1. Players in the Baseball Hall of Fame
2. Players who debuted from 1871 to 1909
3. Players who debuted from 1910 to 1981
4. Umpires who debuted from 1910 to 1981
5. Coaches with no big league playing experience who debuted from 1910 to 1981

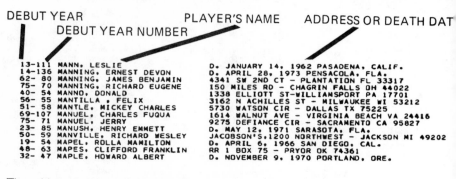

```
DEBUT YEAR              PLAYER'S NAME      ADDRESS OR DEATH DATE
     DEBUT YEAR NUMBER

13-111  MANN, LESLIE              D. JANUARY 14, 1962 PASADENA, CALIF.
14-136  MANNING, ERNEST DEVON     D. APRIL 28, 1973 PENSACOLA, FLA.
62- 80  MANNING, JAMES BENJAMIN   4341 SW 2ND CT - PLANTATION FL 33317
75- 70  MANNING, RICHARD EUGENE   150 MILES RD - CHAGRIN FALLS OH 44022
40- 54  MANNO, DONALD             1338 ELLIOTT ST-WILLIAMSPORT PA 17701
56- 55  MANTILLA , FELIX          3162 N ACHILLES ST - MILWAUKEE WI 53212
51- 58  MANTLE, MICKEY CHARLES    5730 WATSON CIR - DALLAS TX 75225
69-107  MANUEL, CHARLES FUQUA     1614 WALNUT AVE - VIRGINIA BEACH VA 24416
75- 71  MANUEL, JERRY             9275 DEFIANCE CIR - SACRAMENTO CA 95827
23- 85  MANUSH, HENRY EMMETT      D. MAY 12, 1971 SARASOTA, FLA.
50- 59  MANVILLE, RICHARD WESLEY  JACOBSON'S,1200 NORTHWEST - JACKSON MI 49202
19- 54  MAPEL, ROLLA HAMILTON     D. APRIL 6, 1966 SAN DIEGO, CAL.
48- 63  MAPES, CLIFFORD FRANKLIN  RR 1 BOX 75 - PRYOR OK 74361
32- 47  MAPLE, HOWARD ALBERT      D. NOVEMBER 9, 1970 PORTLAND, ORE.
```

The address portion of the listing contains the known current address of the player if the player is now living or information as follows:

> ADDRESS NOT KNOWN—An old address is given for players for whom a current address is not known. In many cases, the year the address was last valid is shown in the data. Birth information is given if no other data is available. If no information is known about a player except his name, a blank space will appear in the address portion of the listing.

> DECEASED PLAYERS—The date and place of a player's death will be listed for deceased players. Incomplete death data is given for some players because complete information is not known. The abbreviation D. with no other information in the address portion of the listing indicates that a player is reportedly deceased, but that no other data is available.

PLEASE NOTE:

> Managers who never appeared in a big league game are listed with the year they first managed in the big leagues.
> Only those coaches who never appeared in a big league game are listed in the coaches section.
> The abbreviations used for states on addresses are standard U.S. Postal Service abbreviations.
> B. indicates born, D. indicates deceased, and other abbreviations are self-explanatory as they are used in normal written communications.

As this nation is known to be a nation of transients, one can expect that the addresses of a considerable number of the ballplayers listed will become invalid over the course of the next year or two.

54-	1	AARON, HENRY LOUIS	1611 ADAMS DR SW - ATLANTA GA 30311
11-	2	ALEXANDER, GROVER CLEVELAND	D. NOVEMBER 4, 1950 ST. PAUL, NEB.
71		ANSON, ADRIAN CONSTANTINE	D. APRIL 14, 1922 CHICAGO, ILL.
30-	1	APPLING, LUCIUS BENJAMIN	RR 7, BRAGG RD - CUMMINGS GA 30130
29-	4	AVERILL, HOWARD EARL	914 4TH # 6 - SNOHOMISH WA 98290
08		BAKER, JOHN FRANKLIN	D. JUNE 28, 1963 TRAPPE, MD.
15-	5	BANCROFT, DAVID JAMES	D. OCTOBER 9, 1972 SUPERIOR, WIS.
53-	7	BANKS, ERNEST	1440 N STATE PKWY #3-D - CHICAGO IL 60610
03		BARROW, EDWARD GRANT	D. DECEMBER 15, 1953 PORT CHESTER, N. Y.
88		BECKLEY, JACOB PETER	D. JUNE 25, 1918 KANSAS CITY, MO.
HOF		BELL, JAMES 'COOL PAPA'	3034 DICKSON - ST. LOUIS MO 63106
03		BENDER, CHARLES ALBERT	D. MAY 22, 1954 PHILADELPHIA, PA.
46-	9	BERRA, LAWRENCE PETER	19 HIGHLAND AVE - MONTCLAIR NJ 07042
22-	13	BOTTOMLEY, JAMES LEROY	D. DECEMBER 11, 1959 SAINT LOUIS. MO.
38-	9	BOUDREAU, LOUIS	15600 ELLIS AVENUE - DOLTON IL 60419
97		BRESNAHAN, ROGER PATRICK	D. DECEMBER 4, 1944 TOLEDO, O.
79		BROUTHERS, DENNIS	D. AUGUST 3, 1932 EAST ORANGE, N. J.
03		BROWN, MORDECAI PETER CENTENNIAL	D. FEBRUARY 14, 1948 TERRE HAUTE, IND.
HOF		BULKELEY, MORGAN G.	D. NOVEMBER 6, 1922 HARTFORD, CONN.
90		BURKETT, JESSE CAIL	D. MAY 27, 1953 WORCESTER, MASS.
48-	22	CAMPANELLA, ROY	1000 ELYSIAN PARK AVE - LOS ANGELES CA 90012
10-	23	CAREY, MAX GEORGE	D. MAY 30, 1976 MIAMI, FLA.
HOF		CARTWRIGHT, ALEXANDER JOY	D. JULY 12, 1892 HONOLULU, HAWAII
HOF		CHADWICK, HENRY	D. APRIL 20, 1908 BROOKLYN, N. Y.
98		CHANCE, FRANK LEROY	D. SEPTEMBER 15, 1924 LOS ANGELES, CAL.
HOF		CHANDLER, ALBERT BENJAMIN "HAPPY"	RR - VERSAILLES KY 40383
HOF		CHARLESTON, OSCAR MCKINLEY	D. OCTOBER 11, 1954 PHILADELPHIA, PA.
99		CHESBRO, JOHN DWIGHT	D. NOVEMBER 6, 1931 CONWAY, MASS.
94		CLARKE, FRED CLIFFORD	D. AUGUST 14, 1960 WINFIELD, KAN.
82		CLARKSON, JOHN GIBSON	D. FEBRUARY 4, 1909 CAMBRIDGE, MASS.
55-	26	CLEMENTE, ROBERTO WALKER	D. DECEMBER 31,1972 SAN JUAN, P. R.
05		COBB, TYRUS RAYMOND	D. JULY 17,1961 ATLANTA, GA.
25-	19	COCHRANE, GORDON STANLEY	D. JUNE 2, 1962 LAKE FOREST, ILL.
06		COLLINS, EDWARD TROWBRIDGE SR.	D. MARCH 25, 1951 BOSTON, MASS.
95		COLLINS, JAMES JOSEPH	D. MARCH 6, 1943 BUFFALO, N. Y.
24-	22	COMBS, EARLE BRYAN	D. JULY 21, 1976 RICHMOND, KY.
82		COMISKEY, CHARLES ALBERT	D. OCTOBER 26,1931 EAGLE RIVER, WIS.
34-	27	CONLAN, JOHN BERTRAND	5937 CHENEY ROAD - SCOTTSDALE AZ 85251
UMP-60		CONNOLLY, THOMAS HENRY	D. APRIL 28, 1961 NATICK, MASS.
80		CONNOR, ROGER	D. JANUARY 4, 1931 WATERBURY, CONN.
12-	39	COVELESKI, STANLEY ANTHONY	1038 W NAPIER - SOUTH BEND IN 46625
99		CRAWFORD, SAMUEL EARL	D. JUNE 15, 1968 HOLLYWOOD, CALIF.

26-	22	CRONIN, JOSEPH EDWARD	BOX 276 - OSTERVILLE MA 02655
72		CUMMINGS, WILLIAM ARTHUR	D. MAY 17, 1924 TOLEDO, O.
21-	19	CUYLER, HAZEN SHIRLEY	D. FEBRUARY 11, 1950 ANN ARBOR, MICH.
30-	16	DEAN, JAY HANNA	D. JULY 17, 1974 RENO, NEV.
88		DELAHANTY, EDWARD JAMES	D. JULY 2, 1903 FORT ERIE, ONT.
28-	29	DICKEY, WILLIAM MALCOLM	114 E. 5TH ST - LITTLE ROCK AR 72203
HOF		DIHIGO, MARTIN	D. MAY 22, 1971 CIENFUEGOS, CUBA
36-	22	DIMAGGIO, JOSEPH PAUL	2150 BEACH ST - SAN FRANCISCO CA 94123

Yours very truly,

Secretary

88	DUFFY, HUGH	D. OCTOBER 19, 1954 BOSTON, MASS.
UMP-06	EVANS, WILLIAM GEORGE	D. JANUARY 23, 1956 MIAMI, FLA.
02	EVERS, JOHN JOSEPH	D. MARCH 28, 1947 ALBANY, N. Y.
80	EWING, WILLIAM BUCKINGHAM	D. OCTOBER 20, 1906 CINCINNATI, O.
14- 61	FABER, URBAN CHARLES	D. SEPTEMBER 25, 1976 CHICAGO, ILL.
36- 24	FELLER, ROBERT WILLIAM ANDREW BOX 157 - GATES MILLS OH 44040	
98	FLICK, ELMER HARRISON	D. JANUARY 9, 1971 BEDFORD, O.
50- 29	FORD, EDWARD CHARLES	38 SCHOOLHOUSE LANE - LAKE SUCCESS NY 11020
HOF	FOSTER, ANDREW "RUBE"	D. DECEMBER 9, 1930 KANKAKEE, ILL.
25- 35	FOXX, JAMES EMORY	D. JULY 21, 1967 MIAMI, FLA.
HOF	FRICK, FORD CHRISTOPHER	D. APRIL 8, 1978 BRONXVILLE, N. Y.
19- 28	FRISCH, FRANK FRANCIS	D. MARCH 12, 1973 WILMINGTON, DEL.
75	GALVIN, JAMES F.	D. MARCH 7, 1902 PITTSBURGH, PA.
23- 50	GEHRIG, HENRY LOUIS	D. JUNE 2, 1941 RIVERDALE, N. Y.
24- 40	GEHRINGER, CHARLES LEONARD	32301 LAHSER RD - BIRMINGHAM MI 48010

HOF	GIBSON, JOSH	D. JANUARY 20, 1947 PITTSBURGH, PA.
59- 30	GIBSON, ROBERT	215 BELLEVIEW BLVD S - BELLEVIEW NE 68005
HOF	GILES, WARREN CHRISTOPHER	D. FEBRUARY 7, 1979 CINCINNATI, O.
30- 26	GOMEZ, VERNON LOUIS	26 SAN BENITO WAY. - NOVATO CA 94947
21- 37	GOSLIN, LEON ALLEN	D. MAY 15, 1971 BRIDGETON, N. J.
30- 27	GREENBERG, HENRY BENJAMIN	1129 MIRADERO RD - BEVERLY HILLS CA 90210
91	GRIFFITH, CLARK CALVIN	D. OCTOBER 27, 1955 WASHINTON, D. C.
16- 35	GRIMES, BURLEIGH ARLAND	%V.TEAS:13955 S INDIANA AVE-CHICAGO IL 60627
25- 41	GROVE, ROBERT MOSES	D. MAY 22, 1975 NORWALK, O.
24- 49	HAFEY, CHARLES JAMES	D. JULY 2, 1973 CALISTOGA, CAL.
18- 23	HAINES, JESSE JOSEPH	D. AUGUST 5, 1978 DAYTON, O.
88	HAMILTON, WILLIAM ROBERT	D. DECEMBER 16, 1940 WORCESTER, MASS.
HOF	HARRIDGE, WILLIAM	D. APRIL 9, 1971 EVANSTON, ILL.
19- 38	HARRIS, STANLEY RAYMOND	D. NOVEMBER 8, 1977 BETHESDA, MD.
22- 52	HARTNETT, CHARLES LEO	D. DECEMBER 20, 1972 PARK RIDGE, ILL.
14- 84	HEILMANN, HARRY EDWIN	D. JULY 9, 1951 DETROIT, MICH.
31- 37	HERMAN, WILLIAM JENNINGS	3111 GARDEN E #33-PALM BEACH GARDENS FL 33410
09	HOOPER, HARRY BARTHOLOMEW	D. DECEMBER 18, 1974 SANTA CRUZ, CALIF.
15- 70	HORNSBY, ROGERS	D. JANUARY 5, 1963 CHICAGO, ILL.
18- 36	HOYT, WAITE CHARLES	3787 ASHWORTH DR - CINCINNATI OH 45208
UMP-36	HUBBARD, ROBERT CAL	D. OCTOBER 16, 1977 ST PETERSBURG, FLA.
28- 49	HUBBELL, CARL OWEN	SUNCREST APT #8,130 N LESEUER #1-MESA AZ83205
04	HUGGINS, MILLER JAMES	D. SEPTEMBER 25, 1929 NEW YORK, N. Y.
49- 39	IRVIN, MONFORD	243 S HARRISON ST #2A-EAST ORANGE NJ 07018
22- 61	JACKSON, TRAVIS CALVIN	WALDO AR 71770
91	JENNINGS, HUGH AMBROSE	D. FEBRUARY 1, 1928 SCRANTON, PA.
HOF	JOHNSON, BYRON BANCROFT	D. MARCH 28, 1931 ST. LOUIS, MO.
07	JOHNSON, WALTER PERRY	D. DECEMBER 10, 1946 WASHINGTON, D. C.
HOF	JOHNSON, WILLIAM JULIUS	3701 KIAMENSI - MARSHALLTOWN DE 19808
02	JOSS, ADRIAN	D. APRIL 14, 1911 TOLEDO, O.
53- 42	KALINE, ALBERT WILLIAM	945 TIMBERLAKE DR - BLOOMFIELD HILLS MI 48013
80	KEEFE, TIMOTHY J.	D. APRIL 23, 1933 CAMBRIDGE, MASS.
92	KEELER, WILLIAM HENRY	D. JANUARY 1, 1923 BROOKLYN, N. Y.

KELLEY   MIZE

91	KELLEY, JOSEPH JAMES	D. AUGUST 14, 1943 BALTIMORE, MD.
15- 80	KELLY, GEORGE LANGE	1151 MILLBRAE AVE - MILLBRAE 94030
78	KELLY, MICHAEL JOSEPH	D. NOVEMBER 8, 1894 BOSTON, MASS.
46- 56	KINER, RALPH MCPHERRAN	BOTE ROAD - GREENWICH CT 06830
28- 55	KLEIN, CHARLES HERBERT	D. MARCH 28, 1958 INDIANAPOLIS, IND.
UMP-05	KLEM, WILLIAM J.	D. SEPTEMBER 16, 1951 MIAMI, FLA.
55- 65	KOUFAX, SANFORD	1000 ELYSIAN AVE - LOS ANGELES CA 90012
96	LAJOIE, NAPOLEON	D. FEBRUARY 7, 1959 DAYTONA BEACH, FLA.
HOF	LANDIS, KENESAW MOUNTAIN	D. NOVEMBER 25, 1944 CHICAGO, ILL.
41- 63	LEMON, ROBERT GRANVILLE	1141 CLAIBORNE DR-LONG BEACH CA 90807
HOF	LEONARD, WALTER FENNER	605 ATLANTIC AVE - ROCKY MOUNT NC 27801
24- 68	LINDSTROM, FRED CHARLES	D. OCTOBER 4, 1981 CHICAGO, ILL.
HOF	LLOYD, JOHN HENRY	D. MARCH 19, 1964
28- 60	LOPEZ, ALFONSO RAMON	3601 BEACH DR - TAMPA FL 33609
23- 84	LYONS, THEODORE AMAR	1401 LOREE ST - VINTON LA 70668
86	MACK, CORNELIUS ALEXANDER	D. FEBRUARY 8, 1956 GERMANTOWN, PA.
HOF	MACPHAIL, LELAND STANFORD	D. OCTOBER 1, 1975 MIAMI, FLA.
51- 58	MANTLE, MICKEY CHARLES	5730 WATSON CIR - DALLAS TX 75225
23- 85	MANUSH, HENRY EMMETT	D. MAY 12, 1971 SARASOTA, FLA.

12-114	MARANVILLE, WALTER JAMES VINCENT	D. JANUARY 5, 1954 NEW YORK, N.Y.
08	MARQUARD, RICHARD WILLIAM	D. JUNE 1, 1980 BALTIMORE, MD.
52- 73	MATHEWS, EDWIN LEE	13744 RECUERDO DR - DEL MAR CA 92014
00	MATHEWSON, CHRISTOPHER	D. OCTOBER 7, 1925 SARANAC LAKE, N.Y.
51- 62	MAYS, WILLIE HOWARD	51 MT VERNON LN - ATHERTON CA 94025
26- 54	MCCARTHY, JOSEPH VINCENT	D. JANUARY 13, 1978 BUFFALO, N.Y.
84	MCCARTHY, THOMAS FRANCIS MICHAEL	D. AUGUST 5, 1922 BOSTON, MASS.
99	MCGINNITY, JOSEPH JEROME	D. NOVEMBER 14, 1929 BROOKLYN, N.Y.
91	MCGRAW, JOHN JOSEPH	D. FEBRUARY 25, 1934 NEW ROCHELLE, N.Y.
07	MCKECHNIE, WILLIAM BOYD	D. OCTOBER 29, 1965 BRADENTON, FLA.
32- 53	MEDWICK, JOSEPH MICHAEL	D. MARCH 21, 1975 ST. PETERSBURG, FLA.
36- 58	MIZE, JOHN ROBERT	BOX 112 - DEMOREST GA 30535

13

```
41- 79  MUSIAL, STANLEY FRANK          85 TRENT DR - LADUE MO 63124
90      NICHOLS, CHARLES AUGUSTUS      D. APRIL 11, 1953 KANSAS CITY, MO.
72      O'ROURKE, JAMES HENRY          D. JANUARY 8, 1919 BRIDGEPORT, CONN.
26- 62  OTT, MELVIN THOMAS             D. NOVEMBER 21, 1958 NEW ORLEANS, LA.
48- 78  PAIGE, LEROY                   2626 EAST 28TH ST - KANSAS CITY MO 64128
```

```
12-154  PENNOCK, HERBERT JEFFERS       D. JANUARY 30, 1948 NEW YORK, N.Y.
01      PLANK, EDWARD STEWART          D. FEBRUARY 24, 1926 GETTYSBURG, PA.
80      RADBOURN, CHARLES              D. FEBRUARY 5, 1897 BLOOMINGTON, ILL.
15-135  RICE, EDGAR CHARLES            D. OCTOBER 13, 1974 ROSSMOR, MD.
05      RICKEY, WESLEY BRANCH          D. DECEMBER 9, 1965 COLUMBIA, MO.
12-165  RIXEY, EPPA                    D. FEBRUARY 28, 1963 TERRACE PARK, O.
48- 85  ROBERTS, ROBIN EVAN            504 TERRACE HILL RD - TEMPLE TERRACE FL 33617
56- 73  ROBINSON, FRANK                15557 AQUA VERDE DR - BEL AIR CA 90024
47- 73  ROBINSON, JACK ROOSEVELT       D. OCTOBER 24, 1972 STAMFORD, CONN.
86      ROBINSON, WILBERT              D. AUGUST 8, 1934 ATLANTA, GA.
13-152  ROUSH, EDD J.                  122 S MAIN ST - OAKLAND CITY IN 47560
24- 92  RUFFING, CHARLES HERBERT       25382 CONCORD DRIVE - CLEVELAND O 44122
89      RUSIE, AMOS WILSON             D. DECEMBER 6, 1942 SEATTLE, WASH.
14-185  RUTH, GEORGE HERMAN            D. AUGUST 16, 1948 NEW YORK, N.Y.
12-171  SCHALK, RAYMOND WILLIAM        D. MAY 19, 1970 CHICAGO, ILL.
20-104  SEWELL, JOSEPH WHEELER         1618 DEARING PLACE - TUSCALOOSA ALA 35401
24-100  SIMMONS, ALOYSIUS HARRY        D. MAY 26, 1956 MILWAUKEE, WIS.
15-154  SISLER, GEORGE HAROLD          D. MARCH 26, 1973 ST. LOUIS, MO.
47- 80  SNIDER, EDWIN DONALD           3037 LAKEMONT DR - FALLBROOK CA 92028
```

```
42- 98  SPAHN, WARREN EDWARD           RR 2 - HARTSHORNE OK 74547
71      SPALDING, ALBERT GOODWILL      D. SEPTEMBER 9, 1915 POINT LOMA, CAL.
07      SPEAKER, TRISTRAM E.           D. DECEMBER 8, 1958 LAKE WHITNEY, TEX.
12-191  STENGEL, CHARLES DILLON        D. SEPTEMBER 29, 1975 GLENDALE, CAL.
23-132  TERRY, WILLIAM HAROLD          BOX 2177 - JACKSONVILLE FL 32203
```

SEE Page 149

85	THOMPSON, SAMUEL L.	D. NOVEMBER 7, 1922 DETROIT, MICH.
02	TINKER, JOSEPH BERT	D. JULY 27, 1948 ORLANDO, FLA.
20-123	TRAYNOR, HAROLD JOSEPH	D. MARCH 16, 1972 PITTSBURGH, PA.
15-166	VANCE, CLARENCE ARTHUR	D. FEBRUARY 16, 1961 HOMOSASSA SPRINGS, FLA.
97	WADDELL, GEORGE EDWARD	D. APRIL 1, 1914 SAN ANTONIO, TEX.
97	WAGNER, JOHN PETER	D. DECEMBER 6, 1955 CARNEGIE, PA.
94	WALLACE, RHODERICK JOHN	D. NOVEMBER 3, 1960 TORRANCE, CAL.
04	WALSH, EDWARD AUGUSTIN	D. MAY 26, 1959 POMPANO BEACH, FLA.
27- 95	WANER, LLOYD JAMES	252 EDGEMERE COURT - OKLAHOMA CITY OK 73118
26- 90	WANER, PAUL GLEE	D. AUGUST 29, 1965 SARASOTA, FLA.
78	WARD, JOHN MONTGOMERY	D. MARCH 4, 1925 AUGUSTA, GA.
HOF	WEISS, GEORGE MARTIN	D. AUGUST 13, 1972 GREENWICH, CONN.
80	WELCH, MICHAEL FRANCIS	D. JULY 30, 1941 NASHUA, N. H.
09	WHEAT, ZACHARY DAVIS	D. MARCH 11, 1972 SEDALIA, MO.
39-126	WILLIAMS, THEODORE SAMUEL	BOX 481 - ISLAMORADA FL 33036

23-144	WILSON, LEWIS ROBERT	D. NOVEMBER 23, 1948 BALTIMORE, MD.
71	WRIGHT, GEORGE	D. AUGUST 31, 1937 BOSTON, MASS.
71	WRIGHT, WILLIAM HARRY	D. OCTOBER 3, 1895 ATLANTIC CITY, N. J.
39-127	WYNN, EARLY	525 BAYVIEW PKWY - NOKOMIS FL 33555
HOF	YAWKEY, THOMAS AUSTIN	D. JULY 9, 1976 BOSTON, MASS.
90	YOUNG, DENTON TRUE	D. NOVEMBER 4, 1955 NEWCOMERSTOWN, O.
17- 93	YOUNGS, ROSS MIDDLEBROOK	D. OCTOBER 22, 1927 SAN ANTONIO, TEX.

Yours very truly,

Geo Wright

Harry Wright
#39 Eliot Street
Boston. Mass.

Cy Young

DEN'S COLLECTORS DEN

Plastic Card Protecting Pages
Largest Selection in Hobby!
16 Different Sizes

FINEST QUALITY PLASTIC SHEETS

FEATURING

* NON—MIGRATING PLASTIC IN ALL SHEETS
* PLASTIC THAT DOES NOT STICK TOGETHER
* STIFFNESS TO PREVENT CARD CURLING
* INTELLIGENT DESIGN
* RESISTANCE TO CRACKING
* FULL COVERAGE OF CARDS, PHOTOS & POSTCARDS

GEORGE HERMAN (BABE) RUTH

BIG LEAGUE CHEWING GUM

SEND $ 1.00 for DEN'S B[...]
48-PAGE CATALOGUE
CATALOGUE WILL BE SEN[...]
FREE WITH ORDER

NO   MIX   &   MATCH

DEN'S COLLECTORS DE[N]

STYLE	POCKETS / CAPACITY	RECOMMENDED FOR	PRICE EACH (DOES NOT INCLUDE P & H)			
			1-24	25-99	100-299	300-600
9	9 / 18	TOPPS (1957—PRESENT), FLEER (1959—63), LEAF (1960), KELLOGG, POST CEREAL, TOPPS CLOTH STICKER CARDS, SSPC (1976), RECENT NON—SPORTS	.25	.23	.21	.19
8	8 / 16	TOPPS (1952—1956), BOWMAN (1953—55)	.25	.23	.21	.19
12	12 / 24	BOWMAN(1948—50), TOPPS (1951 RED AND BLUE BACKS), TICKET STUBS	.25	.23	.21	.19
1	1 / 2	PHOTOGRAPHS (8X10)	.25	.23	.21	.19
2	2 / 4	PHOTOGRAPHS (5X7)	.25	.23	.21	.19
4	4 / 8	POSTCARDS, TOPPS SUPER (1964, 1970, 1971), TOPPS BASKETBALL (1976), EXHIBITS	.25	.23	.21	.19
18	18 / 36	T CARDS, TOPPS COINS, BAZOOKA (1963—67) INDIVIDUAL CARDS)	.35	.35	.30	.27
9G	9 / 18	GOUDEY, DIAMOND STARS, LEAF (1948)	.35	.35	.30	.27
9PB	9 / 18	PLAYBALL, BOWMAN (1951—52), DOUBLE PLAY, 1975 TOPPS MINIS	.35	.35	.30	.27
1C	1 / 2	TURKEY REDS (T—3), 1977 PEPSI GLOVE AND DISC CARDS, PRESS GUIDES, POCKET SIZE 6"X9"	.35	.35	.30	.27
3	3 / 6	HOSTESS PANELS, HIRES ROOT BEER	.30	.25	.25	.20
6V	6 / 12	1955 TOPPS DOUBLE HEADERS, CONNIE MACKS, CURRENT STARS, TEAM CARDS, MECCA DOUBLE FOLDERS, HASSAN TRIPPLE FOLDERS, BAZOOKA PANELS (1963—67)	.35	.35	.30	.27
6D	6 / 12	RED MAN (WITH OR WITHOUT TABS), DISC. KAHN'S (1955—67)	.35	.35	.30	.27
1Y	1 / 1	YEARBOOKS, PROGRAMS, MAGAZINES, HOBBYPAPERS, TABLOIDS, POCKET SIZE 9"X12"	.35	.35	.30	.27
1S	1 / 2	ALL STAR GALLERY INDIVIDUAL PANELS, SMALL PROGRAMS AND OVERSIZED PHOTOS, POCKET SIZE 8½" X 11"	.30	.30	.25	.20
10	10 / 20	MATCHBOOK COVERS, POCKET SIZE 1 3/4" X 4 3/4"	.35	.35	.30	.27

POSTAGE & HANDLING SCHEDULE (P & H)
$ .01 to $ 20.00 add $ 2.00
$ 20.01 to $ 30.00 add $ 2.50
Over $ 30.00 add $ 3.00

MARYLAND RESIDENTS ADD 5% TAX
CANADIAN ORDERS – BOOKS ONLY
CANADIAN BOOK ORDERS ADD 25% postage
Orders outside contiguous U.S.A. add 25% more
U.S. FUNDS ONLY

TRY **DEN'S COLLECTORS DEN**
Dept.   G
P.O. BOX 606, LAUREL, MD 20707

DON'T SETTLE FOR LESS THAN THE BEST. BE SURE THAT THE STYLES 9,8,4,12,1 & 2 HAVE DEN'S COLLECTORS DEN EMBOSSED ON THE BORDER OF THE SHEET.

16

PLAYERS DEBUTING FROM 1871 TO 1909

89	ANDERSON, DAVID S	D. MARCH 22, 1897
89	ANDERSON, VARNEY SAMUEL	D. NOVEMBER 5, 1941 ROCKFORD, ILL
90	ANDREWS, JAMES PRATT	D. DECEMBER 27, 1907 CHICAGO, ILL.
84	ANNIS, WILLIAM PERLEY	D. JUNE 10, 1923 KENNEBUNKPORT, ME.
04	APPLEGATE, FREDERICK ROMAINE	D. APRIL 21, 1968 WILLIAMSPORT, PA.
05	ARMBRUSTER, CHARLES A	D. OCTOBER 7, 1964 GRANTS PASS, ORE.
02	ARMOUR, WILLIAM R	D. DECEMBER 2, 1922 MINNEAPOLIS, MINN.
03	AUBREY, HARRY HERBERT	D. SEPTEMBER 18, 1953 BALTIMORE, MD.
07	AUTRY, WILLIAM ASKEW	D. JANUARY 16, 1976 SANTA ROSA, CALIF.
84	AYDELOTT, JACOB STUART	D. OCTOBER 22, 1926 DETROIT, MICH.
09	BACKMAN, LESTER JOHN	D. NOVEMBER 8, 1975
83	BAKER, NORMAN LESLIE	D. FEBRUARY 20, 1949 HURFFVILLE, N. J.
07	BALL, JAMES CHANDLER	D. APRIL 7, 1963 GLENDALE, CALIF.
80	BANCROFT, FRANK CARTER	D. MAY 31, 1921 CINCINNATI, O.

Yours truly
F. C. Bancroft

05	BARBEAU, WILLIAM JOSEPH	D. SEPTEMBER 10, 1969 MILWAUKEE, WIS.
84	BARRETT, MARTIN F	D. JANUARY 29, 1910 HOLYOKE, MASS.
05	BARRY, EDWARD	D. JUNE 19, 1920 MONTAGUE, MASS.
04	BATCH, EMIL HENRY	D. AUGUST 10, 1926 BROOKLYN, NY
84	BEACH, STONEWALL JACKSON	D. JULY 23, 1896 ALEXANDRIA, VA.
95	BEAM, ERNEST JOSEPH	D. SEPTEMBER 12, 1918 MANSFIELD, O.
71	BEARMAN, CHARLES S	D. AUGUST 4, 1879 HOBOKEN, NJ
09	BECKENDORF, HENRY WARD	D. SEPTEMBER 15, 1949 JACKSON HEIGHTS, NY
84	BEHEL, STEPHEN ARNOLD DOUGLAS	D. FEBRUARY 15, 1945 LOS ANGELES, CALIF.
71	BELLAN, ESTEBAN ENRIQUE	D. AUGUST 8, 1932 HAVANA, CUBA
89	BELLMAN, JOHN HUTCHINS	D. DECEMBER 8, 1931 LOUISVILLE, KY.
83	BENEDICT, ARTHUR M	D. JANUARY 20, 1948 DENVER, COLO.
72	BENTLEY, CYRUS G.	D. FEBRUARY 26, 1873 MIDDLETOWN, CONN.
84	BERRY, CHARLES JOSEPH	D. JANUARY 22, 1940 PHILLIPSBURG, N. J.
04	BERRY, CLAUDE ELZY	D. FEBRUARY 1, 1974 RICHMOND, IND.
03	BERTE, HARRY THOMAS	D. MAY 6, 1952 LOS ANGELES, CALIF.
03	BETTS, HARRY MATTHEW	D. MAY 22, 1946 SAN ANTONIO, TEX.
01	BEVILLE, CLARENCE BENJAMIN	D. JANUARY 5, 1937 YOUNTVILLE, CALIF.
86	BIERBAUER, LOUIS W	D. JANUARY 31, 1926 ERIE, PA.
09	BLANK, FRANK IGNATZ	D. DECEMBER 8, 1961 ST. LOUIS, MO.
90	BLAUVELT, HENRY RUSSELL	D. DECEMBER 28, 1926 PORTLAND, ORE.
83	BLOGG, WESLEY C	D. MARCH 10, 1897
91	BOONE, GEORGE MORRIS	D. SEPTEMBER 24, 1910 LOUISVILLE, KY.
88	BORCHERS, GEORGE BENARD	D. OCTOBER 24, 1938 SACRAMENTO, CAL.
03	BOWCOCK, BENJAMIN JAMES	D. JUNE 16, 1961 NEW BEDFORD, MASS.
94	BOYD, JACOB HENRY	D. AUGUST 12, 1932 GETTYSBURG, PA.
84	BOYLE, HENRY J	D. MAY 25, 1932 PHILADELPHIA, PA.
75	BRADY, THOMAS A.	D. 1921 HARTFORD, CONN.
98	BRANSFIELD, WILLIAM EDWARD	D. MAY 1, 1947 WORCESTER, MASS.
05	BRIDWELL, ALBERT HENRY	D. JANUARY 24, 1969 PORTSMOUTH, O.
90	BRIGGS, GRANT	D. MAY 31, 1928 PITTSBURGH, PA.
80	BRIODY, CHARLES F	D. JUNE 22, 1903 CHICAGO, ILL.
72	BRITT, JAMES EDWARD	D. FEBRUARY 28, 1923 SAN FRANCISCO, CALIF.
06	BROUTHERS, ARTHUR H	D. SEPTEMBER 2, 1959 CHARLESTON, SC
81	BROWN, FREEMAN	D. DECEMBER 27, 1916 WORCESTER, MASS.
84	BROWN, JAMES W. H.	D. APRIL 6, 1908 WILLIAMSPORT, PA.
72	BROWN, OLIVER	D. SEPTEMBER 23, 1932 BROOKLYN, NY
09	BROWN, PAUL PERCIVAL	D. MAY 29, 1955 LOS ANGELES, CAL
05	BRUCKMILLER, ANDREW	D. JANUARY 12, 1970 MCKEESPORT, PA
07	BRUSH, ROBERT	D. APRIL 2, 1944 SAN BERNARDINO, CAL
88	BRYNAN, CHARLES RULEY	D. MAY 10, 1925 PHILADELPHIA, PA.
05	BUCHANAN, JAMES FORREST	D. JUNE 15, 1949 RANDOLPH, NEB.
89	BUCKENBERGER, ALBERT C.	D. JULY 1, 1917 SYRACUSE, N. Y.
95	BUCKINGHAM, EDWARD TAYLOR	D. JULY 30, 1942 BRIDGEPORT, CONN
77	BUNCE, JOSHUA	D. APRIL 28, 1912 BROOKLYN, N. Y.
88	BURDICK, WILLIAM BYRON	D. OCTOBER 23, 1949 SPOKANE, WASH.
88	BURNETT, HERCULES H	D. OCTOBER 4, 1936 LOUISVILLE, KY.
87	BURNHAM, GEORGE WALTER	D. NOVEMBER 18, 1902 DETROIT, MICH.
08	BUSH, OWEN JOSEPH	D. MARCH 28, 1972 INDIANAPOLIS, IND.
84	BUTLER, FRANK E	D. APRIL 9, 1921 SOUTH BOSTON, MASS
02	BUTLER, ISAAC BURR	D. MARCH 17, 1948 OAKLAND, CAL
83	BUTLER, ORMOND HOOK	D. SEPTEMBER 12, 1915 MOUNT HOPE, MD.
01	BUTLER, JOHN ALBERT	D. FEBRUARY 2, 1950 BOSTON, MASS.
04	BYERS, JAMES WILLIAM	D. SEPTEMBER 8, 1948 BALTIMORE, MD.
84	CALDWELL, RALPH GRANT	D. AUGUST 5, 1969 WEST TRENTON, NJ
06	CALLAHAN, PATRICK HENRY	D. FEBRUARY 4, 1940 LOUISVILLE, KY
76	CAMERON, JOHN S	D. AUGUST 17, 1951 BOSTON, MASS.
08	CAMMEYER, WILLIAM HENRY	D. SEPTEMBER 4, 1898 BROOKLYN, N. Y.
73	CAMPBELL, ARTHUR VINCENT	D. NOVEMBER 16, 1969 TOWSON, MD
07	CAMPBELL, HUGH	D. 1881 ELIZABETH, N. J.
07	CAMPBELL, MARC THADDEUS	D. FEBRUARY 13, 1946 NEW BETHLEHEM, PA
75	CANTILLON, JOE	D. JANUARY 31, 1930 HICKMAN, KY
03	CARBINE, JOHN C	D. SEPTEMBER 11, 1915 CHICAGO, ILL
90	CARISCH, FREDERICK BEHLMER	D. APRIL 19, 1977 SAN GABRIEL, CALIF.
04	CARMAN, GEORGE WARTMAN	D. JUNE 16, 1939 LANCASTER, PA.
06	CARNEY, WILLIAM J	D. JULY 31, 1938 HOPKINS, MINN.
91	CARRIGAN, WILLIAM FRANCIS	D. JULY 8, 1969 LEWISTON, ME.
90	CARSEY, WILFRED	D. MARCH 29, 1960 MIAMI, FLA.
01	CARTWRIGHT, EDWARD CHARLES	D. SEPTEMBER 3, 1933 ST. PETERSBURG, FLA.
	CASE, CHARLES EMMETT	D. APRIL 16, 1964 CLERMONT, OH

09	CASEY, JOSEPH FELIX	D. JUNE 2, 1966 MELROSE, MASS
79	CASKIN, EDWARD JAMES	D. OCTOBER 9, 1924 DANVERS, MASS.
04	CASSADY, HARRY DELBERT	D. APRIL 22, 1969 FRESNO, CALIF.
07	CASTLETON, ROYAL EUGENE	D. JUNE 24, 1967 LOS ANGELES, CALIF.
02	CASTRO, LOUIS M.	D. VENEZUELA
85	CAYLOR, OLIVER PERRY	D. OCTOBER 19, 1897 WINONA, MINN.
08	CHARLES, RAYMOND	D. AUGUST 4, 1959 BETHELEHEM, PA
05	CICOTTE, EDWARD VICTOR	D. MAY 5, 1969 DETROIT, MICH.
72	CLARE, DENNIS J.	D. NOVEMBER 26, 1928 BROOKLYN, N. Y.
02	CLARK, ALFRED ROBERT	D. JULY 26, 1956 OGDEN, UTAH
95	CLARK, WILLIAM OTIS	D. NOVEMBER 13, 1932 PITTSBURGH, PA
90	CLARKE, ARTHUR FRANKLIN	D. NOVEMBER 14, 1949 BROOKLINE, MASS
08	CLEMENT, WALLACE OAKES	D. NOVEMBER 1, 1953 CORAL GABLES, FLA
82	CLINE, JOHN	D. SEPTEMBER 23, 1916 LOUISVILLE, KY.
05	COCKMAN, JAMES	D. SEPTEMBER 28, 1947 GUELPH, ONT
97	COLEMAN, PIERCE D	D. FEBRUARY 16, 1948 VAN NUYS, CALIF.
99	COLLIFLOWER, JAMES HARRY	D. AUGUST 14, 1961 WASHINGTON, D.C.
74	COLLINS, DANIEL THOMAS	D. SEPTEMBER 21, 1883 NEW ORLE ANS, LA.
09	COLLINS, RAYMOND WILLISTON	D. JANUARY 9, 1970 BURLINGTON, VT.
90	CONROY, BERNARD PATRICK	D. NOVEMBER 25, 1937 PHILADELPHIA, PA.
84	COOK, PAUL	D. MAY 26, 1905 ROCHESTER, N. Y.
90	CORCORAN, THOMAS WILLIAM	D. JUNE 25, 1960 PLAINFIELD, CONN.
84	COUGHLIN, EDWARD E	D. DECEMBER 25, 1952 HARTFORD, CONN.
02	COURTNEY, ERNEST E	D. FEBRUARY 29, 1920 BUFFALO, N. Y.
03	COVENEY, JOHN PATRICK	D. MARCH 28, 1961 WAYLAND, MASS.
84	COX, FRANK BERNHARDT	D. JUNE 24, 1928 HARTFORD, CONN.
73	CRANE, FREDERICK WILLIAM HOTCHKISS	D. APRIL 27, 1925 BROOKLYN, N. Y.
90	CREELY, AUGUST L	D. APRIL 22, 1934 ST. LOUIS, MO.
01	CROCKETT, DAVID SOLOMON	D. FEBRUARY 23, 1961 CHARLOTTESVILLE, VA.
99	CROFT, HENRY T	D. DECEMBER 11, 1933 OAK PARK, ILL.
09	CROOKE, THOMAS A	D. APRIL 5, 1929 QUANTICO, VA
89	CROOKS, CHARLES JOHN	D. FEBRUARY 2, 1918 ST. LOUIS, MO.
84	CROSBY, GEORGE W. W.	D. JANUARY 9, 1913 SAN FRANCISCO, CALIF.
93	CROSS, GEORGE LEWIS	D. OCTOBER 9, 1930 MANCHESTER, NH
92	CROSS, MONTFORD MONTGOMERY	D. JUNE 21, 1934 PHILADELPHIA, PA.
84	CROTHERS, DOUGLAS	D. MARCH 29, 1907 ST. LOUIS, MO.
82	CROTTY, JOSEPH	D. JUNE 22, 1926 MINNEAPOLIS, MINN.
06	CUNNINGHAM, MODY	D. DECEMBER 10, 1969 LANCASTER, S. C.
99	CURLEY, WALTER JAMES	D. SEPTEMBER 23, 1920 WORCESTER, MASS
02	CURRAN, SIMON FRANCIS	D. MAY 19, 1936 DORCHESTER, MASS.
03	CURTIS, EUGENE HOLMES	D. JANUARY 1, 1919 STEUBENVILLE, O.
05	CURTIS, FREDERICK MARION	D. APRIL 5, 1939 MINNEAPOLIS, MINN.
91	CUSHMAN, CHARLES H.	D. JUNE 29, 1909 MILWAUKEE, WIS.
02	CUSHMAN, HARVEY BARNES	D. DECEMBER 27, 1920 EMSWORTH, PA.
84	CUSICK, ANDREW DANIEL	D. AUGUST 6, 1929 CHICAGO, ILL.
84	DANIELS, CHARLES L	D. FEBRUARY 9, 1938 BOSTON, MASS.
09	DANZIG, HAROLD P	D. JULY 14, 1931 SAN FRANCISCO, CAL.
93	DARBY, GEORGE WILLIAM	D. FEBRUARY 25, 1937 SACRAMENTO, CALIF.
83	DARLING, DELL CONRAD	D. NOVEMBER 20, 1904 ERIE, PA.
88	DAVIDSON, MORDECAI H.	D. SEPTEMBER 6, 1940 LOUISVILLE, KY.
09	DAVIDSON, WILLIAM SIMPSON	D. MAY 23, 1954 LINCOLN, NEB.
84	DAVIS, JAMES J	D. FEBRUARY 14, 1921 ST. LOUIS, MO.
99	DAY, JOHN B.	D. JANUARY 25, 1925 CLIFFSIDE, N. J.
84	DEALY, PATRICK E	D. DECEMBER 17, 1924 BUFFALO, N. Y.
84	DEASLEY, JOHN	D. DECEMBER 25, 1910 PHILADELPHIA, PA.
02	DEININGER, OTTO CHARLES	D. SEPTEMBER 25, 1950 BOSTON, MASS
90	DELANEY, WILLIAM L	D. MARCH 1, 1942 CANTON, O.
09	DENT, ELLIOTT ESTILL	D. NOVEMBER 25, 1974 BIRMINGHAM, ALA.
84	DEPANGHER, MICHAEL ANTHONY	D. JULY 7, 1915 SAN FRANCISCO, CALIF.
85	DERBY, EUGENE A	D. OCTOBER 12, 1928 BUFFALO, N. Y.
90	DEWALD, CHARLES H	D. AUGUST 22, 1904 CLEVELAND, O.
96	DIDDLEBOCK, HENRY H	D. FEBRUARY 5, 1900 PHILADELPHIA, PA.
86	DONAHUE, JAMES AUGUSTUS	D. APRIL 19, 1935 LOCKPORT, ILL.
01	DONOVAN, THOMAS JOSEPH	D. FEBRUARY 20, 1955 WILLIAMSPORT, PA
92	DOOMS, HENRY E	D. DECEMBER 14, 1899 ST. LOUIS, MO.
03	DOSCHER, JOHN HERMAN	D. MAY 27, 1971 RIDGEFIELD PARK, N.J.
09	DOWNEY, THOMAS EDWARD	D. AUGUST 3 1961 PASSAIC, NJ
90	DOWSE, THOMAS JOSEPH	D. DECEMBER 14, 1946 RIVERSIDE, CAL.
89	DOYLE, JOHN JOSEPH	D. DECEMBER 31, 1958 HOLYOKE, MASS.
85	DOYLE, JOSEPH J	D. JANUARY 7, 1906 WHITE PLAINS, N.Y.
07	DOYLE, LAWRENCE JOSEPH	D. MARCH 1, 1974 SARANAC LAKE, N.Y.
02	DRILL, LEWIS L.	D. JULY 4, 1969 ST. PAUL, MINN.
02	DUNHAM, HENRY HUSTON	D. JANUARY 16, 1934 CLEVELAND, O.
03	DUNLEAVY, JOHN FRANCIS	D. APRIL 12, 1944 SOUTH NORWALK, CT
97	DUNN, JOHN JOSEPH	D. OCTOBER 22, 1928 TOWSON, MD.

John Dunn (signature)

84	DUNN, STEPHEN	D. MAY 5, 1933 LONDON, ONT
07	DURBIN, BLAINE ALONZO	D. SEPTEMBER 11, 1943 KIRKWOOD, MO
98	EAGLE, WILLIAM LYCURGUS	D. APRIL 27, 1951 CHURCHTON, MD.
90	EARL, HOWARD J.	D. DECEMBER 22, 1916 NORTH BAY, N. Y.
00	EASON, MALCOLM WAYNE	D. APRIL 16, 1970 DOUGLAS, ARIZ.
84	EASTERDAY, HENRY P	D. MARCH 30, 1895 PHILADELPHIA, PA.
09	EASTERLY, THEODORE HARRISON	D. JULY 6, 1981 CLEAR LAKE HIGHLANDS, CAL
08	EDMONDSON, ROBERT E.	D. AUGUST 14, 1931 LAWRENCE, KAN
06	EDMONDSTON, SAMUEL SHERWOOD	D. APRIL 12, 1979 CORPUS CHRISTI, TEX.
06	EELLS, HARRY ARCHIBALD	D. OCTOBER 15, 1940 LOS ANGELES, CAL

75	ELLICK, JOSEPH	D.	APRIL 21, 1923 KANSAS CITY, MO.
82	EVANS, F. FORD	D.	DECEMBER 15, 1884 AKRON, OH
87	FAGIN, WILLIAM A.	D.	MARCH 21, 1930 TROY, N. Y.
84	FALCH, ANTON C	D.	MARCH 31, 1936 WAUWATOSA, WIS.
79	FARRELL, JOHN A	D.	FEBRUARY 10, 1914 OVERBROOK, N. J.
01	FARRELL, JOHN SEBASTIAN	D.	MAY 13, 1921 KANSAS CITY, MO.
01	FERGUSON, CHARLES AUGUSTUS	D.	MAY 17, 1931 SAULT STE MARIE, MICH.
89	FERSON, ALEXANDER	D.	DECEMBER 5, 1957 BOSTON, MASS.
06	FETZER, WILLIAM MCKINNON	D.	MAY 3, 1959 BUTNER, NC
94	FIGGEMEIER, FRANK Y	D.	APRIL 15, 1915 ST. LOUIS, MO.
84	FIRTH, JOHN E	D.	JUNE 23, 1902 TEWKSBURY, MASS.
02	FISHER, EDWARD FREDERICK	D.	JULY 27, 1951 SPOKANE, WASH.
98	FISHER, NEWTON	D.	FEBRUARY 28, 1947 CHICAGO, ILL
04	FISHER, THOMAS CHALMERS	D.	SEPTEMBER 3, 1972 ANDERSON, IND.
90	FITZGERALD, DENNIS S	D.	OCTOBER 16, 1936 NEW HAVEN, CONN.
91	FITZGERALD, JOHN H	D.	MARCH 31, 1921 BOSTON, MASS.
08	FLATER, JOHN WILLIAM	D.	MARCH 20, 1970 WESTMINSTER, MD
98	FLICK, ELMER HARRISON	D.	JANUARY 9, 1971 BEDFORD, O.
87	FOGEL, HORACE S.	D.	NOVEMBER 15, 1928 PHILADELPHIA, PA.
79	FOLEY, CHARLES JOSEPH	D.	OCTOBER 20, 1898 BOSTON, MASS.
05	FORD, EUGENE WYMAN	D.	AUGUST 23, 1973 DUNEDIN, FLA.
09	FORMAN, WILLIAM ORANGE	D.	OCTOBER 3, 1958 UNIONTOWN, PA.
08	FOSTER, EDDY LEE	D.	MARCH 1, 1929 MONTGOMERY, ALA.
90	FRAZER, GEORGE KASSON	D.	FEBRUARY 5, 1913 SYRACUSE, N. Y.
08	FREEMAN, FRANK ELLSWORTH	D.	SEPTEMBER 30, 1952 LOS ANGELES, CALIF.
88	FREEMAN, JULIUS B	D.	JUNE 10, 1921 ST. LOUIS, MO.
01	FRIEL, WILLIAM EDWARD	D.	DECEMBER 24, 1959 RICHMOND HEIGHTS, MO
09	FROELICH, WILLIAM PALMER	D.	SEPTEMBER 1, 1916 PITTSBURGH, PA.
86	FULLER, EDWARD ASTON WHITE	D.	MARCH 15, 1935 HYATTSVILLE, MD.
84	FULMER, CHRISTOPHER	D.	NOVEMBER 9, 1931 TAMAQUA, PA
82	FUSSELBACK, EDWARD	D.	APRIL 14, 1926 PHILADELPHIA, PA.
86	GAFFNEY, JOHN H	D.	AUGUST 8, 1913 NEW YORK, N. Y.
84	GAGUS, CHARLES FREDERICK	D.	JANUARY 16, 1918 SAN FRANCISCO, CALIF.
08	GAISER, FREDERICK JACOB	D.	OCTOBER 9, 1918 TRENTON, N. J.
89	GALLIGAN, JOHN M	D.	JULY 17, 1901 NEW YORK, N. Y.
72	GALVIN, JOHN	D.	APRIL 20, 1904 BROOKLYN, N. Y.
98	GANNON, WILLIAM G	D.	APRIL 26, 1927 FORT WORTH, TEX
08	GARDNER, WILLIAM LAWRENCE	D.	MARCH 11, 1976 ST. GEORGE, VT.
96	GEIER, PHILIP LOUIS	D.	SEPTEMBER 20, 1967 SPOKANE, WASH.
90	GERMAN, LESTER STANLEY	D.	JUNE 10, 1939 GERMANTOWN, MD.
09	GETZ, GUSTAVE	D.	MAY 28, 1969 KEANSBURG, N.J.
88	GIBSON, LEIGHTON P	D.	OCTOBER 11, 1907 TALMADGE, PA.
84	GIFFORD, JAMES H.	D.	DECEMBER 19, 1901 COLUMBUS, O.
90	GILBERT, HARRY L	D.	APRIL 10, 1906 POTTSTOWN, PA.
90	GILBERT, JOHN G.	D.	NOVEMBER 12, 1903 POTTSTOWN, PA.
09	GILLIGAN, JOHN PATRICK	D.	NOVEMBER 19, 1980 MODESTO, CALIF.
75	GILMORE, JAMES	D.	NOVEMBER 18, 1928 BALTIMORE, MD.
02	GLENDON, MARTIN J	D.	NOVEMBER 6, 1950 NORWOOD PARK, ILL.
01	GOCHNAUR, JOHN PETER	D.	SEPTEMBER 27, 1929 ALTOONA, PA.
99	GOECKEL, WILLIAM JOHN	D.	NOVEMBER 1, 1922 PHILADELPHIA, PA
91	GORMLEY, JOSEPH	D.	JULY 2, 1950 SUMMIT HILL PA
03	GOUZZIE, CLYDE	D.	SEPTEMBER 21, 1907 DENVER, COLO
90	GRAFF, LOUIS GEORGE	D.	APRIL 16, 1955 BRYN MAWR, PA.
07	GRAHAM, OSCAR M	D.	OCYOBER 15, 1931 MOLINE, ILL.
08	GRANEY, JOHN GLADSTONE	D.	APRIL 20, 1978 LOUISIANA, MO.
84	GRAY, JAMES W	D.	JANUARY 31, 1938 PITTSBURGH, PA
03	GREY, RCMER CARL	D.	NOVEMBER 9, 1934 ALTADENA, CALIF.
84	GRIFFIN, THOMAS WILLIAM	D.	APRIL 17, 1933 ROCKFORD, ILL.
09	GROOM, ROBERT	D.	FEBRUARY 19, 1948 BELLEVILLE, ILL.
79	GROSS, EMIL M	D.	AUGUST 24, 1921 EAGLE RIVER, WIS
87	GRUBER, HENRY JOHN	D.	SEPTEMBER 26, 1932 NEW HAVEN , CONN.
84	HACKETT, CHARLES M	D.	AUGUST 1, 1898 HOLYOKE, MASS.
83	HAGAN, ARTHUR CHARLES	D.	MARCH 25, 1936 PROVIDENCE, R. I.
82	HALBRITER, EDWARD L	D.	AUGUST 9, 1936 LOS ANGELES, CALIF.
85	HALLSTROM, CHARLES E	D.	MAY 6, 1949 CHICAGO, ILL.
90	HAMBURG, CHARLES M	D.	MAY 18, 1931 UNION, N. J.
03	HANLON, WILLIAM	D.	MARCH 18, 1951 SACRAMENTO, CALIF.
84	HANNA, JOHN	D.	NOVEMBER 7, 1930 PHILADELPHIA, PA.
06	HANNIFAN, JOHN JOSEPH	D.	OCTOBER 27, 1945 NORTHAMPTON, MASS.
84	HARDIE, LOUIS W	D.	MARCH 5, 1929 OAKLAND, CALIF.
85	HART, JAMES A.	D.	JULY 18, 1919 CHICAGO, ILL.
01	HART, JAMES BURTON	D.	JANUARY 29, 1921 SACRAMENTO, CALIF.
08	HARTMAN, CHARLES OTTO	D.	OCTOBER 22, 1960 LOS ANGELES, CAL
00	HARVEY, ERVIN KING	D.	JUNE 3, 1954 SANTA MONICA, CAL
75	HAUTZ, CHARLES A	D.	JANUARY 24, 1929 ST. LOUIS, MO.
01	HEARNE, HUGH JOSEPH	D.	SEPTEMBER 22, 1932 TROY, N. Y.
00	HEILBRONER, LOUIS WILBUR	D.	DECEMBER 21, 1933 FORT WAYNE, IND.
86	HEINZMAN, JOHN PETER	D.	NOVEMBER 10, 1914 LOUISVILLE, KY
84	HENGLE, EMORY J	D.	DECEMBER 11, 1924 RIVER FOREST, ILL.
87	HERR, EDWARD JOSEPH	D.	JULY 18, 1943 ST. LOUIS, MO
71	HEUBEL, GEORGE A	D.	JANUARY 22, 1896 PHILADELPHIA, PA
88	HEWETT, WALTER F	D.	OCTOBER 7, 1944 WASHINGTON, D. C.
09	HIGGINS, THOMAS EDWARD	D.	FEBRUARY 14, 1959 ELGIN, ILL.
01	HIGH, EDWARD T	D.	FEBRUARY 10, 1926 BALTIMORE, MD.
85	HILAND, JOHN WILLIAM	D.	APRIL 10, 1901 PHILADELPHIA, PA.
02	HILDEBRAND, GEORGE ALBERT	D.	MAY 30, 1960 RESEDA, CALIF.
05	HILLEBRAND, HOMER HILLER HENRY	D.	JANUARY 23, 1974 ELSINORE, CALIF.
83	HILSEY, CHARLES T	D.	OCTOBER 31, 1918 PHILADELPHIA, PA.
05	HIMES, JOHN HERB	D.	DECEMBER 16, 1949 JOLIET, ILL.
01	HINTON, JOHN ROBERT	D.	JULY 19, 1920 BRADDOCK, PA.
08	HOCH, HARRY KELLER	D.	OCTOBER 27, 1981 LEWES, DEL.
88	HOFFNER, JOHN A	D.	NOVEMBER 22, 1946 DANVILLE, PA.
85	HOFFORD, JOHN WILLIAM	D.	DECEMBER 16, 1915 PHILADELPHIA, PA.
01	HOGAN, HARRY S	D.	JANUARY 25, 1934 SYRACUSE, N. Y.
72	HOLDSWORTH, JAMES	D.	MARCH 22, 1918 NEW YORK, N. Y.
92	HOLLISON, JOHN HENRY	D.	AUGUST 19, 1969 CHICAGO, ILL.
06	HOLLY, EDWARD WILLIAM	D.	NOVEMBER 27, 1973 WILLIAMSPORT, PA.

02	HOOKER, WILLIAM EDWARD	D. JULY 2, 1929 RICHMOND, VA.
09	HOOPER, HARRY BARTHOLOMEW	D. DECEMBER 18, 1974 SANTA CRUZ, CALIF.
73	HOOPER, MICHAEL H	D. DECEMBER 1, 1927 BALTIMORE, MD.
07	HOPE, SAMUEL	D. JUNE 30, 1946 GREENPORT, N. Y.
07	HOPKINS, JOHN WINTON	D. OCTOBER 2, 1929 PHOEBUS, VA.
02	HOPKINS, MICHAEL JOSEPH	D. FEBRUARY 5, 1952 PITTSBURGH, PA.
96	HORTON, ELMER E	D. AUGUST 12, 1920 VIENNA, N. Y.
09	HOWARD, PAUL JOSEPH	D. AUGUST 29, 1968 MIAMI, FLA
98	HOWELL, HARRY	D. MAY 22, 1956 SPOKANE, WASH.
02	HUGHES, EDWARD	D. OCTOBER 24, 1933 CHICAGO, ILL.
98	HURST, TIMOTHY CARROLL	D. JUNE 4, 1915 POTTSVILLE, PA.
06	HUSTON, HARRY EMANUEL KRESS	D. OCTOBER 13, 1969 BLACKWELL, OKLA
09	HYATT, ROBERT HAMILTON	D. SEPTEMBER 11, 1963 LIBERTY LAKE, WASH
03	IOTT, FRED JOHN	D. FEBRUARY 17, 1941 ISLAND FALLS, ME.
05	JACKSON, CHARLES BERNARD	D. NOVEMBER 23, 1957 SCOTBLUFF, NEB.
02	JACOBS, MORRIS ELMORE	D. MARCH 26, 1949 LOUISVILLE, KOC
09	JAMES, BERTON HULON	D. JANUARY 2, 1959 ADAIRVILLE, KY.
72	JEWETT, NATHAN W	D. FEBRUARY 23, 1914 BRONX, N. Y.
73	JOHNS, THOMAS PEARCE	D. APRIL 13, 1927 BALTIMORE, MD.
89	JONES, ALEXANDER M	D. APRIL 4, 1941 WOODVILLE, PA.
01	JONES, DAVID JEFFERSON	D. MARCH 30, 1972 MANKATO, MINN.
07	JONES, ELIJAH ALBERT	D. APRIL 29, 1943 PONTIAC, MICH.
03	JORDAN, ADOLF OTTO	D. DECEMBER 23, 1972 PITTSBURGH, PA
94	JORDAN, HARRY J	D. MARCH 1, 1920 PITTSBURGH, PA.
90	JORDAN, MICHAEL HENRY	D. SEPTEMBER 25, 1940 LAWRENCE, MASS
84	JOY, ALCYSIUS C	D. JUNE 28, 1937 WASHINGTON, D. C.
06	JUDE, FRANK	D. MAY 4, 1961 BROWNSVILLE, TEX.
05	JUSTIS, WALTER NEWTON	D. OCTOBER 4, 1941 LAWRENCEBURG, IND
87	KEATING, ROBERT M	D. JANUARY 19, 1922 SPRINGFIELD, MASS
86	KEEFE, GEORGE W	D. AUGUST 24, 1935 WASHINGTON, D.C.
08	KELLOGG, ALBERT CLEMENT	D. JULY 21, 1953 PORTLAND, ORE.
07	KELLY, JOHN B	D. MARCH 19, 1944 BALTIMORE, MD
82	KELLY, JOHN FRANCIS	D. APRIL 13, 1908 PATERSON, N. J.
87	KELLY, JOHN O.	D. MARCH 27, 1926 MALBA, N. Y.
83	KENNEDY, EDWARD	D. MAY 20, 1905 NEW YORK, N. Y.
90	KENNEDY, JAMES C.	D. APRIL 20, 1904 BRIGHTON BEACH, N. Y.
84	KENNEDY, WILLIAM EDWARD	D. DECEMBER 22, 1912 CHEYENNE, WYO.
02	KENNEDY, SHERMAN MONTGOMERY	D. AUGUST 15, 1945 PASADENA, TEX.
03	KERWIN, DANIEL PATRICK	D. JULY 13, 1960 PHILADELPHIA, PA.
84	KILEY, JOHN FREDERICK	D. DECEMBER 18, 1940 NORWOOD, MASS.
05	KINSELLA, EDWARD WILLIAM	D. JANUARY 17, 1976 BLOOMINGTON, ILL.
82	KINZIE, WALTER H	D. NOVEMBER 5, 1909 CHICAGO, ILL.
90	KITTREDGE, MALACHI J	D. JUNE 23, 1928 GARY, IND.
09	KLAWITTER, ALBERT C	D. MAY 2, 1950 MILWAUKEE, WIS
91	KLING, WILLIAM	D. AUGUST 25, 1934 KANSAS CITY, MO.
88	KNELL, PHILIP LOUIS	D. JUNE 5, 1944 SANTA MONICA, CALIF.
09	KNETZER, ELNER ELLSWORTH	D. OCTOBER 3, 1975 PITTSBURGH, PA.
07	KNOTTS, JOSEPH STEVEN	D. SEPTEMBER 15, 1950 PHILADELPHIA, PA.
71	KOHLER, HARRY	D. AUGUST 27, 1934 BALTIMORE, MD.
09	KONNICK, MICHAEL ALOYSIUS	D. JULY 9, 1971 WILKES-BARRE, PA.
96	KOSTAL, JOSEPH	D. OCTOBER 17, 1933 GUELPH, ONTARIO
09	KUSTUS, JOSEPH J.	D. APRIL 27, 1916 ELOISE, MICH.
09	LAFITTE, EDWARD FRANCIS	D. APRIL 12, 1971 JENKINTOWN, PA.
07	LANFORD, LEWIS GROVER	D. SEPTEMBER 14, 1970 WOODRUFF, SC
08	LATTIMORE, WILLIAM HERSHEL	D. OCTOBER 30, 1919 COLORADO SPRINGS, COLO
01	LAWSON, ROBERT BAKER	D. OCTOBER 28, 1952 CHAPEL HILL, NC
98	LEACH, THOMAS WILLIAM	D. SEPTEMBER 29, 1969 HAINES CITY, FLA.
74	LEDWITH, MICHAEL	D. JANUARY 2, 1929 BRONX, N. Y.
05	LEIFIELD, ALBERT PETER	D. OCTOBER 10, 1970 ALEXANDRIA, VA.
84	LEVIS, CHARLES H	D. OCTOBER 16, 1926 ST. LOUIS, MO.
05	LINDSAY, CHRISTIAN H.	D. JANUARY 25, 1941 CLEVELAND, O.
97	LIPP, THOMAS C	D. MAY 30, 1932 BALTIMORE, MD.
01	LIVINGSTON, JACOB M	D. MARCH 22, 1949 WASSAIC, N. Y.
01	LIVINGSTON, PATRICK JOSEPH	D. SEPTEMBER 19, 1977 CLEVELAND, O.
96	LIZOTTE, ABEL	D. DECEMBER 4, 1926 WILKES-BARRE, PA.
99	LOCHHEAD, HARRY ROBERT	D. AUGUST 22, 1909 STOCKTON, CALIF.
01	LOOS, IVAN	D. FEBRUARY 23, 1956 DARBY, PA.
04	LOUDENSLAGER, CHARLES EDWARD	D. OCTOBER 31, 1933 BALTIMORE, MD
03	LOVETT, JOHN	D. DECEMBER 5, 1937 MURRAY CITY, OH
84	LUCAS, HENRY V.	D. NOVEMBER 15, 1910 ST. LOUIS, MO.
93	LUCID, CORNELIUS CECIL	D. JUNE 25, 1931 HOUSTON, TEXAS
01	LUSKEY, CHARLES MELTON	D. DECEMBER 20, 1962 BETHESDA, MD
81	LYNCH, JOHN H	D. APRIL 19, 1923 BRONX, N. Y.
04	LYNCH, MICHAEL JOSEPH	D. APRIL 2, 1927 GARRISON, N. Y.
84	LYNCH, THOMAS	D. MAY 13, 1903 PERU, ILL.
91	LYSTON, WILLIAM EDWARD	D. AUGUST 4, 1944 BALTIMORE, MD
84	MACARTHUR, MALCOLM	D. OCTOBER 18, 1932 DETROIT, MICH.
05	MACGAMWELL, EDWARD	D. MAY 26, 1924 ALBANY, N. Y.
08	MACK, WILLIAM FRANCIS	D. SEPTEMBER 30, 1971 ELMIRA, NY
06	MADDEN, THOMAS JOSEPH	D. JULY 26, 1930 PHILADELPHIA, PA.
86	MADIGAN, WILLIAM	D. DECEMBER 4, 1954 WASHINGTON, D. C.
04	MAGEE, SHERWOOD ROBERT	D. MARCH 13, 1929 PHILADELPHIA, PA.
97	MAGEE, WILLIAM J	D. AUGUST 15, 1922 TUFTONBORO, N. H.
98	MAHAFFEY, LOUIS WOOD	D. OCTOBER 26, 1949 TORRANCE, CALIF.
02	MAHER, THOMAS FRANCIS	D. AUGUST 25, 1929 PHILADELPHIA, PA.
07	MALLOY, HERMAN	D. MAY 9, 1942 MASSILLON, OH
08	MALONEY, CHARLES MICHAEL	D. JANUARY 17, 1967 SOMERVILLE, MASS
84	MANNING, JAMES H	D. OCTOBER 22, 1929 EDINBURG, TEX
05	MANUEL, MARK GARFIELD	D. APRIL 26, 1924 MEMPHIS, TENN
06	MARONEY, JAMES FRANCIS	D. FEBRUARY 26, 1929 PHILADELPHIA, PA.
08	MARQUARD, RICHARD WILLIAM	D. JUNE 1, 1980 BALTIMORE, MD.
03	MARSHALL, JOSEPH ELMER	D. MAY 4, 1934 WALLA WALLA, WASH.
90	MARS, EDWARD M	D. DECEMBER 9, 1941 CHICAGO, ILL.
08	MARTIN, HAROLD WINTHROP	D. APRIL 15, 1935 MILTON, MASS
09	MATHEWS, WILLIAM CALVIN	D. JANUARY 23, 1946 SCHUYLKILL CO., PA
06	MAXWELL, JAMES ALBERT	D. DECEMBER 10, 1961 BRADY, TEX
01	MCALEESE, JOHN JAMES	D. NOVEMBER 15, 1950 NEW YORK, N. Y.

01	MCBRIDE, GEORGE FLORIAN	D.	JULY 2, 1973 MILWAUKEE, WIS.
89	MCCAFFREY, CHARLES P	D.	APRIL 29, 1894 PHILADELPHIA, PA.
72	MCCARTON, FRANCIS	D.	JUNE 17, 1907 NEW YORK, N. Y.
05	MCCARTHY, WILLIAM JOHN	D.	FEBRUARY 4, 1928 WASHINGTON, D. C.
06	MCCARTHY, WILLIAM THOMAS	D.	MAY 29, 1939 CONCORD, MASS.
84	MCCAULEY, ALLEN A	D.	AUGUST 24, 1917 INDIANAPOLIS, IND.
95	MCCLOSKEY, JOHN JAMES	D.	NOVEMBER 17, 1940 LOUISVILLE, KY.
95	MCCORMICK, WILLIAM J	D.	JANUARY 28, 1956 CINCINNATI, O.
09	MCCORRY, WILLIAM CHARLES	D.	MARCH 22, 1973 AUGUSTA, GA.
89	MCCOY, ARTHUR GRAY	D.	MARCH 22, 1904 DANVILLE, PA.
85	MCDERMOTT, THOMAS NATHANIEL	D.	NOVEMBER 23, 1922 MANSFIELD, O.
95	MCDOUGAL, JOHN ARCHANBOLT	D.	OCTOBER 2, 1910 BUFFALO, N. Y.
92	MCFARLAN, ALEXANDER SHEPHERD	D.	MARCH 2, 1939 PEWEE VALLEY, KY.
02	MCFARLAND, CHARLES A	D.	DECEMBER 14, 1924 HOUSTON, TEX.
86	MCGEACHEY, JOHN CHARLES	D.	APRIL 5, 1930 CAMBRIDGE, MASS.
92	MCGRILLIS, MARK A	D.	MAY 16, 1935 PHILADELPHIA, PA.
76	MCGUINNESS, JOHN J	D.	DECEMBER 19, 1916 BINGHAMTON, N. Y.
94	MCGUIRE, MURRAY MASON	D.	SEPTEMBER 1, 1945 RICHMOND, VA
01	MCGUIRE, JAMES A	D.	JANUARY 26, 1917 BUFFALO, NY
98	MCHALE, ROBERT EMMET	D.	JUNE 9, 1952 SACRAMENTO, CALIF.
09	MCINTIRE, JOHN REID	D.	JANUARY 9, 1949 DAYTONA BEACH, FLA.
83	MCINTYRE, FRANK W	D.	JULY 8, 1887 DETROIT, MICH.
98	MCKENNA, JAMES WILLIAM	D.	MARCH 31, 1941 LYNCHBURG, VA
84	MCKNIGHT, HENRY DENNIS	D.	MAY 5, 1900 PITTSBURGH, PA.
08	MCMAHON, HENRY JOHN	D.	DECEMBER 11, 1929 WOBURN, MASS
77	MCMANUS, GEORGE	D.	OCTOBER 2, 1918 NEW YORK, N. Y.
99	MCPARTLIN, FRANK	D.	NOVEMBER 13, 1943 NEW YORK, N. Y.
91	MCSWEENEY, PAUL A	D.	AUGUST 12, 1951 ST. LOUIS, MO.
85	MCTAMANY, JAMES EDWARD	D.	APRIL 16, 1916 LENNI, PA
06	MEIER, ARTHUR ERNST	D.	MARCH 23, 1948 CHICAGO, ILL
84	MEISTER, GEORGE B	D.	AUGUST 24, 1908 GLENWOOD, PA.
86	MEISTER, JOHN F.	D.	JANUARY 17, 1923 PHILADELPHIA, PA.
09	MELTER, STEPHEN BLASIUS	D.	JANUARY 28, 1962 MISHAWAKA, IND.
09	MEYERS, JOHN TORTES	D.	JULY 25, 1971 SAN BERNARDINO, CALIF.
01	MILLER, JAMES MCCURDY	D.	FEBRUARY 8, 1937 PITTSBURGH, PA.
84	MILLER, JOSEPH A.	D.	APRIL 23, 1928 WHEELING, W. VA.
98	MILLER, RALPH DARWIN	D.	MAY 8, 1973 CINCINNATI, O.
09	MILLER, WARREN LEMUEL	D.	AUGUST 12, 1956 PHILADELPHIA, PA.
01	MILLIGAN, WILLIAM J.	D.	OCTOBER 14, 1928 BUFFALO, N. Y.
01	MITCHELL, FREDERICK FRANCIS	D.	OCTOBER 13, 1970 NEWTON, MASS.
09	MITCHELL, WILLIAM	D.	NOVEMBER 23, 1973 SARDIS, MISS.
84	MOFFETT, SAMUEL R	D.	MAY 5, 1907 BUTTE, MONT.
05	MOORE, GEORGE RAYMOND	D.	NOVEMBER 7, 1948 HYANNIS, MASS
84	MOORE, JEREMIAH S	D.	SEPTEMBER 26, 1908 WAYNE, MICH.
03	MORAN, CHARLES BARTHEL	D.	JUNE 13, 1949 HORSE CAVE, KY.
09	MORE, FOREST T.	D.	AUGUST 17, 1968 COLUMBUS, IND.
03	MORIARTY, GEORGE JOSEPH	D.	APRIL 8, 1964 MIAMI, FLA.
09	MORIARTY, WILLIAM JOSEPH	D.	DECEMBER 25, 1916 ELGIN, ILL
01	MORRISSEY, MICHAEL JOSEPH	D.	FEBRUARY 22, 1939 BALTIMORE, MD.
84	MORRISSEY, THOMAS J.	D.	SEPTEMBER 23, 1941 JANESVILLE, WIS.
06	MOSER, WALTER FREDRICK	D.	DECEMBER 10, 1946 PHILADELPHIA, PA
90	MOTZ, FRANK H	D.	MARCH 18, 1944 AKRON, O.
84	MUNDINGER, GEORGE	D.	OCTOBER 12, 1910 COVINGTON, KY.
05	MUNSON, CLARENCE HANFORD	D.	FEBRUARY 19, 1957 MISHAWAKA, IND.
08	MURDOCH, WILBUR EDWIN	D.	OCTOBER 29, 1941 LOS ANGELES, CALIF.
92	MURPHY, DANIEL JOSEPH	D.	DECEMBER 14, 1915 BROOKLYN, NY
05	MURPHY, DAVID FRANCIS	D.	APRIL 8, 1940 ADAMS, MASS
07	MURRAY, WILLIAM JEREMIAH	D.	MARCH 25, 1937 YOUNGSTOWN, O.
83	MUTRIE, JAMES J.	D.	JANUARY 24, 1938 NEW YORK, N. Y.
96	MYERS, JAMES ALBERT	D.	OCTOBER 12, 1915 WASHINGTON, D. C.
86	NEALE, JOSEPH HUNT	D.	DECEMBER 30, 1913 AKRON, O.
01	NELSON, RAYMOND NELSON	D.	JANUARY 8, 1961 MOUNT VERNON, NY
09	NETZEL, MILES A	D.	MARCH 18, 1938 VENTURA CO., CAL.
07	NEUER, JOHN S.	D.	JANUARY 14, 1966 NORTHUMBERLAND, PA.
75	NICHOLS, FREDERICK C	D.	FEBRUARY 8, 1918 BRIDGEPORT, CONN.
06	NORDYKE, LOUIS ELLIS	D.	SEPTEMBER 27, 1945 LOS ANGELES, CAL.
96	NORTON, ELISHA STRONG	D.	MARCH 5, 1950 ASPINWALL, PA
84	NUSZ, EMORY MOBERLY	D.	AUGUST 3, 1898 POINT OF ROCKS, MD.
83	OBERBECK, HENRY A	D.	AUGUST 26, 1921 ST. LOUIS, MO.
87	OBRIEN, JEREMIAH	D.	JULY 4, 1911 BINGHAMTON, N. Y.
84	OBRIEN, JOHN E	D.	DECEMBER 31, 1914 FALL RIVER, MASS.
08	OCONNOR, ANDREW JAMES	D.	SEPTEMBER 26, 1980 NORWOOD, MASS.
93	OCONNOR, FRANK HENRY	D.	DECEMBER 26, 1913 BRATTLEBORO, VT.
09	OHARA, WILLIAM ALEXANDER	D.	JUNE 15, 1931 JERSEY CITY, NJ
83	OLDFIELD, DAVID	D.	AUGUST 28, 1939 PHILADELPHIA, P A.
84	OLIN, FRANKLIN WALTER	D.	MAY 21, 1951 ST. LOUIS, MO.
08	OLMSTEAD, FREDERICK WILLIAM	D.	OCTOBER 22, 1936 MUSKOGEE, OKLA.
05	OLMSTED, HENRY THEODORE	D.	JANUARY 6, 1969 BRADENTON, FLA
75	ORAN, THOMAS	D.	SEPTEMBER 22, 1886 ST. LOUIS, MO.
09	OTIS, HARRY GEORGE	D.	JANUARY 29, 1976 TRENTON, N. J.
87	OTTERSON, WILLIAM JOHN	D.	SEPTEMBER 24, 1940 PITTSBURGH, PA.
84	OXLEY, HENRY HAVELOCK	D.	OCTOBER 12, 1945 SOMERVILLE, MASS.
02	OYLER, ANDREW PAUL	D.	OCTOBER 24, 1970 CUMBERLAND CO., PA.
90	PABST, EDWARD D. A.	D.	JUNE 19, 1940 SAINT LOUIS, MO.
99	PARENT, FREDRICK ALFRED	D.	NOVEMBER 2, 1972 SANFORD, ME.
08	PATTEE, HARRY ERNEST	D.	JULY 17, 1971 LYNCHBURG, VA.
84	PEAK, ELIAS	D.	DECEMBER 17, 1916 PHILADELPHIA, PA.
89	PEARS, FRANK H	D.	NOVEMBER 29, 1923 ST. LOUIS, MO.
76	PEARSON, DAVID P	D.	NOVEMBER 11, 1922 TRENTON, N. J.
02	PEDROES, CHARLES P	D.	AUGUST 6, 1927 CHICAGO, ILL
94	PEITZ, JOSEPH	D.	DECEMBER 4, 1919 ST. LOUIS, MO.
06	PETERSON, ROBERT A	D.	NOVEMBER 27, 1962 MARLTON, N. J.
07	PFYL, MEINHARD CHARLES	D.	OCTOBER 18, 1945 SAN FRANCISCO, CAL
02	PHELPS, EDWARD JOSEPH	D.	JANUARY 31, 1942 ALBANY, N.Y.
98	PICKETT, DAVID T	D.	APRIL 22, 1950 EASTON, MASS.
82	PIERCE, GRAYSON S	D.	AUGUST 28, 1894 NEW YORK, N. Y.
85	PIERSON, EDMUND DANA	D.	JULY 20, 1922 NEWARK, N. J.

02	POLCHOW, LOUIS WILLIAM	D. AUGUST 15, 1912 GOOD THUNDER, MINN
87	POLHEMUS, MARK S	D. NOVEMBER 12, 1923 LYNN, MASS.
02	POPP, WILLIAM PETER	D. SEPTEMBER 5, 1909 ST. LOUIS, MO.
84	PORTER, MATTHEW S.	D. KANSAS CITY, MO.
02	PORTER, ODIE OSCAR	D. MAY 4, 1903 BORDEN, IND.
03	POUNDS, JEARED WELLS	D. JULY 7, 1936 PATERSON, N. J.
09	POWELL, WILLIAM BURRIS	D. SEPTEMBER 28, 1967 EAST LIVERPOOL, OH
90	POWERS, PATRICK THOMAS	D. AUGUST 29, 1925 BELMAR, N. J.
83	PRINCE, WALTER FARR	D. MARCH 2, 1938 BRISTOL, N. H.
79	PURCELL, WILLIAM ALOYSIUS	D. FEBRUARY 20, 1912 TRENTON, NJ
03	PUTTMANN, AMBROSE NICHOLAS	D. JUNE 21, 1936 JAMAICA, N. Y.
03	QUICK, EDWIN S	D. MAY 19, 1913 ROCKY FORD, COLO.
06	QUILLIN, LEON ABNER	D. MARCH 14, 1665 WHITE BEAR LAKE, MINN
02	QUINN, CLARENCE CARR	D. AUGUST 6, 1946 WATERBURY, CONN.
09	RAFTERY, THOMAS FRANCIS	D. DECEMBER 31, 1954 BOSTON, MASS
88	RAYMOND, HARRY H	D. MARCH 21, 1925 SAN DIEGO, CAL.
88	RAY, IRVING BURTON	D. FEBRUARY 21, 1948 HARRINGTON, ME
03	REAGAN, ARTHUR EDGAR	D. JUNE 8, 1953 KANSAS CITY, MO.
82	RECCIUS, J. WILLIAM	D. JANUARY 25, 1911 LOUISVILLE, KY.
83	REID, WILLIAM ALEXANDER	D. JUNE 26, 1940 LONDON, ONT.
77	REIS, LAWRENCE P	D. JANUARY 24, 1921 CHICAGO, ILL.
84	REISING, CHARLES	D. JULY 26, 1915 LOUISVILLE, KY.
04	REMENTER, WILLIS J. H.	D. SEPTEMBER 23, 1922 PHILADELPHIA, PA.
89	REYNOLDS, CHARLES LAWRENCE	D. JULY 3, 1944 DENVER, COLO.
06	RHODES, CHARLES ANDERSON	D. OCTOBER 26, 1918 CANEY, KAN
06	RICHIE, LEWIS A	D. AUGUST 15, 1936 SOUTH MOUNTAIN, PA.
98	RICHTER, JOHN M	D. OCTOBER 4, 1927 LOUISVILLE, KY.
84	RICKLEY, CHRISTIAN	D. OCTOBER 25, 1911 PHILADELPHIA, PA.
84	ROBINSON, CHARLES HENRY	D. MAY 18, 1913 PROVIDENCE, R. I.
03	ROBINSON, WILLIAM CLYDE	D. APRIL 9, 1915 WATERBURY, CONN.
05	ROCKENFIELD, ISAAC B.	D. FEBRUARY 21, 1927 SAN DIEGO, CAL
99	ROTHERMEL, EDWARD HILL	D. FEBRUARY 11, 1927 DETROIT, MICH.
84	ROXBURGH, JAMES A	D. FEBRUARY 21, 1934 SAN FRANCISCO, CALIF.
79	ROWE, JOHN CHARLES	D. APRIL 25, 1911
90	ROAT, FREDERICK	D. SEPTEMBER 24, 1913 OREGON, ILL.
07	RUCKER, GEORGE NAPOLEON	D. DECEMBER 19, 1970 ALPHARETTA, GA.
89	RYAN, JOHN BENNETT	D. AUGUST 21, 1952 BOSTON, MASS.
08	SALVE, AUGUSTUS WILLIAM	D. MARCH 29, 1971 PROVIDENCE, RI
83	SAWYER, WILLARD NEWTON	D. JANUARY 5, 1936 KENT, O.
84	SCANLON, MICHAEL D	D. JANUARY 18, 1929 WASHINGTON, D. C.
09	SCANLAN, FRANK ALOYSIUS	D. APRIL 9, 1969 BROOKLYN, N.Y.
90	SCANLAN, MORTIMER J	D. DECEMBER 29, 1928 CHICAGO, ILL.
88	SCHEFFLER, THEODORE J	D. FEBRUARY 24, 1949 JAMAICA, N. Y.
02	SCHIAPPACASSE, LOUIS JOSEPH	D. SEPTEMBER 20, 1910 ANN ARBOR, MICH.
84	SCHMELZ, GUSTAVUS HEINRICH	D. OCTOBER 14, 1925 COLUMBUS, O.

Yours Truly G A Schmelz

84	SCHOENECK, LOUIS N	D. JANUARY 20, 1930 CHICAGO, ILL.
06	SCHULTE, JOHN HERMAN FRANK	D. AUGUST 17, 1975 ROSEVILLE, MICH.
08	SCHWEITZER, ALBERT CASPAR	D. JANUARY 27, 1969 NEWARK, O.
00	SCOTT, EDWARD	D. NOVEMBER 1, 1933 TOLEDO, OH
09	SCOTT, JAMES	D. APRIL 7, 1957 PALM SPRINGS, CAL.
90	SELEE, FRANK GIBSON	D. JULY 5, 1909 DENVER, COLO.
86	SHAFFER, JOHN W	D. NOVEMBER 21, 1926 ENDICOTT, N. Y.
76	SHANLEY, JAMES H	D. NOVEMBER 4, 1904 BROOKLYN, N. Y.
06	SHANNABROOK, WARREN H	D. MARCH 10, 1964 NORTH CANTON, OH
04	SHANNON, WILLIAM PORTER	D. MAY 16, 1940 MINNEAPOLIS, MINN.
84	SHARSIG, WILLIAM J	D. FEBRUARY 1, 1902 PHILADELPHIA, PA
05	SHAUGHNESSY, FRANCIS JOSEPH	D. MAY 15, 1969 MONTREAL, QUE.
07	SHAW, ALBERT SIMPSON	D. DECEMBER 30, 1974 DANVILLE, ILL.
08	SHAW, ROYAL N.	D. JULY 3, 1969 YAKIMA, WASH.
91	SHEARON, JOHN M	D. FEBRUARY 1, 1923 BRADFORD, PA.
98	SHETTSLINE, WILLIAM JOSEPH	D. FEBRUARY 22, 1933 PHILADELPHIA, PA.
86	SHINDLE, WILLIAM	D. JUNE 3, 1936 LAKELAND, N. J.
87	SHREVE, LEVEN LAWRENCE	D. OCTOBER 18, 1942 DETROIT, MICH
82	SIMMONS, LEWIS	D. SEPTEMBER 2, 1911 ALLENTOWN, PA.
09	SIMON, MICHAEL EDWARD	D. JUNE 10, 1963
84	SLADEN, ARTHUR W	D. FEBRUARY 28, 1914 DRACUT, MASS.
83	SMITH, EDGAR EUGENE	D. NOVEMBER 3, 1892 PROVIDENCE, R. I.
07	SMITH, FREDERICK	D. FEBRUARY 4, 1964 LOS ANGELES, CAL
04	SMITH, LEWIS OSCAR	D. MAY 1, 1928 CHARLESTON, W. VA.
88	SMITH, SAMUEL J	D. APRIL 26, 1916 ST. LOUIS, MO.
73	SMITH, WILLIAM J	D. AUGUST 9, 1886 BALTIMORE, MD
02	SMOOT, HOMER VERNON	D. MARCH 25, 1928 SALISBURY, MD
01	SNODGRASS, AMZIE BEAL	D. SEPTEMBER 9, 1951 NEW YORK, N. Y.
08	SNODGRASS, FRED CARLISLE	D. APRIL 5, 1974 VENTURA, CALIF.
72	SNYDER, JAMES	D. DECEMBER 1, 1922 QUEENS, N. Y.
72	SNYDER, JOSHUA	D. APRIL 21, 1881 BROOKLYN, N. Y.
97	SPARKS, THOMAS FRANK	D. JULY 15, 1937 ANNISTON, ALA.
88	SPENCE, HARRISON L.	D. MAY 19, 1908 CHICAGO, ILL.
08	SPONGBERG, CARL GUSTAV	D. JULY 21, 1938 LOS ANGELES, CAL
89	SPRINGER, EDWARD H	D. APRIL 24, 1926 LOS ANGELES COUNTY FARM, CAL
93	STAFFORD, JOHN HENRY	D. JULY 3, 1940 WORCESTER, MASS
71	STEARNS, WILLIAM F	D. DECEMBER 30, 1898 WASHINGTON, D. C.
94	STEERE, FREDERICK EUGENE	D. MARCH 13, 1942 SAN MATEO, CALIF.
08	STEM, FREDERICK BOOTHE	D. SEPTEMBER 5, 1964 DARLINGTON, SC

93	STOCKSDALE, OTIS HINKLEY	D. MARCH 15, 1933 PENNSVILLE, N. J.
40	STRAUB, JOSEPH J	D. FEBRUARY 13, 1929 PUEBLO, COLO.
08	STRUNK, AMOS AARON	D. JULY 22, 1979 LLANERCH, PA.
72	STUDLEY, SEYMOUR L	D. 1873 OR 1874 WASHINGTON, D. C.
04	STULTZ, GEORGE IRVIN	D. MARCH 19, 1955 LOUISVILLE, KY.
79	SULLIVAN, DENNIS J	D. DECEMBER 31, 1925 BOSTON, MASS.
05	SULLIVAN, DENNIS WILLIAM	D. JUNE 2, 1956 WEST LOS ANGELES, CAL.
08	SULLIVAN, SUTER G	D. APRIL 19, 1925 BALTIMORE, MD.
09	SUTER, HARRY RICHARD	D. JULY 24, 1971 TOPEKA, KAN.
33	SWEENEY, JOHN J	D. JUNE 1, 1889 NEW YORK, N. Y.
01	SWORMSTEDT, LEONARD B.	D. JULY 19, 1964 SALEM, MASS.
85	TATE, EDWARD CHRISTOPHER	D. JUNE 25, 1932 RICHMOND, VA
34	TAYLOR, GEORGE EDWARD	D. FEBRUARY 19, 1888 SAN FRANCISCO, CALIF.
34	TENNEY, FREDERICK CLAY	D. JUNE 15, 1919 FALL RIVER, MASS.
45	THOMAS, FORREST	D. MARCH 18, 1971 ST. JOSEPH, MO
88	THOMAS, WILLIAM WALTER	D. JUNE 6, 1950 ALTOONA, PA.
42	THOMPSON, WILL MCLAIN	D. JUNE 9, 1962 PITTSBURGH, PA
47	TIFT, RAYMOND FRANK	D. MARCH 29, 1945 VERONA, N. J.
46	TOOLE, STEPHEN JOHN	D. MARCH 28, 1919 PITTSBURGH, PA.
72	TRAFFLEY, JOHN	D. JULY 13 OR 14, 1900
44	TRAY, JAMES	D. JULY 28, 1905 JACKSON, MICH.
07	TROTT, SAMUEL W	D. JUNE 5, 1925 CATONSVILLE, MD.
90	TRUAX, FREDERICK W	D. DECEMBER 18, 1899 OMAHA, NEB.
02	TUCKEY, THOMAS H	D. OCTOBER 17, 1950 NEW YORK, N. Y.
03	TURNER, GEORGE A	D. JULY 16, 1945 STATEN ISLAND, NY
	UNDERWOOD, FREDERICK THEODORE	D. JANUARY 26, 1906 KANSAS CITY, MO.
03	URY, LOUIS NEWTON	D. MARCH 4, 1918 KANSAS CITY, MO.
	VAHRENHORST, HARRY HENRY	D. OCTOBER 10, 1943 ST. LOUIS, MO
08	VAIL, ROBERT GARFIELD	D. MARCH 22, 1942 PHILADELPHIA, PA.
33	VALENTINE, JOHN GILL	D. OCTOBER 10, 1903 CENTRAL ISLIP, N. Y.
09	VANDYKE, BENJAMIN HARRISON	D. OCTOBER 22, 1973 SARASOTA, FL
38	VANZANT, RICHARD	D. AUGUST 6, 1912 CENTRE TWP., WAYNE CO.,IND
	VONDERAHE, CHRISTIAN FREDERICK WILHELM	D. JUNE 7, 1913 ST. LOUIS, MO.
90	VONFRICKEN, ANTHONY	D. MARCH 22, 1947 TROY, NY
49	WACKER, CHARLES JAMES	D. AUGUST 7, 1948 EVANSVILLE, IND.
49	WALLER, JOHN FRANCIS	D. FEBRUARY 9, 1915 SECAUCUS, N. J.
43	WALSH, EDWARD AUGUSTIN	D. MAY 26, 1959 POMPANO BEACH, FLA.
01	WALSH, JOHN THOMAS	D. JULY 6, 1938 WILKES-BARRE, PA.
04	WALSH, JOSEPH A.	D. AUGUST 8, 1911 OMAHA, NEB.
09	WALSH, MICHAEL J	D. MARCH 17, 1924 SPRINGFIELD, MO
02	WANNER, CLARENCE CURTIS	D. MAY 28, 1919 GENESEO, ILL
40	WARD, JOHN ANDREW	D. JANUARY 17, 1945 AKRON, OH
07	WASHBURN, LIBE	D. MARCH 22, 1940 MALONE, N. Y.
09	WEIDMAN, GEORGE E	D. MARCH 2, 1905 NEW YORK, N. Y.
02	WESTREBURG, OSCAR W	D. APRIL 17, 1909 ALAMEDA CO., CA.
38	WHEAT, ZACHARY DAVIS	D. MARCH 11, 1972 SEDALIA, MO.
02	WHEELER, EDWARD L	D. AUGUST 15, 1960 FORT WORTH, TEX.
04	WHITAKER, WILLIAM H	D. JULY 15, 1902 ST. LOUIS, MO.
38	WHITE, GUY HARRIS	D. FEBRUARY 17, 1969 SILVER SPRING, MD.
02	WHITE, JOHN WALLACE	D. SEPTEMBER 30, 1963 INDIANAPOLIS, IND
02	WHITING, JESSE W	D. OCTOBER 28, 1937 PHILADELPHIA, PA.
44	WIGGINS, WILLIAM H	D. SEPTEMBER 23, 1926 WILMINGTON, DEL.
04	WILLIAMS, ARTHUR FRANKLIN	D. MAY 16, 1941 ARLINGTON, VA.
44	WILLIAMS, DAVID OWEN	D. APRIL 25, 1918 HOT SPRINGS, ARK.
44	WILLIAMS, JAMES ANDREW	D. OCTOBER 24, 1918 NORTH HEMPSTEAD, N. Y.
42	WILLIAMS, WASHINGTON J	D. JANUARY, 1890 PHILADELPHIA, PA.
49	WILLIGROD, JULIUS	D. NOVEMBER 27, 1906 SAN FRANCISCO, CALIF.
42	WILSON, GEORGE ARCHER	D. NOVEMBER 28, 1914 BROOKLYN, N. Y.
49	WILSON, HOWARD PAUL	D. OCTOBER 16, 1934 HAVRE-DE-GRACE, MD.
03	WILSON, JAMES GARRETT	D. MAY 1, 1969 RANDALLSTOWN, MD.
23	WILSON, PETER ALEC	D. JUNE 5, 1957 ST. PETERSBURG, FLA
03	WINCHELL, FREDERICK RUSSELL	D. AUGUST 8, 1958 TORONTO, ONT.
07	WINHAM, LAFAYETTE SHARKEY	D. SEPTEMBER 11, 1951 BROOKLYN, NY
08	WINKELMAN, GEORGE EDWARD	D. MAY 19, 1960 WASHINGTON, D. C.
90	WISE, WILLIAM E	D. MAY 5, 1940 WASHINGTON, D.C.
76	WOLFE, WILBERT OTTO	D. FEBRUARY 27, 1953 NORTH CHARLEROI, PA.
72	WOLTER, HARRY MEIGS	D. JULY 7, 1970 PALO ALTO, CALIF.
03	WOOD, HAROLD AUSTIN	D. MAY 18, 1935 BETHESDA, MD.
08	WOOD, JOSEPH	90 MARVEL RD - NEW HAVEN CT 06515
72	WORTH, HERBERT	D. APRIL 27, 1914 BROOKLYN, N. Y.
90	WRIGHT, PATRICK FRANCIS	D. MAY 29, 1943 SPRINGFIELD, ILL.
90	WRIGHT, WILLIAM S	D. OCTOBER 14, 1922 DULUTH, MINN
34	WYMAN, FRANK H	D. FEBRUARY 4, 1916 EVERETT, MASS.
36	YAIK, HENRY	D. SEPTEMBER 21, 1935 DETROIT, MICH.
06	YEAGER, GEORGE J	D. JUNE 5, 1940 CINCINNATI, O.
72	YEATMAN, WILLIAM SUTER	D. APRIL 20, 1901 YORK, PA.
01	YERKES, STANLEY LEWIS	D. JULY 28, 1940 BOSTON, MASS.
09	YERKES, STEPHEN DOUGLAS	D. JANUARY 31, 1971 LANSDALE, PA.
04	YEWELL, EDWIN LEONARD	D. SEPTEMBER 15, 1940 WASHINGTON, D.C.
08	YINGLING, JOSEPH GRANVILLE	D. OCTOBER 24, 1946 MANCHESTER, MD.
40	YOUNG, HARLAN EDWARD	D. MARCH 26, 1975 JACKSONVILLE,, FLA.
90	YOUNGMAN, HENRY	D. JANUARY 24, 1936 PITTSBURGH, PA.
07	ZIMMERMAN, HENRY	D. MARCH 14, 1969 NEW YORK, N.Y.

PLAYERS DEBUTING FROM 1910 TO 1981

54-	1	AARON, HENRY LOUIS	1611 ADAMS DR SW - ATLANTA GA 30311
62-	1	AARON, TOMMIE LEE	2404 DENMARK ST - MOBILE AL 36617
77-	1	AASE, DONALD WILLIAM	9902 W BROADWAY #7 - ANAHEIM CA 92804
10-	1	ABBOTT, ODY CLEON	D. APRIL 13, 1933 WASHINGTON, D. C.
73-	1	ABBOTT, WILLIAM GLENN	17511 NE 22ND CT - REDMOND WA 98052
50-	1	ABER, ALBERT JULIUS	7009 MEADOWBROOK AVE - CLEVELAND OH 44144
52-	1	ABERNATHIE, WILLIAM EDWARD	OLD ADD: RR 2 BOX 174A - FYFFE AL
42-	1	ABERNATHY, TALMADGE LAFAYETTE	902 EDGEWOOD CIR - GASTONIA NC 28052
55-	1	ABERNATHY, THEODORE WADE	2211 ARMSTRONG PK RD - GASTONIA NC 28052
46-	1	ABERNATHY, VIRGIL WOODROW	BOX 102 - CHESNEE SC 29323
47-	1	ABERSON, CLIFFORD ALEXANDER	D. JUNE 23, 1973 VALLEJO, CAL.
49-	1	ABRAMS, CALVIN ROSS	HAND LANE - AMAGANSETT NY 11930
23-	1	ABRAMS, GEORGE ALLEN	1375 DREW ST - CLEARWATER FL 33515
42-	2	ABREU, JOSEPH LAWRENCE	26090 REGAL AVE - HAYWARD CA 94544
56-	1	ACKER, THOMAS JAMES	314 EVERS ST - WYCKOFF NJ 07481
63-	1	ACKLEY, FLORIAN FREDERICK	417 W 5TH ST - HAYWARD WI 54843
13-	1	ACOSTA, BALMADERO PEDRO	D. NOVEMBER 17, 1963 MIAMI, FLA.
72-	1	ACOSTA, CECILIO	AUG RAMIREZ 1420,COL GAB LEYVA-CULICAN MEX
70-	1	ACOSTA, EDUARDO ELIXBET	BETANIA 6, 431 X - PANAMA CITY REP OF PANAMA
20-	1	ACOSTA, JOSE	OLD ADD: VUENA BISTA - MARIANAO CUBA
31-	1	ADAIR, JAMES AUBREY	2864 REEDCROFT DR - DALLAS TX 75234
58-	1	ADAIR, KENNETH JERRY	14522 MOCKINGBIRD LN - SAND SPRINGS OK 74063
70-	2	ADAIR, MARION DANNE	1535 PINELLAS POINT S-ST PETERSBURG FL 33705
41-	1	ADAMS, ACE TOWNSEND	1005 SUMMETT DR-ALBANY GA 31705
46-	2	ADAMS, CHARLES DWIGHT	810 FOXKIRK - GLENDALE CA 91206
14-	1	ADAMS, DANIEL LESLIE	D. OCTOBER 6, 1964 ST. LOUIS, MO.
22-	1	ADAMS, EARL JOHN	116 WASHINGTON ST - TREMONT PA 17981
39-	1	ADAMS, ELVIN CLARK	74390 ALLESANDRO - PALM DESERT CA 92260
75-	1	ADAMS, GLENN CHARLES	35 FOWLER RD - NORTHBRIDGE MA 01534
69-	1	ADAMS, HAROLD DOUGLAS	OLD ADD: 20 S PONTIAC #111-JANESVILLE WI
48-	1	ADAMS, HERBERT LOREN	903 S WILLISTON - WHEATON IL 60187
12-	1	ADAMS, JAMES IRVIN	D. JUNE 18, 1937 ALBANY, N.Y.
10-	2	ADAMS, JOHN BERTRAM	D. JUNE 24, 1940 LOS ANGELES, CALIF.
14-	2	ADAMS, KARL TUTWILER	D. SEPTEMBER 17, 1967 EVERETT, WASH.
47-	2	ADAMS, RICHARD LEROY	229 VIA DE AMO - FALLBROOK CA 92028
31-	2	ADAMS, ROBERT ANDREW	D. MARCH 6, 1970 JACKSONVILLE, FLA.
25-	1	ADAMS, ROBERT BURDETTE	314 E UNION ST - SCHUYLKILL HAVEN PA 17972
46-	3	ADAMS, ROBERT HENRY	3828 PUEBLO WAY - SCOTTSDALE AZ 85251
77-	2	ADAMS, ROBERT MELVIN	23277 VALERIO - CANOGA PARK CA 91304
72-	2	ADAMS, ROBERT MICHAEL	2713 CASA DEL NORTE NE - ALBUQUERQUE NM 8711
23-	2	ADAMS, SPENCER DEWEY	D. NOVEMBER 25, 1970 FT. LAUDERDALE, FLA.
67-	1	ADAMSON, JOHN MICHAEL	1122 BARCELONA DR - SAN DIEGO CA 92107
50-	2	ADCOCK, JOSEPH WILBUR	BOX 385 - COUSHATTA LA 71019
50-	3	ADDIS, ROBERT GORDON	7466 HOLLYCROFT LN - MENTOR OH 44060
39-	2	ADERHOLT, MORRIS WOODROW	D. MARCH 18, 1955 SARASOTA, FLA.
28-	1	ADKINS, GRADY EMMETT	D. MARCH 31, 1966 LITTLE ROCK, ARK.
42-	3	ADKINS, JOHN DEWEY	2627 WESTWOOD BLVD-LOS ANGELES CA 90064
42-	4	ADKINS, RICHARD EARL	D. SEPTEMBER 12, 1955 ELECTRA, TEX.
63-	2	ADLESH, DAVID GEORGE	2257 DAISY AVE - LONG BEACH CA 93806
62-	1	AGEE, TOMMIE LEE	11208 ASTORIA BLVD - EAST ELMHURST NY 11369
54-	2	AGGANIS, HARRY	D. JUNE 27, 1955 CAMBRIDGE, MASS.
12-	1	AGLER, JOSEPH ABRAM	D. APRIL 26, 1971 MASSILLON, O.
13-	2	AGNEW, SAMUEL LESTER	D. JULY 19, 1951 SONOMA, CALIF.
81-	1	AGOSTO, JUAN R	VIA LETICIA 4LS8 - CAROLINA PR 00630
80-	1	AGUAYO, LUIS (MURIEL)	BOX 9036, SABANA BRANCH - VEGA BAJA PR 00764
55-	2	AGUIRRE, HENRY JOHN	31101 SUNSET DR - FRANKLIN MI 48025
77-	3	AIKENS, WILLIE MAYS	OLD ADD: RR 4 BOX 369 - SENECA SC
79-	1	AINGE, DANIEL RAY	OLD ADD: 215 JONQUIL ST - EUGENE OR
10-	3	AINSMITH, EDWARD WILBUR	D. SEPTEMBER 6, 1981 FORT LAUDERDALE, FLA.
11-	1	AITCHISON, RALEIGH LEONIDAS	D. SEPTEMBER 26, 1958 COLUMBUS, KAN.
12-	3	AITON, GEORGE WILSON	D. AUGUST 16, 1976 VAN NUYS, CALIF.
64-	1	AKER, JACK DELANE	329 RENO DR - LYNCHBURG VA 24502
12-	4	AKERS, ALBERT EARL	D. MAY 15, 1979 BAY PINES, FLA.
29-	1	AKERS, THOMAS ERNEST	D. APRIL 13, 1962 CHATTANOOGA, TENN.
58-	2	ALBANESE, JOSEPH PETER	54 LONGFELLOW DR - COLONIA NJ 07067
78-	1	ALBERTS, FRANCIS BURT	223 BALTIMORE ST - GETTYSBURG PA 17325
10-	4	ALBERTS, FREDERICK JOSEPH	D. AUGUST 27, 1917 FORT WAYNE, IND.
41-	2	ALBOSTA, EDWARD JOHN	5360 FORT RD-SAGINAW MI 48601
49-	2	ALBRECHT, EDWARD ARTHUR	D. 1979 CENTERVILLE, ILL.
47-	3	ALBRIGHT, JOHN HAROLD	5433 HEWLETT DR - SAN DIEGO CA 92115
73-	2	ALBURY, VICTOR	6205 ALCOT CT - TAMPA FL 33624
76-	1	ALCALA, SANTO	RAMON MOTA #18 - SAN PEDRO DE MARCORIS DOM RE
67-	2	ALCARAZ, ANGEL LUIS	1968 ADD: BOX 423 - HUMACAO PR 00661
14-	3	ALCOCK, JOHN FORBES	D. JANUARY 30, 1973 WOOSTER, O.
43-	1	ALDERSON, DALE LEONARD	D. FEBRUARY 12, 1982 GARDEN GROVE, CALIF.
17-	1	ALDRIDGE, VICTOR EDDINGTON	D. APRIL 17, 1973 TERRE HAUTE, IND.
41-	3	ALENO, CHARLES	601 MARION CT-DELAND FL 32720
29-	2	ALEXANDER, DAVID DALE	D. MARCH 2, 1979 GREENEVILLE, TENN.
71-	1	ALEXANDER, DOYLE LAFAYETTE	2801 MARQUIS CIR E - ARLINGTON TX 76016
75-	2	ALEXANDER, GARY WAYNE	219 W 122ND ST - LOS ANGELES CA 90061

```
11-  2 ALEXANDER, GROVER CLEVELAND  D. NOVEMBER 4, 1950 ST. PAUL, NEB.
37-  1 ALEXANDER, HUGH             BOX 5144 - CLEARWATER FL 33518
73-  3 ALEXANDER, MATTHEW          1310 ROYAL DR #288 - LIBRARY PA 15129
55-  3 ALEXANDER, ROBERT SOMERVILLE 7525 PINTAIL #C1 - CITRUS HEIGHTS CA 95610
12-  5 ALEXANDER, WALTER ERNEST    D. DECEMBER 29, 1978 FORT WORTH, TEXAS
79-  2 ALLARD, BRIAN MARSHALL      110 RICHARD ST - HENRY IL 61537
14-  4 ALLEN, ARTEMUS WARD         D. OCTOBER 16, 1939 HINES, ILL.
52-  3 ALLEN, BERNARD KEITH        OLD ADD: 10918 LARCH CIR - PALM GARDENS FL
26-  1 ALLEN, ETHAN NATHAN         STRATFORD HILL APTS #40C-CHAPEL HIL NC 27514
10-  5 ALLEN, FLETCHER MANSON      D. OCTOBER 16, 1959 LUBBOCK, TEX.
12-  6 ALLEN, FRANK LEON           D. JULY 30, 1933 GAINESVILLE, ALA.
56-  1 ALLEN, HAROLD ANDREW        15 STATON DR - UPPER MARLBORO MD 20870
19-  1 ALLEN, HORACE TANNER        D. JULY 5, 1981 CANTON, N. C.
44-  5 ALLEN, JOHN MARSHALL        D. SEPTEMBER 24, 1967 HAGERSTOWN, MD.
32-  1 ALLEN, JOHN THOMAS          D. MARCH 29, 1959 ST. PETERSBURG, FLA.
80-  2 ALLEN, KIM BRYANT           30 AVENUE 28 #1 - VENICE CA 90291
69-  2 ALLEN, LLOYD CECIL          3867 E THOMAS AVE - FRESNO CA 93702
79-  3 ALLEN, NEIL PATRICK         1402 ARMSTRONG - KANSAS CITY KS 66102
63-  3 ALLEN, RICHARD ANTHONY      OLD ADD: RR 2 BOX 216 - PERKASIE PA
49-  2 ALLEN, ROBERT               B. 1896
37-  2 ALLEN, ROBERT EARL          1888 W AMES CIR CHESAPEAKE VA 23321
61-  1 ALLEN, ROBERT GRAY          515 WOODLAWN - HENDERSON TX 75652
72-  3 ALLEN, RONALD FREDRICK      917 WINONA DR - YOUNGSTOWN OH 44511
79-  4 ALLENSON, GARY MARTIN       4454 W 141ST AVE - HAWTHORNE CA 90250
63-  4 ALLEY, LEONARD EUGENE       8212 NOTRE DAME DR - RICHMOND VA 23228
54-  3 ALLIE, GAIR ROOSEVELT       206 MAPLEWOOD - SAN ANTONIO TX 78216
75-  3 ALLIETTA, ROBERT GEORGE     25 ROBINSON RD - FALMOUTH MA 02540
11-  3 ALLISON, MACK PENDLETON     D. MARCH 13, 1964 ST. JOSEPH, MO.
43-  3 ALLISON, MILO HENRY         D. JUNE 18, 1957 KENOSHA, WIS.
58-  3 ALLISON, WILLIAM ROBERT     6700 GALWAY DR - EDINA MN 55424
33-  1 ALMADA, BALDOMERO MELO      OLD ADD: DICKENS 76, 201-POLANCO 5 MEXICO DF
11-  4 ALMEIDA, RAFAEL D.          D. MARCH, 1968 HAVANA, CUBA
74-  1 ALMON, WILLIAM FRANCIS      88 CLAFLIN CT - WARWICK RI 02886
50-  4 ALOMA, LUIS BARBA           7115 N DAMEN - CHICAGO IL 60645
64-  2 ALOMAR, SANTOS CONDE        BOX 136 - SALINAS PR 00751
58-  4 ALOU, FELIPE ROJAS          CALLE #3 KENNEDY - SANTO DOMINGO DOM REP
63-  5 ALOU, JESUS MARIA ROJAS     CALLE 3-#5,ENS KENNEDY - SANTO DOMINGO DOM RE
60-  1 ALOU, MATEO ROJAS           CALLE 3 NO 5 - ENSANCHE KENNEDY SANTO DOMINGO
54-  4 ALSTON, THOMAS EDISON       616 ELLWOOD DR - HIGH POINT NC 27260
36-  1 ALSTON, WALTER EMMONS       4340 CHERRY ST OXFORD OH 45056
```

```
77-  4 ALSTON, WENDELL             100 RIVERDALE AVE - YONKERS NY 10701
20-  2 ALTEN, ERNEST MATTHIAS      D. SEPTEMBER, 1981
16-  1 ALTENBURG, JESSE HOWARD     D. MARCH 12, 1973 LANSING, MICH.
59-  1 ALTMAN, GEORGE LEE          8401 S M L KING JR DR - CHICAGO IL 60619
55-  4 ALTOBELLI, JOSEPH           17 ADEANE DR W - ROCHESTER NY 14624
58-  5 ALUSIK, GEORGE JOSEPH       581 GARDEN AVE - WOODRIDGE NJ 07095
68-  1 ALVARADO, LUIS CESAR        BOX 853 - LAJAS PR 06667
73-  4 ALVAREZ, JESUS ORLANDO      CUMMUNIDAD DOLORES 37 - RIO GRANDE PR 00745
81-  2 ALVAREZ, JOSE LINO          7813 JAMAICA AVE - TAMPA FL 33614
58-  6 ALVAREZ, OSWALDO GONZALES   SANTUARIO 3137,COL.CHAPALITA-GUADALAJARA MEX
60-  2 ALVAREZ, ROGELIO            5010 NW 183RD ST - CAROL CITY FL 33055
62-  4 ALVIS, ROY MAXWELL          1035 AVE A - JASPER TX 75951
65-  1 ALYEA, GARRABRANT RYERSON   171 SYLVAN ST - RUTHERFORD NJ 07070
54-  5 AMALFITANO, JOHN JOSEPH     434 W 11TH ST - SAN PEDRO CA 90731
58-  7 AMARO, RUBEN                1728 BORBECK ST - PHILADELPHIA PA 19111
37-  3 AMBLER, WAYNE HARPER        913 NOBLE OAKS DR - SAVANNAH GA 31406
55-  5 AMOR, VINCENTE ALVAREZ      CONCEPCION 630 - LAWTON, HAVANA CUBA
22-  2 AMOROS, EDMUNDO ISASI "SANDY" 2128 19TH ST - MIAMI FL 33133
15-  1 ANCKER, WALTER              D. FEBRUARY 13, 1954 ENGLEWOOD, N.J.
75-  4 ANDERSEN, LARRY EUGENE      17016 NE 2ND PL - BELLEVUE WA 98004
41-  4 ANDERSON, ALFRED WALTON     1308 FIFTH AVE - ALBANY GA 31707
48-  2 ANDERSON, ANDY HOLM         7418 E GREENLAKE DR N - SEATTLE WA 98115
37-  4 ANDERSON, ARNOLD REVOLA     D. AUGUST 7, 1972 SIOUX CITY, IA.
71-  2 ANDERSON, DWAIN CLEAVEN     818 SEAVIEW DR - EL CERRITO CA 94532
46-  4 ANDERSON, FERRELL JACK      D. MARCH 12, 1978 JOPLIN, MO.
14-  6 ANDERSON, GEORGE ANDREW JENDRUS D. MAY 28, 1962 CLEVELAND, O.
59-  2 ANDERSON, GEORGE LEE        4077 N VERDE DR - 1000 OAKS CA 91360
32-  2 ANDERSON, HAROLD            D. MAY 1, 1974 ST. LOUIS, MO.
57-  1 ANDERSON, HARRY WALTER      4823 KENNETT PIKE - GREENVILLE DE 19807
78-  2 ANDERSON, JAMES LEA         4158 OLD HAMMER RD - NORCO CA 91760
58-  8 ANDERSON, JOHN CHARLES      1715 CENTRAL AVE - GREAT FALLS MT 59401
74-  2 ANDERSON, LAWRENCE DENNIS   7117 STEWART & GRAY RD - DOWNEY CA 90241
71-  3 ANDERSON, MICHAEL ALLEN     1127 LINDEN MILL APTS - LINDENWOLD NJ 08021
61-  2 ANDERSON, NORMAN CRAIG      814 POPLAR RD - HELLERTOWN PA 18055
```

```
79-  5 ANDERSON, RICHARD LEE        3915 WEST 105TH ST - INGLEWOOD CA 90303
57-  2 ANDERSON, ROBERT CARL        6627 W 28TH ST - GARY IN 46406
17-  2 ANDERSON, WALTER CARL        1811 MORNINGSIDE DR SE - GRAND RAPIDS MI49506
25-  2 ANDERSON, WILLIAM EDWARD     31 CENTURY ST - MEDFORD MA 02155
10-  6 ANDERSON, WINGO CHARLIE      D. DECEMBER 19, 1950 FORT WORTH, TEX.
55-  6 ANDRE, JOHN EDWARD           D. NOVEMBER 25, 1976 CENTERVILLE, MASS.
46-  5 ANDRES, ERNEST HENRY         812 S ROSE - BLOOMINGTON IN 47403
75-  5 ANDREWS, KIM DARRELL         10052 DENSMORE AVE - SEPULVEDA CA 91343
25-  3 ANDREWS, ELBERT DEVORE       D. NOVEMBER 25, 1979 GREENWOOD, S. C.
76-  2 ANDREWS, FRED                8129 S MARYLAND - CHICAGO IL 60619
47-  4 ANDREWS, HERBERT CARL        2305 2ND ST - DODGE CITY KS 67801
31-  3 ANDREWS, IVY PAUL            D. NOVEMBER 23, 1970 DORA, ALA.
73-  5 ANDREWS, JOHN RICHARD        9292 GORDON AVE - LAHABRA CA 90631
66-  2 ANDREWS, MICHAEL JAY         29 PAUL AVE - PEABODY MA 01960
37-  5 ANDREWS, NATHAN HARDY        RR ONE BOX 725 - KING NC 27021
75-  6 ANDREWS, ROBERT PATRICK      9802 BLOOMFIELD #8 - CYPRESS CA 90630
39-  3 ANDREWS, STANLEY JOSEPH      3840 IRONWOOD LN #403 - BRADENTON FL 33505
31-  4 ANDRUS, WILLIAM MORGAN       2117 UNION AV - CHATTANOOGA TN 37404
76-  3 ANDUJAR, JOAQUIN (GARSIA)    JUAN DEACOSTA #10A-SAN PEDRO DE MARCORIS DOMF
```

```
72-  4 ANGELINI, NORMAN STANLEY     16196 E BAILS PL - AURORA CO 80012
29-  3 ANGLEY, THOMAS SAMUEL        D. OCTOBER 26, 1952 WICHITA, KAN.
36-  2 ANKENMAN, FRED NORMAN        4014 UNDERWOOD - HOUSTON TX 77025
44-  1 ANTOLICK, JOSEPH             723 2ND ST - CATASAUQUA PA 18032
48-  3 ANTONELLI, JOHN AUGUST       22 TOBEY WOODS - PITTSFORD NY 14534
44-  2 ANTONELLI, JOHN LAWRENCE     5539 BARFIELD RD - MEMPHIS TN 38117
53-  1 ANTONELLO, WILLIAM JAMES     4054 VALENTINE CT - ST PAUL MN 55112
56-  2 APARICIC, LUIS ERNEST        CALLE 73 #14-53 - MARACAIBO VENEZUELA
73-  6 APODACA, ROBERT JOHN         23 HIGHLAND AVE - GLENWOOD LANDING NY 11547
80-  3 APONTE, LUIS EDUARDO         CALLE BELLA VISTA 48-LA SABANITA,BOLIVAR VENE
15-  2 APPLETON, EDWARD SAMUEL      D. JANUARY 27, 1932 ARLINGTON, TEX.
27-  1 APPLETON, PETER WILLIAM      D. JANUARY 18, 1974 TRENTON, N.J.
30-  1 APPLING, LUCIUS BENJAMIN     RR 7, BRAGG RD - CUMMINGS GA 30130
41-  5 ARAGON, ANGEL VALDES JR      13669 IMPERIAL GROVE N -LARGO FL 33540
14-  7 ARAGON, ANGEL VALDES SR.     D. JANUARY 24, 1952 NEW YORK, N.Y.
23-  3 ARCHDEACON, MAURICE BRUCE    D. SEPTEMBER 5, 1954 ST. LOUIS, MO.
36-  3 ARCHER, FREDERICK MARVIN     RR 1 BOX 203 CHINA GROVE NC 28023
61-  3 ARCHER, JAMES WILLIAM        1414 OLEANDER DR - TARPON SPRINGS FL 33589
38-  1 ARCHIE, GEORGE ALBERT        4007 CLARKSVILLE HIGHWAY NASHVILLE TN 37218
68-  2 ARCIA, JOSE RAIMUNDO         7325 NW 3RD ST - MIAMI FL 33125
61-  4 ARDELL, DANIEL MIERS         15010 VENTURA BLVD #327-SHERMAN OAKS CA 91403
47-  5 ARDIZOLA, RINALDO JOSEPH     130 SANTA ROSA AVE - SAN FRANCISCO CA 94112
48-  4 ARFT, HENRY IRVIN            109 SUNNYSIDE LN - BALLWIN MO 63011
59-  3 ARIAS, RODOLFO MARTINEZ      3911 NW 11TH ST - MIAMI FL 33126
31-  5 ARLETT, RUSSELL LORIS        D. MAY 16, 1964 MINNEAPOLIS, MINN.
65-  2 ARLICH, DONALD LOUIS         6041 GEORGIA BLVD N - ST PAUL MN 55109
69-  3 ARLIN, STEPHEN RALPH         6338 CAMINO CORTO - SAN DIEGO CA 92120
76-  4 ARMAS, ANTONIO RAFAEL        LOS MERCEDES #37,P.PIRITU-EDO.ANZOATEQUI VEN
```

SEE Page 149

```
73-  7  ARMBRISTER, EDISON ROSANDER MCQUAY ST - BOX 2003 - NASSAU BAHAMAS
34-  1  ARMBRUST, ORVILLE MARTIN      D. OCTOBER 2, 1967 MOBILE, ALA.
46-  6  ARMSTRONG, GEORGE NOBLE       16 FRANKLIN ST - EAST ORANGE NJ 07017
11-  5  ARMSTRONG, HOWARD ELMER       D. MARCH 8, 1926 CANISTEO, N.Y.
80-  4  ARMSTRONG, MICHAEL DENNIS     BOX 846 - HALIFAX VA 24558
71-  4  ARNOLD, CHRISTOPHER PAUL      2219 EL CAPITAN - ARCADIA CA 91006
36-  4  ARNOVICH, MORRIS              D. JULY 20, 1959 SUPERIOR, WIS.
43-  2  ARNTZEN, ORIE EDGAR           D. JANUARY 28, 1970 CEDAR RAPIDS, IA.
61-  5  ARRIGO, GERALD WILLIAM        1480 LOCUS LAKE RD S - AMELIA OH 45102
75-  7  ARROYO, FERNANDO              4917 FIRST PKWY - SACRAMENTO CA 95823
55-  7  ARROYO, LUIS ENRIQUE          A-3 SAN ANTONIO - PONCE PR 00731
71-  5  ARROYO, RUDOLPH               828 SIERRA VISTA - MOUNTAIN VIEW CA 94040
38-  2  ASBELL, JAMES MARION          D. JULY 6, 1967 SAN MATEO, CAL.
28-  2  ASBJORNSON, ROBERT ANTHONY    D. JANUARY 21, 1970 WILLIAMSPORT, PA.
25-  4  ASH, KENNETH LOWTHER          D. NOVEMBER 15, 1979 CLARKSBURG, W. VA.
48-  5  ASHBURN, DON RICHARD          GLADWYNNE PA 19035
73-  8  ASHBY, ALAN DEAN              27850 PONTEVEDRA - SAN PEDRO CA 90732
76-  5  ASHFORD, THOMAS STEVEN        5240 GUINDA CT - SAN DIEGO CA 92101
57-  3  ASPROMONTE, KENNETH JOSEPH    % COORS, 10400 HARWIN - HOUSTON TX 77036
56-  5  ASPROMONTE, ROBERT THOMAS     29 CHARLESTON N - SUGARLAND TX 77478
76-  6  ASSELSTINE, BRIAN HANLY       1488 COUNTRY CT - SANTA YNEZ CA 93460
45-  1  ASTROTH, JOSEPH HENRY         151 SOUTH MOYER RD - CHALFONT PA 18914
50-  5  ATKINS, JAMES CURTIS          3221 CLIFF RD - BIRMINGHAM AL 35205
27-  2  ATKINSON, HUBERT BURLEY       D. FEBRUARY 12, 1961 CHICAGO, ILL.
76-  7  ATKINSON,WILLIAM CECIL GLENN  RR 2 - CHATHAM ONTARIO
26-  2  ATTREAU, RICHARD GILBERT      D. JULY 5, 1964 CHICAGO, ILL.
52-  3  ATWELL, MAURICE DAILEY        BOX 686 - PURCELLVILLE VA 22132
36-  5  ATWOOD, WILLIAM FRANKLIN      3100 EL PASO SNYDER TX 79549
71-  6  AUERBACH, FREDERICK STEVEN    4724 ABARGO ST - WOODLAND HILLS CA 91364
73-  9  AUGUSTINE, DAVID RALPH        OLD ADD: 14850 SW 280TH ST #25-HOMESTEAD FL
75-  8  AUGUSTINE, GERALD LEE         569 W 13442 HALES PK CT-HALES CORNER WI 53130
33-  2  AUKER, ELDON LEROY            15 SAILFISH RD - VERO BEACH FL 32960
47-  6  AULDS, LEYCESTER DOYLE        YANCEY STAR RT BOX 16 - HONDO TX 78861
81-  7  AULT, DOUGLAS REAGAN          1450 23RD ST - BEAUMONT TX 77706
65-  3  AUST, DENNIS KAY              4513 AZEELE - TAMPA FL 33609
70-  3  AUSTIN, RICK GERALD           BOX 347 - BROOKFIELD MO 64628
76-  9  AUTRY, ALBERT                 1022 ROBLE AVE - MODESTO CA 95355
24-  1  AUTRY, MARTIN GORDON          D. JANUARY 26, 1950 SAVANNAH, GA.
56-  4  AVERILL, EARL DOUGLAS         8607 71ST ST NW - GIG HARBOR WA 98335
24-  4  AVERILL, HOWARD EARL          914 4TH # 6 - SNOHOMISH WA 98290
49-  3  AVILA, ROBERTO FRANCISCO GONZALEZ NAVEGANTES FR-19 REFORMA-VERACRUZ MEX
77-  5  AVILES, RAMON ANTONIO         26 PADIAL ST - MANATI PR 00701
50-  6  AVREA, JAMES EPHERIUM         927 GLENSTONE - DALLAS TX 75232
74-  3  AYALA, BENIGNO                BOX 814 - BAYAMON PR 00619
47-  7  AYERS, WILLIAM OSCAR          D. SEPTEMBER 24, 1980 NEWNAN, GA.
13-  4  AYERS, YANCEY WYATT           D. MAY 26, 1968 PULASKI, VA.
53-  2  AYLWARD, RICHARD JOHN         9130 BARNVELD - SPRING VALLEY CA 92077
60-  3  AZCUE, JOSE JOAQUIN           10020 CRAIG - SHAWNEE MISSION KS 66212
96-  6  BABCOCK, ROBERT ERNEST        4652 OLD PITTSBURGH RD - NEW CASTLE PA 16101
52-  4  BABE, LOREN ROLLAND           4702 CHICAGO ST - OMAHA NE 68132
22-  3  BABICH, JOHN CHARLES          6111 ROSALIND AV - RICHMOND CA 94803
15-  3  BABINGTON, CHARLES PERCY      D. MARCH 22, 1957 PROVIDENCE, R.I.
80-  5  BABITT, MACK NEAL             2530 MATHEWS ST - BERKELEY CA 94702
17-  3  BACKMAN, WALTER WAYNE         22504 SW RIGGS RD - BEAVERTON OR 97007
75-  9  BACON, EDGAR SUTER            D. OCTOBER 2, 1963 FRANKFORT, KY.
53-  3  BACSIK, MICHAEL JAMES         1608 HANGING CLIFF - DALLAS TX 75224
12-  7  BACZEWSKI, FREDERICK JOHN     D. NOVEMBER 14, 1976 CULVER CITY, CALIF.
29-  5  BADER, LORE VERNE             D. JUNE 2, 1973 LEROY, KAN.
        BADGRO, MORRIS HIRAM          1010 E TEMPERANCE ST - KENT WA 98031
```

```
26-  3  BAECHT, EDWARD JOSEPH         D. AUGUST 15, 1957 QUARRY TWP., ILL.
77-  6  BAEZ, JOSE ANTONIO            27 DEFEBRERO #15 - SAN CRISTOBAL DOMINICAN RP
12-  8  BAGBY, JAMES CHARLES JACOB SR. D. JULY 28, 1954 MARIETTA, GA.
23-  3  BAGBY, JAMES CHARLES JACOB    1910 S COBB DR #4B - MARIETTA GA 30060
23-  4  BAGWELL, WILLIAM MALLORY      D. OCTOBER 5, 1976 CHOUDRANT, LA.
14-  8  BAHNSEN, STANLEY RAYMOND      780 NE 76TH ST - BOCA RATON FL 33431
46-  7  BAHR, EDSON GARFIELD          OLD ADD: STAR RT 1 BOX 51 - ONALASKA WA
14-  8  BAICHLEY, GROVER CLEVELAND    D. JUNE 30, 1956 SAN JOSE, CALIF.
19-  3  BAILEY, ABRAHAM LINCOLN       D. SEPTEMBER 27, 1939 JOLIET, ILL.
17-  4  BAILEY, ARTHUR EUGENE         D. NOVEMBER 14, 1973 HOUSTON, TEX.
76-  2  BAILEY, FRED MIDDLETON        D. AUGUST 16, 1972 HUNTINGTON, W. VA.
```

```
11-  6  BAILEY, HARRY LEWIS           D. OCTOBER 27, 1967 SEATTLE, WASH.
81-  4  BAILEY, HOWARD L              119 SOUTH FIFTH - GRAND HAVEN MI 49417
59-  4  BAILEY, JAMES HOPKINS         3495 SOMERSET TR - ATLANTA GA 30331
53-  4  BAILEY, LONAS EDGAR           642 BROOME RD - KNOXVILLE TN 37919
62-  5  BAILEY, ROBERT SHERWOOD       13450 FAIRFIELD LN #63-A-SEAL BEACH CA 90740
67-  3  BAILEY, STEVEN JOHN           1005 EUCLID AVE - LORAIN OH 44052
75- 10  BAILOR, ROBERT MICHAEL        509 EDNA ST - CONNELLSVILLE PA 15425
45-  2  BAIN, HERBERT LOREN           OLD ADD: 1926 ARTHUR ST NE - MINNEAPOLIS MN
80-  6  BAINES, HAROLD DOUGLAS        107 TRUSTY ST - SAINT MICHAEL MD 21663
76- 10  BAIR, CHARLES DOUGLAS         BOX 86 - MELROSE OH 45861
17-  5  BAIRD, ALBERT WELLS           D. NOVEMBER 27, 1976 SHREVEPORT, LA.
15-  4  BAIRD, HOWARD DOUGLASS        D. JUNE 13, 1967 THOMASVILLE, GA.
62-  6  BAIRD, ROBERT ALLEN           D. APRIL 11, 1974 CHATTANOOGA, TENN.
64-  3  BAKENHASTER, DAVID LEE        3237 MCKINLEY - COLUMBUS OH 43204
38-  4  BAKER, ALBERT JONES           BOX 41 - KENEDY TX 78119
78-  3  BAKER, CHARLES JOSEPH         1521 CHALGROVE DR - CORONA CA 91720
14-  9  BAKER, DELMAR DAVID           D. SEPTEMBER 11, 1973 SAN ANTONIO, TEX.
53-  5  BAKER, EUGENE WALTER          2250 E 48TH ST - DAVENPORT IA 52807
43-  3  BAKER, FLOYD WILSON           3033 IDLEWOOD AVE-YOUNGSTOWN OH 44511
69-  4  BAKER, FRANK                  383 GIRARD AVE - SOMERSET NJ 08873
70-  4  BAKER, FRANK WATTS            BOX 3066 - MERIDIAN MS 39301
12-  9  BAKER, HOWARD FRANCIS         D. JANUARY 16, 1964 BRIDGEPORT, CONN.
76- 11  BAKER, JACK EDWARD            4536 SWALLOW PL - BIRMINGHAM AL 35213
19-  4  BAKER, JESSE EUGENE           D. JULY 25, 1960 POMONA, CALIF.
11-  7  BAKER, JESSE ORMAND           D. SEPTEMBER 26, 1972 TACOMA, WASH.
68-  3  BAKER, JOHNNIE B              4650 MORRO DR - WOODLAND HILLS CA 91364
27-  3  BAKER, NEAL VERNON            1641 COLUMBIA - HOUSTON TX 77008
78-  4  BAKER, STEVEN BYRNE           OLD ADD: 5135 ALZEDA DR - LAMESA CA 92041
35-  1  BAKER, THOMAS CALVIN          2002 GOULD ST FT WORTH TX 76106
63-  6  BAKER, THOMAS HENRY           D. MARCH 9, 1980 PORT TOWNSEND, WASH.
11-  8  BAKER, TRACY LEE              D. MARCH 14, 1975 PLACERVILLE, CAL.
40-  1  BAKER, WILLIAM PRESLEY        412 MELROSE ST SW - LENOIR NC 28645
38-  5  BALAS, MITCHELL FRANCIS       11 LOWELL RD - WESTFORD MA 02181
74-  4  BALAZ, JOHN LARRY             2619 WORDEN ST - SAN DIEGO CA 92110
81-  5  BALBONI, STEPHEN CHARLES      28 CELESTE ST - MANCHESTER NH 03103
56-  5  BALCENA, ROBERT RUDOLPH       2615 CALIFORNIA AVE SW #3 - SEATTLE WA 98116
61-  5  BALDSCHUN, JACK EDWARD        492 BADER ST - GREEN BAY WI 54302
66-  4  BALDWIN, DAVID GEORGE         2002 E RIVER RD #R-11 - TUCSON AZ 85718
53-  6  BALDWIN, FRANK DEWITT         7298 ELKWOOD PL - WESTCHESTER OH 45069
27-  4  BALDWIN, HENRY CLAY           D. FEBRUARY 24, 1964 PHILADELPHIA, PA.
24-  2  BALDWIN, HOWARD EDWARD        D. JANUARY 23, 1958 BALTIMORE, MD.
78-  5  BALDWIN, REGINALD CONRAD      763 LIEBOLD - DETROIT MI 48217
75- 11  BALDWIN, RICKEY ALAN          3304 COLONIAL DR - MODESTO CA 95350
75- 12  BALDWIN, ROBERT HARVEY        878 PACKARD DR - AKRON OH 44320
11-  9  BALENTI, MICHAEL RICHARD      D. AUGUST 4, 1955 ALTUS, OKLA.
66-  5  BALES, WESLEY OWEN            7223 AUGUSTINE - HOUSTON TX 77036
28-  3  BALLENGER, PELHAM ASHBY       D. DECEMBER 8, 1948 WEST GANTT TWP., S. C.
71-  7  BALLINGER, MARK ALAN          XD.BALLINGER:176 DALE - NEWBURY PARK CA 91320
25-  5  BALLOU, NOBLE WINFIELD        D. JANUARY 30, 1963 SAN FRANCISCO, CAL.
62-  7  BALSAMO, ANTHONY FRED         160-15 86TH ST - HOWARD BEACH NY 11414
51-  1  BAMBERGER, GEORGE IRVIN       412 161ST AVE E - REDINGTON BEACH FL 33208
48-  6  BAMBERGER, HAROLD EARL        RR 1 BOX 317 - BIRDSBORO PA 19508
15-  5  BANCROFT, DAVID JAMES         D. OCTOBER 9, 1972 SUPERIOR, WIS.
81-  6  BANDO, CHRISTOPHER MICHAEL    35640 BRUSHWOOD DR - SOLON OH 44139
66-  6  BANDO, SALVATORE LEONARD      104 W JUNIPER LN - MEQUON WI 53092
73- 10  BANE, EDWARD NORMAN           OLD ADD: 6422 APACHE RD - WESTMINSTER CA
69-  5  BANEY, RICHARD LEE            1412 DAMON AVE - ANAHEIM CA 92802
47-  8  BANKHEAD, DANIEL ROBERT       D. MAY 2, 1976 HOUSTON, TEX.
53-  7  BANKS, ERNEST                 1440 N STATE PKWY #3-D - CHICAGO IL 60610
62-  8  BANKS, GEORGE EDWARD          BOX 207 - PACOLET SC 29372
15-  6  BANKSTON, WILBORN EVERETT     D. FEBRUARY 26, 1970 GRIFFIN, GA.
74-  5  BANNISTER, ALAN               2313 S PLAYA - MESA AZ 85202
77-  7  BANNISTER, FLOYD FRANKLIN     10879 26TH AVE S - SEATTLE EA 98168
47-  9  BANTA, JOHN KAY               3215 E 30TH - HUTCHINSON KS 62501
14- 10  BARBARE, WALTER LAWRENCE      D. OCTOBER 28, 1965 GREENVILLE, S.C.
43-  4  BARBARY, DONALD ODELL         402 W CURTIS - SIMPSONVILLE SC 29681
26-  4  BARBEE, DAVID MONROE          D. JULY 1, 1968 ALBEMARLE, N. C.
60-  4  BARBER, STEPHEN DAVID         8324 E LEWIS AVE - SCOTTSDALE AZ 85257
70-  5  BARBER, STEVEN LEE            1517 CUSHMAN DR - SIERRA VISTA AZ 85635
15-  7  BARBER, TYRUS TURNER          D. OCTOBER 20, 1968 MILAN, TENN.
66-  7  BARBIERI, JAMES PATRICK       13619 E 5TH AVE - SPOKANE WA 99216
57-  7  BARCLAY, CURTIS CORDELL       19 VIRGINIA DR - MISSOULA MT 59801
72-  5  BARE, RAYMOND DOUGLAS         911 N IVY ST - JENKS OK 74037
81-  7  BARFIELD, JESSE LEE           5700 BROOKGION #567 - HOUSTON TX 77017
22-  2  BARFOOT, CLYDE RAYMOND        D. MARCH 11, 1971 HIGHLAND PARK, CAL.
76- 12  BARKER, LEONARD HAROLD        5583 RAINER CT - PARMA OH 44134
```

50-	5	BARKER, RAYMOND HAROLD	% GENERAL MOTORS - MARTINSBURG WV 25401
37-	6	BARKLEY, JOHN DUNCAN	1200 LAWRENCE DR - WACO TX 76710
75-	13	BARLOW, MICHAEL ROSWELL	RR 1 BOX 181 - ONEONTA NY 13820
53-	8	BARMES, BRUCE RAYMOND	509 MCDONALD AVE - CHARLOTTE NC 28203
37-	7	BARNA, HERBERT PAUL	D. MAY 18, 1972 CHARLESTON, W. VA.
27-	5	BARNABE, CHARLES EDWARD	D. AUGUST 16, 1977 WACO, TEX.
27-	6	BARNES, EMILE DEERING	D. JULY 3, 1959 MOBILE, ALA.
23-	5	BARNES, EVERETT DUANE	D. NOVEMBER 17, 1980 MINEOLA, N. Y.
57-	5	BARNES, FRANK	507 COMFORT ST - GREENVILLE MS 38701
29-	6	BARNES, FRANK SAMUEL	D. SEPTEMBER 27, 1967 HOUSTON, TEX.
15-	8	BARNES, JESSE LAWRENCE	D. SEPTEMBER 9, 1961 SANTA ROSA, N.MEX.
26-	5	BARNES, JOHN FRANCIS	D. JUNE, 1981
34-	3	BARNES, JUNIE SHOAF	D. DECEMBER 31, 1963 JACKSONVILLE, N. C.
72-	6	BARNES, LUTHER OWEN	5414 34TH AVE SE - LACEY WA 98503
24-	3	BARNES, ROBERT AVERY	LACON ILL 61540
21-	1	BARNES, SAMUEL THOMAS	D. FEBRUARY 19, 1981 MONTGOMERY, ALA.
19-	5	BARNES, VIRGIL JENNINGS	D. JULY 24, 1958 WICHITA, KAN.
15-	9	BARNEY, EDMUND J.	D. OCTOBER 4, 1967 RICE LAKE, WIS.
43-	5	BARNEY, REX EDWARD	4601 HOLLINS FERRY RD - BALTIMORE MD 21227
20-	3	BARNHART, CLYDE LEE	D. JANUARY 21, 1980 HAGERSTOWN, MD.
24-	4	BARNHART, EDGAR VERNON	RR6 BOX 350 - COLUMBIA MO 65201
28-	4	BARNHART, LESLIE EARL	D. OCTOBER 7, 1971 SCOTTSDALE, ARIZ.
24-	3	BARNHART, VICTOR DEE	RR 5 - HAGERSTOWN MD 21741
39-	4	BARNICLE, GEORGE BERNARD	9981 88TH ST N - SEMINOLE FL 33543
65-	4	BARNOWSKI, EDWARD ANTHONY	SILVER STADIUM - ROCHESTER NY 14621
60-	8	BARONE, RICHARD ANTHONY	403 GLENFORD PARK CT - SAN JOSE CA 95136
71-	8	BARR, JAMES LELAND	2129 QUEENS LN - SAN MATEO CA 94402
35-	2	BARR, ROBERT ALEXANDER	OLD ADD: BARRINGTON MOB EST-E BARRINGTON NH
74-	6	BARR, STEVEN CHARLES	550 AVENUE NORTH SE - WINTER HAVEN FL 33880
61-	7	BARRAGAN, FACUNDO ANTHONY	8255 LARIVIERA DR - SACRAMENTO CA 95826
79-	7	BARRANCA, GERMAN MICHAEL	CALLE PINO SUAREZ #1642 - VERACRUZ MEXICO
37-	8	BARRETT, CHARLES HENRY	BOX 427 - TARBORO NC 27886
39-	5	BARRETT, FRANCIS JOSEPH	434 N 3RD ST LEESBURG FL 32748
42-	5	BARRETT, JOHN JOSEPH	D. AUGUST 17, 1974 SEABROOK BEACH, N. H.
23-	6	BARRETT, ROBERT SCHLEY	D. JANUARY 18, 1982 ATLANTA, GA.
33-	3	BARRETT, TRACEY SOUTER	D. NOVEMBER 7, 1966 SEATTLE, WASH.
21-	2	BARRETT, WILLIAM JOSEPH	D. JANUARY 26, 1951 CAMBRIDGE, MASS.
74-	7	BARRIOS, FRANCISCO XAVIER	REFORMA 236 NTE - HERMOSILLO SONORA MEXICO
29-	7	BARRON, DAVID IRENUS	RR 2 - LAWRENCEVILLE GA 30245
14-	11	BARRON, FRANK JOHN	D. SEPTEMBER 18, 1964 PLEASANTS CO., W. VA.
12-	10	BARRY, HARDIN	D. NOVEMBER 5, 1969 CARSON CITY, NEV.
69-	6	BARRY, RICHARD DONOVAN	47275 MIOMIO DR - KANEOHE HI 96744
27-	7	BARTELL, RICHARD WILLIAM	1118 ISLAND DR - ALAMEDA CA 94501
44-	4	BARTHELSON, ROBERT EDWARD	40 MEADOWLARK LN - NORTHFORD CT 06472
28-	5	BARTHOLOMEW, LESTER JUSTIN	D. SEPTEMBER 19, 1972 MADISON, WIS.
53-	5	BARTIROME, ANTHONY JOSEPH	1104 PALMA SOLA BLVD - BRADENTON FL 33505
43-	6	BARTLEY, BOYD OWEN	7500 NOREAST DR - FORT WORTH TX 76118
38-	6	BARTLING, IRVING HENRY	D. JUNE 12, 1973 WESTLAND, MICH.
65-	5	BARTON, ROBERT WILBUR	7956 LOS PINOS CIR - CARLSBAD CA 92008
31-	6	BARTON, VINCENT DAVID	D. SEPTEMBER 13, 1973 TORONTO, ONT.
45-	3	BARTOSCH, DAVID ROBERT	25212 AVENIDA DORENA - NEWHALL CA 91321
48-	7	BASGALL, ROMANUS	1965 LAUREL LN - SIERRA VISTA AZ 85635
12-	11	BASHANG, ALBERT C.	D. JUNE 23, 1967 CINCINNATI, O.
36-	6	BASHORE, WALTER FRANKLIN	4224 KING GEORGE DR - HARRISBURG PA 17109
44-	5	BASINSKI, EDWIN FRANK	6585 SW 67TH ST - PORTLAND OR 97223
11-	10	BASKETTE, JAMES BLAINE	D. JULY 30, 1942 ATHENS, TENN.
61-	8	BASS, NORMAN DELANEY	8814 THIRD AVE - INGLEWOOD CA 90305
77-	8	BASS, RANDY WILLIAM	412 GREEN MEADOW DR - LAWTON OK 73501
39-	6	BASS, RICHARD WILLIAM	2919 LENOX AVE JACKSONVILLE FL 32205
18-	1	BASS, WILLIAM CAPERS	D. JANUARY 12, 1970 MACON, GA.
13-	5	BASSLER, JOHN LANDIS	D. JUNE 29, 1979 SANTA MONICA, CALIF.

23-	7	BATCHELDER, JOSEPH EDMUND	10 MAGNOLIA HOUSE - BEVERLY MA 01915
63-	7	BATEMAN, JOHN ALVIN	OLD ADD: 1911 LINCOLN AVE - LAWTON OK 73505
69-	7	BATES, CHARLES RICHARD	8601 E BONNIE ROSE AVE - SCOTTSDALE AZ 85253
27-	8	BATES, CHARLES WILLIAM	OLD ADD: 5316 W TENTH - TOPEKA KS 66604
70-	6	BATES, DELBERT OAKLEY	8336 133RD NE - REDMOND WA 98052
39-	7	BATES, HUBERT EDGAR	3503 LINDEN AVE - LONG BEACH CA 90807
13-	6	BATES, RAYMOND	D. AUGUST 15, 1970 TUCSON, ARIZ.
73-	11	BATISTA, RAFAEL	P-8 INGENIO CONSUELO-SAN PEDRO DE MACORIS D R
16-	3	BATSCH, WILLIAM MCKINLEY	D. DECEMBER 31, 1963 CANTON, O.

```
12- 12 BATTEN, GEORGE BERNARD          D. AUGUST 4, 1972 NEW PORT RICHEY, FLA.
55-  8 BATTEY, EARL JESSE             %ALLEN, 270 JOY ST - BROOKLYN NY 11201
27-  9 BATTLE, JAMES MILTON           D. SEPTEMBER 30, 1965 CHICO, CAL.
76- 13 BATTON, CHRISTOPHER SEAN       6109 W 77TH ST - LOS ANGELES CA 90045
47- 10 BATTS, MATTHEW DANIEL          838 N ALLYSON - BATON ROUGE LA 70815
48-  8 BAUER, HENRY ALBERT            12705 W 108TH ST - OVERLAND PARK KS 66210
18-  2 BAUER, LOUIS WALTER            D. FEBRUARY 4, 1979 POMONA, N. J.
36-  7 BAUERS, RUSSELL LEE            1924 GARDNER RD WESTCHESTER IL 60156
11- 11 BAUMANN, CHARLES JOHN          D. NOVEMBER 20, 1969 INDIANAPOLIS, IND.
55-  9 BAUMANN, FRANK MATTHEW         7712 SUNRAY LN - ST LOUIS MO 63123
49-  4 BAUMER, JAMES SLOAN            1385 TAREYTON DR - RIVERSIDE CA 92506
12- 13 BAUMGARDNER, GEORGE WASHINGTON D. DECEMBER 13, 1970 BARBOURSVILLE, W. VA
78-  6 BAUMGARTEN, ROSS               1020 BLUFF RD - GLENCOE IL 60022
20-  4 BAUMGARTNER, HARRY E.          D. DECEMBER 3, 1930 AUGUSTA, GA.
53-  9 BAUMGARTNER, JOHN EDWARD       229 FAIRMONT DR - BIRMINGHAM AL 35213
14- 13 BAUMGARTNER, STANWOOD FULTON   D. OCTOBER 4, 1955 PHILADELPHIA, PA.
47- 11 BAUMHOLTZ, FRANK CONRAD        4327 JENNINGS RD - CLEVELAND OH 44109
60-  7 BAUTA, EDUARDO GALVEZ          OLD ADD: 26 NW 58TH AVE - MIAMI FL 33127
59-  5 BAXES, DIMITRIOS S             6211 HUNTLEY AVE - GARDEN GROVE CA 92645
56-  6 BAXES, MICHAEL                 303 WICKMAN DR - MILL VALLEY CA 94941
70-  7 BAYLOR, DONALD EDWARD          260 CAGNEY LN #109 - NEWPORT BEACH CA 92663
```

```
19-  6 BAYNE, WILLIAM LEAR            D. MAY 27, 1981 ST. LOUIS, MO.
13-  7 BEALL, JOHN WOOLF              D. JUNE 13, 1926 EELTSVILLE, MD.
75- 14 BEALL, ROBERT BROOKS          513 BIRCHWOOD RD - HILLSBORO OR 97123
24-  5 BEALL, WALTER ESAU            D. JANUARY 28, 1959 SUITLAND, MD.
56-  7 BEAMON, CHARLES ALONZO         1717 WOODLAND AVE #3-EAST PALO ALTO CA 94303
78-  7 BEAMON, CHARLES ALONZO         421 OAKLAND AVE #6 - OAKLAND CA 94611
30-  2 BEAN, BELVEDORE BENTON         RR 2 BOX 166 - COMANCHE TX 76442
80-  7 BEARD, CHARLES DAVID           3467 REEVES ST - CHAMBLEE GA 30341
48-  9 BEARD, CRAMER THEODORE         RR 13 BOX 258C - INDIANAPOLIS IN 46236
74-  8 BEARD, MICHAEL RICHARD         6200 DENHAM DR - LITTLE ROCK AR 72004
54-  6 BEARD, RALPH WILLIAM           1367 BERKSHIRE DR - WEST PALM BEACH FL 33406
47- 12 BEARDEN, HENRY EUGENE          BOX 176 - HELENA AR 72342
76- 14 BEARE, GARY RAY                2752 ELYSSEE ST - SAN DIEGO CA 92123
63-  8 BEARNARTH, LAWRENCE DONALD     85-18 143RD LN - SEMINOLE FL 33542
77-  9 BEASLEY, LEWIS PAIGE           RR 1 BOX 65 - BOWLING GREEN VA 22427
78-  8 BEATTIE, JAMES LOUIS           161 WILSONS CROSSING RD - AUBURN NH 03032
14- 14 BEATTY, DESMOND A              D. OCTOBER 6, 1969 NORWAY, ME.
63-  9 BEAUCHAMP, JAMES EDWARD        BOX 1790 - PHENIX CITY AL 36867
41-  6 BEAZLEY, JOHN ANDREW           401 BOWLING AVE - NASHVILLE TN 37205
26-  6 BECK, CLYDE EUGENE             BOX 147 - RANDSBURG CA 93554
14- 15 BECK, GEORGE F.               1915 ADD: 22ND AVE- MOLINE ILL
65-  6 BECK, RICHARD HENRY            RR 4 BOX 9528 - WEST RICHLAND WA 99352
24-  6 BECK, WALTER WILLIAM           1925 W FOREST - DECATUR ILL 62522
13-  8 BECK, ZINN BERTRAM            D. MARCH 19, 1981 WEST PALM BEACH, FLA.
11- 12 BECKER, CHARLES S.            D. JULY 30, 1928 WASHINGTON, D.C.
43-  7 BECKER, HEINZ REINHARD         302 CLARENDON DR-DALLAS TX 75208
36-  8 BECKER, JOSEPH EDWARD          15 SUNSET DR - SEBASTIAN FL 32958
15- 10 BECKER, MARTIN HENRY          D. SEPTEMBER 25, 1957 CINCINNATI, O.
65-  7 BECKERT, GLENN ALFRED          870 VIRGINA LAKE CT - PALATINE IL 60067
27- 10 BECKMAN, JAMES JOSEPH          9763 COOPER LANE - CINCINNATI OH 45242
39-  8 BECKMANN, WILLIAM ALOYSIUS     111 FIESTA CIR CREVE COEUR MO 63141
79-  8 BECKWITH, THOMAS JOSEPH        BOX 432 - AUBURN AL 36830
55- 10 BECQUER, JULIO VELLEGAS        829 VINCENT AVE - MINNEAPOLIS MN 55411
62-  9 BEDELL, HOWARD WILLIAM         1187 CRESTWOOD DR - POTTSTOWN PA 19464
25-  6 BEDFORD, JAMES ELDRED         D. JUNE 27, 1962 POUGHKEEPSIE, N. Y.
22-  3 BEDGOOD, PHILIP BURLETTE      D. NOVEMBER 8, 1927 FORT PIERCE, FLA.
12- 14 BEDIENT, HUGH CARPENTER       D. JULY 21, 1965 JAMESTOWN, N.Y.
30-  3 BEDNAR, ANDREW JACKSON        D. NOVEMBER 26, 1937 GRAHAM, TEX.
81-  8 BEDROSIAN, STEPHEN WAYNE       5 CONRAD ST - METHUEN MA 01844
44-  6 BEELER, JOSEPH SAM             3709 NABHOLTZ - MESQUITE TX 75149
68-  4 BEENE, FREDERICK RAY           BOX 143 - OAKHURST TX 77359
48- 10 BEERS, CLARENCE SCOTT          4701 ANDERSON RD #30 - HOUSTON TX 77045
38-  7 BEGGS, JOSEPH STANLEY          9016 WOODMASS LN #1A - INDIANAPOLIS IN 46250
24-  7 BEGLEY, JAMES LAWRENCE        D. FEBRUARY 22, 1957 SAN FRANCISCO, CAL.
21-  3 BEHAN, CHARLES FREDERICK      D. JANUARY 21, 1957 BRADFORD, PA.
70-  8 BEHNEY, MELVIN BRIAN           241 GROVE AVE - VERONA NJ 07042
46-  8 BEHRMAN, HENRY BERNARD         1933 WOODBINE ST - RIDGEWOOD NY 11385
34-  4 BEJMA, ALOYSIUS FRANK          4510 W WASHINGTON #107 - SOUTH BEND IN 46619
65-  8 BELANGER, MARK HENRY           2028 POT SPRING RD - TIMONIUM MD 21093
```

```
50-  7  BELARDI, CARROLL WAYNE        1467 PHANTOM AVE - SAN JOSE CA 95125
62- 10  BELINSKY, ROBERT             OLD ADD: 7110 LAPRESA DR - HOLLYWOOD CA
72-  7  BELL, DAVID GUS "BUDDY"      2200 ENGLISH OAK DR - ARLINGTON TX 76016
50-  8  BELL, DAVID RUSSELL          MINUTEMAN, 1010 RACE ST - CINCINNATI OH 45202
39-  9  BELL, FERN LEE               1975 ADD: 122 W 59TH PL - LOS ANGELES CA
58-  9  BELL, GARY                   40 SAIPAN - SAN ANTONIO TX 78221
24-  8  BELL, HERMAN S.              D. JUNE 7, 1949 GLENDALE, CAL.
71-  9  BELL, JERRY HOUSTON          RR 3 BOX 609 - MOUNT JULIET TN 37122
81-  9  BELL, JORGE ANTONIO          BARIO REST. CLE T #179-SAN PEDRO DE M. DOM RE
76- 15  BELL, KEVIN ROBERT           2341 ALGONQUIN PKWY - ROLLING MEADOWS IL60008
23-  8  BELL, LESTER ROWLAND         615 HIGHLAWN AVE - ELIZABETHTOWN PA 17022
12- 15  BELL, RALPH A.               D. OCTOBER 18, 1959 BURLINGTON, IA.
35-  3  BELL, ROY CHESTER            D. SEPTEMBER 14, 1977 COLLEGE STATION, TEXAS
52-  6  BELL, WILLIAM SAMUEL         D. OCTOBER 11, 1962 DURHAM, N. C.
57-  6  BELLA, JOHN                  24 TAYLOR DR - COS COB CT 06807
75- 15  BELLOIR, ROBERT EDWARD       2666 STONE RD - EAST POINT GA 30344
67-  4  BENCH, JOHN LEE              661 REISLING KNOLL - CINCINNATI OH 45226
78-  9  BENEDICT, BRUCE EDWIN        13810 "Y" CIRCLE - OMAHA NE 68137
31-  7  BENES, JOSEPH ANTHONY        D. MARCH 7, 1975 ELMHURST N. Y.
25-  7  BENGE, RAYMOND ADELPHIA      RR1 BOX 134A - JEWELL TX 75846
23-  9  BENGOUGH, BERNARD OLIVER     D. DECEMBER 22, 1968 PHILADELPHIA, PA.
71- 10  BENIQUEZ, JUAN JOSE          CALLE 99A BLK.87 #12 - CAROLINA PR 00630
39- 10  BENJAMIN, ALFRED STANLEY     140 MARINE CIR - HALLANDALE FL 33009
14- 16  BENN, HOMER OMER             D. JUNE 4, 1967 MENDOTA, WIS.
64-  4  BENNETT, DAVID HANS          408 FAIRCHILD ST - YREKA CA 96097
62- 11  BENNETT, DENNIS JOHN         630 N 5TH - KLAMATH FALLS OR 97601
27- 11  BENNETT, FRANCIS ALLEN       D. MARCH 18, 1966 WILMINGTON, DEL.
23- 10  BENNETT, HERSCHELL EMMETT    D. SEPTEMBER 9, 1964 SPRINGFIELD, MO.
28-  6  BENNETT, JAMES FRED          D. MAY 12, 1957 ATKINS, ARK.
18-  3  BENNETT, JOSEPH HARLEY       D. NOVEMBER 21, 1957 JOEL, MO.
23- 11  BENNETT, JOSEPH ROSENBLUM    148 LEXINGTON CT - RED BANK NJ 07701
34-  5  BENSON, ALLEN WILBERT        HURLEY SD 57036
43-  8  BENSON, VERNON ADAIR         BOX 127-GRANITE QUARRY NC 28072
13-  9  BENTLEY, JOHN NEEDLES        D. OCTOBER 24, 1969 OLNEY, MD.
78- 10  BENTON, ALFRED LEE           OLD ADD: 895 VIL LAKES#102 - ST PETERSBURG FL
34-  6  BENTON, JOHN ALTON           D. APRIL 14, 1968 LYNWOOD, CAL.
10-  7  BENTON, JOHN CLEBON          D. DECEMBER 12, 1937 DOTHAN, ALA.
23- 12  BENTON, LAWRENCE JAMES       D. APRIL 3, 1953 CINCINNATI, O.
22-  4  BENTON, SIDNEY WRIGHT        D. MARCH 8, 1977 FAYETTEVILLE, ARK.
22-  5  BENTON, STANLEY              401 SEQUOIA DR - CHATTANOOGA TN 37411
11- 13  BENZ, JOSEPH LOUIS           D. APRIL 23, 1957 CHICAGO, ILL.
39- 11  BERARDINO, JOHN              1719 AMBASSADOR - BEVERLY HILLS CA 92010
```

54-	7	BERBERET, LOUIS JOSEPH	421 DAROCA AVE - LONG BEACH CA 90814
78-	11	BERENGUER, JUAN BAUTISTA	CLEVMALAMBI AGUADULCE,PROV.COCLE PANAMA
80-	8	BERENYI, BRUCE MICHAEL	BOX 133 - SHERWOOD OH 43556
23-	13	BERG, MORRIS	D. MAY 29, 1972 BELLEVILLE, N. J.
44-	7	BERGAMO, AUGUST SAMUEL	D. AUGUST 19, 1974 GROSSE POINTE CITY, MICH.
14-	17	BERGER, CLARENCE EDWARD	D. JUNE 30, 1959 WASHINGTON, D. C.
22-	6	BERGER, JOHN HENNE	3913 SWANEE ST - LAKE CHARLES LA 70601
13-	10	BERGER, JOSEPH AUGUST	D. MARCH 5, 1956 ROCK ISLAND, ILL.
32-	3	BERGER, LOUIS WILLIAM	11914 RENWOOD LN - ROCKVILLE MD 20852
30-	4	BERGER, WALTER ANTONE	124 21ST ST - MANHATTAN BCH CA 90266
11-	14	BERGHAMMER, MARTIN ANDREW	D. DECEMBER 21, 1957 PITTSBURGH, PA.
16-	4	BERGMAN, ALFRED HENRY	D. JUNE 21, 1961 FORT WAYNE, IND.
75-	16	BERGMAN, DAVID BRUCE	112 PEARTREE LN - ARLINGTON HEIGHTS IL 60004
24-	9	BERLY, JOHN CHAMBERS	D. JUNE 26, 1977 HOUSTON, TEX.
18-	4	BERMAN, ROBERT LEON	105-00 SHORE FRONT PKWY-ROCKAWAY PK NY 11694
77-	10	BERNAL, VICTOR HUGO	4632 ABNER ST - LOS ANGELES CA 90032
78-	12	BERNARD, DWIGHT VERN	RURAL ROUTE 1 - BEKLE RIVE IL 62810
79-	9	BERNAZARD, ANTONIO (GARCIA)	SANTA AV D-25,URB SANTA ELVIRA-CAGUAS PR00625
76-	9	BERNHARDT, JUAN RAMON	4 CALLE IMBERT-SAN PEDRO DE MARCORIS DOM REP
18-	5	BERNHARDT, WALTER JACOB	D. JULY 26, 1958 WATERTOWN, N. Y.
53-	10	BERNIER, CARLOS RODRIGUEZ	OLD ADD: BOX 29, LOMAS VERDI - BAYAMON PR
48-	11	BERO, JOHN GEORGE	14919 S NORMANDIE #30 - GARDENA CA 90249
77-	11	BERRA, DALE ANTHONY	19 HIGHLAND AVE - MONTCLAIR NJ 07042
46-	9	BERRA, LAWRENCE PETER	19 HIGHLAND AVE - MONTCLAIR NJ 07042
12-	16	BERRENS, JOSEPH	
34-	7	BERRES, RAYMOND	111 HAWTHORNE RD - TWIN LAKES WI 53181
62-	12	BERRY, ALLEN KENNETH	1510 MCALISTER - TOPEKA KS 66604
25-	8	BERRY, CHARLES FRANCIS	D. SEPTEMBER 6, 1972 EVANSTON, ILL.
48-	12	BERRY, CORNELIUS JOHN	407 INKSTER AVE - KALAMAZOO MI 49001
42-	6	BERRY, JONAS ARTHUR	D. SEPTEMBER 27, 1958 ANAHEIM, CAL.
21-	4	BERRY, JOSEPH HOWARD JR	D. APRIL 29, 1976 PHILADELPHIA, PA.
64-	5	BERTAINA, FRANK LOUIS	4000 MONTGOMERY DR - SANTA ROSA CA 95405
60-	8	BERTELL, RICHARD GEORGE	25332 REMESA DR - MISSION VIEJO CA 92675
53-	11	BERTOIA, RENO PETER	872 ARGYLE - WINDSOR ONTARIO
36-	9	BERTRAND, ROMAN MATHIAS	4700 MAIN EAST #124 - MESA AZ 85205
56-	8	BESANA, FREDERICK CYRIL	222 DIAMOND OAKS DR - ROSEVILLE CA 95678
40-	2	BESSE, HERMAN	D. AUGUST 13, 1972 LOS ANGELES, CAL.
55-	11	BESSENT, FRED DONALD	1230 LORENTO RD - JACKSONVILLE FL 32211
78-	13	BESWICK, JAMES WILLIAM	12519 DOMINGO RD NE - ALBUQUERQUE NM 87123
10-	8	BETCHER, FRANKLIN LYLE	D. NOVEMBER 27, 1981 WYNNEWOOD, PA.
64-	6	BETHEA, WILLIAM LAMAR	828 W COTTAGE - HOUSTON TX 77009
65-	9	BETHKE, JAMES CHARLES	2003 NE 78TH ST - KANSAS CITY MO 64118
28-	7	BETTENCOURT, LAWRENCE JOSEPH	D. SEPTEMBER 15, 1978 NEW ORLEANS, LA.
20-	5	BETTS, WALTER MARTIN	BOX 326 - MILLSBORO DE 19966
14-	18	BETZEL, CHRISTIAN FREDERICK ALBERT	D. FEBRUARY 7, 1965 WEST HOLLYWOOD,FLA
71-	9	BEVACQUA, KURT ANTHONY	345 WEATHERBEE RD #125 - FORT PIERCE FL 33450
52-	7	BEVAN, HAROLD JOSEPH	D. OCTOBER 5, 1968 NEW ORLEANS, LA.
44-	8	BEVENS, FLOYD CLIFFORD	5067 8TH NE - SALEM OR 97303
42-	7	BEVIL, LOUIS EUGENE	D. FEBRUARY 1, 1973 DIXON, ILL.
17-	6	BEZDEK, HUGH FRANCIS	D. SEPTEMBER 19, 1952 ATLANTIC CITY, N.J.
75-	17	BIANCO, THOMAS ANTHONY	OLD ADD: 353 WERNS AVE - ELMONT NY
49-	5	BIASATTI, HENRY ARCADO	9024 ALLEN RD - ALLEN PARK MI 48101
72-	8	BIBBY, JAMES BLAIR	RR 2 BOX 31B - MADISON HEIGHTS VA 24572
48-	13	BICKFORD, VERNON EDGELL	D. MAY 8, 1960 RICHMOND, VA.
48-	14	BICKNELL, CHARLES STEPHEN	OLD ADD: 5107 WHITEWAY DR - MEMPHIS TN
20-	6	BIEMILLER, HARRY LEE	D. MAY 25, 1965 ORLANDO, FLA.
16-	5	BIGBEE, CARSON LEE	D. OCTOBER 17, 1964 PORTLAND, ORE.
20-	7	BIGBEE, LYLE RANDOLPH	D. AUGUST 5, 1942 PORTLAND, ORE.
29-	8	BIGELOW, ELLIOT ALLARDICE	D. AUGUST 10, 1933 TAMPA, FLA.
32-	4	BIGGS, CHARLES ORVAL	D. MAY 24, 1954 FRENCH LICK, IND.
70-	9	BIITTNER, LARRY DAVID	169 CRESTVIEW CT - BARRINGTON IL 60010
49-	6	BILBREY, JAMES MELVIN	5136 GRELYN DR - TOLEDO OH 43615
37-	9	BILDILLI, EMIL	D. SEPTEMBER 16, 1946 HARTFORD CITY, IND.
49-	7	BILKO, STEPHEN THOMAS	D. MARCH 7, 1978 WILKES-BARRE, PA.

68-	5	BILLINGHAM, JOHN EUGENE	359 ELKHORN CT - WINTER PARK FL 32789
27-	12	BILLINGS, HASKELL CLARK	12 SKYLARK #7 - LARKSPUR, CA 94939
13-	11	BILLINGS, JOHN AUGUSTUS	D. DECEMBER 30, 1981 SANTA MONICA, CALIF.
68-	6	BILLINGS, RICHARD ARLIN	2047 COURTLAND DR - ARLINGTON TX 76017
44-	9	BINKS, GEORGE EUGENE	4803 BELMONT RD - DOWNERS GROVE IL 60515
44-	10	BIRAS, STEPHEN ALEXANDER	D. APRIL 21, 1965 ST. LOUIS, MO.
73-	12	BIRD, JAMES DOUGLAS	OLD ADD: 5542-3 WALT DR - FT MYERS FL
21-	5	BIRD, JAMES EDWARD	D. MARCH 23, 1972 MURFREESBORO, ARK.
33-	4	BIRKOFER, RALPH JOSEPH	D. MARCH 16, 1971 CINCINNATI, O.

```
55- 12 BIRRER, WERNER JOSEPH          115 RANCH TRAIL W - WILLIAMSVILLE NY 14221
42-  8 BISCAN, FRANK STEPHEN          D. MAY 22, 1959 ST. LOUIS, MO.
25-  9 BISCHOFF, JOHN GEORGE          1603 AMOS - GRANITE CITY IL 62040
52-  8 BISHOP, CHARLES TULLER         2705 ADDISON DR - DORAVILLE GA 30040
23- 14 BISHOP, JAMES MORTON           D. SEPTEMBER 20, 1973 MEXICO, MO.
14- 19 BISHOP, LLOYD CLIFTON          D. JUNE 17, 1968 WICHITA, KAN.
24- 10 BISHOP, MAX FREDERICK          D. FEBRUARY 4, 1962 WAYNESBORO, PA.
21-  6 BISHOP, WILLIAM HENRY          D. FEBRUARY 14, 1956 ST. JOSEPH, MO.
12- 17 BISLAND, RIVINGTON MARTIN      D. JANUARY 11, 1973 SALZBURG, AUSTRIA
28-  8 BISSONETTE, DELPHIA LOUIS      D. JUNE 9, 1972 AUGUSTA, ME.
42-  9 BITHORN, HIRAM GABRIEL         D. JANUARY 1, 1952 EL MANTE, MEX.
35-  4 BIVIN, JAMES NATHANIEL         2233 E 8TH ST #251 - PUEBLO CO 81001
14- 20 BLACK, DAVID                   D. OCTOBER 27, 1936 PITTSBURGH, PA.
43-  9 BLACK, DONALD PAUL             D. APRIL 21, 1959 CUYAHOGA FALLS, O.
81- 10 BLACK, HARRY RALSTON           75-707 HWY 111 #C-6 - PALM DESERT CA 92260
11- 15 BLACK, JOHN FALCNOR            D. MARCH 19, 1962 RUTHERFORD, N. J.
24- 11 BLACK, JOHN WILLIAM            D. JANUARY 14, 1968 PHILADELPHIA, PA.
52-  9 BLACK, JOSEPH                  1904 GREYHOUND CORP - PHOENIX AZ 85077
52- 10 BLACK, WILLIAM CARROLL         1233 MT OLIVE AVE - UNIVERSITY CITY MO 63130
62- 13 BLACKABY, ETHAN ALLEN          2308 E ORANGEWOOD - PHOENIX AZ 85020
12- 18 BLACKBURN, EARL STUART         D. AUGUST 4, 1966 MANSFIELD, O.
15- 11 BLACKBURN, FOSTER EDWIN        2542 MAGNOLIA VALLEY DR-NEWPORT RICHEYFL33552
48- 15 BLACKBURN, JAMES RAY           D. OCTOBER 26, 1969 CINCINNATI, O.
58- 10 BLACKBURN, RONALD HAMILTON     RR 10 BOX 67 - MORGANTON NC 28655
10-  9 BLACKBURNE, RUSSELL AUBREY     D. FEBRUARY 29, 1968 RIVERSIDE, N. J.
29-  9 BLACKEREY, GEORGE FRANKLIN     2527 FAIN - WICHITA FALLS TX 76308
42- 10 BLACKWELL, EWELL               84 ULOQUE CT - BREVARD NC 28712
17-  8 BLACKWELL, FREDRICK WILLIAM    D. DECEMBER 8, 1975 MORGANTOWN, KY.
74-  9 BLACKWELL, TIMOTHY P           8854 WHITEPORT LANE - SAN DIEGO CA 92106
27-  2 BLADES, FRANCIS RAYMOND        D. MAY 18, 1979 LINCOLN, ILL.
69-  8 BLADT, RICHARD ALAN            15175 QUAIL RD - SILVERTON OR 97381
25- 10 BLAEHOLDER, GEORGE FRANKLIN    D. DECEMBER 29, 1947 GARDEN GROVE, CALIF.
41-  7 BLAEMIRE, RAE BERTRAM          OLD ADD: 17 SANDALWOOD - CHAMPAIGN IL
29-  9 BLAIR, CLARENCE VICK           312 JEROME - TEXARKANA TX 75501
74- 10 BLAIR, DENNIS HERMAN           612 FAIRWAY - REDLANDS CA 92373
42- 11 BLAIR, LOUIS NATHAN            700 FILHALL-MONROE LA 71205
64-  7 BLAIR, FAUL L. D.              OLD ADD: 3 OBERLEIN CT - TOWSON MD 21204
51-  2 BLAKE, EDWARD JAMES            20 VIEUX CARRE DR - EAST ST LOUIS IL 62203
20-  8 BLAKE, JOHN FREDERICK          OLD ADD: 310 VALLEY DR N - BECKLEY W VA
34-  8 BLAKELY, LINCOLN HOWARD        D. SEPTEMBER 28, 1976 OAKLAND, CALIF.
55- 13 BLANCHARD, JOHN EDWIN          15541 LARKIN DR - MINNETONKA MN 55343
```

```
35-  5 BLANCHE, PROSPER ALBERT        81 EVERETT ST - ARLINGTON MA 02174
72-  9 BLANCO, DAMASO                 OLD ADD: 659 CATAMARAN ST #2 - FOSTER CITY CA
65- 10 BLANCO, GILBERT HENRY          360 E MONTE VISTA RD - PHOENIX AZ 85004
70- 10 BLANCO, OSVALDO CARLOS         OLD ADD: DE LOZADA B1 E16.SAN JOSE DE AVILAVZ
10- 10 BLANDING, FRED JAMES           D. JULY 16, 1950 SALEM, VA.
22-  8 BLANKENSHIP, HOMER             D. JUNE 22, 1974 LONGVIEW, TEX.
22-  9 BLANKENSHIP, THEODORE          D. JANUARY 14, 1945 ATOKA, OKLA.
72- 10 BLANKS, LARVELL                102 INSPIRATION WAY - DEL RIO TX 78840
34-  9 BLANTON, DARRELL ELIJAH        D. SEPTEMBER 13, 1945 NORMAN, OKLA.
55- 14 BLASINGAME, DONALD LEE         % W.COOPER, RR 1 - BUCKNER MO 64016
63- 10 BLASINGAME, WADE ALLEN         BOX 1960 - FAIRBANKS AK 99707
44-  8 BLASS, STEPHEN ROBERT          1756 QUIGG DR - PITTSBURGH PA 15241
71- 12 BLATERIC, STEPHEN LAWRENCE     1662 S UTICA - DENVER CO 80219
48- 16 BLATNIK, JOHN LOUIS            5 CHERMONT RD - LANSING CH 43934
42- 12 BLATTNER, ROBERT GARNETT       RR 2 BOX 205 - LAKE OZARK MO 65049
52-  6 BLAYLOCK, GARY NELSON          BOX 395 - MALDEN MO 63860
50-  9 BLAYLOCK, MARVIN EDWARD        1309 COOLHURST - SHERWOOD AR 72116
56-  9 BLAYLOCK, ROBERT EDWARD        RR2 BOX 235 - MULDROW OK 74948
65- 11 BLEFARY, CURTIS LEROY          39 IROQUOIS AVE - OCEANPORT NJ 07757
60-  9 BLEMKER, RAYMOND               2363 DUNDEE DR - HENDERSON KY 42420
72- 11 BLESSITT, ISAIAH               19712 ANGLIN - DETROIT MI 48234
23- 15 BLETHEN, CLARENCE WALDO        D. APRIL 11, 1973 FREDERICK, MD.
42- 13 BLOCK, SEYMOUR                 4 OLDFIELD LN-LAKESUCCESS NY 11020
49-  9 BLOMBERG, RONALD MARK          3442 SPRING CREEK DR - CONYERS GA 30207
37- 10 BLOODWORTH, JAMES HENRY        BOX 232 APALACHICOLA FL 32320
63- 11 BLOOMFIELD, CLYDE STALCUP      RR2 - ROGERS AR 72756
24- 12 BLOTT, JACK LEONARD            D. JUNE 11, 1964 ANN ARBOR, MICH.
21-  7 BLUE, LUZERNE ATWELL           D. JULY 28, 1958 ALEXANDRIA, VA.
69- 10 BLUE, VIDA ROCHELLE            10285 ROYAL OAK DR - OAKLAND CA 94605
```

22-	10	BLUEGE, OSWALD LOUIS	4429 ELLSWORTH DR - EDINA MN 55435
32-	5	BLUEGE, OTTO ADAM	D. JUNE 28, 1977 CHICAGO, ILL.
14-	21	BLUEJACKET, JAMES	D. MARCH 26, 1947 PEKIN, ILL.
18-	6	BLUHM, HARVEY FRED	D. MAY 7, 1952 FLINT, MICH.
22-	11	BLUME, CLINTON WILLIS	D. JUNE 12, 1973 ISLIP, N.Y.
70-	11	BLYLEVEN, RIKALBERT BERT	18992 CANYON DR - VILLA PARK CA 92667
53-	12	BLYZKA, MICHAEL JOHN	OLD ADD: 2590 BIRCH ST - DENVER CO
60-	10	BOAK, CHESTER ROBERT	816 BONZO ST - NEW CASTLE PA 16101
13-	12	BOARDMAN, CHARLES LOUIS	D. AUGUST 10, 1968 SACRAMENTO, CALIF.
68-	7	BOBB, MARK RANDALL	11036 WESCOTT AVE - SUNLAND CA 91040
63-	12	BOCCABELLA, JOHN DOMINIC	1035 LEA DR - SAN RAFAEL CA 94903
33-	5	BOCEK, MILTON FRANK	2342 S 61ST CT - CICERO IL 60650
74-	11	BOCHTE, BRUCE ANTON	19734 NE 191ST ST - WOODINVILLE WA 98072
78-	14	BOCHY, ERUCE DOUGLAS	115 E AVENUE B - MELBOURNE FL 32901
46-	10	BOCKMAN, JOSEPH EDWARD	BOX 97 - DANVILLE CA 94526
80-	9	BODDICKER, MICHAEL JAMES	BOX 21 - NORWAY IA 52318
11-	16	BODIE, FRANK STEPHAN	D. DECEMBER 12, 1961 SAN FRANCISCO, CALIF.
17-	9	BOECKEL, NORMAN DOXIE	D. FEBRUARY 16, 1924 TORREY PINES, CALIF.
12-	19	BOEHLER, GEORGE HENRY	D. JUNE 23, 1958 LAWRENCEBURG, IND.
12-	20	BOEHLING, JOHN JOSEPH	D. SEPTEMBER 8, 1941 RICHMOND, VA.
67-	5	BOEHMER, LEONARD JOSEPH	FLINT HILLS MO 63346
32-	6	BOERNER, LAWRENCE HYER	D. OCTOBER 16, 1969 STAUNTON, VA.
20-	9	BOGART, JOHN RENZIE	580 W WASHINGTON ST - GENEVA NY 14456
28-	10	BOGGS, RAYMOND JOSEPH	1135 HILL AVE - GRAND JUNCTION CO 81501
76-	17	BOGGS, THOMAS WINSTON	8805 POINT WEST - AUSTIN TX 78759
68-	8	BOGLE, WARREN FREDERICK	11605 SW 103RD AVE - MIAMI FL 33156
13-	13	BOHEN, LEO IGNATIUS	D. APRIL 8, 1942 NAPA, CALIF.
16-	6	BOHEN, SAMUEL ARTHUR	D. MAY 23, 1977 PALO ALTO, CALIF.
74-	12	BOISCLAIR, BRUCE ARMAND	2828 29TH AVE N - ST PETERSBURG FL 33713
78-	15	BOITANO, DANNY JON	15400 WINCHESTER BLVD #43-LOS GATOS CA 95030
51-	3	BOKELMANN, RICHARD WERNER	629 N BELMONT AV - ARLINGTON HEIGHTS IL 60004
33-	6	BOKEN, ROBERT ANTHONY	4011 TACOMA - LAS VEGAS NV 89121
36-	10	BOKINA, JOSEPH	1901 E 25TH ST CHATTANOOGA TN 37404
15-	12	BOLAND, BERNARD ANTHONY	D. SEPTEMBER 12, 1973 DETROIT, MICH.
34-	10	BOLAND, EDWARD JOHN	4813 IMPERIAL PALM DR - LARGO FL 33541
14-	22	BOLD, CHARLES DICKENS	D. JULY 29, 1978 CHELSEA, MASS.
19-	7	BOLDEN, WILLIAM HORACE	D. DECEMBER 8, 1966 JEFFERSON CITY, TENN.
26-	7	BOLEN, STEWART O'NEAL	D. AUGUST 30, 1969 JACKSON, ALA.
62-	14	BOLES, CARL THEODORE	9086 BROADWAY TER - OAKLAND CA 94611
27-	13	BOLEY, JOHN PETER	D. DECEMBER 30, 1962 MAHANOY CITY, PA.
50-	10	BOLGER, JAMES CYRIL	5524 SIDNEY RD - CINCINNATI OH 45238
61-	9	BOLIN, BOBBY DONALD	BOX E - SIX MILE SC 29682
54-	8	BOLLING, FRANK ELMORE	171 FENWICK RD - MOBILE AL 36608
39-	12	BOLLING, JOHN EDWARD	BOX 9266 - PANAMA CITY BEACH FL 32407
52-	11	BOLLING, MILTON JOSEPH	2752 FONTAINEBLEAU DR S - MOBILE AL 36606
65-	12	BOLLO, GREGORY GENE	15207 REGINA ST - ALLEN PARK MI 48101
50-	11	BOLLWEG, DONALD RAYMOND	513 TIMBER RIDGE #206-CAROL STREAM IL 60187
28-	11	BOLTON, CECIL GLENFORD	419 S MAIN ST - GREENVILLE MS 38701

31-	8	BOLTON, WILLIAM CLIFTON	D. APRIL 21, 1979 LEXINGTON, N.C.
78-	16	BOMBACK, MARK VINCENT	%H.BOMBACK, 145 DULUTH ST-FALL RIVER MA 0272?
60-	11	BOND, WALTER FRANKLIN	D. SEPTEMBER 14, 1967 HOUSTON, TEX.
68-	9	BONDS, BOBBY LEE	175 LYNDHURST - SAN CARLOS CA 94076
37-	11	BONETTI, JULIO G	D. JUNE 17, 1952 BELMONT, CAL.
27-	14	BONEY, HENRY TATE	BOX 906 - LAKE WORTH FL 33460
38-	8	BONGIOVANNI, ANTHONY THOMAS	416 ROSEWOOD AVE SAN JOSE CA 95117
40-	3	BONHAM, ERNEST EDWARD	D. SEPTEMBER 15, 1949 PITTSBURGH, PA.
71-	13	BONHAM, WILLIAM GORDON	1605 SYCAMORE WAY - SOLVANG CA 93463
62-	15	BONIKOWSKI, JOSEPH PETER	5109 COTTAGE ST - PHILADELPHIA PA 19124
81-	11	BONILLA, JUAN GUILLERMO	RR 3 BOX 262 - QUINCY FL 32351
13-	14	BONIN, ERNEST LUTHER	D. JANUARY 3, 1965 SYCAMORE, O.
77-	12	BONNELL, ROBERT BARRY	5805 PRICE RD - MILFORD OH 45140
80-	10	BONNER, ROBERT AVERILL	1214 BERNICE ST - CORPUS CHRISTI TX 78412
44-	11	BONNESS, WILLIAM JOHN	D. DECEMBER 3, 1977 CLEVELAND, O.
20-	10	BONO, ACLAI WENDELL	D. DECEMBER 3, 1948 DEARBORN, MICH.
34-	11	BONURA, HENRY JOHN	7441 BENSON - NEW ORLEANS LA 70127
13-	15	BOOE, EVERETT LITTLE	D. MAY 21, 1969 KENNEDY, TEX.
66-	8	BOOKER, RICHARD LEE	BOX 59 - BROOKNEAL VA 24528
28-	12	BOOL, ALBERT	D. SEPTEMBER 27, 1981 LINCOLN, NEB.
81-	12	BOONE, DANIEL HUGH	4615 FELTON #1 - SAN DIEGO CA 92116
22-	12	BOONE, ISAAC MORGAN	D. AUGUST 1, 1958 NORTHPORT, ALA.
19-	8	BOONE, JAMES ALBERT	D. MAY 11, 1968 TUSCALOOSA, ALA.

3- 16	BOONE, LUTE JOSEPH	2810 BRENTWOOD AVE - PITTSBURGH PA 15227
8- 17	BOONE, RAYMOND OTIS	15420 OLDE HWY 80 #137 - EL CAJON CA 92021
2- 12	BOONE, ROBERT RAYMOND	51 SUNRISE CT - MEDFORD NJ 08055
2- 16	BOOZER, JOHN MORGAN	RR 4 - LEXINGTON SC 29072
9- 11	BORBON, PEDRO RODRIGUEZ	LAS PALMAS,CORRAZONO DEJESUS#2-STO DOMINGO DR
4- 12	BORDAGARAY, STANLEY GEORGE	395 CRESTWOOD AV - VENTURA CA 93003
0- 11	BORDI, RICHARD ALBERT	206 ARROYO DR - SOUTH SAN FRANCISCO CA 94080
0- 12	BORDLEY, WILLIAM CLARKE	15521 CHADRON AVE - GARDENA CA 90249
2- 13	BORGMANN, GLENN DENNIS	16 LUNDY TER - BUTLER NJ 07405
4- 9	BORK, FRANK BERNARD	725 FAIRWAY BLVD - COLUMBUS OH 43227
0- 12	BORKOWSKI, ROBERT VILARIAN	1031 GERHARD ST - DAYTON OH 45404
0- 12	BORLAND, THOMAS BRUCE	624 CHEROKEE DR - STILLWATER OK 74074
4- 12	BOROM, EDWARD JONES	827 HIGHLAND OAKS - DALLAS TX 75232
7- 7	BOROS, STEPHEN	2130 WELLS ST - SARASOTA FL 33580
2- 14	BOROWY, HENRY LUDWIG	375 BROAD ST-BLOOMFIELD NJ 07003
2- 21	BORTON, WILLIAM BAKER	D. JULY 29, 1954 BERKELEY, CALIF.
6- 9	BOSCH, DONALD JOHN	1600 MCKINLEY RD - NAPA CA 94558
6- 18	BOSETTI, RICHARD ALAN	1233 HILL ST - ANDERSON CA 96007
7- 13	BOSLEY, THADDIS	1965 VALLEY RD - OCEANSIDE CA 92054
6- 10	BOSMAN, RICHARD ALLAN	%JKJ CHEVROLET - VIENNA VA 22180
8- 13	BOSS, ELMER HARLEY	D. MAY 15, 1964 NASHVILLE, TENN.
5- 4	BOSSER, MELVIN EDWARD	RR 8 BOX 228 - CROSSVILLE TN 38555
5- 13	BOSTICK, HENRY LANDERS	D. SEPTEMBER 16, 1968 DENVER, COLO.
5- 18	BOSTOCK, LYMAN WESLEY	D. SEPTEMBER 24, 1978 GARY, IND.
4- 10	BOSWELL, DAVID WILSON	309 ROXBURY CT - JOPPA MD 21085
7- 6	BOSWELL, KENNETH GEORGE	2306-B ARPDALE - AUSTIN TX 78704
7- 12	BOTTARINI, JOHN CHARLES	303 PLACITAS RD NW ALBUQUERQUE NM 87107
9- 10	BOTTING, RALPH WAYNE	1154 THOMPSON AVE - GLENDALE CA 91201
2- 13	BOTTOMLEY, JAMES LEROY	D. DECEMBER 11, 1959 SAINT LOUIS, MO.
2- 17	BOTZ, ROBERT ALLEN	4592 MONCHES RD - COLGATE WI 53017
6- 10	BOUCHEE, EDWARD FRANCIS	2036 SPRUCE AVE - DES PLAINES IL 60018
4- 23	BOUCHER, ALEXANDER FRANCIS	D. JUNE 23, 1974 TORRANCE, CALIF.
4- 24	BOUCHER, MEDRIC T.	B. 1889
8- 9	BOUDREAU, LOUIS	15600 ELLIS AVENUE - DOLTON IL 60419
1- 10	BOULDIN, CARL EDWARD	37 AUDUBON - FORT THOMAS KY 41075
0- 13	BOURJOS, CHRISTOPHER	4425 N ST. LOUIS - CHICAGO IL 60625
1- 14	BOURQUE, PATRICK DANIEL	2013 E HARVARD DR - TEMPE AZ 85283
2- 18	BOUTON, JAMES ALAN	6 MYRON CT - TEANECK NJ 07666

70- 12	BOWA, LAWRENCE ROBERT	240 MCCLENAGHAN MILL RD - WYNNEWOOD PA 19096
14- 25	BOWDEN, DAVID TIMON	D. OCTOBER 25, 1949 EMORY UNIVERSITY, GA.
19- 9	BOWEN, EMMONS JOSEPH	D. AUGUST 9, 1948 NEW HAVEN, CONN.
77- 14	BOWEN, SAMUEL THOMAS	8 HIGH HILL DR - BRUNSWICK GA 31520
63- 13	BOWENS, SAMUEL EDWARD	RR 4 BOX 27 NATIONAL AVE - LELAND NC 28451
49- 8	BOWERS, GROVER BILL	1007 N FALLS ST - WYNNE AR 72396
35- 6	BOWERS, STEWART COLE	NEW FREEDOM PA 17349
31- 9	BOWLER, GRANT TIERNEY	D. JUNE 25, 1968 DENVER, COLO.

see page 149

```
43- 10  BOWLES, CHARLES JAMES          3004 N CENTER ST-HICKORY NC 28601
22- 14  BOWLES, EMMETT JEROME          D. SEPTEMBER 3, 1959 FLAGSTAFF, ARIZ.
67-  7  BOWLIN, LOIS WELDON            BOX 1026 - LIVINGSTON AL 35470
76- 19  BOWLING, STEPHEN SHADDON       OLD ADD: RR 1 BOX 377A - BIXBY OK 74008
14- 26  BOWMAN, ALVAH EDSON            D. OCTOBER 11, 1979 LONGVIEW, TEXAS
20- 11  BOWMAN, ELMER WILHELM          846 ROBINSON ST - LOS ANGELES CA 90026
61- 11  BOWMAN, ERNEST FERRELL         LAKE SHORE APTS #3 - JOHNSON CITY TN 37601
32-  7  BOWMAN, JOSEPH EMIL            2001 W 83RD ST - LEAWOOD KS 66206
39- 13  BOWMAN, ROBERT JAMES           D. SEPTEMBER 4, 1972 BLUEFIELD, W. VA.
55- 15  BOWMAN, ROBERT LEROY           2911 VIA CARMEN - SAN JOSE CA 95124
49-  9  BOWMAN, ROGER CLINTON          2210 S SEPULVEDA BLVD - LOS ANGELES CA 90064
10- 11  BOWSER, JAMES H                B. 1886 GREENSBURG, PA.
58- 11  BOWSFIELD, EDWARD OLIVER       BOX 4100 - SEATTLE WA 98104
69- 12  BOYD, GARY LEE                 15227 CHANERA AVE - GARDENA CA 90249
10- 12  BOYD, RAYMOND C.               D. FEBRUARY 11, 1920 FRANKFORT, IND.
51-  4  BOYD, ROBERT RICHARD           2811 N VASSAR AVE - WICHITA KS 67220
55- 16  BOYER, CLETIS LEROY            3142 CHAMBLEE TUCKER RD NE - ATLANTA GA 3030
49- 10  BOYER, CLOYD VICTOR            RR ONE BOX 231-A - WEBB CITY MO 64870
55- 17  BOYER, KENTON LLOYD            1254 N KIRKWOOD - SAINT ANN MO 63074
78- 17  BOYLAND, DORIAN SCOTT          8130 S SAGINAW - CHICAGO IL 60617
26-  8  BOYLE, JAMES JOHN              D. DECEMBER 24, 1958 CINCINNATI, O.
12- 22  BOYLE, JOHN BELLEW             D. APRIL 3, 1971 FORT LAUDERDALE, FLA.
29- 10  BOYLE, RALPH FRANCIS           D. NOVEMBER 12, 1978 CINCINNATI, O.
38- 10  BOYLES, HARRY                  BOX 119 - MANNFORD OK 74044
66- 11  BRABENDER, EUGENE MATHEW       % ZESPY, 43 SKIVIEW DR - BELOIT WI 53511
37- 13  BRACK, GILBERT HERMAN          D. JANUARY 20, 1960 GREENVILLE, TEX.
64- 11  BRADEY, DONALD EUGENE          3686 OAKLEY RD - WEST BLOOMFIELD MI 48033
66- 12  BRADFORD, CHARLES WILLIAM      6440 SPRING PARK AVE - LADERA HEIGHTS CA90050
43- 11  BRADFORD, HENRY VICTOR         RR 4-PARIS KY 40361
77- 15  BRADFORD, LARRY                7441 S WABASH AVE - CHICAGO IL 60619
56- 11  BRADFORD, WILLIAM D            BOX 3043 - FAIRFIELD BAY AR 72153
```

```
48- 18  BRADLEY, FREDERICK LANGDON     4540 SOUTH LAYMAN AVE - PICO RIVERA CA 90660
46- 11  BRADLEY, GEORGE WASHINGTON     525 GLEN CROSSING RD - GLEN CARBON IL 62034
27- 15  BRADLEY, HERBERT THEODORE      D. OCTOBER 16, 1959 CLAY CENTER, KAN.
10- 13  BRADLEY, HUGH FREDERICK        D. JANUARY 26, 1949 WORCESTER, MASS.
16-  7  BRADLEY, JOHN THOMAS           D. MARCH 18, 1969 TULSA, OKLA.
81- 13  BRADLEY, MARK ALLEN            COUNTRY SIDE MANOR #9-ELIZABETHTOWN KY 42701
69- 13  BRADLEY, THOMAS WILLIAM        3220 KENNEY DR - FALLS CHURCH VA 22042
17- 10  BRADSHAW, DALLAS CARL          D. DECEMBER 11, 1939 HERRIN, ILL.
52- 12  BRADSHAW, GEORGE THOMAS        RR 2 BOX 6A - HORSE SHOE NC 28742
29- 11  BRADSHAW, JOSEPH SIAH          42 TAMMI DR - TAVARES FL 32778
20- 12  BRADY, CLIFFORD FRANCIS        D. SEPTEMBER 25, 1974 BELLEVILLE, ILL.
15- 14  BRADY, CORNELIUS JOSEPH        D. JUNE 19, 1947 FORT MITCHELL, KY.
56- 12  BRADY, JAMES JOSEPH            OLD ADD: 1027 CAMBRIDGE CRES - NORFOLK VA
46- 12  BRADY, ROBERT JAY             42 OVERLAND ST - MANCHESTER CT 06040
12- 23  BRADY, WILLIAM A.
40-  4  BRAGAN, ROBERT RANDALL         4337 CALMONT ST-FORT WORTH TX 76107
14- 27  BRAINARD, FREDERICK            D. APRIL 17, 1959 GALVESTON, TEX.
15- 15  BRAITHWOOD, ALFRED             D. NOVEMBER 24, 1960 ROWLESBURG, W. VA.
28- 14  BRAME, ERVIN BECKHAM           D. NOVEMBER 22, 1949 HOPKINSVILLE, KY.
35-  7  BRAMHALL, ARTHUR WASHINGTON    1417 ANNEN LN MADISON WI 53715
44- 13  BRANCA, RALPH THEODORE JOS.    791 NORTH ST - WHITE PLAINS NY 10605
39- 14  BRANCATO, ALBERT               108 GREEN VALLEY RD UPPER DARBY PA 19082
62- 19  BRANCH, HARVEY ALFRED          4995 JOLLY DR - MEMPHIS TN 38101
41-  8  BRANCH, NORMAN DOWNS           D. NOVEMBER 21, 1971 NAVASOTA, TEX.
79- 11  BRANCH, ROY                    5322 TERRY AVE - SAINT LOUIS MO 63120
63- 14  BRAND, RONALD GEORGE           1500 PINE VALLEY CIR - ROSEVILLE CA 95678
66- 13  BRANDON, DARRELL G             196 OLD FARM RD - HANOVER MA 02339
28- 15  BRANDT, EDWARD ARTHUR          D. NOVEMBER 1, 1944 SPOKANE, WASH.
56- 13  BRANDT, JOHN GEORGE            611 OSAGE DR - PAPILLION NE 68046
41-  9  BRANDT, WILLIAM GEORGE         D. MAY 16, 1968 FORT WAYNE, IND.
28- 16  BRANNAN, OTIS OWEN             D. JUNE 6, 1967 LITTLE ROCK, ARK.
27- 16  BRANNON, EDGAR DUDLEY          D. FEBRUARY 4, 1980 SUN CITY, ARIZ.
80- 14  BRANT, MARSHALL LEE            301 OAK ST - PENNGROVE CA 94951
21-  8  BRATCHE, FREDERICK OSCAR       D. JANUARY 7, 1962 MASSILLON, O.
24- 13  BRATCHER, JOSEPH WARLICK       OLD ADD: 2519 ROGERS - FORT WORTH TX 76109
64- 12  BRAUN, JOHN PAUL               5101 ACADEMY DR - MADISON WI 53716
71- 15  BRAUN, STEPHEN RUSSELL         FERNRIDGE LN - TITUSVILLE NJ 08560
69- 14  BRAVO, ANGEL ALFONSO           OLD ADD: CALLE CAMINO NUEVO #208-MARACAIBO VZ
21-  9  BRAXTON, EDGAR GARLAND         D. FEBRUARY 25, 1966 NORFLOK, VA.
```

```
41- 10  BRAY, CLARENCE WILBUR              3017 SHERIDAN RD-EVANSVILLE IN 47710
21- 10  BRAZILL, FRANK LEO                 D. NOVEMBER 3, 1976 OAKLAND, CALIF.
43- 12  BRAZLE, ALPHA EUGENE               D. OCTOBER 24, 1973 GRAND JUNCTION , COL.
69- 15  BREAZEALE, JAMES LEO               717 BOLLING - HOUSTON TX 77022
40-  5  BRECHEEN, HARRY DAVID              1134 S HIGHSCHOOL - ADA OK 74820
29- 12  BRECKINRIDGE, WILLIAM ROBERTSON D. AUGUST 23, 1958 TULSA, OKLA.
69- 16  BREEDEN, DANNY RICHARD             DRAWER F - ROBERTSDALE AL 36567
71- 16  BREEDEN, HAROLD NOEL               RR1 BOX 311 - LEESBURG GA 31763
60- 13  BREEDING, MARVIN EUGENE            BOX 1061 - DECATUR AL 35601
80- 15  BREINING, FRED LAWRENCE            1218 33RD AVE - SAN FRANCISCO CA 94122
37- 14  BREMER, HERBERT FREDERICK          D. NOVEMBER 28, 1979 COLUMBUS, GA.
14- 28  BRENEGAN, OLAF SELMAR              D. APRIL 20, 1956 GALESVILLE, WIS.
81- 14  BRENLY, ROBERT EARL                936 ORANGE ST - COSHOCTON OH 43812
10- 14  BRENNAN, ADDISON FOSTER            D. JANUARY 7, 1962 KANSAS CITY, MO.
33-  7  BRENNAN, JAMES DONALD              D. APRIL 2L, 1953 BOSTON, MASS.
81- 15  BRENNAN, THOMAS MARTIN             5500 OAK CENTER DR - OAK LAWN IL 60453
65- 13  BRENNEMAN, JAMES LEROY             16800 PFEIFFER WAY - PERRIS CA 92370
12- 24  BRENNER, DELBERT HENRY             D. APRIL 11, 1971 ST. LOUIS PARK, MINN.
13- 17  BRENTON, LYNN DAVIS                D. OCTOBER 14, 1968 LOS ANGELES, CALIF.
32-  8  BRENZEL, WILLIAM RICHARD           D. JUNE 12, 1979 OAKLAND, CALIF.
14- 29  BRESSLER, RAYMOND BLOOM            D. NOVEMBER 7, 1966 MT. WASHINGTON, O.
56- 14  BRESSOUD, EDWARD FRANCIS           10455 CRESTON DR - LOS ALTOS CA 94022
13- 18  BRETON, JOHN FREDERICK             D. MAY 30, 1973 BELOIT, WIS.
73- 13  BRETT, GEORGE HOWARD               LOT E KAW LN/LAKE QUIVIRA-KANSAS CITY KS66106
24- 14  BRETT, HERBERT JAMES               D. NOVEMBER 25, 1974 ST PETERSBURG, FLA.
67-  8  BRETT, KENNETH ALVEN               1504 STRAND - HERMOSA BEACH CA 90254
39- 15  BREUER, MARVIN HOWARD              1106 JOYCE AVE ROLLA MO 65401
60- 14  BREWER, JAMES THOMAS               23104 E 75TH - BROKEN ARROW OK 74012
44- 14  BREWER, JOHN HERNDON               605 N DEL NORTE AVE - ONTARIO CA 91762
54-  9  BREWER, THOMAS AUSTIN              409 STATE RD - CHERAW SC 29520
43- 13  BREWSTER, CHARLES LAWRENCE         RR 2 BOX 165A - BLACKSEAR GA 31516
61- 12  BRICE, ALAN HEALEY                 7807 16TH AVE NW - BRADENTON FL 33505
58- 12  BRICKELL, FRITZ DARRELL            D. OCTOBER 15,1965 WICHITA, KAN.
26-  9  BRICKELL, GEORGE FREDERICK         D. APRIL 8, 1961 WICHITA, KAN.
13- 19  BRICKLEY, GEORGE VINCENT           D. FEBRUARY 23, 1947 EVERETT, MASS.
52- 13  BRICKNER, RALPH HAROLD             3967 ROBINHILL DR - CINCINNATI OH 45211
51-  5  BRIDEWESER, JAMES EHRENFELD        24326 PARK PLACE DR - LAGUNA NIGUEL CA 92677
51-  6  BRIDGES, EVERETT LAMAR             RR3 BOX 522 L-1 - COEUR D'ALENE ID 83814
59-  7  BRIDGES, MARSHALL                  1908 RIDGEWAY - JACKSON MS 39206
30-  5  BRIDGES, THOMAS JEFFERSON DAVIS D. APRIL 19, 1968 NASHVILLE, TENN.
12- 25  BRIEF, ANTHONY VINCENT             D. FEBRUARY 10, 1963 MILWAUKEE, WIS.
75- 19  BRIGGS, DANIEL LEE                 7575 E ARKANSAS #9-205 - DENVER CO 80231
64- 13  BRIGGS, JOHN EDWARD                BOX 1885 - PATERSON NJ 07509
56- 15  BRIGGS, JOHN TIFT                  8724 SHERRY DR - ORANGEVALE CA 95662
58- 13  BRIGHT, HARRY JAMES                2048 50TH AVE - SACRAMENTO CA 95827
65- 14  BRILES, NELSON KELLEY              1324 CLEARVIEW DR - GREENSBURG PA 15501
22- 15  BRILLHEART, JAMES BENSON           D. SEPTEMBER 2, 1972 RADFORD, VA.
12- 26  BRINKER, WILLIAM HUTCHINSON        D. FEBRUARY 5, 1965 ARCADIA, CAL.
69- 17  BRINKMAN, CHARLES ERNEST           332 INGALLS ST - CINCINNATI OH 45204
61- 13  BRINKMAN, EDWIN ALBERT             7106 WYANDOTTE DR - CINCINNATI OH 45238
52- 14  BRINKOPF, LEON CLARENCE            915 S MINNESOTA - CAPE GIRARDEAU MO 63701
47- 13  BRISSIE, LELAND VICTOR             653 CRESTLYN DR - NORTH AUGUSTA SC 29841
66- 14  BRISTOL, JAMES DAVID               RR1 - ANDREWS NC 28901
37- 15  BRITTAIN, AUGUST SCHUSTER          D. FEBRUARY 16, 1974 WILMINGTON, N. C.
50- 13  BRITTIN, JOHN ALBERT               1036 FRANCELLA CT - SPRINGFIELD IL 62702
67-  9  BRITTON, JAMES ALAN                10455 SW 112TH ST - MIAMI 33176
13- 20  BRITTON, STEPHEN GILBERT           2404 STEVENS - PARSONS KS 67357
79- 12  BRIZZOLARA, ANTHONY JOHN           %T.BRIZZOLARA,640 CLAIRMONT - ATLANTA GA30333
34- 13  BROACA, JOHN JOSEPH                123 GARDEN ST - LAWRENCE MA 01841
71- 17  BROBERG, PETER SVEN                1010 LOCUST ST - WEST PALM BEACH FL 33405
17- 11  BROCK, JOHN RAY                    D. OCTOBER 27, 1951 CLAYTON, MO.
61- 14  BROCK, LOUIS CLARK                 12595 DURBIN DR - ST LOUIS MO 63141
```

John Brower

```
52- 15  BRODOWSKI, RICHARD STANLEY         90 FORD ST - LYNN MA 01904
59-  8  BROGLIO, ERNEST GILBERT            2838 VIA CARMEN - SAN JOSE CA 95124
72- 14  BROHAMER, JOHN ANTHONY             1060-4 VALE TER - VISTA CA 92083
44- 15  BRONDELL, KENNETH LEROY            7029 DECELIS PL - VAN NUYS CA 91401
10- 15  BRONKIE, HERMAN CHARLES            D. MAY 27, 1968 SOMERS, CONN.
59-  9  BRONSTAD, JAMES WARREN             6101 KENWICK - FT WORTH TX 76116
75- 20  BROOKENS, EDWARD DWAIN             92 FIFTH AVE - FAYETTEVILLE PA 17222
79- 13  BROOKENS, THOMAS DALE              120 HILLSIDE DR - FAYETTEVILLE PA 17222
80- 16  BROOKS, HUBERT                     1502 SPRING AVE - COMPTON CA 90221
25- 11  BROOKS, JONATHAN JOSEPH            D. JUNE 17, 1962 KIRKWOOD, MO.
69- 18  BROOKS, ROBERT                     1130 W 252ND ST - HARBOR CITY CA 90710
40-  6  BROSKIE, SIGMUND THEODORE          D. MAY 17, 1975 CANTON, O.
54- 10  BROSNAN, JAMES PATRICK             7742 W CHURCHILL ST - MORTON GROVE IL 60053
69- 19  BROSSEAU, FRANKLIN LEE             41 ISLAND RD - SAINT PAUL MN 55110
16-  8  BROTTEM, ANTON CHRISTIAN           D. AUGUST 5, 1929 CHICAGO, ILL.
80- 17  BROUHARD, MARK STEVEN              6289 JACKIE AVE - WOODLAND HILLS CA 91367
55- 18  BROVIA, JOSEPH JOHN                142 ACADIA ST - SANTA CRUZ CA 95060
20- 13  BROWER, FRANK WILLARD              D. NOVEMBER 20, 1960 BALTIMORE, MD.
```

BROWER   BRYANT

```
31- 10 BROWER, LOUIS LESTER          RR 4 BOX 974 - LINDALE TX 75771
51-  7 BROWN, ALTON LEO              253 CONSUL AVE - VIRGINIA BEACH VA 23462
11- 17 BROWN, CARROLL WILLIAM        D. FEBRUARY 8, 1977 BURLINGTON, N. J.
11- 18 BROWN, CHARLES ROY            D. JUNE 10, 1968 SPRING HILL, KAN.
28- 17 BROWN, CLINTON HAROLD         D. DECEMBER 31, 1955 ROCKY RIVER,O.
73- 14 BROWN, CURTIS                 3745 HAYWOOD ST - SACRAMENTO CA 95838
81- 16 BROWN, DARRELL WAYNE          5843 FIFTH AVE - LOS ANGELES CA 90043
14- 30 BROWN, DELOS HIGHT            D. DECEMBER 21, 1964 CARBONDALE, ILL.
13- 21 BROWN, DRUMMOND NICOL         D. JANUARY 27, 1927 PLATTE CO., MO.
20- 14 BROWN, EDWARD WILLIAM         D. SEPTEMBER 10, 1956 VALLEJO, CAL.
69- 20 BROWN, EDWIN RANDOLPH         OLD ADD: 1119 EDWARD ST - LEESBURG FL 32749
11- 19 BROWN, ELMER YOUNG            D. JANUARY 23, 1955 INDIANAPOLIS, IND.
51-  8 BROWN, HECTOR HAROLD          BOX 1626 - GREENSBORO NC 27402
69- 21 BROWN, ISAAC                  LINCOLN CT #A-4 - LAKELAND FL 33805
70- 13 BROWN, JACKIE GENE            RR 3 BOX 50B - HOLDENVILLE OK 74848
15- 16 BROWN, JAMES DONALDSON        1917 ADD: 712 ELLAS ST - BEATRICE NE
37- 16 BROWN, JAMES ROBERSON         D. DECEMBER 29, 1977 BATH, N. C.
75- 21 BROWN, JERALD RAY             9023 TILE ST - HOUSTON TX 77029
37- 17 BROWN, JOHN LINDSAY           D. JANUARY 1, 1967 SAN ANTONIO, TEX.
68- 10 BROWN, JOPHERY CLIFFORD       3008 W 81ST ST - INGLEWOOD CA 90305
27- 17 BROWN, JOSEPH HENRY           D. MARCH 7, 1950 LOS ANGELES, CALIF.
63- 15 BROWN, LARRY LESLEY           1428 NORTH O ST - LAKE WORTH FL 33460
76- 20 BROWN, LEON                   1209 E FREMONT - TEMPE AZ 85282
25- 12 BROWN, LLOYD ANDREW           D. JANUARY 14, 1974 OPALOCKA, FLA.
35-  8 BROWN, MACE STANLEY           305 N HOLDEN ROAD GREENSBORO NC 27410
22- 16 BROWN, MYRL LINCOLN           D. FEBRUARY 23, 1981 HARRISBURG, PA.
43- 14 BROWN, NORMAN                 106 E MAIN ST-BENNETTSVILLE SC 29512
65- 15 BROWN, OLLIE LEE              8462 COUNTRY CLUB DR - BUENA PARK CA 90621
69- 22 BROWN, OSCAR LEE              19113 GUNLOCK AVE - CARSON CA 90746
61- 15 BROWN, PAUL DWAYNE            RR 4 - HOLDENVILLE OK 74848
57-  8 BROWN, RICHARD ERNEST         D. APRIL 12, 1970 BALTIMORE, MD.
14- 31 BROWN, ROBERT M.              B. 1891
30-  6 BROWN, ROBERT MURRAY          53 QUEEN ANNES DR-EAST WEYMOUTH MA 02189
46- 13 BROWN, ROBERT WILLIAM         1324 THOMAS PL - FT WORTH TX 76107
79- 14 BROWN, ROGERS LEE             BOX 874 - EASTVILLE VA 23307
81- 17 BROWN, SCOTT EDWARD           BOX 608 - DEQUINCY LA 70633
78- 18 BROWN, THOMAS DALE            248 GLORIA DR - BATON ROUGE LA 70815
44- 16 BROWN, THOMAS MICHAEL         315 SHADY PL - BRENTWOOD TN 37027
63- 16 BROWN, THOMAS WILLIAM         9104 WOODLAND DR - SILVER SPRING MD 20910
25- 13 BROWN, WALTER GEORGE          D. OCTOBER 2, 1966 FREEPORT, N. Y.
47- 14 BROWN, WALTER IRVING          RR ORIENTAL PARK - BEMUS POINT NY 14712
47- 15 BROWN, WILLARD JESSE          2217 BRECKENRIDGE - HOUSTON TX 77026
63- 17 BROWN, WILLIAM JAMES          17206 SANTA BARBARA - DETROIT MI 48221
12- 27 BROWN, WILLIAM VERNA          D. MAY 15, 1965 LUBBOCK, TEX.
65- 16 BROWNE, BYRON ELLIS           2223 SYLVANIE - SAINT JOSEPH MO 64501
35-  9 BROWNE, EARL JAMES            1405 FAIR PARK BLVD LITTLE ROCK AZ 72204
62- 20 BROWNE, PRENTICE ALMONT       187-23 CASPER DR - SPRING TX 77373
60- 15 BROWNING, CALVIN DUANE        1000 CAMELOT - CLINTON OK 73601
10- 16 BROWNING, FRANK               D. MAY 19, 1948 SAN ANTONIO, TEX.
67- 10 BRUBAKER, BRUCE ELLSWORTH     OLD ADD: 6622 RED HORSE PIKE - EVANSVILLE IN
32-  9 BRUBAKER, WILBUR LEE          D. APRIL 2, 1978 LAGUNA HILLS, CALIF.
59- 10 BRUCE, ROBERT JAMES           OLD ADD: 30607 BOBRICH ST - LIVONIA MI
61- 16 BRUCKBAUER, FREDERICK JOHN    OLD ADD: 3215 15TH AVE S - GREAT FALLS MT
48- 19 BRUCKER, EARLE FRANCIS JR     303 S WESTWIND DR - EL CAJON CA 92020
37- 18 BRUCKER, EARLE FRANCIS SR     D. MAY 8, 1981 SAN DIEGO, CALIF.
```

```
21- 11 BRUGGY, FRANK LEO             D. APRIL 5, 1959 ELIZABETH, N. J.
78- 19 BRUHERT, MICHAEL EDWIN        143-35 95TH AVE - JAMAICA NY 11435
64- 14 BRUMLEY, TONY MIKE            OLD ADD: 5605 S KENTUCKY AVE - OKLAHOMA CITY
81- 18 BRUMMER, GLENN EDWARD         RR 1 - MOUNTAIN GROVE MO 65711
81- 19 BRUNANSKY, THOMAS ANDREW      1319 S HILLWARD AVE - WEST COVINA CA 91791
49- 11 BRUNER, JACK RAYMOND          1641 N 76TH - LINCOLN NE 68505
39- 16 BRUNER, WALTER ROY            305 S LYNDON LN LOUISVILLE KY 40222
56- 16 BRUNET, GEORGE STUART         4674 FALCON AVE - LONG BEACH CA 90807
76- 21 BRUNO, THOMAS MICHAEL         4609 LINSCOTT - DOWNERS GROVE IL 60515
66- 15 BRUNSBERG, ARLO ADOLPH        1164 128TH AVE N - BLAINE MN 55434
77- 16 BRUSSTAR, WARREN SCOTT        3320 REDWOOD RD - NAPA CA 94558
53- 13 BRUTON, WILLIAM HARON         6122 W OUTER DR - DETROIT MI 48235
61- 17 BRYAN, WILLIAM RONALD         3313 GRACE DR - OPELIKA AL 36801
35- 10 BRYANT, CLAIBORNE HENRY       1380 NW 43RD TER #102-FORT LAUDERDALE FL33313
79- 15 BRYANT, DEREK ROSZELL         OLD ADD: C-12 COOPERSTOWN - LEXINGTON KY
```

BRYANT

66- 16	BRYANT, DONALD RAY	RR 24 BOX 34 - BALDWIN FL 32234
67- 11	BRYANT, RONALD RAYMOND	423 ALVARADO - DAVIS CA 95616
70- 14	BRYE, STEPHEN ROBERT	200 STANTONVILLE RD - OAKLAND CA 94619
22- 17	BUBSER, HAROLD FRED	D. JUNE 22, 1959 MELROSE PARK, ILL.
48- 20	BUCHA, JOHN GEORGE	RR 1 - DANIELSVILLE PA 18038
61- 18	BUCHEK, GERALD PETER	3950A WILMINGTON AVE - ST. LOUIS MO 63116
34- 14	BUCHER, JAMES QUINTER	BOX 308 - PALMYRA PA 17078
18- 7	BUCKEYE, GARLAND MAIERS	D. NOVEMBER 14, 1975 STONE LAKE, WIS.
16- 9	BUCKLES, JESS ROBERT	D. AUGUST 2, 1975 WESTMINSTER, CAL.
69- 23	BUCKNER, WILLIAM JOSEPH	555 W BELDEN AVE - CHICAGO IL 60614
78- 20	BUDASKA, MARK DAVID	10855 BATON ROUGE - NORTHRIDGE CA 91326
56- 17	BUDDIN, DONALD THOMAS	BOX 186 - FOUNTAIN INN SC 29644
46- 14	BUDNICK, MICHAEL JOE	307 WEST BLAINE - SEATTLE WA 98119
13- 22	BUES, ARTHUR FREDERICK	D. NOVEMBER 7, 1954 WHITEFISH BAY, WIS.
63- 18	BUFORD, DONALD ALVIN	15412 VALLEY VISTA BLVD-SHERMAN OAKS CA 91403
53- 14	BUHL, ROBERT RAY	8550 SPACECOAST PKWY - KISSIMMEE FL 32741
45- 5	BUKER, CYRIL OWEN	108 CENTRAL AVE - GREENWOOD WI 54437
54- 11	BULLARD, GEORGE DONALD	7 DYER COURT - DANVERS MA 01923
77- 17	BULLING, TERRY CHARLES	15591 ASTER ST - WESTMINSTER CA 92683
36- 11	BULLOCK, MALTON JOSEPH	BOX 727 - MOSS POINT MS 39563
72- 15	BUMBRY, ALONZA BENJAMIN	311 HOMETOWN WAY - COCKEYSVILLE MD 21030
63- 19	BUNKER, WALLACE EDWARD	OLD ADD: 11201 GREENWOOD N - SEATTLE WA
55- 19	BUNNING, JAMES PAUL DAVID	30 WINSTON HILL RD - FT THOMAS KY 41075
69- 24	BURBACH, WILLIAM DAVID	BOX 3 - DICKEYVILLE WI 53808
55- 20	BURBRINK, NELSON EDWARD	9895 88TH WAY N - SEMINOLE FL 33543
69- 25	BURCHART, LARRY WAYNE	6305 SOUTH 114 EAST AVE - TULSA OK 74133
62- 21	BURDA, EDWARD ROBERT	8737 E KEIM DR - SCOTTSDALE AZ 85253
62- 22	BURDETTE, FREDDIE THOMASON	1200 KINGSTON CT - ALBANY GA 31707
50- 14	BURDETTE, SELVA LEWIS	2837 GULF OF MEXICO DR - LONGBOAT KEY FL33548
10- 17	BURG, JOSEPH PETER	D. APRIL 28, 1969 JOLIET, ILL.
49- 12	BURGESS, FORREST HARRILL	717 CAROLEEN RD - FOREST CITY NC 28043
54- 12	BURGESS, THOMAS ROLAND	3101 WALNUT ST NE - ST PETERSBURG FL 33704
68- 11	BURGMEIER, THOMAS HENRY	12104 W 100TH ST - LENEXA KS 66215
43- 15	BURGO, WILLIAM ROSS	231 GLENWOOD ST-MORGAN CITY LOUISIANA 70380
42- 15	BURICH, WILLIAM MAX	1175 LAMOREE RD #62 - SAN MARCOS CA 92069
10- 18	BURK, CHARLES SANFORD	D. OCTOBER 11, 1934 BROOKLYN, N.Y.
56- 18	BURK, MACK EDWIN	4310 BRAZIL CIR - PASADENA TX 77502
15- 17	BURKAM, CHAUNCEY DEPEW	D. MAY 9, 1964 KALAMAZOO, MICH.
36- 12	BURKART, ELMER ROBERT	139 OTHORIDGE RD LUTHERVILLE MA 21093
76- 22	BURKE, BARRY LAWRENCE	279 COLLINGWOOD - SAN FRANCISCO CA 94114
58- 14	BURKE, LEO PATRICK	RR 10 BOX 29F - HAGERSTOWN MD 21740
23- 16	BURKE, LESLIE KINGSTON	D. MAY 6, 1975 DANVERS, MASS.
24- 15	BURKE, PATRICK EDWARD	D. JULY 7, 1965 ST. LOUIS, MO.
27- 18	BURKE, ROBERT JAMES	D. FEBRUARY 8, 1671 JOLIET, ILL.

BURRUS

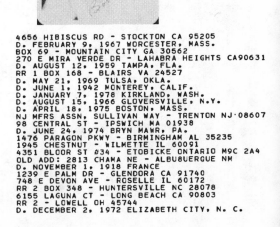

77- 18	BURKE, STEVEN MICHAEL	4656 HIBISCUS RD - STOCKTON CA 95205
10- 19	BURKE, WILLIAM IGNATIUS	D. FEBRUARY 9, 1967 WORCESTER, MASS.
45- 6	BURKHART, WILLIAM KENNETH	BOX 69 - MOUNTAIN CITY GA 30562
74- 13	BURLESON, RICHARD PAUL	270 E MIRA VERDE DR - LAHABRA HEIGHTS CA90631
27- 19	BURNETT, JOHN HENDERSON	D. AUGUST 12, 1959 TAMPA, FLA.
56- 19	BURNETTE, WALLACE HARPER	RR 1 BOX 168 - BLAIRS VA 24527
23- 17	BURNS, DENNIS	D. MAY 21, 1969 TULSA, OKLA.
12- 28	BURNS, EDWARD JAMES	D. JUNE 1, 1942 MONTEREY, CALIF.
14- 32	BURNS, GEORGE HENRY	D. JANUARY 7, 1978 KIRKLAND, WASH.
11- 20	BURNS, GEORGE JOSEPH	D. AUGUST 15, 1966 GLOVERSVILLE, N.Y.
30- 7	BURNS, JOHN IRVING	D. APRIL 18, 1975 BOSTON, MASS.
24- 16	BURNS, JOSEPH FRANCIS	NJ MFRS ASSN, SULLIVAN WAY - TRENTON NJ 08607
10- 20	BURNS, JOSEPH FRANCIS	98 CENTRAL ST - IPSWICH MA 01938
43- 16	BURNS, JOSEPH JAMES	D. JUNE 24, 1974 BRYN MAWR, PA.
78- 21	BURNS, ROBERT BRITT	1476 PARAGON PKWY - BIRMINGHAM AL 35235
55- 21	BURNSIDE, PETER WILLITS	1945 CHESTNUT - WILMETTE IL 60091
78- 22	BURNSIDE, SHELDON JOHN	4351 BLOOR ST #34 - ETOBICKE ONTARIO M9C 2A4
46- 15	BURPO, GEORGE HARVIE	OLD ADD: 2813 CHAMA NE - ALBUQUERQUE NM
14- 33	BURR, ALEXANDER THOMSON	D. NOVEMBER 1, 1918 FRANCE
62- 23	BURRIGHT, LARRY ALLEN	1239 E PALM DR - GLENDORA CA 91740
73- 15	BURRIS, BERTRAM RAY	748 E DEVON AVE - ROSELLE IL 60172
48- 21	BURRIS, PAUL ROBERT	RR 2 BOX 348 - HUNTERSVILLE NC 28078
70- 15	BURROUGHS, JEFFREY ALAN	6155 LAGUNA CT - LONG BEACH CA 90803
43- 17	BURROWS, JOHN	RR 2 - LOWELL OH 45744
19- 10	BURRUS, MAURICE LENNON	D. DECEMBER 2, 1972 ELIZABETH CITY, N. C.

```
58- 15 BURTON, ELLIS NARRINGTON      13555 FIJI WAY - MARINA DEL REY CA 90291
75- 22 BURTON, JAMES SCOTT           700 PEACH TREE LN - ROCHESTER MI 48063
50- 15 BURTSCHY, EDWARD FRANK        620 PEDRETTE APT A-6 - CINCINNATI OH 45238
60- 16 BURWELL, RICHARD MATTHEW      BOX 1153 - MESA AZ 85201
20- 15 BURWELL, WILLIAM EDWIN        D. JUNE 11, 1973 ORMOND BEACH, FLA.
50- 16 BUSBY, JAMES FRANKLIN         BOX 97 - YALAHA FL 32797
41- 11 BUSBY, PAUL MILLER            2011 35TH AVE-MERIDIAN MS 39301
72- 16 BUSBY, STEVEN LEE             OLD ADD: BOX 783 - BLUE SPRINGS MO
43- 18 BUSCH, EDGAR JOHN             508 E WASHINGTON-O'FALLON IL 62269
65- 17 BUSCHHORN, DONALD LEE         17804 E 26TH ST - INDEPENDENCE MO 64057
23- 18 BUSH, GUY TERRELL             BOX 177 - SHANNON MS 38868
12- 29 BUSH, LESLIE AMBROSE          D. NOVEMBER 1, 1974 FORT LAUDERDALE, FLA.
```

```
27- 20 BUSHEY, FRANCIS CLYDE         D. MARCH 18, 1972 TOPEKA, KAN.
26- 10 BUSKEY, JOSEPH HENRY          D. APRIL 11, 1949 CUMBERLAND, MD.
77- 19 BUSKEY, MICHAEL THOMAS        315 OXFORD ST - SAN FRANCISCO CA 94134
73- 16 BUSKEY, THOMAS WILLIAM        476 ALLEGHENY DR - HARRISBURG PA 17111
71- 18 BUSSE, RAYMOND EDWARD         %WM.BUSSE-501 MYRTLE LN S-DAYTONA BCH FL32014
36- 13 BUTCHER, ALBERT MAXWELL       D. SEPTEMBER 15, 1957 LOGAN, W. VA.
11- 21 BUTCHER, HENRY JOSDPH         D. DECEMBER 28, 1979 HAZEL CREST, ILL.
80- 18 BUTCHER, JOHN DANIEL          3826 SAN AUGUSTINE DR - GLENDALE CA 91206
80- 19 BUTERA, SALVATORE PHILIP      38 HILL DR- BOHEMIA NY 11716
43- 19 BUTKA, EDWARD LUKE            131 W COLLEGE ST-CANONSBURG PA 15317
40-  7 BUTLAND, WILBURN RUE          2735 CRUFT-TERRE HAUTE IN 47803
11- 22 BUTLER, ARTHUR EDWARD         732 JUNE ST - FALL RIVER MA 02720
81- 20 BUTLER, BRETT MORGAN          624 W AUSTIN - LIBERTYVILLE IL 60048
62- 24 BUTLER, CECIL DEAN            RR4 - DALLAS GA 30132
33-  8 BUTLER, CHARLES THOMAS        D. MAY 10, 1964 SIMON'S ISLAND, GA.
26- 11 BUTLER, JOHN STEPHEN          D. APRIL 29, 1967 LONG BEACH, CAL.
69- 26 BUTLER, WILLIAM FRANKLIN      RR 2 BOX F-13 - STEPHENS CITY VA 22655
62- 25 BUTTERS, THOMAS ARDEN         ATH DEPT, DUKE UNIV - DURHAM NC 27706
38- 11 BUXTON, RALPH STANLEY         348 BOWLING GREEN SAN LEANDRO CA 94577
45-  7 BUZAS, JOSEPH JOHN            BOX 1030 - ALPHA NJ 08865
58- 16 BUZHARDT, JOHN WILLIAM        RR 2 BOX 141A - PROSPERITY SC 29127
43- 20 BYERLY, ELDRED WILLIAM        8611 SAPPINGTON RD-ST LOUIS MO 63126
50- 17 BYRD, HARRY GLADWIN           110 HELTON ST - DARLINGTON SC 29532
77- 20 BYRD, JEFFREY ALAN            11085 MORNING DOVE RD - LAKESIDE CA 92040
29- 13 BYRD, SAMUEL DEWEY            D. MAY 11, 1981 MESA, ARIZ.
29- 14 BYRNE, GERALD WILFORD         D. AUGUST 11, 1955 LANSING, MICH.
43- 21 BYRNE, THOMAS JOSEPH          442 PINEVIEW AVE-WAKE FOREST NC 27587
43- 22 BYRNES, MILTON JOHN           D. FEBRUARY 1, 1979 ST. LOUIS, MO.
80- 20 BYSTROM, MARTIN EUGENE        17071 SW 86TH AVE - MIAMI FL 33157
44- 17 CABALLERO, RALPH JOSEPH       6773 MILNE ST - NEW ORLEANS LA 70119
72- 17 CABELL, ENOS MILTON           10031 SAGEDOWNE - HOUSTON TX 77034
13- 23 CABRERA, ALFREDO A            D. HAVANA, CUBA
77- 21 CACEK, CRAIG THOMAS           8916 GLORIA AVE - SEPULVEDA CA 91343
15- 18 CADORE, LEON JOSEPH           D. MARCH 16, 1958 SPOKANE, WASH.
12- 30 CADY, FORREST LEROY           D. MARCH 3, 1946 CEDAR RAPIDS, IA.
37- 19 CAFEGO, THOMAS                D. OCTOBER 29, 1961 DETROIT, MICH.
56- 20 CAFFIE, JOSEPH CLIFFORD       447 3RD ST - WARREN OH 44483
78- 23 CAGE, WAYNE LEVELL            RURAL ROUTE 2 BOX 182 - CHOUDRANT LA 71227
68- 12 CAIN, LESLIE                  4516 CYPRESS AVE - RICHMOND CA 91804
32- 10 CAIN, MERRITT PATRICK         D. APRIL 3, 1975 ATLANTA, GA.
49- 13 CAIN, ROBERT MAX              161 EAST 226TH ST - EUCLID ON 44123
34- 15 CAITHAMER, GEORGE THEODORE    D. JUNE 1, 1954 CHICAGO, ILL.
50- 18 CALDERONE, SAMUEL FRANCIS     1000 S COOPER ST - BEVERLY NJ 08010
28- 18 CALDWELL, BRUCE               D. FEBRUARY 15, 1959 WEST HAVEN, CONN.
25- 14 CALDWELL, CHARLES WILLIAM     D. NOVEMBER 1, 1957 PRINCETON, N. J.
28- 19 CALDWELL, EARL WELTON         1110 OAK DR - MISSION TX 78572
71- 19 CALDWELL, RALPH MICHAEL       1645 BROOK RUN DR - RALEIGH NC 27614
10- 21 CALDWELL, RAYMOND BENJAMIN    D. AUGUST 17, 1967 SALAMANCA, N. Y.
13- 24 CALHOUN, WILLIAM DAVITTE      D. FEBRUARY 11, 1955 SANDERSVILLE, GA.
41- 12 CALIGIURI, FREDERICK JOHN     RIMERSBURG PA 16248
22- 18 CALLAGHAN, MARTIN FRANCIS     D. JUNE 24, 1975 NORWOOD, MASS.
10- 22 CALLAHAN, DAVID JOSEPH        D. OCTOBER 28, 1969 OTTAWA, ILL.
39- 17 CALLAHAN, JOSEPH THOMAS       D. MAY 24, 1949 SOUTH BOSTON, MASS.
13- 25 CALLAHAN, LEO DAVID           611 MARYLAND AVE - ERIE PA 16502
15- 19 CALLAHAN, RAYMOND JAMES       D. JANUARY 23, 1973 OLYMPIA, WASH.
13- 26 CALLAHAN, WESLEY LEROY        D. SEPTEMBER 13, 1953 DAYTON,O.
21- 12 CALLAWAY, FRANK BURNETT       919 SCENIC DR - KNOXVILLE TN 37919
58- 17 CALLISON, JOHN WESLEY         2316 OAKDALE ST - GLENSIDE PA 19038
```

CALMUS   CARLTON

```
63- 20  CALMUS, RICHARD LEE           3823 S 28TH WEST AVE - TULSA OK 74107
42- 16  CALVERT, PAUL LEO EMILE       364 RUE CHAPLAINE #7-SHERBROOKE QUEBEC
13- 27  CALVO, JACINTO                D. JUNE 15, 1965 MIAMI, FLA.
80- 21  CAMACHO, ERNEST CARLOS        OLD ADD: 746 ST REGIS - AVON LAKE OH 44012
70- 16  CAMBRIA, FREDERICK DENNIS     12 IRIS CT - NORTHPORT NY 11768
43- 23  CAMELLI, HENRY RICHARD        6 LARCH RD-WELLESLEY MA 02181
33-  9  CAMILLI, ADOLF LOUIS          2831 HACIENDA ST - SAN MATEO CA 94403
60- 17  CAMILLI, DOUGLAS JOSEPH       %B.CAMILLI,1119 WINDING RDG-SANTAROSA CA95404
69- 27  CAMILLI, LOUIS STEVEN         4700 OAHU DR NE - ALBUQUERQUE NM 87111
17- 12  CAMP, HOWARD LEE              D. MAY 8, 1950 EASTABOGA, ALA.
76- 23  CAMP, RICK LAMAR              37 MOORE ST - TRION GA 30753
48- 22  CAMPANELLA, ROY               1000 ELYSIAN PARK AVE - LOS ANGELES CA 90012
64- 15  CAMPANERIS, DAGOBERTO         BOX 16901 - RAYTOWN MO 64133
43- 24  CAMPANIS, ALEXANDER SEBASTIAN 3113 CORONADO DR-FULLERTON CA 92632
66- 17  CAMPANIS, JAMES ALEXANDER     17082 CASCADES AVE - YORBA LINDA CA 92686
28- 20  CAMPBELL, ARCHIBALD STEWART   800 E NICHOLS BLVD #7 - SPARKS NV 89431
30-  8  CAMPBELL, BRUCE DOUGLAS       4011 BAYSIDE RD - FT MYERS BEACH FL 33931
40-  8  CAMPBELL, CLARENCE            SPARTA VA 22552
77- 22  CAMPBELL, DAVID ALAN          RR 10 LYNN TER #2 - JOHNSON CITY TN 37601
67- 12  CAMPBELL, DAVID WILSON        11154 IRONWOOD RD - SAN DIEGO CA 92131
70- 17  CAMPBELL, JAMES ROBERT        RR 1 - LAMAR SC 29069
62- 26  CAMPBELL, JAMES ROBERT        411 WAVERLEY AVE - MENLO PARK CA 94025
33- 10  CAMPBELL, JOHN MILLARD        100 SILVER BEACH #4-DAYTONA BEACH FL 32081
67- 13  CAMPBELL, JOSEPH EARL         RR 9 BOX 738 - BOWLING GREEN KY 42101
41- 13  CAMPBELL, PAUL MCLAUGHLIN     BOX 1724 - FAIRFIELD GLADE TN 38555
64- 16  CAMPBELL, RONALD THOMAS       MEADOWVIEW DR - DECATUR TN 37322
33- 11  CAMPBELL, WILLIAM GILTHORPE   D. FEBRUARY 21, 1973 LOS ANGELES, CAL.
73- 17  CAMPBELL, WILLIAM RICHARD     16812 ALGONQUIN - HUNTINGTON BEACH CA 92649
77- 23  CAMPER, CARDELL               BOX 1652 AVONDALE AZ 85323
69- 28  CAMPISI, SALVATORE JOHN       3303 LAKEWOOD DR - HOLIDAY FL 33590
51-  9  CAMPOS, FRANCISCO JOSE LOPEZ  2840 NW 4TH ST - MIAMI FL 33125
18-  8  CANAVAN, HUGH EDWARD          D. SEPTEMBER 4, 1967 BOSTON, MASS.
75- 23  CANDELARIA, JOHN ROBERT       312 32ND AVE E - BRADENTON FL 33505
43- 25  CANDINI, MILO CAIN            641 MANOR - MANTECA CA 95336
77- 24  CANEIRA, JOHN CASCAES         18 SPRUCE ST - NAUGATUCK CT 06770
60- 18  CANNIZZARO, CHRISTOPHER JOHN  6615 RIDGE MANOR AVE - SAN DIEGO CA 92120
77- 25  CANNON, JOSEPH JEROME         6426 WAGNER RD - PENSACOLA FL 32505
25- 15  CANTRELL, DEWEY GUY           D. JANUARY 31, 1961 MCALESTER, OKLA.
27- 21  CANTWELL, BENJAMIN CALDWELL   D. DECEMBER 4, 1962 SALEM, MO.
16- 10  CANTWELL, MICHAEL JOSEPH      D. JANUARY 9, 1953 OTEEN, N.C.
76- 24  CAPILLA, DOUGLAS EDMOND       3178 MANDA DR - SAN JOSE CA 95124
81- 21  CAPPUZZELLO, GEORGE ANGELO    2345 COLLINS LN - LAKELAND FL 33803
71- 20  CAPRA, LEE WILLIAM            7111 RIVERSIDE - BERWYN IL 60402
44- 18  CAPRI, FATRICK NICHOLAS       935 41ST ST - BROOKLYN NY 11219
12- 31  CAPRON, RALPH EARL            D. SEPTEMBER 19, 1980 LOS ANGELES, CALIF.
30-  9  CARAWAY, CECIL BRADFORD       D. JUNE 9, 1974 EL PASO, TEX.
69- 29  CARBO, BERNARDO               14578 MARKESE - ALLEN PARK MI 48101
46- 16  CARDEN, JOHN BRUTON           D. FEBRUARY 8, 1949 MEXIA, TEX.
63- 21  CARDENAL, JOSE ROSARIO        2818 FARMINGTON LN - NORTHBROOK IL 60062
60- 19  CARDENAS, LEONARDO LAZARO     6700 STOLL LN - CINCINNATI OH 45236
63- 22  CARDINAL, CONRAD SETH         212 HILLCREST DR - NORTH LAS VEGAS NV 89030
43- 26  CARDONI, ARMAND JOSEPH        D. APRIL 2, 1969 JESSUP, PA.
57-  9  CARDWELL, DONALD EUGENE       BOX 474 - CLEMMONS NC 27012
67- 14  CAREW, RODNEY CLINE           5144 CRESCENT DR - ANAHEIM CA 92807
52- 16  CAREY, ANDREW ARTHUR          4411 E EMBERWOOD LN - ANAHEIM CA 92807
10- 23  CAREY, MAX GEORGE             D. MAY 30, 1976 MIAMI, FLA.
35- 11  CAREY, THOMAS FRANCIS ALOYSIUS D. FEBRUARY 21, 1970 ROCHESTER, N. Y.
32- 11  CARLETON, JAMES OTTO          D. JANUARY 11, 1977 FORT WORTH, TEX.
41- 14  CARLIN, JAMES ARTHUR          1215 33RD ST-BIRMINGHAM AL 35218
67- 15  CARLOS, FRANCISCO MANUEL      1229 SESMAS ST - DUARTE CA 91010
48- 23  CARLSEN, DONALD HERBERT       3600 E EASTER AVE - LITTLETON CO 80120
17- 13  CARLSON, HAROLD GUST          D. MAY 28, 1930 CHICAGO, ILL.
20- 16  CARLSON, LEON ALTON           D. SEPTEMBER 15, 1961 JAMESTOWN, N. Y.
11- 23  CARLSTROM, ALBIN OSCAR        D. APRIL 23, 1935 ELIZABETH, N.J.
65- 18  CARLTON, STEVEN NORMAN        16240 HOLTS LAKE DR - CHESTERFIELD MO 63017
```

27- 22	CARLYLE, HIRAM CLEO	D. NOVEMBER 12, 1967 LOS ANGELES, CAL.
25- 16	CARLYLE, ROY EDWARD	D. NOVEMBER 22, 1956 NORCROSS, GA.
59- 11	CARMEL, LEON JAMES	10 PLEASANT VALLEY DR - CORAM NY 11727
41- 15	CARNETT, EDWIN ELLIOTT	1010 INDIAN CREEK DR - LEBANON MO 65536
43- 27	CARPENTER, LEWIS EMMETT	D. APRIL 25, 1979 MARIETTA, GA.
16- 11	CARPENTER, PAUL CALVIN	D. MARCH 14, 1968 NEWARK, O.
40- 9	CARPENTER, ROBERT LOUIS	9321 S SACRAMENTO AVE-EVERGREEN PK IL 60642
65- 19	CARPIN, FRANK DOMINIC	BOX 1758 - RICHMOND VA 23214
39- 18	CARRASQUEL, ALEJANDRO ALEXANDER APARICIO D. AUGUST 19, 1969 CARACAS,VEN.
50- 19	CARRASQUEL, ALFONSO COLON	SAN NARCISO A SANTA INEZ #67 CARACAS VEN
59- 12	CARREON, CAMILO GARCIA	4450 E COOPER ST - TUCSON AZ 85711
70- 18	CARRITHERS, DONALD GEORGE	1851 HARRIS AVE - SAN JOSE CA 95124
64- 17	CARROLL, CLAY PALMER	4515 26TH AVE - BRADENTON FL 33503
19- 11	CARROLL, DORSEY LEE	8066 BUFFALO AVE - JACKSONVILLE FL 32208
29- 15	CARROLL, EDGAR FLEISCHER	1709 ABERDEEN RD - BALTIMORE MD 21234
25- 17	CARROLL, OWEN THOMAS	D. JUNE 8, 1975 ORANGE, N. J.
16- 12	CARROLL, RALPH ARTHUR	BOX 1354 - WORCESTER MA 01601
55- 22	CARROLL, THOMAS EDWARD	607 BAYSIDE - ROCKAWAY POINT NY 11697
74- 14	CARROLL, THOMAS MICHAEL	1447 TOWLSON RD - VIENNA VA 22180
10- 24	CARSON, ALEXANDER JAMES	D. AUGUST 18, 1954 LOS ANGELES, CALIF.
34- 16	CARSON, WALTER LLOYD	788 ORIZABA AVE - LONG BEACH CA 90804
53- 15	CARSWELL, FRANK WILLIS	BOX 153 - CARMINE TX 78932
44- 19	CARTER, ARNOLD LEE	8102 PEBBLE BROOK LN - LOUISVILLE KY 40219
74- 15	CARTER, GARY EDMUND	3090 MOUNTAINVIEW DR - KIRKLAND QUE H9J 2E2
26- 12	CARTER, JOHN HOWARD	430 E 86TH ST - NEW YORK NY 10028
25- 18	CARTER, OTIS LEONARD	D. SEPTEMBER 8, 1978 GREENVILLE, S. C.
14- 34	CARTER, PAUL WARREN	RR 1 BOX 266A - LAKE PARK GA 31636
31- 11	CARTER, SOLOMON MOBLEY DR	2402 GALE PL - EL DORADO TX 71730
63- 23	CARTY, RICARDO ADOLFO JACABO	5 ENS ENRIQUILLO-SAN PEDRO DE MACORIS DOM RE
47- 16	CARY, SCOTT RUSSELL	RR 4 - BRONSON MI 49028
58- 18	CASALE, JERRY JOSEPH	145 DURANT AVE - STATEN ISLAND NY 10306
65- 20	CASANOVA, ORTIZ PAULINO	1312 EDENVILLE DR - DISTRICTS HEIGHTS MD20028
34- 17	CASCARELLA, JOSEPH THOMAS	LAUREL RACE COURSE - LAUREL MD 20810
37- 20	CASE, GEORGE WASHINGTON	1108 EVERGREEN RD MORRISVILLE PA 19068
35- 12	CASEY, HUGH THOMAS	D. JULY 3, 1951 ATLANTA, GA.
69- 30	CASH, DAVID	937 VISTA DEL MONTE WAY - EL CAJON CA 92021
58- 19	CASH, NORMAN DALTON	OLD ADD: 7426 AZALEA CT - WEST BLOOMFIELD MI
73- 18	CASH, RONALD FOREST	118 CHERYWOOD DR - WOODSTOCK GA 30188
11- 24	CASHION, JAY CARL	D. NOVEMBER 17, 1935 LAKE MILLICENT, WIS.
73- 19	CASKEY, CRAIG DOUGLAS	836 YVONNE PL - ANAHEIM CA 92801
49- 14	CASSINI, JACK DEMPSEY	4600 N 19TH - PALM HARBOR FL 33565
34- 18	CASTER, GEORGE JASPER	D. DECEMBER 18, 1955 LAKEWOOD, CAL.
42- 17	CASTIGLIA, JAMES VINCENT	5301 WESTBARD CIR #313 - WASHINGTON DC 20016
47- 17	CASTIGLIONE, PETER PAUL	1320 NE 26TH TERRACE - POMPANO BEACH FL 33062

Duke Carmel

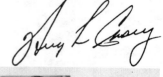

Dear Friend,
Thanks very much for
your interest in me and
the Cardinals. All the
players appreciate it very
much.

Sincerely,

Pete Castiglione

78- 24	CASTILLO, ANTHONY BELTRAN	10300 JOYCE CT - SAN JOSE CA 95127
80- 22	CASTILLO, ESTEBAN MANUEL	COSTA RICA 112,ENS. OZAMA-SANTO DOMINGO DOM R
81- 22	CASTILLO, MARTIN HORACE	2669 BAYLOR ST - ANAHEIM CA 92801
77- 26	CASTILLO, ROBERT ERNIE	2837 SIERRA ST - LOS ANGELES CA 90031
79- 16	CASTINO, JOHN ANTHONY	256 KENILWORTH AVE - KENILWORTH IL 60043
43- 28	CASTINO, VINCENT CHARLES	D. MARCH 6, 1967 SACRAMENTO, CAL.
73- 20	CASTLE, DONALD HARDY	RR 2 BOX 34A - COLDWATER MS 28618
10- 25	CASTLE, JOHN FRANCIS	D. APRIL 15, 1929 PHILADELPHIA, PA.
34- 19	CASTLEMAN, CLYDELL	3211 LAKELAND DR - NASHVILLE TN 37211
54- 13	CASTLEMAN, FOSTER EPHRAIM	5 JUSTICIA LN - CINCINNATI OH 45218
23- 19	CASTNER, PAUL HENRY	1999 DE SOTA - ST. PAUL MN 55117
74- 16	CASTRO, WILLIAMS RADHAMES	DANIEL GORIS #39, VILLA BISONO-SANTIAGO DOM R
64- 18	CATER, DANNY ANDERSON	608 CLIFF DR - AUSTIN TX 78745
12- 33	CATHER, THEODORE P.	D. APRIL 9, 1945 ELKTON, MD.
42- 18	CATHEY, HARDIN	561 ELAINE DR - NASHVILLE TN 37211
17- 14	CATON, JAMES HOWARD	D. JANUARY 8, 1948 ZANESVILLE, O.
79- 17	CAUDILL, WILLIAM HOLLAND	1200 MANHATTAN BEACH BLVD - MANHATTAN BCH CA
46- 17	CAULFIELD, JOHN JOSEPH	557 28TH AVE - SAN FRANCISCO CA 94121
18- 9	CAUSEY, CECIL ALGERNON	D. NOVEMBER 11, 1960 TAMPA, FLA.
55- 23	CAUSEY, JAMES WAYNE	2905 PAYNTER DR - RUSTON LA 71270
19- 12	CAVANAUGH, JOHN J.	D. JANUARY 14, 1961 NEW BRUNSWICK, N. J.
34- 20	CAVARRETTA, PHILIP JOSEPH	2206 PORTSIDE PASSAGE - PALM HARBOR FL 33563
22- 19	CAVENEY, JAMES CHRISTOPHER	D. JULY 6, 1949 SAN FRANCISCO, CAL.

Jimmy Caveney

41- 25 CAVET, TILLER   D. AUGUST 4, 1966 SAN LUIS OBISPO, CALIF.
55- 24 CECCARELLI, ARTHUR EDWARD   63 HALL DR - ORANGE CT 06477
44- 20 CECIL, REX HOLSTON   D. OCTOBER 30, 1966 LONG BEACH, CAL.
70- 19 CEDENO, CESAR EUGENITO   9919 SAGE DOWNE - HOUSTON TX 77034
42- 19 CENTER, MARVIN EARL   BOX 64 - CAMPTON KY 41301
58- 20 CEPEDA, ORLANDO MANUEL   1974 ADD: 45-3 23RD ST - BAYAMON PR 00619
75- 25 CERONE, RICHARD ALDO   OLD ADD: 332 CLIFTON AVE - NEWARK NJ
51- 10 CERV, ROBERT HENRY   1314 TENTH ST - HAWARDEN IA 51023
71- 21 CEY, RONALD CHARLES   22714 CREOLE RD - WOODLAND HILLS CA 91364
60- 20 CHACON, ELIO RODRIGUEZ   OLD ADD: AVE ANDALUCIA,ED. MARICAY-CARACAS VZ
29- 16 CHAGNON, LEON WILBUR   D. JULY 30, 1953 AMESBURY, MASS.
51- 11 CHAKALES, ROBERT EDWARD   206 MORELAND DR - RICHMOND VA 23229
73- 21 CHALK, DAVID LEE   748 W JEFFERSON - DALLAS TX 75208
10- 26 CHALMERS, GEORGE W.   D. AUGUST 5, 1960 BRONX, N.Y.
79- 18 CHAMBERLAIN, CRAIG PHILIP   9057 COBBLESTONE - CYPRESS CA 90630
32- 12 CHAMBERLAIN, WILLIAM VINCENT   404 SPADARO DR - VENICE FL 33595
34- 21 CHAMBERLIN, JOSEPH JEREMIAH   1737 NEWCOMB AVE - SAN FRANCISCO CA 94124

48- 24 CHAMBERS, CLIFFORD DAY   PRAIRIE RD RR 1 - BOISE ID 83702
37- 21 CHAMBERS, JOHNNIE MONROE   D. MAY 11, 1977 PALATKA, FLA.
10- 27 CHAMBERS, WILLIAM CHRISTOPHER   D. MARCH 27, 1962 FORT WAYNE, IND.
71- 22 CHAMBLISS, CARROLL CHRISTOPHER   19 ORATAM - UPPER SADDLE RIVER NJ 07458
69- 31 CHAMPION, BUFORD BILLY   1899 HARPER AVE SW - LENOR NC 28645
76- 25 CHAMPION, ROBERT MICHAEL   84 PORT OF SPAIN - CORONADO CA 92118
63- 24 CHANCE, ROBERT   OLD ADD: 2255 OAK RIDGE DR - CHARLESTON WV
61- 19 CHANCE, WILMER DEAN   1413 TR 13 RD 2 - JEROMESVILLE OH 44840
47- 18 CHANDLER, EDWARD OLIVER   5839 GREEN VALLEY #107-CULVER CITY CA 90230
37- 22 CHANDLER, SPURGEON FERDINAND   1591 77TH ST N - ST PETERSBURG FL 33710
69- 32 CHANEY, DARREL LEE   5196 CLEARWATER DR - STONE MOUNTAIN GA 30087
13- 28 CHANEY, ESTEY CLEON   D. FEBRUARY 5, 1952 CLEVELAND, O.
10- 28 CHANNELL, LESTER CLARK   D. MAY 7, 1954 DENVER, COLO.
75- 24 CHANT, CHARLES JOSEPH   1219 W 212TH ST - TORRANCE CA 90502
20- 17 CHAPLIN, BERT EDGAR   D. AUGUST 15, 1978 SANFORD, FLA.
28- 21 CHAPLIN, JAMES BAILEY   D. MARCH 25, 1939 NATIONAL CITY, CAL.
55- 13 CHAPMAN, CALVIN LOUIS   CHARLESTON MS 38921
33- 12 CHAPMAN, EDWIN VOLNEY   LAMBERT MS 38643
34- 22 CHAPMAN, GLENN JUSTICE   418 E ARBOR AVE - SUNNYVALE CA 94086
12- 34 CHAPMAN, HARRY E.   D. OCTOBER 21, 1918 NEVADA, MO.
24- 17 CHAPMAN, JOHN JOSEPH   D. NOVEMBER 3, 1953 PHILADELPHIA, PA.
79- 19 CHAPMAN, KELVIN KEITH   300 ROAD NORTH - REDWOOD VALLEY CA 94570
12- 35 CHAPMAN, RAYMOND JOHNSON   D. AUGUST 17, 1920 NEW YORK, N.Y.
38- 12 CHAPMAN, SAMUEL BLAKE   11 ANDREW DR #39 - TIBURON CA 94920
30- 10 CHAPMAN, WILLIAM BENJAMIN   401 SHADESWOOD CIR - BIRMINGHAM AL 35226
39- 19 CHAPMAN, WILLIAM FRED   210 MAIN ST - KANNAPOLIS NC 28081
78- 25 CHAPPAS, HARRY PERRY   1440 NW 52ND AVE - LAUDERHILL FL 33313
13- 29 CHAPPELL, LAVERNE ASHFORD   D. NOVEMBER 8, 1918 SAN FRANCISCO, CALIF.
80- 23 CHARBONEAU, JOSEPH   32363 LAKE RD -AVON LAKE OH 44012
62- 27 CHARLES, EDWIN DOUGLAS   5208 LISTER AVE - KANSAS CITY MO 64130
40- 10 CHARTAK, MICHAEL GEORGE   D. JULY 25, 1967 OAKDALE, IA.
36- 19 CHARTON, FRANK LANE   RR 4 BOX 183 - ROCKWOOD TN 37854
36- 14 CHASE, KENDALL FAY   RR 4, WEST STREET RD - ONEONTA NY 13820

30- 11 CHATHAM, CHARLES L	D. DECEMBER 15, 1975 WACO, TEXAS
66- 18 CHAVARRIA, OSWALDO QUIJANO	5771 WINCH ST - NORTH BARNEBY BRITISH COLUMB
67- 16 CHAVEZ, NESTOR ISAIAS SILVA	D. MARCH 16, 1969 MARACAIBO, VENEZ.
73- 22 CHEADLE, DAVID BAIRD	38 WOODWARD AVE - ASHEVILLE NC 28804
10- 29 CHEEK, HARRY G.	B. KANSAS CITY, MO.
20- 18 CHEEVES, VIRGIL EARL	OLD ADD: BOX 571 - CARROLLTON TX
35- 14 CHELINI, ITALO VINCENT	D. AUGUST 25, 1972 SAN FRANCISCO, CAL.
11- 26 CHENEY, LAURANCE RUSSELL	D. JANUARY 6, 1969 DAYTONA BEACH, FLA.
57- 10 CHENEY, THOMAS EDGAR	2307-B AUSTIS DR - ALBANY GA 31707
37- 23 CHERVINKO, PAUL	D. JUNE 3, 1976 DANVILLE, ILL.
48- 25 CHESNES, ROBERT VINCENT	D. MAY 23, 1979 EVERETT, WASH.
45- 8 CHETKOVICH, MITCHELL	D. AUGUST 24, 1971 GRASS VALLEY, CAL.
77- 27 CHEVEZ, ANTONIO SILVIO	TELIA D. PTO. - LEON NICARAGUA
30- 12 CHILD, HARRY PATRICK	D. NOVEMBER 8, 1972 ALEXANDRIA, VA.
71- 23 CHILES, RICHARD FRANCIS	4501 SAN RAMON DR - DAVIS CA 95616
35- 15 CHIOZZA, DINO JOSEPH	D. APRIL 23, 1972 MEMPHIS, TENN.
34- 23 CHIOZZA, LOUIS PEO	D. FEBRUARY 28, 1971 MEMPHIS, TENN.
41- 16 CHIPMAN, ROBERT HOWARD	D. NOVEMBER 8, 1973 HUNTINGTON, N.Y.
45- 9 CHIPPLE, WALTER JOHN	52 RAMSDELL AVE - BUFFALO NY 14216
79- 20 CHISM, THOMAS RAYMOND	1311 ELSON ROAD - CHESTER PA 19013
50- 20 CHITI, HARRY	3897 WORDSWORTH ST - RALEIGH TN 38128
58- 21 CHITTUM, NELSON BOYD	2312 TEROVA - TROY MI 48098
70- 20 CHLUPSA, ROBERT JOSEPH	RR1 - SOUND BEACH NY 11789
60- 21 CHOATE, DONALD LEON	109 N 5TH - DESLOGE MO 63601
10- 30 CHOUINARD, FELIX GEORGE	D. APRIL 28, 1955 HINES, ILL.
10- 31 CHOUNEAL, WILLIAM	D. SEPTEMBER 17, 1948 CLOQUET, MINN.
37- 24 CHOZEN, HARRY KENNETH	2208 20TH ST - LAKE CHARLES LA 70601
79- 21 CHRIS, MICHAEL	12437 WOODGREEN ST - LOS ANGELES CA 90066
57- 11 CHRISLEY, BARBRA O'NEIL	104 WOODLAND WAY - GREENWOOD SC 29646
19- 13 CHRISTENBURY, LLOYD REID	D. DECEMBER 13, 1944 BIRMINGHAM, ALA.

71- 24 CHRISTENSEN, BRUCE RAY	BOX 178 - MORONI UT 84646
26- 13 CHRISTENSEN, WALTER NIELS	611 JUNIPERO SERRA - STANFORD CA 94305
79- 22 CHRISTENSON, GARY RICHARD	1610 WASHINGTON AVE - NEW HYDE PARK NY 11040
73- 23 CHRISTENSON, LARRY RICHARD	2120 BRYN MAWR PL - ARDMORE PA 19003
68- 13 CHRISTIAN, ROBERT CHARLES	D. FEBRUARY 20, 1974 SAN DIEGO, CAL.
38- 13 CHRISTMAN, MARQUETTE JOSEPH	D. OCTOBER 9, 1976 ST. LOUIS, MO.
59- 13 CHRISTOPHER, JOSEPH O'NEAL	1970 ADD: CALLE CHILE 108 - MAYAGUEZ PR 00708
45- 10 CHRISTOPHER, LOYD EUGENE	747 GOLDEN GATE AVE - RICHMOND CA 94801
42- 20 CHRISTOPHER, RUSSELL ORMAND	D. DECEMBER 5, 1954 POINT RICHMOND, CAL.
50- 21 CHURCH, EMORY NICHOLAS	1926-F TREETOP - BIRMINGHAM AL 35216
66- 19 CHURCH, LEONARD	%OSHMAN'S, PROMENADE CTR-RICHARDSON TX 75080
57- 12 CHURN, CLARENCE NOTTINGHAM	BOX 112 - TOWNSEND VA 23443
24- 18 CHURRY, JOHN	D. FEBRUARY 8, 1970 ZANESVILLE, O.
51- 12 CIAFFONE, LAWRENCE THOMAS	240 LAKE ST - BROOKLYN NY 11223
29- 17 CICERO, JOSEPH FRANCIS	2266 GULF TO BAY BLVD - CLEARWATER FL 33515
57- 13 CICOTTE, ALVA WARREN	45473 LILAC LN - BELLEVILLE MI 4811
44- 21 CIESLAK, THADDEUS WALTER	6244 S 20TH ST - MILWAUKEE WI 53221
45- 11 CIHOCKI, ALBERT JOSEPH	124 W GREEN - NANTICOKE PA 18634
32- 13 CIHOCKI, EDWARD JOSEPH	23 BOXWOOD AV - WILMINGTON DE 19804
65- 21 CIMINO, PETER WILLIAM	14 FILLMORE ST - BRISTOL PA 19007
56- 21 CIMOLI, GINO NICHOLAS	30 LINDA VISTA - TIBURON CA 94920
43- 29 CIOLA, LOUIS ALEXANDER	2105 8TH AVE NW-AUSTIN MN 55912
61- 20 CIPRIANI, FRANK DOMINICK	62 BARLOW - LACKAWANNA NY 14218
37- 25 CISAR, GEORGE JOSEPH	2520 S 56TH COURT CICERO IL 60650
61- 21 CISCO, GALEN BERNARD	RR 1 BOX 150 - SAINT MARYS OH 45885
28- 22 CISSELL, CHALMER WILLIAM	D. MARCH 15, 1949 CHICAGO, ILL.
26- 14 CLABAUGH, JOHN WILLIAM	132 LOS ARCOS - GREEN VALLEY AZ 85614
20- 19 CLAIRE, DAVID MATTHEW	D. JANUARY 7, 1956 LAS VEGAS, NEV.
11- 27 CLANCY, ALBERT HARRISON	D. OCTOBER 17, 1951 LAS CRUCES, N. MEX.
77- 28 CLANCY, JAMES	11244 S ST LOUIS - CHICAGO IL 60655
24- 19 CLANCY, JOHN WILLIAM	D. SEPTEMBER 26, 1968 OTTUMWA, IA.
22- 20 CLANTON, UCAL CURT	D. FEBRUARY 24, 1960 ANTLERS, OKLA.
76- 26 CLAREY, DOUGLAS WILLIAM	11521 ROCHESTER #4 - LOS ANGELES CA 90025
47- 19 CLARK, ALFRED ALOYSIUS	250 N STEVENS AVE - SOUTH AMBOY NJ 08879
27- 23 CLARK, BAILEY EARL	D. JANUARY 16, 1938 WASHINGTON, D. C.
81- 23 CLARK, BRYAN DONALD	508 N CLARK ST - MADERA CA 93637
22- 21 CLARK, DANIEL CURRAN	D. MAY 23, 1937 MERIDIAN, MISS.
13- 30 CLARK, GEORGE MYRON	D. NOVEMBER 14, 1940 SIOUX CITY, IA.
67- 17 CLARK, GLEN ESTER	3110 E 14TH - AUSTIN TX 78702
75- 26 CLARK, JACK ANTHONY	1125 FARRAGUT - FOSTER CITY CA 94404
48- 26 CLARK, JAMES	1518 7TH ST #4 - SANTA MONICA CA 90401
71- 25 CLARK, JAMES EDWARD	1322 W ECKERMAN - WEST COVINA CA 91790
11- 28 CLARK, JAMES FRANCIS	D. MARCH 20, 1969 BEAUMONT, TEX.

44

```
38- 14  CLARK, JOHN CARROLL              D. FEBRUARY 16, 1957 FAYETTEVILLE, N. C.
51- 13  CLARK, MELVIN EARL              BOX 97 - WEST COLUMBIA WV 25287
52- 17  CLARK, MICHAEL JOHN             3 ASPEN AVE - BELLMAWR NJ 08030
58- 22  CLARK, PHILIP JAMES             1103 6TH ST - ALBANY GA 31701
67- 18  CLARK, RICKEY CHARLES           16132 MEADOWBROOK - DETROIT MI 48240
79- 23  CLARK, ROBERT CALE              1030 PERVISITO ST - PERRIS CA 92370
20- 20  CLARK, ROBERT WILLIAM           D. MAY 18, 1944 CARLSBAD, N. M.
66- 20  CLARK, RONALD BRUCE             OLD ADD: 2008 EDGEBROOK CT - DALLAS TX
45- 12  CLARK, WILLIAM OTIS             2735 E BASS LAKE RD - GRAND RAPIDS MN 55744
24- 20  CLARK, WILLIAM WATSON           D. MARCH 4, 1972 CLEARWATER, FLA.
21- 13  CLARKE, ALAN THOMAS             D. MARCH 11, 1975 CHEVERLY, MD.
65- 22  CLARKE, HORACE MEREDITH         BOX 891 - FREDERIKSTED VI 00840
44- 22  CLARKE, RICHARD GREY            2122 GLENWOOD ST - KANNAPOLIS NC 28081
23- 20  CLARKE, RUFUS RIVERS            3600 CHATEAU DR #207 - COLUMBIA SC 29204
20- 21  CLARKE, SUMPTER MILLS           D. MARCH 16, 1962 KNOXVILLE, TENN.
55- 25  CLARKE, VIBERT ERNESTO          21252 TYEE ST - CASTRO VALLEY CA 94546
29- 18  CLARKE, WILLIAM STUART          D. JUNE 14, 1970 CRISTOBAL, CANAL ZONE
52- 18  CLARKSON, JAMES BUSTER          639 SIXTH ST - JEANETTE PA 15644
27- 24  CLARKSON, WILLIAM HENRY         D. AUGUST 27, 1971 RALEIGH, N. C.
42- 21  CLARY, ELLIS                    206 W ALDEN ST-VALDOSTA GA 31603
33- 13  CLASET, GOWELL SYLVESTER        D. MARCH 8, 1981 ST. PETERSBURG, FLA.
13- 31  CLAUSS, ALBERT STANLEY          D. SEPTEMBER 13, 1952 NEW HAVEN, CONN.
43- 30  CLAY, DAIN ELMER                462 PARKWAY - CHULA VISTA CA 92010
77- 29  CLAY, KENNETH EARL              14518 NE 6TH PL #4 - BELLEVUE WA 98007
79- 24  CLEAR, MARK ALAN                18608 NUBIA - COVINA CA 91722
45- 13  CLEARY, JOSEPH CHRISTOPHER      OLD ADD: 15 JACOBUS PL - BRONX NY 10463
39- 20  CLEMENS, CHESTER SPURGEON       423 CRESPI - SAN CLEMENTE CA 92672
14- 35  CLEMENS, CLEMENT LAMBERT        D. NOVEMBER 18 1967 ST PETERSBURG, FLA.
60- 22  CLEMENS, DOUGLAS HORACE         218 GREEN DR - CHURCHVILLE PA 18966
14- 36  CLEMENS, ROBERT BAXTER          D. APRIL 5, 1964 LOS ANGELES, CALIF.
39- 21  CLEMENSEN, WILLIAM MELVILLE     7555 MYRTLE VISTA AVE - SACRAMENTO CA 95831
55- 26  CLEMENTE, ROBERTO WALKER        D. DECEMBER 31,1972 SAN JUAN, P. R.
71- 26  CLEMONS, LANCE LEVIS            1634 LODGE CIR - SPRING HILL FL 33512
16- 13  CLEMONS, VERNE JAMES            D. MAY 5, 1959 BAY PINES, FLA.
61- 22  CLENDENON, DONN ALVIN           5932 CULZEAN DR #702 - DAYTON OH 45426
69- 33  CLEVELAND, REGINALD LESLIE      506 WALNUT CREEK DR - MANSFIELD TX 76063
54- 14  CLEVENGER, TRUMAN EUGENE        74 N CARMELITA - PORTERVILLE CA 93257
80- 24  CLIBURN, STANLEY GENE           727 NIMITZ DR - JACKSON MS 39209
34- 24  CLIFT, HARLOND BENTON           915 N 15TH AVE #5 - YAKIMA WA 98907
34- 25  CLIFTON, HERMAN EARL            4077 RACE RD - CINCINNATI OH 45211
60- 23  CLINE, TYRONE ALEXANDER         676 AYERS - CHARLESTON SC 29412
70- 21  CLINES, EUGENE ANTHONY          245 DARLENE ST - YORK PA 17402
60- 24  CLINTON, LUCIEAN LOUIS          CLINTON OIL CO. W. HWY 54 - WICHITA KS 67213
61- 23  CLONINGER, TONY LEE             RR 1 - IRON STATION NC 28080
66- 21  CLOSTER, ALAN EDWARD            CREIGHTON NE 68729
24- 21  CLOUGH, EDGAR GEORGE            D. JANUARY 30, 1944 HARRISBURG, PA.
26- 15  CLOWERS, WILLIAM PERRY          D. JANUARY 13, 1978 SWEENY, TEX.
73- 24  CLYDE, DAVID EUGENE             402 HICKORY POST - HOUSTON TX 77024
43- 31  CLYDE, THOMAS KNOX              3612 GARDEN BROOK DR - DALLAS TX 75234
46- 18  COAN, GILBERT FITZGERALD        BOX 668 - BREVARD NC 28712
56- 22  COATES, JAMES ALTON             BOX 57 - LANCASTER VA 22503
29- 19  COBB, HERBERT EDWARD            OLD ADD: 334 N CONFEDERATE - ROCK HILL SC
18- 10  COBB, JOSEPH STANLEY            D. DECEMBER 24, 1947 ALLENTOWN, PA.
39- 22  COBLE, DAVID LAMAR              D. OCTOBER 15, 1971 ORLANDO, FLA.
15- 20  COCHRAN, ALVAH JACKSON          D. MAY 23, 1947 ATLANTA, GA.
18- 11  COCHRAN, GEORGE LESLIE          D. MAY 21, 1960 HARBOR CITY, CALIF.
25- 19  COCHRANE, GORDON STANLEY        D. JUNE 2, 1962 LAKE FOREST, ILL.
13- 32  COCREHAM, EUGENE                D. DECEMBER 27, 1945 LULING, TEX.
12- 36  COFFEY (JOHN JOSEPH SMITH)      D. DECEMBER 4, 1962 NEW YORK, N. Y.
37- 26  COFFMAN, GEORGE DAVID           BOX 254 ATHENS AL 35611
```

```
27- 25  COFFMAN, SAMUEL RICHARD         D. MARCH 24, 1972 ATHENS, ALA.
67- 19  COGGINS, FRANKLIN               106 ARMSTEDD CIR - GRIFFIN GA 30223
72- 18  COGGINS, RICHARD ALLEN          2565 HAYES - LAVERNE CA 91750
31- 12  COHEN, ALBERT                   338 WARWICK AVE - SOUTH ORANGE NJ 07079
26- 16  COHEN, ANDREW HOWARD            4341 N STANTON - EL PASO TX 79902
55- 27  COHEN, HYMAN                    22610 FLAMINGO ST - WOODLAND HILLS CA 91364
34- 26  COHEN, SYDNEY HARRY             1121 RIM RD - EL PASO TX 79902
58- 23  COKER, JIMMIE GOODWIN           BOX TWO - THROCKMORTON TX 76083
55- 28  COLAVITO, ROCCO DOMENICO        520 N TEMPLE BLVD - TEMPLE PA 19560
78- 26  COLBERN, MICHAEL MALLOY         1059 E FAIRMONT - TEMPE AZ 85282
66- 22  COLBERT, NATHAN                 OLD ADD: 4170 MT ALIFAN PL E - SAN DIEGO CA
```

70- 22	COLBERT, VINCENT NORMAN	1417 "E" ST SE - WASHINGTON DC 20003
69- 34	COLBORN, JAMES WILLIAM	2932 SOLIMAR BEACH DR - VENTURA CA 93001
21- 14	COLE, ALBERT GEORGE	D. MAY 30, 1975 SAN MATEO, CAL.
50- 22	COLE, DAVID BRUCE	30 S CONOCOCHEAGUE ST - WILLIAMSPORT MD 21795
38- 15	COLE, EDWARD WILLIAM	OLD ADD: 1422 STEMMONS AVE - DALLAS TX
51- 14	COLE, RICHARD ROY	3149 MADEIRA AVE - COSTA MESA CA 92626
61- 24	COLEMAN, CLARENCE	726 CORNELIA CT - ORLANDO FL 32807
12- 37	COLEMAN, CURTIS HANCOCK	D. JULY 1, 1980 NEWPORT, ORE.
77- 30	COLEMAN, DAVID LEE	1410 FALKE DR - DAYTON OH 45432
49- 15	COLEMAN, GERALD FRANCIS	1004 HAVENHURST DR - LAJOLLA CA 92037
59- 14	COLEMAN, GORDON CALVIN	8698 ZENITH CT - CINCINNATI OH 45231
65- 23	COLEMAN, JOSEPH HOWARD	16502 NE 46TH - REDMOND WA 98052
42- 22	COLEMAN, JOSEPH PATRICK	2422 N WESTWOOD DR - NORTH FT MYERS FL 33901
32- 14	COLEMAN, PARKE EDWARD	D. AUGUST 5, 1964 OREGON CITY, ORE.
47- 20	COLEMAN, RAYMOND LEROY	RR 6 BOX 2 - MAYFIELD KY 42066
13- 33	COLEMAN, ROBERT HUNTER	D. JULY 16, 1959 BOSTON, MASS.
55- 29	COLEMAN, WALTER GARY	173 PINEWOODS AVE - TROY NY 12180
14- 37	COLES, CADWALLADER R.	D. JUNE 30, 1942 MIAMI, FLA.
58- 24	COLES, CHARLES EDWARD	BOX 32 - JEFFERSON PA 15344
72- 19	COLETTA, CHRISTOPHER MICHAEL	1062 BAILEY DR - COVENTRY RI 02816
11- 29	COLLAMORE, ALLAN EDWARD	D. AUGUST 8, 1980 BATTLE CREEK, MI.
27- 26	COLLARD, EARL CLINTON	D. JULY 14, 1968 JAMESTOWN, N. Y.
31- 13	COLLIER, ORLIN EDWARD	D. SEPTEMBER 9, 1944 MEMPHIS, TENN.
13- 34	COLLINS, CYRIL WILSON	D. FEBRUARY 28, 1941 KNOXVILLE, TENN.
75- 27	COLLINS, DAVID SCOTT	95 SPRINGWOOD - SPRINGBORO OH 45066
77- 31	COLLINS, DONALD EDWARD	3771 ROSWELL RD NE - ATLANTA GA 30305
39- 23	COLLINS, EDWARD TROWBRIDGE	BOX 206 - KENNETT SQUARE PA 19348
20- 22	COLLINS, HARRY WARREN	D. MAY 27, 1968 BRYAN, TEX.
31- 14	COLLINS, JAMES ANTHONY	D. APRIL 16, 1970 NEW HAVEN, N. Y.
14- 38	COLLINS, JOHN EDGAR	B. MAY 2, 1892 BROOKLYN, N. Y.
10- 32	COLLINS, JOHN FRANCIS	D. SEPTEMBER 10, 1955 NEWTON, MASS.
48- 27	COLLINS, JOSEPH EDWARD	731 SUBURBAN RD - UNION NJ 07083
65- 24	COLLINS, KEVIN MICHAEL	BOX 1 - HAZEL PARK MI 48030
23- 21	COLLINS, PHILIP EUGENE	D. AUGUST 14, 1948 CHICAGO, ILL.
40- 11	COLLINS, ROBERT JOSEPH	D. APRIL 19, 1969 PITTSBURGH, PA.
19- 14	COLLINS, THARON LESLIE	D. MAY 19, 1960 KANSAS CITY, KAN.
10- 33	COLLINS, WILLIAM SHIRLEY	D. JUNE 26, 1961 SAN BERNARDINO, CALIF.
51- 15	COLLUM, JACK DEAN	1305 SUMMER ST - GRINNELL IA 50112

42- 23	COLMAN, FRANK LOYD	512 GREY ST-LONDON ONTARIO
70- 23	COLPAERT, RICHARD CHARLES	47412 ELDON - UTICA MI 48087
70- 24	COLSON, LOYD ALBERT	RR ONE - GOULD OK 73544
68- 14	COLTON, LAWRENCE ROBERT	5623 NE CLEVELAND - PORTLAND OR 97211
73- 25	COLUCCIO, ROBERT PASQUALI	RR 3 BOX 763 - OLYMPIA WA 98506
80- 25	COMBE, GEOFFREY WADE	1762 E AVE DE LOS FLORES - 100 OAKS CA 91360
24- 22	COMBS, EARLE BRYAN	D. JULY 21, 1976 RICHMOND, KY.
47- 21	COMBS, MERRILL RUSSELL	D. JULY 8, 1981 RIVERSIDE, CALIF.
45- 14	COMELLAS, JORGE	13015 SW 50TH ST - MIAMI FL 33165
67- 20	COMER, HARRY WAYNE	RR 1 BOX 4F - SHENANDOAH VA 22849
78- 27	COMER, STEVEN MICHAEL	20500 SUMMERVILLE RD - EXCELSIOR MN 55331
54- 15	COMMAND, JAMES DALTON	1743 MATILDA ST NE - GRAND RAPIDS MI 49503
26- 17	COMORSKY, ADAM ANTHONY	D. MARCH 2, 1951 SWOYERSVILLE, PA.
11- 30	COMPTON, ANNA SEBASTIAN	D. FEBRUARY 3, 1978 KANSAS CITY, MO.
11- 31	COMPTON, HARRY LEROY	D. JULY 4, 1974 LANCASTER, O.
70- 25	COMPTON, MICHAEL LYNN	2511 N GOLDEN - ODESSA TX 79762
72- 20	COMPTON, ROBERT CLINTON	OLD ADD: 45 KENT ST - MONTGOMERY AL
13- 35	COMSTOCK, RALPH REMICK	D. SEPTEMBER 13, 1966 TOLEDO, O.
48- 28	CONATSER, CLINTON ASTOR	16375 BOLSA CHICA - HUNTINGTON BCH CA 92649
70- 26	CONCEPCION, DAVID ISMAEL	URB LOS CAOBOS BOTALON 5D, 5PISO-MARACAY VEN
80- 26	CONCEPCION, ONIX (CARDONA)	PARCELA 61AA-BO.HIGUILLAR - DORADO PR 00646
62- 28	CONDE, RAMON LUIS	BOX 57 - JUANA DIAZ PUERTO RICO 00665
15- 21	CONE, ROBERT EARL	D. MAY 24, 1955 GALVESTON, TEX.
40- 12	CONGER, RICHARD	D. FEBRUARY 16, 1970 LOS ANGELES, CAL.
64- 20	CONIGLIARO, ANTHONY RICHARD	25 KNOLL WAY - SAN RAFAEL CA 94903
69- 35	CONIGLIARO, WILLIAM MICHAEL	ROSEMARY RD - NAHANT MA 01908
20- 23	CONKWRIGHT, ALLEN HOWARD	7835 COWLES MT CT #B-2 - SAN DIEGO CA 92119
34- 27	CONLAN, JOHN BERTRAND	5937 CHENEY ROAD - SCOTTSDALE AZ 85251
52- 19	CONLEY, DONALD EUGENE	4 BIRCHTREE RD - FOXBORO MA 02035
14- 39	CONLEY, JAMES PATRICK	D. JANUARY 7, 1978 DESOTO, TEX.
58- 25	CONLEY, ROBERT BURNS	3531 PETERS CREEK RD#408 - ROANOKE VA 24019
23- 22	CONLON, ARTHUR JOSEPH	374 COMMONWEALTH AV - BOSTON MA 02116
21- 15	CONNALLY, GEORGE WALTER	D. JANUARY 27, 1978 TEMPLE, TEXAS
31- 15	CONNATSER, BROADUS MILBURN	D. JANUARY 27, 1971 TERRE HAUTE, IND.

31- 16 CONNELL, EUGENE JOSEPH	D. AUGUST 31, 1937 WAVERLY, N. Y.
26- 18 CONNELL, JOSEPH BERNARD	D. SEPTEMBER 21, 1977 TREXLERTOWN, PA.
20- 24 CONNELLY, THOMAS MARTIN	OLD ADD: 18W-218 STANDISH LN-VILLA PARK IL
45- 15 CONNELLY, WILLIAM WIRT	D. NOVEMBER 27, 1980 RICHMOND, VA.
64- 17 CONNOLLY, EDWARD JOSEPH JR	56 PALOMINO DR - PITTSFIELD MA 01201
29- 20 CONNOLLY, EDWARD JOSEPH	D. NOVEMBER 14, 1963 PITTSFIELD, MASS.
13- 36 CONNOLLY, JOSEPH ALOYSIUS	D. SEPTEMBER 1, 1943 SPRINGFIELD, R.I.
21- 16 CONNOLLY, JOSEPH GEORGE	D. MARCH 30, 1960 SAN FRANCISCO, CALIF.
25- 20 CONNOLLY, MERVIN THOMAS	D. JUNE 12, 1964 BERKELEY, CAL.
15- 22 CONNOLLY, THOMAS FRANCIS	D. MAY 14, 1966 BOSTON, MASS.
49- 16 CONNORS, KEVIN JOSEPH	STAR RT BOX 73 - TEHACHAPI CA 93561
37- 27 CONNORS, MERVYN JAMES	1131 ADDISON ST BERKELEY CA 94702
66- 23 CONNORS, WILLIAM JOSEPH	895 N VILLAGE DR - ST PETERSBURG FL 33702
78- 28 CONROY, TIMOTHY JAMES	416 LUZERNE DR - MONROEVILLE PA 15146
23- 23 CONROY, WILLIAM FREDERICK	D. JANUARY 23, 1970 CHICAGO, ILL.
35- 16 CONROY, WILLIAM GORDON	7194 CRAIL CT - CITRUS HEIGHTS CA 95610
53- 16 CONSOLO, WILLIAM ANGELO	1266 WILLSBROOK CT - WESTLAKE VILLAGE CA91360
56- 23 CONSTABLE, JAMES LEE	RR 14 - BOX 540 - JONESBORO TN 37659
50- 23 CONSUEGRA, SANDALIO SIMEON	1200 SW FIRST ST - MIAMI FL 33135
80- 27 CONTRERAS, ARNALDO JUAN	1540 RIVER LN - TAMPA FL 33603
11- 32 CONWAY, CHARLES CONNELL	D. SEPTEMBER 12, 1968 YOUNGSTOWN, O.
41- 17 CONWAY, JACK CLEMENTS	3545 PINE - WACO TX 76708
20- 25 CONWAY, JEROME PATRICK	D. APRIL 16, 1980 HOLYOKE, MASS.
15- 23 CONWAY, OWEN SYLVESTER	D. MARCH 13, 1942 PHILADELPHIA, PA.
18- 12 CONWAY, RICHARD DANIEL	D. DECEMBER 3, 1971 ST PAUL, MINN.
11- 33 CONWELL, EDWARD JAMES	D. MAY 1, 1926 NORWOOD PARK, ILL.
50- 24 CONYERS, HERBERT LEROY	D. SEPTEMBER 16, 1964 CLEVELAND, O.
13- 37 CONZELMAN, JOSEPH HARRISON	D. APRIL 17, 1979 MOUNTAIN BROOK, ALA.
50- 25 COOGAN, DALE ROGER	600 E MAIN ST - SAN JACINTO CA 92383
41- 18 COOK, EARL DAVIS	RR 4 - STOUFFVILLE ONTARIO
13- 38 COOK, LUTHER ALMUS	D. JUNE 30, 1973 LAWRENCEBURG, TENN.
59- 15 COOK, RAYMOND CLIFFORD	605 WILLIAMSBURG MANOR - ARLINGTON TX 76014
15- 24 COOK, ROLLIN EDWARD	D. AUGUST 11, 1975 TOLEDO, O.
70- 27 COOK, RONALD WAYNE	114 E HOYT - LONGVIEW TX 75602
30- 13 COOKE, ALLEN LINDSEY	BOX 65 - FUQUAY-VARINA NC 27526
14- 40 COOMBS, CECIL LYSANDER	D. NOVEMBER 25, 1975 FORT WORTH, TEX.
63- 25 COOMBS, DANIEL BERNARD	6202 LEAF ARBOR - HOUSTON TX 77092
33- 14 COOMBS, RAYMOND FRANKLIN	BOX 782 - OGUNQUIT ME 03907
17- 15 COONEY, JAMES EDWARD	34 WOODSIA RD - SAUNDERSTOWN RI 02874
21- 17 COONEY, JOHN WALTER	818 WHITFIELD AVE - SARASOTA FL 33580
31- 17 COONEY, ROBERT DANIEL	D. MAY 4, 1976 GLEN FALLS, N. Y.
12- 38 COOPER, ARLEY WILBUR	D. AUGUST 7, 1973 ENCINO, CALIF.
48- 29 COOPER, CALVIN ASA	330 POPLAR ST - CLINTON SC 29325
71- 27 COOPER, CECIL CELESTER	9716 LAMPLIGHTER - MEQUON WI 53092
13- 39 COOPER, CLAUDE WILLIAM	D. JANUARY 21, 1974 PLAINVIEW, TEX.
81- 24 COOPER, DONALD JAMES	66-10 52ND AVE - MASPETH NY 11378
80- 28 COOPER, GARY NATHANIEL	468A OGLESBY AVE - GARDEN CITY GA 31408
14- 41 COOPER, GUY EVANS	D. AUGUST 2, 1951 SANTA MONICA, CALIF.
38- 16 COOPER, MORTON CECIL	D. NOVEMBER 17, 1958 LITTLE ROCK, ARK.
46- 19 COOPER, ORGE PATTERSON	4424 HOBBS HILL DR - CHARLOTTE NC 28212
40- 13 COOPER, WILLIAM WALKER	RR 1-BUCKNER MO 64016

Johnny Cooney

John M. Corriden

Walter Cooper

35- 17 COPELAND, MAYS	78-491 AVE 41 INDIO CA 92201
35- 18 COPPOLA, HENRY PETER	42 PLEASANT STREET MILFORD MA 01757
80- 29 CORBETT, DOUGLAS MITCHELL	2647 CANTERCLUB TR - APOPKA FL 32703
36- 15 CORBETT, EUGENE LOUIS	BOX 904 - SALISBURY MD 21801
71- 28 CORBIN, ALTON RAY	922 LIBERTY ST - LIVE OAK FL 32060
45- 16 CORBITT, CLAUDE ELLIOTT	D. MAY 1, 1978 CINCINNATI, O.
15- 25 CORCORAN, ARTHUR ANDREW	D. JULY 27, 1958 CHELSEA, MASS.
10- 34 CORCORAN, MICHAEL JOSEPH	4014 N WALNUTHAVEN DR - COVINA CA 91722
77- 32 CORCORAN, TIMOTHY MICHAEL	D. SEPTEMBER 17, 1970 KENOSHA, WIS.
18- 13 COREY, EDWARD NORMAN	RR 5 BOX 686 - EVERGREEN CO 80439
79- 25 COREY, MARK MUNDELL	D. JUNE 13, 1928 WAGONER, OKLA.
25- 21 CORGAN, CHARLES HOWARD	D. NOVEMBER 24, 1958 SAN FRANCISCO, CALIF.
11- 34 CORHAN, ROY GEORGE	407 E VAN KOUVERING AVE - RIALTO CA 92376
69- 36 CORKINS, MICHAEL PATRICK	121 NORTH G ST - WELLINGTON KS67152
78- 29 CORNEJO, NEIVES MARDIE	122 SE MILLER ST - ROSEBURG OR 97470
77- 33 CORNUTT, TERRY STANTON	1837 CEDAR ELM DR E - ARLINGTON TX 76012
64- 22 CORRALES, PATRICK	9 E MOORE ST - STATESBORO GA 30458
72- 21 CORRELL, VICTOR CROSBY	5441 E 17TH ST - INDIANAPOLIS IN 46218
46- 20 CORRIDEN, JOHN MICHAEL JR	D. SEPTEMBER 28, 1959 INDIANAPOLIS, IND.
10- 35 CORRIDEN, JOHN MICHAEL SR.	OLD ADD: 8707 SEAHAWK LN - TAMPA FL
77- 34 CORT, BARRY LEE	

23- 24	CORTAZZO, JOHN FRANK	D. MARCH 4, 1963 PITTSBURGH, PA.
51- 16	CORWIN, ELMER NATHAN	919 REDWING DR - GENEVA IL 60134
35- 19	COSCARART, JOSEPH MARVIN	1929 SW 164TH ST - SEATTLE WA 98166
38- 17	COSCARART, PETER JOSEPH	2808 JULINDA WAY - ESCONDIDO CA 92025
80- 30	CCSEY, DONALD RAY	139 BYXBEE ST - SAN FRANCISCO CA 94132
72- 22	COSGROVE, MICHAEL JOHN	2226 W PALO VERDE DR - PHOENIX AZ 85015
66- 24	COSMAN, JAMES HENRY	4327 PRESCOTT DR - NASHVILLE TN 37204
13- 40	COSTELLC, DANIEL FRANCIS	D. MARCH 26, 1936 PITTSBURGH, PA.
26- 19	CCTE, WARREN PETER	22 VENUS RD - SOUTH YARMOUTH MA 02664
26- 20	CCTTER, EDWARD CHRISTOPHER	D. JUNE 14, 1959 HARTFORD, CONN.
22- 22	COTTER, HARVEY LOUIS	D. AUGUST 6, 1955 LOS ANGELES, CAL.
11- 35	COTTER, RICHARD RAPHAEL	D. APRIL 4, 1945 BROOKLYN, N. Y.
59- 16	COTTIER, CHARLES KEITH	1404 E BALDWIN - ORANGE CA 92667
11- 36	COTTRELL, ENSIGN STOVER	D. FEBRUARY 27, 1947 SYRACUSE, N.Y.
17- 16	COUCH, JOHN DANIEL	D. DECEMBER 8, 1975 PALO ALTO, CALIF.
60- 25	COUGHTRY, JAMES MARLAN	OLD ADD: 5713 LOS ALTOS LN - YORBA LINDA CA
69- 37	COULTER, THOMAS LEE	809 TRENTON ST - TORONTO OH 43964
14- 42	COUMBE, FREDERICK NICHOLAS	D. MARCH 21, 1978 PARADISE, CALIF.
51- 17	COURTNEY, CLINTON DAWSON	D. JUNE 16, 1975 ROCHESTER, N. Y.
19- 15	COURTNEY, HENRY SEYMOUR	D. DECEMBER 11, 1954 LYME, CT.
23- 25	COUSINEAU, ED	D. JULY 14, 1951 WATERTOWN, MASS.
12- 39	COVELESKI, STANLEY ANTHONY	1038 W NAPIER - SOUTH BEND IN 46625
44- 23	CCVINGTON, CHESTER ROGERS	D. JUNE 11, 1976 PEMBROKE PARK, FLA.
13- 41	CCVINGTON, CLARENCE CALVERT	D. JANUARY 4, 1963 DENISON, TEX.
56- 24	COVINGTCN, JOHN WESLEY	1969 ADD: 4521 BALTIMORE AVE - PHILADELPHIA P
11- 37	COVINGTCN, WILLIAM WILKES	D. DECEMBER 10, 1931 DENISON, TEX.
63- 26	COWAN, BILLY ROLAND	1539 VIA CORONEL-PALOS VERDES ESTATES CA90274
74- 17	COWENS, ALFRED EDWARD	5723 KENISTON AVE - LOS ANGELES CA 90043
25- 22	COX, ELMER JOSEPH	D. JUNE 1, 1966 MORRO BAY, CALIF.
22- 22	COX, ERNEST THOMPSON	D. APRIL 29, 1974 BIRMINGHAM, ALA.
28- 23	COX, GECRGE MELVIN	1525 N WHARTON - SHERMAN TX 75090
55- 30	COX, GLENN MELVIN	BOX 487 - LOS MOLINOS CA 96055
73- 26	COX, JAMES CHARLES	916 SOUTH VALE - BLOOMINGTON IL 61701
80- 31	COX, JEFFREY LINDON	2727 VANDERHOOF DR - WEST COVINA CA 91791
66- 25	COX, JOSEPH CASEY	630 GRAND AVE - LONG BEACH CA 90814
73- 27	COX, LARRY EUGENE	OLD ADD: 26 TERRACE CT - LIMA OH
26- 21	COX, LESLIE WARREN	D. OCTOBER 14, 1934 SAN ANGELO, TEX.
20- 26	COX, PLATEAU REX	RR 3 BOX 356 - VINTON VA 24179
68- 15	COX, ROBERT JOE	48 PLEASANT DR - MARIETTA GA 30067
70- 28	COX, TERRY LEE	2166 LEDGEWOOD - WEST JORDON UT 84084
36- 16	COX, WILLIAM DONALD	45 CIRCLE DR CHARLESTON IL 61920
41- 19	COX, WILLIAM RICHARD	D. MARCH 30, 1978 HARRISBURG, PA.
77- 35	COX, WILLIAM TED	113 W PRATT DR - MIDWEST CITY OK 73110
14- 43	COYNE, "TOOTS"	
45- 17	COZART, CHARLES RHUBIN	RR 2 BOX 212-A - HUDSON NC 28638
12- 40	CRABB, JAMES ROY	D. MARCH 30, 1940 LEWISTON, MONT.
10- 36	CRABLE, GEORGE E	B. 1886 BROOKLYN, N.Y.
29- 21	CRABTREE, ESTEL CRAYTON	D. JANUARY 4, 1967 LOGAN, O.
55- 31	CRADDOCK, WALTER ANDERSON	D. JULY 6, 1980 PARMA HEIGHTS OHIO
37- 28	CRAFT, HARRY FRANCIS	716 GLEN HAVEN DR - CONROE TX 77301
16- 14	CRAFT, MAURICE MONTAGUE	D. OCTOBER 25, 1978 LOS ANGELES, CALIF.
31- 18	CRAGHEAD, HOWARD OLIVER	D. JULY 15, 1962 SAN ZIELOE, CAL.
64- 23	CRAIG, PETER JOEL	801 SILVERLEAF PL - RALEIGH NC 27609
79- 26	CRAIG, RODNEY PAUL	23230 SESAME ST - TORRANCE CA 90504
55- 32	CRAIG, ROGER LEE	2453 CANORA AVE - ALPINE CA 92331
69- 38	CRAM, GERALD ALLEN	2748 N 121ST AVE - OMAHA NE 68164
29- 22	CRAMER, ROGER MAXWELL	5 HILLIARD DR - MANAHAWKIN NJ 08050
12- 41	CRAMER, WILLIAM WENDELL	D. SEPTEMBER 11, 1966 FORT WAYNE, IND.
49- 17	CRANDALL, DELMAR WESLEY	623 ROSARITA DR - FULLERTON CA 92632

14- 44	CRANE, SAMUEL BYREN	D. NOVEMBER 12, 1955 PHILADELPHIA, PA.
37- 29	CRAWFORD, CHARLES LOWRIE	B. APRIL 27, 1914 SWISSVALE, PA.
29- 23	CRAWFORD, CLIFFORD RANKIN	1201 N QUEEN ST - KINSTON NC 28501
45- 18	CRAWFORD, GLENN MARTIN	D. JANUARY 2, 1972 SAGINAW, MICH.
73- 28	CRAWFORD, JAMES FREDERICK	OLD ADD: 48621 I-94 S'CE DR DR-BELLKEVILLE MI
15- 26	CRAWFORC, KENNETH DANIEL	D. NOVEMBER 11, 1976 PITTSBURGH, PA.
52- 20	CRAWFORD, RUFUS	2928 WESTBROOK - FORT WORTH TX 76111
80- 32	CRAWFORD, STEVEN RAY	407 W ALLEN RD #22 - TAHLEQUAH OK 74464
64- 24	CRAWFORD, WILLIE MURPHY	879 LINDA FLORA DR - LOS ANGELES CA 90049
43- 32	CREEDEN, CORNELIUS STEPHEN	D. NOVEMBER 30, 1969 SANTA ANA, CAL.
31- 19	CREEDON, PATRICK FRANCIS	622 N MAIN ST - BROCKTON MA 02401
45- 19	CREEL, JACK DALTON	7119 OAK ARBOR - HOUSTON TX 77018
47- 22	CREGER, BERNARD ODELL	15 GREENWELL CT - LYNCHBURG VA 24502

```
27- 27  CREMINS, ROBERT ANTHONY        415 MANOR RIDGE RD - PELHAM NY 10803
38- 18  CRESPI, FRANK ANGELO JOSEPH    2647 DALTON AVE - ST LOUIS MO 63139
48- 30  CRESS, WALKER JAMES            BOX 2292 - BATON ROUGE LA 70821
69- 39  CRIDER, JERRY STEPHEN          821 KENSINGTON DR - ORLANDO FL 32808
51- 18  CRIMIAN, JOHN MELVIN           3012 GREEN ST - CLAYMONT DE 19703
78- 30  CRIPE, DAVID GORDON            40657 OAKLAND AVE - HEMET CA 92343
77- 36  CRISCIONE, DAVID GERALD        87 HAMLET ST - FREDONIA NY 14063
42- 24  CRISCOLA, ANTHONY PAUL         4025 BAYARD-SAN DIEGO CA 92109
10- 37  CRISP, JOSEPH SHELBY           D. FEBRUARY 5, 1939 KANSAS CITY, MO.
51- 19  CRISTANTE, LEO DANTE           D. AUGUST 24, 1977 DEARBORN, MICH.
24- 23  CRITZ, HUGH MELVILLE           D. JANUARY 10, 1980 GREENWOOD, MISS.
44- 24  CROCKER, CLAUDE ARTHUR         MERRIE OAKS - CLINTO SC 29325
74- 18  CROMARTIE, WARREN LIVINGSTON   %BOOTH,1751 NW 36TH ST - MIAMI FL 33142
37- 30  CROMPTON, HERBERT BRYAN        D. AUGUST 5, 1963 MOLINE, ILL.
54- 16  CRONE, RAYMOND HAYES           RR 1 PANORAMA LOOP - WAXAHACHIE TX 75165.
29- 24  CRONIN, JAMES JOHN             431 LIBERTY ST - EL CERRITO CA 94531
26- 22  CRONIN, JOSEPH EDWARD          BOX 276 - OSTERVILLE MA 02655
28- 24  CRONIN, WILLIAIM PATRICK       D. OCTOBER 26, 1966 NEWTON, MASS.
70- 29  CROSBY, EDWARD CARLTON         11463 ANTICOST WAY - CYPRESS CA 90630
75- 28  CROSBY, KENNETH STEWART        OLD ADD: 484 N MAIN - OREM UT 84057
32- 15  CROSETTI, FRANK PETER JOSEPH   65 W MONTEREY AV - STOCKTON CA 95204
42- 25  CROSS, JOFFRE JAMES            6154 LONGMONT-HOUSTON TX 77027
12- 42  CROSSIN, FRANK PATRICK         D. DECEMBER 6, 1965 KINGSPORT, PA.
30- 14  CROUCH, JACK ALBERT            D. AUGUST 25, 1972 LEESBURG, FLA.
39- 24  CROUCH, WILLIAM ELMER          D. DECEMBER 26, 1980 HOWELL, MICH.
10- 38  CROUCH, WILLIAM HENRY          D. DECEMBER 22, 1945 HIGHLAND PARK, MICH.
39- 25  CROUCHER, FRANK DONALD         D. MAY 21, 1980 HOUSTON, TEXAS
23- 26  CROUSE, CLYDE ELLSWORTH        905 W WASHINGTON ST - MUNCIE IN 47303
26- 23  CROWDER, ALVIN FLOYD           D. APRIL 3, 1972 WINSTON-SALEM, N. C.
52- 21  CROWE, GEORGE DANIEL           BOX 22 - LONG EDDY NY 12760
15- 27  CROWELL, MINOT JOY             D. SEPTEMBER 30, 1962 CENTRAL FALLS, R.I.
28- 25  CROWLEY, EDGAR JEWEL           D. APRIL 14, 1970 BIRMINGHAM, ALA.
69- 40  CROWLEY, TERRENCE MICHAEL      41 DUDLEY AVE - STATEN ISLAND NY 10301
45- 20  CROWSON, THOMAS WOODROW WILSON D. AUGUST 14, 1947 MAYODAN, N. C.
14- 45  CRUISE, WALTON EDWIN           D. JANUARY 9, 1975 TUSCALUGA ALA.
17- 17  CRUM, CALVIN CARL              D. DECEMBER 7, 1945 TULSA, OKLA.
45- 21  CRUMLING, EUGENE LEON          RR 11, HELLAN BRANCH - YORK PA 17406
24- 24  CRUMP, ARTHUR ELLIOTT          D. SEPTEMBER 7, 1976 RALEIGH, N. C.
20- 27  CRUMPLER, RAY MAXTON           D. OCTOBER 6, 1969 FAYETTEVILLE, N. C.
14- 46  CRUTCHER, RICHARD LOUIS        D. JUNE 19, 1952 FRANKFORT, KY.
13- 42  CRUTHERS, CHARLES PRESTON      D. DECEMBER 27, 1976 KENOSHA, WISC.
75- 29  CRUZ (ACOSTA), HENRY           MONTE BRISAS CALLE I-O-6 - FAJARDO PR 00648
73- 29  CRUZ, CIRILO                   CALLE H-E-8 - ARROYO PR 00615
73- 30  CRUZ, HECTOR LUIS              CALLE H-E-8 - ARROYO PR 00615
70- 30  CRUZ, JOSE DELAN               B-15 JARDINES LAFAYETTE - ARROYO PR 00615
77- 37  CRUZ, JULIO LOUIS              4027 145TH NE - BELLEVUE WA 98007
78- 31  CRUZ, TODD RUBEN               OLD ADD: 1046 20TH ST - DETROIT MI
78- 32  CRUZ, VICTOR MANUEL            ALEXANDER FLEMING NO. 67-SANTO DOMINGO DOM RE
74- 19  CUBBAGE, MICHAEL LEE           BOX 126 - RUCKERSVILLE VA 22968
35- 20  CUCCINELLO, ALFRED EDWARD      7 CRYSTAL ST ELMONT NY 11003
30- 15  CUCCINELLO, ANTHONY FRANCIS    3610 BEACH DR - TAMPA FL 33609
43- 33  CUCCURULLO, ARTHUR JOSEPH      37 PARK AVE - WEST ORANGE NJ 07052
50- 26  CUELLAR, CHARLES JESUS PATRICK 3209 GRACE ST - TAMPA FL 33607
59- 17  CUELLAR, MIGUEL ANGEL          5219 TRAIL LAKE DR - HOUSTON TX 77045
77- 38  CUELLAR, ROBERT                823 S CAMERON - ALICE TX 78332
61- 25  CUETO, DAGOBERTO CONCEPCION    EL COROJO - SAN LUIS PINAR DEL RIO CUBA
14- 47  CUETO, MANUEL MELO             D. JUNE 29, 1942 REGLA, HAVANA CUBA
43- 34  CULBERSON, DELBERT LEON        7 CONASAUGA CT - ROME GA 30161
62- 29  CULLEN, JOHN PATRICK           164 ALEXANDER AVE - NUTLEY NJ 07110
66- 26  CULLEN, TIMOTHY LEO            789 SOLANA DR - LAFAYETTE CA 94549
38- 19  CULLENBINE, ROY JOSEPH         24638 MEADOW LN - MOUNT CLEMENS MI 48043
```

```
36- 17  CULLER, RICHARD BROADUS        D. JUNE 16, 1964 CHAPEL HILL, N. C.
26- 24  CULLOP, HENRY                  D. DECEMBER 8, 1978 WESTERVILLE, O.
13- 43  CULLOP, NORMAN ANDREW          D. APRIL 15, 1961 TAZEWELL, VA.
25- 23  CULLOTON, BERNARD ALOYSIUS     D. NOVEMBER 9, 1976 KINGSTON, N. Y.
42- 26  CULP, BENJAMIN BALDY           3827 KAREN ST-PHILADELPHIA PA 19114
63- 27  CULP, RAY LEONARD              7400 WATERLINE - AUSTIN TX 78731
10- 39  CULP, WILLIAM EDWARD           D. SEPTEMBER 3, 1969 ARNOLD, PA.
66- 27  CULVER, GEORGE RAYMOND         3200 FLEUR ST - BAKERSFIELD CA 93301
68- 16  CUMBERLAND, JOHN SHELTON       36 ARLINGTON AVE - WESTBROOK ME 04092
```

26-	25	CUMMINGS, JOHN WILLIAM	D. OCTOBER 5, 1962 WEST MIFFLIN, PA.
29-	25	CUNNINGHAM, BRUCE LEE	22400 ROCKAWAY LANE #311 - HAYWARD CA 94541
16-	15	CUNNINGHAM, GEORGE HAROLD	D. MARCH 10, 1972 CHATTANOOGA, TENN.
54-	17	CUNNINGHAM, JOSEPH ROBERT	14426 LADUE RD - CHESTERFIELD MO 63017
31-	20	CUNNINGHAM, RAYMOND LEE	1007 CHRISTINE - HOUSTON TX 77017
21-	18	CUNNINGHAM, WILLIAM ALOYSIUS	D. SEPTEMBER 26, 1953 COLUSA, CAL.
10-	40	CUNNINGHAM, WILLIAM JAMES	D. FEBRUARY 21, 1946 SCHENECTADY, N. Y.
75-	30	CURRENCE, DELANCY LAFAYETTE	1238 STANLEY DR - ROCK HILL SC 29730
16-	16	CURRIE, MURPHY ARCHIBALD	D. JUNE 22, 1939 ASHEBORO, N.C.
55-	33	CURRIE, WILLIAM CLEVELAND	ARLINGTON GA 31713
47-	23	CURRIN, PERRY GILMORE	1967 ADD: 1615 SIGMON NW - ROANOKE VA 24017
60-	26	CURRY, GEORGE ANTHONY	BOX 7054 - NASSAU BAHAMAS
11-	38	CURRY, GEORGE JAMES	D. OCTOBER 5, 1963 STRATFORD, CONN.
61-	26	CURTIS, JACK PATRICK	RR1 BOX 326 - GRANITE FALLS NC 28630
70-	31	CURTIS, JOHN DUFFIELD	858 ANDROMEDA LN - FOSTER CITY CA 94404
43-	35	CURTIS, VERNON EUGENE	724 21ST ST - CAIRO IL 62914
43-	36	CURTRIGHT, GUY PAXTON	1868 S ALKIRE CT - LAKEWOOD CO 80228
51-	20	CUSICK, JOHN PETER	46 MORTHWOOD AVE - DEMAREST NJ 07627
12-	43	CUTSHAW, GEORGE WILLIAM	D. AUGUST 22, 1973 SAN DIEGO, CALIF.
21-	19	CUYLER, HAZEN SHIRLEY	D. FEBRUARY 11, 1950 ANN ARBOR, MICH.
22-	24	CVENGROS, MICHAEL JOHN	D. AUGUST 2, 1970 HOT SPRINGS, ARK.
14-	48	CYPERT, ALFRED BOYD	D. JANUARY 9, 1973 WASHINGTON, D.C.
73-	31	DACQUISTO, JOHN FRANCIS	3440 FIR ST - SAN DIEGO CA 92104
75-	31	DADE, LONNIE PAUL	15829 SE 171ST PL - RENTON WA 98055
43-	37	DAGENHARD, JOHN DOUGLAS	BOX 337-SAXONBURY PA 16056
32-	16	DAGLIA, PETER GEORGE	D. MARCH 11, 1952 WILLITS, CAL.
55-	34	DAGRES, ANGELO GEORGE	GREENTREE LN RFD - ROWLEY MA 01969
63-	28	DAHL, JAY STEVEN	D. JUNE 20, 1965 SALISBURY, N. C.
35-	21	DAHLGREN, ELLSWORTH TENNEY	17 WOODLYN LN - BRADBURY CA 91010
56-	25	DAHLKE, JEROME ALEXANDER	3643 HALLBROOK ST - MEMPHIS TN 38127
29-	26	DAILEY, SAMUEL LAURENCE	D. DECEMBER 2, 1979 COLUMBIA, MO.
61-	27	DAILEY, WILLIAM GARLAND	OLD ADD: 3419 S 14TH ST - ARLINGTON VA
67-	21	DAL CANTON, JOHN BRUCE	624 RAY DR - CARNEGIE PA 15106
11-	39	DALE, EMMETT EUGENE	D. MARCH 20, 1958 ST. LOUIS, MO.
55-	35	DALEY, BUDDY LEO	RR 62-C BOX 205 - LANDER WY 82520
12-	44	DALEY, JOHN FRANCIS	470 W 3RD ST - MANSFIELD OH 44903
11-	40	DALEY, JUD LAWRENCE	D. JANUARY 26, 1967 GADSDEN, ALA.
55-	36	DALEY, PETER HARVEY	502 W MAIN ST - GRASS VALLEY CA 95945
37-	31	DALLESSANDRO, NICHOLAS DOMINIC	4821 OAKKNOLL DR - INDIANAPOLIS IN 46241
60-	27	DALRYMPLE, CLAYTON ERROL	2506 ALBERT RILL RD - WESTMINSTER MD 21157
15-	28	DALRYMPLE, MICHAEL	B. ST. LOUIS, MO.
10-	41	DALTON, TALBOT PERCY	1940 ADD: 2 PROSPECT AVE - CATONSVILLE MD
13-	44	DALY, THOMAS DANIEL	D. NOVEMBER 7, 1946 MEDFORD, MASS.
63-	29	DAMASKA, JACK LLOYD	252 BLACKHAWK RD - BEAVER FALLS PA 15010
15-	29	DAMRAU, HARRY ROBERT	D. AUGUST 21, 1957 STATEN ISLAND, N. Y.
28-	26	DANEY, ARTHUR LEE	7523 CULVER ST #326 - SCOTTSDALE AZ 85257
11-	41	DANFORTH, DAVID CHARLES	D. SEPTEMBER 19, 1970 BALTIMORE, MD.
57-	14	DANIEL, CHARLES EDWARD	1640 BABS RD - MEMPHIS TN 38116
37-	32	DANIEL, HANDLEY JACOB	505 PINE ST - WEST POINT GA 31833
57-	15	DANIELS, BENNIE	1671 E 122ND - LOS ANGELES CA 90059
10-	42	DANIELS, BERNARD ELMER	D. JUNE 6, 1958 CEDAR GROVE, N.J.
45-	22	DANIELS, FREDERICK CLINTON	522 SALISBURY RD - STATESVILLE NC 28677
52-	22	DANIELS, HAROLD JACK	3715 ELMRIDGE DR - EVANSVILLE IN 47711
15-	30	DANNER, HENRY FREDERICK	D. SEPTEMBER 19, 1949 BOSTON, MASS.
33-	15	DANNING, HARRY	1150 BOWER HILL RD #301N-MT LEBANON PA 15243
28-	27	DANNING, IKE	5805 W 8TH ST #209 - LOS ANGELES CA 90036
44-	25	DANTONIC, JOHN JAMES	430 S CLARK ST - NEW ORLEANS LA 70119
42-	27	DAPPER, CLIFFORD ROLAND	733 BURMA RD-FALLBROOK CA 92028
74-	20	DARCY, PATRICK LEONARD	515 S COLUMBUS BLVD - TUCSON AZ 85711
14-	49	DARINGER, CLIFFORD CLARENCE	D. DECEMBER 12, 1971 SACRAMENTO, CALIF.
14-	50	DARINGER, ROLLA HARRISON	D. MAY 23, 1974 SEYMOUR, IND.
46-	21	DARK, ALVIN RALPH	608 NEPTUNE AVE - LEUCADIA CA 92024
80-	33	DARK, MARK WILLIAM	1620 READING BLVD - WYOMISSING PA 19610
54-	18	DARNELL, ROBERT JACK	1442 OVERO CIR - SPRINGDALE AR 72764
77-	39	DARR, MICHAEL EDWARD	5862B FULLERTON AVE - BUENA PARK CA 90621
34-	28	DARROW, GEORGE OLIVER	10052 CONCORD AVE - SUN CITY AZ 85151
62-	30	DARWIN, ARTHUR BOBBY LEE	OLD ADD: 12902 GLENDA - CERRITOS CA 90701
78-	33	DARWIN, DANNY WAYNE	1404 MORRISON - DENISON TX 75020
24-	25	DASHIELL, JOHN WALLACE	D. MAY 20, 1972 PENSACOLA, FLA.
13-	45	DASHNER, LEE CLAIRE	D. DECEMBER 16, 1960 EL DORADO, KAN.
45-	23	DASSO, FRANCIS JOSEPH NICHOLAS	1413 MADISON - WENATCHEE WA 98801
15-	31	DAUBERT, HARRY J.	D. JANUARY 8, 1944 DETROIT, MICH.
10-	43	DAUBERT, JACOB ELSWORTH	D. OCTOBER 9, 1924 CINCINNATI, O.
76-	27	DAUER, RICHARD FREMONT	7087 TIPPICANOE - SAN BERNARDINO CA 92404

51-	21	DAUGHERTY, HAROLD RAY	66 ELDRED AVE - BEDFORD OH 44014
37-	33	DAUGHTERS, ROBERT FRANCIS	35 OLD PARISH RD DARIEN CO 06820
12-	45	DAUSS, GEORGE AUGUST	D. JULY 27, 1963 ST. LOUIS, MO.
53-	17	DAVALILLO, POMPEYO ANTONIO	CENTRO COMMERCIAL #8-MAIQUETIA VENEZUELA
63-	30	DAVALILLO, VICTOR JOSE	CLE TRUJILLO 7,MARIPEREZ,Q.V.--CARACAS VENEZ
69-	41	DAVANON, FRANK GERALD	4161 37TH ST #10 - SAN DIEGO CA 92104

```
20- 28  DAVENPORT, CLAUDE EDWIN       D. JUNE 13, 1976 CORPUS CHRISTI, TEX.
14- 51  DAVENPORT, DAVID W.           D. OCTOBER 16, 1954 EL DORADO, ARK.
58- 26  DAVENPORT, JAMES HOUSTON      1016 HEWITT DR - SAN CARLOS CA 94070
21- 20  DAVENPORT, JOUBERT LUM        D. APRIL 21, 1961 DALLAS, TEX.
77- 40  DAVEY, MICHAEL GERALD         3022 E 19TH ST - SPOKANE WA 99203
62- 31  DAVIAULT, RAYMOND JOSEPH ROBERT 12116 ONTARIO E-POINTES AUX TREMBLES QUE
18- 14  DAVIDSON, CLAUDE BOUCHER      D. APRIL 18, 1956 WEYMOUTH, MASS.
55- 25  DAVIDSON, THOMAS EUGENE       515 DE ARMOND PLACE - SANTA MARIA CA 93454
59- 18  DAVIE, GERALD LEE             14390 DIX - SOUTHGATE MI 48192
14- 52  DAVIES, LLOYD GARRISON        D. SEPTEMBER 5, 1973 MIDDLETOWN, CONN.
65- 26  DAVIS, ARTHUR WILLARD         6638 KNOX AVE S - MINNEAPOLIS MN 55423
63- 31  DAVIS, BRYSHEAR BARNETT       227 E 94TH ST - LOS ANGELES CA 90003
81- 25  DAVIS, CHARLES THEODORE       142 E 85TH ST - LOS ANGELES CA 90003
34- 29  DAVIS, CURTIS BENTON          D. OCTOBER 12, 1965 COVINA, CAL.
12- 46  DAVIS, FRANK TALMADGE         D. FEBRUARY 4, 1944 RALEIGH, N.C.
12- 47  DAVIS, GEORGE ALLEN          D. JUNE 4, 1961 BUFFALO, N.Y.
26- 26  DAVIS, GEORGE WILLIS          370 LAUREL AVE - BRIDGEPORT CT 06605
32- 17  DAVIS, HARRY ALBERT           BOX 27 - SHREVEPORT LA 71161
59- 19  DAVIS, HERMAN THOMAS "TOMMY"  1514 S FAIRFAX - LOS ANGELES CA 90019
19- 16  DAVIS, ISAAC MARION           OLD ADD: 524 S OZARK - SAN DIEGO CA
62- 32  DAVIS, JACKE SYLVESTA         1131 LYNNWOOD DR - CARTHAGE TX 75633
54- 19  DAVIS, JAMES BENNETT          3327 COUNTRYSIDE DR - SAN MATEO CA 94403
81- 26  DAVIS, JODY RICHARD           RR 1 BEN HILL DR - OAKWOOD GA 30566
41- 20  DAVIS, JOHN HUMPHREY          OLD ADD: HOTEL LAWRENCE - DALLAS TEX 75202
15- 32  DAVIS, JOHN WILBUR            D. MAY 26, 1967 LIGHTFOOT, VA.
40- 14  DAVIS, LAWRENCE COLUMBUS      4767 CHAMPION CT - GREENSBORO NC 27410
80- 34  DAVIS, MICHAEL DWAYNE         3606 47TH ST - SAN DIEGO CA 92105
80- 35  DAVIS, ODIE ERNEST            1014 MONTANA ST - SAN ANTONIO TX 78203
46- 22  DAVIS, OTIS ALLEN            183 BAYBERRY LANE - ROCHESTER NY 14616
36- 18  DAVIS, RAY THOMAS            1802 BEECH ST DUNCAN OK 73533
77- 41  DAVIS, RICHARD EARL          2415 W ALONDRA - COMPTON CA 90220
52- 23  DAVIS, ROBERT BRANDON        222 CHELTENHAM RD - NEWARK DE 19712
58- 27  DAVIS, ROBERT EDWARD         OLD ADD: 101 W 12TH ST #15E - NEW YORK NY
73- 32  DAVIS, ROBERT JOHN EUGENE    BOX 132 - LOCUST GROVE OK 74352
62- 33  DAVIS, RONALD EVERETTE       OLD ADD: 15331 E BARBARA CIR - HOUSTON TX
78- 34  DAVIS, RONALD GENE           8103 COYTON - HOUSTON TX 77061
79- 27  DAVIS, STEVEN MICHAEL        1377 ANTONIO LANE - SAN JOSE CA 95117
49- 18  DAVIS, THOMAS OSCAR          D. DECEMBER 31, 1978 WEST COVINA, CALIF.
28- 28  DAVIS, VIRGIL LAWRENCE       RR 5 BOX 186- ALEXANDER CITY AL 35010
60- 28  DAVIS, WILLIAM HENRY         OLD ADD: 8515 HOLLYWOOD BLVD - HOLLYWOOD CA
38- 20  DAVIS, WOODROW WILSON        BOX 87 ODUM GA 31555
69- 42  DAVISON, MICHAEL LYNN        110U ARMSTRONG BLVD N - ST JAMES MN 56081
76- 28  DAWSON, ANDRE NOLAN          6295 SW 58TH PL - MIAMI FL 33143
24- 26  DAWSON, RALPH FENTON         D. JANUARY 4, 1978 LONGVIEW, TEX.
13- 46  DAWSON, REXFORD PAUL         D. OCTOBER 20, 1958 INDIANAPOLIS, IND.
69- 43  DAY, CHARLES FREDERICK       140 KIMBER LN - EVANSVILLE IN 47715
24- 27  DAY, CLYDE HENRY             D. MARCH 21, 1934 KANSAS CITY, MO.
12- 48  DEAL, CHARLES ALBERT         D. SEPTEMBER 16, 1979 COVINA, CALIF.
47- 24  DEAL, ELLIS FERGUSON         4751 NW 24TH #114N - OKLAHOMA CITY OK 73127
39- 26  DEAL, LINDSAY FRED           D. APRIL 18, 1979 LITTLE ROCK, ARK.
36- 19  DEAN, ALFRED LOVILL          D. DECEMBER 21, 1970 RIVERSIDE, N. J.
41- 21  DEAN, JAMES HARRY            D. JUNE 1, 1960 ROCKMART, GA.
30- 16  DEAN, JAY HANNA              D. JULY 17, 1974 RENO, NEV.
34- 30  DEAN, PAUL DEE               D. MARCH 17, 1981 SPRINGDALE, ARK.
67- 22  DEAN, TOMMY DOUGLAS          RR2 - IUKA MS 38852
24- 28  DEAN, WAYLAND OGDEN          D. APRIL 10, 1930 HUNTINGTON, W. VA.
27- 28  DEAR, PAUL STANFORD          BOX 2475 - CHRISTIANSBURG VA 24073
77- 42  DEBARR, DENNIS LEE           35481 CLAREMONT DR - NEWARK CA 94560
16- 17  DEBERRY, JOHN HERMAN         D. SEPTEMBER 10, 1951 SAVANNAH, TENN.
20- 29  DEBERRY, JOSEPH GADDY        D. OCTOBER 9, 1944 SOUTHERN PINES, N. C.
17- 18  DEBUS, ADAM JOSEPH           D. MAY 13, 1977 CHICAGO, ILL.
62- 34  DEBUSSCHERE, DAVID ALBERT    90 3RD ST - GARDEN CITY NY 11530
22- 25  DECATUR, ARTHUR RUE          D. APRIL 25, 1966 TALLADEGA, ALA.
73- 33  DECINCES, DOUGLAS VERNON     2437 STILL FOREST RD - BALTIMORE MD 21208
```

```
69- 44  DECKER, GEORGE HENRY "JOE"   2605 W VAN BUREN - PHOENIX AZ 85009
16- 18  DEDE, ARTHUR RICHARD         D. SEPTEMBER 6, 1971 KEENE, N.H.
35- 22  DEDEAUX, RAOUL MARTIAL       1430 S EASTMAN AVE - LOS ANGELES CA 90023
15- 33  DEE, MAURICE LEO             D. AUGUST 12, 1971 JAMAICA PLAINS, MASS.
63- 32  DEES, CHARLES HENRY          23412 DORSET PL - HARBOR CITY CA 90710
17- 19  DEFATE, CLYDE HERBERT        D. SEPTEMBER 3, 1963 NEW ORLEANS, LA.
78- 35  DEFREITES, ARTURO SIMON      HERMONOS MIRABAL #21 SAN PEDRO DE MARCORIS DR
```

DEGERICK · DeVIVEIROS

Code	Name	Address
61- 28	DEGERICK, MICHAEL ARTHUR	353 RIDGEDALE AVE - EAST HANOVER NJ 07936
74- 21	DEIDEL, JAMES LAWRENCE	OLD ADD: 2545 S PATTON CT - DENVER CO
40- 15	DEJAN, MIKE DAN	D. FEBRUARY 2, 1953 WEST LOS ANGELES, CALIF.
74- 22	DEJESUS, IVAN	758 ENEAS ST - RIO PIEDRAS PR 00926
45- 24	DEKONING, WILLIAM CALLAHAN	D. JULY 26, 1979 PALM HARBOR, FLA.
44- 26	DELACRUZ, TOMAS	D. SEPTEMBER 6, 1958 HAVANA, CUBA
60- 29	DELAHOZ, MIGUEL ANGEL	OLD ADD: 5011 SW 127TH CT - MIAMI FL 33165
32- 18	DELANCEY, WILLIAM PINKNEY	D. NOVEMBER 28, 1946 PHOENIX, ARIZ.
24- 29	DELANEY, ARTHUR DEWEY	D. MAY 2, 1970 HAYWARD, CALIF.
75- 32	DELAROSA, JESUS	34 SHERMAN AVE - NEW YORK NY 10034
81- 27	DELEON, LUIS ANTONIO	SAN ANTON 120,CLE E.CABRERRA - PONCE PR 00731
77- 25	DELGADO, LUIS FELIPE	URB. BRISAS LE HATILLO #A-Y-HATILLO PR 00659
52- 24	DELGRECC, ROBERT GEORGE	625 SOUTHVIEW DR - PITTSBURGH PA 15226
12- 49	DELHI, LEE WILLIAM	D. MAY 9, 1966 GREENBRAE, CALIF.
55- 37	DELIS, JUAN FRANCISCO	1963 ADD:3A #24508, REPARTO DOLORES - HAVANA
29- 27	DELKER, EDWARD ALBERTS	1 S FRONT ST - ST CLAIR PA 17970
12- 50	DELL, WILLIAM GEORGE	D. AUGUST 24, 1966 INDEPENDENCE, CALIF.
33- 16	DELMAS, ALBERT CHARLES	D. DECEMBER 4, 1979 HUNTINGTON BEACH, CALIF.
52- 25	DELCCK, IVAN MARTIN	PARKER RD - NEEDHAM MA 02194
74- 23	DELCS SANTOS, RAMON GENERO	OZAMA ESTE #13 - SANTO DOMINGO DOM REP
43- 38	DELSAVIC, GARTON ORVILLE	48 ROOSEVELT DR-BLAUVELT NY 10913
48- 31	DELSING, JAMES HENRY	449 CAMERON RD - ST LOUIS MO 63137
51- 22	DEMAESTRI, JOSEPH PAUL	50 FAIRWAY - NOVATO CA 94947
12- 51	DEMAREE, ALBERT WENTWORTH	D. MAY 2, 1962 LONG BEACH, CALIF.
32- 19	DEMAREE, JOSEPH FRANKLIN	D. AUGUST 30, 1958 LOS ANGELES, CAL.
48- 32	DEMARS, WILLIAM LESTER	224 BEECHTREE LN - WAYNE PA 19087
57- 16	DEMERIT, JOHN STEPHEN	550 W WALTER ST - PORT WASHINGTON WI 53074
74- 24	DEMERY, LAWRENCE CALVIN	2024 W 66TH ST - LOS ANGELES CA 90047
56- 26	DEMETER, DONALD LEE	1521 SW 56TH ST - OKLAHOMA CITY OK 73119
59- 20	DEMETER, STEVEN	2805 MARIONCLIFF DR - PARMA OH 44134
74- 25	DEMOLA, DONALD JOHN	460 VILLAGE DR - HAUPPAUGE NY 11787
10- 44	DEMOTT, BENYEW HARRISON	D. JULY 5, 1963 SOMERVILLE, N.J.
51- 23	DEMPSEY, CORNELIUS FRANCIS	1530 CORDILLEURS RD - REDWOOD CITY CA 94062
69- 45	DEMPSEY, JOHN RIKARD "RICK"	3081 TOWNSHIP - SANTA SUSANA CA 93063
67- 23	DENEHY, WILLIAM FRANCIS	OLD ADD: SIMSBURY CT 06070
23- 27	DENNEHEY, THOMAS FRANCIS	D. AUGUST 8, 1977 PHILADELPHIA, PA.
42- 28	DENNING, OTTO GEORGE	3434 W MELROSE-CHICAGO IL 60618
65- 27	DENNIS, DONALD RAY	RR2 - UNIONTOWN KS 66779
74- 26	DENNY, JOHN ALLEN	14551 BURNLEY ST - CHESTERFIELD MO 63017
73- 34	DENT, RUSSELL EARL	19925 NE 14TH CT - NORTH MIAMI BEACH FL 33162
47- 25	DENTE, SAMUEL JOSEPH	19 REDMAN TER - WEST CALDWELL NJ 07006
43- 39	DEPHILLIPS, ANTHONY ANDREW	3808 221ST ST-BAYSIDE NY 11361
80- 36	DERNIER, ROBERT EUGENE	9509 E 77TH ST - RAYTOWN MO 64138
10- 45	DERRICK, CLAUD LESTER	D. JULY 15, 1974 CLAYTON, GA.
70- 32	DERRICK, JAMES MICHAEL	1117 ONTARIO AVE - WEST COLUMBIA SC 29169
31- 21	DERRINGER, PAUL	2017 OAK TER - SARASOTA FL 33580
56- 27	DERRINGTON, CHARLES JAMES	10509 BRYSON AVE - SOUTH GATE CA 90281
44- 27	DERRY, ALVA RUSSELL	PRINCETON MO 64673
80- 37	DESA, JOSEPH	642A N VINEYARD BLVD - HONOLULU HI 96817
30- 17	DESAUTELS, EUGENE ABRAHAM	2802 MANSFIELD AV - FLINT MI 48503
32- 20	DESHONG, JAMES BROOKLYN	99 S 31ST ST - HARRISBURG PA 17109
16- 19	DESJARDIEN, PAUL RAYMOND	D. MARCH 7, 1956 MONROVIA, CALIF.
80- 38	DETHERAGE, ROBERT WAYNE	2325 N BENTON - SPRINGFIELD MO 65803
30- 18	DETORE, GEORGE FRANCIS	RR 1 - NEW HARTFORD NY 13413
73- 35	DETTORE, THOMAS ANTHONY	1120 MCEWEN AVE - CANONSBURG PA 15317
42- 29	DETWEILER, ROBERT STERLING	312 HOLT ST-FEDERALSBURG MD 21632
46- 23	DEUTSCH, MELVIN ELLIOTT	1701 W HWY 21 - CALDWELL TX 77836
32- 21	DEVENS, CHARLES	265 FRANKLIN ST - BOSTON MA 02110
73- 36	DEVINE, PAUL ADRIAN	3410 WOODFORD DR - ARLINGTON TX 76103
18- 15	DEVINE, WILLIAM PATRICK	D. OCTOBER 1, 1957 ALBANY, N. Y.
20- 30	DEVINEY, JOHN HAROLD	D. JANUARY 4, 1933 WESTWOOD, MASS.
24- 30	DEVIVEIROS, BERNARD JOHN	3520 REDDING ST - OAKLAND CA 94619

44- 28	DEVLIN, JAMES RAYMOND	130 WORMAN ST. ESPY - BLOOMSBURG PA 17815
13- 47	DEVOGT, REX EUGENE	D. NOVEMBER 9, 1935 ALMA, MICH.
18- 16	DEVORMER, ALBERT E.	D. AUGUST 29, 1966 GRAND RAPIDS, MICH.
77- 44	DIAZ, BAUDILIO JOSE	LA VEGA #40 - CUA., ESTADO MIRANDA VENEZUELA
24- 31	DIBUT, PEDRO	D. DECEMBER 4, 1979 HIALEAH, FLA.
64- 25	DICKEN, PAUL FRANKLIN	7253 ST ANDREWS RD - LAKE WORTH FL 33460
23- 28	DICKERMAN, LEO LOUIS	206 4TH AVE NE - ATKINS AR 72823
17- 20	DICKERSON, GEORGE CLARK	D. JULY 9, 1938 LOS ANGELES, CALIF.
35- 23	DICKEY, GEORGE WILLARD	D. JUNE 16, 1976 DEWITT, ARK.
28- 29	DICKEY, WILLIAM MALCOLM	114 E. 5TH ST - LITTLE ROCK AR 72203
36- 20	DICKMAN, GEORGE EMERSON	D. APRIL 27, 1981 NEW YORK, N. Y.
36- 21	DICKSHOT, JOHN OSCAR	1530 JENKINSON CT - WAUKEGAN IL 60085
63- 33	DICKSON, JAMES EDWARD	685 FRANKLIN - ASTORIA OR 97103
39- 27	DICKSON, MURRY MONROE	505 TERRANCE RD - LEAVENWORTH KS 66048
10- 46	DICKSON, WALTER R.	D. DECEMBER 9, 1918 ARDMORE, OKLA.
69- 46	DIDIER, ROBERT DANIEL	4601 ONTARIO ST - VANCOUVER BC V5V 3H4
42- 30	DIEHL, GEORGE KRAUSE	717 CHIPPENDALE - KINGSPORT TN 37660
47- 26	DIERING, CHARLES EDWARD ALLEN	1 NOB HILL DR - ST LOUIS MO 63138
64- 26	DIERKER, LAWRENCE EDWARDS	9019 COLLEEN - HOUSTON TX 77035
33- 17	DIETRICH, WILLIAM JOHN	D. JUNE 20, 1978 PHILADELPHIA, PA.
27- 29	DIETRICK, WILLIAM ALEXANDER	D. MAY 6, 1946 BETHESDA, MD.
40- 16	DIETZ, LLOYD ARTHUR	D. OCTOBER 29, 1972 BEAUMONT, TEX.
66- 28	DIETZ, RICHARD ALLEN	406 LEYSWOOD DR - GREENVILLE SC 29607
54- 20	DIETZEL, LEROY LOUIS	2331 CARTWIGHT PL - CHARLOTTE NC 28208
48- 33	DIFANI, CLARENCE JOSEPH	808 N MILL - FESTUS MO 63028
34- 31	DIGGS, REESE WILSON	D. OCTOBER 30, 1978 BALTIMORE, MD.
69- 47	DILAURO, JACK EDWARD	168 E MOHAWK - MALVERN OH 44644
59- 21	DILLARD, DAVID DONALD	RR1 - WATERLOO SC 29384
75- 33	DILLARD, STEPHEN BRADLEY	RR 2 BOX 162 - SALTILLO MS 38866
17- 21	DILLHOEFER, WILLIAM MARTIN	D. FEBRUARY 22, 1922 ST. LOUIS, MO.
14- 54	DILLINGER, HARLEY HUGH	D. JANUARY 8, 1959 CLEVELAND, O.
46- 24	DILLINGER, ROBERT BERNARD	15380 RHODODENDRON DR-CANYON COUNTY CA 91351
67- 24	DILLMAN, WILLIAM HOWARD	44 HOLLY HILL RD - RICHBORO PA 18954
63- 34	DILLON, STEPHEN EDWARD	130 W 228TH ST - BRONX NY 10463
74- 27	DILONE, MIGUEL ANGEL	CALLE EL SOL #190 - SANTIAGO DOM REPUBLIC
40- 17	DIMAGGIO, DOMINIC PAUL	90 BEACON ST - BOSTON MA 02108
36- 22	DIMAGGIO, JOSEPH PAUL	2150 BEACH ST - SAN FRANCISCO CA 94123
37- 34	DIMAGGIO, VINCENT PAUL	7528 BECK AVE - NORTH HOLLYWOOD CA 91605
77- 45	DIMMEL, MICHAEL WAYNE	1817 BROOKSIDE CIR - ALBERT LEA MN 56007
75- 34	DINEEN, KERRY MICHAEL	702 ELDER AVE - CHULA VISTA CA 92010
45- 25	DINGES, VANCE GEORGE	274 S HIGH ST - HARRISONBURG VA 22801
73- 37	DIORIC, RONALD MICHAEL	83 GILES ST - WATERBURY CT 06704
51- 24	DIPIETRO, ROBERT LOUIS PAUL	909 CARRIAGE HILL DR - YAKIMA WA 98902
81- 28	DIPINO, FRANK MICHAEL	141 NORTHWOOD WAY - CAMILLUS NY 13031
69- 48	DISTASO, ALEC JOHN	9450 1/2 SIERRA WAY - SAUGUS CA 91350
18- 17	DISTEL, GEORGE ADAM	D. FEBRUARY 12, 1967 MADISON, IND.
54- 21	DITMAR, ARTHUR JOHN	13629 STARLITE DR - BROOK PARK OH 44142
52- 26	DITTMER, JOHN DOUGLAS	200 N MAIN ST - ELKADER IA 52043
53- 18	DIXON, JOHN CRAIG	RR 2 BOX 344 - CHARLOTTE NC 28210
25- 24	DIXON, LEO MICHAEL	6639 S CAMPBELL - CHICAGO IL 60629
77- 46	DIXON, THOMAS EARL	2945 S DELANEY ST - ORLANDO FL 32806
12- 52	DOAK, WILLIAM LEOPOLD	D. NOVEMBER 26, 1954 BRADENTON, FLA.
24- 32	DOBB, JOHN KENNETH	973 HAMPDEN RD - MUSKEGON MI 49441
59- 22	DOBBEK, DANIEL JOHN	300 GREENLAND RD - ONTONAGON MI 49953
29- 28	DOBENS, RAYMOND JOSEPH	D. APRIL 21, 1980 STUART, FLA.
39- 28	DOBERNIC, ANDREW JOSEPH	2906 MO ST LOUIS MO 63118
66- 29	DOBSON, CHARLES THOMAS	4208 LOCUST ST - KANSAS CITY MO 64110
39- 29	DOBSON, JOSEPH GORDON	BOX 298 - TOMBSTONE AZ 85638
67- 25	DOBSON, PATRICK EDWARD	BOX 23290 - NASHVILLE TN 37202
47- 27	DOBY, LAWRENCE EUGENE	NISHUANE RD 45 - MONTCLAIR NJ 07042
45- 26	DOCKINS, GEORGE WOODROW	BOX 3 - CLYDE KS 66938
12- 53	DODD, ONA MELVIN	D. MARCH 31, 1929 NEWPORT, ARK.
12- 54	DODGE, JOHN LEWIS	D. JUNE 19, 1916 MOBILE, ALA.
21- 21	DODGE, SAMUEL EDWARD	1940 ADD: WYALUSING, PA.
37- 35	DOERR, ROBERT PERSHING	33705 ILLAMO-AGNESS RD - AGNESS OR 97406
74- 28	DOHERTY, JOHN MICHAEL	109 WAKEFIELD ST - READING MA 01867
14- 55	DOLAN, E. L.	
30- 19	DOLJACK, FRANK JOSEPH	D. JANUARY 23, 1948 CLEVELAND, O.
35- 24	DOLL, ARTHUR JAMES	D. APRIL 28, 1978 CALUMET CITY, ILL.
23- 29	DONAHUE, JOHN FREDERICK	D. OCTOBER 3, 1949 BOSTON, MASS.
43- 40	DONAHUE, JOHN STEPHEN MICHAEL	415 N BELMONT AVE-ARLINGTON HGTS IL 60004
38- 21	DONALD, RICHARD ATLEY	RR 2 BOX 132 CHOUDRANT LA 71227

```
12- 55  DONALDS, EDWARD ALEXANDER     D. JULY 3, 1950 COLUMBUS, O.
66- 30  DONALDSON, JOHN DAVID          3331 BENARD AVE - CHARLOTTE NC 28206
29- 29  DONDERO, LEONARD PETER         38861 MISSION BLVD #2224 - FREMONT CA 94536
11- 42  DONNELLY, EDWARD               D. NOVEMBER 28, 1957 RUTLAND, VT.
59- 23  DONNELLY, EDWARD VINCENT       823 ROPER - HOUSTON TX 77034
44- 29  DONNELLY, SYLVESTER URBAN      D. JUNE 20, 1976 OLIVIA, MINN.
61- 29  DONOHUE, JAMES THOMAS          16 HUNTLEIGH DOWNS - ST LOUIS MO 63131
21- 22  DONOHUE, PETER JOSEPH          8713 S NORMANDALE ST #261 - FT WORTH TX 7611#
79- 28  DONOHUE, THOMAS JAMES          249 LIBERTY AVE - WESTBURY NY 11590
55- 38  DONOSO, LINO GALATA            1971 ADD: CALLE SANTA MARIA - HAVANA CUBA
50- 27  DONOVAN, RICHARD EDWARD        61 DEEP RUN RD - COHASSET MA 02025
42- 31  DONOVAN, WILLARD EARL          1611 S 10TH AVE-MAYWOOD IL 60153
22- 26  DORAN, WILLIAM JAMES           D. MARCH 9, 1978 SANTA MONICA, CALIF.
47- 28  DORISH, HARRY                  68 ELEY ST - KINGSTON PA 18704
23- 30  DORMAN, CHARLES WILLIAM        D. NOVEMBER 15, 1928 SAN FRANCISCO, CAL.
28- 30  DORMAN, DWIGHT DEXTER          D. DECEMBER 7, 1974 ANAHEIM, CAL.
40- 18  DORSETT, CALVIN LEAVELLE       D. OCTOBER 22, 1970 ELK CITY, OKLA.
80- 39  DORSEY, JAMES EDWARD           8409 SHIRLEY AVE - NORTHRIDGE CA 91324
11- 43  DORSEY, JEREMIAH               B. 1885 OAKLAND, CALIF.
79- 29  DOTSON, RICHARD ELLIOTT        8147 FOREST RD - CINCINNATI OH 45230
61- 30  DOTTER, GARY RICHARD           1639 HURSCH - WICHITA FALLS TX 76302
57- 17  DOTTERER, HENRY JOHN JR.       2706 GRANT BLVD - SYRACUSE NY 13208
21- 23  DOUGLAS, ASTYANAX SAUNDERS     D. JANUARY 26, 1975
57- 18  DOUGLAS, CHARLES WILLIAM       OLD ADD: RR 6 BOX 536 #C5 - GREENSBORO NC
45- 27  DOUGLAS, JOHN FRANKLIN         536 MENDOZA AVE - CORAL GABLES FL 33134
12- 56  DOUGLAS, PHILIPS BROOKS        D. AUGUST 1, 1952 SEQUATCHIE VALLEY, TENN.
15- 34  DOUGLASS, HOWARD LAWRENCE      D. NOVEMBER 4, 1949 JELLICO, TENN.
23- 31  DOUTHIT, TAYLOR LEE            6020 BULLARD DR - OAKLAND CA 94611
10- 47  DOWD, JAMES JOSEPH             D. DECEMBER 20, 1960 HOLYOKE, MASS.
19- 17  DOWD, RAYMOND BERNARD          D. APRIL 4, 1962 SPRINGFIELD, MASS.
64- 27  DOWLING, DAVID BARCLAY         1802 24TH - LONGVIEW WA 98632
61- 31  DOWNING, ALPHONSO ERWIN        2800 NEILSON WAY #412 - SANTA MONICA CA 90405
73- 38  DOWNING, BRIAN JAY             6750 LEAFWOOD DR - ANAHEIM CA 92807
72- 23  DOWNS, DAVID RALPH             925 EAST 1050 NORTH - BOUNTIFUL UT 84010
78- 36  DOYLE, BRIAN REED              BOX 9156 - WINTER HAVE FL 33880
43- 41  DOYLE, HOWARD JAMES            322 S PAYNE - STILLWATER OK 74074
10- 48  DOYLE, JAMES FRANCIS           D. FEBRUARY 1, 1912 SYRACUSE, N.Y.
25- 25  DOYLE, JESSE HERBERT           D. APRIL 15, 1961 BELLEVILLE, ILL.
69- 49  DOYLE, PAUL SINNOTT            5832 WOODBORO DR - HUNTINGTON BEACH CA 92649
70- 33  DOYLE, ROBERT DENNIS           6617 FARMINGTON LN - CRESTWOOD KY 40014
35- 25  DOYLE, WILLIAM CARL            D. SEPTEMBER 4, 1951 KNOXVILLE, TENN.
47- 29  DOZIER, WILLIAM JOSEPH         2609 BRAEMAR - WACO TX 76710
56- 28  DRABOWSKY, MYRON WALTER        530 AUDUBON PLACE - HIGHLAND PARK IL 60035
69- 50  DRAGO, RICHARD ANTHONY         RR 2 BOX 2253 - LAND O'LAKES FL 33539
11- 44  DRAKE, CELOS DANIEL            D. OCTOBER 3, 1965 FINDLAY, O.
45- 28  DRAKE, LAWRENCE FRANKLIN       16302 EL CAMINO REAL - HOUSTON TX 77062
22- 27  DRAKE, LOGAN GAFFNEY           D. JUNE 1, 1940
60- 30  DRAKE, SAMUEL HARRISON         6302 OVERHILL DR #2 - LOS ANGELES CA 90034
56- 29  DRAKE, SOLOMON LOUIS           1732 CORNING ST - LOS ANGELES CA 90035
39- 30  DRAKE, THOMAS KENDALL          4121 50TH AVE N BIRMINGHAM AL 35217
31- 22  DREESEN, WILLIAM RICHARD       D. NOVEMBER 9, 1971 MOUNT VERNON, N. Y.
44- 30  DREISEWERD, CLEMENT JOHN       45 SNIPE ST - NEW ORLEANS LA 70124
44- 31  DRESCHER, WILLIAM CLAYTON      D. MAY 15, 1968 CONGERS, N. Y.
25- 26  DRESSEN, CHARLES WALTER        D. AUGUST 10, 1966 DETROIT, MICH.
14- 56  DRESSEN, LEO AUGUST            D. JUNE 30, 1931 DILLER, NEB.
75- 35  DRESSLER, ROBERT ALAN          3002 N 46TH ST - PHOENIX AZ 85018
44- 32  DREWS, FRANK JOHN              D. APRIL 22, 1972 BUFFALO, N. Y.
46- 25  DREWS, KARL AUGUST             D. AUGUST 15, 1963 DANIA, FLA.
73- 39  DRIESSEN, DANIEL               BOX 1001 - HILTON HEAD ISLAND SC 29928
70- 34  DRISCOLL, JAMES BERNARD        948 S ALMA SCHOOL RD #48- MESA AZ 85202
17- 22  DRISCOLL, JOHN LEO             D. JUNE 28, 1968 CHICAGO, ILL.
16- 20  DRISCOLL, MICHAEL COLUMBUS     D. MARCH 21, 1953 FOXBORO, MASS.
13- 48  DROHAN, THOMAS F.              D. SEPTEMBER 17, 1926 KEWANEE, ILL.
49- 19  DROPO, WALTER                  7 GRANT RD - MARBLEHEAD MA 01945
```

```
57- 19  DROTT, RICHARD FRED            425 E MCFETRIDGE - CHICAGO IL 60601
78- 37  DRUMRIGHT, KEITH ALAN          1450 CREEKSIDE DR #45 - WALNUT CREEK CA 94596
56- 30  DRYSDALE, DONALD SCOTT         78 COLGATE - RANCHO MIRAGE CA 92270
44- 33  DUBIEL, WALTER JOHN            D. OCTOBER 25, 1969 HARTFORD, CONN.
63- 35  DUCKWORTH, JAMES RAYMOND       5568 TAMRES DR - SAN DIEGO CA 92110
29- 30  DUDLEY, ELISE CLISE            BOX 186 - FOLLY BEACH SC 29439
41- 22  DUDRA, JOHN JOSEPH             D. OCTOBER 24, 1965 PANA, ILL.
77- 47  DUES, HAL JOSEPH               DRAWER R - DICKINSON TX 77539
22- 28  DUFF, CECIL ELBA               D. NOVEMBER 10, 1969 BEND, ORE.
```

```
61- 32  DUFFALO, JAMES FRANCIS        1508 DUBERRY - LANCASTER TX 75134
67- 26  DUFFIE, JOHN BROWN            3453 GLEN RD - DECATUR GA 30032
13- 49  DUFFY, BERNARD ALLEN          D. FEBRUATY 9, 1962 ABILENE, TEX.
70- 35  DUFFY, FRANK THOMAS           23656 SHADOW DR - AUBURN CA 95603
28- 31  DUGAN, DANIEL PHILLIP         D. JUNE 25, 1968 GREEN BROOK, N. J.
17- 23  DUGAN, JOSEPH ANTHONY         38 HIGH ST - WALPOLE MA 02081
30- 20  DUGAS, AUGUSTIN JOSEPH        46 SOUTH "A" ST - TAFTVILLE CT 06380
13- 50  DUGEY, CSCAR JOSEPH           D. JANUARY 1, 1966 DALLAS, TEX.
11- 45  DUGGAN, JAMES ELMER           D. DECEMBER 5, 1951 INDIANAPOLIS, IND.
69- 51  DUKES, JAN NOBLE              1242 MILLBRAE AVE - MILLBRAE CA 94030
67- 27  DUKES, THOMAS EARL            325 MONTE VISTA RD - ARCADIA CA 91007
59- 24  DULIBA, ROBERT JOHN           113 GROVE ST - EXETER PA 18643
15- 35  DUMONT, GEORGE HENRY          D. OCTOBER 13, 1956 MINNEAPOLOS, MINN.
77- 48  DUMOULIN, DANIEL LYNN         304 IVY DR - KOKOMO IN 46902
23- 32  DUMOVICH, NICHOLAS            D. DECEMBER 12, 1979 LAGUNA HILLS, CALIF.
64- 28  DUNCAN, DAVID EDWIN           6425 N FOOTHILLS DR - TUCSON AZ 85718
15- 36  DUNCAN, LOUIS BAIRD           D. JULY 17, 1960 COLUMBUS, O.
77- 49  DUNCAN, TAYLOR MCDOWELL       1528 NORTH AVE - SACRAMENTO CA 95838
13- 51  DUNCAN, VERNON VAN DYKE       D. JUNE 1, 1954 DAYTONA BEACH, FLA.
70- 36  DUNEGAN, JAMES WILLIAM        1405 S 12TH ST - BURLINGTON IA 52601
26- 27  DUNHAM, LELAND HUFFIELD       D. MAY 11, 1961 ATLANTA, ILL.
53- 19  DUNLAP, GRANT LESTER          1881 CAMPUS RD - LOS ANGELES CA 90041
29- 31  DUNLAP, WILLIAM JAMES         D. NOVEMBER 29, 1980 READING, PA.
13- 52  DUNLOP, GEORGE HENRY          D. DECEMBER 12, 1972 MERIDEN, CONN.
52- 27  DUNN, JAMES WILLIAM           1656 SUMMIT DR - GADSDEN AL 35901
74- 29  DUNN, RONALD RAY              1831 HOMARK CT - SAN JOSE CA 95125
70- 37  DUNNING, STEVEN JOHN          1435 W CERRITOS #40 - ANAHEIM CA 92802
76- 29  DUPREE, MICHAEL DENNIS        1648 S RECREATION AVE - FRESNO CA 93702
81- 29  DURAN, DANIEL JAMES           201 DEL NORTE - SUNNYVALE CA 94086
54- 22  DUREN, RINOLD GEORGE          RR 1 BOX 444 - STOUGHTON WI 53589
72- 24  DURHAM, DONALD GARY           710 MAGNOLIA ST - BOWLING GREEN KY 42101
29- 32  DURHAM, EDWARD FANT           D. APRIL 27, 1976 CHESTER, S. C.
54- 23  DURHAM, JOSEPH VANN           9715 MENDOZA RD - RANDALLSTOWN MD 21133
80- 40  DURHAM, LEON                  3932 DICKSON AVE - CINCINNATI OH 45229
57- 20  DURNBAUGH, ROBERT EUGENE      1638 N CENTRAL DR - DAYTON OH 45432
25- 27  DURNING, GEORGE WARREN        OLD ADD: 2131 SABLE ST - PHILADELPHIA PA
17- 24  DURNING, RICHARD KNOTT        D. SEPTEMBER 23, 1948 CASTLE POINT, N. Y.
25- 28  DUROCHER, LEO ERNEST          1400 E PALM CANYON #210-PALM SPRINGS CA 92262
44- 34  DURRETT, ELMER CHARLES        1012 MAPLE - LANCASTER TX 75146
22- 29  DURST, CEDRIC MONTGOMERY      D. FEBRUARY 16, 1971 SAN DIEGO, CAL.
41- 23  DUSAK, ERVIN FRANK            241 E PRAIRIE AVE - LOMBARD IL 60148
56- 31  DUSER, CARL ROBERT            3021 CORMWALL RD - BETHLEHEM PA 18017
63- 36  DUSTAL, ROBERT ANDREW         4919 CACHET BLVD - LAKELAND FL 33806
73- 40  DWYER, JAMES EDWARD           7607 W 159TH PL - TINLEY PARK IL 60477
37- 36  DWYER, JOSEPH MICHAEL         56 HIGH ST W ORANGE NJ 07052
80- 41  DYBZINSKI, JEROME MATTHEW     9956 JOHNNYCANE RIDGE D5-PAINESVILLE OH 44077
51- 25  DYCK, JAMES ROBERT            1505 5TH ST - CHENEY WA 99004
14- 57  DYER, BENJAMIN FRANKLIN       D. AUGUST 7, 1959 KENOSHA, WIS.
68- 17  DYER, DONALD ROBERT           742 W LAS PALMARITAS - PHOENIX AZ 85021
22- 30  DYER, EDWIN HAWLEY            D. APRIL 20, 1964 HOUSTON, TEX.
18- 18  DYKES, JAMES JOSEPH           D. JUNE 15, 1976 PHILADELPHIA, PA.
59- 25  EADDY, DONALD JOHNSON         %J.EADDY-3440 POINSETTIA-GRAND RAPIDS MI49508
15- 37  EAKLE, CHARLES EMORY          D. JUNE 15, 1959 BALTIMORE, MD.
60- 31  EARLEY, ARNOLD CARL           4341 CAPTAINS LN - FLINT MI 48507
38- 22  EARLEY, THOMAS FRANCIS ALOYSIUS 51 CEDAR ST - NEW BRITAIN CT 06052
29- 31  EARLY, JACOB WILLARD          1608 S MITCHELL ST #2 - MELBOURNE FL 32901
28- 32  EARNSHAW, GEORGE LIVINGSTON   D. DECEMBER 1, 1976 LITTLE ROCK, ARK.
73- 41  EASLER, MICHAEL ANTHONY       14901 MILVERTON - CLEVELAND OH 44120
15- 38  EAST, CARLTON WILLIAM         D. JANUARY 15, 1953 CLEM, GA.
41- 24  EAST, GORDON HUGH             1049 OVERHILL RD SE-BESSEMER AL 35022
49- 20  EASTER, LUSCIOUS LUKE         D. MARCH 29, 1979 EUCLID, O.
28- 33  EASTERLING, PAUL              BOX 392 - REIDSVILLE GA 30453
74- 30  EASTERLY, JAMES MORRIS        1306 PLANTATION - CROCKETT TX 75835
44- 35  EASTERWCOD, ROY CHARLES       BURGER RD - GRAHAM TX 76046
55- 39  EASTON, JOHN DAVID            SCOTCH RD BOX 418 RR1 - PENNINGTON NJ 08534
74- 31  EASTWICK, RAWLINS JACKSON     224 CHESTNUT ST - HADDONFIELD NJ 08033
79- 30  EATON, CRAIG                  5444 LEE CT - WEST PALM BEACH FL 33406
44- 36  EATON, ZEBULON VANCE          131 LINCOLN BLVD - KENMORE NY 14217
```

```
35- 26  EAVES, VALLIE ENNIS           D. APRIL 19, 1960 NORMAN, OKLA.
13- 53  EAYRS, EDWIN                  D. NOVEMBER 30, 1969 WARWICK, R.I.
15- 39  ECCLES, HARRY JOSIAH          D. JUNE 28, 1955 JAMESTOWN, N.Y.
39- 32  ECHOLS, JOHN GRESHAM          D. NOVEMBER 13, 1972 ATLANTA, GA.
75- 36  ECKERSLEY, DENNIS LEE         711 OHIO SAVINGS PLACE - CLEVELAND OH 44114
```

```
30- 21 ECKERT, ALBERT GEORGE         D. APRIL 20, 1974 MILWAUKEE, WIS.
19- 18 ECKERT, CHARLES WILLIAM       4936 RIDGE AVE - TREVOSE PA 19047
32- 22 ECKHARDT, OSCAR GEORGE        D. APRIL 22, 1651 YORKTOWN, TEX.
70- 38 EDDY, DONALD EUGENE           BOX 412 - ROCKWELL IA 50469
79- 31 EDDY, STEVEN ALLEN            OLD ADD: 2332 14TH AVE - MOLINE IL 61265
81- 30 EDELEN, BENNY JOE             BOX 13 - GRACEMONT OK 73042
32- 23 EDELEN, EDWARD JOSEPH         VALLEY RD - PORT TOBACCO MD 20646
55- 40 EDELMAN, JOHN ROGERS          922 MONTE VISTON DR - WEST CHESTER PA 19380
76- 30 EDEN, EDWARD MICHAEL          862 HARD RD - WEBSTER NY 14620
79- 32 EDGE, CLAUDE LEE              910 REED LN - AUBURN CA 95603
66- 31 EDGERTON, WILLIAM ALBERT      56339 NORTH CEDAR - MISHAWAKA IN 46544
12- 57 EDINGTON, JACOB FRANK         D. NOVEMBER 29, 1969 BASTROP.LA.
80- 42 EDLER, DAVID DELMAR           1504 S 34TH AVE - YAKIMA W A 98902
13- 54 EDMONDSON, EDWARD EARL        D. MAY 10, 1971 LEESBURG, FLA.
22- 31 EDMONDSON, GEORGE HENDERSON   D. JULY 11, 1973 WACO, TEX.
69- 52 EDMONDSON, PAUL MICHAEL       D. FEBRUARY 13, 1970 SANTA BARBARA, CALIF.
15- 40 EDWARDS, ALBERT              B. 1896 FREEPORT, N.Y.
46- 26 EDWARDS, CHARLES BRUCE        D. APRIL 25, 1975 SACRAMENTO, CALIF.
78- 38 EDWARDS, DAVID LEONARD        3216 WADSWORTH AVE - LOS ANGELES CA 90011
25- 29 EDWARDS, FOSTER HAMILTON      D. JANUARY 4, 1980 ORLEANS, MASS.
41- 25 EDWARDS, HENRY ALBERT         1815 W CERRITOS-ANAHEIM CA 92804
62- 35 EDWARDS, HOWARD RODNEY        345 S WHITEHALL DR - ROCHESTER NY 14616
22- 32 EDWARDS, JAMES CORBETTE       D. JANUARY 19, 1965 CALHOUN COUNTY, MISS.
61- 33 EDWARDS, JOHN ALBAN           10118 SPRINGWOOD FOREST DR - HOUSTON TX 77055
81- 31 EDWARDS, MARSHALL LYNN        3216 WADSWORTH AVE - LOS ANGELES CA 90011
77- 50 EDWARDS, MICHAEL LEWIS        3216 WADSWORTH AVE - LOS ANGELES CA 90011
34- 32 EDWARDS, SHERMAN STANLEY      1223 W 1ST - ELDORADO AR 71730
63- 37 EGAN, RICHARD WALLIS          861 PALISADE CIR - GARDNERVILLE NV 89410
65- 28 EGAN, THOMAS PATRICK          16318 E HALBURTON RD-HACIENDA HEIGHTS CA91745
27- 30 EGGERT, ELMER ALBERT          D. APRIL 9, 1971 ROCHESTER, N. Y.
15- 41 EHMKE, HOWARD JONATHAN        D. MARCH 17, 1959 PHILADELPHIA, PA.
24- 33 EHRHARDT, WELTON CLAUDE       D. APRIL 27, 1980 CHICAGO HEIGHTS, ILL.
12- 58 EIBEL, HENRY HACK             D. OCTOBER 16, 1945 MACON, GA.
78- 39 EICHELBERGER, JUAN TYRONE     12728 COACHMAN CT - POWAY CA 92064
25- 30 EICHRODT, FREDERICK GEORGE    D. JULY 14, 1965 INDIANAPOLIS, IND.
64- 29 EILERS, DAVID LOUIS           1500 LEE - BRENHAM TX 77833
44- 37 EISENHART, JACOB HENRY        24 OLIVIA DR - YARDLEY PA 19068
35- 27 EISENSTAT, HARRY              3333 WARRENSVILLE CTR. RD SHAKER HTS OH 44122
49- 21 ELDER, GEORGE REZIN           40200 BROOKSIDE AVE - CHERRY VALLEY CA 92223
13- 55 ELDER, HENRY KNOX             D. NOVEMBER 13, 1958 LONG BEACH, CALIF.
66- 32 ELIA, LEE CONSTANTINE         1201 NORWOOD AVE - CLEARWATER FL 33516
43- 42 ELKO, PETER                   133 MADISON ST - WILKES-BARRE PA 18702
17- 25 ELLER, HORACE OWEN            D. JULY 18, 1961 INDIANAPOLIS, IND.
19- 19 ELLERBE, FRANCIS ROGERS       LATTA SC 29565
74- 32 ELLINGSEN, H. BRUCE           5873 DANELAND - LAKEWOOD CA 90713
62- 36 ELLIOT, LAWRENCE LEE          1475 RUBENSTEIN - ENCINITAS CA 92024
23- 33 ELLIOTT, ALLEN CLIFFORD       D. MAY 6, 1979 ST. LOUIS, MO.
21- 24 ELLIOTT, CARTER WARD          D. MAY 21, 1959 PALM SPRINGS, CAL.
11- 46 ELLIOTT, EUGENE BIRMINGHOUSE  D. JANUARY 5, 1976 HUNTINGDON, PA.
10- 49 ELLIOTT, HAROLD B.            D. FEBRUARY 12, 1934 SAN FRANCISCO, CALIF.
29- 33 ELLIOTT, HAROLD WILLIAM       D. APRIL 25, 1963 HONOLULU, HAW.
53- 20 ELLIOTT, HARRY LEWIS          1154 RANDOM - EL CAJON CA 92020
47- 30 ELLIOTT, HERBERT GLENN        D. JULY 27, 1969 PORTLAND, ORE.
23- 34 ELLIOTT, JAMES THOMPSON       D. JANUARY 7, 1970 TERRE HAUTE, IND.
72- 25 ELLIOTT, RANDY LEE            89 NANCY - CAMARILLO CA 93010
39- 33 ELLIOTT, ROBERT IRVING        D. MAY 4, 1966 SAN DIEGO, CAL.
68- 18 ELLIS, COCK PHILIP            OLD ADD: 8155-1202 JEFFERSON-BATON ROUGE LA
67- 28 ELLIS, JAMES RUSSELL          13608 AVE 224 - TULARE CA 93274
69- 53 ELLIS, JOHN CHARLES           15 WHITNEY LN - EAST LYME CT 06333
71- 29 ELLIS, ROBERT WALTER          8139 E OSBORN - SCOTTSDALE AZ 85251
62- 37 ELLIS, SAMUEL JOSEPH          6111 WHITEWAY - TEMPLE TERRACE FL 33617
20- 31 ELLISON, GEORGE RUSSELL       D. JANUARY 20, 1978 SAN FRANCISCO, CALIF.
16- 21 ELLISON, HERBERT SPENCER      D. AUGUST 11, 1955 SAN FRANCISCO, CALIF.
58- 28 ELLSWORTH, RICHARD CLARK      1099 W MORRIS - FRESNO CA 93705
24- 34 ELMORE, VERDO WILSON          D. AUGUST 5, 1969 BIRMINGHAM, ALA.
23- 35 ELSH, EUGENE ROY             D. NOVEMBER 12, 1978 PHILADELPHIA, PA.
53- 21 ELSTON, DONALD RAY            2436 MAPLE ST - NORTHBROOK IL 60062
41- 26 EMBREE, CHARLES WILLARD "RED" 5500 N BANK RD - CRESCENT CITY CA 95531
```

```
23- 36 EMBRY, CHARLES AKIN           D. OCTOBER 10, 1947 NASHVILLE, TENN.
11- 47 EMERSON, CHESTER ARTHUR       D. JULY 2, 1971 AUGUSTA, ME.
63- 38 EMERY, CALVIN WAYNE           2600 BARKSDALE CT - CLEARWATER FL 33519
24- 35 EMERY, HERRICK SMITH          D. JUNE 2, 1975 CAPE CANAVERAL, FLA.
```

```
16- 22  EMMER, FRANK WILLIAM              D. OCTOBER  18, 1963 HOMESTEAD, FLA.
23- 37  EMMERICH, ROBERT G.              D. NOVEMBER 23, 1948 BRIDGEPORT, CONN.
45- 29  EMMERICH, WILLIAM PETER          257 EAST FAIRVIEW ST - ALLENTOWN PA 18103
46- 27  ENDICOTT, WILLIAM FRANKLIN       14219 OAK KNOLL RD - SONORA CA 95370
12- 59  ENGEL, JOSEPH WILLIAM            D. JUNE 12, 1969 CHATTANOOGA, TENN.
25- 31  ENGLE, CHARLES                   223 PASCHAL ST #2 - SAN ANTONIO TX 78212
81- 32  ENGLE, RALPH DAVID               727 ISMUS CT - SAN DIEGO CA 92109
81- 33  ENGLE, RICHARD DOUGLAS           2634 JACKSON PIKE - BATAVIA OH 45103
32- 24  ENGLISH, CHARLES DEWIE           915 MOUT OLIVE DR - DUARTE CA 91010
27- 31  ENGLISH, ELWOOD GEORGE           14 N ELEVENTH ST - NEWARK OH 43055
31- 23  ENGLISH, GILBERT RAYMOND         RR 2 - TRINITY NC 27370
46- 28  ENNIS, DELMAR                    712 WOODSIDE RD - JENKINTOWN PA 19046
25- 28  ENNIS, RUSSELL ELWOOD            D. JANUARY 29, 1949 SUPERIOR, WIS.
76- 31  ENRIGHT, GEORGE ALBERT           6046 LAKE WORTH RD #969-LAKE WORTH FL 33463
17- 26  ENRIGHT, JOHN PERCY              D. AUGUST 18, 1975 POMPANO BEACH, FLA.
12- 60  ENS, ANTON                       D. JUNE 28, 1950 ST. LOUIS, MO.
22- 33  ENS, JEWEL WINKLEMEYER           D. JANUARY 17, 1950 SYRACUSE, N. Y.
74- 33  ENYART, TERRY GENE               520 SEAL AVE - PIKETON OH 45661
14- 58  ENZENROTH, CLARENCE HERMAN       D. FEBRUARY 21, 1944
14- 59  ENZMANN, JOHN                    1910 SW 85TH LN - FT LAUDERDALE FL 33314
38- 23  EPPERLY, ALBERT PAUL             2621 IOWA ST - DAVENPORT IA 52803
35- 28  EPPS, AUBREY LEE                 478 HAYNES - MEMPHIS TN 38111
38- 24  EPPS, HAROLD FRANKLIN            8121 GARLAND DR HOUSTON TX 77017
66- 33  EPSTEIN, MICHAEL PETER           712 S LINN ST - LUSK WY 82225
77- 51  ERARDI, JOSEPH GREGORY           204 HANOVER AVE - LIVERPOOL NY 13088
47- 31  ERAUTT, EDWARD LORENZ            7252 WAITE DR - LAMESA CA 92041
50- 28  ERAUTT, JOSEPH MICHAEL           D. OCTOBER 6, 1976 PORTLAND, ORE.
58- 29  ERICKSON, DON LEE                2717 INTERLACHEN - SPRINGFIELD IL 62704
14- 60  ERICKSON, ERIC GEORGE ADOLPH D. MAY 19, 1965 JAMESTOWN, N. Y.
53- 22  ERICKSON, HAROLD JAMES           333 BAYSHORE DR - OSPREY FL 33559
35- 29  ERICKSON, HENRY NELS             D. DECEMBER 13, 1964 LOUISVILLE, KY.
41- 27  ERICKSON, PAUL WALFORD           363 BOYD ST - FOND DU LAC WI 54935
29- 34  ERICKSON, RALPH LEIF             5770 WINFIELD BLVD #153 - SAN JOSE CA 95123
78- 40  ERICKSON, ROGER FARRELL          1104 N FIRST - SPRINGFIELD IL 62702
47- 32  ERMER, CALVIN COOLIDGE           1009 PANORAMA DR - CHATTANOOGA TN 37421
57- 21  ERNAGA, FRANK JOHN               50 N ROOP ST - SUSANVILLE CA 96130
38- 25  ERRICKSON, RICHARD MERRIWELL 1406 S MAIN RD - VINELAND NJ 08360
48- 34  ERSKINE, CARL DANIEL             6214 S MADISON AVE - ANDERSON IN 46013
54- 24  ESCALERA, SATURNINO CUADRADO 141 ST. - C-G #12 - CAROLINA PR 00630
15- 42  ESCHEN, JAMES GODRICH            D. SEPTEMBER 27, 1960 SLOATSBURG, N.Y.
42- 32  ESCHEN, LAWRENCE EDWARD          9 B 4 MAYFIELD APTS - POTSDAM NY 13676
11- 48  ESMOND, JAMES J.                 D. JUNE 26, 1948 TROY, N.Y.
74- 34  ESPINOSA, ARNULFO ACEVEDO        27 DEBEBREO #10 - VILLA ALTAGRACIA DOM REP
52- 28  ESPOSITO, SAMUEL                 ATH DEPT N. C. ST U - RALEIGH NC 27607
58- 30  ESSEGIAN, CHARLES ABRAHAM        144 N HOBART BLVD - LOS ANGELES CA 90004
79- 33  ESSER, MARK GERALD               4 JACKSON DR - POUGHKEEPSIE NY 12603
73- 42  ESSIAN, JAMES SARKIS             22959 GAUKLER - ST CLAIR SHORES MI 48080
35- 30  ESTALELLA, ROBERTO MENDEZ        3297 W 14TH LN - HIALEAH FL 33012
54- 30  ESTELLE, RICHARD HARRY           2221 TAYLOR AVE - POINT PLEASANT NJ 08742
51- 26  ESTOCK, GEORGE JOHN              6 BURNS RD - CLAYMONT DE 19703
60- 32  ESTRADA, CHARLES LEONARD         .8308 CARLTON OAKS DR - SANTEE CA 92071
71- 30  ESTRADA, FRANCISCO               605 MANUEL DOBLADO - NAVAJOA SONORA
29- 35  ESTRADA, OSCAR                   D. JANUARY 2, 1978 HAVANA, CUBA
52- 38  ETCHEBARREN, ANDREW AUGUSTE 15851 DODRILL DR - HACIENDA HEIGHTS CA 91745
43- 41  ETCHISON, CLARENCE HAMPTON       D. JANUARY 24, 1980 EAST NEW MARKET, MD.
57- 29  ETHERIDGE, BOBBY LAMAR           BOX 5624 - GREENVILLE MS 38701
38- 26  ETTEN, NICHOLAS RAYMOND TOM 21 SPINNING WHEEL RD - HINSDALE IL 60521
```

```
22- 34  EUBANKS, UEL MELVIN              D. NOVEMBER 21, 1954 DALLAS, TEX.
17- 27  EUNICK, FERNANDES BOWEN          D. DECEMBER 9, 1959 BALTIMORE, MD.
39- 34  EVANS, ALFRED HUBERT             D. APRIL 6, 1979 WILSON, N. C.
78- 41  EVANS, BARRY STEVEN              5657 ASH ST - FOREST PARK GA 30050
69- 54  EVANS, DARRELL WAYNE             11 CASTLEDOWN RD - PLEASANTON CA 94566
72- 26  EVANS, DWIGHT MICHAEL            3 JORDAN RD - LYNNFIELD MA 01940
15- 43  EVANS, JOSEPH PATTON             D. AUGUST 9, 1953 GULFPORT, MISS.
36- 23  EVANS, RUSSELL EARL              BOX 92 - LAKEVIEW AR 72642
32- 25  EVANS, WILLIAM ARTHUR            D. JANUARY 8, 1952 WICHITA, KANS.
16- 23  EVANS, WILLIAM JAMES             D. DECEMBER 21, 1946 BURLINGTON, N. C.
49- 22  EVANS, WILLIAM LAWRENCE          312 PINE ST - GRAND JUNCTION CO 81501
69- 55  EVERITT, EDWARD LEON             RR 1 BOX 417 - MARSHALL TX 75670
13- 56  EVERS, JOSEPH FRANCIS            D. JANUARY 4, 1949 ALBANY, N.Y.
41- 28  EVERS, WALTER ARTHUR             637 S RIPPLE CREEK - HOUSTON TX 77057
21- 25  EWING, REUBEN                    D. OCTOBER 5, 1970 WEST HARTFORD, CONN.
73- 43  EWING, SAMUEL JAMES              RR 4, POWELL RD - LEWISBURG TN 37091
```

```
19- 20  EWOLDT, ARTHUR LEE              D. DECEMBER 8, 1977 DES MOINES, IA.
43- 44  EYRICH, GEORGE LINCOLN          565 S 15TH ST-READING PA 19602
23- 38  EZZELL, HOMER ESTELL            D. AUGUST 3, 1976 SAN ANTONIO, TEX.
14- 61  FABER, URBAN CHARLES            D. SEPTEMBER 25, 1976 CHICAGO, ILL.
16- 24  FABRIQUE, ALBERT LAVERNE        D. JANUARY 10, 1960 ANN ARBOR, MICH.
53- 23  FACE, ELROY LEON                3917 MAIN ST - MCKEESPORT PA 15132
80- 43  FAEDO, LEONARDO LAGO            2920 COLLINS ST - TAMPA FL 33607
19- 21  FAETH, ANTHONY JOSEPH           111 E KELLOGG BLVD #2701 - ST PAUL MN 55101
43- 45  FAGAN, EVERETT JOSEPH           BOX 70 - GLADSTONE NJ 07934
18- 19  FAHEY, FRANCIS RAYMOND          D. MARCH 19, 1954 UXBRIDGE, MASS.
12- 61  FAHEY, HOWARD SIMPSON           D. OCTOBER 24, 1971 CLEARWATER, FLA.
71- 31  FAHEY, WILLIAM ROGER            5720 MONA LN - DALLAS TX 75236
51- 27  FAHR, GERALD WARREN             816 WEST PARK ST - PARAGOULD AR 72450
14- 62  FAHRER, CLARENCE WILLIE         D. JUNE 10, 1967 FREMONT, MICH.
47- 33  FAIN, FERRIS ROY                STAR ROUTE 5 - GEORGETOWN CA 95634
19- 22  FAIRCLOTH, JAMES LAMAR          OLD ADD: BOX 254 - SUNLAND CA 91040
68- 19  FAIREY, JAMES BURKE             218 STRAWBERRY ST - CLEMSON SC 29361
58- 31  FAIRLY, RONALD RAY              23140 PARK SORRENTO - CALABASAS CA 90302
75- 37  FALCONE, PETER FRANK            12 PONY CIR - ROSLYN HEIGHTS NY 11577
20- 32  FALK, BIBB AUGUST               4213 AVE 'D ' - AUSTIN TX 78751
25- 32  FALK, CHESTER EMANUEL           5924 HIGHLAND HILLS DR - AUSTIN TX 78731
31- 24  FALLENSTIN, EDWARD JOSEPH       D. NOVEMBER 24, 1971 ORANGE, N.J.
37- 37  FALLON, GEORGE DECATUR          71 PLAINVIEW DR - STRATFORD CT 06497
14- 63  FALSEY, PETER JAMES             D. MAY 23, 1976 LOS ANGELES, CALIF.
45- 30  FANNIN, CLIFFORD BRYSON         D. DECEMBER 11, 1966 SANDUSKY, O.
54- 25  FANNING, WILLIAM JAMES          BOX 500 STATION M - MONTREAL QUE H1V 3P2
63- 39  FANOK, HARRY MICHAEL            BOX 154 - WHIPPANY NJ 07981
49- 23  FANOVICH, FRANK JOSEPH          7 BLOSSOM RD - SUFFERN NY 10901
10- 50  FANWELL, HARRY CLAYTON          D. JULY 15, 1965 BALTIMORE, MD.
70- 39  FANZONE, CARMEN RONALD          12360 WHITEHALL - DETROIT MI 48224
61- 34  FARLEY, ROBERT JACOB            RR 3 - MONTOURSVILLE PA 17754
71- 32  FARMER, EDWARD JOSEPH           1215 19TH ST "C" - SANT A MONICA CA 90404
16- 25  FARMER, FLOYD HASKELL           D. MAY 21, 1970 COLUMBIA, LA.
25- 33  FARRELL, EDWARD STEPHEN         D. DECEMBER 20, 1966 LIVINGSTON, N. J.
14- 64  FARRELL, JOHN J.                D. MARCH 24, 1918 CHICAGO, ILL.
43- 46  FARRELL, MAJOR KERBY            D. DECEMBER 17, 1975 NASHVILLE, TENN.
56- 32  FARRELL, RICHARD JOSEPH         D. JUNE 11, 1977 GREAT YARMOUTH, ENGLAND
68- 20  FAST, DARCY RAE                 7012 TIMBERLAKE DR - LACEY WA 98503
53- 24  FASZHOLZ, JOHN EDWARD           7108 GENEVA - AUSTIN TX 78723
62- 39  FAUL, WILLIAM ALVAN            RR1 BOX 7 - PLEASANT PLAIN OH 45162
27- 32  FAULKNER, JAMES LEROY           D. JUNE 2, 1962 WEST PALM BEACH, FLA.
44- 38  FAUSETT, ROBERT SHAW            120 LUTHER #121 - COLLEGE STATION TX 77840
11- 49  FAUST, CHARLES VICTOR           D. JUNE 18, 1915 FORT STEILACOOM, WASH.
16- 26  FAUTSCH, JOSEPH ROAMON          D. MARCH 16, 1971 NEW HOPE, MINN.
62- 40  FAZIO, ERNEST JOSEPH            2310 ROYAL OAKS DR - ALAMO CA 94507
52- 29  FEAR, LUVERN CARL               D. SEPTEMBER 6, 1976 SPENCER, IA.
51- 28  FEDEROFF, ALFRED                604 RIVERBANK - LINCOLN PARK MI 48146
34- 33  FEHRING, WILLIAM PAUL           1735 POPPY AVE - MENLO PARK CA 94023
38- 27  FEINBERG, EDWARD                7712 ALGON AVE PHILADELPHIA PA 19111
42- 33  FELDERMAN, MARVIN WILFRED       4342 W 177TH ST-TORRANCE CA 90504
41- 29  FELDMAN, HARRY                  D. MARCH 16, 1962 FORT SMITH, ARK.
23- 39  FELIX, AUGUST GUENTHER          D. MAY 12, 1960 MONTGOMERY, ALA.
58- 32  FELLER, JACK LELAND             111 GREENLEAF - ONSTED MI 49265
36- 24  FELLER, ROBERT WILLIAM ANDREW   BOX 157 - GATES MILLS OH 44040
15- 44  FELSCH, OSCAR EMIL              D. AUGUST 17, 1964 MILWAUKEE, WIS.
68- 21  FELSKE, JOHN FREDRICK           600 LIVINGSTON - MCHENRY IL 60050
79- 34  FELTON, TERRY LANE              BOX 533 - BAKER LA 70714
21- 26  FENNER, HORACE ALFRED           D. NOVEMBER 20, 1954 DETROIT, MICH.
72- 27  FENWICK, ROBERT RICHARD         932 BLACKOAKS LN - ANOKA MN 55303
42- 34  FERENS, STANLEY                 BOX 261-YUKON PA 15698
18- 20  FERGUSON, JAMES ALEXANDER       D. APRIL 28, 1976 SEPULVEDA, CALIF.
70- 40  FERGUSON, JOSEPH VANCE          2041 VIRAZON DR - LAHABRA HEIGHTS CA 90631
44- 39  FERGUSON, ROBERT LESTER         3320 FOUNTAIN LN #B - MONTGOMERY AL 36111
40- 19  FERNANDES, EDWARD PAUL          D. NOVEMBER 27, 1968 HAYWARD, CAL.
67- 30  FERNANDEZ, FRANK                37 COUGHLAN AVE - STATEN ISLAND NY 10310
42- 35  FERNANDEZ, FROILAN              26229 MONTE VISTA-LOMITA CA 90717
56- 33  FERNANDEZ, HUMBERTO PEREZ       3322 24TH ST - DETROIT MI 48208
68- 22  FERNANDEZ, LORENZO MARTO        1310 SW 97TH AVE - MIAMI FL 33175
63- 40  FERRARA, ALFRED JOHN            BOX 69263 - LOS ANGELES CA 90069
55- 41  FERRARESE, DONALD HUGH          14140 GAYHEAD RD - APPLE VALLEY CA 92307
66- 34  FERRARO, MICHAEL DENNIS         1009 N OCEAN BLVD #405 - POMPANO BEACH FL
35- 31  FERRAZZI, WILLIAM JOSEPH        RR 1 BOX 46 HAWTHORNE FL 32640
29- 36  FERRELL, RICHARD BENJAMIN       2121 TRUMBULL AVE - DETROIT MI 48216
```

FERRELL   FLANAGAN

```
27- 33  FERRELL, WESLEY CHEEK          D. DECEMBER 9, 1976 SARASOTA, FLA.
74- 35  FERRER, SERGIO                 PEDRO ARCILAGOS HX8 - CATTARO PR 00632
41- 30  FERRICK, THOMAS JEROME         517 HARRINGTON RD-HAVERTOWN PA 19083
79- 35  FERRIS, ROBERT EUGENE          8628 SPRING CREEK CT - SPRINGFIELD VA 22153
45- 31  FERRISS, DAVID MEADOW          510 ROBINSON DR - CLEVELAND MS 38732
10- 51  FERRY, JOHN FRANCIS            D. AUGUST 29, 1954 PITTSFIELD, MASS.
37- 38  FETTE, LOUIS HENRY WILLIAM     D. JANUARY 3, 1981 WARRENSBURG, MO.
17- 28  FEWSTER, WILSON LLOYD          D. APRIL 16, 1945 BALTIMORE, MD.
81- 34  FIALA, NEIL STEPHEN            4929 DEVONSHIRE - ST LOUIS MO 63109
44- 40  FICK, JOHN RALPH               D. JUNE 9, 1958 SOMERS POINT, N. J.
76- 32  FIDRYCH, MARK STEVEN           16 CHESTERFIELD RD - MARLBORO MA 01752
32- 26  FIEBER, CLARENCE THOMAS        BOX 821 - PALO ALTO CA 93402
73- 44  FIFE, DANNY WAYNE              OLD ADD: 5553 DVORAK - CLARKSTON MI
74- 36  FIGUEROA, EDUARDO             CALLE 41 A-N15 - SANTA JUANITA PR 00619
80- 44  FIGUEROA, JESUS MARIA         SANTA CRUZ VILLA MELLA KM 8-SANTO DOMINGO D R
40- 20  FILE, LAWRENCE SAMUEL          171/2 W ROLAND RD-CHESTER PA 19015
44- 41  FILIPOWICZ, STEPHEN CHARLES   D. FEBRUARY 21, 1975 WILKES-BARRE, PA.
34- 34  FILLEY, MARCUS LUCIUS          43 FIRST ST - TROY NY 12180
15- 45  FILLINGIM, DANA               D. FEBRUARY 3, 1961 TUSKEGEE, ALA.
79- 36  FINCH, JOEL D                 68571 OAK SPRING RD - EDWARDSBURG MI 49112
16- 27  FINCHER, WILLIAM ALLEN        D. MAY 8, 1946 SHREVEPORT, LA.
47- 34  FINE, THOMAS MORGAN            1731 ROGERS PLACE - BURBANK CA 91504
68- 23  FINGERS, ROLAND GLEN           1437 DE LA WARR CIR - MEQUON WI 53092
54- 26  FINIGAN, JAMES LEROY           D. MAY 16, 1981 QUINCY, ILL.
35- 32  FINK, HERMAN ADAM             D. AUGUST 24, 1980 SALISBURY, N. C.
43- 47  FINLEY, ROBERT EDWARD          6810 HAMMOND AVE-DALLAS TX 75223
30- 22  FINN, CORNELIUS FRANCIS        D. JULY 7, 1933 ALLENTOWN, PA.
12- 62  FINNERAN, JOSEPH IGNATIUS      D. FEBRUARY 3, 1942 ORANGE, N.J.
31- 25  FINNEY, HAROLD WILSON          RR 2 - LAFAYETTE AL 36862
31- 26  FINNEY, LOUIS KLOPSCHE         D. APRIL 22, 1966 LAFAYETTE, ALA.
68- 30  FIORE, MICHAEL GARY JOSEPH     17 SILVER ST - MALVERNE NY 11565
81- 35  FIREOVID, STEPHEN JOHN         RR 5 - BRYAN OH 43506
81- 36  FIROVA, DANIEL MICHAEL         202 ST JOHN - REFUGIO TX 78377
19- 23  FISBURN, SAMUEL               D. APRIL 11, 1965 BETHLEHEM, PA.
30- 23  FISCHER, CHARLES WILLIAM      D. DECEMBER 10, 1963 MEDINA, N. Y.
62- 41  FISCHER, HENRY WILLIAM         BOX 301 - MOUNT ARLINGTON NJ 07856
41- 31  FISCHER, REUBEN WALTER         2453 DORN DR - GREEN BAY WI 54301
56- 34  FISCHER, WILLIAM CHARLES       4849 HAWAIIAN TER - CINCINNATI OH 45223
13- 57  FISCHER, WILLIAM CHARLES      D. SEPTEMBER 4, 1945 RICHMOND, VA.
77- 52  FISCHLIN, MICHAEL THOMAS       9523 COLTON AVE - ELK GROVE CA 95624
11- 50  FISHER, AUGUSTUS HARRIS        D. APRIL 8, 1972 PORTLAND, ORE.
19- 24  FISHER, CLARENCE HENRY         D. NOVEMBER 2, 1965 POINT PLEASANT, W. VA.
45- 32  FISHER, DONALD RAYMOND         D. JULY 29, 1973 MAYFIELD HEIGHTS, O.
59- 26  FISHER, EDDIE GENE             408 CARDINAL CIRCLE S - ALTUS OK 73521
64- 31  FISHER, FREDERICK BROWN        11730 ECKEL JUNCTION - PERRYSBURG OH 43551
23- 40  FISHER, GEORGE ALOYS           AVON MINN 56310
51- 29  FISHER, HARRY DEVEREAUX        OLD ADD: WARDSVILLE ONTARIO
10- 52  FISHER, JOHN GUS              D. JANUARY 1, 1940 LOUISVILLE, KY.
59- 27  FISHER, JOHN HOWARD            611 HAMILTON ST - EASTON PA 18042
55- 42  FISHER, MAURICE WAYNE          15920 LUCERNE RD - FREDERICKTOWN OH 43019
10- 53  FISHER, RAYMOND LYLE           2112 BROCKMAN BLVD - ANN ARBOR MI 48104
12- 63  FISHER, ROBERT TAYLOR          D. AUGUST 4, 1963 JACKSONVILLE, FLA.
67- 31  FISHER, THOMAS GENE            7225 N TUXEDO - INDIANAPOLIS IN 46240
16- 28  FISHER, WILBUR MCCULLOUGH      D. OCTOBER 24, 1960 WELCH, W. VA.
69- 56  FISK, CARLTON ERNEST           RR1 LONG HILL RD - RAYMOND NH 03077
14- 65  FISKE, MAXIMILIAN PATRICK      D. MAY 15, 1928 CHICAGO, ILL.
14- 66  FITTERY, PAUL CLARENCE         D. JANUARY 28, 1974 CARTERSVILLE, GA.
48- 35  FITZ GERALD, EDWARD RAYMOND    3028 WHITNEY AVE - SACRAMENTO CA 95821
11- 51  FITZ GERALD, JUSTIN HOWARD     D. JANUARY 17, 1945 SAN MATEO, CALIF.
28- 34  FITZBERGER, CHARLES CASPAR     D. JANUARY 25, 1965 BALTIMORE, MD.
22- 35  FITZGERALD, HOWARD CHUMNEY     D. FEBRUARY 26, 1959 EAGLE FALLS, TEX.
58- 33  FITZGERALD, JOHN FRANCIS       846 BAY RIDGE AVE - BROOKLYN NY 11220
31- 27  FITZGERALD, RAYMOND FRANCIS    D. SEPTEMBER 6, 1977 WESTFIELD, MASS.
24- 36  FITZKE, PAUL FREDERICK HERMAN  D. JUNE 30, 1950 SACRAMENTO, CAL.
66- 35  FITZMAURICE, SHAUN EARLE       6253 NICOLET RD - RICHMOND VA 23225
69- 57  FITZMORRIS, ALAN JAMES         3545 MT EVEREST AVE - SAN DIEGO CA 92111
15- 46  FITZPATRICK, EDWARD HENRY      D. OCTOBER 23, 1965 BETHLEHEM, PA.
25- 34  FITZSIMMONS, FREDERICK LANDIS D. NOVEMBER 18, 1979 YUCCA VALLEY, CALIF.
19- 25  FITZSIMMONS, THOMAS WILLIAM   D. DECEMBER 20, 1971 OAKLAND, CALIF.
14- 67  FLACK, MAX JOHN               D. JULY 31, 1975 BELLEVILLE, ILL.
45- 33  FLAGER, WALTER LEONARD         3215 PORTLAND RD NE - SALEM OR 97303
17- 29  FLAGSTEAD, IRA JAMES           D. MARCH 13, 1940 OLYMPIA, WASH.
41- 32  FLAIR, ALBERT DELL             2538 CALHOUN ST-NEW ORLEANS LA 70118
75- 38  FLANAGAN, MICHAEL KENDALL      30 GORDON RD - DERRY NH 03038
```

59

```
13- 58  FLANIGAN, CHARLES JAMES        D. JANUARY 8, 1930 SAN FRANCISCO, CALIF.
46- 29  FLANIGAN, RAYMOND ARTHUR       1416 GLENDALE RD - BALTIMORE MD 21239
54- 27  FLANIGAN, THOMAS ANTHONY       5845 CADILLAC DR - INDEPENDENCE KY 41015
77- 53  FLANNERY, JOHN MICHAEL         9652 LENORE DR - GARDEN GROVE CA 92641
79- 37  FLANNERY, TIMOTHY EARL         2007 FIGWOOD LANE - ANAHEIM CA 92806
27- 34  FLASKAMFER, RAYMOND HAROLD     D. FEBRUARY 3, 1978 SAN ANTONIO, TEX.
64- 32  FLAVIN, JOHN THOMAS            5744 NORTH BOND - FRESNO CA 93710
48- 36  FLEITAS, ANGEL FELIX           101 SW 52ND CT - MIAMI FL 33134
40- 21  FLEMING, LESLIE FLETCHERD      401 COLLEGE DR #106 - RENO NV 89503
39- 35  FLEMING, LESLIE HARVEY         D. MARCH 5, 1980
34- 35  FLETCHER, ELBURT PRESTON       131 OTIS AVE - MILTON MA 02186
14- 68  FLETCHER, O. FRANK             D. OCTOBER 7, 1974 ST. PETERSBURG, FLA.
81- 37  FLETCHER, SCOTT BRIAN          360 ELM ST - WADSWORTH OH 44281
62- 42  FLETCHER, THOMAS WAYNE         RR ONE - OAKWOOD IL 61858
55- 43  FLETCHER, VANOIDE              YADKINVILLE NC 27055
43- 48  FLICK, LEWIS MILLER            1712 ECHO DR - KINGSPORT TN 37665
17- 30  FLINN, CON RAPHIEL            D. MARCH 9, 1959 WACO, TEX.
78- 42  FLINN, JOHN RICHARD            9412 NATICK AVE - SEPULVEDA CA 91343
42- 36  FLITCRAFT, HILDRETH MILTON     WOODSTOWN NJ 08098
34- 36  FLOHR, MORITZ HERMAN           ORDWAY LANE - CANISTEO NY 14823
56- 35  FLOOD, CURTIS CHARLES          2368 MONTICELLO AVE - OAKLAND CA 94611
26- 29  FLORENCE, PAUL ROBERT          BOX 670 - WILLISTON FL 32696
77- 54  FLORES, GILBERTO               BDA SALAZAR 1 #38 - PONCE PR 00731
42- 37  FLORES, JESSE SANDEVAL         1930 EL PORTAL DR-LAHABRA CA 90632
51- 30  FLOWERS, BENNETT               901 TREMONT RD - WILSON NC 27895
40- 22  FLOWERS, CHARLES WESLEY        1622 DODD DR - WYNNE AR 72396
23- 41  FLOWERS, D'ARCY RAYMOND        D. DECEMBER 27, 1962 CLEARWATER, FLA.
44- 42  FLOYD, LESLIE ROE              6306 PRESTONCREST - DALLAS TX 75230
68- 25  FLOYD, ROBERT NATHAN           5009 WALNUT - KANSAS CITY MO 64112
15- 47  FLUHRER, JOHN L.               D. JULY 17, 1946 COLUMBUS, O.
10- 54  FLYNN, JOHN ANTHONY            D. MARCH 23, 1935 PROVIDENCE, R.I.
75- 39  FLYNN, ROBERT DOUGLAS          428 MCKENNA CT - LEXINGTON KY 40505
36- 25  FLYTHE, STUART MCGUIRE         D. OCTOBER 18, 1963 DURHAM, N. C.
58- 34  FODGE, EUGENE ARLEN            1505 N CHICAGO ST - SOUTH BEND IN 46628
53- 25  FOILES, HENRY LEE              1019 FLEMING CIR - VIRGINIA BEACH VA 23451
78- 43  FOLEY, MARVIS EDWIN            2900 YELLOWSTONE PKWY - LEXINGTON KY 40502
28- 35  FOLEY, RAYMOND KIRWIN          BOX 149 - MIDDLEBURY CT 06762
70- 41  FOLI, TIMOTHY JOHN             105 WILLOW ROAD LN - ORMOND BEACH FL 32074
70- 42  FOLKERS, RICHARD NEVIN         1805 PASS-A-GRILLE WAY-PASSA-A-GRILLE FL3374?
51- 31  FONDY, DEE VIRGIL              1422 BELLA VISTA CIR - REDLANDS CA 92373
```

DEE FONDY
Cincinnati Redlegs

```
21- 27  FONSECA, LEWIS ALBERT          525 HAWTHORNE PL #904 - CHICAGO IL 60657
71- 33  FOOR, JAMES EMERSON            42 S SCHLUETER - ST LOUIS MO 63135
73- 45  FOOTE, BARRY CLIFTON           5300 CASTLEBROOK DR - RALEIGH NC 27604
75- 40  FORD, DARNELL GLENN            7080 E COLUMBUS DR - ANAHEIM CA 92801
78- 44  FORD, DAVID ALAN               2923 MARVIN - CLEVELAND OH 44109
50- 29  FORD, EDWARD CHARLES           38 SCHOOLHOUSE LANE - LAKE SUCCESS NY 11020
36- 26  FORD, EUGENE MATTHEW           D. SEPTEMBER 7, 1970 EMMETSBURG, IA.
19- 26  FORD, HORACE HILLS             D. JANUARY 29, 1977 WINCHESTER, MASS.
73- 46  FORD, PERCIVAL EDMUND WENTWORTH - D. JULY 8, 1980 NASSAU BAHAMAS
70- 43  FORD, THEODORE HENRY           967 SW AVE - VINELAND NJ 00360
24- 37  FOREMAN, AUGUST                D. FEBRUARY 13, 1953 NEW YORK, N. Y.
52- 30  FORNIELES, JOSE MIGUEL         29 OAK SQUARE AVE - BRIGHTON MA 02135
70- 44  FORSCH, KENNETH ROTH           3311 ROLLING GREEN - MISSOURI CITY TX 77459
74- 37  FORSCH, ROBERT HERBERT         428 HICKORY GLEN LN - ST LOUIS MO 63141
71- 34  FORSTER, TERRY JAY             1947 TRUNBULL CANYON-HACIENDA HGTS CA 91745
15- 48  FORSYTHE, CLARENCE D           B. ST. LOUIS, MO.
16- 29  FORTUNE, GARRETT REESE         D. SEPTEMBER 23, 1955 WASHINGTON, D. C.
64- 33  FOSNOW, GERALD EUGENE          OLD ADD: RR ONE - DESHLER OH 43516
21- 28  FOSS, GEORGE DUEWARD           D. NOVEMBER 10, 1969 MIAMI, FLA.
61- 35  FOSS, LAWRENCE CURTIS          125 N BELMONT ST - WICHITA KS 67211
67- 32  FOSSE, RAYMOND EARL            7950 W BATES RD - TRACY CA 95376
67- 33  FOSTER, ALAN BENTON            1515 STALKER CT - EL CAJON CA 92020
10- 55  FOSTER, EDWARD CUNNINGHAM      D. JANUARY 15, 1937 WASHINGTON, D.C.
13- 59  FOSTER, GEORGE                 D. MARCH 1, 1976 BOKOSHE, OKLA.
69- 58  FOSTER, GEORGE ARTHUR          14400 CEROSE - HAWTHORNE CA 90250
63- 41  FOSTER, LARRY LYNN             BOX 97 - WHITEHALL MI 49461
71- 35  FOSTER, LEONARD NORRIS         36 JACOB PRICE APTS - COVINGTON KY 41012
70- 45  FOSTER, ROY                    1421 N MADISON PL - TULSA OK 74106
22- 36  FOTHERGILL, ROBERT ROY         D. MARCH 20, 1938 DETROIT, MICH.
73- 47  FOUCAULT, STEVEN RAYMOND       2102 WOODSIDE DR - ARLINGTON TX 76013
12- 64  FOURNIER, JOHN FRANK           D. SEPTEMBER 5, 1973 TACOMA, WASH.
24- 38  FOWLER, JESSE                  D. SEPTEMBER 23, 1973 COLUMBIA, S. C.
```

54- 28	FOWLER, JOHN ARTHUR	3046 E MAIN EXTENSION - SPARTANBURG SC 29301
23- 42	FOWLER, JOSEPH CHESTER	6116 LBJ FWY #126 - DALLAS TX 75240
41- 33	FOWLER, RICHARD JOHN	D. MAY 22, 1972 ONEONTA, N. Y.
42- 38	FOX, CHARLES FRANCIS	5721 N 20TH ST-PHOENIX AR 85016
33- 18	FOX, ERVIN	D. JULY 5, 1966 DETROIT, MICH.
44- 43	FOX, HOWARD FRANCIS	D. OCTOBER 9, 1955 SAN ANTONIO, TEX.
47- 35	FOX, JACOB NELSON	D. DECEMBER 1, 1975 BALTIMORE, MD.
60- 33	FOX, TERRENCE EDWARD	STAR ROUTE A BOX 196-D - NEW IBERIA LA 70560
25- 35	FOXX, JAMES EMORY	D. JULY 21, 1967 MIAMI, FLA.
66- 36	FOY, JOSEPH ANTHONY	1655 UNDERCLIFF DR - BRONX NY 10453
53- 26	FOYTACK, PAUL EUGENE	5590 TADWORTH PL - WEST BLOOMFIELD MI 48033
72- 28	FRAILING, KENNETH DOUGLAS	4137 PRESCOTT - SARASOTA FL 33582
60- 34	FRANCIS, EARL COLEMAN	28 QUAIL HILL RD - PITTSBURGH PA 15214
22- 37	FRANCIS, RAY JAMES	D. JULY 14, 1932 ATLANTA, GA.
56- 36	FRANCONA, JOHN PATSY	2206 MERCER RD - NEW BRIGHTON PA 15066
81- 38	FRANCONA, TERRY JON	2206 MERCER RD - NEW BRIGHTON PA 15066
27- 35	FRANKHOUSE, FREDRICK MELOY	BOX 297 - PORT ROYAL PA 17082
44- 44	FRANKLIN, JAMES WILFORD	1211 MARSHALL ST - PARIS IL 61944
71- 36	FRANKLIN, JOHN WILLIAM	OLD ADD: 2305 STRYKER AVE - VIENNA VA
41- 34	FRANKLIN, MURRAY ASHER	D. MARCH 16, 1978 HARBOR CITY, CALIF.
39- 36	FRANKS, HERMAN LOUIS	2745 COMANCHE DR SALT LAKE CITY UT 84108
31- 28	FRASIER, VICTOR PATRICK	D. JANUARY 10, 1977 JACKSONVILLE, TEX.
78- 45	FRAZIER, GEORGE ALLEN	7701 S 80TH E AVE - TULSA OK 74133
47- 36	FRAZIER, JOSEPH FILMORE	519 FAIRWAY DR - BROKEN ARROW OK 74012
29- 37	FREDERICK, JOHN HENRY	D. JUNE 18, 1977 TIGARD, ORE.
42- 39	FREED, EDWIN CHARLES	840 MCDOW DR-ROCK HILL SC 29730
70- 46	FREED, ROGER VERNON	1329 S WILLOW AVE - WEST COVINA CA 91790
61- 36	FREEHAN, WILLIAM ASHLEY	4248 SUNNINGDALE - BLOOMFIELD HILLS MI 48013
21- 29	FREEMAN, ALEXANDER VERNON	D. FEBRUARY 21, 1953 FORT SAM HOUSTON, TEXAS
21- 30	FREEMAN, HARVEY BAYARD	D. JANUARY 10, 1970 KALAMAZOO, MICH.
52- 31	FREEMAN, HERSHELL BASKIN	5437 SAN MARINO PL - ORLANDO FL 32807
72- 29	FREEMAN, JIMMY LEE	2164 S URBANA - TULSA OK 74114
27- 36	FREEMAN, JOHN EDWARD	D. APRIL 14, 1958 WASHINGTON, D. C.
59- 28	FREEMAN, MARK PRICE	6 BROOKSIDE DR - LITTLETON CO 80120
55- 44	FREESE, EUGENE LEWIS	3031 8TH ST - METAIRIE LA 70002
53- 27	FREESE, GEORGE WALTER	3341 SW MARIGOLD ST - PORTLAND OR 97219
25- 36	FREEZE, CARL ALEXANDER	630 S BISHOP - SAN ANGELO TX 76903
61- 37	FREGOSI, JAMES LOUIS	18772 WINNWOOD LN - SANTA ANA CA 92705
41- 35	FREIBERGER, VERNON DONALD	15490 DEVONSHIRE CIR-WESTMINSTER, CA 92683
22- 38	FREIGAU, HOWARD EARL	D. JULY 18, 1932 CHATTANOOGA, TENN.
74- 38	FREISLEBEN, DAVID JAMES	2119 PEACH LN - PASADENA TX 77502
32- 27	FREITAS, ANTONIO	5648 GREENACRES WAY - ORANGEVALE CA 95662
17- 31	FRENCH, FRANK ALEXANDER	D. JULY 13, 1969 BATH, ME.
29- 38	FRENCH, LAWRENCE ROBERT	3520 FENELON ST - SAN DIEGO CA 92106
20- 33	FRENCH, RAYMOND EDWARD	D. APRIL 3, 1978 ALAMEDA, CALIF.
65- 29	FRENCH, RICHARD JAMES	6960 GLORIA DR - PENNGROVE CA 94951
23- 43	FRENCH, WALTER EDWARD	120 VISTA DR - LA SELVA BEACH CA 95076
29- 39	FREY, BENJAMIN RUDOLPH	D. NOVEMBER 1, 1937 JOCKSON, MICH.
80- 45	FREY, JAMES GOTTFRIED	1805 REUTER RD - TIMONIUM MD 21093
33- 19	FREY, LINUS REINHARD	14424 127TH AVE SE - SNOHOMISH WA 98290
73- 48	FRIAS, JESUS MARIA	CALLE 4 #9 - SAN PEDRO DE MACORIS DOM REP
19- 27	FRIBERG, AUGUSTAF BERNHARD	D. DECEMBER 8, 1958 SWAMPSCOTT, MASS.
52- 32	FRICANO, MARION JOHN	D. MAY 18, 1976 TIJUANA, MEX.
23- 44	FRIDAY, GRIER WILLIAM	D. AUGUST 25, 1962 GASTONIA, N. C.
52- 33	FRIDLEY, JAMES RILEY	540 JOSMINE NW AVE - PORT CHARLOTTE FL 33952
20- 34	FRIED, ARTHUR EDWIN	D. OCTOBER 10, 1970 SAN ANTONIO, TEX.
32- 28	FRIEDRICHS, ROBERT GEORGE	1972 ADD: 9808 DALY RD - CINCINNATI OH 45231
49- 24	FRIEND, OWEN LACEY	2917 HALSTED - WICHITA KS 67204
51- 32	FRIEND, ROBERT BARTMESS	4 SALEM CIR - FOX CHAPEL PA 15238

LINUS
FREY

41- 36	FRIERSON, ROBERT LAWRENCE	RR 1-ARTHUR CITY TX 75411
10- 56	FRILL, JOHN EDMOND	D. SEPTEMBER 29, 1918 WESTERLY, R. I.
34- 37	FRINK, FRED FERDINAND	340 NE 54TH ST - MIAMI FL 33137
19- 28	FRISCH, FRANK FRANCIS	D. MARCH 12, 1973 WILMINGTON, DEL.
67- 34	FRISELLA, DANIEL VINCENT	D. JANUARY 1, 1977 PHOENIX, ARIZ.
13- 60	FRITZ, HARRY KOCH	D. NOVEMBER 4, 1974 COLUMBUS, O.
75- 41	FRITZ, LAURENCE JOSEPH	2632 SCHRAGE AVE - WHITING IN 46394
55- 45	FROATS, WILLIAM JOHN	OLD ADD: 16 ASHTON RD - YONKERS NY 10705
77- 55	FROST, CARL DAVID	7136 S MARINA PACIFIC DR-LONG BEACH CA 90803
78- 46	FRY, JERRY RAY	405 E MULBERRY #12 - CHATHAM IL 62629
23- 45	FRY, JOHNSON	D. APRIL 7, 1959 CARMI, ILL.
40- 23	FRYE, CHARLES ANDREW	D. MAY 25, 1945 HICKORY, N. C.
66- 37	FRYMAN, WOODROW THOMPSON	RR 1 BOX 21 - EWING KY 41039

42- 40	FUCHS, CHARLES RUDOLPH	D. JUNE 10, 1969 WEEHAWKEN, N. J.
29- 40	FUCHS, EMIL EDWIN	D. DECEMBER 5, 1961 BOSTON, MASS.
69- 59	FUENTES, MIGUEL	D. JANUARY 29, 1970 LOIZA ALDEA, P. R.
65- 30	FUENTES, RIGOBERTO PEAT	1080 HATTERAS - FOSTER CITY CA 94404
21- 31	FUHR, OSCAR LAWRENCE	D. MARCH 27, 1975 DALLAS, TEX.
22- 39	FUHRMAN, ALFRED GEORGE	D, JANUARY 11, 1969 PEORIA, ILL.
21- 32	FULGHUM, JAMES LAVOISIER	D. NOVEMBER 11, 1947 MIAMI, FLA.
79- 38	FULGHUM, JOHN THOMAS	2703 ARROW HEIGHTS - MARYLAND HEIGHTS MO6304
15- 49	FULLER, FRANK EDWARD	D. OCTOBER 29, 1965 WARREN, MICH.
73- 49	FULLER, JAMES H	2844 POINSETTIA DR - SAN DIEGO CA 92106
74- 39	FULLER, JOHN EDWARD	OLD ADD: 3916 MAGNOLIA - LYNWOOD CA
64- 34	FULLER, VERNON GORDON	OLD ADD: EXECUTIVE HOUSE - DENVER CO 80301
21- 33	FULLERTON, CURTIS HOOPER	D. JANUARY 2, 1975 WINTHROP, MASS.
28- 36	FULLIS, CHARLES PHILIP	D. MARCH 28, 1946 ASHLAND, PA.
81- 39	FUNDERBURK, MARK CLIFFORD	3128 STANCIL PL - CHARLOTTE NC 28205
29- 41	FUNK, ELIAS CALVIN	D. JANUARY 17, 1968 OKLAHOMA CITY, OKLA.
60- 35	FUNK, FRANKLIN RAY	4452 E BELLVIEW ST - PHOENIX AZ 85008
46- 30	FURILLO, CARL ANTHONY	1415 CARSONIA AVE - STONY CREEK MILLS PA1960
22- 40	FUSSELL, FREDERICK MORRIS	D. OCTOBER 23, 1966 SYRACUSE, N. Y.
52- 34	FUSSELMAN, LESTER LEROY	D. MAY 21, 1970 CLEVELAND, O.
35- 33	GABLER, FRANK HAROLD	D. NOVEMBER 1, 1967 LONG BEACH, CAL.
59- 29	GABLER, JOHN RICHARD	8606 W 81ST ST - OVERLAND PARK KS 66204
58- 35	GABLER, WILLIAM LOUIS	2519 ST LOUIS AVE - ST LOUIS MO 63106
45- 34	GABLES, KENNETH HARLIN	D. JANUARY 2, 1960 WALNUT GROVE, MO.
60- 36	GABRIELSON, LEONARD GARY	24230 HILLVIEW DR - LOS ALTOS HILLS CA 94022
39- 37	GABRIELSON, LEONARD HILBOURN	1387 GLEN DR - SAN LEANDRO CA 94577
38- 28	GADDY, JOHN WILSON	D. MAY 3, 1966 ALBEMARLE, N. C.
51- 33	GAEDEL, EDWARD CARL	D. JUNE 19, 1961 CHICAGO, ILL.
81- 40	GAETTI, GARY JOSEPH	201 MONROE AVE #278 - MAITLAND FL 32751
36- 27	GAFFKE, FABIAN SEBASTIAN	4305 S PENNSYLVANIA AVE MILWAUKEE WI 53207
63- 42	GAGLIANO, PHILIP JOSEPH	723 GARLYN CT - ST LOUIS MO 63123
65- 31	GAGLIANO, RALPH MICHAEL	845 DICKINSON ST - MEMPHIS TN 38107
14- 69	GAGNIER, EDWARD J.	D. SEPTEMBER 13, 1946 DETROIT, MICH.
22- 41	GAGNON, HAROLD DENNIS	D. APRIL 30, 1970 WILMINGTON, DEL.
60- 37	GAINES, ARNESTA JOE	4759 MELDON AVE - OAKLAND CA 94619
21- 34	GAINES, WILLARD ROLAND	D. JANUARY 26, 1979 WARRENTON, VA.
34- 38	GALAN, AUGUST JOHN	1345 NOB HILL - PINOLE CA 94564
77- 56	GALASSO, ROBERT JOSE	BOX 493-A - CONNELSVILLE PA 15425
33- 20	GALATZER, MILTON	D. JANUARY 29, 1976 SAN FRANCISCO, CALIF.
78- 47	GALE, RICHARD BLACKWELL	13 SCHOOL ST - LITTLETON NH 03561
34- 39	GALEHOUSE, DENNIS WARD	121 HUFFMAN AVE - DOYLESTOWN OH 44230
70- 47	GALLAGHER, ALAN MITCHELL	1852 BEVERLY AVE - CLOVIS CA 93612
62- 43	GALLAGHER, DOUGLAS EUGENE	1690 MAPLE LN - FREMONT OH 43420
32- 29	GALLAGHER, EDWARD MICHAEL	D. DECEMBER 22, 1981 HYANNIS PORT, MASS.
15- 50	GALLAGHER, JOHN C.	B. 1894 PITTSBURGH, PA.
23- 46	GALLAGHER, JOHN LAWRENCE	14 RIALTO ST - PROVIDENCE RI 02908
39- 38	GALLAGHER, JOSEPH EMMETT	2323 MCCUE #17 HOUSTON TX 77027
22- 42	GALLAGHER, LAWRENCE KIRBY	D. JANUARY 6, 1957 WASHINGTON, D. C.
72- 30	GALLAGHER, ROBERT COLLINS	315 FAIR AVE - SANTA CRUZ CA 95060
42- 41	GALLE, STANLEY JOSEPH	7 N REED AVE - MOBILE AL 36604
12- 65	GALLIA, MELVIN ALLYS	D. MARCH 19, 1976 DEVINE, TEX.
31- 29	GALLIVAN, PHILIP JOSEPH	D. NOVEMBER 24, 1969 ST. PAUL, MINN.
19- 29	GALLOWAY, CLARENCE EDWARD	D. NOVEMBER 7, 1969 CLINTON, S. C.
12- 66	GALLOWAY, JAMES CATO	D. MAY 3, 1950 FORT WORTH, TEX.
30- 24	GALVIN, JAMES JOSEPH	D. SEPTEMBER 30, 1969 MARIETTA, GA.
72- 31	GAMBLE, JOHN ROBERT	3740 AMADOR WAY - RENO NV 89502
35- 34	GAMBLE, LEE JESSE	237 JENKS AVE PUNXATAWNEY PA 15767
69- 60	GAMBLE, OSCAR CHARLES	4127 GASTON CT - MONTGOMERY AL 36105
10- 57	GANDIL, CHARLES ARNOLD	D. DECEMBER 12, 1970 CALISTOGA, CALIF.
16- 30	GANDY, ROBERT BRINKLEY	D. JUNE 19, 1945 JACKSONVILLE, FLA.
39- 39	GANTENBEIN, JOSEPH STEPHEN	535 ORANGE AVE S SAN FRANCISCO CA 94080
76- 33	GANTNER, JAMES ELMER	BOX 156 - EDEN WI 53019
27- 37	GANZEL, FOSTER PIRIE	D. FEBRUARY 6, 1978 JACKSONVILLE FLA.
46- 31	GARAGIOLA, JOSEPH HENRY	4514 DESERT PARK PL - PARADISE VALLEY AZ8525
44- 45	GARBARK, NATHANIEL MICHAEL	2321 CHARLOTTE DR - CHARLOTTE NC 28203
34- 40	GARBARK, ROBERT MICHAEL	267 JEFFERSON ST - MEADVILLE PA 16335
69- 61	GARBER, HENRY EUGENE	RR1 BOX 331 - ELIZABETHTOWN PA 17022
56- 37	GARBER, ROBERT MITCHELL	101 ACACIA LN - REDWOOD CITY CA 94062
52- 35	GARBOWSKI, ALEXANDER	110 ELLIOTT ST - YONKERS NY 10705
76- 34	GARCIA, ALFONSO RAFAEL	526A N CIVIC DR - WALNUT CREEK CA 94596

78- 48	GARCIA, DAMASO DOMINGO	SANCHEZ NO. 104 - MOCA DOMINICAN REPUBLIC
81- 41	GARCIA, DANIEL RAPHAEL	90-64 184TH PL - HOLLIS NY 11423
77- 57	GARCIA, DAVID	15420 OLDE HWY 80 #129 - EL CAJON CA 92021
48- 37	GARCIA, EDWARD MIGUEL	4229 VIRGINIA DR - FAIRVIEW PARK OH 44126
73- 50	GARCIA, PEDRO MODESTO	OLD ADD: BARRIOS PUENTO DE JOBOS-GUAYAMA PR
72- 32	GARCIA, RALPH	2247 DUVALL ST - LOS ANGELES CA 90031
48- 38	GARCIA, RAMON GARCIA	FALGUERAS 256 - HAVANA CUBA
54- 29	GARCIA, VINICIO UZCANGA	R CAMPOAMOR 805 COL ANAHUAC - MONTEREY NL MEX
45- 35	GARDELLA, ALFRED STEVE	3160 BERRY LN SW #93 - ROANOKE VA 24018
44- 46	GARDELLA, DANIEL LEWIS	16 MORSEMERE PL - YONKERS NY 10701

```
81- 42 GARDENHIRE, RONALD CLYDE      7701 QUAIL - WICHITA KS 67212
23- 47 GARDINER, ARTHUR CECIL        D. OCTOBER 21, 1954 COPIAGUE, N. Y.
75- 42 GARDNER, ARTHUR JUNIOR        RR 2 BOX 41 - WALNUT GROVE MS 39189
45- 36 GARDNER, GLENN MILESO         D. JULY 7, 1964 ROCHESTER, N. Y.
11- 52 GARDNER, HARRY RAY            D. AUGUST 2, 1961 CANBY, ORE.
29- 42 GARDNER, RAYMOND VINCENT      D. MAY 3, 1968 FREDERICK, MD.
65- 32 GARDNER, RICHARD FRANK        OLD ADD: 129 CHAPIN ST - BINGHAMTON NY 13905
54- 30 GARDNER, WILLIAM FREDERICK    35 DAYTON RD - WATERFORD CT 06385
36- 28 GARIBALDI, ARTHUR EDWARD      D. OCTOBER 20, 1967 SACRAMENTO, CAL.
62- 44 GARIBALDI, BOB ROY            2443 OREGON AVE - STOCKTON CA 95204
31- 30 GARLAND, LOUIS LYMAN          BOX 492 - IDAHO FALLS ID 83401
73- 51 GARLAND, MARCUS WAYNE         7123 CEDAR RD - CHESTERLAND OH 44026
69- 62 GARMAN, MICHAEL DOUGLAS       3806 AIRPORT AVE - CALDWELL ID 83605
32- 30 GARMS, DEBS                   # 51 GLEN ROSE TX 76043
73- 52 GARNER, PHILIP MASON          BOX 288 - HOUSTON TX 77001
68- 26 GARR, RALPH ALLAN             7819 CHASEWAY DR - MISSOURI CITY TX 77459
15- 51 GARRETT, CLARENCE RAYMOND     D. FEBRUARY 11, 1977 MOUNDSVILLE, W. VA.
70- 48 GARRETT, GREGORY              14963 SANDRA - SAN FERNANDO CA 91340
66- 38 GARRETT, HENRY ADRIAN         3353 LUNAR ST - NAPLES FL 33940
69- 63 GARRETT, RONALD WAYNE         CHALET VLG,WILEY OAKLY DR-GATLINBURG TN 37738
64- 35 GARRIDO, GIL GONZALO          APARTADO 1119 O - PANAMA CITY 6 PANAMA
46- 32 GARRIOTT, CECIL VIRGIL        31750 MACHADO #71 - LAKE ELSINORE CA 92330
28- 37 GARRISON, CLIFFORD WILLIAM    815 CAPAY ST - ESPARTO CA 95627
53- 49 GARRISON, ROBERT FORD         5075 65TH AVE N - PINELLAS PARK FL 33565
31- 31 GARRITY, FRANCIS JOSEPH       D. SEPTEMBER 3, 1962 BOSTON, MASS.
48- 39 GARVER, NED FRANKLIN          BOX 114 - NEY OH 43549
69- 64 GARVEY, STEVEN PATRICK        4393 PARK VICENTE - CALABASA CA 91302
```

```
77- 58 GARVIN, THEODORE JARED        7642 WEST 2940 SOUTH - MAGNA UT 84044
69- 65 GASPAR, RODNEY EARL           26535 VIA CONCHITA - MISSION VIEJO CA 92675
44- 47 GASSAWAY, CHARLES CASON       10925 WESTWOOD LAKE DR - MIAMI FL 33165
55- 46 GASTALL, THOMAS EVERETT       D. SEPTEMBER 20, 1956 CHESAPEAKE BAY, MD.
20- 35 GASTON, ALEXANDER NATHANIEL   D. FEBRUARY 8, 1979 SANTA MONICA, CALIF.
67- 35 GASTON, CLARENCE EDWIN        4106 SPRINGVIEW - SAN ANTONIO TX 78223
24- 39 GASTON, NATHANIEL MILTON      5064 WHITE OAK CT - BRADENTON FL 33507
78- 49 GATES, JOSEPH DANIEL          1517 EAST NINETEENTH AVE - GARY IN 46407
81- 43 GATES, MICHAEL GRANT          8149 GARDEN GROVE - RESEDA CA 91335
63- 43 GATEWOOD, AUBREY LEE          OLD ADD: 2021 SANFORD - LITTLE ROCK AR
78- 50 GAUDET, JAMES JENNINGS        BOX 387 - LIVINGSTON MANOR NY 12758
25- 37 GAUTREAL, WALTER PAUL         D. AUGUST 23, 1970 SALT LAKE CITY, UTAH
36- 29 GAUTREALX, SIDNEY ALLEN       D. APRIL 19, 1980 MORGAN CITY, LA.
20- 36 GAW, GEORGE JOSEPH            D. MAY 26, 1968 BOSTON, MASS.
23- 48 GAZELLA, MICHAEL              D. SEPTEMBER 11, 1978 ODESSA, TEX.
47- 37 GEARHART, LLOYD WILLIAM       DIAMOND ACRES - XENIA OH 45385
23- 49 GEARIN, DENNIS JOHN           D. MARCH 11, 1959 PROVIDENCE, R. I.
42- 42 GEARY, EUGENE FRANCIS JOSEPH  D. JANUARY 27, 1981 CUBA, N. Y.
18- 21 GEARY, ROBERT NORTON          D. JANUARY 31, 1980 CINCINNATI, O.
71- 37 GEBHARD, ROBERT HENRY         117 MARQUETTE AVE -NORTH MANKATO MN 56001
47- 38 GEBRIAN, PETER                512 BLOOMFIELD AVE - CALDWELL NJ 07006
72- 33 GEDDES, JAMES LEE             4129 ZUBER RD - ORIENT OH 43146
39- 40 GEDEON, ELMER JOHN            D. APRIL 15, 1944 FRANCE
13- 61 GEDEON, ELMER JOSEPH          D. MAY 19, 1941 SAN FRANCISCO, CALIF.
80- 46 GEDMAN, RICHARD LEO           32 LAFAYETTE - WORCESTER MA 01608
39- 41 GEE, JOHN ALEXANDER           71 HICKORY PARK RD - CORTLAND NY 13045
23- 50 GEHRIG, HENRY LOUIS           D. JUNE 2, 1941 RIVERDALE, N. Y.
24- 40 GEHRINGER, CHARLES LEONARD    32301 LAHSER RD - BIRMINGHAM MI 48010
37- 39 GEHRMAN, PAUL ARTHUR          1535 AWBREY RD BEND OR 97701
58- 36 GEIGER, GARY MERLE            7327 S 69TH E CT - TULSA OK 74133
78- 51 GEISEL, JOHN DAVID            59 COSHWAY PLACE - TONAWANDA NY 14150
69- 66 GEISHERT, VERNON WILLIAM      RR 3 BOX 32 - RICHLAND CENTER WI 53581
29- 43 GELBERT, CHARLES MAGNUS       D. JANUARY 13, 1967 EASTON, PA.
64- 36 GELNAR, JOHN RICHARD          312 S ROBINSON - MANGUM OK 73554
22- 43 GENEWICH, JOSEPH EDWARD       77 MAIN ST #514 - LOCKPORT NY 14810
50- 30 GENOVESE, GEORGE MICHAEL      11615 KILLION ST - NORTH HOLLYWOOD CA 91606
57- 22 GENTILE, JAMES EDWARD         1016 NEPTUNE - EDMOND OK 73034
43- 50 GENTILE, SAMUEL CHRISTOPHER   123 CENTRAL AVE-EVERETT MA 02149
69- 67 GENTRY, GARY EDWARD           6590 N SCOTTSDALE - SCOTTSDALE AZ 85257
54- 31 GENTRY, HARVEY WILLIAM        109 EATON LN - BRISTOL TN 37620
43- 51 GENTRY, JAMES RUFFUS          4929 FULP ST-WINSTON-SALEM NC 27105
55- 47 GEORGE, ALEXANDER THOMAS      311 W 72ND ST - KANSAS CITY MO 64114
35- 33 GEORGE, CHARLES PETER         RR 2 BOX 39E - BRUNSWICK GA 31520
11- 53 GEORGE, THOMAS EDWARD         D. MAY 13, 1955 YORK, PA.
38- 29 GEORGY, OSCAR JOHN            6878 VICKSBURG ST NEW ORLEANS LA 70124
```

36- 30 GERAGHTY, BENJAMIN RAYMOND   D. JUNE 18, 1963 JACKSONVILLE, FLA.
62- 45 GERARD, DAVID FREDERICK   318 DOONE PL - FAIRLESS HILLS PA 19030
14- 70 GERBER, WALTER   D. JUNE 19 , 1951 COLUMBUS, O.
62- 46 GERBERMAN, GEORGE ALOIS   RR 3 BOX 382-B - EL CAMPO TX 77437
74- 40 GERHARDT, ALLEN RUSSELL   2931 HISS AVE - PARKVILLE MD 21234
43- 52 GERHEAUSER, ALBERT   D. MAY 28, 1972 SPRINGFIELD, MO.
27- 38 GERKEN, GEORGE HERBERT   D. OCTOBER 23, 1977 ARCAIDA, CALIF.

George Gerken

THE SPORT AMERICANA BASEBALL CARD PRICE GUIDE
IS "THE" AUTHORITATIVE SOURCE FOR CURRENT
PRICES OF BASEBALL CARDS. NO SERIOUS COLLECTOR
OF BASEBALL CARDS SHOULD BE WITHOUT A COPY.
SEE DETAILS ON THE INSIDE FRONT COVER.

45- 37 GERKIN, STEPHEN PAUL   D. NOVEMBER 8, 1978 BAY PINES, FLA.
38- 30 GERLACH, JOHN GLENN   5721 DOGWOOD PL - MADISON WI 53705
19- 30 GERNER, EDWIN FREDERICK   D. MAY 15, 1970 PHILADELPHIA, PA.
52- 36 GERNERT, RICHARD EDWARD   1420 ROSE VIRGINIA RD - READING PA 19615
69- 68 GERONIMO, CESAR FRANCISCO   TEFADA FLO. #56 - SANTO DOMINGO DR
13- 62 GERVAIS, LUCIEAN EDWARD   D. OCTOBER 19, 1950 LOS ANGELES, CALIF.
45- 38 GETTEL, ALLEN JONES   5620 PARLIAMENT DR - VIRGINIA BEACH VA 23452
10- 58 GEYER, JACOB BOWMAN   D. OCTOBER 12, 1962 WAHKON, MINN.
24- 41 GEYGAN, JAMES EDWARD   D. MARCH 16, 1966 COLUMBUS, O.
16- 31 GHARRITY, EDWARD PATRICK   D. OCTOBER 10, 1966 BELOIT, WIS.
58- 37 GIALLOMBARDO, ROBERT PAUL   1340 E FIFTH - BROOKLYN NY 11230
11- 54 GIANNINI, JOSEPH FRANCIS   D. SEPTEMBER 26, 1942 SAN FRANCISCO, CALIF.
25- 38 GIARD, JOSEPH OSCAR   D. JULY 10, 1956 WORCESTER, MASS.
60- 38 GIBBON, JOSEPH CHARLES   RR2 NEWTON MS 39345
62- 47 GIBBS, JERRY DEAN   ST ANDREWS CIR - OXFORD MS 38655
24- 42 GIBSON, CHARLES GRIFFIN   713 RIDGECREST RD - LAGRANGE GA 30241
13- 63 GIBSON, FRANK GILBERT   D. APRIL 27, 1961 AUSTIN, TEX.
67- 36 GIBSON, JOHN RUSSELL   %WHIRLPOOL,2880 BARNES - SANTA CLARA CA 95051
79- 39 GIBSON, KIRK HAROLD   4955 CURTIS LN - WATERFORD MI 48095
59- 30 GIBSON, ROBERT   215 BELLEVIEW BLVD S - BELLEVIEW NE 68005
26- 30 GIBSON, SAMUEL BRAXTON   OLD ADD: RR 2 BOX 65 - PALMETTO FL 33561
37- 40 GICK, GEORGE EDWARD   3 BRADY CT - LAFAYETTE IN 47905
75- 43 GIDEON, JAMES LESLIE   5623 BRAESVALLEY - HOUSTON TX 77035
13- 64 GIEBEL, JOSEPH HENRY   D. MARCH 17, 1981 SILVER SPRING, MD.
39- 42 GIEBELL, FLOYD GEORGE   38 SAN REMO CIR - NAPLES FL 33982
54- 32 GIEL, PAUL ROBERT   13400 MCGINTZ RD - MINNEAPOLIS MN 55343
59- 31 GIGGIE, ROBERT THOMAS   89 MCANDREW RD - BRAINTREE MA 02184
67- 37 GIGON, NORMAN PHILLIP   205 PAXINOSA RD E - EASTON PA 18042
67- 38 GIL, TOMAS GUSTAVO   9766 NW 4TH ST - CORAL SPRINGS FL 33065
42- 43 GILBERT, ANDREW   803 WALNUT DR-LATROBE PA 15650
40- 24 GILBERT, CHARLES MADER   6875 VICKSBURG ST-NEW ORLEANS LA 70124
59- 32 GILBERT, DREW EDWARD   1913 BELCARO DR - KNOXVILLE TN 37918
50- 31 GILBERT, HAROLD JOSEPH   D. JUNE 23, 1967 NEW ORLEANS, LA.
72- 34 GILBERT, JOE DENNIS   1952 N BOWIE ST - JASPER TX 75951
14- 71 GILBERT, LAWRENCE WILLIAM   D. FEBRUARY 17, 1965 NEW ORLEANS, LA.
28- 38 GILBERT, WALTER JOHN   D. SEPTEMBER 8, 1959 DULUTH, MINN.
72- 35 GILBREATH, RODNEY JOE   1438 RIDGELAND WAY - LILBURN GA 30247
71- 38 GILBRETH, WILLIAM FREEMAN   690 E N 16TH ST - ABILENE TX 79601
59- 33 GILE, DONALD LOREN   2474 BROADMOOR - LIVERMORE CA 94550
81- 44 GILES, BRIAN JEFFREY   8607 GLEN HAVEN ST - SAN DIEGO CA 92125
20- 37 GILHAM, GEORGE LEWIS   D. APRIL 25, 1937 LANSDOWNE, PA.
11- 55 GILHOOLEY, FRANK PATRICK   D. JULY 11, 1959 TOLEDO, O.
19- 31 GILL, EDWARD JAMES   27 FEDERICO CIR - STOUGHTON MA 02072
37- 41 GILL, GEORGE LLOYD   RAYMOND MS 39154
23- 51 GILL, HAROLD EDMUND   D. AUGUST 1, 1932
27- 39 GILL, JOHN WESLEY   1901 SWEETBRIAR AV - NASHVILLE TENN 37212
40- 25 GILLENWATER, CARDEN EDISON   8703 BARDMOOR BLVD #203-E - LARGO FL 33543
23- 52 GILLENWATER, CLARAL LEWIS   D. FEBRUARY 26, 1978 PENSACOLA, FLA.
22- 44 GILLESPIE, JOHN PATRICK   D. FEBRUARY 15, 1954 VALLEJO, CAL.
42- 44 GILLESPIE, PAUL ALLEN   D. AUGUST 11, 1970 ANNISTON, ALA.
44- 48 GILLESPIE, ROBERT WILLIAM   123 CAROL RD - WINSTON-SALEM NC 27106
53- 28 GILLIAM, JAMES WILLIAM   D. OCTOBER 8, 1978 INGLEWOOD, CALIF.
67- 39 GILLIFORD, PAUL GANT   7 WOODLAND DR - MALVERN PA 19355
27- 40 GILLIS, GRANT   D. FEBRUARY 4, 1981 THOMASVILLE, ALA.
14- 72 GILMORE, ERNEST GROVER   D. NOVEMBER 25, 1919 SIOUX CITY, IA.
44- 49 GILMORE, LEONARD PRESTON   RR 2 BOX 213C - JONES OK 73049
68- 27 GILSON, HAROLD   OLD ADD: 1509 JULIE ST #B - BERKELEY CA 94703
15- 52 GINGRAS, JOSEPH ELZEAD JOHN   D. SEPTEMBER 6, 1947 JERSEY CITY, N.J.
14- 73 GINN, TINSLEY RUCKER   D. AUGUST 30, 1931 ATLANTA, GA.
48- 40 GINSBERG, MYRON NATHAN   520 GRISWOLD - NORTHVILLE MI 48067
44- 50 GIONFRICDO, ALBERT FRANCIS   7367 FREEMAN PL #A - GOLETA CA 93017
53- 29 GIORDANO, THOMAS ARTHUR   BOX 806 - AMITYVILLE NY 11701
10- 59 GIRARD, CHARLES AUGUST   D. AUGUST 6, 1936 BROOKLYN, N. Y.
36- 31 GIULIANI, ANGELO JOHN   1985 NORFOLK AVE - ST PAUL MN 55116
62- 48 GIUSTI, DAVID JOHN   524 CLAIR DR - PITTSBURGH PA 15241

```
46- 33  GLADD, JAMES WALTER          2109 KALLIN AVE - LONG BEACH CA 90815
61- 38  GLADDING, FRED EARL          4721 MACMONT CIR - POWELL TN 37819
44- 51  GLADU, ROLAND EDOUARD        OLD ADD: 1130 JEAN DE BREBEUF-DUVERNAY QUE
20- 38  GLAISER, JOHN BURKE          D. MARCH 7, 1959 HOUSTON, TEX.
25- 39  GLASS, THOMAS JOSEPH         RR 14 BOX 225 - GREENSBORO NC 27406
13- 65  GLAVENICH, LUKE FRANK        D. MAY 22, 1935 STOCKTON, CALIF.
49- 25  GLAVIANO, THOMAS GIATANO     1733 HERITAGE LN #374 - SACR AMENTO CA 95815
20- 39  GLAZNER, CHARLES FRANKLIN    705 1/2 LAKE ADAIR BLVD - ORLANDO FL 32704
20- 40  GLEASON, JOSEPH PAUL         18 EXCHANGE - PHELPS NY 14532
63- 44  GLEASON, ROY WILLIAM         1115 WILCOX AVE - MONTEREY PARK CA 91754
16- 32  GLEASON, WILLIAM PATRICK     D. JANUARY 9, 1957 HOLYOKE, MASS.
79- 40  GLEATON, JERRY DON           121 GARMAN DR - EARLY TX 76801
36- 32  GLEESON, JAMES JOSEPH        545 E 129TH TER - KANSAS CITY MO 64145
19- 32  GLEICH, FRANK ELMER          D. MARCH 27, 1949 COLUMBUS, O.
20- 41  GLENN, BURDETTE              D. JUNE 3, 1977 RICHMOND, CALIF.
15- 53  GLENN, HARRY MELVILLE        D. OCTOBER 12, 1918 ST. PAUL, MINN.
60- 39  GLENN, JOHN                  502 5TH AVE NW - MOULTRIE GA 31768
32- 31  GLENN, JOSEPH CHARLES        RR 2 - TUNKHANNOCK PA 18657
30- 25  GLIATTO, SALVADOR MICHAEL    15517 PRESTON RD #1197 - DALLAS TX 75240
14- 74  GLOCKSON, NORMAN STANLEY     D. AUGUST 5, 1955 MAYWOOD, ILL.
39- 43  GLOSSOP, ALBAN               1429 PHIL MAR LN - VISTA CA 92083
75- 44  GLYNN, EDWARD PAUL           16205 45TH AVE - FLUSHING NY 11355
49- 26  GLYNN, WILLIAM VINCENT       6916 51ST - SAN DIEGO CA 92120
74- 41  GODBY, DANNY RAY             RR 2 BOX 28A - CHAPMANVILLE WV 25508
72- 36  GODDARD, JOSEPH HAROLD       CHERRYWOOD TER #A-4 - BEAVER WI 25813
22- 45  GOEBEL, EDWIN                D. AUGUST 12, 1959 BROOKLYN, N. Y.
60- 40  GOETZ, JOHN HARDY            3253 MYDDLETON - TROY MI 48084
72- 37  GOGGIN, CHARLES FRANCIS      1206 DAVIDSON RD - NASHVILLE TN 37205
70- 49  GOGOLEWSKI, WILLIAM JOSEPH   512 STANLEY AVE - OSHKOSH WI 54901
60- 41  GOLDEN, JAMES EDWARD         827 LINDENWOOD AVE - TOPEKA KS 66606
10- 60  GOLDEN, ROY KRAMER           D. OCTOBER 4, 1961 CINCINNATI, O.
28- 39  GOLDMAN, JONAH JOHN          D. AUGUST 17, 1980 PALM BEACH, FLA.
49- 27  GOLDSBERRY, GORDON FREDERICK 22772 BAY FRONT LN - LAKE FOREST CA 92630
26- 31  GOLDSMITH, HAROLD EUGENE     BOX 383 - SOUTHOLD NY 11971
32- 32  GOLDSTEIN, ISADORE           OLD ADD: 2161 SOUTHERN BLVD - BRONX NY 10460
43- 53  GOLDSTEIN, LESLIE ELMER      6516 SABROSA CT W - FORT WORTH TX 76133
62- 49  GOLDY, FURNAL WILLIAM        1318 CHERRYVILLE RD - LITTLETON CO 80120
41- 37  GOLETZ, STANLEY              B3X 157-SIBLEY LA 71073
49- 28  GOLIAT, MIKE MITCHEL         2650 GREEN LAWN DR - SEVEN HILLS OH 44131
72- 38  GOLTZ, DAVID ALLAN           RR 6 BOX 230 - FERGUS FALLS MN 56537
22- 46  GOLVIN, WALTER GEORGE        D. JUNE 11, 1973 GARDENA, CALIF.
35- 36  GOMEZ, JOSE LUIS RODRIGUEZ   GONZALEZ DE COSIO 359-3 MEXICO CITY D F MEX
74- 42  GOMEZ, LUIS JOSE             12408 ROSE ST - CERRITOS CA 90701
44- 52  GOMEZ, PEDRO MARTINEZ        404 SAN VICENTE BLVD - SANTA MONICA CA 95401
53- 30  GOMEZ, RUBEN                 T2-8 IGUAZA PARK GARDENS-RIO PIEDRAS PR 00928
30- 26  GOMEZ, VERNON LOUIS          26 SAN BENITO WAY - NOVATO CA 94947
60- 42  GONDER, JESSE LEMAR          5937 WHITNEY ST - OAKLAND CA 94609
79- 41  GONZALES, DANIEL DAVID       OLD ADD: 12319 CULLMAN AVE-WHITTIER CA 90604
18- 22  GONZALES, EUSEBIO MIGUEL     D. FEBRUARY 14, 1976 HAVANA, CUBA
37- 42  GONZALES, JOE MADRID         30715 COCOS PALM AVE - HOMELAND CA 92348
77- 59  GONZALES, JULIO CESAR        BO. RIO CANAS, BOX 86 - CAGUAS PR 00625
49- 29  GONZALES, JULIO ENRIQUE      OLD ADD: CALIXTO GARCIA 37 - ORIENTE CUBA
55- 48  GONZALES, WENCESLAO O'REILLY D. 1981
60- 43  GONZALEZ, ANDRES ANTONIO     OLD ADD: 3501 WOODHAVE - PHILADELPHIA PA
72- 39  GONZALEZ, JOSE FERNANDO      URB VISTA ANGEL CALLE 4-A-48-ARECIBO PR 00612
12- 67  GONZALEZ, MIGUEL ANGEL CORDERO D. FEBRUARY 19, 1977 HAVANA, CUBA
76- 35  GONZALEZ, ORLANDO EUGENE     OLD ADD: 2352 SW 26TH LN - MIAMI FL
63- 45  GONZALEZ, PEDRO              104 GEN CABRAL - SAN PEDRO DE MACORIS DOM REP
29- 44  GOOCH, CHARLES FURMAN        6509 LANDOVER RD - CHEVERLY MD 20785
21- 35  GOOCH, JOHN BEVERLEY         D. MAY 15, 1975 NASHVILLE, TENN.
```

```
15- 54  GOOCH, LEE CURRIN            D. MAY 18, 1966 RALEIGH, N.C.
10- 61  GOOD, RALPH NELSON           D. NOVEMBER 24, 1965 WATERVILLE, ME.
28- 40  GOODELL, JOHN HENRY WILLIAM  OLD ADD: 3701 SAN BAR LN-FORT WORTH TX
35- 37  GOODMAN, IVAL RICHARD        4377 SCHENCK AVE - CINCINNATI OH 45236
47- 39  GOODMAN, WILLIAM DALE        4525 NORTHLAKE DR - SARASOTA FL 33582
70- 50  GOODSON, JAMES EDWARD        RR 2 BOX 12-0 - INDEPENDENCE VA 24348
14- 75  GOODWIN, CLAIRE VERNON       D. FEBRUARY 15, 1972 OAKLAND, CALIF.
75- 45  GOODWIN, DANNY KAY           2001 N BOURLAND - PEORIA IL 61601
48- 41  GOODWIN, JAMES PATRICK       11533 FRANCETTA LN - ST LOUIS MO 63138
16- 33  GOODWIN, MARVIN MARDO        D. OCTOBER 21, 1925 HOUSTON, TES.
46- 34  GOOLSBY, RAYMOND DANIEL      OLD ADD: 1101 LEE RD #3 - WINTER PARK FL
65- 33  GOOSSEN, GREGORY BRYANT      OLD ADD: 12723 RIVERSIDE DR - NORTH HOLLYWOOD
```

```
55- 49  GORBOUS, GLEN EDWARD            BOX 630 - VULCAN ALBERTA TOL 2B0
38- 31  GORDON, JOSEPH LOWELL           D. APRIL 14, 197, SACRAMENTO, CALIF.
77- 60  GORDON, MICHAEL WILLIAM         OLD ADD: 263 BELMONT ST - BROCKTON MA
41- 38  GORDON, SIDNEY                  D. JUNE 17, 1975 NEW YORK, N.Y.
21- 36  GORDONIER, RAYMOND CHARLES      D. NOVEMBER 15, 1960 ROCHESTER, N. Y.
54- 33  GORIN, CHARLES PERRY            2617 FISET DR - AUSTIN TX 78731
77- 61  GORINSKI, ROBERT JOHN           BOX 133 - CALUMET PA 15621
52- 37  GORMAN, HERBERT ALLEN           D. APRIL 5, 1953 SAN DIEGO, CAL.
37- 43  GORMAN, HOWARD PAUL             4720 NORMA DR PITTSBURGH PA 15236
52- 38  GORMAN, THOMAS ALOYSIUS         474 W VLY STRM BLVD - VALLEY STREAM NY 11581
39- 44  GORMAN, THOMAS DAVID            697 CLOSTER DOCK RD CLOSTER NJ 37624
81- 45  GORMAN, THOMAS PATRICK          2523 N BOONES FERRY RD - WOODBURN OR 97071
41- 39  GORNICKI, FRANK T               5510 TAMBERLANE DR-PALM BCH GARDENS FL 33480
40- 26  GORSICA, JOHN JOSEPH PERRY      BOX 1518 - BECKLEY WV 25801
57- 23  GORYL, JOHN ALBERT              504 HARLAND AVE - MELBOURNE BEACH FL 32951
63- 46  GOSGER, JAMES CHARLES           OLD ADD: 1431 WHIPPLE ST - PORT HURON MI
21- 37  GOSLIN, LEON ALLEN              D. MAY 15, 1971 BRIDGETON, N. J.
62- 50  GOSS, HOWARD WAYNE              BOX 70 - FORT MYERS FL 33902
72- 10  GOSSAGE, RICHARD MICHAEL        32 N FOOTE - COLORADO SPRINGS CO 80909
13- 66  GOSSETT, JOHN STAR              D. OCTOBER 6, 1962 MASSILLON, O.
60- 44  GOTAY, JULIO ENRIQUE            OLD ADD: BELGICA 2 NO. 12 - PONCE PR 00731
12- 68  GOULAIT, THEODORE LEE           D. JULY 15, 1936 ST. CLAIR, MICH.
16- 34  GOULD, ALBERT FRANK             117 HOLLYCREST DR - LOS GATOS CA 95030
44- 53  GOULISH, NICHOLAS EDWARD        36 LAKE SHORE DR - YOUNGSTOWN OH 44511
10- 62  GOWDY, HARRY                    D. AUGUST 1, 1966 COLUMBUS, O.
72- 41  GOWELL, LAWRENCE CLYDE          45 7TH ST - AUBURN MAINE 04210
69- 69  GRABARKEWITZ, BILLY CORDELL     12133 MISSION TRACE - SAN ANTONIO TX 78234
58- 38  GRABER, RODNEY BLAINE           4674 MOUNT ARMET DR - SAN DIEGO CA 92117
29- 45  GRABOWSKI, ALFONS FRANCIS       D. OCTOBER 29, 1966 MEMPHIS, N. Y.
24- 43  GRABOWSKI, JOHN PATRICK         D. MAY 23, 1946 ALBANY, N. Y.
32- 33  GRABOWSKI, REGINALD JOHN        D. APRIL 2, 1955 SYRACUSE, N. Y.
38- 32  GRACE, JOSEPH LAVERNE           D. SEPTEMBER 18, 1969 MURPHYSBORO, ILL.
78- 52  GRACE, MICHAEL LEE              3514 SHELBY - PONTIAC MI 48054
29- 46  GRACE, ROBERT EARL              D. DECEMBER 23, 1980 PHOENIX, ARIZ.
13- 67  GRAF, FREDERICK GOTTLIEB        D. OCTOBER 4, 1979 CHATTANOOGA, TENN.
57- 24  GRAFF, MILTON EDWARD            249 MAGNOLIA PL - PITTSBURGH PA 15225
34- 41  GRAHAM, ARTHUR WILLIAM          D. JULY 10, 1967 ARLINGTON, MASS.
```

```
10- 63  GRAHAM, BERT                    D. JUNE 17, 1971 COTTONWOOD, ARIZ.
79- 42  GRAHAM, DANIEL JAY              BOX 728 - WINKELMAN AZ 85298
14- 76  GRAHAM, DAWSON FRANK            D. DECEMBER 29, 1962 NASHVILLE, TENN.
46- 35  GRAHAM, JOHN BERNARD            3240 E 10TH ST - LONG BEACH CA 90804
24- 44  GRAHAM, KYLE                    D. DECEMBER 1, 1973 OAK GROVE, ALA.
22- 47  GRAHAM, ROY VINCENT             D. APRIL 26, 1933 MANILLA, PHILLIPINES
63- 47  GRAHAM, WAYNE LEON              6419 PINESHADE LN - HOUSTON TX 77008
66- 39  GRAHAM, WILLIAM ALBERT          RR 2 BOX 275 - FLEMINGSBURG KY 41041
68- 28  GRAMLY, BERT THOMAS             643 LADING LN - ALLEN TX 75002
54- 34  GRAMMAS, ALEXANDER PETER        3432 OAKDALE DR - BIRMINGHAM AL 35223
27- 41  GRAMPP, HENRY ERCHARDT          73-20 AUSTIN ST #2A - FOREST HILLS NY 11370
68- 29  GRANGER, WAYNE ALLEN            BOX 134, ALDRICH AVE - HUNTINGTON MA 01050
23- 53  GRANT, GEORGE ADDISON           RR 2 BOX 445 - PRATTVILLE AL 36067
42- 45  GRANT, JAMES CHARLES            D. JULY 8, 1970 ROCHESTER, MINN.
23- 54  GRANT, JAMES RONALD             MADRID IA 50156
58- 39  GRANT, JAMES TIMOTHY            16632 SCOTTSDALE BLVD-SHAKER HEIGHTS OH 44120
22- 48  GRANTHAM, GEORGE FARLEY         D. MARCH 16, 1954 KINGMAN, ARIZ.
48- 42  GRASMICK, LOUIS JUNIOR          303 VALDINE CT - TIMONIUM MD 21093
46- 36  GRASSO, NEWTON MICHAEL          D. DECEMBER 15, 1975 MIAMI FLA.
45- 39  GRATE, DONALD                   1245 NW 203RD ST - MIAMI FL 33169
26- 32  GRAVES, JOSEPH EBENEZER         D. DECEMBER 22, 1980 SALEM, MASS.
27- 42  GRAVES, SAMUEL SIDNEY           103 CAT MOSAM - KENNEBUNK ME 04043
64- 37  GRAY, DAVID ALEXANDER           539 BRINKER AVE - OGDEN UT 84404
77- 62  GRAY, GARY GEORGE               95 OLD BROADWAY - NEW YORK NY 10027
54- 35  GRAY, JOHN LEONARD              3323 PONCIANA - MIAMI FL 33133
37- 44  GRAY, MILTON MARSHALL           D. JUNE 30, 1969 QUINCY, FLA.
45- 40  GRAY, PETER                     203 PHILLIPS ST - NANTICOKE PA 18634
58- 40  GRAY, RICHARD BENJAMIN          503 S HAMPTON - ANAHEIM CA 92804
24- 45  GRAY, SAMUEL DAVID              D. APRIL 16, 1953 MCKINNEY, TEX.
12- 69  GRAY, STANLEY OSCAR             D. OCTOBER 11, 1964 SNYDER, TEX.
46- 37  GRAY, THEODORE GLENN            21 E WASHINGTON - CLARKSTON MI 48016
59- 34  GRBA, ELI                       OLD ADD: 9628 S COMMERCIAL - CHICAGO IL
54- 36  GREASON, WILLIAM HENRY          4536 HILLMAN DR SW - BIRMINGHAM AL 35221
81- 46  GREEN, DAVID ALEJANDRO          COLINIA MANAGUA GRUPO H#47-MANAGUA NICARAGUA
59- 35  GREEN, ELIJAH JERRY             BERKELEY H.S. 2246 MILVA-BERKELEY CA 94704
59- 36  GREEN, FRED ALLAN               BOX 161 - TITUSVILLE NJ 08560
```

```
57- 25  GREEN, GENE LEROY              D. MAY 23, 1981 ST. LOUIS, MO.
60- 45  GREEN, GEORGE DALLAS           RR 1 BOX 227A - WEST GROVE PA 19390
35- 38  GREEN, HARVEY GEORGE           D. JULY 24, 1970 FRANKLIN, LA.
24- 46  GREEN, JOSEPH HENRY            D. FEBRUARY 4, 1972 BRYN MAWR, PA.
28- 41  GREEN, JULIUS FOUST            D. MARCH 19, 1974 GLENDORA, CALIF.
57- 26  GREEN, LEONARD CHARLES         18693 SUNSET ST - DETROIT MI 48234
63- 48  GREEN, RICHARD LARRY           525 38TH - RAPID CITY SD 57701
30- 27  GREENBERG, HENRY BENJAMIN      1129 MIRADERO RD - BEVERLY HILLS CA 90210
79- 43  GREENE, ALTAR ALPHONSE         18294 MARLOWE - DETROIT MI 48235
24- 47  GREENE, NELSON GEORGE          212 E GRANT ST - LEBANON PA 17042
24- 48  GREENFIELD, KENT               D. MARCH 14, 1978 GUTHRIE, KY.
52- 39  GREENGRASS, JAMES RAYMOND      2930 OCTAVIA CIR - MARIETTA GA 30062
54- 37  GREENWOOD, ROBERT CHANDLER     35800 MOLINA CT - FREMONT CA 94536
77- 63  GREER, BRIAN KEITH             914 CARLSON DR - BREA CA 92621
13- 68  GREGG, DAVID CHARLES           D. NOVEMBER 12, 1965 CLARKSTON, WASH.
43- 54  GREGG, HAROLD DANA             BOX 1322 - BULLHEAD CITY AZ 86430
11- 56  GREGG, SYLVEANUS AUGUSTUS      D. JULY 29, 1964 ABERDEEN, WASH.
12- 70  GREGORY, FRANK ERNST           D. NOVEMBER 5, 1955 BELOIT, WIS.
64- 38  GREGORY, GROVER LEROY          6456 N TEILMAN - FRESNO CA 93705
11- 57  GREGORY, HOWARD WATTERSON      D. MAY 30, 1970 TULSA, OKLA.
32- 34  GREGORY, PAUL EDWIN            ATH DEPT, MISSISSIPPI ST-STATE COLLEGEMS39762
71- 39  GREIF, WILLIAM BRILEY          807 E 31ST - AUSTIN TX 78705
20- 42  GREISENBECK, CARLOS TIMOTHY    D. MARCH 25, 1953 SAN ANTONIO, TEX.
40- 27  GREMP, LOUIS EDWARD            1229 BRIGHTON AVE #150 - MODESTO CA 95350
19- 33  GREVELL, WILLIAM               D. JUNE 21, 1923 SPRINGFIELD TWP., PA.
70- 51  GRICH, ROBERT ANTHONY          210 BELMONT AVE - LONG BEACH CA 90803
70- 52  GRIEVE, THOMAS ALAN            3206 HERITAGE CT - ARLINGTON TX 76016
46- 38  GRIFFETH, LEON CLIFFORD        RR TWO - PATTERSON NY 12563
73- 53  GRIFFEY, GEORGE KENNETH        5654 LITTLEFLOWER AVE - CINCINNATI OH 45239
76- 36  GRIFFIN, ALFREDO CLAUDINO      B#3 B HATOMAYOR ING CONS-SAN PED DE MARC.DOMR
70- 53  GRIFFIN, DOUGLAS LEE           164 S PINE ST - ORANGE CA 92666
17- 32  GRIFFIN, FRANCIS ARTHUR        D. OCTOBER 12, 1951 COLORADO SPRINGS COLO.
19- 34  GRIFFIN, IVY MOORE             D. AUGUST 25, 1957 GAINESVILLE, FLA.
11- 58  GRIFFIN, JAMES LINTON          D. FEBRUARY 11, 1950 TERRELL, TEX.
28- 42  GRIFFIN, MARTIN JOHN           D. NOVEMBER 19, 1951 LOS ANGELES, CAL.
79- 44  GRIFFIN, MICHAEL LEROY         1620 GROVE AVE - WOODLAND CA 95695
14- 77  GRIFFIN, PATRICK RICHARD       D. JUNE 7, 1927 YOINGSTOWN, O.
69- 70  GRIFFIN, THOMAS JAMES          OLD ADD: 13147 AVE LAVELENCIA-POWAY CA 92064
22- 49  GRIFFITH, BARTHOLOMEW JOSEPH   D. MAY 5, 1973 BISHOP, CALIF.
63- 49  GRIFFITH, ROBERT DERRELL       515 W TEXAS - ANADARKO OK 73005
13- 69  GRIFFITH, THOMAS HERMAN        D. APRIL 13, 1967 CINCINNATI, O.
56- 38  GRIGGS, HAROLD LLOYD           1100 NE 4TH ST - POMPANO BEACH FL 33060
23- 55  GRIGSBY, DENVER CLARENCE       D. NOVEMBER 10, 1973 SAPULPA, OKLA.
66- 40  GRILLI, GUIDO JOHN             4636 LORECE - MEMPHIS TN 38117
75- 46  GRILLI, STEPHEN JOSEPH         1834 RELYEA DR - MERRICK NY 11566
54- 38  GRIM, ROBERT ANTON             7118 CODY - OVERLAND PARK KS 66203
16- 35  GRIMES, BURLEIGH ARLAND        %V.TEAS,13955 S INDIANA AVE-CHICAGO IL 60627
31- 32  GRIMES, EDWARD ADELBERT        D. OCTOBER 4, 1974 CHICAGO, ILL.
38- 33  GRIMES, OSCAR RAY JR.          25151 BROOKPARD RD #203 - N. OLMSTED OH 44070
20- 43  GRIMES, OSCAR RAY SR.          D. MAY 25, 1953 MINERVA, O.
20- 44  GRIMES, ROY AUSTIN             D. SEPTEMBER 13, 1954 HANOVERTON, O.
16- 36  GRIMM, CHARLES JOHN            1149 N 92ND ST #18 - SCOTTSDALE AZ 85257
51- 34  GRIMSLEY, ROSS ALBERT          1538 FRAYSER BLVD - MEMPHIS TN 38127
71- 40  GRIMSLEY, ROSS ALBERT II       2987 S ATLANTIC #506-DAYTONA BCH SHRS FL32018
12- 71  GRINER, DONALD DEXTER          D. JUNE 3, 1950 BISHOPVILLE, S.C.
34- 42  GRISSOM, LEE THEO              BOX 875 - CORNING CA 96021
46- 39  GRISSOM, MARVIN EDWARD         BOX 3007 - RED BLUFF CA 96080
52- 40  GROAT, RICHARD MORROW          320 BEACH ST - PITTSBURGH PA 15218
56- 39  GROB, CONRAD GEORGE            2311 MAPLE ST - CROSS PLAINS WI 53528
41- 40  GRODZICKI, JOHN                RR 2 BOX 346 - DAYTONA BEACH FL 32019
12- 72  GROH, HENRY KNIGHT             D. AUGUST 22, 1968 CINCINNATI,O.
19- 35  GROH, LEWIS CARL               D. OCTOBER 20, 1960 ROCHESTER, N. Y.
41- 41  GROMEK, STEPHEN JOSEPH         21455 CORSAUT - BIRMINGHAM MI 48010
```

```
55- 50  GROSS, DONALD JOHN             2868 S COLDWATER RD - MOUNT PLEASANT MI 48858
25- 40  GROSS, EWELL                   D. JANUARY 22, 1936 DALLAS, TEX.
73- 54  GROSS, GREGORY EUGENE          556 WOODLEA LN - BERWYN PA 19312
76- 37  GROSS, WAYNE DALE              1550 REGAL COURT - RIVERSIDE CA 92506
30- 28  GROSSKLOS, HOWARD HOFFMAN      7210 OLD CUTLER RD - CORAL GABLES FL 33143
52- 41  GROSSMAN, HARLEY JOSEPH        2926 HARTIG AVE - EVANSVILLE IN 47712
63- 50  GROTE, GERALD WAYNE            148-26 WILLOW BEND - SAN ANTONIO TX 78232
47- 40  GROTH, ERNEST WILLIAM          BLACKHAWK-NEGLY RD - BEAVER FALLS PA 15010
46- 40  GROTH, JOHN THOMAS             177 QUEENS LN - PALM BEACH FL 33480
40- 28  GROVE, ORVAL LEROY             2743 POPE AVE - SACRAMENTO CA 95821
```

```
25- 41  GROVE, ROBERT MOSES            D. MAY 22, 1975 NORWALK, O.
13- 70  GROVER, CHARLES BERT           D. MAY 24, 1971 EMMETT TWP., CALHOUN CO.,MIC
16- 37  GROVER, ROY ARTHUR             D. FEBRUARY 7, 1978 MILWAUKIE, ORE.
12- 73  GRUBB, HARVEY HARRISON         D. JANUARY 25, 1970 CORPUS CHRISTI, TEX.
72- 42  GRUBB, JOHN MAYWOOD            3920 COGBILL RD - RICHMOND VA 23234
20- 45  GRUBBS, THOMAS DILLARD         N MAYSVILLE ST - MT STERLING KY 40353
31- 33  GRUBE, FRANKLIN THOMAS         D. JULY 2, 1945 NEW YORK, N. Y.
55- 51  GRUNWALD, ALFRED HENRY         7120 BOTHWELL RD - RESEDA CA 91335
38- 34  GRYSKA, SIGMUND STANLEY        4527 S DRAKE CHICAGO IL 60632
61- 39  GRZENDA, JOSEPH CHARLES        GOULDSBORO PA 18424
29- 47  GUDAT, MARVIN JOHN             D. MARCH 2, 1954 LOS ANGELES, CAL.
37- 45  GUERRA, FERMIN ROMERO          CRISTINA NO 24 ARROYO APOLO HAVANA CUBA
73- 55  GUERRERO, MARIO MIGUEL         CALLE DUARTE #450 - SANTO DOMINGO DOM REP
78- 53  GUERRERO, PEDRO                VILLA MAGDALENA #20 - SAN PEDRO DE MACORIS D
75- 47  GUIDRY, RONALD AMES            109 CONWAY - LAFAYETTE LA 70507
64- 39  GUINDON, ROBERT JOSEPH         1220 OAK TRAIL DR - LIBERTYVILLE IL 60048
68- 30  GUINN, CRANNON EUGENE          5270 ESTRADE LN - SAN JOSE CA 95118
46- 41  GUINTINI, BENJAMIN JOHN        119A ESTATES DR - ROSEVILLE CA 95678
40- 29  GUISE, WITT ORISON             D. AUGUST 13, 1968 NORTH LITTLE ROCK, ARK.
16- 38  GUISTO, LOUIS JOSEPH           2037 WAVERLY - NAPA CA 94558
78- 54  GULDEN, BRADLEY LEE            BOX 254 (LIME STREET) - CARVER MN 55315
70- 54  GULLETT, DONALD EDWARD         P.O. BOX - SOUTH PORTSMOUTH KY 41174
23- 56  GULLEY, THOMAS JEFFERSON       D. NOVEMBER 24, 1966 ST. CHARLES, ARK.
30- 29  GULLIC, TEDD JOSEPH            BOX 703 - WEST PLAINS MO 65775
79- 45  GULLICKSON, WILLIAM LEE        1290 S LINCOLN ST - KANKAKEE IL 60901
35- 39  GUMBERT, HARRY EDWARD          BOX 377 - WIMBERLEY TX 78676
36- 33  GUMPERT, RANDALL PENNINGTON    MONOCACY STATION PA 19542
16- 39  GUNKEL, WOODROW WILLIAM        D. APRIL 19, 1974 NORTH CHICAGO, ILL.
11- 59  GUNNING, HYLAND               D. MARCH 28, 1975 TOGUS, ME.
70- 55  GURA, LARRY CYRIL              9 NW CIRCLE DR - JOLIET IL 60432
11- 60  GUST, ERNEST HERMAN FRANK      D. OCTOBER 26, 1945 MAUPIN, ORE.
39- 45  GUSTINE, FRANK WILLIAM         3911 FORBES AVE PITTSBURGH PA 15213
72- 43  GUTH, CHARLES HENRY            202 MORRIS DR - SALISBURY MD 21801
67- 40  GUTIERREZ, CESAR DARIO         PINTO A MISERIA #100 - CARACAS VEN
36- 34  GUTTERIDGE, DONALD JOSEPH      804 LAKEVIEW DR - PITTSBURG KS 66762
69- 71  GUZMAN, SANTIAGO DONOVAN       ENS RESTAUROSIN M4TA#12-SAN PEDRO DE MAR, D
81- 47  GWOSDZ, DOUGLAS WAYNE          2822 MONTICELLO - HOUSTON TX 77045
33- 21  GYSELMAN, RICHARD RENALD       5212 54TH AV S - SEATTLE WA 98118
37- 46  HAAS, BERTHOLD JOHN            4604 KENSINGTON AVE TAMPA FL 33609
15- 55  HAAS, BRUNO PHILIP             D. JUNE 5, 1952 SARASOTA, FLA.
76- 38  HAAS, BRYAN EDMOND             5 WENGATE RD - OWINGS MILLS MD 21117
57- 27  HAAS, GEORGE EDWIN            100 HILLMONT DR, RR 10 - PADUCAH KY 42001
25- 42  HAAS, GEORGE WILLIAM           D. JUNE 30, 1974 NEW ORLEANS, LA.
51- 35  HABENICHT, ROBERT JULIUS       D. DECEMBER 24, 1980 RICHMOND, VA.
32- 35  HACK, STANLEY CAMFIELD         D. DECEMBER 15, 1979 DIXON, ILL.
71- 41  HACKER, RICHARD WARREN         930 E MAIN - BELLEVILLE IL 62220
48- 43  HACKER, WARREN LOUIS           P. O. BOX 4 - LENZBURG IL 62255
```

WARREN HACKER
CINCINNATI REDLEGS

```
52- 42  HADDIX, HARVEY                 4001 VERNON ASHBURY RD-SOUTH VIENNA OH 45369
26- 33  HADLEY, IRVING DARIUS          D. FEBRUARY 15,1963 LYNN, MASS.
58- 41  HADLEY, KENT WILLIAM           549 HYDE - POCATELLO ID 83201
15- 56  HAEFFNER, WILLIAM BERNHARD     D. JANUARY 27, 1982 DELAWARE CO., PA.
43- 55  HAEFNER, MILTON ARNOLD         504 JACKSON-NEW ATHENS IL 62264
24- 49  HAFEY, CHARLES JAMES           D. JULY 2, 1973 CALISTOGA, CAL.
35- 40  HAFEY, DANIEL ALBERT           BOX 701 SIERRA CITY CA 96125
39- 46  HAFEY, THOMAS FRANCIS          7747 TERRACE DR EL CERRITO CA 94532
11- 61  HAGEMAN, KURT MORITZ           D. APRIL 1, 1964 NEW BEDFORD, PA.
68- 31  HAGUE, JOE CLARENCE            OLD ADD: 10157 SUEZ ST - EL PASO TX 79925
69- 72  HAHN, DONALD ANTONE            1046 BOISE DR - CAMPBELL CA 95008
52- 43  HAHN, FREDERICK ALOYS          23 VAN WARDT PL - TAPPAN NY 10983
40- 30  HAHN, RICHARD FREDERICK        1968 ADD: 1304 TANAGER DR - ORLANDO FL 32803
19- 36  HAID, HAROLD AUGUSTINE         D. AUGUST 13, 1952 LOS ANGELES, CAL.
23- 57  HAINES, HENRY LUTHER           D. JANUARY 9, 1979 SHARON HILL, PA.
18- 23  HAINES, JESSE JOSEPH           D. AUGUST 5, 1978 DAYTON, O.
73- 56  HAIRSTON, JERRY WAYNE          3770 1ST ST W - BIRMINGHAM AL 32507
69- 73  HAIRSTON, JOHN LOUIS           3612 4TH ST W - BIRMINGHAM AL 35207
51- 36  HAIRSTON, SAMUEL               3770 1ST ST W - BIRMINGHAM AL 35207
13- 71  HAISLIP, JAMES CLIFTON         D. JANUARY 22, 1970 DALLAS, TEX.
41- 42  HAJDUK, CHESTER                6838 CONCORD LN-NILES IL 60648
19- 37  HALAS, GEORGE STANLEY          5555 N SHERIDAN RD - CHICAGO ILL 60640
31- 34  HALE, ARVEL ODELL              D. JUNE 9, 1980 EL DORADO, ARK.
14- 78  HALE, GEORGE WAGNER            D. NOVEMBER 1, 1945 WICHITA, KAN.
74- 43  HALE, JOHN STEVEN             2309 9TH ST - WASCO CA 93280
```

55- 52	HALE, ROBERT HOUSTON	1105 GRANVILLE - PARK RIDGE IL 60068
20- 46	HALE, SAMUEL DOUGLAS	D. SEPTEMBER 6, 1974 WHEELER, TEX.
15- 57	HALEY, RAYMOND TIMOTHY	D. OCTOBER 8, 1973 BRADENTON, FLA.
74- 44	HALICKI, EDWARD LOUIS	615 BARBARA WAY - HILLSBOROUGH CA 94010
81- 48	HALL, ALBERT	1628 SPAULDING RD - BIRMINGHAM AL 35211
11- 62	HALL, HERBERT ERNEST	D. JULY 18, 1948 SEATTLE, WASH.
18- 24	HALL, HERBERT SILAS	D. JULY 1, 1970 FRESNO, CAL.
43- 56	HALL, IRVIN GLADSTONE	1153 DEANWOOD RD - BALTIMORE MD 21234
63- 51	HALL, JIMMIE RANDOLPH	OLD ADD: BOX 342 - MOUNT HOLLY NC 28120
48- 44	HALL, JOHN SYLVESTER	300 BELL DR - MIDWEST CITY OK 73110
10- 64	HALL, MARCUS	D. FEBRUARY 24, 1915 JOPLIN, MO.
81- 49	HALL, MELVIN	RR 1 ROUTE 90 - CAYAGA NY 13034
52- 44	HALL, RICHARD WALLACE	2131 FOLKSTONE RD - TIMONIUM MD 21093
49- 30	HALL, ROBERT LEWIS	116 26TH AVE NE - ST PETERSBURG FL 33704
68- 32	HALL, THOMAS EDWARD	3592 LILLIAN AVE - RIVERSIDE CA 92504
13- 72	HALL, WILLIAM BERNARD	D. AUGUST 15, 1947 NEWPORT, KY.
54- 39	HALL, WILLIAM LEMUEL	RR1 - HARTSFIELD GA 31756
25- 43	HALLAHAN, WILLIAM ANTHONY	D. JULY 8, 1981 BINGHAMTON, N. Y.
61- 40	HALLER, THOMAS FRANK	745 COLUMBIA DR - SAN MATEO CA 94402
40- 31	HALLETT, JACK PRICE	2005 GLEN ARBOR DR-TOLEDO OH 43614
16- 40	HALLIDAY, NEWTON R	OLD ADD: 4401 KEOKUK AVE - CHICAGO IL 60601
11- 63	HALLINAN, EDWARD S	D. AUGUST 24, 1940 SAN FRANCISCO, CALIF.
14- 79	HALT, ALVA WILLIAM	D. JANUARY 22, 1973 SANDUSKY, O.
22- 50	HAMANN, ELMER JOSEPH	D. JANUARY 11, 1973 MILWAUKEE, WIS.
71- 42	HAMBRIGHT, ROGER DEE	OLD ADD: 523 N 39 TH ST - SPRINGFIELD OR
26- 34	HAMBY, JAMES SANFORD	1117 S 11TH ST - SPRINGFIELD IL 62703
72- 46	HAMILTON, DAVID EDWARD	9464 CHERRY HILLS LN - SAN RAMON CA 94583
11- 64	HAMILTON, EARL ANDREW	D. NOVEMBER 17, 1968 ANAHEIM, CALIF.
62- 51	HAMILTON, JACK EDWIN	MORNING SUN IOWA 52640
61- 41	HAMILTON, STEVE ABSHER	RR 5 - MOREHEAD KY 40351
52- 45	HAMILTON, THOMAS BALL	D. NOVEMBER 29, 1973 TYLER, TEX.
57- 28	HAMLIN, KENNETH LEE	TALL TIMBERS - CLIMAX MI 49034
33- 22	HAMLIN, LUKE DANIEL	D. FEBRUARY 18,1978 CLARE, MICH.
70- 56	HAMM, PETER WHITFIELD	525 LOCKHART BULCH RD - SANTA CRUZ CA 95060
81- 50	HAMMAKER, CHARLTON ATLEE	RR 5 - LENOIR CITY TN 37771
15- 58	HAMMOND, WALTER CHARLES	D. MARCH 4, 1942 KENOSHA, WIS.
44- 54	HAMNER, GRANVILLE WILBUR	OLD ADD: 1118 AMBLE LN - CLEARWATER FL 33515
46- 42	HAMNER, RALPH CONANT	BOX 236 - BRADLEY AR 71826
45- 41	HAMNER, WESLEY GARVIN	4306 AUGUSTA AVE - RICHMOND VA 23230
74- 45	HAMPTON, ISAAC GEORGE	1604 LEE ST - CAMDEN SC 29020
55- 53	HAMRIC, ODBERT HERMAN	115 W STATE ST - SPRINGBORO OH 45066
43- 57	HAMRICK, RAYMOND BERNARD	3125 SHANE DR-RICHMOND CA 94806
40- 32	HANCKEN, MORRIS MEDLOCK	BOX 288 - HOUSTON TX 77001
49- 31	HANCOCK, FRED JAMES	703 4TH AVE SE - ROCHESTER MN 55901
78- 55	HANCOCK, RONALD GARRY	15806 ASHBURY PL - TAMPA FL 33624
70- 57	HAND, RICHARD ALLEN	RR 2 BOX 2467 #15 - LA GRANDE OR 97850
11- 65	HANDIBOE, ALOYSIUS JAMES	D. JANUARY 31, 1953 SAVANNAH, GA.
46- 43	HANDLEY, EUGENE LOUIS	8933-223F BISCAYNE CT-HUNTINGTON BCH CA 92646
36- 35	HANDLEY, LEE ELMER	D. APRIL 8, 1970 PITTSBURGH, PA.
64- 40	HANDRAHAN, JAMES VERNON	23 SEAVIEW BLVD - CHARLOTTETOWN PRINCE EDW IS
65- 34	HANDS, WILLIAM ALFRED	320 REYNOLDS AVE - PARSIPPANY NJ 07054
53- 31	HANEBRINK, HARRY ALOYSIUS	10400 RENFREW DR - ST LOUIS MO 63137
22- 51	HANEY, FRED GIRARD	D. NOVEMBER 9, 1977 BEVERLY HILLS, CALIF.
66- 41	HANEY, WALLACE LARRY	BOX 97 - BARBOURSVILLE VA 22923
14- 80	HANFORD, CHARLES JOSEPH	D. JULY 19, 1963 TRENTON, N.J.
27- 43	HANKINS, DONALD WAYNE	D. MAY 16, 1963 WINSTON-SALEM, N. C.
61- 42	HANKINS, JAY NELSON	9309 E 84TH TER - RAYTOWN MO 64138
13- 73	HANLEY, JOSEPH PATRICK	D. MAY 1, 1961 ELMHURST, N. Y.
75- 48	HANNA, PRESTON LEE	7602 HARVEY ST - PENSACOLA FL 32506
18- 25	HANNAH, JAMES HARRISON	104 PIGEON LN - FOUNTAIN VALLEY CA 92708
76- 39	HANNAHS, GERALD ELLIS	26 LORNA DR - LITTLE ROCK AR 72205
62- 52	HANNAN, JAMES JOHN	3907 CHERRY HILL DR - ANNANDALE VA 22003
39- 47	HANNING, LOY VERNON	RR 2 BOX 256B - SAINT CLAIR MO 63077
44- 55	HANSEN, ANDREW VIGGO	362 YORKTOWN CIR - ATLANTIS FL 33462
51- 37	HANSEN, DOUGLAS WILLIAM	16796 E ROCKY KNOLL RD - HACIENDA HGTSCA91745
74- 46	HANSEN, ROBERT JOSEPH	19 N KELSEY AVE - EVANSVILLE IN 47711
58- 42	HANSEN, RONALD LAVERN	BOX 247 ALLISTON DR - BALDWIN MD 21013
30- 30	HANSEN, ROY EMIL FREDERICK	D. SEPTEMBER 11, 1978 CHICAGO, ILL.
18- 26	HANSEN, ROY INGLOF	D. FEBRUARY 9, 1977 BELOIT, WIS.
43- 58	HANSKI, DONALD THOMAS	D. SEPTEMBER 2, 1957 WORTH, ILL.
21- 38	HANSON, EARL SYLVESTER	D. AUGUST 19, 1951 CLIFTON, N.J.
13- 74	HANSON, JOSEPH	B. ST. LOUIS, MO.
42- 46	HANYZEWSKI, EDWARD MICHAEL	1941 INGLEWOOD PL - SOUTH BEND IN 46616
23- 58	HAPPENNY, JOHN CLIFFORD	2908 NE CENTER AV - FT LAUDERDALE FL 33308
28- 43	HARDER, MELVIN LEROY	11643 RIO VISTA DR - SUN CITY AZ 85351

```
18- 27  HARDGROVE, WILLIAM PATRICK     OLD ADD: 1546 S WICHITA - WICHITA KS 67213
67- 41  HARDIN, JAMES WARREN           9606 DUNDAWAN RD - BALTIMORE MD 21236
52- 46  HARDIN, WILLIAM EDGAR          8135 ENCINO AVE - NORTHRIDGE CA 91324
13- 75  HARDING, CHARLES HAROLD        D. OCTOBER 30, 1971 BOLD SPRINGS, TENN.
58- 43  HARDY, CARROLL WILLIAM         213 VAQUERO DR - BOULDER CO 80302
51- 38  HARDY, FRANCIS JOSEPH          5620 N 12TH ST - PHOENIX AZ 85014
74- 47  HARDY, HOWARD LAWRENCE         5300 PATRICK HENRY - BELLAIRE TX 77401
65- 35  HARGAN, STEVEN LOWELL          2502 MORANGO TRAIL - PALM SPRINGS CA 92262
80- 47  HARGESHEIMER, ALAN ROBERT      7400 W MYRTLE - CHICAGO IL 60631
79- 46  HARGIS, GARY LYNN              157 GEMINI AVE - LOMPOC CA 93436
13- 76  HARGRAVE, EUGENE FRANKLIN      D. FEBRUARY 23, 1969 CINCINNATI, O.
23- 59  HARGRAVE, WILLIAM MCKINLEY     D. OCTOBER 3, 1942 FT. WAYNE, IND.
23- 60  HARGREAVES, CHARLES RUSSELL    D. MAY 9, 1979 NEPTUNE, N. J.
74- 48  HARGROVE, DUDLEY MICHAEL       20738 PARKWOOD LN - STRONGSVILLE OH 44136
10- 65  HARKNESS, FREDERICK HARVEY     D. MAY 18, 1952 COMPTON, CALIF.
61- 43  HARKNESS, THOMAS WILLIAM       222 PEARSON RD #42 - OSHAWA ONTARIO
75- 49  HARLOW, LARRY DUANE            1002 TOWNSEND AVE - AZTEC NM 87410
41- 43  HARMAN, WILLIAM BELL           9 GUYENNE RD - WILMINGTON DE 19807
54- 41  HARMON, CHARLES BYRON          6035A RIDGEACRE DR - CINCINNATI OH 45237
67- 42  HARMON, TERRY WALTER           OAKWOOD DR - MEDFORD NJ 08055
79- 47  HARPER, BRIAN DAVID            6 SILVERLEAF DR - ROLLING HILLS CA 90274
16- 41  HARPER, GEORGE WASHINGTON      D. AUGUST 18, 1978 MAGNOLIA, ARK.
13- 77  HARPER, HARRY CLAYTON          D. APRIL 23, 1963 LAYTON, N.J.
15- 59  HARPER, JOHN WESLEY            D. JUNE 18, 1927 HALSTEAD, KAN.
80- 48  HARPER, TERRY JOE             1685 DORRIS RD - DOUGLAS GA 30134
62- 53  HARPER, THOMAS                 3 CHRISTOPHER DR - STOUGHTON MA 02072
11- 66  HARPER, WILLIAM HOMER          D. JUNE 17, 1951 SOMERVILLE, TENN.
69- 74  HARRAH, COLBERT DALE           824 CHAPARRAL - BEDFORD TX 76021
69- 75  HARRELL, JOHN ROBERT           2555 LANCASTER CT - SANTA CLARA CA 95051
12- 74  HARRELL, OSCAR MARTIN          D. APRIL 30, 1971 HILLSBORO, TEX.
35- 41  HARRELL, RAYMOND JAMES         JULIA COURT #102 - PINEVILLE LA 71360
55- 54  HARRELL, WILLIAM               128 OAKWOOD AVE - TROY NY 12180
65- 36  HARRELSON, DERRELL MCKINLEY    "BUD" 31 FALCON DR - HAUPPAUGE NY 11787
63- 52  HARRELSON, KENNETH SMITH       WSBK-TV - BOSTON MA 02101
68- 33  HARRELSON, WILLIAM CHARLES     5804 FAIR OAKS DR - BAKERSFIELD CA 93306
13- 78  HARRINGTON, ANDREW FRANCIS     D. NOVEMBER 12, 1938 MALDEN, MASS.
25- 44  HARRINGTON, ANDREW MATTHEW     D. JANUARY 26, 1979 BOISE, IDAHO
63- 53  HARRINGTON, CHARLES MICHAEL    1107 WEST PINE ST - HATTIESBURG MS 39401
53- 32  HARRINGTON, WILLIAM WOMBLE     RR1 - GARNER NC 27529
67- 43  HARRIS, ALONZO                 1254 E 78TH ST - LOS ANGELES CA 90001
25- 46  HARRIS, ANTHONY SPENCER        330 OAK GROVE #3 - MINNEAPOLIS MN 55403
14- 81  HARRIS, BENJAMIN FRANKLIN      D. APRIL 29, 1927 ST. LOUIS, MO.
55- 55  HARRIS, BOYD GAIL              7583 MARGATE CT #004 - MANASSAS VA 22110
41- 44  HARRIS, CHALMER LUMAN          RR 1 BOX 385 - VINCENT AL 35178
48- 45  HARRIS, CHARLES               4730 MAINE ST - LAKE WORTH FL 33460
25- 45  HARRIS, DAVID STANLEY          D. SEPTEMBER 18, 1973 ATLANTA, GA.
81- 51  HARRIS, GREG ALLEN            11248 BARBI LANE - LOS ALAMITOS CA 90720
36- 36  HARRIS, HERBERT                1973 ADD: 5805 N FOREST GLEN - CHICAGO IL
68- 34  HARRIS, JAMES WILLIAM          626 N COLLEGE RD - WILMINGTON NC 28401
79- 48  HARRIS, JOHN THOMAS            3609 LINKWOOD - CLOVIS NM 88101
14- 82  HARRIS, JOSEPH                 D. DECEMBER 10, 1959 RENTON, PA.
40- 33  HARRIS, MAURICE CHARLES        D. APRIL 15, 1971 FARMINGTON, MICH.
38- 35  HARRIS, ROBERT ARTHUR          BOX 492 N PLATTE NE 69101
41- 45  HARRIS, ROBERT NED             D. DECEMBER 18, 1976 WEST PALM BEACH, FLA.
19- 38  HARRIS, STANLEY RAYMOND        D. NOVEMBER 8, 1977 BETHESDA, MD.
72- 45  HARRIS, VICTOR LANIER          6625 GREEN VALLEY CIR - CULVER CITY CA 90230
70- 58  HARRIS, WALTER FRANCIS         3343 W SCHOOL HOUSE LN - PHILADELPHIA PA19144
23- 61  HARRIS, WILLIAM MILTON         D. AUGUST 21, 1965 INDIAN TRAIL, N. C.
57- 29  HARRIS, WILLIAM THOMAS         322 S REED - KENNEWICK WA 99336
65- 37  HARRISON, CHARLES WILLIAM      1958 WILLOW DR - ABILENE TX 79602
55- 56  HARRISON, ROBERT LEE           253 BRIERLEY WAY - INDIANAPOLIS IN 46032
72- 46  HARRISON, RORIC EDWARD         1103 CONCORDA DR - TEMPE AZ 85251
65- 38  HARRISON, THOMAS JAMES         6822 SHERMAN WAY - BELL CA 90203
20- 47  HARRISS, WILLIAM JENNINGS BRYAN D. SEPTEMBER 19, 1963 TEMPLE, TEX.
45- 42  HARRIST, EARL                  BOX 238 - SIMSBORO LA 71275
37- 47  HARSHANEY, SAMUEL              419 THELMA DR SAN ANTONIO TX 78212
48- 46  HARSHMAN, JOHN ELVIN           OLD ADD: 265 S MAIN UNIT - WAREHOUSE PT CT
15- 60  HARSTAD, OSCAR THEANDER        129 ORCHARD - MILTON-FREEWATER OR 97862
80- 49  HART, JAMES MICHAEL            409 LARKSPUR - PORTAGE MI 49081
63- 54  HART, JAMES RAYMOND           %GEARY FORD,4041 GEARY-SAN FRANCISCO CA 94118
43- 59  HART, WILLIAM WOODROW          D. JULY 29, 1968 LYKINS,PA.
65- 39  HARTENSTEIN, CHARLES OSCAR     6815 DEPAUL COVE - AUSTIN TX 78723
12- 75  HARTER, FRANKLIN PIERCE        D. APRIL 14, 1959 BREESE, ILL.
14- 83  HARTFORD, BRUCE DANIEL         D. MAY 25, 1975 LOS ANGELES, CAL.
39- 48  HARTJE, CHRISTIAN HENRY        D. JUNE 26, 1946 SEATTLE, WASH.
11- 67  HARTLEY, GROVER ALLEN          D. OCTOBER 19, 1964 DAYTONA BEACH, FLA.
62- 54  HARTMAN, J. C.                 61 RIESNER ST - HOUSTON TX 77002
```

```
59- 37  HARTMAN, ROBERT LOUIS          2002 35TH ST - KENOSHA WI 53140
22- 52  HARTNETT, CHARLES LEO          D. DECEMBER 20, 1972 PARK RIDGE, ILL.
13- 79  HARTRANFT, RAYMOND CHARLES     D. FEBRUARY 10, 1955 CHESTER CO., PA.
73- 57  HARTS, GREGORY RUDOLPH         OLD ADD: 160 WOODARD AVE SE - ATLANTA GA
50- 32  HARTSFIELD, ROY THOMAS         160 WOODHAVEN WAY - ALPHARETTA GA 30201
47- 41  HARTUNG, CLINTON CLARENCE      BOX 554 - SINTON TX 78387
76- 40  HARTZELL, PAUL FRANKLIN        610 NEWPORT CT- I-8 290-NEWPORT BCH CA 92660
28- 44  HARVEL, LUTHER RAYMOND         7609 MADISON - KANSAS CITY MO LJUUJ
16- 42  HASBROOK, ROBERT LYNDON        D. FEBRUARY 9, 1976 GARLAND, TEX.
45- 43  HASENMAYER, DONALD IRVIN       12 BARBARA ST - HATBORO PA 19040
40- 34  HASH, HERBERT HOWARD           BOSTON VIRGINIA 22713
33- 23  HASLIN, MICHAEL JOSEPH         171 GEORGE AV - PLAINS PA 18705
36- 37  HASSETT, JOHN ALOYSIUS         114 STONY RIDGE DR HILLSDALE NJ 07642
78- 56  HASSEY, RONALD WILLIAM         3849 CALLE ALTAR - TUCSON AZ 85716
71- 43  HASSLER, ANDREW EARL           OLD ADD: BOX 17101 - TUCSON AZ
28- 45  HASSLER, JOSEPH FREDERICK      D. SEPTEMBER 4, 1971 DUNCAN, OKLA.
37- 48  HASSON, CHARLES EUGENE         830 E KINGSLEY AVE #63 - POMONA CA 91767
19- 39  HASTY, ROBERT KELLER           D. MAY 28, 1972 DALLAS, GA.
79- 49  HATCHER, MICHAEL VAUGHN        1941 EAST DANA AVE - MESA AZ 85204
50- 33  HATFIELD, FRED JAMES           BOX 348 7611 DAVIS HWY - RICHMOND VA 23234
45- 44  HATHAWAY, RAY WILSON           25 LEISURE MOUNT RD - ASHEVILLE NC 28804
46- 44  HATTEN, JOSEPH HILARIAN        RR 2 BOX 678 - SHINGLETOWN CA 96088
35- 42  HATTER, CLYDE MELNO            D. OCTOBER 16, 1937 YOSEMITE, KY.
46- 45  HATTON, GRADY EDGEBERT         BOX 97 - WARREN TX 77664
12- 76  HAUGER, JOHN ARTHUR            D. AUGUST 2, 1944 REDWOOD CITY, CALIF.
43- 60  HAUGHEY, CHRISTOPHER FRANCIS   45-12 215TH PL - BAYSIDE NY 11361
47- 42  HAUGSTAD, PHILIP DONALD        RR 4 BOX 180 - BLACK RIVER FALLS WI 54615
10- 66  HAUSER, ARNOLD GEORGE          D. MAY 22, 1956 AURORA, ILL.
22- 53  HAUSER, JOSEPH JOHN            914 N 8TH ST - SHEBOYGAN WI 53081
```

```
75- 50  HAUSMAN, THOMAS MATTHEW        3165 WESTFIELD CIR - LAS VEGAS NV 89121
44- 56  HAUSMANN, CLEMENS RAYMOND      D. AUGUST 29, 1972 BAYTOWN, TEX.
44- 57  HAUSMANN, GEORGE JOHN          OLD ADD: 6430 DEW DR - SAN ANTONIO TX 78239
81- 52  HAVENS, BRADLEY DAVID          1526 E WOODLAWN - ROYAL OAK MI 48073
51- 39  HAWES, ROY LEE                 BOX 912 - RINGGOLD GA 30736
11- 68  HAWK, EDWARD                   D. MARCH 26, 1936 NEOSHO, MO.
60- 46  HAWKINS, WYNN FIRTH            5326 COTTAGE LN - CORTLAND OH 44410
21- 39  HAWKS, NELSON LOUIS            D. MAY 26, 1973 SAN RAFAEL, CAL.
15- 61  HAWORTH, HOMER HOWARD          D. JANUARY 28, 1953 TROUTDALE, ORE.
70- 59  HAYDEL, JOHN HAROLD            304 LYNWOOD DR - HOUMA LA 70360
58- 44  HAYDEN, EUGENE FRANKLIN        1597 ALAMO DR #188 - VACAVILLE CA 95688
33- 24  HAYES, FRANKLIN WITMAN         D. JUNE 22, 1955 POINT PLEASANT, N. J.
35- 43  HAYES, JAMES MILLARD           OLD ADD: CLANTON ALA 35045
27- 44  HAYES, WINTER CARNEY           BOX 613 - CLANTON ALA 35045
81- 53  HAYES, VON FRANCIS             129 WHITBURN CT - STOCKTON CA 95210
80- 50  HAYES, WILLIAM ERNEST          8 SOUTH ASH ST - NORTH PLATTE NE 69101
39- 49  HAYNES, JOSEPH WALTER          D. JANUARY 6, 1967 HOPKINS, MINN.
68- 35  HAYWOOD, WILLIAM KIERNAN       BOX 1213 - CULLOWHEE NC 28723
44- 58  HAYWORTH, MYRON CLAUDE         507 OAK VIEW RD - HIGH POINT NC 27260
26- 35  HAYWORTH, RAYMOND HALL         RR 1 BOX 160 - HIGH POINT NC 27260
80- 51  HAZEWOOD, DRUNGO LARUE         5130 DEL NORTE BLVD - SACRAMENTO CA 95820
55- 57  HAZLE, ROBERT SIDNEY           164 DORSET DR - COLUMBIA SC 29210
40- 35  HEAD, EDWARD MARVIN            D. JANUARY 31, 1980 BASTROP, LA.
23- 62  HEAD, RALPH                    D. OCTOBER 8, 1962 MUSCADINE, ALA.
30- 31  HEALEY, FRANCIS XAVIER PAUL    13 SCHOOL ST - HOLYOKE MA 01040
69- 76  HEALY, FRANCIS XAVIER          1 PRIMROSE LN - HOLYOKE MA 01040
15- 62  HEALY, THOMAS FITZGERALD       D. JANUARY 15, 1974 CLEVELAND, O.
54- 41  HEARD, JEHOSIE                 OLD ADD: 1348 RICHMOND AVE - MEMPHIS TN 38106
10- 67  HEARN, BUNN                    D. OCTOBER 11, 1959 WILSON, N.C.
10- 68  HEARN, EDMUND                  D. SEPTEMBER 8, 1952 SANTELLE, CALIF.
26- 36  HEARN, ELMER LAFAYETTE         D. MARCH 31, 1974 VENICE, FLA.
47- 43  HEARN, JAMES TOLBERT           1678 BEVERLY WOOD CT - CHAMBLEE GA 30341
36- 38  HEATH, JOHN GEOFFREY           D. DECEMBER 9, 1975 SEATTLE, WASH.
78- 57  HEATH, MICHAEL THOMAS          2203 EAST IDLEWILD - TAMPA FL 33610
31- 35  HEATH, MINOR WILSON            2650 HARLA AVE #C-113 - COSTA MESA CA 92627
20- 48  HEATH, SPENCER PAUL            D. JANUARY 25, 1930 CHICAGO, ILL.
35- 44  HEATH, THOMAS GEORGE           D. FEBRUARY 26, 1967 LOS GATOS, CAL.
65- 40  HEATH, WILLIAM CHRIS           %R.HEATH,106 BRYANT CT - EXETER CA 93221
```

```
18- 28  HEATHCOTE, CLIFTON EARL        D. JANUARY 19, 1939 YORK, PA.
75- 51  HEAVERLC, DAVID WALLACE        8436 NE 21ST PL - BELLEVUE WA 98004
31- 36  HEBERT, WALLACE ANDREW         3408 WESTWOOD RD - WEST LAKE LA 70665
68- 36  HEBNER, RICHARD JOSEPH         510 NATHAN ST - NORWOOD MA 02062
12- 77  HECHINGER, MICHAEL VINCENT     D. AUGUST 13, 1967 CHICAGO, ILL.
13- 80  HEDGEPETH, HARRY MALCOLM       D. JULY 30, 1966 RICHMOND, VA.
65- 41  HEDLUND, MICHAEL DAVID         714 CARSWELL TER - ARLINGTON TX 76010
79- 50  HEEP, DANIEL WILLIAM           327 TEAKWOOD LN - SAN ANTONIO TX 78216
34- 43  HEFFNER, DONALD HENRY          816 SOUTHVIEW - ARCADIA CA 91006
63- 55  HEFFNER, ROBERT FREDERIC       1817 LIBERTY - ALLENTOWN PA 18104
45- 45  HEFLIN, RANDOLPH RUTHERFORD    509 HANSON AVE - FREDERICKSBURG VA 22401
41- 46  HEGAN, JAMES EDWARD            10 BAY VIEW AVE-SWAMPSCOTT MA 01907
64- 41  HEGAN, JAMES MICHAEL           9648 OLD BARN RD - MEQUON WI 53092
18- 29  HEHL, HERMAN JACOB             D. JULY 4, 1961 BROOKLYN, N. Y.
69- 77  HEIDEMANN, JACK SEALE          1303 CHAPPELL HILL - BRENHAM TX 77833
14- 84  HEILMANN, HARRY EDWIN          D. JULY 9, 1951 DETROIT, MICH.
42- 47  HEIM, VAL RAYMOND              1050 LOUDON - SUPERIOR NE 68978
20- 49  HEIMACH, FRED AMOS             D. JUNE 1, 1973 FORT MYERS, FLA.
21- 40  HEINE, WILLIAM HENRY           D. SEPTEMBER 2, 1976 FORT LAUDERDALE, FLA.
37- 49  HEINTZELMAN, KENNETH ALPHONSE  406 S CHURCH - ST PETERS MO 63376
73- 58  HEINTZELMAN, THOMAS KENNETH    406 S CHURCH - ST PETERS MO 63376
34- 44  HEISE, CLARENCE EDWARD         5 W NIGHTINGALE ST - APOPKA FL 32703
57- 30  HEISE, JAMES EDWARD            4021 HARGILL DR - ORLANDO FL 32806
67- 44  HEISE, ROBERT LOWELL           160 QUIETWOOD DR - VACAVILLE CA 95688
61- 44  HEISER, LEROY BARTON           1038 GROVE HILL RD - BALTIMORE MD 21227·
60- 47  HEIST, ALFRED MICHAEL          900 W FOX #15 - TAHLEQUAH OK 74464
18- 30  HEITMANN, HENRY ANTON          D. DECEMBER 15, 1958 BROOKLYN, N. Y.
56- 40  HELD, MELVIN NICHOLAS          BOX 204 - EDON OH 43518
54- 42  HELD, WOODSON GEORGE           BIG DIAMOND RANCH - DUBOIS WY 82513
38- 36  HELF, HENRY HARTZ              719 POSTOAK ST AUSTIN TX 78704
15- 63  HELFRICH, EMORY WILBUR         D. MARCH 18, 1955 PLEASANTVILLE, N.J.
64- 42  HELMS, TOMMY VAN               7116 WHITESIDE LN - CHARLOTTE NC 28214
43- 61  HELTZEL, WILLIAM WADE          RR 2-YORK PA 17403
61- 45  HEMAN, RUSSELL FREDRICK        1410 N MARLES DR - SANTA ANA CA 92706
14- 85  HEMINGWAY, EDSON MARSHALL      D. JULY 5, 1969 EAST GRAND RAPIDS, MICH
28- 46  HEMSLEY, RALSTON BURDETT       D. JULY 31, 1972 WASHINGTON, D. C.
49- 32  HEMUS, SOLOMON JOSEPH          4506 BRIARBEND DR - HOUSTON TX 77035
30- 32  HENDERSON WILLIAM MAXWELL      D. OCTOBER 6, 1966 PENSACOLA, FLA.
21- 41  HENDERSON, BERNARD            D. JUNE 4, 1966 LINDEN, TEXAS
81- 54  HENDERSON, DAVID LEE           41690 W VALERIA - DOS PALOS CA 93620
14- 86  HENDERSON, EDWARD J.           D. JANUARY 15, 1964 NEW YORK, N. Y.
74- 49  HENDERSON, JOSEPH LEE          OLD ADD: 125 INQUERO LN #38 - EL PASO TX
65- 42  HENDERSON, KENNETH JOSEPH      13225 VIA BLANC CT - SARATOGA CA 95070
79- 51  HENDERSON, RICKEY HENLEY       7237 SKYLINE - OAKLAND CA 94611
77- 64  HENDERSON, STEPHEN CURTIS      OLD ADD: 4701 JOSEPH CT #248 - TAMPA FL 33614
61- 46  HENDLEY, CHARLES ROBERT        645 WIMBISH - MACON GA 31204
71- 46  HENDRICK, GEORGE ANDREW        8917 8TH AVE - INGLEWOOD CA 90305
23- 63  HENDRICK, HARVEY LEE           D. OCTOBER 29, 1941 COVINGTON, TENN.
10- 69  HENDRICKS, EDWARD              D. NOVEMBER 28, 1930 JACKSON, MICH.
68- 37  HENDRICKS, ELROD FEROME        3709 BROWNBROOK CT - BALTIMORE MD 21133
45- 46  HENDRICKSON, DONALD WILLIAMSON D. JANUARY 19, 1977 NORFOLK, VA.
11- 69  HENDRIX, CLAUDE RAYMOND        D. MARCH 22, 1944 ALLENTOWN, PA.
11- 70  HENDRYX, TIMOTHY GREEN         D. AUGUST 14, 1957 CORPUS CHRISTI, TEX.
19- 40  HENION, LAFAYETTE M.           D. JULY 22, 1955 SAN LUIS OBISPO, CALIF.
54- 43  HENLEY, GAIL CURTICE           10150 DAINES DR - TEMPLE CITY CA 91780
21- 42  HENLINE, WALTER JOHN           D. OCTOBER 9, 1957 SARASOTA, FLA.
37- 50  HENNESSEY, GEORGE              POSSUM RD SKILLMAN NJ 08558
13- 81  HENNESSY, LESTER BAKER         D. NOVEMBER 20, 1976 NEW YORK, N. Y.
69- 78  HENNIGAN, PHILIP WINSTON       RR 1 BOX 178-D - JASPER TX 75951
14- 87  HENNING, ERNEST HERMAN         D. NOVEMBER 9, 1939 DYER, IND.
73- 59  HENNINGER, RICHARD LEE         BOX 271 RR1 - HASTINGS NE 68901
24- 50  HENRICH, FRANK WILDE           D. MAY 1, 1959 PHILADELPHIA, PA.
57- 31  HENRICH, ROBERT EDWARD         1531 VIA LOS COYOTES - LAHABRA CA 90631
37- 51  HENRICH, THOMAS DAVID          150 CEMETERY W - YELLOW SPRINGS OH 45387
11- 71  HENRIKSEN, OLAF                D. OCTOBER 17, 1962 CANTON, MASS.
44- 59  HENRY, EARL CLIFFORD           BOX 43 - WHITE COTTAGE OH 43791
21- 43  HENRY, FRANK JOHN              D. AUGUST 23, 1968 EAST CLEVELAND, O.
22- 54  HENRY, FREDERICK MARSHALL      BOX 333 WENDELL NC 27591
36- 39  HENRY, JAMES FRANCIS           D. AUGUST 15, 1976 MEMPHIS, TENN.
10- 70  HENRY, JOHN PARK               D. NOVEMBER 24, 1941 FORT HUACHUCA, ARIZ.
61- 47  HENRY, RONALD BAXTER           316 TOWNSEND ST - CHESTER PA 19013
```

```
66- 42  HENRY, WILLIAM FRANCIS         725 HUTCHINSON - FLOSSMOR IL 60422
52- 47  HENRY, WILLIAM RODMAN          302 CHRISTINE - HOUSTON TX 77017
33- 25  HENSHAW, ROY K                 4221 GARDEN AV - WESTERN SPRINGS IL 60558
35- 45  HENSIEK, PHILIP FRANK          D. FEBRUARY 21, 1972 ST. LOUIS, MO.
66- 43  HEPLER, WILLIAM LEWIS          OLD ADD: 217 E GORDON ST - COVINGTON VA
63- 56  HERBEL, RONALD SAMUEL          116 CRESTWOOD DR - TACOMA WA 98498
13- 82  HERBERT, ERNIE ALBERT          D. JANUARY 13, 1968 DALLAS, TEX.
15- 64  HERBERT, FREDERICK             D. MAY 29, 1963 TICE, FLA.
50- 34  HERBERT, RAYMOND ERNEST        13995 MELVIN ST - LIVONIA MI 48154
26- 37  HERMAN, FLOYD CAVES            1622 HIGHLAND AVE - GLENDALE CA 91202
31- 37  HERMAN, WILLIAM JENNINGS       3111 GARDEN E #33-PALM BEACH GARDENS FL 33410
23- 64  HERMANN, ALBERT BARTEL         D. AUGUST 21, 1980 LEWES, DEL.
43- 62  HERMANSKI, EUGENE VICTOR       25 WASHINGTON AVE - NORTH PLAINFIELD NJ 07060
67- 45  HERMOSO, ANGEL REMIGIO         CALLE BOUKTON #7 - CARABOBO VEN
74- 50  HERNAIZ, JESUS RAFAEL          24 ST BLOCK 76 #47 VILLA - CAROLINA PR 00630
71- 45  HERNANDEZ, ENZO OCTAVIO        VEREDA N 5E-4,GUANTRA-PUERTA LACRUZ ANZ, VENE
56- 41  HERNANDEZ, GREGORIO EVELIO     3004 SW 113TH AVE - MIAMI FL 33165
77- 65  HERNANDEZ, GUILLERMO           BO ESPINA CALLE C BOX 125 - AGUADA PR 00602
65- 43  HERNANDEZ, JACINTO             1391 NW 95TH ST - MIAMI FL 33147
74- 51  HERNANDEZ, KEITH               BOX 137 - CHESTERFIELD MO 63017
```

```
79- 52  HERNANDEZ, PEDRO JULIO         EUGENE A. MIRARDO #35- LA ROMANO DOM REP
67- 46  HERNANDEZ, RAMON GONZALEZ      REPARTO. ROSAMARIA CLE 5F-19-CAROLINA PR00630
72- 47  HERNANDEZ, RODOLFO             LOTA 9 NANZAMA 38 COLMIA ORIENTE-EMPALME MEX
60- 48  HERNANDEZ, RUDOLPH ALBERT      8 CALLE RODRIGUEZ SERRA - CONDADO PR 00907
42- 48  HERNANDEZ, SALVADOR RAMOS      1944 ADD: COCHA Y VELAZQUEZ-LUYANO, HAVANA
74- 52  HERNDON, LARRY DARNELL         3550 CARTER DR #8-SOUTH SAN FRANCISCO CA94080
79- 53  HERR, THOMAS MITCHELL          2058 MILLER ROAD - EAST PETERSBURG PA 17520
11- 72  HERRELL, WALTER W              B. WASHINGTON, D.C.
67- 47  HERRERA, JOSE CONCEPCION       MARAVEN ADRI 12.CEN.COM.LAGUNILLAS-E.ZULIA VZ
58- 45  HERRERA, JUAN FRANCISCO        2930 NW 21ST AVE - MIAMI FL 33142
51- 40  HERRERA, PROCOPIO RODRIGUEZ    APDO POSTAL 257, CD. SATELITE, EDO. DE MEXICO
25- 47  HERRERA, RAMON                 D. FEBRUARY 3, 1978 HAVANA, CUBA
56- 42  HERRIAGE, WILLIAM TROY         1340 PONTIAC ST - OAKDALE CA 95361
54- 44  HERRIN, THOMAS EDWARD          BOX 550 - SAN JOSE CA 95125
29- 48  HERRING, ARTHUR L              1307 W 54TH ST - MARION IN 46952
12- 78  HERRING, HERBERT LEE           D. APRIL 22, 1964 TUCSON, ARIZ.
15- 65  HERRING, WILLIAM FRANCIS       D. SEPTEMBER 10, 1962 HONESDALE, PA.
67- 48  HERRMANN, EDWARD MARTIN        13431 ST ANDREWS PL - POWAY CA 92064
32- 36  HERRMANN, LEROY GEORGE         D. JULY 3, 1972 LIVERMORE, CAL.
18- 31  HERRMANN, MARTIN JOHN          D. SEPTEMBER 11, 1956 CINCINNATI, O.
62- 55  HERRNSTEIN, JOHN ELLETT        603 SEMINOLE RD - CHILLICOTHE OG 45602
62- 56  HERRSCHER, RICHARD FRANKLIN    4024 DRUID - DALLAS TX 75205
56- 43  HERSH, EARL WALTER             3201 MURKLE RD - WESTMINSTER MD 21157
61- 48  HERSHBERGER, NORMAN MICHAEL    4130 MEADOWVIEW DR - CANTON OH 44709
38- 37  HERSHBERGER, WILLARD MCKEE     D. AUGUST 3, 1940 BOSTON, MASS.
52- 48  HERTWECK, NEAL CHARLES         3030 ST CLAIRE RD - WINSTON-SALEM NC 27106
64- 43  HERTZ, STEVE ALLAN             10211 SW 96TH TER - MIAMI FL 33156
56- 44  HERZOG, DORREL HORMAN ELVERT   9939 CODDINGTON WAY - ST LOUIS MO 63132
16- 43  HESSELBACHER, GEORGE EDWARD    D. FEBRUARY 18, 1980 RYDAL, PA.
45- 47  HETKI, JOHN EDWARD             4004 STARY DR - PARMA OH 44134
35- 46  HEUSSER, EDWARD BURLETON       D. MARCH 1, 1956 AURORA, COLO.
20- 50  HEVING, JOHN ALOYSIUS          D. DECEMBER 24, 1968 SALISBURY, N. C.
30- 33  HEVING, JOSEPH WILLIAM         D. APRIL 11, 1970 COVINGTON, KY.
73- 60  HEYDEMAN, GREGORY GEORGE       61 VIA PARAISO - MONTEREY CA 93940
64- 44  HIATT, JACK E                  26825 W PICO CANYON RD - NEWHALL CA 91321
67- 49  HIBBS, JAMES KERR              2821 S MAIN ST - VENTURA CA 93003
42- 49  HICKEY, JAMES ROBERT           163 CHESTER ST-E HARTFORD CT 06108
81- 55  HICKEY, KEVIN JOHN             2732 W 36TH ST - CHICAGO IL 60632
15- 66  HICKMAN, DAVID JAMES           D. DECEMBER 30, 1958 BROOKLYN, N. Y.
62- 57  HICKMAN, JAMES LUCIUS          BOX  355 - HENNING TN 38041
65- 44  HICKMAN, JESSE OWENS           114 MYRTLEWOOD DR - PINEVILLE LA 71360
56- 45  HICKS, CLARENCE WALTER         7600 COOLGROVE DR - DOWNEY CA 90240
64- 45  HICKS, JAMES EDWARD            3717 EUCLID AVE - EAST CHICAGO IN 46312
59- 38  HICKS, WILLIAM JOSEPH          2707 BROOKMERE RD - CHARLOTTESVILLE VA 22901
37- 52  HIGBE, WALTER KIRBY            BOX 4814 - COLUMBIA SC 29240
22- 55  HIGBEE, MAHLON JESSE           D. APRIL 7, 1968 DEPAUW, IND.
49- 33  HIGDON, WILLIAM TRAVIS         1428 SHADES CREST RD - BIRMINGHAM AL 35226
66- 44  HIGGINS, DENNIS DEAN           2204 ANDERSON DR - JEFFERSON CITY MO 65101
30- 34  HIGGINS, MICHAEL FRANKLIN      D. MARCH 21, 1969 DALLAS, TEX.
22- 56  HIGH, ANDREW AIRD              D. FEBRUARY 22, 1981 TOLEDO, O.
19- 41  HIGH, CHARLES EDWIN            D. SEPTEMBER 11, 1960 PORTLAND, ORE.
13- 83  HIGH, HUGH JENKEN              D. NOVEMBER 16, 1962 ST. LOUIS CO., MO.
```

31- 38	HILCHER, WALTER FRANK	D. NOVEMBER 21, 1962 MINNEAPOLIS, MINN.
31- 39	HILDEBRAND, ORAL CLYDE	D. SEPTEMBER 8, 1977 SOUTHPORT, IND.
13- 84	HILDEBRAND, PALMER MARION	D. JANUARY 25, 1960 NORTH CANTON, O.
69- 79	HILGENDRF, THOMAS EUGENE	% MCAULEY, RR 1 - DEARBORN MO 64439
15- 67	HILL, CARMEN PROCTOR	2913 BROADWAY - INDIANAPOLIS IN 46205
17- 33	HILL, CLIFFORD JOSEPH	D. AUGUST 11, 1938 EL PASO, TEX.
57- 32	HILL, DAVID BURNHAM	2677 GROSSE POINT RD - EVANSTON IL 60201
69- 80	HILL, GARRY ALTON	401 PATRICIA AVE.- HARRISBURG NC 28075
15- 68	HILL, HERBERT LEE	D. SEPTEMBER 2, 1970 FARMERS BRANCH, TEX.
69- 81	HILL, HERMAN ALEXANDER	D. DECEMBER 14, 1970 MAGALLANES, VEN.
35- 47	HILL, JESSE TERRILL	1616 FAIROAKS AVE #11-SOUTH PASADENA CA 91030
39- 50	HILL, JOHN CLINTON	D. SEPTEMBER 20, 1970 DECATUR, GA.
73- 61	HILL, MARC KEVIN	707 ELLIS ST - ELSBERRY MO 63343
61- 49	HILLER, CHARLES JOSEPH	6435 28TH AVE N - ST PETERSBURG FL 33710
46- 46	HILLER, FRANK WALTER	848 FARRAGUT RD - BERWYN PA 19312
20- 51	HILLER, HARVEY MAX	D. DECEMBER 27, 1956 LEHIGHTON, PA.
65- 45	HILLER, JOHN FREDERICK	102 W ARROWHEAD RD - DULUTH MN 55803
24- 51	HILLIS, MALCOLM DAVID	D. JUNE 16, 1961 CAMBRIDGE, MASS.
55- 58	HILLMAN, DARIUS DUTTON	849 MIMOSA DR - KINGSPORT TN 37660
14- 88	HILLY, WILLIAM EDWARD	D. JULY 25, 1953 EUREKA, MO.
72- 48	HILTON, JOHN DAVID	5205 CAMDEN LANE - PEARLAND TX 77581
61- 50	HIMSL, AVITUS BERNARD	1060 W ADDISON ST - CHICAGO IL 60613
77- 66	HINDS, SAMUEL RUSSELL	3290 W ASHLAN #156 - FRESNO CA 93705
34- 45	HINKLE, DANIEL GORDON	D. MARCH 19, 1972 HOUSTON, TEX.
51- 41	HINRICHS, PAUL EDWIN	1100 E CLAYTON RD - BALLWIN MO 63011
10- 71	HINRICHS, WILLIAM LOUIS	D. AUGUST 18, 1972 SELMA, CALIF.
64- 46	HINSLEY, JERRY DEAN	RR 1 BOX 1048 - LAS CRUCES NM 88001
28- 47	HINSON, JAMES PAUL	D. SEPTEMBER 23, 1960 MUSKOGEE, OKLA.
61- 51	HINTON, CHARLES EDWARD	6330 16TH ST NW - WASHINGTON DC 20011
71- 46	HINTON, RICHARD MICHAEL	730 AGAVE PL - TUCSON AZ 85718
66- 45	HIPPAUF, HERBERT AUGUST	1791 KIMBERLY DR - SUNNYVALE CA 94087
71- 47	HISER, GENE TAYLOR	1107 LITCHFIELD RD - BALTIMORE MD 21239
68- 38	HISLE, LARTY EUGENE	1111 11TH ST - PORTSMOUTH OH 45662
51- 42	HISNER, HARLEY PARNELL	RR 2 BOX 253A - MONROEVILLE IN 46773
38- 38	HITCHCOCK, JAMES FRANKLIN	D. JUNE 23, 1959 MONTGOMERY, ALA.
42- 50	HITCHCOCK, WILLIAM CLYDE	1117 W COLLINWOOD CIR-OPELIKA AL 36801
17- 34	HITT, BRUCE SMITH	D. NOVEMBER 10, 1973 PORTLAND, ORE.
49- 34	HITTLE, LLOYD ELDON	2031 WEST ELM ST - LODI CA 95240
31- 40	HOAG, MYRIL OLIVER	D. JULY 28, 1971 HIGH SPRINGS, FLA.

54- 45	HOAK, DONALD ALBERT	D. OCTOBER 9, 1969 PITTSBURGH, PA.
61- 52	HOBAUGH, EDWARD RUSSELL	527 5TH AVE - FORD CITY PA 16226
57- 33	HOBBIE, GLEN FREDERICK	RR 2, NORTHWOOD HEIGHTS - HILLSBORO IL 62049
81- 56	HOBBS, JOHN DOUGLAS	3 WADE DR - CHERRY HILL NJ 08034
13- 85	HOBBS, WILLIAM LEE	D. JANUARY 5, 1945 HAMILTON, O.
75- 52	HOBSON, CLELL LAVERN	1422 CLARENDON AVE - BESSEMER AL 35020
20- 52	HOCK, EDWARD FRANCIS	D. NOVEMBER 21, 1963 PORTSMOUTH, O.
75- 53	HOCKENBERY, CHARLES MARION	1112 PIERCE ST - ONALASKA WI 54650
38- 39	HOCKETT, ORIS LEON	D. MARCH 23, 1969 HAWTHORNE, CAL.
34- 46	HOCKETTE, GEORGE EDWARD	D. JANUARY 20, 1974 PLANTATION, FLA.
25- 48	HODAPP, URBAN JOHN	D. JUNE 14, 1980 CINCINNATI, O.
51- 43	HODERLEIN, MELVIN ANTHONY	535 CINTI BATAVIA PIKE - CINCINNATI OH 45244
20- 53	HODGE, CLARENCE CLEMET	D. DECEMBER 31, 1967 FORT WALTON BEACH, FLA.
42- 51	HODGE, EDWARD BURTON	RR 19-KNOXVILLE TN 37920
71- 48	HODGE, HAROLD MORRIS	RR 5 BOX 206 - RUTHERFORDTON NC 28139
43- 63	HODGES, GILBERT RAYMOND	D. APRIL 2, 1972 WEST PALM BEACH, FLA.
73- 62	HODGES, RONALD WRAY	239 LAW ST - ROCKY MOUNT VA 24151
39- 51	HODGIN, ELMER RALPH	3203 FARMINGTON DR GREENSBORO NC 27407
80- 52	HODGSON, PAUL JOSEPH DENIS	5 MCGLOIN ST - FREDERICTON NEW BRUNSWICK
46- 47	HOOKEY, ALOYSIUS JOSEPH	5163 BROADWAY - LORAIN OH 44052
52- 49	HOEFT, WILLIAM FREDERICK	36427 SHERWOOD - LIVONIA MI 48154
63- 57	HOERNER, JOSEPH WALTER	6344 TIDEWATER DR - FLORISSANT MO 63033
40- 36	HOERST, FRANK JOSEPH	OLD ADD: 124 BONCOWER RD - CHELTENHAM PA
11- 73	HOFF, CHESTER CORNELIUS	133 LAURIE DR - ORMOND BEACH FL 32074
44- 60	HOFFERTH, STEWART EDWARD	BOX 283 - KOUTS IN 46347
29- 49	HOFFMAN, CLARENCE CASPER	D. DECEMBER 6, 1962 BELLEVILLE, ILL.
15- 69	HOFFMAN, EDWARD ADOLPH	D. MAY 19, 1947 NEW ORLEANS, LA.
80- 53	HOFFMAN, GLENN EDWARD	217 N DALE ST - ANAHEIM CA 92801
79- 54	HOFFMAN, GUY ALAN	1111 WALNUT - OTTAWA IL 61350
64- 47	HOFFMAN, JOHN EDWARD	17316 SE 133RD ST - RENTON WA 98055
42- 52	HOFFMAN, RAYMOND LAMONT	18553 SHADYSIDE-LIVONIA MI 48152
39- 52	HOFFMAN, WILLIAM JOSEPH	3234 N 25TH ST-PHILADELPHIA PA 19129
49- 35	HOFMAN, ROBERT GEORGE	1332 N CUMBERLAND DR - ST LOUIS MO 63137
19- 42	HOFMANN, FRED	D. NOVEMBER 19, 1964 ST. HELENA, CAL.

14- 89	HOGAN, GEORGE A.	D. FEBRUARY 28, 1922 BARTLESVILLE, OKLA.
25- 49	HOGAN, JAMES FRANCIS	D. APRIL 7, 1967 BOSTON, MASS.
21- 44	HOGAN, KENNETH SYLVESTER	D. JANUARY 2, 1980 CLEVELAND, O.
11- 74	HOGAN, WILLIAM HENRY	D. SEPTEMBER 28, 1974 SAN JOSE, CALIF.
11- 75	HOGG, CARTER BRADLEY	D. APRIL 2, 1935 BUENA VISTA, GA.
34- 47	HOGG, WILBERT GEORGE	22914 BEACONSFIELD - EAST DETROIT MI 48021
29- 50	HOGSETT, ELON CHESTER	115 W 16TH ST - HAYS KS 67601
52- 50	HOGUE, CALVIN GREY	1512 E SCHANTZ - DAYTON OH 45419
48- 47	HOGUE, ROBERT CLINTON	BOX 2501 - KEY WEST FL 33040
27- 45	HOHMAN, WILLIAM HENRY	D. OCTOBER 29, 1968 BALTIMORE, MD.
10- 72	HOHNHURST, EDWARD HENRY	D. MARCH 26, 1916 COVINGTON, KY.
44- 61	HOLBROOK, WALTER ALBERT	OLD ADD: 15-28 147TH ST - WHITESTONE NY 11357
35- 48	HOLBROOK, JAMES MARBURY	1215 21ST AVE - MERIDIAN MS 39301
45- 48	HOLCOMBE, KENNETH EDWARD	32 BOTANY DR - ASHEVILLE NC 28803
34- 48	HOLDEN, JOSEPH FRANCIS	424 S 2ND ST - ST CLAIR PA 17970
13- 86	HOLDEN, WILLIAM PAUL	D. SEPTEMBER 14, 1971 PENSACOLA, FLA.
72- 49	HOLDSWORTH, FREDRICK WILLIAM	47300 W MAIN ST - NORTHVILLE MI 48167
14- 90	HOLKE, WALTER HENRY	D. OCTOBER 12, 1954 ST LOUIS, MO.
20- 54	HOLLAHAN, WILLIAM JAMES	D. NOVEMBER 27, 1965 NEW YORK, NEW YORK
77- 67	HOLLAND, ALFRED WILLIS	BOX 417 - LOWELL NC 28098
26- 38	HOLLAND, HOWARD ARTHUR	D. FEBRUARY 16, 1969 WESTCHESTER, VA.
32- 37	HOLLAND, ROBERT CLYDE	D. JUNE 16, 1967 LUMBERTON, N.C.
39- 53	HOLLAND, WILLIAM DAVID	SMITH HARDWARE - GOLDSBORO NC 27530
79- 55	HOLLE, GARY CHARLES	820 FIFTH AVE - WATERVLIET NY 12189
28- 48	HOLLEY, EDWARD EDGAR	SUPERIOR CARE HOME,3100 CLAY-PADUCAH KY 42001
21- 45	HOLLING, CARL	D. JULY 28, 1962 SONOMA, CAL.
35- 49	HOLLINGSWORTH, ALBERT WAYNE	8901 BISSONNET #69 - HOUSTON TX 77074
22- 57	HOLLINGSWORTH, JOHN BURNETT	RR 2 - STRAWBERRY PLAINS TN 37871
49- 36	HOLLMIG, STANLEY ERNEST	D. DECEMBER 4, 1981 SAN ANTONIO, TEXAS
18- 32	HOLLOCHER, CHARLES JACOB	D. AUGUST 14, 1940 STRATMAN, MO.
53- 33	HOLLOMAN, ALVA LEE	650 RIVERMONT RD - ATHENS GA 30601
29- 51	HOLLOWAY, JAMES MADISON	RR 1 BOX 308 - MARINGOVIN LA 70757
22- 58	HOLLOWAY, KENNETH EUGENE	D. SEPTEMBER 25, 1968 THOMASVILLE, GA.
77- 68	HOLLY, JEFFREY OWEN	15228 CORDARY AVE - LAWNDALE CA 90260
24- 52	HOLM, ROSCOE ALBERT	D. MAY 19, 1950 EVERLY, IA.
43- 64	HOLM, WILLIAM FRED	D. JULY 27, 1977 EAST CHICAGO, IND.
68- 39	HOLMAN, GARY RICHARD	800 E DATE - BREA CA 92621
80- 54	HOLMAN, RANDY SCOTT	5662 SHOSHONE - SIMI VALLEY CA 93065
18- 33	HOLMES, ELWOOD MARTER	D. APRIL 15, 1954 CAMDEN, N. J.
42- 53	HOLMES, THOMAS FRANCIS	1 PINE DR-WOODBURY NJ 11797
30- 35	HOLSHAUSER, HERMAN ALEXANDER	90 WINECOFF AVE NE - CONCORD NC 28025
25- 50	HOLT, JAMES EMMETT MADISON	D. FEBRUARY 2, 1961 BIRMINGHAM, ALA.
68- 40	HOLT, JAMES WILLIAM	RR 3 BOX 335 - GRAHAM NC 27253
80- 55	HOLT, ROGER BOYD	625 OAK TERRACE DR - LEESBURG FL 32748
65- 46	HOLTGRAVE, LAVERN GEORGE	389 N 8TH ST - BREESE IL 62230
65- 47	HOLTZMANN, KENNETH DALE	44 FOX TRAIL - LINCOLNSHIRE IL 60015
77- 69	HONEYCUTT, FREDERICK WAYNE	207 FORREST RD - FORT OGLETHORPE GA 30742
25- 51	HOOD, ALBIE LARRISON	1126 HAZEL AVE - CHESAPEAKE VA 23324
73- 63	HOOD, DONALD HARRIS	708 FIRESTONE DR - FLORENCE SC 29501
49- 37	HOOD, WALLACE JAMES JR.	966 EILINITA AVE - GLENDALE CA 91208
20- 55	HOOD, WALLACE JAMES SR.	D. MAY 2, 1965 HOLLYWOOD, CAL.
57- 34	HOOK, JAMES WESLEY	768 SUFFIELD - BIRMINGHAM MI 48009
35- 50	HOOKS, ALEXANDER MARCUS	BOX 123 EDGEWOOD TX 75117
50- 35	HOOPER, ROBERT NELSON	D. MARCH 17, 1980 NEW BRUNSWICK, N. J.
74- 53	HOOTEN, MICHAEL LEON	461 N 11TH ST - COOS BAY OR 97420
71- 49	HOOTON, BURT CARLTON	3619 GRANBY CT - SAN ANTONIO TX 78217
52- 51	HOOVER, RICHARD LLOYD	D. APRIL 12, 1981 LAKE PLACID, FLA.
43- 65	HOOVER, ROBERT JOE	D. SEPTEMBER 2, 1965 LOS ANGELES, CAL.
75- 54	HOPKINS, DONALD	3257 REGAL LN - CINCINNATI OH 45237
68- 41	HOPKINS, GAIL EASON	1026 S NORTON AVE - LOS ANGELES CA 90019
34- 49	HOPKINS, MEREDITH HILLIARD	D. NOVEMBER 20, 1963 DALLAS, TEX.
27- 46	HOPKINS, PAUL HENRY	CHESTER CONN 06412
39- 54	HOPP, JOHN LEONARD	715 E 5TH ST-HASTINGS NE 68901

46- 48	HOPPER, JAMES MCDANIEL	2608 PINCKNEY ST - CHARLOTTE NC 28205
13- 87	HOPPER, WILLIAM BOOTH	D. JANUARY 14, 1965 ALLEN PARK, MICH.
24- 53	HORAN, JOSEPH PATRICK	D. FEBRUARY 13, 1969 LOS ANGELES, CAL.
61- 53	HORLEN, JOEL EDWARD	302 ANTLER DR - SAN ANTONIO TX 78213
29- 52	HORNE, BERLYN DALE	D.
78- 58	HORNER, JAMES ROBERT	4145 W AUGUSTA - PHOENIX AZ 85021
15- 70	HORNSBY, ROGERS	D. JANUARY 5, 1963 CHICAGO, ILL.
12- 79	HORSEY, HANSON	D. DECEMBER 1, 1949 MILLINGTON, MD.
17- 35	HORSTMAN, OSCAR THEODORE	D. MAY 11, 1977 SALINA, KAN.
64- 48	HORTON, ANTHONY DARRIN	17001 LIVORNO DR - PACIFIC PALISADES CA 90272

63- 58 HORTON, WILLIAM WATTERSON	19312 STEEL ST - DETROIT MI 48235
53- 34 HOSKINS, DAVID TAYLOR	D. APRIL 2, 1970 FLINT, MICH.
70- 60 HOSLEY, TIMOTHY KENNETH	401 W HENRY ST - SPARTANBURG SC 29301
56- 46 HOST, EUGENE EARL	1415 FULTON ST - NASHVILLE TN 37206
44- 62 HOSTETLER, CHARLES CLOYD	D. FEBRUARY 18, 1971 FORT COLLINS, COLO.
81- 57 HOSTETLER, DAVID ALAN	424 W NORMAN - ARCADIA CA 91006
71- 50 HOTTMAN, KENNETH ROGER	7960 BAR DU LN - SACRAMENTO CA 95828
12- 50 HOUCK, BYRON SIMON	D. JUNE 17, 1969 SANTA CRUZ, CALIF.
70- 61 HOUGH, CHARLES OLIVER	2266 SHADE TREE CIR - BREA CA 92621
47- 44 HOUK, RALPH GEORGE	2941 NE 23RD CT - POMPANO BEACH FL 33062
50- 36 HOUSE, HENRY FRANKLIN	727 SOMERSET BLVD - SKYVIEW AL 35020
67- 50 HOUSE, PATRICK LORY	4205 GREEN MEADOWS DR - MERIDIAN ID 83642
71- 51 HOUSE, THOMAS ROSS	26 BAHAMA BEND - CORONADO CA 92118
13- 88 HOUSE, WILLARD EDWIN	D. NOVEMBER 16, 1923 KANSAS CITY, MO.
80- 56 HOUSEHOLDER, PAUL WESLEY	1 ALLENDALE DR - NORTH HAVEN CT 06473
10- 73 HOUSER, BENJAMIN FRANKLIN	D. JANUARY 15, 1952 AUGUSTA, ME.
14- 91 HOUSER, JOSEPH WILLIAM	D. JANUARY 3, 1953 ORLANDO, FLA.
45- 49 HOUTTEMAN, ARTHUR JOSEPH	1755 W BUELL RD - LAKE ORION MI 48035
69- 82 HOVLEY, STEPHEN EUGENE	925 E OJAI AVE - OJAI CA 93023
18- 34 HOVLIK, EDWARD C.	D. MARCH 20, 1955 PAINESVILLE, O.
63- 59 HOWARD, BRUCE ERNEST	3114 BOUGAINVILLEA - SARASOTA FL 33580
12- 81 HOWARD, DAVID AUSTIN	D. JANUARY 26, 1966 DALLAS, TEX.
72- 50 HOWARD, DOUGLAS LYNN	352 SOUTH 1200 EAST - SALT LAKE CITY UT 84102
18- 35 HOWARD, EARL NYCUM	D. APRIL 4, 1937 EVERETT, PA.
55- 59 HOWARD, ELSTON GENE	D. DECEMBER 14, 1980 NEW YORK, N.Y.
58- 46 HOWARD, FRANK OLIVER	14528 HILL-N-DALE WAY - POWAY CA 92064
79- 56 HOWARD, FRED IRVING	88 SCAMMAN ST - SOUTH PORTLAND MA 04106
14- 92 HOWARD, IVAN CHESTER	D. MARCH 30, 1967 MEDFORD, ORE.
70- 62 HOWARD, LARRY RAYFORD	1165 LUTHER DR - ROCKLEDGE FL 32955
46- 49 HOWARD, LEE VINCENT	570 S ROSEMEAD BLVD - PASADENA CA 91107
81- 58 HOWARD, MICHAEL FREDRIC	4981 46TH ST - SACRAMENTO CA 95820
73- 64 HOWARD, WILBUR LEON	BOX 372 - LOWELL NC 28098
71- 52 HOWARTH, JAMES EUGENE	108 VIA NICOLA - WATSONVILLE CA 95076
74- 54 HOWE, ARTHUR HENRY	109 TOWNVIEW RD - PITTSBURGH PA 15209
52- 52 HOWE, CALVIN EARL	1104 MAYBELL NE - GRAND RAPIDS MI 49503
23- 65 HOWE, LESTER CURTIS	D. JULY 16, 1976 WOODMERE, N.Y.
80- 57 HOWE, STEVEN ROY	28844 GARNET HILL CT - AGOURA CA 91301
47- 45 HOWELL, HOMER ELLIOTT	216 STONEHENGE DR - LOUISVILLE KY 40207
80- 58 HOWELL, JAY CANFIELD	4720 HANCOCK DR - BOULDER CO 80303
40- 37 HOWELL, MILLARD FILLMORE	D. MARCH 18, 1960 HOLLYWOOD, FLA.
41- 47 HOWELL, MURRAY DONALD	D. OCTOBER 1, 1950 GREENVILLE, S.C.
12- 82 HOWELL, ROLAND BOATNER	D. MARCH 31, 1973
74- 55 HOWELL, ROY LEE	%GILMAN,436CARDINAL - SATELLITE BCH FL 32927
49- 38 HOWERTON, WILLIAM RAY	1430 BUCKINGHAM WAY - HAYWARD CA 94544
13- 89 HOWLEY, DANIEL PHILIP	D. MARCH 10, 1944 EAST WEYMOUTH, MASS.
61- 54 HOWSER, RICHARD DALTON	6425 JET PILOT TR - TALLAHASSEE FL 32308
52- 53 HOYLE, ROLAND EDISON	695 CHURCH ST - CARBONDALE PA 18407
79- 57 HOYT, DEWEY LAMARR	329 PINECLIFF CT - COLUMBIA SC 29209
18- 36 HOYT, WAITE CHARLES	3787 ASHWORTH DR - CINCINNATI OH 45208
70- 63 HRABOSKY, ALAN THOMAS	8800 PLEASANT HILL RD - LITHONIA GA 30058
81- 59 HRBEK, KENT ALAN	9109 4TH AVE S - BLOOMINGTON MN 55420
68- 42 HRINIAK, WALTER JOHN	44 BARNSDALE RD - NATICK MA 01762
78- 59 HUBBARD, GLENN DEE	3828 VALLEY BROOK RD - SNELLVILLE GA 30278
28- 49 HUBBELL, CARL OWEN	SUNCREST APT #8,130 N LESEUER #1-MESA AZ83205
19- 43 HUBBELL, WILBERT WILLIAM	D. AUGUST 3, 1980 LAKEWOOD, CO.
61- 55 HUBBS, KENNETH DOUGLASS	D. FEBRUARY 15, 1964 UTAH LAKE, UTAH
20- 56 HUBER, CLARENCE BILL	D. FEBRUARY 22, 1965 LAREDO, TEX.
39- 55 HUBER, OTTO	7 FRANKLIN AVE - GARFIELD NJ 07026
35- 51 HUCKLEBERRY, EARL EUGENE	RR 2 MAUD OK 74854
23- 66 HUDGENS, JAMES PRICE	D. AUGUST 26, 1955 ST. LOUIS, MO.
26- 39 HUDLIN, GEORGE WILLIS	14 BETSEY LN - LITTLE ROCK AR 72205
72- 51 HUDSON, CHARLES	RR 5 BOX 50 - COALGATE OK 74538
52- 54 HUDSON, HAL CAMPBELL	1974 ADD: 5535 BALFOUR - DETROIT MI 48224
69- 83 HUDSON, JESSIE JAMES	1101 ELOISE - MANSFIELD LA 71052
36- 40 HUDSON, JOHN WILSON	D. NOVEMBER 7, 1970 BRYAN, TEX.
74- 56 HUDSON, REX HAUGHTON	1639 S LEWIS PL - TULSA OK 74104
40- 38 HUDSON, SIDNEY CHARLES	1309 WESTWOOD DR - WACO TX 76710
14- 93 HUENKE, ALBERT A.	D. SEPTEMBER 20, 1974 SAINT MARYS, O.
37- 53 HUFFMAN, BENJAMIN FRANKLIN	2 CEDAR LN LURAY VA 22835
79- 58 HUFFMAN, PHILLIP LEE	334 CALADIUM ST - LAKE JACKSON TX 77566
74- 57 HUGHES, JAMES MICHAEL	7526 EL MANOR AVE - LOS ANGELES CA 90045
52- 55 HUGHES, JAMES ROBERT	4521 W 83RD ST - CHICAGO IL 60652
66- 46 HUGHES, RICHARD HENRY	BOX 598 - STEPHENS AZ 71764
35- 52 HUGHES, ROY JOHN	4730 BRANDT PIKE DAYTON OH 45424
70- 64 HUGHES, TERRY WAYNE	432 PIERPONT AVE EXT - SPARTANBURG SC 29303
59- 39 HUGHES, THOMAS EDWARD	1971 ADD: 5921 SOUTHCREST ST - HOUSTON TX
30- 36 HUGHES, THOMAS FRANKLIN	790 19TH ST - BEAUMONT TX 77706

41- 48	HUGHES, THOMAS OWEN	RR 4-MOUNTAINTOP PA 18707
14- 94	HUGHES, VERNON ALEXANDER	D. SEPTEMBER 26, 1961 SEWICKLEY, PA.
21- 46	HUGHES, WILLIAM NESBERT	D. FEBRUARY 25, 1963 BIRMINGHAM, ALA.
41- 49	HUGHSON, CECIL CARLTON	BLANCO ROUTE BOX 7-SAN MARCOS TX 78666
15- 71	HUHN, EMIL HUGO	D. SEPTEMBER 5, 1925 CAMDEN, S.C.
22- 59	HULIHAN, HARRY JOSEPH	117 LAUREL DR - NEEDHAM MA 02192
23- 67	HULVEY, JAMES HENSEL	RR 1 BOX 201 - MOUNT SIDNEY VA 24467
77- 70	HUME, THOMAS HUBERT	1803 W 7TH ST - PAMETTO FL 33561
11- 76	HUMPHREY, ALBERT	D. MAY 13, 1961 ASHTABULA, O.
38- 40	HUMPHREY, BYRON WILLIAM	619 NORRIS DR JEFFERSON CITY MO 65101
71- 53	HUMPHREY, TERRYAL GENE	21 ENSUENO WEST - IRVINE CA 92701
62- 58	HUMPHREYS, ROBERT WILLIAM	ATH DEPT, VIRGINIA TECH-BLACKSBURG VA 24061
10- 74	HUMPHRIES, ALBERT	D. SEPTEMBER 21, 1945 ORLANDO, FLA.
38- 41	HUMPHRIES, JOHN WILLIAM	D. JUNE 24, 1965 NEW ORLEANS, LA.
64- 49	HUNDLEY, CECIL RANDOLPH	122 E FOREST LN - PALATINE IL 60067
22- 60	HUNGLING, BERNARD HERMAN	D. MARCH 30, 1968 DAYTON, O.
26- 40	HUNNEFIELD, WILLIAM FENTON	D. AUGUST 28, 1976 NANTUCKET, MASS.
10- 75	HUNT, BENJAMIN FRANKLIN	1913 ADD: 730 K ST - SACRAMENTO CA
59- 40	HUNT, KENNETH LAWRENCE	1464 W 170TH ST - GARDENA CA 90247
61- 56	HUNT, KENNETH RAYMOND	268 EAST 300 NORTH - MORGAN UT 84050
31- 41	HUNT, OLIVER JOEL	D. JULY 24, 1978 TEAGUE, TEXAS
63- 60	HUNT, RONALD KENNETH	RR3 - WENTZVILLE MO 63385
33- 26	HUNTER, EDISON FRANKLIN	D. MARCH 14, 1967 COLERAIN TWP., O.
11- 77	HUNTER, FREDERICK CREIGHTON	D. OCTOBER 26, 1963 COLUMBUS, O.
53- 35	HUNTER, GORDON WILLIAM	104 E SEMINARY AVE - LUTHERVILLE MD 21093
71- 54	HUNTER, HAROLD JAMES	5407 S 15TH ST - OMAHA NE 68107
16- 44	HUNTER, HERBERT HARRISON	D. JULY 26, 1970 ORLANDO, FLA.
65- 48	HUNTER, JAMES AUGUSTUS	RR ONE BOX 895 - HERTFORD NC 27944
62- 59	HUNTER, WILLARD MITCHELL	2562 POPPLETON AVE - OMAHA NE 68105
12- 83	HUNTER, WILLIAM ELLSWORTH	D. APRIL 10, 1934 BUFFALO, N.Y.
67- 51	HUNTZ, STEPHEN MICHAEL	4425 FAIRVIEW PKWY - CLEVELAND OH 44126
23- 68	HUNTZINGER, WALTER HENRY	D. AUGUST 11, 1981 UPPER DARBY, PA.
54- 46	HURD, THOMAS CARR	3710 VERALTA DR - CEDAR FALLS IA 50613
77- 71	HURDLE, CLINTON MERRICK	515 MARGARET ST - MERRITT ISLAND FL 32952
80- 59	HURST, BRUCE VEE	471 EAST 650 SOUTH - ST GEORGE UT 84770
28- 50	HURST, FRANK O'DONNELL	D. DECEMBER 6, 1952 LOS ANGELES, CAL.
25- 52	HUSTA, CADRL LAWRENCE	D. NOVEMBER 6, 1951 KINGSTON, N. Y.
37- 54	HUSTON, WARREN LLEWELLYN	29 ROBINWOOD RD - BUZZARD BAY MA 02538
33- 27	HUTCHESON, JOSEPH JOHNSON	2400 BELL AVE - DENTON TX 76201
40- 39	HUTCHINGS, JOHN RICHARD JOSEPH	D. APRIL 27, 1963 INDIANAPOLIS, IND.
39- 56	HUTCHINSON, FREDERICK CHARLES	D. NOVEMBER 12, 1964 BRADENTON, FLA.
33- 28	HUTCHINSON, IRA KENDALL	D. AUGUST 21, 1973 CHICAGO, ILL.
74- 58	HUTSON, GEORGE HERBERT	1101 E 67TH ST - SAVANNAH GA 31404
25- 53	HUTSON, ROY LEE	D. MAY 20, 1957 LAMESA, CAL.
70- 65	HUTTO, JAMES NEAMON	OLD ADD: 11051 SUNDAY RD - CANTONMENT FL
66- 47	HUTTON, THOMAS GEORGE	1694 HARBOR CIR W - LARGO FL 3354/
55- 60	HYDE, RICHARD ELDE	1506 CAMBRIDGE - CHAMPAIGN IL 61820
73- 65	IGNASIAK, GARY RAYMOND	2276 ROSEWOOD - PONTIAC MI 48055
13- 90	IMLAY, HARRY MILLER	D. OCTOBER 7, 1948 BORDENTOWN, N.J.
14- 95	INGERSOLL, ROBERT RANDOLPH	D. JANUARY 13, 1927 MINNEAPOLIS, MINN.
11- 78	INGERTON, WILLIAM JOHN	D. JUNE 15, 1956 CLEVELAND, O.
29- 53	INGRAM, MELVIN DAVID	D. OCTOBER 28, 1979 MEDFORD, ORE.
77- 72	IORG, DANE CHARLES	730 EAST 950 NORTH - OREM UT 84017
78- 60	IORG, GARTH RAY	BOX 495 - BLUE LAKE CA 95525
41- 50	IOTT, CLARENCE EUGENE	D. AUGUST 17, 1980 ST. PETERSBURG, FLA.
14- 96	IRELAN, HAROLD	D. JULY 16, 1944 CARMEL, IND.
81- 60	IRELAND, TIMOTHY NEAL	20932 TIMES AVE - HAYWARD CA 94541
49- 39	IRVIN, MONFORD	243 S HARRISON ST #2A-EAST ORANGE NJ 07018
12- 84	IRVIN, WILLIAM EDWARD	D. FEBRUARY 18, 1916 PHILADELPHIA, PA.
38- 42	IRWIN, THOMAS ANDREW	508 50TH ST ALTOONA PA 16602
21- 47	IRWIN, WALTER KINGSLEY	D. AUGUST 18, 1976 SPRING LAKE, MICH.
80- 60	ISALES, ORLANDO (PIZARRO)	1171 16TH SE CAPARRA TER-HATO REY PR 00921
71- 55	IVIE, MICHAEL WILSON	1125 FARRAGUT BLVD - FOSTER CITY CA 94404
67- 52	IZQUIERDO, ENRIQUE ROBERTO	6011 SW 97TH AVE - MIAMI FL 33173
53- 36	JABLONSKI, RAYMOND LEO	4457 S SACRAMENTO AVE - CHICAGO IL 60632
59- 41	JACKSON, ALVIN NEIL	ONE SAINT M ARKS PL - DIX HILLS NY 11746
15- 72	JACKSON, CHARLES HERBERT	D. MAY 27, 1968 RATFORD, VA.
78- 61	JACKSON, DARRELL PRESTON	13107 JARVIS AVE - LOS ANGELES CA 90061
11- 79	JACKSON, GEORGE CHRISTOPHER	D. NOVEMBER 25, 1972 CLEBURNE, TEX.
65- 49	JACKSON, GRANT DWIGHT	212 MESA CIR - UPPERST CLAIR PA 15241
33- 29	JACKSON, JOHN LEWIS	D. OCTOBER 24, 1956 SOMERS POINT, N. J.
55- 61	JACKSON, LAWRENCE CURTIS	3300 BOGUS BASIN RD - BOISE ID 83702
58- 47	JACKSON, LOUIS CLARENCE	D. MAY 27, 1969 TOKYO, JAPAN
70- 66	JACKSON, MICHAEL WARREN	6-8 ANGELA PL - PATERSON NJ 07502
50- 37	JACKSON, RANSOM JOSEPH	250 HUNNICUT DR - ATHENS GA 30601
67- 53	JACKSON, REGINALD MARTINEZ	22 YANKEE HILL - OAKLAND CA 94616

```
63- 61  JACKSON, ROLAND THOMAS           3377 BOBOLINK DR - ATLANTA GA 30311
54- 47  JACKSON, RONALD ALLEN            2828 SPRINGBROOK DR - KALAMAZOO MI 49004
75- 55  JACKSON, RONNIE D                RR 4 BOX 216 - BESSEMER AL 35020
77- 73  JACKSON, ROY LEE                 711 DOGWOOD AVE - OPELIKA AL 36801
22- 61  JACKSON, TRAVIS CALVIN           WALDO AR 71770
14- 97  JACKSON, WILLIAM RILEY           D. SEPTEMBER 26, 1958 PEORIA, ILL.
48- 48  JACOBS, ANTHONY ROBERT           D. DECEMBER 21, 1980 NASHVILLE, TENN.
39- 57  JACOBS, ARTHUR EVAN              D. JUNE 8, 1967 INGLEWOOD, CAL.
54- 48  JACOBS, FORREST VANDERGRIFT      BOX 66 - MILFORD DE 19963
60- 49  JACOBS, LAMAR GARY               5500 MARKET ST #201 - YOUNGSTOWN OH 44512
37- 55  JACOBS, NEWTON SMITH             1437 GREYCOURT AVE RICHMOND VA 23227
18- 37  JACOBS, OTTO ALBERT              D. NOVEMBER 19, 1955 CHICAGO, ILL.
28- 51  JACOBS, RAYMOND F.               D. APRIL 5, 1952 LOS ANGELES, CAL.
14- 98  JACOBS, WILLIAM ELMER            D. FEBRUARY 10, 1958 SALEM, MO.
15- 73  JACOBSON, MERWIN JOHN WILLIAM    D. JANUARY 13, 1978 BALTIMORE, MD.
15- 74  JACOBSON, WILLIAM CHESTER        D. JANUARY 16, 1977 ORION, ILL.
18- 38  JACOBUS, STUART LOUIS            D. AUGUST 19, 1965 NORTH COLLEGE HILL, OHIO
81- 61  JACOBY, BROOK WALLACE            1521 RACCOON DR - VENTURA CA 93003
71- 56  JACQUEZ, PATRICK THOMAS          8351 COLONIAL - STOCKTON CA 95209
64- 50  JAECKEL, PAUL HENRY              250 S ROSE DR #141 - PLACENTIA CA 92690
20- 57  JAEGER, JOSEPH PETER             D. DECEMBER 13, 1963 HAMPTON, IA.
25- 54  JAHN, ARTHUR CHARLES             D. JANUARY 9, 1948 LITTLE ROCK, ARK.
36- 41  JAKUCKI, SIGMUND                 D. MAY 28, 1979 GALVESTON, TEXAS
24- 54  JAMERSON, CHARLEY DEWEY          MAPLE ST - MOCKSVILLE NC 27028
75- 56  JAMES, ARTHUR                    4531 GARLAND AVE - DETROIT MI 48214
60- 50  JAMES, CHARLES WESLEY            104 COLLIER ST - FULTON MO 62521
68- 43  JAMES, CLEO JOEL                 6020 KITTYHAWK DR - RIVERSIDE CA 92504
68- 44  JAMES, JEFFREY LYNN              2531 JASMINE - EUGENE OR 97404
58- 48  JAMES, JOHN PHILLIP              6037 E LARKSPUR - SCOTTSDALE AZ 85254
77- 74  JAMES, PHILIP ROBERT             1759 E DECATUR - MESA AZ 85203
67- 54  JAMES, RICHARD LEE               1206 AMHERST DR - DOTHAN AL 36301
29- 54  JAMES, ROBERT BYRNE              LOOKOUT RD - SAN ANTONIO TX 78228
78- 62  JAMES, ROBERT HARVEY             7833 KYLE - SUNLAND CA 91040
12- 85  JAMES, WILLIAM A                 D. MAY 3, 1933 PORTSMOUTH, O.
11- 80  JAMES, WILLIAM HENRY             D. MAY 24, 1942 VENICE, CALIF.
13- 91  JAMES, WILLIAM LAWRENCE          D. MARCH 10, 1971 OROVILLE, CALOF.
15- 75  JAMIESON, CHARLES DEVINE         D. OCTOBER 27, 1969 PATERSON, N.J.
70- 67  JANESKI, GERALD JOSEPH           317 N MISSION DR - SAN GABRIEL CA 91711
53- 37  JANOWICZ, VICTOR FELIX           1966 JERVIS RD - COLUMBUS OH 43221
47- 46  JANSEN, LAWRENCE JOSEPH          RR 2 BOX 413A - FOREST GROVE OR 97116
10- 76  JANSEN, RAYMOND WILLIAM          D. MARCH 19, 1934 ST. LOUIS, MO.
12- 86  JANTZEN, WALTER C                D. APRIL 1, 1948 HINES, ILL.
11- 81  JANVRIN, HAROLD CHANDLER         D. MARCH 2, 1962 BOSTON, MASS.
44- 63  JARVIS, LEROY GILBERT            524 GREENLEA CHASE - OKLAHOMA CITO OK 73160
69- 84  JARVIS, RAYMOND ARNOLD           15 BERKLEY ST - PROVIDENCE RI 02908
66- 48  JARVIS, ROBERT PATRICK           4425 E KINGSPOINTS CIR - DUNWOOD GA 30338
14- 99  JASPER, HARRY W.                 D. MAY 22, 1937 ST. LOUIS, MO.
65- 50  JASTER, LARRY EDWARD             1306 WHITEHOUSE DR-COLORADO SPRINGS CO 80904
72- 52  JATA, PAUL                       35-25 34TH ST - LONG ISLAND CITY NY 11101
40- 40  JAVERY, ALVA WILLIAM             D. SEPTEMBER 13, 1977 WOODSTOCK, CONN.
76- 41  JAVIER, IGNACIO ALFREDO          BARRIO LIBRE #96ING CON-SAN PEDRO DE MARC D R
60- 51  JAVIER, MANUEL JULIAN            BOX 71 - SAN FRANCISCO DE MARCORIS DOM REP
53- 38  JAY, JOSEPH RICHARD              3660 STATE RD 580 - CLEARWATER FL 33519
21- 48  JEANES, ERNEST LEE               D. APRIL 5, 1973 LONGVIEW, TEX.
36- 42  JEFFCOAT, GEORGE EDWARD          D. OCTOBER 13, 1978 LEESVILLE, S. C.
48- 49  JEFFCOAT, HAROLD BENTLEY         4016 WISCONSIN AVE - TAMPA FL 33616
73- 66  JEFFERSON, JESSE HARRISON        1421 RAILROAD AVE - MIDLOTHIAN VA 23113
30- 37  JEFFRIES, IRVINE FRANKLIN        1101 LYNDON LN - LYNDON KY 40222
41- 51  JELINCICH, FRANK ANTHONY         170 W RINCON ST #4 - CAMPBELL CA 95008
65- 51  JENKINS, FERGUSON ARTHUR         BOX 275 - BLENHEIM ONTARIO
22- 62  JENKINS, JOHN ROBERT             D. AUGUST 3, 1968 COLUMBIA, MO.
14-100  JENKINS, JOSEPH DANIEL           D. JUNE 21, 1974 FRESNO, CALIF.
25- 55  JENKINS, THOMAS GRIFFIN          D. MAY 3, 1979 WEYMOUTH, MASS.
62- 60  JENKINS, WARREN WASHINGTON       3810 OBISPO - TAMPA FL 33609
51- 44  JENNINGS, WILLIAM LEE            7065 FOXCROFT DR - AFFTON MO 63123
31- 42  JENSEN, FORREST DOCENUS          1311 N PARKWOOD LN - WICHITA KS 67208
50- 38  JENSEN, JACK EUGENE              RR 2 BOX 170A2 - SCOTTSVILLE VA 24590
12- 87  JENSEN, WILLIAM CHRISTIAN        D. MARCH 27, 1917 PHILADELPHIA, PA.
29- 55  JESSEE, DANIEL EDWARD            D. APRIL 30, 1970 VENICE, FLA.
69- 85  JESTADT, GARRY ARTHUR            825 PARNELL PL - SUNNYVALE CA 94087
52- 56  JESTER, VIRGIL MILTON            8130 RALEIGH PL - WESTMINSTER CO 80030
69- 86  JETER, JOHN                      OLD ADD: 5717 MCALPINE - SHREVEPORT LA
```

50- 39	JETHROE, SAMUEL	340 E 14TH ST - ERIE PA 16503
64- 51	JIMENEZ, FELIX ELVIO	SIMON BOLIVAR #24 - MACORIS DOM REPUBLIC
62- 61	JIMENEZ, MANUEL EMILIO	24 SIMON BOLIVAR - SAN PEDRO DE MARCORIS DR
74- 59	JIMINEZ, JUAN ANTONIO	CLE 9,CASA 1N EL ENSUENO-SANTIAGO DOM REP
63- 62	JOHN, THOMAS EDWARD	845 SHADOW RIDGE RD - FRANKLIN LAKES NJ 07417
26- 41	JOHNS, AUGUSTUS FRANCIS	D. SEPTEMBER 12, 1975 SAN ANTONIO, TEX.
15- 76	JOHNS, WILLIAM R.	D. AUGUST 9, 1964 CLEVELAND, O.
41- 52	JOHNSON, ADAM RANKIN JR	1306 WARREN AVE-WILLIAMSPORT PA 17706
14-101	JOHNSON, ADAM RANKIN SR	D. JULY 2, 1972 WILLIAMSPORT, PA.
46- 52	JOHNSON, ALEXANDER	OLD ADD: 19474 BIRWOOD - DETROIT MI 48221
81- 62	JOHNSON, ANTHONY CLAIR	4446 JANSSEN DR - MEMPHIS TN 38101
27- 47	JOHNSON, ARTHUR GILBERT	3100 HAWTHORNE ST - SARASOTA FL 33580
40- 41	JOHNSON, ARTHUR HENRY	23 HEMLOCK DR-HOLDEN MA 01520
59- 42	JOHNSON, BENJAMIN FRANKLIN	112 LOCKSLEY DR - GREENWOOD SC 29646
81- 63	JOHNSON, BOBBY EARL	3423 W ILLINOIS #258 - DALLAS TX 75211
46- 50	JOHNSON, CHESTER LILLIS	627 NW 90TH - SEATTLE WA 98117
69- 87	JOHNSON, CLAIR BARTH	22355 N 5TH - CASTRO VALLEY CA 94546
53- 39	JOHNSON, CLIFFORD	1900 E 54TH ST - KANSAS CITY MO 64130
72- 53	JOHNSON, CLIFFORD	318 GLEN OAK - SAN ANTONIO TX 78220
52- 57	JOHNSON, DARRELL DEAN	2792 HAMILTON DR - PINOLE CA 94564
65- 52	JOHNSON, DAVID ALLEN	RR 1 BOX 64 - MAITLAND FL 32751
74- 60	JOHNSON, DAVID CHARLES	2402 MARCHALL ST - ABILENE TX 79605
60- 52	JOHNSON, DERON ROGER	13847 TWIN PEAKS RD - POWAY CA 92064
47- 47	JOHNSON, DONALD ROY	711 W 24TH ST - VANCOUVER WA 98665
43- 66	JOHNSON, DONALD SPORE	580 BROOKS - LAGUNA BEACH CA 92651
40- 42	JOHNSON, EARL DOUGLAS	9541 25TH AVE NW-SEATTLE WA 98107
20- 58	JOHNSON, EDWIN CYRIL	D. JULY 3, 1975 MORGANFIELD, KY.
12- 88	JOHNSON, ELLIS WATT	D. JANUARY 14, 1965 MINNEAPOLIS, MINN.
14-102	JOHNSON, ELMER ELLSWORTH	D. OCTOBER 31, 1966 HOLLYWOOD, FLA.
12- 89	JOHNSON, ERNEST RUDOLPH	D. MAY 1, 1952 MCNROVIA, CALIF.
50- 40	JOHNSON, ERNEST THORWALD	BOX 4064 - ATLANTA GA 30302
66- 49	JOHNSON, FRANK HERBERT	568 N CENTER ST - MESA AZ 85201
22- 63	JOHNSON, FREDERICK EDWARD	D. JUNE 14, 1973 KERRVILLE, TEX.
13- 92	JOHNSON, GEORGE HOWARD	D. JUNE 12, 1922 DES MOINES, IA.
25- 56	JOHNSON, HENRY WARD	117 29TH ST W - BRADENTON FL 33506
70- 68	JOHNSON, JAMES BRIAN	1459 MADISON ST - MUSKEGON MI 49442
68- 45	JOHNSON, JERRY MICHAEL	505 STATE ST - SAN MATEO CA 94401
44- 64	JOHNSON, JOHN CLIFFORD	OLD ADD: 120 MUNSON - YPSILANTI MI 48197
78- 63	JOHNSON, JOHN HENRY	3830 CREEKSIDER DR - SAN LEANDRO CA 94578
58- 49	JOHNSON, KENNETH TRAVIS	791 CAROLINE AVE - W PALM BEACH FL 33406
47- 48	JOHNSON, KENNETH WANDERSEE	326 BROOKFIELD - WICHITA KS 67206
74- 61	JOHNSON, LAMAR	2960 VALLEY FORD RD - LISLE IL 60532
72- 54	JOHNSON, LARRY DOBY	3115 E 98TH ST - CLEVELAND OH 44104
34- 50	JOHNSON, LLOYD WILLIAM	45 N BUENA VISTA - SAN JOSE CA 95126
60- 53	JOHNSON, LOUIS BROWN	976 GLADWICK ST - CARSON CA 90746
74- 62	JOHNSON, MICHAEL NORTON	RR ONE - FARIBAULT MN 55021
11- 82	JOHNSON, OTIS L.	D. NOVEMBER 9, 1915 BINGHAMTON, N.Y.
20-136	JOHNSON, PAUL OSCAR	D. FEBRUARY 14, 1973 MCALLEN, TEX.
80- 61	JOHNSON, RANDALL STUART	40 W 64TH ST - HIALEAH FL 33012
58- 50	JOHNSON, RICHARD ALLAN	808-B N BEELINE - PAYSON AZ 85541
69- 88	JOHNSON, ROBERT DALE	3559 SYDNEY DR - SAN JOSE CA 95132
33- 30	JOHNSON, ROBERT LEE	219 E 61ST ST - TACOMA WA 98404
60- 54	JOHNSON, ROBERT WALLACE	1474 BARCLAY ST - ST PAUL MN 55106
18- 40	JOHNSON, ROY	5749 GRANITE REEF RD - SCOTTSDALE AZ 85251
29- 56	JOHNSON, ROY CLEVELAND	D. SEPTEMBER 10, 1973 TACOMA, WASH.

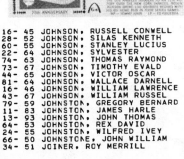

16- 45	JOHNSON, RUSSELL CONWELL	D. DECEMBER 6, 1950 POTTSTOWN, PA.
28- 52	JOHNSON, SILAS KENNETH	600 W CHURCH ST - SHERIDAN ILL 60551
60- 55	JOHNSON, STANLEY LUCIUS	56 MORNINGSIDE DR - DALY CITY CA 94015
22- 64	JOHNSON, SYLVESTER	944 SE 168TH AV - PORTLAND OR 97233
74- 63	JOHNSON, THOMAS RAYMOND	1575 HURON ST - ST PAUL MN 55108
73- 67	JOHNSON, TIMOTHY EVALD	1025 DOE LN - LAS CRUCES NM 88001
44- 65	JOHNSON, VICTOR OSCAR	1515 DRURY AVE - EAU CLAIRE WI 54701
81- 64	JOHNSON, WALLACE DARNELL	2512 ADAMS ST - GARY IN 46407
16- 46	JOHNSON, WILLIAM LAWRENCE	D. NOVEMBER 5, 1950 LOS ANGELES, CALIF.
43- 67	JOHNSON, WILLIAM RUSSEL	2903 LAKE FOREST DR-AUGUSTA GA 30904
79- 59	JOHNSTON, GREGORY BERNARD	20528 BUCKLAND AVE - WALNUT CA 91789
11- 83	JOHNSTON, JAMES HARLE	D. FEBRUARY 14, 1967 CHATTANOOGA, TENN.
13- 93	JOHNSTON, JOHN THOMAS	D. MARCH 7, 1940 SAN DIEGO, CALIF.
64- 53	JOHNSTON, REX DAVID	15117 ILLINOIS ST - PARAMOUNT CA 90723
24- 55	JOHNSTON, WILFRED IVEY	D. JULY 14, 1959 TYLER, TEX.
66- 50	JOHNSTONE, JOHN WILLIAM	1365 ST ALBANS - SAN MARINO CA 91108
34- 51	JOINER, ROY MERRILL	#153 - VINA CA 96092

54- 49	JCK, STANLEY EDWARD	D. MARCH 6, 1972 BUFFALO, N. Y.
30- 38	JOLLEY, SMEAD POWELL	1940 FRANCISCAN WAY #311 - ALAMEDA CA 94501
53- 40	JOLLY, DAVID	D. MAY 27, 1963 DURHAM, N. C.
32- 38	JONES, ARTHUR LENOX	#1 - KERSHAW SC 29067
16- 47	JONES, CARROLL ELMER	D. DECEMBER 28, 1952 PITTSBURG, KAN.
67- 55	JONES, CLARENCE WOODROW	435 S SPRUCE - SANTA ANA CA 92703
63- 63	JONES, CLEON JOSEPH	751 EDWARD ST - MOBILE AL 36610
28- 53	JONES, COBURN DYAS	D. JUNE 3, 1969 DENVER, COLO.
41- 53	JONES, DALE ELDON	D. NOVEMBER 8, 1980 ORLANDO, FLA.
79- 60	JONES, DARRYL LEE	2240 CRANSTON RD - UNIVERSITY HGTS OH 44118
26- 42	JONES, DECATUR POINDEXTER	125 MCAULEY DR - VICKSBURG MS 39180
45- 50	JONES, EARL LESLIE	4054 MONTECITO AVE - FRESNO CAL 93702
70- 69	JONES, GARY HOWELL	4919 BROMPTON - BELL CA 90201
54- 50	JONES, GORDON BASSETT	53 MOONLIT CIR - SACRAMENTO CA 95831
62- 62	JONES, GROVER WILLIAM	1814 MILLBURY DR - MISSOURI CITY TX 77459
61- 57	JONES, HAROLD MARION	4125 PALMYRA RD - LOS ANGELES CA 90008
21- 49	JONES, HOWARD	D. JULY 15, 1972 JEANNETTE, PA.
64- 54	JONES, JAMES DALTON	5290 WYANDOTTE ST - BATON ROUGE LA 70805
41- 54	JONES, JAMES MURRELL	BOX 156-EPPS LA 71237
80- 62	JONES, JEFFREY ALLEN	15626 DRAKE - SOUTHGATE MI 48198
23- 69	JONES, JESSE	D. SEPTEMBER 7, 1977 LEWES, DEL.
24- 56	JONES, JOHN JOSEPH	D. MAY 13, 1961 ST. LOUIS, MO.
19- 44	JONES, JOHN PAUL	D. JUNE 5, 1980 RUSTON, LA.
23- 70	JONES, JOHN WILLIAM	D. NOVEMBER 3, 1956 BALTIMORE, MD.
24- 57	JONES, KENNETH FREDERICK	45 BRISTOL DR - CANTON CT 06019
79- 61	JONES, LYNN MORRIS	12727 KINGSTON - HUNTINGTON WOODS MI 48070
61- 58	JONES, MACK	184 NATHAN RD - ATLANTA GA 30331
80- 63	JONES, MICHAEL CARL	16 WASHINGTON RD - PITTSFORD NY 14534
40- 43	JONES, MORRIS E	D. JUNE 30, 1975 LINCOLN, CALIF.
75- 57	JONES, ODELL	17800 LYSANDER DR - CARSON CA 90746
20- 59	JONES, PERCY LEE	606 CLERMONT AVE - DALLAS, TX 75223
73- 68	JONES, RANDALL LEO	15417 POWAY RD - POWAY CA 92064
74- 64	JONES, ROBERT OLIVER	2107 ABEYTA CT - LOVELAND CO 80537
17- 36	JONES, ROBERT WALTER	D. AUGUST 30, 1964 SAN DIEGO, CAL.
76- 42	JONES, RUPPERT SANDERSON	5800 LAKE MURRAY #13 - LAMESA CA 92041
51- 45	JONES, SAMUEL	D. NOVEMBER 5, 1971 MORGANTOWN, W. VA.
14-103	JONES, SAMUEL POND	D. JULY 6, 1966 BARNESVILLE, O.
46- 51	JONES, SHELDON LESLIE	1975 ADD: 56 FAIRFIELD BEACH RD-FAIRFIELD CT
60- 56	JONES, SHERMAN JARVIS	WEAVER DR - KANSAS CITY KS 66104
67- 56	JONES, STEVEN HOWELL	8116 KINGSDALE DR - KNOXVILLE TN 37919
76- 43	JONES, THOMAS FREDERICK	4835 MANVILLE CIR - JACKSONVILLE FL 37210
77- 75	JONES, TIMOTHY BYRON	6204 GREENEYES WAY - ORANGEVALE CA 95662
46- 52	JONES, VERNAL LEROY	7322 ALCEDO CIR - SACRAMENTO CA 95823
11- 84	JONES, WILLIAM DENNIS	D. OCTOBER 10, 1946 BOSTON, MASS.
11- 85	JONES, WILLIAM RODERICK	D. FEBRUARY 26, 1938 WICHITA, KAN.
47- 49	JONES, WILLIE EDWARD	BOX 30223 - CINCINNATI OH 45230
20- 60	JONNARD, CLARENCE JAMES	D. AUGUST 23, 1977 NEW YORK, N. Y.
21- 50	JONNARD, CLAUDE ALFRED	D. AUGUST 27, 1959 NASHVILLE, TENN.
36- 43	JOOST, EDWIN DAVID	BOX 11515-ZEPHYR COVE NV 89448
27- 48	JORDAN, BAXTER BYERLY	2004-D LINCOLNTON RD - SALISBURY NC 28144
33- 31	JORDAN, JAMES WILLIAM	D. DECEMBER 4, 1957 CHARLOTTE, N. C.
53- 41	JORDAN, MILTON MIGNOT	57 LAKESHORE RD - LANSING NY 14881
51- 46	JORDAN, NILES CHAPMAN	1114 METCALF - SEDRO-WOOLLEY WA 98284
12- 90	JORDAN, RAYMOND WILLIS	D. JUNE 5, 1960 MERIDEN, CONN.
44- 66	JORDAN, THOMAS JEFFERSON	1604 E BLAND - ROSWELL NM 88201
29- 57	JORGENS, ARNDT LUDWIG	D. MARCH 1, 1980 WILMETTE, ILL.
35- 53	JORGENS, ORVILLE EDWARD	129 S SPRUCE ST WOOD DALE IL 60191
47- 50	JORGENSEN, JOHN DONALD	8267 KIRKWOOD CT - CUCAMONGA CA 91730
68- 46	JORGENSEN, MICHAEL	1316 19 TH ST - CHESAPEAKE VA 23327
37- 56	JORGENSCN, CARL	119 MINNIE ST - SANTA CRUZ CA 95062
64- 55	JOSEPH, RICARDO EMELINDO	D. SEPTEMBER 8, 1979 SANTIAGO DOM REP
65- 53	JOSEPHSCN, DUANE CHARLES	RR 3 - NEW HAMPTON IA 50659
69- 89	JOSHUA, VON EVERETT	1896 REDDING AVE - UPLAND CA 91786
16- 48	JOURDAN, THEODORE CHARLES	D. SEPTEMBER 23, 1961 NEW ORLEANS, LA.
62- 63	JOYCE, MICHAEL LEWIS	1609 WHITMAN LN - WHEATON IL 60187
65- 54	JOYCE, RICHARD EDWARD	20 HILLSIDE AVE - UPPER SADDLE RIVER NJ 07458
39- 58	JOYCE, ROBERT EMMETT	D. DECEMBER 10, 1981 SAN FRANCISCO, CALIF.
27- 49	JUDD, RALPH WESLEY	D. MAY 6, 1957 LAPEER, MICH.
41- 55	JUDD, THOMAS WILLIAM OSCAR	CATERBURY ST 64-INGERSOLL ONTARIO
15- 77	JUDGE, JOSEPH IGNATIUS	D. MARCH 11, 1963 WASHINGTON, D.C.
40- 44	JUDNICH, WALTER FRANKLIN	D. JULY 12, 1971 GLENDALE, CAL.
48- 50	JUDSON, HOWARD KOLLS	12107 MCKINLEY - HEBRON IL 60034
35- 54	JUDY, LYLE LEROY	410 FLAGLER BLVD ST AUGUSTINE FL 32084
39- 59	JUELICH, JOHN WALTER	D. DECEMBER 25, 1970 ST. LOUIS, MO.
40- 45	JUMONVILLE, GEORGE BENEDICT	2459 SALVIA N - MOBILE AL 36606
37- 57	JUNGELS, KENNETH PETER	D. SEPTEMBER 9, 1975 WEST BEND, WIS.
65- 55	JUREWICZ, MICHAEL ALLEN	17826 IXONIA AVE W - LAKEVILLE MN 55044
31- 43	JURGES, WILLIAM FREDERICK	2048 BEL OMBRE CIR - LAKE WALES FL 33853
44- 67	JURISICH, ALVIN JOSEPH	6549 LOUIS XIV - NEW ORLEANS LA 70124
44- 68	JUST, JOSEPH ERWIN	1001 W MORGAN AVE - MILWAUKEE WI 53221
72- 55	JUTZE, ALFRED HENRY	3395 ZEPHYR CT - WHEAT RIDGE CO 80033
14-104	JUUL, EARL HERBERT	D. JANUARY 4, 1942 CHICAGO, ILL.
11- 86	JUUL, HERBERT VICTOR	D. NOVEMBER 14, 1928 CHICAGO, ILL.
59- 43	KAAT, JAMES LEE	SWEETWATER FARM - GLEN MILLS PA 19342
10- 77	KADING, JOHN FREDERICK	D. JUNE 2, 1964 CHICAGO, ILL.
13- 94	KAFORA, FRANK JACOB	D. MARCH 23, 1928 CHICAGO, ILL.
22- 65	KAHDOT, ISAAC LEONARD	18161/2 NW 37TH - OKLAHOMA CITY OK 73104
38- 43	KAHLE, ROBERT WAYNE	5311 GLASGOW CT LOS ANGELES CA 90045
10- 78	KAHLER, GEORGE RANNELS	D. FEBRUARY 14, 1924 BATTLE CREEK, MICH.
30- 39	KAHN, OWEN EARLE	504 DUNRAY DR - RICHMOND VA 23222
80- 64	KAINER, DONALD WAYNE	8800 BROADWAY #5370 - HOUSTON TX 77061
11- 87	KAISER, ALFRED EDWARD	D. APRIL 11, 1969 CINCINNATI, O.
55- 62	KAISER, CLYDE DONALD	2901 EAST 12TH - ADA OK 74820
71- 57	KAISER, ROBERT THOMAS	2625 RUSTIC MEADOWS - SOUTH JORDAN UT 84065
14-105	KAISERLING, GEORGE	D. MARCH 2, 1918 STEUBENVILLE, O.
37- 58	KALFASS, WILLIAM PHILIP	D. SEPTEMBER 8, 1968 BROOKLYN, N. Y.
40- 46	KALIN, FRANK BRUNO	D. JANUARY 12, 1975 WEIRTON, W. VA.

43- 42	KALINE, ALBERT WILLIAM	945 TIMBERLAKE DR - BLOOMFIELD HILLS MI 48013
8- 41	KALLIO, RUDOLPH	D. APRIL 6, 1979 NEWPORT, ORE.
3- 71	KAMM, WILLIAM EDWARD	2021 DEVEREUX DRIVE - BURLINGAME CA 94011
78- 64	KAMMEYER, ROBERT LYNN	10021 SIERRA GLEN WAY - SACRAMENTO CA 95827
74- 58	KAMP, ALPHONSE FRANCIS	D. FEBRUARY 26, 1955 BOSTON, MASS.
54- 52	KAMPOURIS, ALEX WILLIAM	2776 17TH ST - SACRAMENTO CA 95818
25- 78	KANE, FRANCIS THOMAS	D. DECEMBER 2, 1962 BROCKTON, MASS.
25- 57	KANE, JOHN FRANCIS	1975 ADD: 952 W GARFIELD BLVD - CHICAGO IL
38- 44	KANE, THOMAS JOSEPH	D. NOVEMBER 26, 1973 CHICAGO, ILL.
52- 64	KANEHL, RODERICK EDWIN	10338 WILKINS - LOS ANGELES CA 90024
14-106	KANTLEHNER, ERVINE LESLIE	OLD ADD: 502 1/2 HIGHLAND W-SIERRA MADRE CA
36- 44	KARDOW, PAUL OTTO	D. APRIL 27, 1968 SAN ANTONIO, TEXAS
43- 68	KARL, ANTON ANDREW	RR 3 HOLLYWYLE PK-NEWFAIRFIELD CT 06810
30- 40	KARLON, WILLIAM JOHN	D. DECEMBER 7, 1964 MONSON, MASS.
27- 50	KAROW, MARTIN GREGORY	RR 3 BOX 428 - BRYAN TX 77801
46- 53	KARPEL, HERBERT	6922 BABCOCK AVE - NORTH HOLLYWOOD CA 91605
20- 61	KARR, BENJAMIN JOYCE	D. DECEMBER 8, 1968 MEMPHIS, TENN.
15- 79	KARST, JOHN GOTTLIEB	D. MAY 21, 1976 CAPE MAY COURT HOUSE, N. J.
57- 35	KASKO, EDWARD MICHAEL	317 BURNWICK RD - RICHMOND VA 23227
52- 58	KATT, RAYMOND FREDERICK	522 LAUREL LN - NEW BRAUNFELS TX 78130
44- 69	KATZ, ROBERT CLYDE	D. DECEMBER 14, 1962 ST. JOSEPH, MICH.
12- 91	KAUFF, BENJAMIN MICHAEL	D. NOVEMBER 17, 1961 COLUMBUS,O.
14-107	KAUFFMAN, HOWARD RICHARD	D. APRIL 17, 1948 LEWISBURG, PA.
21- 51	KAUFMAN, ANTHONY CHARLES	6203 N TALMAN AV - CHICAGO ILL 60645
14-108	KAVANAGH, CHARLES HUGH	D. SEPTEMBER 6, 1973 REEDSBURG, WIS.
14-109	KAVANAGH, LEO DANIEL	D. AUGUST 10, 1950 CHICAGO, ILL.
14-110	KAVANAGH, MARTIN JOSEPH	D. JULY 28, 1960 TAYLOR, MICH.
48- 51	KAZAK, EDWARD TERRANCE	802 NEWMAN DR - AUSTIN TX 78703
53- 43	KAZANSKI, THEODORE STANLEY	27 S PLAZA DR - ROCHESTER MI 48063
68- 47	KEALEY, STEVEN WILLIAM	RR ONE - CEDAR POINT KS 66843
61- 59	KEANE, JOHN JOSEPH	D. JANUARY 6, 1967 HOUSTON, TEX.
79- 62	KEARNEY, ROBERT HENRY	7839 GALLOP - SAN ANTONIO TX 78227
24- 59	KEARNS, EDWARD PAUL	D. DECEMBER 21, 1949 TRENTON, N. J.
54- 54	KEARSE, EDWARD PAUL	D. JULY 15, 1968 EUREKA, CALIF.
12- 92	KEATING, RAYMOND HERBERT	D. DECEMBER 28, 1963 SACRAMENTO, CALIF.
13- 95	KEATING, WALTER FRANCIS	D. JULY 13, 1959 PHILADELPHIA, PA.
81- 65	KEATLEY, GREGORY STEVEN	120 LONGITUDE LN - LEXINGTON SC29072
22- 66	KECK, FRANK JOSEPH	D. FEBRUARY 6, 1981 ST. LOUIS, MO.
17- 37	KEEFE, DAVID EDWIN	D. FEBRUARY 4, 1978 KANSAS CITY, MO.
59- 44	KEEGAN, EDWARD CHARLES	24 W CHESTNUT ST - CLAYTON NJ 08312
53- 44	KEEGAN, ROBERT CHARLES	101 SANDSTONE DR - ROCHESTER NY 14616
44- 70	KEELY, ROBERT WILLIAM	313 BRYN MAWR ISLAND - BRADENTON FL 33505

SEE PAGE 149

18- 42	KEEN, HOWARD VICTOR	D. DECEMBER 10, 1976 SALISBURY, MD.
11- 88	KEEN, WILLIAM BROWN	D. JULY 16, 1947 SOUTH POINT, O.
20- 62	KEENAN, JAMES WILLIAM	D. JUNE 5, 1980 SEMINOLE, FLA.
76- 44	KEENER, JOSEPH DONALD	STAR ROUTE 79 - ADELANTO CA 92301
25- 58	KEESEY, JAMES WARD	D. SEPTEMBER 5, 1951 BOISE, IDA.
80- 65	KEETON, RICKEY	3433 STATHEM AVE - CINCINNATI OH 45211
42- 55	KEHN, CHESTER LAURENCE	8249 BONNIE OAK WAY - CITRUS HEIGHTS CA 95610
14-111	KEIFER, SHERMAN C.	B. 1892
55- 56	KEKICH, MICHAEL DENNIS	RR 3 PATTIE CANYON - MISSOULA MT 59801
11- 89	KELIHER, MAURICE MICHAEL	D. SEPTEMBER 7, 1930 WASHINGTON, D.C.
52- 59	KELL, EVERETT LEE	4918 STEVENS DR - PINE BLUFF AR 71605
43- 69	KELL, GEORGE CLYDE	BOX 158-SWIFTON AK 72471
16- 49	KELLEHER, ALBERT ALOYSIUS	D. SEPTEMBER 28, 1947 STATEN ISLAND, N. Y.
42- 56	KELLEHER, FRANCIS EUGENE	D. APRIL 13, 1979 STOCKTON, CALIF.
35- 55	KELLEHER, HAROLD JOSEPH	%H.KELLEHER,2620 MASSEY ST-PHILADE'A PA 19142
12- 93	KELLEHER, JOHN PATRICK	D. AUGUST 21, 1960 BOSTON, MASS.
72- 56	KELLEHER, MICHAEL DENNIS	2429 ANACAPA ST - SANTA BARBARA CA 93105
39- 60	KELLER, CHARLES ERNEST	8238 YELLOW SPRING RD - FREDERICK MD 21701
49- 40	KELLER, HAROLD KEFAUVER	620 MELROSE - SEGUIN TX 78155
66- 51	KELLER, RONALD LEE	7050 NORTH PENN - INDIANAPOLIS IN 46260
53- 45	KELLERT, FRANK WILLIAM	D. NOVEMBER 19, 1976 OKLAHOMA CITY, OKLA.
23- 72	KELLETT, ALFRED HENRY	D. JULY 14, 1960 NEW YORK, N. Y.
34- 53	KELLETT, DONALD STAFFORD	D. NOVEMBER 5, 1970 FT. LAUDERDALE, ALA.
25- 59	KELLEY, HARRY LEROY	D. MARCH 23, 1958 PARKIN, ARK.
64- 56	KELLEY, RICHARD ANTHONY	1091 LEHIGH VALLEY CIR - DANVILLE CA 94526
64- 57	KELLEY, THOMAS HENRY	7036 NORTHWAY DR NW - ROANOKE VA 24019
19- 45	KELLIHER, FRANCIS MORTIMER	D. MARCH 4, 1956 SOMERVILLE, MASS.
48- 52	KELLNER, ALEXANDER RAYMOND	3716 N JACKSON AVE - TUCSON AZ 85719
52- 60	KELLNER, WALTER JOSEPH	3737 N TUCSON BLVD - TUCSON AZ 85716
14-112	KELLOGG, WILLIAM DEARSTYNE	D. DECEMBER 12, 1971 BALTIMORE, MD.
10- 79	KELLY, ALBERT MICHAEL	D. JANUARY 29, 1961 ZEPHYRHILLS, FLA.

```
80- 66 KELLY, DALE PATRICK          5176 SAN SIMEON DR - SANTA BARBARA CA 93111
14-113 KELLY, EDWARD L.             1914 ADD: 2818 DAKOTA ST - SPOKANE WA
15- 80 KELLY, GEORGE LANGE          1151 MILLBRAE AVE - MILLBRAE 94030
67- 57 KELLY, HAROLD PATRICK        836 E HAINES ST - PHILADELPHIA PA 19138
14-114 KELLY, HERBERT BARRETT       D. MAY 18, 1973 TORRANCE, CALIF.
14-115 KELLY, JAMES ROBERT          D. APRIL 10, 1961 KINGSPORT, TENN.
75- 58 KELLY, JAY THOMAS            25 EVELYN TER - SOUTH AMBOY NJ 08879
14-116 KELLY, JOSEPH HENRY          D. AUGUST 16, 1977 ST. JOSEPH, MO.
26- 43 KELLY, JOSEPH JAMES          D. NOVEMBER 24, 1967 LYNBROOK, N. Y.
26- 44 KELLY, MICHAEL J.            OLD ADD: 5853 VON VESSEN AVE - ST LOUIS MO
23- 73 KELLY, REYNOLDS JOSEPH       D. AUGUST 24, 1963 MILLBRAE, CAL.
51- 47 KELLY, ROBERT EDWARD         9 MOHAWK DR - NIENTIC CT 06359
69- 90 KELLY, VAN HOWARD            338 WILLIAM IVEY RD - LILBURN GA 30247
20- 63 KELLY, WILLIAM HENRY         37 QUEENS WAY - CAMILLUS NY 13031
10- 80 KELLY, WILLIAM JOSEPH        D. JUNE 3, 1940 DETROIT, MICH.
64- 58 KELSO, WILLIAM EUGENE        OLD ADD: 5316 NW 33RD TER - KANSAS CITY MO
37- 59 KELTNER, KEN FREDERICK       3220 KING ARTHURS CT W - GREENFIELD WI 53221
54- 51 KEMMERER, RUSSELL PAUL       RR 4, HICKORY HILLS - NORTH VERNON IN 47265
29- 58 KEMNER, HERMAN JOHN          2215 OAK - QUINCY ILL 62301
77- 76 KEMP, STEVEN F               103 W SANTA ANITA TER - ARCADIA CA 91006
69- 91 KENDALL, FRED LYN            3223 VIA VIEJAS - ALPINE CA 92001
61- 60 KENDERS, ALBERT DANIEL GEORGE 8744 MATILIJA AVE - VAN NUYS CA 91402
28- 54 KENNA, EDWARD ALOYSIUS       D. AUGUST 21, 1972 SAN FRANCISCO, CALIF.
70- 70 KENNEDY, JAMES EARL          23060 SW 83RD AVE - PORTLAND OR 97225
62- 65 KENNEDY, JOHN EDWARD         2 RODNEY RD - WEST PEABODY MASS 01960
57- 36 KENNEDY, JOHN IRVIN          XE.WHITE,4166 LOCKHART-JACKSONVILLE FL 32209
74- 65 KENNEDY, JUNIOR RAYMOND      25459 JUDITH ST - ARVIN CA 93203
34- 54 KENNEDY, LLOYD VERNON        #176 - MENDON MO 64660
46- 54 KENNEDY, MONTIA CALVIN       5735 BERRYWOOD - RICHMOND VA 23224
16- 50 KENNEDY, RAYMAND LINCOLN     D. JANUARY 18, 1969 CASSELBERRY, FLA.
39- 61 KENNEDY, ROBERT DANIEL       1060 W ADDISON ST - CHICAGO IL 60613
78- 65 KENNEDY, TERRENCE EDWARD     8223 PARK - BURR RIDGE IL 60521
48- 53 KENNEDY, WILLIAM AULTON      OLD ADD: CHURCH ST - ROCKY MOUNT NC 27802
42- 57 KENNEDY, WILLIAM GORMAN      OLD ADD: 104 E MASON AVE - ALEXANDRIA VA
38- 45 KENNEY, ARTHUR JOSEPH        #3 TIMBER LANE N READING MA 01864
67- 58 KENNEY, GERALD T             1980 HARRISON - BELOIT WI 53511
12- 94 KENT, MAURICE ALLEN          D. APRIL 19, 1966 IOWA CITY, IA.
62- 66 KENWORTHY, RICHARD LEE       3745 TADE LN - INDIANAPOLIS IN 46234
12- 95 KENWORTHY, WILLIAM JENNINGS  D. SEPTEMBER 21, 1950 EUREKA, CALIF.
68- 48 KEOUGH, JOSEPH WILLIAM       10320 BUBB RD - CUPERTINO CA 95014
77- 77 KEOUGH, MATTHEW LON          433 VISTA SUERTE - NEWPORT BEACH CA 92660
56- 47 KEOUGH, RICHARD MARTIN       433 VISTA SUERTE - NEWPORT BEACH CA 92660
50- 41 KERIAZAKOS, CONSTANTINE NICHOLAS 6. SUMMIT RD - BROOKSIDE NJ 07926
39- 62 KERKSIECK, WAYMAN WILLIAM    D. MARCH 11, 1970 LITTLE ROCK, ARK.
15- 81 KERLIN, ORIE MILTON          D. OCTOBER 29, 1974 SHREVEPORT, LA.
74- 66 KERN, JAMES LESTER           6009 AMBERWOOD CT - ARLINGTON TX 76016
```

JERRY KENNEY

```
62- 67 KERN, WILLIAM GEORGE         625 GREEN ST - ALLENTOWN PA 18102
65- 57 KERNEK, GEORGE BOYD          210 NORTH GULF - HOLDENVILLE OK 74848
20- 64 KERNS, DANIEL P.             B. PHILADELPHIA, PA.
45- 51 KERNS, RUSSELL ELDON         3000 NAPOLEON RD - FREMONT OH 43420
23- 74 KERR, JOHN FRANCIS           2812 E 220TH PL - LONG BEACH CA 90810
14-117 KERR, JOHN JONAS             D. JUNE 9, 1937 BALTIMORE, MD.
43- 70 KERR, JOHN JOSEPH            341 GROVE ST-ORADELL NJ 07649
25- 60 KERR, JOHN MELVILLE          D. AUGUST 9, 1980 VERO BEACH, FLA.
19- 46 KERR, RICHARD HENRY          D. MAY 4, 1963 HOUSTON, TEX.
76- 45 KERRIGAN, JOSEPH THOMAS      5148 LEIPER ST - PHILADELPHIA PA 19124
64- 59 KESSINGER, DONALD EULON      1010 JUNE RD - MEMPHIS TN 38119
68- 49 KESTER, RICHARD LEE          BOX 623 - GARDNERVILLE NV 89410
22- 67 KETCHUM, AUGUSTUS FRANKLIN   4409 NW 16TH PLACE - OKLAHOMA CITY OK 73107
12- 96 KETTER, PHILIP               B. HUTCHINSON, KAN.
14-118 KEUPPER, HENRY J.            D. AUGUST 14 1960 MARION, ILL.
25- 61 KIBBIE, HORACE KENT          D. OCTOBER 19, 1975 FORT WORTH, TEX.
12- 97 KIBBLE, JOHN WESTLY          D. DECEMBER 13, 1969 ROUNDUP, MONT.
20- 65 KIEFER, JOSEPH WILLIAM       3264 ONEIDA ST - CHADWICKS NY 13319
51- 48 KIELY, LEO PATRICK           31-U RIVERVIEW GARDENS - N ARLINGTON NJ 07032
17- 38 KILDUFF, PETER JOHN          D. FEBRUARY 14, 1930 PITTSBURG, KAN.
14-119 KILHULLEN, JOSEPH ISADORE    D. NOVEMBER 2, 1922 OAKLAND, CA.
69- 92 KILKENNY, MICHAEL DAVID      274 HOLLAND ST W - BRADFORD ONTARIO
54- 52 KILLEBREW, HARMON CLAYTON    BOX 626 - ONTARIO OR 97914
59- 45 KILLEEN, EVANS HENRY         123 MAIN ST - WESTHAMPTON NY 11978
11- 90 KILLILAY, JOHN WILLIAM       D. OCTOBER 21, 1968 TULSA, OKLA.
```

```
7- 60 KIMBALL, NEWELL W
16- 45 KIMBERLIN, HARRY LYDLE
5- 52 KIMBLE, RICHARD LOUIS
0- 66 KIME, HAROLD LEE
6- 46 KIMM, BRUCE EDWARD
9- 47 KIMMICK, WALTER LYONS
59- 59 KIMSEY, CLYDE ELIAS
16- 48 KINDALL, GERALD DONALD
16- 55 KINDER, ELLIS RAYMOND
6- 56 KINER, RALPH MCPHERRAN
64- 53 KING, CHARLES GILBERT
4- 71 KING, CLYDE EDWARD
16- 51 KING, EDWARD LEE
7- 59 KING, HAROLD
5- 63 KING, JAMES HUBERT
6- 52 KING, LEE
35- 56 KING, LYNN PAUL
54- 54 KING, NELSON JOSEPH
32- 39 KINGDON, WESCOTT WILLIAM
79- 63 KINGMAN, BRIAN PAUL
71- 58 KINGMAN, DAVID ARTHUR
14-120 KINGMAN, HENRY LEES
78- 66 KINNEY, DENNIS PAUL
18- 43 KINNEY, WALTER WILLIAM
80- 67 KINNUNEN, MICHAEL JOHN
19- 48 KINSELLA, ROBERT FRANCIS
34- 55 KINZY, HENRY HENSEL
57- 37 KIPP, FRED LEO
53- 46 KIPPER, THORNTON JOHN
14-121 KIPPERT, EDWARD AUGUST
69- 93 KIRBY, CLAYTON LAWS
49- 41 KIRBY, JAMES HERSCHEL
12- 98 KIRBY, LARUE
19- 49 KIRCHER, MICHAEL ANDREW
47- 51 KIRK, THOMAS DANIEL
61- 61 KIRK, WILLIAM PARTHEMORE
10- 81 KIRKE, JUDSON FABIAN
58- 51 KIRKLAND, WILLIE CHARLES
62- 68 KIRKPATRICK, EDGAR LEON
12- 99 KIRKPATRICK, ENOS CLAIRE
74- 67 KIRKWOOD, DONALD PAUL
50- 42 KIRRENE, JOSEPH JOHN
10- 82 KIRSCH, HARRY LOUIS
45- 53 KISH, ERNEST ALEXANDER
57- 59 KISON, BRUCE EUGENE
54- 55 KITSOS, CHRISTOPHER ANESTOS
34- 56 KLAERNER, HUGO EMIL
66- 52 KLAGES, FRED ANTHONY
64- 60 KLAUS, ROBERT FRANCIS
52- 61 KLAUS, WILLIAM JOSEPH
25- 62 KLEE, OLLIE CHESTER
28- 55 KLEIN, CHARLES HERBERT
44- 72 KLEIN, HAROLD JOHN
43- 71 KLEIN, LOUIS FRANK
34- 57 KLEINHANS, THEODORE OTTO
35- 57 KLEINKE, NORBERT GEORGE
11- 91 KLEPFER, EDWARD LLOYD
76- 47 KLEVEN, JAY ALLEN
43- 72 KLIEMAN, EDWARD FREDERICK
58- 52 KLIMCHOCK, LOUIS STEPHEN
69- 94 KLIMKOWSKI, RONALD BERNARDO
55- 64 KLINE, JOHN ROBERT
30- 41 KLINE, ROBERT GEORGE
52- 62 KLINE, RONALD LEE
```

```
1425 GRIFFITH AVE - LAS VEGAS NV 89104
OLD ADD: 203 N 7TH - POPLAR BLUFF MO
3733 LARCHMONT PARKWAY - TOLEDO OH 43613
D. MAY 16, 1939 COLUMBUS, O.
BOX 298 - NORWAY IA 52318
3333 NE 34TH ST #320 - FT LAUDERDALE FL 33308
D. DECEMBER 3, 1942 PRYOR, OKLA.
ATH DEPT, UNIV OF ARIZONA - TUCSON AZ 85721
D. OCTOBER 16, 1968 JACKSON, TENN.
BOTE ROAD - GREENWICH CT 06830
BOX 741 - PARIS TN 38242
103 STRATFORD RD - GOLDSBORO NC 27530
D. SEPTEMBER 16, 1967 SHINNSTOWN, W. VA.
OLD ADD: 518 FOREST AVE - CINCINNATI OH 45229
RR 2 BOX 15 - ELKINS AR 72727
D. SEPTEMBER 7, 1938 NEWTON CENTRE, MASS.
D. MAY 11, 1972 ATLANTIC, IA.
126 JAMES PL - PITTSBURGH PA 15228
D. APRIL 19, 1975 CAPISTRANO, CALIF.
11 TOKENEKE TRAIL - DARIEN CT 06820
818 W BUSSE AVE - MOUNT PROSPECT IL 60056
33 LINDA ST #2211 - OAKLAND CA 94611
1114 NORTH PARK DR - TEMPERANCE MI 48182
D. JULY 1, 1971 ESCONDIDO, CAL.
5818 MCKINLEY PL N - SEATTLE WA 98103
D. DECEMBER 30, 1951 LOS ANGELES, CALIF.
3721 ARROYO RD - FT WORTH TX 76109
6510 W 69TH ST - OVERLAND PARK KS 66204
8780 E MCKELLOPS #340 - SCOTTSDALE AZ 85257
D. JUNE 3, 1960 DETROIT, MICH.
2256 VIA DIEQUENOS - ALPINE CA 92001
729 DOVER RD - NASHVILLE TN 37211
D. JUNE 10, 1961 LANSING, MICH.
D. JUNE 26, 1972 ROCHESTER, N.Y.
D. AUGUST 1, 1974 PHILADELPHIA, PA.
550 SOUTH PINE ST - YORK PA 17403
D. AUGUST 31, 1968 NEW ORLEANS, LA.
16549 PARKSIDE ST - DETROIT MI 48221
24791 VIA LARGA - LAGUNA NIGUEL CA 92677
D. APRIL 14, 1964 PITTSBURGH, PA.
455 W ELMWOOD - CLAWSON MI 48017
2340 MARSHALL WAY - SACRAMENTO CA 95819
D. DECEMBER 25, 1925 PITTSBURGH, PA.
6619 SOUTH CENTER RD - SOLON OH 44187
2509 NIGHTENGALE LN #61 - BRADENTON FL 33505
1219 ANCHOR DR - MOBILE AL 36609
D. JANUARY 3, 1982 FREDERICKSBURG, TEXAS
418 MELLON AVE - BADEN PA 15005
2632 PALACE DR - SAN DIEGO CA 92123
1655 SOUTH DR - SARASOTA FL 33579
D. FEBRUARY 9, 1977 TOLEDO, O.
D. MARCH 28, 1958 INDIANAPOLIS, IND.
D. DECEMBER 10, 1957 ST. LOUIS, MO.
D. JUNE 20, 1976 METAIRIE, LA.
16011 5TH ST E - REDINGTON BEACH FL 33708
D. MARCH 16, 1950 MARIN, CAL.
D. AUGUST 9, 1950 TULSA, OKLA.
118 VIA BOLSA - SAN LORENZO CA 94580
D. NOVEMBER 15, 1979 HOMOS ASSA, FLA.
BOX 56 - LOYALHANNA PA 15661
791 EDGEWOOD DR - WESTBURY NY 11590
5924 47TH AVE N -ST PETERSBURG FL 33703
7513 RIVERSIDE DR - POWELL OH 43065
MAIN ST BOX 155 - CALLERY PA 16024
```

```
70- 71 KLINE, STEVEN JACK            BOX 429 - CHELAN WA 98816
27- 51 KLINGER, JOSEPH JOHN          D. JULY 31, 1960 LITTLE ROCK, ARK.
38- 46 KLINGER, ROBERT HAROLD        D. AUGUST 19, 1977 VILLA RIDGE, MO.
50- 43 KLIPPSTEIN, JOHN CALVIN       1176 ABERDEEN RD - PALATINE IL 60067
44- 73 KLOPP, STANLEY HAROLD         D. MARCH 11, 1980 ROBESONIA, PA.
31- 44 KLOZA, JOHN CLARENCE          D. JUNE 11, 1962 MILWAUKEE, WIS.
21- 52 KLUGMANN, JOSIE               D. JULY 18, 1951 MOBERLY, MO.
34- 58 KLUMPP, ELMER EDWARD          N67 W27085 HWY 74 - SUSSEX WI 53089
47- 52 KLUSZEWSKI, THEODORE BERNARD  8353 ISLAND LN - MAINEVILLE OH 45039
```

```
76- 48  KLUTTS, GENE ELLIS               20701 BEACH BLVD - HUNTINGTON BEACH CA 92648
42- 58  KLUTTZ, CLYDE FRANKLIN           D. MAY 12, 1979 SALISBURY, N. C.
75- 59  KNAPP, ROBERT CHRISTIAN          1415 CASTLE CT - ST JOSEPH MI 49085
10- 83  KNAUPP, HENRY ANTONE             D. JULY 6, 1967 NEW ORLEANS, LA.
26- 45  KNEISCH, RUDOLPH FRANK           D. APRIL 6, 1965 BALTIMORE, MD.
76- 49  KNEPPER, ROBERT WESLEY           18026 N CAVE CREEK RD #127 - PHOENIX AZ 85032
45- 54  KNERR, WALLACE LUTHER            D. MARCH 23, 1980 LANCASTER, P A.
79- 64  KNICELY, ALAN LEE                BOX 433 - DAYTON VA 22721
47- 53  KNICKERBOCKER, AUSTIN JAY        CLINTON CORNERS NY 12514
33- 32  KNICKERBOCKER, WILLIAM HART      D. SEPTEMBER 8, 1963 SEBASTOPOL, CALIF.
74- 68  KNIGHT, CHARLES RAY              RR2 BOX 380C - ALBANY GA 31707
22- 68  KNIGHT, ELMA RUSSELL             D. JULY 30, 1976 SAN ANTONIO, TEX.
12-100  KNISELY, PETER C.                D. JULY 1, 1948 BROWNSVILLE,PA.
20- 67  KNODE, KENNETH THOMSON           D. DECEMBER 20, 1980 SOUTH BEND, IND.
23- 75  KNODE, ROBERT TROXELL            561 GARRISON RD #3 - BATTLE CREEK MI 49017
64- 61  KNOOP, ROBERT FRANK              1655 SHERRINGTON #2104-SANTA MONICA CA 92260
32- 40  KNOTHE, GEORGE BERTRAM           #1099 E 514 VAUGHN - FORKED RIVER NJ 08731
32- 41  KNOTHE, WILFRED EDGAR            D. MARCH 22, 1963 PASSAIC, N. J.
33- 33  KNOTT, JOHN HENRY                D. OCTOBER 13, 1981 BROWNWOOD, TEXAS
65- 58  KNOWLES, DAROLD DUANE            1004 RAINBOW LN - BLUE SPRINGS MO 64015
15- 82  KNOWLSON, THOMAS HERBERT         D. APRIL 11, 1943 MIAMI SHORES, FLA.
20- 68  KNOWLTON, WILLIAM YOUNG          D. FEBRUARY 25, 1944 PHILADELPHIA, PA.
24- 60  KNOX, CLIFFORD HIRAM             D. SEPTEMBER 24, 1965 OSKALOOSA, IA.
72- 57  KNOX, JOHN CLINTON               492 TROUTWOOD DR - PITTSBURGH PA 15237
53- 47  KOBACK, NICHOLAS NICHOLIA        52 STONEHEDGE DR - NEWINGTON CT 06111
73- 69  KOBEL, KEVIN RICHARD             EDDY RD - COLDEN NY 14033
63- 64  KOCH, ALAN GOODMAN               8 CLOVER RIDGE DR - DEMOPOLIS AL 36732
44- 74  KOCH, BARNETT                    OLD ADD: 1505 N DEFIANCE #Q105-TACOMA WA
12-101  KOCHER, BRADLEY WILSON           D. JANUARY 13, 1965 WHITE HAVEN, PA.
46- 57  KOECHER, RICHARD FINLAY          2000 VALLEY FORGE CIR-KING OF PRUSSIA PA19406
70- 72  KOEGEL, PETER JOHN               OLD ADD: 1205 N 48TH - PHOENIX AZ 85008
25- 63  KOEHLER, HORACE LEVERING         1018 S SPRAGUE AVE - TACOMA WA 98405
32- 42  KOENECKE, LEONARD GEORGE         D. SEPTEMBER 17, 1935 TORONTO, ONT.
25- 64  KOENIG, MARK ANTHONY             4295 WARM SPRINGS - GLEN ELLEN CA 95442
19- 50  KOENIGSMARK, WILLIS THOMAS       D. JULY 1, 1972 WATERLOO, ILL.
10- 84  KOESTNER, ELMER JOSEPH           D. OCTOBER 27, 1959 FAIRBURY, ILL.
37- 61  KOHLMAN, JOSEPH JAMES            1968 ADD: 4532 CHESTNUT - PHILADELPHIA PA
48- 54  KOKOS, RICHARD JEROME            2537 N MAJOR AVE - CHICAGO IL 60639
60- 57  KOLB, GARY ALAN                  XJ-KOLB,1201 DIXON #F - ROCK FALLS IL 61071
40- 47  KOLLOWAY, DONALD MARTIN          2236 W 121ST STREET PL - BLUE ISLAND IL 60406
21- 53  KCLP, RAYMOND CARL               D. JULY 29, 1967 NEW ORLEANS, LA.
15- 83  KOLSETH, KARL DICKEY             D. MAY 3, 1956 CUMBERLAND, MD.
62- 63  KOLSTAD, HAROLD EVERETTE         15149 BEL ESCOU DR - SAN JOSE CA 95124
13- 96  KOMMERS, FRED RAYMOND            D. JUNE 14, 1943 CHICAGO, ILL.
73- 70  KONIECZKY, DOUGLAS JAMES         40304 SPITZ DR- STERLING HEIGHTS MI 48078
48- 55  KONIKOWSKI, ALEXANDER JAMES      BANK ST - SEYMOUR CT 06483
42- 59  KONOPKA, BRUCE BRUNO             3212 S ADAMS - DENVER CO 80210
44- 75  KONSTANTY, CASIMIR JAMES         D. JUNE 11, 1976 ONEONTA, N. Y.
15- 84  KOOB, ERNEST GERALD              D. NOVEMBER 12, 1941 LEMAY, MO.
62- 70  KOONCE, CALVIN LEE               3646 GOLFVIEW DR - HOPE MILLS NC 28348
67- 60  KOOSMAN, JERRY MARTIN            RR 2 BOX 67E - CHASKA MN 55318
66- 53  KOPACZ, GEORGE FELIX             4120 S RICHMOND - CHICAGO IL 60623
21- 54  KOPF, WALTER HENRY               D. APRIL 30, 1979 CINCINNATI, O.
13- 97  KOPF, WILLIAM LORENZ             7177 STONINGTON RD - CINCINNATI OH 45230
61- 62  KOPLITZ, HOWARD DEAN             623 BOYD ST - OSHKOSH WI 54901
15- 85  KOPPE, MERLIN HENRY              D. MAY 7, 1960 SACRAMENTO, CALIF.
58- 53  KOPPE, JOSEPH                    7887 BEATRICE ST - WESTLAND MI 48185
23- 76  KOPSHAW, GEORGE KARL             D. DECEMBER 26, 1934 LYNCHBURG, VA.
54- 56  KORCHECK, STEPHEN JOSEPH         8018 WILLOW AVE - SARASOTA FL 33580
15- 86  KORES, ARTHUR EMIL               D. MARCH 26, 1974 MILWAUKEE, WIS.
66- 54  KORINCE, GEORGE EUGENE           OLD ADD: 172 DORCHESTER BLVD-ST CATHERINES ON
65- 59  KOSCO, ANDREW JOHN               9329 NEW SPRINGFIELD RD - POLAND OH 44514
52- 63  KOSHOREK, CLEMENT JOHN           3951 ANHERST - ROYAL OAK MI 48072
51- 49  KOSKI, WILLIAM JOHN              2656 EL GRECO DR - MODESTO CA 95351
41- 56  KOSLO, GEORGE BERNARD            D. DECEMBER 1, 1975 MENASHA, WIS.
44- 76  KOSMAN, MICHAEL THOMAS           2110 S 6TH LAFAYETTE IN 47904
31- 46  KOSTER, FREDERICK CHARLES        D. APRIL 24, 1979 SAINT MATTHEWS, KY.
62- 71  KOSTRO, FRANK JERRY              3161 S JASMINE WAY - DENVER CO 80222
55- 65  KOUFAX, SANFORD                  1000 ELYSIAN AVE - LOS ANGELES CA 90012
25- 65  KOUPAL, LOUIS LADDIE             D. DECEMBER 8, 1961 SAN GABRIEL, CAL.
32- 43  KOWALIK, FABIAN LORENZ           D. AUGUST 14, 1954 KARNES CITY, TEX.
38- 47  KOY, ERNEST ANYZ                 BOX 476 1047 S OAK BELLVILLE TX 77418
```

```
48- 56 KOZAR, ALBERT KENNETH           3004 VINCENT RD - WEST PALM BEACH FL 33405
39- 63 KRACHER, JOSEPH PETER           1515 CADDO - SAN ANGELO TX 76901
14-122 KRAFT, CLARENCE OTTO            D. MARCH 26, 1958 FORT WORTH, TEX.
37- 62 KRAKAUSKAS, JOSEPH VICTOR LAWRENCE D. DECEMBER 8, 1960 HAMILTON, ONT.
59- 46 KRALICK, JOHN FRANCIS           BOX 3006 - SOLDOTNA AK 99669
53- 48 KRALY, STEVEN CHARLES           2246 SCHRAGE - WHITING IN 46354
39- 64 KRAMER, JOHN HENRY              2126 PAULINE ST-NEW ORLEANS LA 70117
62- 72 KRANEPOOL, EDWARD EMIL          LANE 1, BROOKVILLE - JERICHO NY 11753
11- 92 KRAPP, EUGENE H.                D. APRIL 13, 1923 DETROIT, MICH.
43- 73 KRAUS, JOHN WILLIAM             D. JANUARY 2, 1976 SAN ANTONIO, TEX.
61- 63 KRAUSSE, LOUIS BERNARD JR       RR 1 BOX 572C - HOLT MO 64048
31- 46 KRAUSSE, LOUIS BERNARD SR       3206 CAMBRIDGE AVE - BRADENTON FL 33507
75- 60 KRAVEC, KENNETH PETER           13599 MOHAWK TRAIL - MIDDLEBURG HGTS OH 44130
56- 49 KRAVITZ, DANIEL                 RR1 - DUSHORE PA 18614
31- 47 KREEVICH, MICHAEL ANDREAS       3S637 TERRACE DR - AURORA IL 60504
11- 93 KREITZ, RALPH WESLEY            D. JULY 20, 1941 PORTLAND, ORE.
24- 61 KREMER, REMY PETER              D. FEBRUARY 8, 1965 PINOLE, CAL.
73- 71 KREMMEL, JAMES LOUIS            2704 S BLAKE RD - SPOKANE WA 99216
79- 65 KRENCHICKI, WAYNE RICHARD       53 FARRELL AVE - TRENTON NJ 08618
47- 54 KRESS, CHARLES STEVEN           RUSH LAKE RESORT - OTTERTAIL MN 56571
27- 52 KRESS, RALPH                    D. NOVEMBER 29, 1962 LOS ANGELES, CALIF.
46- 58 KRETLOW, LOUIS HENRY            3213 W MAINE - ENID OK 73701
75- 61 KREUGER, RICHARD ALLEN          985 DEN HARTOG - WYOMING MI 49509
62- 73 KREUTZER, FRANK JAMES           305 HERRINGTON DR - LARGO MD 20870
11- 94 KRICHELL, PAUL BERNARD          D. JUNE 4, 1957 NEW YORK, N.Y.
49- 42 KRIEGER, KURT FERDINAND         D. AUGUST 16, 1970 ST. LOUIS, MO.
43- 74 KRIETNER, ALBERT JOSEPH         313 CHURCH ST-NASHVILLE TN 37201
37- 63 KRIST, HOWARD WILBUR            44 GROVE ST - DELAVAN NY 14042
78- 67 KROL, JOHN THOMAS               3012 FLEET ST - WINSTON-SALEM NC 27107
64- 62 KROLL, GARY MELVIN              9038 E 40TH ST - TULSA OK 74145
55- 58 KRONER, JOHN HAROLD             D. AUGUST 26, 1968 ST. LOUIS, MO.
60- 58 KRSNICH, MICHAEL                6818 W LINCOLN AVE - WEST ALLIS WI 53219
49- 43 KRSNICH, ROCCO PETER            5420 E HARRY - WICHITA KS 67218
13- 98 KRUEGER, ERNEST GEORGE          D. APRIL 22, 1976 WAUKEGAN, ILL.
65- 60 KRUG, EVERETT BEN               4125 ALLOTT AVE - SHERMAN OAKS CA 91423
81- 66 KRUG, GARY EUGENE               1327 BAYLOR DR - COLORADO SPRINGS CO 80909
12-102 KRUG, MARTIN JOHN               D. JUNE 27, 1966 GLENDALE, CALIF.
76- 50 KRUKOW, MICHAEL EDWARD          221 COUNTRY CLUB DR - SAN GABRIEL CA 91775
49- 44 KRYHOSKI, RICHARD DAVID         18855 WARWICK RD - BIRMINGHAM MI 48009
57- 38 KUBEK, ANTHONY CHRISTOPHER      3311 N MCDONALD - APPLETON WI 54911
57- 61 KUBIAK, THEODORE ROGER          327 BONITA AVE - PIEDMONT CA 94611
61- 64 KUBISZYN, JACK JOSEPH           186 WOODLAND - TUSCALOOSA AL 35401
80- 68 KUBSKI, GILBERT THOMAS          OLD ADD: 11647 DURRY -GRANADA HILLS CA
50- 44 KUCAB, JOHN ALBERT              D. MAY 26, 1977 YOUNGSTOWN, O.
74- 69 KUCEK, JOHN ANDREW CHARLES      1219 WARREN RD - NEWTON FALLS OH 44444
55- 66 KUCKS, JOHN CHARLES             15 OAKLAND ST - HILLSDALE NJ 07642
49- 45 KUCZEK, STANISLAW LEO           769 SACANDAGA RD - SCOTIA NY 12302
43- 75 KUCZYNSKI, BERNARD CARL         RR 4 - ALLENTOWN PA 18103
76- 51 KUEHL, KARL OTTO                4395 50TH AVE S - ST PETERSBURG FL 33711
52- 64 KUENN, HARVEY EDWARD            5527 W NATIONAL-WEST MILWAUKEE WI 53214
77- 78 KUHAULUA, FRED MAHELE           BOX 2539 - NANAKULI HI 96792
30- 42 KUHEL, JOSEPH ANTHONY           437 W 87TH PL - KANSAS CITY MO 64114
24- 62 KUHN, BERNARD DANIEL            D. NOVEMBER 20, 1956 LANSING, MICH.
55- 67 KUHN, KENNETH HAROLD            OLD ADD: CLAYBROOK & MAINE - DOVER MA 02030
12-103 KUHN, WALTER CHARLES            D. JUNE 14, 1935 FRESNO, CALIF.
74- 70 KUIPER, DUANE EUGENE            5507-A SUTTON LN - WILLOUGHBY OH 44094
55- 68 KUME, JOHN MIKE                 RR2 WOODARD RD - ANDOVER OH 44003
61- 65 KUNKEL, WILLIAM GUSTAVE JAMES 1 NAUTILUS DR - LEONARDO NJ 07737
```

```
79- 66 KUNTZ, RUSSELL JAY              1254 LANA ST - PASO ROBLES CA 93446
23- 77 KUNZ, EARL DEWEY               D. APRIL 14, 1963 SACRAMENTO, CAL.
75- 62 KUROSAKI, RYAN YOSHITOMO        1324 HIGH VIEW PL - HONOLULU HI 96816
41- 57 KUROWSKI, GEORGE JOHN           310 SPRINGSIDE DR-SHILLINGTON PA 19607
68- 50 KURTZ, HAROLD JAMES             RR GLENN DALE MD 20769
41- 58 KUSH, EMIL BENEDICT             D. NOVEMBER 26, 1969 RIVER GROVE, ILL.
73- 72 KUSICK, CRAIG ROBERT            %D.BAERTSCHY,RR 1 - ST GERMAIN WI 54558
70- 73 KUSNYER, ARTHUR WILLIAM         419 ROYAL AVE - AKRON OH 44303
11- 95 KUTINA, JOSEPH PETER            D. APRIL 13, 1945 CHICAGO, ILL.
59- 47 KUTYNA, MARION JOHN             2711 EAST CAMBRIA ST - PHILADELPHIA PA 19134
```

```
46- 59  KUZAVA, ROBERT LEROY            1118 VINEWOOD ST - WYANDOTTE MI 48192
42- 60  KVASNAK, ALEXANDER             3265 HEMPSTEAD AVE-ARCADIA CA 91006
12-104  KYLE, ANDREW EWING             D. SEPTEMBER 6, 1971 TORONTO, ONT.
37- 64  LAABS, CHESTER PETER           8401 WERMUTH - CENTER LINE MI 48015
50- 45  LABINE, CLEMENT WALTER         BOX 643 - WOONSOCKET RI 02895
69- 95  LABOY, JOSE ALBERTO            CLE 30 BLQ 29-#26V.ASTORIUS-CAROLINA PR 00630
77- 79  LACEY, ROBERT JOSEPH           2525 E FOUNTAIN - MESA AZ 85201
69- 96  LACHEMANN, MARCEL ERNEST       1449 BOOKMAN AVE - WALNUT CA 91789
65- 61  LACHEMANN, RENE GEORGE         2736 W PLATA AVE - MESA AZ 85202
14-128  LACLAIRE, GEORGE LEWIS         D. OCTOBER 10, 1918 FARNHAM, QUE.
72- 58  LACOCK, RALPH PIERRE           9722 BRIAR - OVERLAND PARK KS 66207
75- 63  LACORTE, FRANK JOSEPH          791 ESCHENBURG DR - GILROY CA 95020
78- 68  LACOSS, MICHAEL JAMES          4110 LAVIDA - VISALIA CA 93277
72- 59  LACY, LEONDAUS                 3939 BLACKBIRD WAY - CALABASA CA 91203
26- 46  LACY, OSCEOLA GUY              D. NOVEMBER 19, 1953 CLEVELAND, TENN.
79- 67  LADD, PETER LINWOOD            79 STEVENS AVE - PORTLAND ME 04102
46- 60  LADE, DOYLE MARION             445 N 12TH ST - GENEVA NE 68361
47- 55  LAFATA, JOSEPH JOSEPH          4172 DEVONSHIRE - DETROIT MI 48224
45- 55  LAFOREST, BYRON JOSEPH         D. MAY 5, 1947 ARLINGTON, MASS.
34- 59  LAGGER, EDWIN JOSEPH           D. NOVEMBER 10, 1981 JOLIET, ILL.
70- 74  LAGROW, LERRIN HARRIS          12271 E TURQUOISE - SCOTTSDALE AZ 85259
68- 51  LAHOUD, JOSEPH MICHAEL         13 AUSTIN ST - DANBURY CT 06810
46- 65  LAJESKIE, RICHARD EDWARD       D. AUGUST 15, 1976 RAMSEY, N. J.
39- 65  LAKE, EDWARD ERVING            1840 NELSON ST - SAN LEANDRO CA 94578
42- 74  LAKEMAN, ALBERT WESLEY         D. MAY 25, 1976 SPARTANBURG, S.C .
62- 74  LAMABE, JOHN ALEXANDER         48 BALCOM RD - FARMINGDALE NY 11735
43- 76  LAMACCHIA, ALFRED ANTHONY      354 SANDALWOOD LN-SAN ANTONIO TX 78216
40- 48  LAMANNA, FRANK                 D. SEPTEMBER 1, 1980 SYRACUSE, N. Y.
41- 59  LAMANNO, RAYMOND SIMON         827 POLK ST-ALBANY CA 94706
35- 59  LAMANSKE, FRANK JAMES          D. AUGUST 4, 1971 OLNEY,ILL.
17- 39  LAMAR, WILLIAM HARMONG         D. MAY 24, 1970 ROCKPORT, MASS.
37- 65  LAMASTER, WAYNE LEE            2525 E ELM ST NEW ALBANY IN 47150
70- 75  LAMB, JOHN ANDREW              HILLTOP RD - SHARON CT 06069
20- 69  LAMB, LAYMAN RAYMOND           D. OCTOBER 5, 1955 FAYETTEVILLE, ARK.
69- 97  LAMB, RAYMOND RICHARD          1512 E BALBOA BLVD - BALBOA CA 92661
46- 62  LAMBERT, CLAYTON PATRICK       454 EAST 3100 N - OGDEN UT 84404
41- 60  LAMBERT, EUGENE MARION         268 MONTELO-MEMPHIS TN 38117
16- 53  LAMBETH, OTIS SAMUEL           D. JUNE 5, 1976 MORAN, KAN.
12-105  LAMLINE, FREDERICK ARTHUR      D. SEPTEMBER 20, 1970 PORT HURON, MICH.
70- 76  LAMONT, GENE WILLIAM           500 SOUTH 4TH ST - KIRKLAND IL 60146
20- 70  LAMOTTE, ROBERT EUGENE         D. NOVEMBER 2, 1970 CHATHAM, MA.
77- 80  LAMP, DENNIS PATRICK           12100 MONTECITO RD #161-LOS ALAMITOS CA 90720
69- 98  LAMPARD, CHRISTOPHER KEITH     842 NE 74TH AVE - PORTLAND OR 97213
35- 60  LANAHAN, RICHARD ANTHONY       D. MARCH 12, 1975 ROCHESTER, MINN.
77- 81  LANCE, GARY DEAN               1802 OMEGA DR - COLUMBIA SC 29206
29- 60  LAND, WILLIAM GILBERT          RR 1 BOX G-31 - EMELLE AL 35459
52- 65  LANDENBERGER, KENNETH HENRY    D. JULY 28, 1960 CLEVELAND, O.
77- 82  LANDESTCY,RAFAEL SIVIALDO CAMILO M.GOMEZ 56,BANI-PROV PERAVIA DOM REP
57- 39  LANDIS, JAMES HENRY            2439 STONEHOUSE CT - NAPA CA 94558
63- 65  LANDIS, WILLIAM HENRY          525 SYCAMORE - HANFORD CA 93230
77- 83  LANDREAUX, KENNETH FRANCIS     1211 N CHESTER AVE - COMPTON CA 94520
76- 52  LANDRETH, LARRY ROBERT         951 COMMISSIONERS RD E #609- LONDON ONTARIO
50- 46  LANDRITH, HOBERT NEAL          1462 NOME CT - SUNNYVALE CA 94087
57- 40  LANDRUM, DONALD LEROY          19 BARRIE COURT - PITTSBURG CA 94565
38- 48  LANDRUM, JESSE GLENN           3445 ELDER ST BEAUMONT TX 77703
50- 47  LANDRUM, JOSEPH BUTLER         RR 5 BOX 339 - COLUMBIA SC 29203
80- 69  LANDRUM, TERRY LEE             1121 KENTUCKY SE - ALBUQUERQUE NM 87108
24- 63  LANE, JAMES HUNTER             5720 HERALD SQUARE - MEMPHIS TN 38119
53- 49  LANE, JERALD HAL               7306 ELAINE DR - CHATTANOOGA TN 37421
71- 61  LANE, MARVIN                   17191 ARDMORE - DETROIT MI 48235
49- 46  LANE, RICHARD HARRISON         26609 ACADEMY DR-PALOS VERDES PENIN CA 90274
41- 61  LANFRANCONI, WALTER OSWALD     19 PERRIO ST - BARRE VT 05641
38- 49  LANG, DONALD CHARLES           5700 KIRKSIDE DR #F - BAKERSFIELD CA 93309
30- 43  LANG, MARTIN JOHN              D. JANUARY 13, 1968 LAKEWOOD, COLO.
75- 64  LANG, ROBERT DAVID             985 HOMER AVE - PITTSBURGH PA 15237
14-123  LANGE, ERWIN HENRY             D. APRIL 24, 1971 MAYWOOD, ILL.
10- 85  LANGE, FRANK HERMAN            D. DECEMBER 26, 1945 MADISON, WIS.
72- 60  LANGE, RICHARD OTTO            3387 BROOKS RD, RR 2 - FREELAND MI 48623
26- 47  LANGFORD, ELTON L.             1003 OAKLAND ST - PLAINVIEW TX 79072
76- 53  LANGFORD, JAMES RICK           1119 59TH ST NW - BRADENTON FL 33505
64- 63  LANGFORD, HAROLD CLIFTON       2365 WOODLAWN CIR E - ST PETERSBURG FL 33704
38- 50  LANIER, HUBERT MAX             RR 4 BOX 27 - DUNNELLON FL 32630
71- 61  LANIER, LORENZO                2928 WOODHILL AVE - CLEVELAND OH 44104
```

5- 46 LANNING, JOHN YOUNG   28 DEANWOOD CIR - ASHEVILLE NC 28803
5- 54 LANNING, LESTER ALFRED   D. JUNE 13, 1962 BRISTOL, CONN.
8- 51 LANNING, THOMAS NEWTON   D. NOVEMBER 4, 1967 MARIETTA, GA.
8- 69 LANSFORD, CARNEY RAY   OLD ADD: 2001 DEERPARK PL #718-FULLERTON CA
4- 69 LANSING, EUGENE HEWETT   D. JANUARY 18, 1945 RENSSELAER, N. Y.
4- 50 LAPALME, PAUL EDMORE   167 SMITH ST - LEOMINSTER MA 01453
2- 70 LAPAN, PETER NELSON   D. JANUARY 5, 1953 NORWALK, CAL.
2- 62 LAPIHUSKA, ANDREW   900 MULBERRY STREET-MILLVILLE NJ 08332
6- 70 LAPOINT, DAVID JEFFREY   5 ELSMERE AVE #D1 - DELMAR NY 12054
7- 56 LAPOINTE, RALPH JOHN   D. SEPTEMBER 13, 1967 BURLINGTON, VT.
8- 54 LARKER, NORMAN HOWARD JOHN   4701 VILLAGE RD - LONG BEACH CA 90808
4- 60 LARKIN, STEPHEN PATRICK   D. MAY 2, 1969 NORRISTOWN, PA.
8- 44 LARMORE, ROBERT MCCAHAN   D. JANUARY 15, 1964 ST. LOUIS, MO.
0- 77 LAROCHE, DAVID EUGENE   36 HARBOR SIGHT DR-ROLLING HLS E'TES CA 90274
8- 70 LAROSE, HENRY JOHN   99 ROLAND - CUMBERLAND RI 02864
8- 52 LAROSE, VICTOR RAYMOND   2908 E SYLVIA ST - PHOENIX AZ 85028
4-124 LAROSS, HARRY RAYMOND   D. MARCH 22, 1954 HINES, ILL.
3- 50 LARSEN, DONALD JAMES   17090 COPPER HILL DR - MORGAN HILL CA 95037
6- 47 LARSEN, ERLING ADELI   33 PROSPECT AVE #1B - HACKENSACK NJ 07601
6- 54 LARSON, DANIEL JAMES   1616 MONTEREY AVE - HERMOSA BEACH CA 90254
3- 66 LARUSSA, ANTHONY   2010 N MACDILL AVE - TAMPA FL 33607
4- 57 LARY, ALFRED ALLEN   RR 4 BOX 171-A - NORTHPORT AL 35476
4- 58 LARY, FRANK STRONG   RR 8 BOX 142 - NORTHPORT AL 35476
9- 61 LARY, LYNFORD HOBART   D. JANUARY 9, 1973 DOWNEY, CAL.

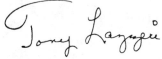

3- 67 LASHER, FREDERICK WALTER   RASSIGA RD 2 ROUTE 17 - MIDDLETOWN NY 10940
4- 64 LASLEY, WILLARD ALMOND   163 S JACKSON ST - SEATTLE WA 98104
4- 59 LASORDA, THOMAS CHARLES   1473 W MAXZIM - FULLERTON CA 92633
7- 41 LASSETTER, DONALD O'NEAL   406 GORDY ST - PERRY GA 31069
0- 86 LATHERS, CHARLES TEN EYCK   D. JULY 26, 1971 PETOSKEY, MICH.
3- 99 LATHROP, WILLIAM GEORGE   D. NOVEMBER 20, 1958 JANESVILLE, WIS.
7- 42 LATMAN, ARNOLD BARRY   OLD ADD: 19205 KNAPP ST - NORTHRIDGE CA
6- 50 LAU, CHARLES RICHARD   99 CORAL LN - KEY COLONY BAY FL 33051
7- 67 LAUDNER, TIMOTHY JON   1801 PEARSON PKWY - MINNEAPOLIS MN 55444
7- 62 LAUZERIQUE, GEORGE ALBERT   4390 SW 10TH ST - MIAMI 33134
4- 61 LAVAGETTO, HARRY ARTHUR   46 TARA RD - ORINDA CA 94563
4-100 LAVAN, JOHN LEONARD   D. MAY 29, 1952 DETROIT, MICH.
4- 71 LAVELLE, GARY ROBERT   1015 E LINDEN ST - ALLENTOWN PA 18103
2-106 LAVENDER, JAMES SANFORD   D. JANUARY 12, 1960 CARTERSVILLE, GA.
4-125 LAVIGNE, ARTHUR DAVID   D. JULY 18, 1950 WORCESTER, MASS.
9- 99 LAW, RONALD DAVID   OLD ADD: 9000 YUCCA WAY - THORNTON CO
8- 71 LAW, RUDY KARL   2206 MENATO ST - EAST PALO ALTO CA 94303
0- 71 LAW, VANCE AARON   1760 WILLOWBROOK DR - PROVO UT 84601
0- 48 LAW, VERNON SANDERS   3885 N LITTLE ROCK DR - PROVO UT 84601
6- 63 LAWING, GARLAND FREDERICK   5710 ORR RD #20 - CHARLOTTE NC 28213
3- 68 LAWRENCE, BROOKS ULYSSES   OLD ADD: 2451 ASHBURN RD - CINCINNATI OH
4- 65 LAWRENCE, JAMES ROSS   BOX 851 - CALEDONIA ONTARIO
4- 65 LAWRENCE, ROBERT ANDREW   73-48 181ST ST - FLUSHING NY 11366
2- 44 LAWRENCE, WILLIAM HENRY   135 GRAND ST - REDWOOD CITY CA 94062
6- 55 LAWRY, OTIS CARROLL   D. OCTOBER 23, 1965 CHINA, ME.
0- 44 LAWSON, ALFRED VOYLE   D. APRIL 9, 1977 STOCKPORT, IA.
2- 61 LAWSON, STEVEN GEORGE   2906 STRONG ST - SAN LEANDRO CA 94578
0- 78 LAXTON, WILLIAM HARRY   262 MANSION AVE - AUDUBON NJ 08106
5- 87 LAYDEN, EUGENE FRANCIS   OLD ADD: 1801 PIONEER AVE - PITTSBURGH PA
8- 57 LAYDEN, PETER JOHN   506 S GILBERT - EDNA TX 77957
7- 53 LAYNE, HERMAN   D. AUGUST 27, 1973 GALLIPOLIS, O.
1- 62 LAYNE, IVORIA HILLIS   4623 DORISA AVE-CHATTANOOGA TN 37411
8- 58 LAYTON, LESTER LEE   8780 E MCKELLIPS RD #27 - SCOTTSDALE AZ 85257
8- 53 LAZAR, JOHN DAN   1007 RIVER DR - MUNSTER IN 46321
3- 77 LAZAR, JOHN PAUL   8054 S 116TH ST-SEATTLE WASHINGTON 98178
6- 48 LAZZERI, ANTHONY MICHAEL   D. AUGUST 6, 1946 SAN FRANCISCO, CAL.
0- 72 LEA, CHARLES WILLIAM   4237 FAIRMONT AVE - MEMPHIS TN 38108
3- 78 LEACH, FREDERICK M   BLISS IDAHO 83314
1- 68 LEACH, RICHARD MAX   4033 WEST COURT - FLINT MI 48504
1- 69 LEACH, TERRY HESTER   603 HOWELL AVE - SELMA AL 36701
3- 73 LEAL, LUIS ENRIQUE   CALLE 28 #30-60 - BARQUISIMETO,EDO. LARA VENEZ
4-126 LEAR, CHARLES BERNARD   D. OCTOBER 31, 1976 GREENCASTLE, PA.
5- 88 LEAR, FREDERICK FRANCIS   D. OCTOBER 13, 1955 EAST ORANGE, N.J.
7- 40 LEARD, WILLIAM WALLACE   D. JANUARY 15, 1970 SAN FRANCISCO, CAL.
4-127 LEARY, JOHN LOUIS   D. AUGUST 18, 1961 WALTHAM, MASS.
1- 70 LEARY, TIMOTHY JAMES   218 25TH ST - SANTA MONICA CA 90402
0- 71 LEATHERS, HAROLD LANGFORD   D. APRIL 12, 1977 MODESTO, CALIF.
9- 51 LEBOURVEAU, DEWITT WILEY   D. DECEMBER 19, 1947 NEVADA CITY, CAL.

```
15- 89 LEDBETTER, RALPH OVERTON      D. FEBRUARY 1, 1969 WEST PALM BEACH, FLA.
19- 52 LEE, CLIFFORD WALKER          D. AUGUST 25, 1980 DENVER, COLO.
57- 43 LEE, DONALD EDWARD            9101 PALM TREE DR - TUCSON AZ 85710
20- 72 LEE, ERNEST DUDLEY            D. JANUARY 7, 1971 DENVER, COLO.
30- 45 LEE, HAROLD BURNHAM           4118 RIVER RD - MOSS POINT MS 39563
69-100 LEE, LERON                    111 SOUTH AVE - SACRAMENTO CA 95838
78- 72 LEE, MARK LINDEN              5019 W 133RD ST - HAWTHORNE CA 90250
60- 59 LEE, MICHAEL RANDALL          33202 PIEDRAS GRANDE-GREEN VALLEY LK CA 9234
64- 64 LEE, ROBERT DEAN              16116 CRYSTAL CREEK LN - CERRITOS CA 90701
45- 56 LEE, ROY EDWIN                42 VIOLA DR - TROY IL 62294
33- 34 LEE, THORNTON STARR           509 W VIRGINIA AV - PHOENIX AZ 85003
34- 62 LEE, WILLIAM CRUTCHER         D. JUNE 15, 1977 PLAQUEMINE, LA.
69-101 LEE, WILLIAM FRANCIS          1030 PIEDMONT - BELLINGHAM WA 98225
15- 90 LEE, WILLIAM JOSEPH           207 N BROAD ST - WEST HAZELTON PA 18201
59- 48 LEEK, ELGENE HAROLD           3327 BANCROFT ST - SAN DIEGO CA 92104
21- 55 LEES, GEORGE EDWARD           D. JANUARY 2, 1980 MECHANICSBURG, PA.
65- 62 LEFEBVRE, JAMES KENNETH       7715 ST BERNARD ST - MARINA DEL REY CA 9029
80- 74 LEFEBVRE, JOSEPH HENRY        1 CARTER HILL RD - PENCOOK NH 03301
38- 52 LEFEBVRE, WILFRID HENRY       7200 ULMERTON RD #1379--LARGO FL 33541
20- 73 LEFEVRE, ALFREDO MODESTO      D. JANUARY 21, 1982 GLEN COVE, N. Y.
24- 66 LEFLER, WADE HAMPTON          D. MARCH 6, 1981
74- 72 LEFLORE, RONALD               10448 SOMERSET - DETROIT MI 48224
29- 62 LEGETT, LOUIS ALFRED          20 SNIPE ST - NEW ORLEANS LA 70124
32- 45 LEHENY, REGIS FRANCIS         D. NOVEMBER 2, 1976 PITTSBURGH, PA.
61- 66 LEHEW, JAMES ANTHONY          398 ARMSTRONG LN - BALTIMORE MD 21221
52- 66 LEHMAN, KENNETH KARL          447 COIN LAKE RD - SEDRO-WOOLLEY WA 98294
46- 64 LEHNER, PAUL EUGENE           D. DECEMBER 27, 1967 BIRMINGHAM, ALA.
11- 96 LEHR, CLARENCE EMANUEL        D. JANUARY 31, 1948 DETROIT, MICH.
26- 49 LEHR, NORMAN CARL MICHAEL     D. JULY 17, 1968 CONESUS LAKE, N. Y.
33- 35 LEIBER, HENRY EDWARD          RR2 #811 - TUCSON AZ 85715
13-101 LEIBOLD, HARRY LORAN          D. FEBRUARY 4, 1977 DETROIT, MICH.
79- 68 LEIBRANDT, CHARLES LOUIS      1424 OVERLOOK DR - GOLF IL 60029
21- 56 LEIFER, ELMER EDWIN           D. SEPTEMBER 26, 1948 EVERETT, WASH.
12-107 LEINHAUSER, WILLIAM CHARLES   D. APRIL 14, 1978 ELKINS PARK, PA.
39- 66 LEIP, EDGAR ELLSWORTH         329 JOY RD - SOUTH DAYTONA FL 32019
54- 61 LEJA, FRANK JOHN              118 WILSON RD - NAHANT MA 01908
11- 97 LEJEUNE, SHELDON ALDENBERT    D. APRIL 21, 1952 CHATTANOOGA, TENN.
65- 63 LEJOHN, DONALD EVERETT        154 EDWARDS ST - BROWNSVILLE PA 15417
73- 73 LEMANCZYK, DAVID LAWRENCE     OLD ADD: 1766 VICTORIA ST - BALDWIN NY
62- 75 LEMASTER, DENVER CLAYTON      4424 RIVERCLIFF CR - LILBURN GA 30247
```

Best Wishes
Bob Lemon

```
75- 65 LEMASTER, JOHNNIE LEE         372 4TH ST - PAINTSVILLE KY 41240
61- 67 LEMAY, RICHARD PAUL           4821 S FLORENCE AVE - TULSA OK 74105
50- 49 LEMBO, STEPHEN NEAL           133-22 124TH ST - SOUTH OZONE PARK NY 11420
75- 66 LEMON, CHESTER EARL           1388 GROTON LN - WHEATON IL 60187
50- 50 LEMON, JAMES ROBERT           6824 PINEWAY - HYATTSVILLE MD 20782
41- 63 LEMON, ROBERT GRANVILLE       1141 CLAIBORNE DR-LONG BEACH CA 90807
69-102 LEMONDS, DAVID LEE            207 JACKSON DR - CHARLOTTE NC 28213
76- 55 LEMONGELLO, MARK              %STAPLETON,251 ATLANTIC #30A-KEYPORT NJ 0773
50- 51 LENHARDT, DONALD EUGENE       5569 BARONRIDGE DR #1 - ST LOUIS MO 63129
28- 56 LENNON, EDWARD FRANCIS        D. SEPTEMBER 13, 1947 PHILADELPHIA, PA.
54- 62 LENNON, ROBERT ALBERT         8 DUDLEY LN - DIX HILLS NY 11743
78- 73 LENTINE, JAMES MATTHEW        512 MALTBY - BIR BEAR CITY CA 90605
68- 54 LEON, EDUARDO ANTONIO         1312 W NIAGARA ST - TUCSON AZ 85705
45- 57 LEON, ISIDORO JUAN            CALLE O NO. 260, APT 5 - VADARO HAVANA CUBA
73- 74 LEON, MAXIMINO                VENUSTIANO CARRANZA #97 - CUITLAHUAC MEXICO
74- 73 LEONARD, DENNIS PATRICK       2034 TEAL AVE - SARASOTA FL 33580
11- 98 LEONARD, ELMER ELLSWORTH      D. MAY 27, 1981 NAPA, CALIF.
33- 36 LEONARD, EMIL JOHN            RR1 #23 - AUBURN ILLINOIS 62615
13-102 LEONARD, HUBERT BENJAMIN      D. JULY 11, 1952 FRESNO, CALIF.
77- 84 LEONARD, JEFFREY N            1626 N FELTON ST - PHILADELPHIA PA 19151
14-129 LEONARD, JOSEPH HOWARD        D. MAY 1, 1920 WASHINGTON, D.C.
67- 63 LEONARD, DAVID PAUL           87 CORNING ST - BEVERLY MA 01915
28- 57 LEOPOLD, RUDOLPH MATAS        D. SEPTEMBER 3, 1965 BATON ROUGE, LA.
41- 64 LEOVICH, JOHN JOSEPH          CAPT JOHNS, 2130 HWY 101-LINCOLN CITY OR9736
52- 67 LEPCIO, THADDEUS STANLEY      263 GREENLODGE ST - DEDHAM MA 02026
55- 69 LEPPERT, DON EUGENE           5130 DURANT - MEMPHIS TN 38116
61- 68 LEPPERT, DONALD GEORGE        ROAD #1 BOX AA-7 - NINEVAH IN 46164
75- 67 LERCH, RANDY LOUIS            ONE BARBET DR - VOORHEES NJ 08043
10- 87 LERCHEN, BERTRAM ROE          D. JANUARY 7, 1962 DETROIT, MICH.
52- 68 LERCHEN, GEORGE EDWARD        354 EAST ROSE - GARDEN CITY MI 48135
28- 58 LERIAN, WALTER IRVIN          D. OCTOBER 22, 1929 BALTIMORE, MD.
69-103 LERSCH, BARRY LEE             OLD ADD: 1617 1/2 PALMER ST - PUEBLO CO 8100
```

```
72- 62  LESHNOCK, DONALD LEE          464 LORA AVE - YOUNGSTOWN OH 44504
47- 41  LESLIE, ROY REID              D. APRIL 9, 1972 SHERMAN, TEX.
29- 63  LESLIE, SAMUEL ANDREW         D. JANUARY 21, 1979 PASCAGOULA, MISS.
39- 67  LETCHAS, CHARLIE              1121 HIGHLAND ST - THOMASVILLE GA 31792
47- 57  LEVAN, JESSE ROY              255 LINCOLN RD - READING PA 19606
43-103  LEVERENZ, WALTER FRED         D. MARCH 19, 1973 ATASCADERO, CALIF.
22- 71  LEVERETT, GORHAM VANCE        D. FEBRUARY 20, 1957 BEAVERTON, ORE.
20- 74  LEVERETTE, HORACE WILBUR      D. APRIL 10, 1958 ST. PETERSBURG, FLA.
30- 46  LEVEY, JAMES JULIUS           D. MARCH 14, 1970 DALLAS, TEX.
23- 79  LEVSEN, EMIL HENRY            D. MARCH 12, 1972 MINNEAPOLIS, MINN.
40- 49  LEVY, EDWARD CLARENCE         312 BROAD ST-LAGRANGE GA 30240
75- 68  LEWALLYN, DENNIS DALE         320 EDGEWATER DR - PENSACOLA FL 32507
51- 51  LEWANDOWSKI, DANIEL WILLIAM   1974 ADD: 1277 BROADWAY - BUFFALO NY 14212
57- 64  LEWIS, ALLAN SYDNEY           PUERTO ARMUELLAS - CHIRIGUI PANAMA
40- 88  LEWIS, GEORGE EDWARD          D. JUNE 17, 1979 SALEM, N. H.
79- 69  LEWIS, JAMES MARTIN           16049 NE 8TH AVE - NORTH MIAMI BEACH FL 33162
41- 99  LEWIS, JOHN DAVID             D. FEBRUARY 25, 1956 STEUBENVILLE, O.
35- 61  LEWIS, JOHN KELLY             BOX 788 GASTONIA NC 28052
54- 65  LEWIS, JOHNNY JOE             1133 URSULA ST - UNIVERSITY CITY MO 63130
24- 67  LEWIS, WILLIAM BURTON         D. MARCH 24, 1950 TONAWANDA, N. Y.
33- 37  LEWIS, WILLIAM HENRY          D. OCTOBER 24, 1977 MEMPHIS, TENN.
71- 62  LEY, TERRENCE RICHARD         4443 NE PRESCOTT ST - PORTLAND OR 97218
30- 75  LEZCANO, CARLOS MANUEL        962 ALAMEDA VILLA-GRANADA,RIO PIEDRAS PR00923
74- 74  LEZCANO, SIXTO JOAQUIN        OLD ADD: 437 S HAWLEY RD #69-MILWAUKEE WI
45- 58  LIBKE, ALBERT WALTER          1117 SOUTH APPELAND DR - WENATCHEE WA 98801
59-104  LIBRAN, FRANCISCO             CALLE DR ESCADE #202 - MAYAGUEZ PR 00708
31- 71  LICKERT, JOHN WILBUR          922 WILHELM ST - PITTSBURGH PA 15220
53- 51  LIDDLE, DONALD EUGENE         1022 CHERRY - MOUNT CARMEL IL 62863
35- 62  LIEBER, CHARLES EDWIN         D. DECEMBER 31, 1961 LOS ANGELES, CAL.
40- 47  LIEBHARDT, GLENN IGNATIUS     2460 TANTELON PL - WINSTON-SALEM NC 27107
40- 89  LIESE, FREDERICK RICHARD      D. JUNE 30, 1967 LOS ANGELES, CALIF.
36- 48  LILLARD, ROBERT EUGENE        5676 ENCINA RD - GOLETA CA 93117
39- 68  LILLARD, WILLIAM BEVERLY      5290 PAREJO DR - SANTA BARBARA CA 93111
38- 55  LILLIS, ROBERT PERRY          14265 MISTY MEADOW - HOUSTON TX 77079
51- 52  LIMMER, LOUIS                 100-11 DEBS PL - BRONX NY 10475
31- 72  LINARES, RUFINO DELACRUZ      ING QUIS QUEYA - SPM BARRIO GUACHUPITA DOM R
27- 54  LIND, HENRY CARL              D. AUGUST 2, 1946 NEW YORK, N. Y.
74- 75  LIND, JACKSON HUGH            OLD ADD: 735 S BARKLEY - MESA AZ
50- 60  LINDBECK, EMERIT DESMOND      347 E GARFIELD ST - KEWANNEE IL 61443
55- 64  LINDBLAD, PAUL AARON          6203 LAKE RIDGE RD - ARLINGTON TX 76016
57- 58  LINDE, LYMAN GILBERT          607 W BURNETT ST - BEAVER DAM WI 53916
41- 65  LINDELL, JOHN HARLAN          8811 COAST HWY - LAGUNA BEACH CA 92651
50- 52  LINDEN, WALTER CHARLES        4432 HARVEY AVE - WESTERN SPRINGS IL 60558
43- 78  LINDQUIST, CARL EMIL          BOX 5 - EMPORIUM PA 15834
41-100  LINDSAY, WILLIAM GIBBONS      D. JULY 14, 1963 GREENSBORO, N.C.
22- 72  LINDSEY, JAMES KENDRICK       D. OCTOBER 25, 1963 JACKSON, LA.
16- 56  LINDSTROM, AXEL OLAF          D. JUNE 25, 1940 ASHEVILLE, N. C.
48- 56  LINDSTROM, CHARLES WILLIAM    605 LINCOLN AVE - LINCOLN IL 62656
24- 68  LINDSTROM, FRED CHARLES       D. OCTOBER 4, 1981 CHICAGO, ILL.
26- 55  LINES, RICHARD GEORGE         OLD AD: 1161 SW 45TH TER-FT LAUDERDALE FL
42- 69  LINHART, CARL JAMES           2647 DELMAR AVE - GRANITE CITY IL 62040
40- 90  LINK, FREDERICK THEODORE      D. MAY 22, 1939 HOUSTON, TEXAS
22- 38  LINKE, EDWARD KARL            4830 N MULLIGAN AVE - CHICAGO IL 60630
44- 63  LINT, ROYCE JAMES             6814 SE JACK RD - MILWAUKIE OR 97222
29- 64  LINTON, CLAUD CLARENCE        D. APRIL 3, 1980 DESTIN, FLA.
73- 75  LINTZ, LARRY                  2548 SLEEPY HOLLOW LN - SAN JOSE CA 95116
52- 76  LINZ, PHILIP FRANCIS          1189 FIRST AVE - NEW YORK NY 10021
53- 69  LINZY, FRANK ALFRED           RR 2 BOX 395 - COWETA OK 74429
56- 51  LIPIETRI, MICHAEL ANGELO      150 YOAKUM AVE - FARMINGDALE NY 11735
62- 63  LIPON, JOHN JOSEPH            13315 ALCHESTER - HOUSTON TX 77024
37- 66  LIPSCOMB, GERARD              D. FEBRUARY 27, 1978 HUNTERSVILLE, N. C.
53- 70  LIPSKI, ROBERT PETER          1 SNOOK ST - SCRANTON PA 18505
50- 79  LIS, JOSEPH ANTHONY           107 KIMBERLY RD - SOMERVILLE NJ 08876
27- 55  LISENBEE, HORACE MILTON       RR 5 - CLARKSVILLE TN 37042
51- 73  LISI, RICCARDO PATRICK EMIL   32 RIVERVIEW W APTS #2 - PITTSFIELD MA 01201
29- 65  LISKA, ADOLPH JAMES           3831 NE WASCO - PORTLAND OR 97232
23- 76  LITTELL, MARK ALAN            1780 CANYON VIEW - CHESTERFIELD MO 63017
77- 59  LITTLE, DONALD JEFFREY        5550 C. R. 44 - WOODVILLE OH 43469
42-108  LITTLE, WILLIAM ARTHUR        D. JULY 27, 1961 DALLAS, TEX.
50- 77  LITTLEFIELD, JOHN ANDREW      ALAMEDA ST - AZUSA CA 91702
60- 53  LITTLEFIELD, RICHARD BERNARD  14838 KENTFIELD - DETROIT MI 48223
47- 56  LITTLEJOHN, CHARLES CARLISLE  IRENE TX 76650
78- 74  LITTLEJOHN, DENNIS GERALD     OLD ADD: 2244 W FREMONT DR - TEMPE AZ
81- 74  LITTLETON, LARRY MARVIN       2318 ARMAND RD NE - ATLANTA GA 30324
42- 70  LITTRELL, JACK NAPIER         7510 FLOYDSBURG RD - CRESTWOOD KY 40014
40- 70  LITWHILER, DANIEL WEBSTER     MSU ATH DEPT-E LANSING MI 48823
77- 59  LIVELY, EVERETT ADRIAN        8605 ESSLINGER CT - HUNTSVILLE AL 35802
41-101  LIVELY, HENRY EVERETT         D. DECEMBER 5, 1967 ARAB, ALA.
49- 69  LIVENGOOD, WESLEY AMOS        2220 ELGIN RD-WINSTON-SALEM NC 27103
48- 53  LIVINGSTON, THOMPSON ORVILLE  BOX 44 - GILCHRIST TX 77617
38- 55  LLENAS, WINSTON ENRIQUILLO    APARTADO #92 - SANTIAGO DOM REP
52- 73  LLEWELLYN, CLEMENT MANLEY     D. NOVEMBER 27, 1969 CHARLOTTE, N. C.
42-109  LOAN, WILLIAM JOSEPH          D. NOVEMBER 12, 1966 SPRINGFIELD, PA.
79- 70  LOANE, ROBERT KENNETH         BOX 67 - DANVILLE CA 94526
44-130  LOBERT, FRANK JOHN            D. MAY 29, 1932 PITTSBURGH, PA.
52- 77  LOCK, DONALD WILSON           1330 N WALNUT - KINGMAN KS 67068
55- 70  LOCKE, CHARLES EDWARD         BOX 276 - POPLAR BLUFF MO 63901
49- 49  LOCKE, LAWRENCE DONALD        RR 1 BOX 400 - DUNBAR PA 15431
54- 66  LOCKE, RONALD THOMAS          LEWISTON AVE - KENYON RI 02836
45- 65  LOCKER, ROBERT AWTRY          1167 MONTRIELLO RD - LAFAYETTE CA 94549
```

73- 77 LOCKLEAR, GENE   RR1 BOX 213 - PEMBROKE NC 28382
55- 71 LOCKLIN, STUART CARLTON   1823 S BOUTEN - APPLETON WI 54911
45- 59 LOCKMAN, CARROLL WALTER   8234 N 75TH ST - SCOTTSDALE AZ 85253
65- 66 LOCKWOOD, CLAUDE EDWARD "SKIP" 131 BUCKSKIN DR-WESTON MA 02193
38- 54 LODIGIANI, DARIO ANTHONY   1864 GRANT ST SAN FRANCISCO CA 94133
28- 59 LOEPP, GEORGE HERBERT   D. SEPTEMBER 4, 1967 LOS ANGELES, CAL.
50- 54 LOES, WILLIAM   33-08 84TH ST - JACKSON HEIGHTS NY 11372
26- 50 LOFTUS, FRANCIS PATRICK   D. OCTOBER 27, 1980 BELCHERTOWN, MASS.
24- 69 LOFTUS, RICHARD JOSEPH   D. JANUARY 21, 1972 CONCORD, MASS.
51- 53 LOGAN, JOHN   6115 W CLEVELAND AVE - MILWAUKEE WI 53219
35- 63 LOGAN, ROBERT DEAN   D. MAY 20, 1978 INDIANAPOLIS, IND.
14-131 LOHR, HOWARD SYLVESTER   D. JUNE 9, 1977 PHILADELPHIA, PA.
47- 60 LOHRKE, JACK WAYNE   2817 LUCENA DR - SAN JOSE CA 95132
34- 63 LOHRMAN, WILLIAM LEROY   250 ROUTE 208 - NEW PALTZ NY 12561
78- 75 LOIS, ALBERTO   ING CONSUELO CALLE5 #12 SANPEDRO DEMACORIS D
63- 71 LOLICH, MICHAEL STEPHEN   6252 ROBINHILL - WASHINGTON MI 48094
71- 63 LOLICH, RONALD JOHN   2436 NW SAVIER - PORTLAND OR 97210
46- 65 LOLLAR, JOHN SHERMAN   D. SEPTEMBER 24, 1977 SPRINGFIELD, MO.
80- 78 LOLLAR, WILLIAM TIMOTHY   316 N JEFFERSON - FARMINGTON MO 63640
31- 48 LOMBARDI, ERNEST NATALI   D. SEPTEMBER 26, 1977 SANTA CRUZ, CALIF.
45- 60 LOMBARDI, VICTOR ALVIN   5164 E ASHLAN #103 - FRESNO CA 93727
48- 59 LOMBARDO, LOUIS   3905 MEEK DR - JACKSONVILLE FL 32211
65- 67 LONBORG, JAMES REYNOLD   498 FIRST PARISH RD - SCITUATE MA 02066
11-102 LONERGAN, WALTER E.   D. JANUARY 23, 1958 LEXINGTON, MASS.
22- 74 LONG, JAMES ALBERT   D. SEPTEMBER 14, 1970 FORT DODGE, IA.
63- 72 LONG, JEOFFREY KEITH   11 FLOWER CT - LAKESIDE PARK KY 41017
11-103 LONG, LESTER   D. OCTOBER 21, 1958 BIRMINGHAM, ALA.
51- 54 LONG, RICHARD DALE   22 WALDEN GLEN - BALLSTON LAKE NY 12019
81- 75 LONG, ROBERT EARL   250 GLADIOLIS - ANNA MARIA FL 33501
11-104 LONG, THOMAS AUGUSTUS   D. JUNE 15, 1972 MOBILE, ALA.
24- 70 LONG, THOMAS FRANCIS   D. SEPTEMBER 16, 1973 LOUISVILLE, KY.
56- 52 LONNETT, JOSEPH PAUL   126 DUNCAN CIR - BEAVER PA 15009
68- 56 LOOK, BRUCE MICHAEL   3863 HEMMINGWAY - OKEMOS MI 48864
61- 69 LOOK, DEAN ZACHARY   2103 BUTTERNUT - OKEMOS MI 48864
44- 77 LOPAT, EDMUND WALTER   99 OAK TRAIL RD - HILLSDALE NJ 07642
48- 60 LOPATA, STANLEY EDWARD   1518 ELKINS AVE - ABINGTON PA 19001
45- 61 LOPATKA, ARTHUR JOSEPH   7310 N HARLEM - CHICAGO IL 60648
72- 63 LOPES, DAVID EARL   16984 AVE DE SANTA YNEZ-PAC PALISADES CA9027
28- 60 LOPEZ, ALFONSO RAMON   3601 BEACH DR - TAMPA FL 33609
65- 68 LOPEZ, ARTURO   3 COUNTRY LN - HILLSDALE NJ 07642
74- 76 LOPEZ, AURELIO RIOS   5 PONIENTE #8 - TECAMACHALCO PUEBLA MEXICO
76- 56 LOPEZ, CARLOS ANTONIO   MEXICI #33A, POINTE - MAZATLAN SINALOA MEXIC
55- 72 LOPEZ, HECTOR HEADLEY   666 JANOS LN - WEST HEMPSTEAD NY 11552
66- 56 LOPEZ, JOSE RAMON   2250 SW 21ST TER - MIAMI FL 33145
63- 73 LOPEZ, MARCELINO PONS   841 NW LITTLE RIVER DR - MIAMI FL 33150
23- 80 LORD, WILLIAM CARLTON   D. AUGUST 15, 1947 CHESTER, PA.
13-104 LORENZEN, ADOLPH ANDREAS   D. MARCH 5, 1963 DAVENPORT, IA.
16- 57 LOTZ, JOSEPH PETER   D. JANUARY 1, 1971 HAYWARD, CAL.
80- 79 LOUCKS, SCOTT GREGORY   1801 VIOLA DR - SIERRA VISTA AZ 85635
10- 91 LOUDELL, ARTHUR   D. FEBRUARY 19, 1961 KANSAS CITY, MO.
67- 65 LOUGHLIN, LAWRENCE JOHN   410 S 57TH - TACOMA WA 98408
64- 67 LOUN, DONALD NELSON   3102 BARNARD CT - FAIRFAX VA 22030
13-105 LOVE, EDWARD HAUGHTON   D. NOVEMBER 30, 1942 MEMPHIS, TENN.
22- 75 LOVELACE, THOMAS RIVERS   D. JULY 12, 1979 DALLAS, TEX.
55- 73 LOVENGUTH, LYNN RICHARD   7575 SW 101ST COURT - BEAVERTON OR 97005
33- 39 LOVETT, MERRITT MARWOOD   407 ASHLAND AVE #1H - RIVER FOREST IL 60305
80- 80 LOVIGLIC, JOHN PAUL   96 COUNTRY VILLAGE LN - EAST ISLIP NY 11730
72- 64 LOVITTO, JOSEPH   1401 FOREST EDGE #6 - ARLINGTON TX 76012
63- 74 LOVRICH, PETER   19626 BEECHNUT DR - MOKENA IL 60448
15- 91 LOW, FLETCHER   D. JUNE 6, 1973 HANOVER, N.H.
11-105 LOWDERMILK, LOUIS BAILEY   D. DECEMBER 27, 1975 CENTRALIA, ILL.
20- 75 LOWE, GEORGE WESLEY   D. SEPTEMBER 2, 1981 SOMERS POINT, N. J.
70- 80 LOWENSTEIN, JOHN LEE   4540 S BRIGHTON DR - LAS VEGAS NV 89121
51- 55 LOWN, OMAR JOSEPH   1106 VAN BUREN - PUEBLO CO 81004
42- 64 LOWREY, HARRY LEE   OLD ADD: 802 EDGEWOOD ST #3-INGLEWOOD CA
42- 65 LOWRY, SAMUEL JOSEPH   4716 FOWLER - PHILADELPHIA PA 19127
81- 76 LUBRATICH, STEVEN GEORGE   910 CASTLE - SAN LEANDRO CA 94578
36- 49 LUBY, HUGH MAX   1730 W 28TH AVE EUGENE OR 97405
38- 55 LUCADELLO, JOHN   103 OAKWOOD DR SAN ANTONIO TX 78228
23- 81 LUCAS, CHARLES FRED   1124 GREENFIELD AV - NASHVILLE TN 37216
35- 64 LUCAS, FREDERICK WARRINGTON   711 MARYLAND CAMBRIDGE MA 21613
80- 81 LUCAS, GARY PAUL   11754 PAPAGALLO CT - SAN DIEGO CA 92124

```
31- 49  LUCAS, JOHN CHARLES            D. OCTOBER 31, 1970 MARYVILLE, ILL.
29- 66  LUCAS, RAY WESLEY              D. OCTOBER 9, 1969 HARRISON, MICH.
70- 81  LUCCHESI, FRANK JOSEPH         3027 GLASGOW DR - ARLINGTON TX 76013
23- 82  LUCE, FRANK EDWARD             D. FEBRUARY 3, 1942 MILWAUKEE, WIS.
20- 76  LUCEY, JOSEPH EARL             D. JULY 30, 1980 HOLYOKE, MASS.
43- 79  LUCIER, LOUIS JOSEPH           579 HIGHLAND ST - NORTHBRIDGE MA 01534
24- 71  LUDOLPH, WILLIAM FRANCIS       D. APRIL 8, 1952 OAKLAND, CAL.
25- 66  LUEBBE, ROY JOHN               6476 PIERCE - OMAHA NE 68106
71- 64  LUEBBER, STEPHEN LEE           RR 1 BOX 252 - CARL JUNCTION MO 64834
62- 78  LUEBKE, RICHARD RAYMOND        D. DECEMBER 4, 1974 SAN DIEGO, CALIF.
13-106  LUHRSEN, WILLIAM FERDINAND     D. AUGUST 15, 1973 NORTH LITTLE ROCK, ARK.
41- 66  LUKON, EDWARD PAUL             RR 3, CHERRY VALLEY RD - BURGETTSTOWN PA15021
67- 66  LUM, MICHAEL KEN-WAI           2831 LAOLA PL - HONOLULU HI 96813
57- 44  LUMENTI, RALPH ANTHONY         9 TOMASSO - MILFORD MA 01757
56- 53  LUMPE, JERRY DEAN              732 PEARSON DR - SPRINGFIELD MO 65801
54- 64  LUNA, GUILLERMO ROMERO         CARDENAS 50 OTE. - LOS MOCHIS, SINOLOA MEXICO
45- 62  LUND, DONALD ANDREW            1000 S STATE ST - ANN ARBOR MI 48109
67- 67  LUND, GORDON T                 1717 ROBBIE LN - MOUNT PROSPECT IL 60056
24- 72  LUNDGREN, EBIN DELMAR          423 N 3RD ST - LINDSBORG KS 67456
73- 78  LUNDSTEDT, THOMAS ROBERT       245 RIVERWOODS LN - BURNSVILLE MN 55337
19- 53  LUNTE, HARRY AUGUST            BOX 351 - NORWICH VT 05055
40- 51  LUPIEN, ULYSSES JOHN           2450 STARLITE DR - SAGINAW MI 48603
61- 70  LUPLOW, ALVIN DAVID            D. JULY 3, 1957 HAVANA, CUBA
14-132  LUQUE, ADOLFO                  D. FEBRUARY 26, 1937 DETROIT, MICH.
10- 92  LUSH, ERNEST BENJAMIN          2308 MARCO CIR - CHATTANOOGA TN 37421
56- 54  LUTTRELL, LYLE KENNETH         93 MAYO DR - NEWPORT KY 41071
22- 76  LUTZ, LOUIS WILLIAM            1411 QUAIL DR - SARASOTA FL 33581
51- 56  LUTZ, ROLLIN JOSEPH            D. MARCH 6, 1938 MILWAUKEE, WIS.
23- 83  LUTZKE, WALTER JOHN            84 SWEETBRIER CT - MEDFORD NJ 08055
70- 82  LUZINSKI, GREGORY MICHAEL      107 PINE TERRACE DR - DEMAREST NJ 07627
67- 68  LYLE, ALBERT WALTER            D. OCTOBER 10, 1977 WILLIAMSPORT, PA.
25- 67  LYLE, JAMES CHARLES            D. MARCH 16, 1934 DAVENPORT, IA.
20- 77  LYNCH, ADRIAN RYAN             5940 SW 120TH ST - MIAMI FL 33156
80- 82  LYNCH, EDWARD FRANCIS          RR1 - BOLIVER PA 15923
54- 65  LYNCH, GERALD THOMAS           D. JUNE 30, 1978 PLANO, TEXAS
48- 61  LYNCH, MATT DANNY              D. DECEMBER 21, 1976 DAYTONA BEACH, CALIF.
22- 77  LYNCH, WALTER EDWARD           D. FEBRUARY 5, 1940 NAPA, CAL.
16- 58  LYNN, BYRD                     6961 E VIA EL ESTRIBO-ANAHEIM HILLS CA 92807
74- 77  LYNN, FREDRIC MICHAEL          D. OCTOBER 27, 1977 BELLVILLE, TEX.
39- 71  LYNN, JAPHET MONROE            D. SEPTEMBER 25, 1972 SCRANTON, PA.
37- 67  LYNN, JEROME EDWARD            #366 - CALHOUN FALLS SC 29628
44- 78  LYON, RUSSELL MAYO             D. DECEMBER 20, 1965 INGLEWOOD, CAL.
47- 61  LYONS, ALBERT HAROLD           1466 EBERT ST - WINSTON-SALEM NC 27103
20- 78  LYONS, EDWARD HOYT             D. AUGUST 12, 1981 NEVADA, MO.
41- 67  LYONS, GEORGE TONY             7900 DUNBARTON AVE-LOS ANGELES CA 90045
29- 67  LYONS, HERSCHEL E              D. SEPTEMBER 9, 1959 DAYTON, O.
23- 84  LYONS, TERENCE HILBERT         1401 LOREE ST - VINTON LA 70668
80- 83  LYONS, THEODORE AMAR           B. FEBRUARY 21, 1953 HUNTINGTON PARK, CALIF.
69-105  LYSANDER, RICHARD EUGENE       110 LIPONA RD - TALLAHASSEE FL 32304
55- 74  LYTTLE, JAMES LAWRENCE         D. DECEMBER 7, 1976 MOUNT CLEMENS, MICH.
58- 57  MAAS, DUANE FREDRICK           90 BISHOP AVE - DANVILLE VA 24541
18- 46  MABE, ROBERT LEE               D. APRIL 11, 1950 BUFFALO, N. Y.
76- 57  MACCABE, RICHARD JAMES         2 SCHMIDT PL - SECAUCUS NJ 07094
28- 61  MACCORMACK, FRANK LOUIS        D. OCTOBER 4, 1965 MANOA, MA.
50- 55  MACDONALD, HARVEY FORSYTH      524 BANYAN CIR - WALNUT CREEK CA 94598
26- 51  MACDONALD, WILLIAM PAUL        D. AUGUST 26, 1972 BRUNSWICK, ME.
74- 78  MACFAYDEN, DANIEL KNOWLES      876 PATTON ST - MONROEVILLE PA 15146
79- 70  MACHA, KENNETH EDWARD          117 PERTH - VICTORIA TX 77901
71- 65  MACHA, MICHAEL WILLIAM         RR 5 BOX 234 - BRENHAM TX 77833
78- 76  MACHEMEHL, CHARLES WALTER      1861 EDISON - SAINT JOSEPH MI 49085
10- 93  MACHEMER, DAVID RITCHIE        D. FEBRUARY 4, 1967 UPPER DARBY, PA.
22- 78  MACK, EARLE THADDEUS           D. JULY 2, 1971 SACRAMENTO, CALIF.
45- 63  MACK, FRANK GEORGE             2038 MULBERRY LN - ARLINGTON HEIGHTS IL 60004
38- 56  MACK, JOSEPH JOHN              D. MAY 7, 1969 BUCYRUS, O.
        MACK, RAYMOND JAMES
```

```
73- 79  MACKANIN, PETER               327 LAVAL BLVD - ST ROSE, LAVAL QUEBEC
55- 75  MACKENZIE, ERIC HUGH          1224 EMILY ST - MOORETOWN ONT
61- 71  MACKENZIE, HENRY GORDON       RR1 BOX 411C - LEESBURG FL 32748
60- 61  MACKENZIE, KENNETH PURVIS     819 S MAIN AVE - SIDNEY OH 45365
41- 68  MACKIEWICZ, FELIX THADDEUS    33 NANTUCKET LN-OLIVETTE MO 63132
53- 52  MACKINSON, JOHN JOSEPH        OLD ADD: SNYDERTOWN PA 17877
79- 71  MACKO, STEVEN JOSEPH          D. NOVEMBER 15, 1981 ARLINGTON, TEX.
62- 79  MACLEOD, WILLIAM DANIEL       62 SOUTH ST - WEST NEWBURY MA 01985
38- 57  MACON, MAX CULLEN             825 W CENTER ST #16D - JUPITER FL 33458
```

22- 79 MACPHEE, WALTER SCOTT	3826 NW 53RD ST - FT LAUDERDALE FL 33309
44- 80 MACPHERSON, HARRY WILLIAM	GAGE HILL RD - PELHAM NH 03076
80- 84 MACWHORTER, KEITH	18 SALEM DR - NORTH PROVIDENCE RI 03030
14-133 MADDEN	B. PITTSBURGH, PA.
16- 59 MADDEN, EUGENE	D. APRIL 6, 1949 UTICA, N. Y.
12-110 MADDEN, LEONARD JOSEPH	D. SEPTEMBER 9, 1949 TOLEDO, O.
46- 66 MADDERN, JAMES CLARENCE	BOX 1656 - BISBEE AZ 85603
70- 83 MADDOX, ELLIOTT	330 E 33RD ST - NEW YORK NY 10016
72- 65 MADDOX, GARRY LEE	49 NEW POND LN - WILLINGBORO NJ 08046
78- 77 MADDOX, JERRY GLENN	15513 DOMART - NORWALK CA 90650
50- 56 MADISON, DAVID PLEDGER	BOX 63 - BROOKVILLE MS 39739
32- 46 MADJESKI, EDWARD WILLIAM	47 DE HART - ELIZABETH NJ 07202
73- 80 MADLOCK, BILL	453 E DECATUR ST - DECATUR IL 62521
47- 62 MADRID, SALVADOR	D. FEBRUARY 24, 1977 FORT WAYNE, IND.
60- 62 MAESTRI, HECTOR ANIBAL	2360 SW 3RD ST - MIAMI FL 33135
11-106 MAGEE, LEO CHRISTOPHER	D. MARCH 14, 1966 COLUMBUS, O.
38- 58 MAGGERT, HARL WARREN	2127 PEACH AVE #1 - CLOVIS CA 93612
45- 64 MAGLIE, SALVATORE ANTHONY	77 MORNINGSIDE DR - GRAND ISLAND NY 14072
11-107 MAGNER, EDMUND BURKE	D. SEPTEMBER 9, 1956 CHILLICOTHE, O.
70- 84 MAGNUSON, JAMES ROBERT	641 STATE ST - MARINETTE WI 54143
66- 57 MAGRINI, PETER ALEXANDER	2402 RANCHO CABEZA DR - SANTA ROSA CA 95404
22- 80 MAGUIRE, FRED EDWARD	D. NOVEMBER 3, 1961 BRIGHTON, MASS.
50- 57 MAGUIRE, JACK	BOX 13947 - GAINESVILLE FL 32604
21- 57 MAHADY, JAMES BERNARD	D. AUGUST 9, 1936 CORTLAND, N. Y.
60- 63 MAHAFFEY, ARTHUR	105 CAMERON MANOR - BROOMALL PA 19008
26- 52 MAHAFFEY, LEE ROY	D. JULY 23, 1969 ANDERSON, S. C.
40- 52 MAHAN, ARTHUR LEO	1002 KENWYN ST-PHILADELPHIA PA 19124
12-111 MAHARG, WILLIAM	1921 ADD: PHILADELPHIA PA
78- 78 MAHLBERG, GREGORY JOHN	5100 N. PLACITA DEL LAZO - TUCSON AZ 85715
77- 85 MAHLER, MICHAEL JAMES	8911 QUIRT DR - SAN ANTONIO TX 78227
79- 72 MAHLER, RICHARD KEITH	7911 QUIRT DR - SAN ANTONIO TX 78227
30- 48 MAHON, ALFRED GWIN	OLD ADD: 87 E PEARL ST - NEW HAVEN CT 0651
10- 94 MAHONEY, CHRISTOPHER JOHN	D. JULY 15, 1954 VISALIA, CALIF.
11-108 MAHONEY, DANIEL JOSEPH	D. SEPTEMBER 28, 1960 UTICA, N.Y.
59- 50 MAHONEY, JAMES THOMAS	150 SYCAMORE TER - GLEN ROCK NJ 07452
51- 57 MAHONEY, ROBERT PAUL	6901 LAYN - LINCCLN NE 68505
45- 65 MAIER, ROBERT PHILIP	334 DUNELLEN AVE - DUNELLAN NJ 08812
36- 50 MAILHO, EMIL PIERRE	566 SCOTT ST - FREMONT CA 94538
15- 92 MAILS, JOHN WALTER	D. JULY 5, 1974 SAN FRANCISCO, CALIF.
48- 62 MAIN, FORREST HARRY	2028 N FRESNO ST #E - FRESNO CA 93703
14-134 MAIN, MILES GRANT	D. DECEMBER 29, 1965 ROYAL OAK, MICH.
43- 80 MAINS, JAMES ROYAL	D. MARCH 17, 1969 BRIDGTON, ME.
15-105 MAISEL, CHARLES LOUIS	D. AUGUST 25, 1953 BALTIMORE, MD.
13-107 MAISEL, FREDERICK CHARLES	D. APRIL 22, 1967 BALTIMORE, MD.
13-108 MAISEL, GEORGE JOHN	D. NOVEMBER 20, 1968 BALTIMORE, MD.
39- 72 MAJESKI, HENRY	12 ROOSEVELT ST - STATEN ISLAND NY 10304
37- 68 MAKOSKY, FRANK	916 MAIN - BOONTON NJ 07005

SEE PAGE 149

75- 69 MAKOWSKI, THOMAS ANTHONY	195 ROESCH AVE - BUFFALO NY 14201
33- 40 MALAY, JOSEPH CHARLES	233 SUCCESS PARK - BRIDGEPORT CT 06610
81- 77 MALDONACO, CANDIDO	BUZON G-27,BO. DOMINGUITO-ARECIBO PR 06612
81- 78 MALER, JAMES MICHAEL	6951 SW 105TH ST - MIAMI FL 33156
37- 69 MALINOSKY, ANTHONY JOSEPH	5540 W FIFTH ST #60 - OXNARD CA 93030
34- 64 MALIS, CYRUS SOL	D. JANUARY 12, 1971 NORTH HOLLYWOOD, FLA.
57- 45 MALKMUS, ROBERT EDWARD	400 WALLINGFORD TER - UNION NJ 07083
59- 51 MALLETT, GERALD GORDON	7610 FOREST PARK DR - BEAUMONT TX 77707
50- 58 MALLETTE, MALCOLM FRANCIS	2419 SILVER FOX LN - RESTON VA 22091
31- 50 MALLON, LESLIE CLYDE	2641 RAINTREE - ABILENE TX 79605
21- 58 MALLONEE, HOWARD BENNETT	D. FEBRUARY 19, 1978 BALTIMORE, MD.
25- 68 MALLONEE, JULIUS NORRIS	D. DECEMBER 26, 1934 CHARLOTTE, N. C.
40- 53 MALLORY, JAMES BAUGH	1905 FOREST HILLS DR - GREENVILLE SC 27834
77- 86 MALLORY, SHELDON	7516 W 63RD PL - ARGO IL 60501
10- 95 MALLOY, ARCHIBALD ALEXANDER	D. MARCH 1, 1961 FERRIS, TEX.
43- 81 MALLOY, ROBERT PAUL	3850 KIRKUP AVE-CINCINNATI OH 45213
55- 76 MALMBERG, HARRY WILLIAM	D. OCTOBER 29, 1976 SAN FRANCISCO, CALIF.
49- 47 MALONE, EDWARD RUSSEL	8340 OCEAN VIEW - WHITTIER CA 90602
15- 93 MALONE, LEWIS ALOYSIUS	D. FEBRUARY 17, 1972 BROOKLYN, N.Y.
28- 62 MALONE, PERCE LEIGH	D. MAY 13, 1943 ALTOONA, PA.
60- 64 MALONEY, JAMES WILLIAM	2217 W KEATS - FRESNO CA 93705
12-112 MALONEY, PATRICK WILLIAM	D. JUNE 27, 1979 PAWTUCKET, R. I.
13-109 MALOY, PAUL AUGUSTUS	D. MARCH 18, 1976 SANDUSKY, O.
43- 82 MALTZBERGER, GORDON RALPH	D. DECEMBER 11, 1974 RIALTO, CALIF.
55- 77 MALZONE, FRANK JAMES	16 ALETHA RD - NEEDHAM MA 02192
13-110 MAMAUX, ALBERT LEON	D. JANUARY 2, 1963 SANTA MONICA, CALIF.

```
28- 63  MANCUSO, AUGUST RODNEY        10103 KEMPWOOD - HOUSTON TX 77055
44- 81  MANCUSO, FRANK OCTAVIUS       5126 CRIPPLE CREEK - HOUSTON TX 77017
14-135  MANDA, CARL ALAN              1115 S FOURTH - ARTESIA NM 88210
41- 69  MANDERS, HAROLD CARL          RR 3-ADEL IA 50003
52- 71  MANGAN, JAMES DANIEL          6878 TRINIDAD - SAN JOSE CA 95120
69-106  MANGUAL, ANGEL LUIS           LAS DELICIAS R10,RCD.DEL VALLE-PONCE PR 00731
72- 66  MANGUAL, JOSE MANUEL          CALLE 41,AC19 LOS CAOBOS - PONCE PR 00731
24- 73  MANGUM, LEON ALLEN            D. JULY 9, 1974 LIMA, O.
12-113  MANGUS, GEORGE GRAHAM         D. AUGUST 10, 1933 RUTLAND, MASS.
20- 79  MANION, CLYDE JENNINGS        D. SEPTEMBER 4, 1967 DETROIT, MICH.
76- 58  MANKOWSKI, PHILIP ANTHONY     106 AVERY PL - CHEEKTOWAGA NY 14225
44- 82  MANN, BEN GARTH               RR 1 BOX 14 - ITALY TEX 76651
28- 64  MANN, JOHN LEO                D. MARCH 31, 1977 TERRE HAUTE, IND.
13-111  MANN, LESLIE                  D. JANUARY 14, 1962 PASADENA, CALIF.
14-136  MANNING, ERNEST DEVON         D. APRIL 28, 1973 PENSACOLA, FLA.
62- 80  MANNING, JAMES BENJAMIN       4341 SW 2ND CT - PLANTATION FL 33317
55- 70  MANNING, RICHARD EUGENE       150 MILES RD - CHAGRIN FALLS OH 44022
40- 54  MANNO, DONALD                 1338 ELLIOTT ST-WILLIAMSPORT PA 17701
81- 79  MANRIQUE, FRED ELOI           CARRERA 6 #21 SANTA FE - CD. BOLIVAR VENEZUEL
56- 55  MANTILLA , FELIX              2585 N CRAMER #101 - MILWAUKEE WI 53211
51- 58  MANTLE, MICKEY CHARLES        5730 WATSON CIR - DALLAS TX 75225
69-107  MANUEL, CHARLES FUQUA         234 BOWER RD - ROANOKE VA 24018
55- 71  MANUEL, JERRY                 9275 DEFIANCE CIR - SACRAMENTO CA 95827
23- 85  MANUSH, HENRY EMMETT          D. MAY 12, 1971 SARASOTA, FLA.
50- 59  MANVILLE, RICHARD WESLEY      OLD ADD:  112 E LIBERTY ST-ANN ARBOR MI 48108
19- 54  MAPEL, ROLLA HAMILTON         D. APRIL 6, 1966 SAN DIEGO, CAL.
48- 63  MAPES, CLIFFORD FRANKLIN      RR 1 BOX 75 - PRYOR OK 74361
32- 47  MAPLE, HOWARD ALBERT          D. NOVEMBER 9, 1970 PORTLAND, ORE.
60- 65  MARANDA, GEORGES HENRI        OLD ADD: 21 AVENUE PLANTE - LEVIS QUEBEC
12-114  MARANVILLE, WALTER JAMES VINCENT D. JANUARY 5, 1954 NEW YORK, N.Y.
23- 86  MARBERRY, FREDRICK           D. JUNE 30, 1976 MEXIA, TEX.
13-112  MARBET, WALTER WILLIAM        D. SEPTEMBER 24, 1956 HOHENWALD, TENN.
40- 55  MARCHILDON, PHILIP JOSEPH     3 COURTWRIGHT RD - ETOBICOKE ONT
33- 41  MARCUM, JOHN ALFRED           RR 2 - EMINENCE KY 40019
65- 69  MARENTETTE, LEO JOHN          4246 HERMAN PL - TOLEDO OH 43623
56- 56  MARGONERI, JOSEPH EMANUEL     RR1 - WEST NEWTON PA 15089
60- 66  MARICHAL, JUAN ANTONIO        170 JOOST AVE - SAN FRANCISCO CA 94131
14-137  MARION, DONALD G              D. JANUARY 18, 1933 MILWAUKEE, WIS.
35- 65  MARION, JOHN WYETH            D. MARCH 13, 1975 SAN JOSE, CALIF.
40- 56  MARION, MARTIN WHITEFORD      201 S BROADWAY - ST LOUIS MO 63102
57- 46  MARIS, ROGER EUGENE           3820 NE 49TH DR - GAINESVILLE FL 32601
51- 59  MARKELL, HARRY DUQUESNE       249 BRANDYWINE CT - ROYAL PALM BEACH FL 33411
50- 60  MARKLAND, CLENETH EUGENE      918 NW 13TH ST - FT LAUDERDALE FL 33311
15- 94  MARKLE, CLIFFORD MONROE       D. MAY 24, 1974 TEMPLE CITY, CALIF.
51- 60  MARLOWE, RICHARD BURTON       D. DECEMBER 30, 1968 TOLEDO, O.
40- 57  MARNIE, HARRY SYLVESTER       2715 S SMETLEY-PHILADELPHIA PA 19145
53- 53  MAROLEWSKI, FRED DANIEL       298 BENSLEY - CALUMET CITY IL 60409
69-108  MARONE, LOUIS STEPHEN         663 TYRONE ST - EL CAJON CA 92020
31- 51  MARQUARDT, ALBERT LUDWIG      D. FEBRUARY 7, 1968 PORT CLINTON, O.
72- 67  MARQUEZ, GONZALO ENRIQUE      LIRB EL CARIBE #3A CLE#11-CATIA CARACAS VENEZ
61- 61  MARQUEZ, LUIS ANGEL           113 MERCADO ST - AGUADILLO PUERTO RICO 00603
25- 69  MARQUIS, JAMES MILBURN        BOX F - WEST POINT CA 95255
53- 54  MARQUIS, ROBERT RUDOLPH       2075 LONGFELLOW DR - BEAUMONT TX 77706
55- 78  MARQUIS, ROGER J              5 LINDBERGH AVE - HOLYOKE MA 01040
50- 61  MARRERO, CONRADO EUGENIO RAMOS 205 AVONTAMIENTO #1 - CERRO HAVANA CUBA
17- 42  MARRIOTT, WILLIAM EARL        D. AUGUST 11, 1969 BERKELEY, CALIF.
32- 48  MARROW, CHARLES KENNON        203 RIVER RD - NEWPORT NEWS VA 23601
```

```
11-109  MARSANS, ARMANDO              D. SEPTEMBER 3, 1960 HAVANA, CUBA
49- 48  MARSH, FRED FRANCIS           RR4 - CORRY PA 16407
41- 70  MARSHALL, CHARLES ANDREW      1 RADCLIFF CT-WILMINGTON DE 19804
46- 67  MARSHALL, CLARENCE WESTLY     2732 N LICIA PL - SIMA CA 93065
67- 69  MARSHALL, DAVID LEWIS         4433 CHARLEMAGNE - LONG BEACH CA 90808
29- 68  MARSHALL, EDWARD HERBERT      1840 FAIRWAY CIR CR - SAN MARCOS CA 92069
58- 58  MARSHALL, JIM RUFE            5761 N CASA BLANCA - SCOTTSDALE AZ 88253
73- 81  MARSHALL, KEITH ALAN          113 DURLAND AVE - ELMIRA NY 14905
81- 80  MARSHALL, MICHAEL ALLEN       427 HIAWATHA DR - BUFFALO GROVE IL 60090
67- 70  MARSHALL, MICHAEL GRANT       25360 BIRCH BLUFF RD - SHOREWOOD MN 55331
42- 66  MARSHALL, MILO MAX            OLD ADD: 4520 MONROE AVE - SALEM OR
12-115  MARSHALL, ROY DEVERNE         D. JUNE 11, 1980 DOVER, O.
42- 67  MARSHALL, WILLARD WARREN      204 MAIN ST-FORT LEE NJ 07024
31- 52  MARSHALL, WILLIAM HENRY       D. MAY 5, 1977 SACRAMENTO, CALIF.
50- 62  MARTIN, ALFRED MANUEL         20 EAST 69TH - NEW YORK NY 10021
53- 55  MARTIN, BARNEY ROBERT         1617 TALL PINES CIR - COLUMBIA SC 29205
```

```
44- 83 MARTIN, BORIS MICHAEL          OLD ADD: 10816 LEEBUR - ST LOUIS MO
79- 73 MARTIN, DONALD RENIE           504 FAIRVIEW AVE - DOVER DE 19901
17- 43 MARTIN, ELWOOD GOOD            2003 GRANADA AVE - SAN DIEGO CA 92104
46- 68 MARTIN, FRED TURNER            D. JUNE 11, 1979 CHICAGO, ILL.
37- 70 MARTIN, HERSHEL RAY            D. NOVEMBER 17, 1980 CUBA, MO.
74- 79 MARTIN, JERRY LINDSEY          918 S BONHAM RD - COLUMBIA SC 29205
12-116 MARTIN, JOHN CHRISTOPHER       D. JULY 4, 1980 BRONX, N. Y.
28- 65 MARTIN, JOHN LEONARD ROOSEVELT D. MARCH 5, 1965 MCALESTER, OKLA.
80- 85 MARTIN, JOHN ROBERT            1901 WASHYENAW - YPSILANTI MI 48197
59- 52 MARTIN, JOSEPH CLIFTON         2234 HIGH RIDGE PKWY - HILLSIDE IL 60162
49- 49 MARTIN, MORRIS WEBSTER         244 POTTERY RD - WASHINGTON MO 63090
19- 55 MARTIN, PATRICK FRANCIS        D. FEBRUARY 4, 1949 BROOKLYN, N. Y.
55- 79 MARTIN, PAUL CHARLES           OLD ADD: BOX 221 - FAYETTE CITY PA
43- 83 MARTIN, RAYMOND JOSEPH         107 PELLANA RD-NORWOOD MA 02062
36- 51 MARTIN, STUART MCGUIRE         BOX 184 - SEVERN NC 27877
68- 57 MARTIN, THOMAS EUGENE          110 STANLEY DR - LEESBURG GA 31763
14-138 MARTIN, WILLIAM GLOYD          D. SEPTEMBER 15, 1949 WASHINGTON, D.C.
36- 52 MARTIN, WILLIAM JOSEPH         D. SEPTEMBER 28, 1960 BUFFALO, N. Y.
24- 74 MARTINA, JOSEPH JOHN           D. MARCH 22, 1962 NEW ORLEANS, LA.
80- 86 MARTINEZ, ALFREDO             2346 THOMAS - LOS ANGELES CA 90031
74- 80 MARTINEZ, FELIX ANTHONY        216 HARRIET - LAJUNTA CO 81050
63- 75 MARTINEZ, GABRIEL ANTONIO      7800 SW 28TH ST - MIAMI FL 33155
69-109 MARTINEZ, JOHN ALBERT          6213 VISTA AVE - SACRAMENTO CA 95824
69-110 MARTINEZ, JOSE AZCUIZ          11813 E 59TH TER CIR - KANSAS CITY MO 64133
76- 59 MARTINEZ, JOSE DENNIS          IG.JALTEVA.CUADRAS 2.5-ALNOTRE GRANADA NICAR
62- 82 MARTINEZ, ORLANDO OLIVO        748 N 23RD WEST AVE - TULSA OK 74127
62- 81 MARTINEZ, RODOLFO HECTOR       OLD ADD: MARIANOA - HAVANA CUBA
50- 63 MARTINEZ, ROGELIO ULLOA        209 NICHOLS AVE - BROOKLYN NY 11208
77- 87 MARTINEZ, SILVIO RAMON         CARLOS DELORA 25,BELLE VISTA-SANTIAGO DOM RE
70- 85 MARTINEZ, TEODORO NOEL         CALLE ABREU 150 - SANTO DOMINGO DOM REPUBLIC
35- 66 MARTINI, GUIDO JOE             D. OCTOBER 28, 1970
37- 71 MARTY, JOSEPH ANTON            1316 24TH ST - SACRAMENTO CA 95816
57  47 MARTYN, ROBERT GORDON          3365 SW 123RD - BEAVERTON OR 97005
75- 72 MARIZ, GARY ARTHUR             E 8003 EUCLID - SPOKANE WA 99206
80- 87 MARTZ, RANDY CARL              RR 6 BOX 551 - PIEDMONT SC 29673
69-111 MASHORE, CLYDE WAYNE           14680 MARSH CREEK RD - CLAYTON CA 94517
39- 73 MASI, PHILIP SAMUEL            1 N MAIN-MT PROSPECT IL 60056
66- 58 MASON, DONALD STETSON          1605 HOTEL CIR S #B211 - SAN DIEGO CA 92108
58- 59 MASON, HENRY                   1136 S LINCOLN - MARSHALL MO 65340
71- 66 MASON, JAMES PERCY             RR 1 BOX 308 - THEODORE AL 36582
57- 48 MASSA, GORDON RICHARD          5905 KIMBERLY AVE - CINCINNATI OH 45213
18- 45 MASSEY, ROY HARDEE             D. JUNE 23, 1954 ATLANTA, GA.
17- 44 MASSEY, WILLIAM HERBERT        D. OCTOBER 17, 1971 SHREVEPORT, LA.
31- 53 MASTERS, WALTER THOMAS         151 METCALFE ST APT 404 - OTTAWA ONT K2P 1N8
40- 58 MASTERSON, PAUL NICKALIS       3003 W 53RD ST-CHICAGO IL 60632
39- 74 MASTERSON, WALTER EDWARD       BOX 36-WOODVILLE VA 22749
52- 72 MATARAZZO, LEONARD             5 CATHERINE ST - LYNBROOK NY 11563
67- 71 MATCHICK, JOHN THOMAS          135 MIDDLETON, RR 1 - FREELAND PA 18224
12-117 MATHES, JOSEPH JOHN            D. DECEMBER 21, 1978 ST. LOUIS, MO.
52- 73 MATHEWS, EDWIN LEE             13744 RECUERDO DR - DEL MAR CA 92014
60- 67 MATHEWS, NELSON ELMER          211 CRESTVIEW - COLUMBIA IL 62236
60- 68 MATHIAS, CARL LYNWOOD          RR 2 - OLEY PA 19567
70- 86 MATIAS, JOHN ROY               98-1616 HAOLANAE - ALEA HI 96701
71- 67 MATLACK, JONATHAN TRUMPBOUR    502 BEADY RD - ARLINGTON TX 76012
14-139 MATTESON, HENRY EDSON          D. AUGUST 31, 1943 BROCTON, N.Y.
72- 68 MATTHEWS, GARY NATHANIEL       5025 GREENTREE TR SW - ATLANTA GA 30331
22- 81 MATTHEWS, JAMES VINCENT        1923 ADD: 127 LOCUST ST - WAYNESBORO PA
23- 87 MATTHEWS, WID CURRY            D. OCTOBER 5, 1965 HOLLYWOOD, CAL.
43- 84 MATTHEWSON, DALE WESLEY        7685 W LASALLE BLVD-MIRAMAR FL 33023
38- 59 MATTICK, ROBERT JAMES          1045 BYERS - GILROY CA 95020
12-118 MATTICK, WALTER JOSEPH         D. NOVEMBER 5, 1968 LOS ALTOS, CALIF.
31- 54 MATTINGLY, LAURENCE EARL       4007 BEDFORD PL - SUITLAND MD 20023
14-140 MATTIS, RALPH L.               D. SEPTEMBER 13, 1960 WILLIAMSPORT, PA.
29- 69 MATTCX, CLOY MITCHELL          RR 4 BASSETT VA 24055
22- 82 MATTCX, JAMES POWELL           D. OCTOBER 12, 1973 MYRTLE BEACH, S. C.
79- 74 MATULA, RICHARD CARLTON        RR 3 BOX 320 - WHARTON TX 77488
81- 81 MATUSZEK, LEONARD JAMES        OLD ADD: 434 W ALEXIS RD #29 - TOLEDO OH
34- 65 MATUZAK, HARRY GEORGE          D. NOVEMBER 26, 1978 HOPE, ALA.
```

```
44- 84 MAUCH, EUGENE WILLIAM          46 LA RONDA DR - RANCHO MIRAGE CA 92270
34- 66 MAULDIN, MARSHALL REESE        6545 HANEN ST - UNION CITY GA 30291
24- 75 MAUN, ERNEST GERALD            RR 1 BOX 129 - FALFURRIAS TX 78355
45- 66 MAUNEY, RICHARD                D. FEBRUARY 6, 1970 ALBEMARLE, N. C.
58- 60 MAURIELLO, RALPH               23644 DEL CER CIR - CANOGA PARK CA 91304
```

48- 64	MAURO, CARMEN LOUIS	536 STANFORD DR - SAN LUIS OBISPO CA 93401
49- 50	MAVIS, ROBERT HENRY	300 MARKWOOD DR - LITTLE ROCK AR 72205
69-112	MAXIE, LARRY HANS	1515 N MONTERREY - ONTARIO CA 91762
62- 83	MAXVILL, CHARLES DALLAN	6745 RYAN CREST RD - FLORISSANT MO 63031
50- 64	MAXWELL, CHARLES RICHARD	RR2 MAPLE LAKE - PAW PAW MI 49079
68- 58	MAY, CARLOS	2413 TEMPEST DR SW - BIRMINGHAM AL 35211
67- 72	MAY, DAVID LAFRANCE	915 GRAY ST - NEW CASTLE DE 19720
17- 45	MAY, FRANK SPRUIELL	D. JUNE 3, 1970 WENDELL, N. C.
64- 68	MAY, JERRY LEE	RR 2 BOX 318 - BRIDGEWATER VA 22812
65- 70	MAY, LEE ANDREW	5533 HILL & DALE - CINCINNATI OH 45210
39- 75	MAY, MERRILL GLEND	615 LINCOLN - NEW ALBANY IN 47150
70- 87	MAY, MILTON SCOTT	2305 QUAIL CT - BRADENTON FL 33529
65- 71	MAY, RUDOLPH	960 CALLE PLANTADOR - THOUSAND OAKS CA 91360
24- 76	MAY, WILLIAM HERBERT	3000 BAYLOR - BAKERSFIELD CA 93305
68- 59	MAYBERRY, JOHN CLAIBORN	15710 SORRENTO - DETROIT MI 48227
59- 53	MAYE, ARTHUR LEE	867 E 52ND ST - LOS ANGELES CA 90011
57- 49	MAYER, EDWIN DAVID	440 OAKDALE AVE - CORTE MADERA CA 94925
12-119	MAYER, ERSKINE JOHN	D. MARCH 10, 1957 LOS ANGELES. CALIF.
15- 95	MAYER, SAMUEL FRANKEL	D. JULY 1, 1962 ATLANTA, GA.
11-110	MAYER, WALTER A.	D. NOVEMBER 18, 1951 MINNEAPOLIS, MINN.
11-111	MAYES, ADAIR BUSHYHEAD	D. MAY 28, 1962 FAYETTEVILLE, ARK.
40- 59	MAYNARD, JAMES WALTER	904 NICHOLAS ST-HENDERSON NC 27536
22- 83	MAYNARD, LEROY EVANS	D. JANUARY 31, 1957 BANGOR, ME.
36- 53	MAYO, EDWARD JOSEPH	825 OCEAN PINES - BERLIN MD 21811
48- 65	MAYO, JOHN LEWIS	719 MAPLERIDGE DR - YOUNGSTOWN OH 44512
15- 96	MAYS, CARL WILLIAM	D. APRIL 4, 1971 EL CAJON, CALIF.
51- 62	MAYS, WILLIE HOWARD	51 MT VERNON LN - ATHERTON CA 94025
56- 57	MAZEROSKI, WILLIAM STANLEY	RR6 BOX 130 - GREENSBURG PA 15601
35- 67	MAZZERA, MELVIN LEONARD	6 WEST DUNMAR LN - STOCKTON CA 95207
76- 60	MAZZILLI, LEE LOUIS	2555 E 12TH ST - BROOKLYN NY 11235
11-112	MCADAMS, GEORGE D.	D. MAY 21, 1937 SAN FRANCISCO, CALIF.
30- 49	MCAFEE, WILLIAM FORT	D. JULY 8, 1958 CULPEPPER, VA.
13-113	MCALLESTER, WILLIAM LUSK	D. MARCH 3, 1970 CHATTANOOGA, TENN.
71- 68	MCANALLY, ERNEST LEE	RR 4 BOX 61-A - MOUNT PLEASANT TX 75455
58- 61	MCANANY, JAMES	11066 RHODA WAY - CULVER CITY CA 90230
68- 60	MCANDREW, JAMES CLEMENT	5749 N STETSON CT - PARKER CO 80134
14-141	MCARTHUR, OLAND ALEXANDER	2602 MCARTHUR DR - COLUMBUS MS 39701
14-142	MCAULEY, JAMES EARL	D. APRIL 6, 1928 DES MOINES, IA.
60- 69	MCAULIFFE, RICHARD JOHN	BOX 211 - WEST SIMSBURY CT 06092
14-143	MCAVOY, GEORGE H	OLD ADD: ARDMORE OK 73401
13-114	MCAVOY, JAMES EUGENE	D. JULY 5, 1973 ROCHESTER, N. Y.
59- 54	MCAVOY, THOMAS JOHN	CLINTON COURT - STILLWATER NY 12118
61- 72	MCBEAN, ALVIN O'NEAL	BOX 4475 - ST THOMAS VI 00801
26- 53	MCBEE, PRYOR EDWARD	D. APRIL 19, 1963 ROSEVILLE, CALIF.
73- 82	MCBRIDE, ARNOLD RAY "BAKE"	5210 N HWY 67 - FLORISSANT MO 63033
59- 55	MCBRIDE, KENNETH FAYE	OLD ADD: 3118 W 155TH ST - CLEVELAND OH
43- 85	MCBRIDE, THOMAS RAYMOND	2100 SANTE FE - WICHITA FALLS TX 76309
64- 69	MCCABE, JOSEPH ROBERT	409 MEADOW DR - GREENCASTLE IN 46135

46- 69	MCCABE, RALPH HERBERT	D. MAY 4, 1974 WINDSOR, ONT.
15- 97	MCCABE, TIMOTHY	D. APRIL 12, 1971 IRONTON, MO.
18- 47	MCCABE, WILLIAM FRANCIS	D. SEPTEMBER 2, 1966 CHICAGO, ILL.
46- 70	MCCAHAN, WILLIAM GLENN	8 PENINSULA DR - GRANBURY TX 76048
62- 84	MCCALL, BRIAN ALLEN	120 MONCURE DR - ALEXANDRIA VA 22314
48- 66	MCCALL, JOHN WILLIAM	299330 OAKMONT DR - SIERRA VISTA AZ 85635
77- 88	MCCALL, LARRY STEPHEN	RR 5 BOX 354 - CANDLER NC 28715
48- 67	MCCALL, ROBERT LEONARD	2600 ASHLEY #A107-NORTH LITTLE ROCK AR 72114
27- 57	MCCALLISTER, JOHN	D. OCTOBER 18, 1946 COLUMBUS, O.
14-144	MCCANDLESS, SCOTT COOK	D. AUGUST 17, 1961 PITTSBURGH, PA.
20- 80	MCCANN, ROBERT EMMETT	D. APRIL 15, 1937 PHILADELPHIA, PA.
59- 56	MCCARDELL, ROGER MORTON	16 W MAIN ST - RISING SUN MD 21911
23- 88	MCCARREN, WILLIAM JOSEPH	515 KIMBARK - LONGMONT CO 80501
10- 96	MCCARTHY, ALEXANDER GEORGE	D. MARCH 12, 1978 SALISBURY, MD.
48- 68	MCCARTHY, JEROME FRANCIS	D. OCTOBER 3, 1965 OCEANSIDE, N. Y.
34- 67	MCCARTHY, JOHN JOSEPH	D. SEPTEMBER 13, 1973 MUNDELEIN, ILL.
26- 54	MCCARTHY, JOSEPH VINCENT	D. JANUARY 13, 1978 BUFFALO,N. Y.
13-115	MCCARTY, GEORGE LEWIS	D. JUNE 9, 1930 READING, PA.
59- 57	MCCARVER, JAMES TIMOTHY	RR 1 - MILLINGTON TN 38053
77- 89	MCCATTY, STEVEN EARL	692 TENNYSON - ROCHESTER MI 48063
61- 73	MCCLAIN, JOE FRED	RR 8 BOX 109 - JOHNSON CITY TN 37601
31- 55	MCCLANAHAN, PETE	BOX 157 - MONT BELVIOU TX 77580
19- 56	MCCLELLAN, HERVEY MCDOWELL	D. NOVEMBER 6, 1925 CYNTHIANA, KY.
13-116	MCCLESKEY, JEFFERSON LAMAR	D. MAY 11, 1971 AMERICUS, GA.
36- 54	MCCLOSKEY, JAMES ELLWOOD	D. AUGUST 18, 1971 JERSEY CITY, N. J.

```
10- 97  MCCLURE, LAWRENCE LEDWITH        D. AUGUST 31, 1948 HUNTINGTON, W. VA.
75- 73  MCCLURE, ROBERT CRAIG            1515 SUNSET LOOP - WALNUT CREEK CA 94595
15- 98  MCCLUSKEY, HARRY ROBERT          D. JUNE 7, 1962 TOLEDO, O.
33- 42  MCCOLL, ALEXANDER BOYD           1203 SHERMAN ST - GENEVA OH 44041
14-145  MCCONNAUGHEY, RALPH J.           D. JUNE 4, 1966 DETROIT, MICH.
15- 99  MCCONNELL, SAMUEL FAULKNER       D. JUNE 27, 1981 PHOENIXVILLE, PA.
64- 70  MCCOOL, WILLIAM JOHN             863 FERNSHIRE DR - CENTERVILLE OH 45459
80- 88  MCCORMACK, DONALD ROSS           RR 2 BOX 93 - OMAK WA 98841
34- 68  MCCORMICK, FRANK ANDREW          14 VANDERBILT RD - MANHASSET NY 11030
56- 58  MCCORMICK, MICHAEL FRANCIS       464 CHESLEY - MOUNTAIN VIEW CA 94040
40- 60  MCCORMICK, MYRON WINTHROP        D. APRIL 14, 1976 LOS ANGELES, CALIF.
39- 76  MCCOSKY, WILLIAM BARNEY          811 CLAVEMONT-DEARBORN MI 48124
59- 58  MCCOVEY, WILLIE LEE              220 CREST RD - WOODSIDE CA 94062
38- 60  MCCOY, BENJAMIN JENISON          3932 E OMAHA DR SW GRANDVILLE MI 49418
39- 77  MCCRABB, LESTER WILLIAM          OLD ADD: 212 S BRIDGE - CHRISTIANA PA 17509
63- 76  MCCRAW, TOMMY LEE                2102 SOUTHLINE DR - HUNTSVILLE AL 35810
25- 70  MCCREA, FRANCIS WILLIAM          10 LEHIGH ST - DOVER NJ 07801
14-146  MCCREERY, EDWARD P.              D.
22- 84  MCCUE, FRANK ALOYSIUS            D. JULY 5, 1953 EVERGREEN PARK, ILL.
40- 61  MCCULLOUGH, CLYDE EDWARD         931 ROUN BAY RD #E - NORFOLK VA 23503
```

THE SPORT AMERICANA PRICE GUIDE TO THE NON—
SPORTS CARDS IS THE BEST SOURCE FOR INFORMA—
TION AND PRICES FOR NON—SPORTS CARDS. SEE THE
INSIDE BACK COVER FOR DETAILS.

```
29- 70  MCCULLOUGH, PAUL WILLARD         D. NOVEMBER 7, 1970 NEWCASTLE, PA.
42- 68  MCCULLOUGH, PHILIP LAMAR         25 EXETER RD-AVONDALE ESTATES GA 30002
22- 85  MCCURDY, HARRY HENRY             D. JULY 21, 1972 HOUSTON, TEX.
55- 80  MCDANIEL, LYNDALL DALE           5024 SOUTH OSAGE - KANSAS CITY MO 64133
57- 50  MCDANIEL, MAX VON                33202 ROLLING WOOD - PINEHURST TX 77361
12-120  MCDERMOTT, FRANK A               D. SEPTEMBER 11, 1964 PHILADELPHIA, PA.
48- 69  MCDERMOTT, MAURICE JOSEPH        4950 BRILL - PHOENIX AZ 85008
72- 69  MCDERMOTT, TERRENCE MICHAEL      407 N VILLAGE AVE - ROCKVILLE CENTRE NY 11552
57- 51  MCDEVITT, DANIEL EUGENE          2991 SALEM RD SE - CONYERS GA 30207
12-121  MCDONALD, CHARLES E              D. MARCH 31, 1943 HOUSTON, TEX.
69-113  MCDONALD, DAVID BRUCE            2480 SE 6TH ST - POMPANO BEACH FL 33067
11-113  MCDONALD, EDWARD C.              D. MARCH 11, 1946 ALBANY, N.Y.
31- 56  MCDONALD, HENRY MONROE           BOX 275 - HOMELAND CA 92348
50- 65  MCDONALD, JIMMIE LEROY           3012 KNOXVILLE AVE - LONG BEACH CA 90808
10- 98  MCDONALD, MALCOLM JOSEPH         D. MAY 30, 1963 BAYTOWN, TEXAS
43- 86  MCDONNELL, JAMES WILLIAM         14238 SEYMOUR-DETROIT MICHIGAN 48205
51- 63  MCDOUGALD, GILBERT JAMES         10 WARREN AVE - SPRING LAKE NJ 07762
61- 74  MCDOWELL, SAMUEL EDWARD          201 PENN CENTER BLVD - PITTSBURGH PA 15235
16- 60  MCELWEE, LELAND STANFORD         D. FEBRUARY 8, 1957 UNION, ME.
42- 69  MCELYEA, FRANK                   722 E MARYLAND ST - EVANSVILLE IN 47711
74- 81  MCENANEY, WILLIAM HENRY          1038 ROYAL PALM DR - ELLENTON FL 33532
30- 50  MCEVOY, LOUIS ANTHONY            D. DECEMBER 16, 1953 WEBSTER GROVE, MO.
68- 61  MCFADDEN, LEON                   701 E 102ND ST - LOS ANGELES CA 90002
45- 67  MCFARLAND, HOWARD ALEXANDER      8321 WILLOWBROOK - WICHITA KS 67207
62- 85  MCFARLANE, ORLANDO DE JESUS      1971 ADD: 33 TAFT AVE - ASHEVILLE NC 28803
81- 82  MCGAFFIGAN, ANDREW JOSEPH        262 SW 63RD AVE - PLANTATION FL 33317
17- 46  MCGAFFIGAN, MARK ANDREW          D. DECEMBER 22, 1940 CARLYLE, ILL.
46- 71  MCGAH, EDWARD JOSEPH             3732 MT DIABLO BLVD #390 - LAFAYETTE CA 94549
62- 86  MCGAHA, FRED MELVIN              3220 JUNIOR PLACE - SHREVEPORT LA 71109
12-122  MCGARR, JAMES VINCENT            D. JULY 21, 1981 MIAMI, FLA.
12-123  MCGARVEY, DANIEL
34- 69  MCGEE, DANIEL ALOYSIUS           252 BUTTRICK AVE - BRONX NY 10465
25- 71  MCGEE, FRANCIS D.                D. JANUARY 30, 1934 COLUMBUS, O.
35- 68  MCGEE, WILLIAM HENRY             RR 1 HARDIN IL 62047
11-114  MCGEEHAN, DANIEL DESALES         D. JULY 12, 1955 HAZELTON, PA.
 2-124  MCGEEHEE, PATRICK HENRY          D. DECEMBER 30, 1946 PADUCAH, KY.
 0- 66  MCGHEE, WARREN EDWARD            5415 RAPPAHANNOCK - MEMPHIS TN 38134
 4- 85  MCGHEE, WILLIAM MAC              MUSTANG RD - GULF BREEZE FL 32561
 7- 90  MCGILBERRY, RANDALL KENT         23 NORTHPOINT APTS - SARALAND AL 36571
 4- 86  MCGILLEN, JOHN JOSEPH            1214 5TH AVE - WOODLYN PA 19094
 8- 62  MCGINN, DANIEL MICHAEL           1340 S 163RD ST - OMAHA NE 68120
 2- 70  MCGLOTHEN, LYNN EVERATT          RR 2 BOX 54 - SIMSBORO LA 71275
 9- 51  MCGLOTHIN, EZRA MAC              2317 COREFIELD RD - KNOXVILLE TN 37919
35- 72  MCGLOTHIN, JAMES MILTON          D. DECEMBER 23, 1975 UNION, KY.
22- 86  MCGOWAN, FRANK BERNARD           80 ROLLING RIDGE RD - MOUNT CARMEL CT 06518
18- 70  MCGOWAN, TULLIS EARL             618 SPRATT ST - WAYCROSS GA 31501
12-125  MCGRANER, HOWARD                 D. OCTOBER 22, 1952 ZALESKI, O.
55- 73  MCGRAW, FRANK EDWIN              COLESHILL ROSE VALLEY RD - MEDIA PA 19063
14-147  MCGRAW, JOHN                     D. NOVEMBER 14, 1918 CLEVELAND, O.
17- 47  MCGRAW, ROBERT EMMETT            D. JUNE 2, 1978 BOISE, ID.
76- 61  MCGREGOR, SCOTT HOUSTON          641 W SYCAMORE - EL SEGUNDO CA 90245
22- 87  MCGREW, WALTER HOWARD            D. AUGUST 21, 1967 PORT ARTHUR, TEX.
```

62- 87 MCGUIRE, MC ADOLFUS	1471 BENSON DR - DAYTON OH 45406
14-148 MCGUIRE, THOMAS PATRICK	D. DECEMBER 8, 1959 PHOENIX, AZ.
43- 87 MCHALE, JOHN JOSEPH	BOX 500 STATION R-MONTRIAL QUE H25 3G7
10- 99 MCHALE, MARTIN JOSEPH	D. MAY 7, 1979 HEMPSTEAD, N. Y.
18- 48 MCHENRY, AUSTIN BUSH	D. NOVEMBER 27, 1922 MT. OREB, O.
81- 83 MCHENRY, VANCE LOREN	290 BROWN ST - DURHAM CA 95938
21- 59 MCILREE, VANCE ELMER	D. MAY 6, 1959 KANSAS CITY, MO.
57- 52 MCILWAIN, WILLIAM STOVER	D. JANUARY 15, 1966 BUFFALO, N. Y.
74- 82 MCINTOSH, JOSEPH ANTHONY	1002 PARKHILL - BILLINGS MT 59102
11-115 MCIVER, EDWARD OTTO	D. MAY 4, 1954 DALLAS, TEX.
37- 72 MCKAIN, ARCHIE RICHARD	515 CONCORD ST MINNEAPOLIS KS 67467
27- 58 MCKAIN, HAROLD LEROY	D. JANUARY 24, 1970 SACRAMENTO, CAL.
75- 74 MCKAY, DAVID LAWRENCE	4981 ST CATHERINE - VANCOUVER BRITISH COLUMB
15-100 MCKAY, REEVE STEWART	D. JANUARY 18, 1946 DALLAS, TEX.
72- 71 MCKEE, JAMES MARION	RR, LITHOPLIS RD - GROVEPORT OH 43125
13-117 MCKEE, RAY	D. AUGUST 5, 1972 SAGINAW, MICH.
43- 88 MCKEE, ROGERS HORNSBY	BOX 61-SHELBY NC 28150
32- 49 MCKEITHAN, EMMETT JAMES	D. AUGUST 20, 1969 FOREST CITY, N. C.
15-101 MCKENRY, FRANK GORDON	D. NOVEMBER 1, 1956 FRESNO, CALIF.
73- 83 MCKEON, JOHN ALOYSIUS	2418 MORNINGSIDE DR - BURLINGTON NC 27215
70- 88 MCKINNEY, CHARLES RICHARD	1633 EAST PETERSON - TROY OH 45373
60- 70 MCKNIGHT, JAMES ARTHUR	RR2 - BEE BRANCH AR 72013
63- 77 MCLAIN, DENNIS DALE	OLD ADD: 1 EARLY MAXWELL BLVD - MEMPHIS TN
32- 50 MCLARNEY, ARTHUR JAMES	303 FILLMORE - PORT TOWNSEND WA 98368
12-126 MCLARRY, HOWARD ZELL	D. NOVEMBER 4, 1971 BONHAM, TEX.
77- 91 MCLAUGHLIN, BYRON SCOTT	1343 MONUMENT - PACIFIC PALISADES CA 90272
14-149 MCLAUGHLIN, JAMES ANSON	D. NOVEMBER 13, 1934 ALLEGANY, N.Y.
32- 51 MCLAUGHLIN, JAMES ROBERT	D. DECEMBER 18, 1968 MOUNT VERNON, ILL.
77- 92 MCLAUGHLIN, JOEY RICHARD	1611 S TROOST - TULSA OK 74120
31- 57 MCLAUGHLIN, JUSTIN THEODORE	D. SEPTEMBER 27, 1964 CAMBRIDGE, MASS.
76- 62 MCLAUGHLIN, MICHAEL DUANE	3708 OAKWOOD - AMELIA OH 45102
37- 73 MCLAUGHLIN, PATRICK ELMER	1535 CHANTILLY LN - HOUSTON TX 77018
35- 69 MCLEAN, ALBERT ELDON	B. SEPTEMBER 20, 1912 CHICAGO, ILL.
51- 64 MCLELAND, WAYNE GAFFNEY	6622 BELDART - HOUSTON TX 77017
38- 61 MCLEOD, RALPH ALTON	30 ACTON ST WOLLASTON MA 02170
30- 51 MCLEOD, SOULE JAMES	D. AUGUST 3, 1981 LITTLE ROCK, ARK.
44- 87 MCLISH, CALVIN COOLIDGE	BOX 753 - EDMOND OK 73034
56- 59 MCMAHAN, JACK WALLY	70 BRISTOL - BRYANT AR 72022
57- 53 MCMAHON, DONALD JOHN	11131 FRALEY ST - GARDEN GROVE CA 92641
60- 71 MCMANUS, JAMES MICHAEL	334 CORNELL ST - ROSLINDALE MA 02131
13-118 MCMANUS, JOAB LOGAN	D. DECEMBER 23, 1955 SKELTON, W. VA.
20- 81 MCMANUS, MARTIN JOSEPH	D. FEBRUARY 18, 1966 ST. LOUIS, MO.
68- 63 MCMATH, JIMMY LEE	3321 22ND ST - TUSCALOOSA AL 35401
22- 88 MCMILLAN, NORMAN ALEXIS	D. SEPTEMBER 28, 1969 LATTA, S. C.
51- 65 MCMILLAN, ROY DAVID	1200 E 9TH ST - BONHAM TX 75418
77- 93 MCMILLAN, THOMAS ERWIN	3810 W COOPER LAKE DR - SMYRNA GA 30080
25- 72 MCMULLEN, HUGH RAPHAEL	1051 SITE DR #42 - BREA CA 92621
62- 88 MCMULLEN, KENNETH LEE	10 ESTABAN - CAMARILLO CA 93010
14-150 MCMULLIN, FREDERICK WILLIAM	D. NOVEMBER 21, 1952 LOS ANGELES, CALIF.
45- 68 MCNABB, CARL MAC	BOX 203 - JASPER TN 37347
29- 71 MCNAIR, DONALD ERIE	D. MARCH 11, 1949 MERIDIAN, MISS.
62- 89 MCNALLY, DAVID ARTHUR	3305 RAMADA DR - BILLINGS MT 59102
15-102 MCNALLY, MICHAEL JOSEPH	D. MAY 29, 1965 BETHLEHEM, PA.
22- 89 MCNAMARA, GEORGE FRANCIS	3627 ARTHUR AVE - MARKHAM IL 60426
69-114 MCNAMARA, JOHN FRANCIS	40 TRISTEN CIR - SACRAMENTO CA 95823
27- 59 MCNAMARA, JOHN RAYMOND	D. DECEMBER 20, 1963 LEXINGTON, MASS.
39- 78 MCNAMARA, ROBERT MAXEY	1633 DAVID DR - ESCONDIDO CA 92026
22- 90 MCNAMARA, THOMAS HENRY	D. MAY 5, 1974 DANVERS, MASS.
22- 91 MCNAMARA, TIMOTHY AUGUSTINE	21 SUMMIT AV - WOONSOCKET RI 02895
32- 52 MCNAUGHTON, GORDON JOSEPH	D. AUGUST 6, 1942 CHICAGO, ILL.
24- 77 MCNEELY, GEORGE EARL	D. JULY 16, 1971 SACRAMENTO, CAL.
19- 57 MCNEIL, NORMAN FRANCIS	D. APRIL 11, 1942 BUFFALO, N.Y.
64- 71 MCNERTNEY, GERALD EDWARD	918 RIDGEWOOD AVE - AMES IA 50010
22- 92 MCNULTY, PATRICK HOWARD	D. MAY 4, 1963 HOLLYWOOD, CAL.
69-115 MCNULTY, WILLIAM FRANCIS	5408 TIBURON WAY - SACRAMENTO CA 95841
23- 89 MCQUAID, HERBERT GEORGE	D. APRIL 5, 1966 RICHMOND, CAL.
34- 70 MCQLAIG, GERALD JOSEPH	110 SCHOOL DR - BUFORD GA 30518
69-116 MCQUEEN, MICHAEL ROBERT	3206 CAMEO DR - HOUSTON TX 77055
18- 49 MCQUILLAN, HUGH A.	D. AUGUST 26, 1947 NEW YORK, N. Y.
38- 62 MCQUILLEN, GLENN RICHARD	4400 ANNTANA AVE - BALTIMORE MD 21206
36- 55 MCQUINN, GEORGE HARTLEY	D. DECEMBER 24, 1978 ALEXANDRIA, VA.

68- 64	MCRAE, HAROLD ABRAHAM	1312 63RD ST NW - BRADENTON FL 33505
69-117	MCRAE, NORMAN	OLD ADD: 1009 LAURA ST - ELIZABETH NJ 07206
11-116	MCTIGUE, WILLIAM PATRICK	D. MAY 11, 1920 NASHVILLE, TENN.
21- 60	MCWEENY, DOUGLAS LAWRENCE	D. JANUARY 1, 1953 CHICAGO, ILL.
78- 79	MCWILLIAMS, LARRY DEAN	736 HENSON DR - HURST TX 76053
31- 58	MCWILLIAMS, WILLIAM HENRY	OLD ADD: 559 SURF ST - CHICAGO IL 60651
43- 89	MEAD, CHARLES RICHARD	16350 FREMONTIA - HESPERIA CA 92345
20- 82	MEADOR, JOHN DAVIS	D. APRIL 11, 1970 WINSTON-SALEM, N. C.
15-103	MEADOWS, HENRY LEE	D. JANUARY 29, 1963 DAYTONA BEACH, FLA.
26- 55	MEADOWS, RUFUS RIVERS	D. MAY 10, 1970 WICHITA, KAN.
12-127	MEANEY, PATRICK	D. OCTOBER 20, 1922 PHILADELPHIA,PA.
14-151	MEARA, CHARLES EDWARD	D. FEBRUARY 8, 1962 KINGSBRIDGE, N. Y.
45- 69	MEDEIROS, RAY ANTON	313 SAN MIGUEL WAY - SAN MATEO CA 94403
72- 72	MEDICH, GEORGE FRANCIS	2332 LINDEN AVE - ALIQUIPPA PA 15001
49- 52	MEDLINGER, IRVING JOHN	D. SEPTEMBER 3, 1975 WHEELING, ILL.
32- 53	MEDWICK, JOSEPH MICHAEL	D. MARCH 21, 1975 ST. PETERSBURG, FLA.
10-100	MEE, THOMAS WILLIAM	D. MAY 16, 1981 CHICAGO, ILL.
15-104	MEEHAN, WILLIAM THOMAS	B. SEPTEMBER 3, 1891 OSCEOLA, PA.
23- 90	MEEKER, CHARLES ROY	D. MARCH 25, 1929 ORLANDO, FLA.
48- 71	MEEKS, SAMUEL MACK	4963 HELENE - MEMPHIS TN 38117
72- 73	MEELER, CHARLES PHILLIP	OLD ADD: 108 HAWTHORNE LN - LENOIR NC 28645
41- 71	MEERS, RUSSELL HARLAN	4568 SUDBURY RD NE - ATLANTA GA 30340
22- 93	MEINE, HENRY WILLIAM	D. MARCH 18, 1968 ST. LOUIS, MO.
13-119	MEINERT, WALTER HENRY	D. NOVEMBER 9, 1958 DECATUR, ILL.
10-101	MEINKE, ROBERT BERNARD	D. DECEMBER 29, 1952 CHICAGO, ILL.
13-120	MEISTER, KARL DANIEL	D. AUGUST 15, 1967 MARIETTA, O.
12-128	MEIXELL, MERTEN MERRILL	1449 S WELLESLEY - WEST LOS ANGELES CA 90025
55- 81	MEJIAS, ROMAN GEORGE	3242 W 59TH ST - LOS ANGELES CA 90043
76- 63	MEJIAS, SAMUEL ELIAS	AVE ENRIQUILLO 31 - SANTIAGO DOMINICAN REP.
37- 74	MELE, ALBERT ERNEST	D. FEBRUARY 12, 1975 HOLLYWOOD, FLA.
47- 63	MELE, SABATH ANTHONY	340 ADAMS ST - QUINCY MA 02169
70- 89	MELENDEZ, LUIS ANTONIO	BO. RABANAL - AIBONITO PR 00609
26- 56	MELILLO, OSCAR DONALD	D. NOVEMBER 14, 1963 CHICAGO, ILL.
27- 60	MELLANA, JOSEPH PETER	D. NOVEMBER 1, 1969 SAN RAFAEL, CALIF.
10-102	MELOAN, PAUL	D. FEBRUARY 11, 1950 TAFT, CALIF.
37- 75	MELTON, CLIFFORD GEORGE	1525 ARGONNE DR BALTIMORE MARYLAND 21218
56- 60	MELTON, DAVID OLIN	10253 RICHWOOD DR - CUPERTINO CA 95014
41- 72	MELTON, REUBEN FRANKLIN	D. SEPTEMBER 11, 1971 GREER, S. C.
68- 65	MELTON, WILLIAM EDWIN	695 TOWN CENTER DR - COSTA MESA CA 92626
70- 90	MENDOZA, CRISTOBAL RIGOBERTO	4110 BROADVIEW DR - CHARLOTTE NC 28208
74- 83	MENDOZA, MARIO	LATERAL DE PACUAL OROZEO #1123-CHIHUAHUA MEX
79- 75	MENDOZA, MICHAEL JOSEPH	12812 ELMFIELD LN - POWAY CT 92064
62- 90	MENKE, DENIS JOHN	780 MAPLE RIDGE RD - PALM HARBOR FL 33563
14-152	MENOSKY, MICHAEL WILLIAM	8522 CANFIELD DR #206 - DEARBORN HGTS MI48127
12-129	MENSOR, EDWARD	D. APRIL 20, 1970 SALEM, ORE.
18- 50	MENZE, THEODORE CHARLES	D. DECEMBER 23, 1969 ST. LOUIS, MO.
33- 43	MEOLA, EMILE MICHAEL	D. SEPTEMBER 1, 1976 FAIR LAWN, N. J.
71- 66	MEOLI, RUDOLPH BARTHOLOMEW	3233 GREENLEAF - BREA CA 92624
10-103	MERCER, JOHN	
12-224	MERCER, JOHN LOCKE	OLD ADD: FOUNTAIN TOWERS - SHREVEPORT LA
81- 84	MERCER, MARK KENNETH	OLD ADD: 2732 2ND AVE S #302-MINNEAPOLIS MN
75- 75	MERCHANT, JAMES ANDERSON	716 EUCLID AVE - MOBILE AL 36601
34- 71	MERENA, JOHN JOSEPH	D. MARCH 8, 1977 BRIDGEPORT, CONN.
22- 94	MEREWETHER, ARTHUR FRANCIS	37-02 222ND ST - BAYSIDE NY 11361
49- 53	MERRIMAN, LLOYD ARCHER	6691 N DEWOLF - CLOVIS CA 93612
21- 61	MERRITT, HERMAN G.	D. MAY 26, 1927 KANSAS CITY, MO.
65- 74	MERRITT, JAMES JOSEPH	12530 OAK CREEK - CERRITOS CA 90701
13-121	MERRITT, JOHN HOWARD	D. NOVEMBER 3, 1955 TUPELO, MISS.
57- 56	MERRITT, LLOYD WESLEY	260 HEATHERCREST DR - CHESTERFIELD MO 63017
14-153	MERSON	
51- 66	MERSON, JOHN WARREN	6264 OLD WASHINGTON RD - ELK RIDGE MD 21227
43- 90	MERTZ, JAMES VERLIN	5116 EMORY CIR - JACKSONVILLE FL 32207
41- 73	MERULLO, LEONARD RICHARD	BOX E - READING MA 01867
38- 63	MESNER, STEPHEN MATHIAS	D. APRIL 6, 1981 SAN DIEGO, CALIF.
24- 78	MESSENGER, ANDREW WARREN	D. NOVEMBER 4, 1971 LANSING, MICH.
68- 66	MESSERSMITH, JOHN ALEXANDER	200 LAGUNITA DR - SOQUEL CA 95073
63- 78	METCALF, THOMAS JOHN	1390 WISCONSIN RIVER DR-PORT EDWARDS WI 54469
40- 62	METHA, FRANK JOSEPH	D. MARCH 2, 1975 FOUNTAIN VALLEY, CALIF.
43- 91	METHENY, ARTHUR BEAUREGARD	2424 N SANDPIPER RD - VIRGINIA BEACH VA 23456
22- 95	METIVIER, GEORGE DEWEY	D. MARCH 2, 1947 CAMBRIDGE, MASS.
43- 92	METKOVICH, GEORGE MICHAEL	18191 DEVONWOOD CIR-FOUNTAIN VALLEY CA 92708
43- 93	METRO, CHARLES	7890 INDIANA ST-GOLDEN CO 80401
23- 91	METZ, LEONARD RAYMOND	D. FEBRUARY 24, 1953 DENVER, COLO.
74- 84	METZGER, CLARENCE EDWARD	OLD ADD: 6109 24TH ST - SACRAMENTO CA 95822
70- 91	METZGER, ROGER HENRY	OLD ADD: 202 WESTMORELAND - SAN ANTONIO TX
44- 88	METZIG, WILLIAM ANDREW	2129 57TH ST - LUBBOCK TX 79412
25- 73	METZLER, ALEXANDER	D. NOVEMBER 30, 1973 FRESNO, CAL.
14-154	MEUSEL, EMIL FREDERICK	D. MARCH 1, 1963 LONG BEACH, CALIF.
20- 83	MEUSEL, ROBERT WILLIAM	D. NOVEMBER 28, 1977 DOWNEY, CALIF.
13-122	MEYER, BENJAMIN	D. FEBRUARY 6, 1974 FESTUS, MO.
74- 85	MEYER, DANIEL THOMAS	18339 NE 153RD ST - WOODINVILLE WA 98072
38- 64	MEYER, GEORGE FRANCIS	B. AUGUST 22, 1912 CHICAGO, ILL.
55- 82	MEYER, JOHN ROBERT	D. MARCH 9, 1967 PHILADELPHIA, PA.

```
37- 76  MEYER, LAMBERT DANIEL           OLD ADD: 3908 THISTLE LN - FORT WORTH TX
64- 72  MEYER, ROBERT BERNARD           4204 WESTWAY AVE - TOLEDO OH 43612
46- 72  MEYER, RUSSELL CHARLES          5921 JUNIPER - GARY IN 46403
78- 80  MEYER, SCOTT WILLIAM            15243 S HAMLIN AVE - MIDLOTHIAN IL 60445
13-123  MEYER, WILLIAM ADAM            D. MARCH 31, 1957 KNOXVILLE, TENN.
54- 66  MICELOTTA, ROBERT PETER        295 SAVILLE RD - MINEOLA NY 11501
66- 59  MICHAEL, GENE RICHARD          30 FARRINGTON ST - CLOSTER NJ 07624
43- 94  MICHAELS, CASIMIR EUGENE       1171 N RENAUD - GROSSE POINTE WOODS MI 48236
32- 54  MICHAELS, JOHN JOSEPH          3190 63RD ST - FT LAUDERDALE FL 33309
24- 79  MICHAELS, RALPH JOSEPH         123 LOCUST ST - PITTSBURGH PA 15223
21- 62  MICHAELSON, JOHN AUGUST        D. APRIL 16, 1968 WOODRUFF, WIS.
50- 67  MICKELSON, EDWARD ALLEN        12620 FEE FEE RD - CREVE COUER MO 63141
53- 56  MICKENS, GLENN ROGER           7241 WHITE OAK AVE BOX 583 - RESEDA CA 91335
17- 48  MIDDLETON, JAMES BLAINE        D. JANUARY 12, 1974 ARGOS, IND.
22- 96  MIDDLETON, JOHN WAYNE          2026 ONG ST - AMARILLO TX 79109
12-223  MIDKIFF, EZRA MILLINGTON       D. MARCH 21, 1957 HUNTINGTON, W. VA.
38- 65  MIDKIFF, RICHARD JAMES         D. OCTOBER 30, 1956 TEMPLE, TEX.
45- 70  MIERKOWICZ, EDWARD FRANK       7530 MACOMB - GROSSE ILE MI 48138
48- 72  MIGGINS, LAWRENCE EDWARD       2405 KINGSTON DR - HOUSTON TX 77019
35- 70  MIHALIC, JOHN MICHAEL          120 BELLE MEADE BLVD - NASHVILLE TN 37205
64- 73  MIKKELSEN, PETER JAMES         RR 1 BOX 1667--PROSSER WA 99350
44- 89  MIKLOS, JOHN JOSEPH            19701 S 115TH AVE - MOKENA IL 60448
44- 90  MIKSIS, EDWARD THOMAS          3906 WHITMAN RD - HUNTINGDON VALLEY PA 19006
15-106  MILAN, HORACE ROBERT           D. JUNE 29, 1955 TEXARKANA, TEX.
74- 86  MILBOURNE, LAWRENCE WILLIAM    128 W MAIN ST - PORT NORRIS NJ 08349
40- 63  MILES, CARL THOMAS             806 AUSTIN RD - HORSESHOE BEND AR 72512
58- 62  MILES, DONALD RAY              1975 ADD: 9826 HARWYN - HOUSTON TX 77036
68- 67  MILES, JAMES CHARLIE           RR2 - BATESVILLE MS 38606
35- 71  MILES, WILSON DANIEL           D. NOVEMBER 2, 1976 BIRMINGHAM, ALA.
75- 76  MILEY, MICHAEL WILFRED         D. JANUARY 6, 1977 BATON ROUGE, LA.
15-107  MILJUS, JOHN KENNETH           D. FEBRUARY 11, 1976 POLSON, MONT.
66- 60  MILLAN, FELIX BERNARDO         CALLE 1-336, SABANA LLANA-RIO PIEDRAS PR 00928
73- 84  MILLER, CHARLES BRUCE          5715 DARTMOUTH DR - FORT WAYNE IN 46825
12-130  MILLER, CHARLES ELMER          D. APRIL 23, 1972 WARRENSBURG, MO.
15-108  MILLER, CHARLES HESS           D. JANUARY 13, 1951 MILLERSVILLE, PA.
13-124  MILLER, CHARLES MARION         D. JUNE 16, 1961 HOUSTON, TEX.
75- 77  MILLER, DYAR K                 8 RUSSELL DR - GREENSBURG IN 47240
21- 63  MILLER, EDMUND JOHN            D. MAY 7, 1966 PHILADELPHIA, PA.
77- 94  MILLER, EDWARD LEE             5014 HARTNETT - RICHMOND CA 94804
36- 56  MILLER, EDWARD ROBERT          204 CYPRESS DR LAKE WORTH FL 33460
12-131  MILLER, EDWIN                  D. APRIL 17, 1980 LEBANON, PA.
12-132  MILLER, ELMER                  D. NOVEMBER 28, 1944 BELOIT, WIS.
29- 72  MILLER, ELMER LEROY            20402 POWERS - DEARBORN HEIGHTS MI 48127
13-125  MILLER, FRANK LEE              D. FEBRUARY 19, 1974 ALLEGAN, MICH.
10-104  MILLER, FREDERICK HOLMAN       D. MAY 2, 1953 BROOKVILLE, IND.
11-117  MILLER, HUGH STANLEY           D. DECEMBER 24, 1945 ST. LOUIS, MO.
22- 97  MILLER, JACOB GEORGE           B. FEBRUARY 5, 1897 BALTIMORE, MD.
44- 91  MILLER, JAMES ELDRIDGE         D. NOVEMBER 21, 1966 DALLAS, TEX
66- 61  MILLER, JOHN ALLEN             5105 RIVER AVE - NEWPORT BEACH CA 92660
43- 95  MILLER, JOHN ANTHONY           STAR RT - GEORGE WEST TX 78022
62- 91  MILLER, JOHN ERNEST            1216 REDCHIEF RD - BALTIMORE MD 21228
44- 92  MILLER, KENNETH ALBERT         9344 RAMBLER DR - AFFTON MO 63123
64- 74  MILLER, LARRY DON              11221 N 73RD ST - SCOTTSDALE AZ 85254
16- 61  MILLER, LAWRENCE H.            D. SEPTEMBER 17, 1971 OAKLAND, CAL.
23- 92  MILLER, LEO ALPHONSO           D. OCTOBER 20, 1973 ORLANDO, FL.
10-105  MILLER, LOWELL OTTO            D. MARCH 29, 1962 BROOKLYN, N.Y.
65- 75  MILLER, NORMAN CALVIN          OLD ADD: 3006 BROADMOOR - SUGARLAND TX
27- 61  MILLER, OTIS LOUIS             D. JULY 26, 1959 BELLEVILLE, ILL.
21- 64  MILLER, RALPH HENRY            D. FEBRUARY 18, 1967 WHITE BEAR LAKE, MINN.
20- 84  MILLER, RALPH JOSEPH           D. MARCH 18, 1939 FORT WAYNE, IND.
77- 95  MILLER, RANDALL SCOTT          321 E PEDREGOSA - SAN TA BARBARA CA 93101
17- 49  MILLER, RAYMOND PETER          D. APRIL 7, 1927 PITTSBURGH, PA.
71- 70  MILLER, RICHARD ALAN           804 LAKE ALBERT CT NE - WINTER HAVEN FL 33880
53- 57  MILLER, ROBERT GERALD          1813 SCHOOL AVE - LOMBARD IL 60148
```

```
49- 54  MILLER, ROBERT JOHN           17397 GLENMORE - DETROIT MI 48240
57- 55  MILLER, ROBERT LANE           14550 VICTORIA ESTATES LN - POWAY CA 92064
57- 56  MILLER, RODNEY CARTER         8459 SOUTHGATE AVE - SOUTH GATE CA 90280
74- 87  MILLER, ROGER WESLEY          RR 1 BOX 130 - MILL RUN PA 15464
41- 74  MILLER, ROLLAND ARTHUR        3827-A HUMPHREY - ST LOUIS MO 63116
10-106  MILLER, ROY OSCAR             D. JULY 31, 1938 JERSEY CITY, N. J.
29- 73  MILLER, RUDEL CHARLES         2246 TIPPERARY RD - KALAMAZOO MI 49001
27- 62  MILLER, RUSSELL LEWIS         D. AUGUST 30, 1962 BUCYRUS, O.
52- 74  MILLER, STUART LEONARD        252 DEVONSHIRE BLVD - SAN CARLOS CA 94070
```

```
18- 51  MILLER, THOMAS ROYALL          D. AUGUST 13, 1980 RICHMOND, VA.
24- 80  MILLER, WALTER JACOB           D. AUGUST 20, 1975 VENICE, FLA.
11-118  MILLER, WALTER W.              D. MARCH 1, 1956 MARION, IND.
37- 77  MILLER, WILLIAM FRANCIS        260 N LOCUST HANNIBAL MO 63401
52- 75  MILLER, WILLIAM PAUL           501 EXTON RD - HATBORO PA 19040
34- 72  MILLIES, WALTER LOUIS          5312 W 96TH ST - OAK LAWN IL 60453
28- 66  MILLIGAN, JLHN ALEXANDER       D. MAY 15, 1972 FORT PIERCE, FLA.
53- 58  MILLIKEN, ROBERT FOGLE         1875 SOUTHWOOD LN - CLEARWATER FL 33516
11-119  MILLS, ABBOTT PAIGE            D. JUNE 3, 1973 WASHINGTON, D.C.
27- 63  MILLS, ARTHUR GRANT            D. JULY 23, 1975 UTICA, N. Y.
34- 73  MILLS, COLONEL BUSTER          BOX 13081 ARLINGTON TX 76016
14-155  MILLS, FRANK LEMOYNE           1216 5TH AVE - YOUNGSTOWN OH 44504
34- 74  MILLS, HOWARD ROBERTSON        BOX 5176 CANYON LAKE CA 92380
80- 89  MILLS, JAMES BRADLEY           BOX 54 - LEMONCOVE CA 93244
70- 92  MILLS, RICHARD ALAN            44 WOOD AVE - SCITUATE MA 02060
15-109  MILLS, RUPERT FRANK            D. JULY 20, 1929 LAKE HOPATCONG, N. J.
44- 93  MILLS, WILLIAM HENRY           BOX 43 - EL JOBEAN FL 33927
36- 57  MILNAR, ALBERT JOSEPH          19520 SHAWNEE AVE CLEVELAND OH 44119
48- 73  MILNE, WILLIAM JAMES           BOX 160566 - MOBILE AL 36616
78- 81  MILNER, BRIAN TATE             1401 CAIRN CIR - FORT WORTH TX 76134
80- 90  MILNER, EDDIE JAMES            491 STAMBAUGH - COLUMBUS OH 43207
71- 71  MILNER, JOHN DAVID             1821 CAVENDISH PL - PITTSBURGH PA 15220
44- 94  MILOSEVICH, MICHAEL            D. FEBRUARY 3, 1966 EAST CHICAGO, IND.
24- 81  MILSTEAD, GEORGE EARL          D. AUGUST 9, 1977 CLEBURNE, TEX.
55- 83  MINARCIN, RUDY ANTHONY         37 N FIRST ST - NORTH VANDERGRIFT PA 15690
60- 72  MINCHER, DONALD RAY            BOX 120 - MERIDIANVILLE AL 35759
21- 65  MINER, RAYMOND THEADORE        D. SEPTEMBER 15, 1963 GLENRIDGE SAN., N. Y.
78- 82  MINETTO, CRAIG STEPHEN         206 W MONTEREY - STOCKTON CA 95204
70- 93  MINGORI, STEPHEN BERNARD       5723 N COLORADO - KANSAS CITY MO 64119
46- 73  MINNER, PAUL EDISON            115 GREEN LANE DR - CAMP HILL PA 17011
57- 57  MINNICK, DONALD ATHEY          FRANKLIN HGTS - ROCKY MOUNT VA 24151
49- 55  MINOSO, SATURNINO ORESTES      DAN RYAN AT 35TH - CHICAGO IL 60616
```

```
74- 88  MINSHALL, JAMES EDWARD              2602 10TH ST SW - PALMETTO FL 33561
75- 78  MINTON, GREGORY BRIAN               112 MARSH PL - SAN RAMON CA 94583
78- 83  MIRABELLA, PAUL THOMAS              550 KNOLL RD - BOONTON MANOR NJ 0700K
51- 67  MIRANDA, GUILLERMO PEREZ            5502 WHITWOOD RD - BALTIMORE MD 21206
14-156  MISSE, JOHN BEVERLY                 D. MARCH 18, 1970 ST. JOSEPH, MO.
10-107  MITCHELL, ALBERT ROY                D. SEPTEMBER 8, 1959 TEMPLE, TEX.
11-120  MITCHELL, CLARENCE ELMER            D. NOVEMBER 6, 1963 GRAND ISLAND, NEB.
75- 79  MITCHELL, CRAIG SETON               BOX 174 - ELK CA 95432
21- 66  MITCHELL, JOHN FRANKLIN             D. NOVEMBER 4, 1965 OAKLAND CO., MICH.
46- 74  MITCHELL, LOREN DALE                3434 E 75TH PL S - TULSA OK 74136
23- 93  MITCHELL, MONROE BARR               D. SEPTEMBER 4, 1976 VALDOSTA, GA.
75- 80  MITCHELL, PAUL MICHAEL              7 WABASH AVE - WORCESTER MA 0160J
80- 91  MITCHELL, ROBERT VAN                18844 TULSA ST - NORTHRIDGE CA 91326
70- 94  MITCHELL, ROBERT VANCE              38 E ELM ST - NORRISTOWN PA 19401
16- 62  MITTERLING, RALPH                   D. JANUARY 22, 1956 PITTSBURGH, PA.
66- 62  MITTERWALD, GEORGE EUGENE           1721 MURDOCK BLVD - ORLANDO FL 32807
36- 58  MIZE, JOHN ROBERT                   BOX 112 - DEMOREST GA 30535
52- 76  MIZELL, WILMER DAVID                RR 5 BOX 333 - WINSTON-SALEM NC 27107
23- 94  MIZEUR, WILLIAM FRANCIS             D. AUGUST 27, 1976 DANVILLE, ILL.
74- 89  MOATES, DAVID ALLAN                 4715 18TH AVE N - BRADENTON FL 33505
45- 71  MODAK, MICHAEL JOSEPH ALOYSIUS      235 COITSVILLE - CAMPBELL OH 44405
62- 92  MOELLER, JOSEPH DOUGLAS             OLD ADD: 331 CARRIAGE PL - MANHATTAN BEACH CA
56- 61  MOELLER, RONALD RALPH               3560 GAILYNN DR - CINCINNATI OH 45211
72- 74  MOFFITT, RANDALL JAMES              506 ISABELLA - EL GRANADA CA 94018
55- 84  MOFORD, HERBERT                     RR 1 - DOVER KY 41034
11-121  MOGRIDGE, GEORGE ANTHONY            D. MARCH 4, 1962 ROCHESTER, N.Y.
22- 98  MOHARDT, JOHN HENRY                 D. NOVEMBER 24, 1961 SAN DIEGO, CAL.
20- 85  MOHART, GEORGE BENJAMIN             D. OCTOBER 2, 1970 SILVER CREEK, N.Y.
53- 59  MOISAN, WILLIAM JOSEPH              BOX 41 - NEWTON NH 03858
21- 67  MOKAN, JOHN LEO                     5076 BROADWAY - DEPEW NY 14043
49- 56  MOLE, FENTON LEROY                  349 ALOHA DR - SAN LEANDRO CA 94578
75- 81  MOLINARO, ROBERT JOSEPH             6 DUNN RD - WEST ORANGE NJ 07052
78- 84  MOLITOR, PAUL LEO                   1037 PORTLAND AVE - SAINT PAUL MN 55104
14-157  MOLLENKAMP, FREDERICK HENRY         D. NOVEMBER 1, 1948 CINCINNATI, O.
13-126  MOLLWITZ, FREDERICK AUGUST          D. OCTOBER 3, 1967 BRADENTON, FLA.
70- 95  MOLONEY, RICHARD HENRY              95 GRANT ST #7 - WALTHAM MA 02154
17- 50  MOLYNEAUX, VINCENT LEO              D. MAY 4, 1950 STAMFORD, CONN.
37- 78  MONACO, BLAS                        410 FROST DR - SAN ANTONIO TX 78201
53- 60  MONAHAN, EDWARD FRANCIS             165 83RD ST - BROOKLYN NY 11209
58- 63  MONBOUQUETTE, WILLIAM CHARLES CLARK HILL RD - NEW BOSTON NH 03070
```

```
28- 67  MONCEWICZ, FRED ALFRED          D. APRIL 23, 1969 BROCKTON, MASS.
40- 64  MONCHAK, ALEX                   2404 BRANCH PIKE-RIVERTON NJ 08077
66- 63  MONDAY, ROBERT JAMES            5447 ROBIN LN - YORBA LINDA CA 92686
68- 68  MONEY, DONALD WAYNE             282 OLD FOREST RD - VINELAND NJ 08360
15- 82  MONGE, ISIDRO PEDROZA           3510 LOUISVILLE - EL PASO TX 79924
17- 51  MONROE, EDWARD OLIVER           D. APRIL 29, 1969 LOUISVILLE, KY.
21- 68  MONROE, JOHN ALLEN              D. JUNE 19, 1956 CONROE, TEX.
76- 64  MONROE, LAWRENCE JAMES          2101 HAVEN ST - MOUNT PROSPECT IL 60056
58- 64  MONROE, ZACHARY CHARLES         10 SANDALWOOD LN - BARTONVILLE IL 61607
28- 68  MONTAGUE, EDWARD FRANCIS        396 EL DORADO DR - DALY CITY CA 94015
73- 85  MONTAGUE, JOHN EVANS            BOX 159 - GLENWOOD AL 36034
66- 64  MONTANEZ, GUILLERMO NARANJO     ZONA RURAL 142 BUZON 36# - CAGUAS PR 00625
63- 79  MONTEAGUDO, AURELIO FAUNTINO    BOX 468 - BARQUISIMETO LARA VENEZ
38- 66  MONTEAGUDO, RENE MIRANDA        D. SEPTEMBER 14, 1973 HIALEAH, FL.
74- 90  MONTEFUSCO, JOHN JOSEPH         386 EL GRANADA BLVD - EL GRANADA CA 94018
61- 75  MONTEJO, MONTEJO                LEONCIO VIDAL #21,CARBARIIN-LAS VILLAS CUBA
53- 61  MONTEMAYOR, FELIPE ANGEL        TORREON #308 MITRAS - MONTERREY, N L, MEXICO
41- 75  MONTGOMERY, ALVIN ATLAS         D. APRIL 26, 1942 WAVERLY, VA.
71- 72  MONTGOMERY, MONTY BRYSON        BOX 1314 - ALBEMARLE NC 28001
70- 96  MONTGOMERY, ROBERT EDWARD       107 PAINE DR SE - WINTER HAVEN FL 33880
72- 75  MONTREUIL, ALLAN ARTHUR         2016 LAUREL ST - GRETNA LA 70053
54- 67  MONZANT, RAMON SEGUNDO          CALLE 87 NRO 2A-33 MARACAIBO - EDO ZULIA VEN
72- 76  MONZON, DANIEL FRANCISCO        912 OLMSTEAD AVE - BRONX NY 10473
67- 73  MOOCK, JOSEPH GEOFFREY          12432 PECOS AVE - GREENWELL LA 70739
32- 55  MOON, LEO                       D. AUGUST 25, 1970 NEW ORLEANS, LA.
54- 68  MOON, WALLACE WADE              BOX 28268 - SAN ANTONIO TX 78228
31- 59  MOONEY, JAMES IRVING            D. APRIL 27, 1979 JOHNSON CITY, TENN.
25- 74  MOORE, ALBERT JAMES             D. NOVEMBER 29, 1974 ATLANTIC OCEAN
72- 65  MOORE, ALVIN EARL               3728 WALL AVE - RICHMOND CA 94804
46- 75  MOORE, ANSELM WINN              245 MARILYN DR - JACKSON MS 39208
64- 75  MOORE, ARCHIE FRANCIS           69 TOWNSEND DR - FLORHAM PARK NJ 07932
70- 97  MOORE, BALOR LILBON             3317 BOND - PASADENA TX 77503
30- 52  MOORE, CARLOS WHITMAN           D. JULY 2, 1958 NEW ORLEANS, LA.
12-133  MOORE, CHARLES WESLEY           D. JULY 29, 1970 PORTLAND, ORE.
73- 86  MOORE, CHARLES WILLIAM          1636 CIRCLEWOOD DR - BIRMINGHAM AL 35214
36- 59  MOORE, D C                      53 MOBILE VLG - WILLISTON ND 58801
75- 83  MOORE, DONNIE RAY               12339 INLETRIDGE DR - MARYLAND HGTS MO 63043
34- 75  MOORE, EUEL WALTON              OLD ADD: TISHOMINGO OK 73460
31- 60  MOORE, EUGENE JR.               D. MARCH 12, 1978 JACKSON, MISS.
14-158  MOORE, FERDINAND DEPAGE         D. MAY 6, 1947 ATLANTIC CITY, N.J.
70- 98  MOORE, GARY DOUGLAS             OLD ADD: 5408 AIRLINE - DALLAS TX
23- 95  MOORE, GRAHAM EDWARD            D. FEBRUARY 10, 1976 FORT MYERS, FLA.
65- 76  MOORE, JACKIE SPENCER           2708 HILLDALE - ARLINGTON TX 76010
28- 69  MOORE, JAMES STANFORD           D. MAY 19, 1973 SEATTLE, WASH.
30- 53  MOORE, JAMES WILLIAM            475 N HIGHLAND ST #10B - MEMPHIS TN 38122
30- 54  MOORE, JOE GREGG                GAUSE TX 77857
28- 70  MOORE, JOHN FRANCIS             4-A SWAN LAKE VLG - BRADENTON FL 33507
81- 85  MOORE, KELVIN ORLANDO           RR 1 BOX 132 - LEROY AL 36548
36- 60  MOORE, LLOYD ALBERT             144 WASHINGTON AVE UHRICHSVILLE OH 44683
27- 64  MOORE, RANDOLPH EDWARD          BOX 757 - OMAHA TX 75571
52- 77  MOORE, RAYMOND LEROY            BOX 4214 - UPPER MARLBORO MD 20870
65- 77  MOORE, ROBERT BARRY             RR1 BOX 174 - CLEVELAND NC 27013
20- 86  MOORE, ROY DANIEL               D. APRIL 5, 1951 SEATTLE, WASH.
35- 72  MOORE, TERRY BLUFORD            501 RIDGEMONT DR - COLLINSVILLE IL 62234
72- 77  MOORE, TOMMY JOE                13-129 LIGGETT ST - NORWALK CA 90650
17- 52  MOORE, WILLIAM ALLEN            D. OCTOBER 13, 1964 LITTLE ROCK, ARK.
29- 74  MOORE, WILLIAM AUSTIN           D. MARCH 28, 1972 AUGUSTA, GA.
25- 75  MOORE, WILLIAM CHRISTOPHER      197 W FIRST ST - CORNING NY 14830
26- 57  MOORE, WILLIAM HENRY            D. MAY 24, 1972 KANSAS CITY, MO.
27- 65  MOORE, WILLIAM WILEY            D. MARCH 29, 1963 HOLLIS, OKLA.
62- 93  MOORHEAD, CHARLES ROBERT        3413 MARKET ST - CAMP HILL PA 17011
67- 74  MOOSE, ROBERT RALPH             D. OCTOBER 9, 1976 MARTINS FERRY, O.
36- 61  MOOTY, J. T.                    D. APRIL 20, 1970 FORT WORTH, TEX.
76- 66  MORA, ANDRES (IBARRA)           GALEANO 567,PTE. LOS MOCHIS MEXICO
73- 87  MORALES, JOSE MANUEL            BOX 3458 - MAYAGUEZ PR 00708
69-118  MORALES, JULIO RUBEN            VILLA NUEVA CALLE 16-C5 - CAGUAS PR 00625
67- 75  MORALES, RICHARD ANGELO         1650 ROSITA RD - PACIFICA CA 94044
38- 67  MORAN, ALBERT THOMAS            2515 FIRST ST #4 - FORT MYERS FL 33901
74- 91  MORAN, CARL WILLIAM             200 SHORE DR - PORTSMOUTH VA 23701
12-134  MORAN, HARRY EDWIN              D. NOVEMBER 28, 1962 BECKLEY, W VA
63- 80  MORAN, RICHARD ALAN             OLD ADD: 24236 LEEWIN - DETROIT MI 48219
12-135  MORAN, ROY ELLIS                D. JULY 18, 1966 ATLANTA, GA.
58- 65  MORAN, WILLIAM NELSON           2845 HOGAN RD - EAST POINT GA 30044
24- 82  MOREHART, RAYMOND ANDERSON      5939 VANDERBILT - DALLAS TX 75206
63- 81  MOREHEAD, DAVID MICHAEL         1342 TIKI CIR - TUSTIN CA 92680
57- 58  MOREHEAD, SETH MARVIN           8675 GROVER PL - SHREVEPORT LA 71105
```

see PAGE 149

```
58- 66  MOREJON, DANIEL TORRES            4041 SW 117TH AVE - MIAMI FL 33165
78- 85  MORELAND, BOBBY KEITH             RR 1 BOX 146 CA - LEWISVILLE TX 75067
81- 86  MORENO, ANGEL                     GOMEZ FARIAZ #604-AGUASCALIENTES MEXICO
80- 92  MORENO, JOSE DE LOS SANTOS        CORREA Y CIDRON 9-SANTO DOMINGO DOMINICAN RE
50- 68  MORENO, JULIO GONZALES            1000 SW 96TH AVE - MIAMI FL 33144
75- 84  MORENO, OMAR RENAN (QUINTERO)     SILVER CITY #4503 - PUERTO ARMUELLES PANAMA
70- 99  MORET, ROGELIO                    BARRIO PUERTO JOBOS - GUAYAMA PR 00654
13-127  MOREY, DAVID BEALE                BOX 296 - OAK BLUFF MA 02557
35- 73  MORGAN, CHESTER COLLINS           602 ORIOLE LA PASADENA TX 77502
21- 69  MORGAN, CYRIL ARLON               D. SEPTEMBER 11, 1946 LAKEVILLE, MASS.
28- 71  MORGAN, EDWARD CARRE              D. APRIL 9, 1980 NEW ORLEANS, LA.
36- 62  MORGAN, EDWIN WILLIS              1290 GRANGER AVE - LAKEWOOD OH 44107
16- 63  MORGAN, JOHN P
63- 82  MORGAN, JOSEPH LEONARD            5588 FERNHOFF RD - OAKLAND CA 94619
59- 59  MORGAN, JOSEPH MICHAEL            15 OAK HILL DRIVE - WALPOLE MA 02081
```

```
78- 86  MORGAN, MICHAEL THOMAS            2008 JANSEN ST - LAS VEGAS NV 89101
11-122  MORGAN, RAYMOND CARYLL            D. FEBRUARY 15, 1940 BALTIMORE, MD.
50- 69  MORGAN, ROBERT MORRIS             2212 BARCLAY RD - OKLAHOMA CITY OK 83120
51- 68  MORGAN, TOM STEPHEN               2724 CLE AVENTURA-RANCHO PALOS VERDE CA 90274
54- 69  MORGAN, VERNON THOMAS             D. NOVEMBER 8, 1975 MINNEAPOLIS, MINN.
61- 76  MORHARDT, MEREDITH GOODWIN        182 WILLIAMS AVE - WINSTED CT 06098
35- 74  MORIARTY, EDWARD JEROME           150 LINDEN ST - HOLYOKE MA 01040
73- 88  MORLAN, JOHN GLEN                 2348 SALEM AVE - GROVE CITY OH 43123
13-128  MORLEY (WILLIAM MORLEY JENNINGS)  3109 21ST ST - LUBBOCK TX 79410
26- 58  MORRELL, WILLARD BLACKMER         D. AUGUST 5, 1975 BIRMINGHAM, ALA.
68- 69  MORRIS, DANNY WALKE               216 WILSON ST - GREENVILLE KY 42345
37- 79  MORRIS, DOYT THEODORE             BOX 548 - STANLEY NC 28164
77- 96  MORRIS, JOHN SCOTT                292 S SARATOGA - ST PAUL MN 55116
66- 65  MORRIS, JOHN WALLACE              4620 E ARCADIA LN - PHOENIX AZ 85018
22-100  MORRIS, WALTER EDWARD             D. MARCH 3, 1932 CENTURY, FLA.
15-110  MORRISETTE, WILLIAM LEE           D. MARCH 25, 1966 VIRGINIA BEACH, VA.
77- 97  MORRISON, JAMES FOREST            6566 DEER PATH CT - LISLE IL 60532
20- 87  MORRISON, JOHN DEWEY              D. MARCH 20, 1966 LEXINGTON, KY.
21- 70  MORRISON, PHILIP MELVIN           D. JANUARY 18, 1955 LEXINGTON, KY.
27- 66  MORRISON, WALTER GUY              D. AUGUST 14, 1934 GRAND RAPIDS, MICH.
32- 56  MORRISSEY, JOSEPH ANSELM          D. MAY 2, 1950 WORCESTER, MASS.
29- 75  MORSE, NEWELL OBEDIAH             2015 IVES AVE - RENO NA 89503
11-123  MORSE, PETER RAYMOND              D. JUNE 19, 1974 ST. PAUL, MINN.
69-119  MORTON, CARL WENDLE               1927 W 41ST ST - TULSA OK 74107
54- 70  MORTON, GUY JR                    RR1 - WOOSTER OH 44691
14-159  MORTON, GUY SR.                   D. OCTOBER 18, 1934 SHEFFIELD, ALA.
61- 77  MORTON, WYCLIFFE NATHAN           3332 MONACO PARKWAY - DENVER CO 80207
54- 71  MORYN, WALTER JOSEPH              545 CHARLES ST - GLENDALE HEIGHTS IL 60137
65- 78  MOSCHITTO, ROSAIRO ALLEN          32 MORTON ST - GARNERSVILLE NY 10923
80- 93  MOSEBY, LLOYD ANTHONY             850 37TH ST - OAKLAND CA 94608
13-129  MOSELEY, EARL VICTOR              D. JULY 1, 1963 ALLIANCE, O.
37- 80  MOSER, ARNOLD ROBERT              7714 ANTOINE - HOUSTON TX 77088
65- 79  MOSES, GERALD BRAHEEN             1712 JACKSON AVE - YAZOO CITY MS 39194
35- 75  MOSES, WALLACE                    OLD ADD: 300 E LANCASTER #403 - WYNNEWOOD PA
77- 98  MOSKAU, PAUL RICHARD              4152 E SECOND ST - TUCSON AZ 85711
10-108  MOSKIMAN, WILLIAM BANKHEAD        D. JANUARY 11, 1953 SAN LEANDRO, CALIF.
29- 76  MOSOLF, JAMES FREDERICK           D. DECEMBER 28, 1979 DALLAS, ORE.
34- 76  MOSS, CHARLES CROSBY              2400 40TH AVE - MERIDIAN MS 39304
30- 55  MOSS, CHARLES MALCOLM             7200 SEARS TOWER - CHICAGO IL 60606
42- 70  MOSS, HOWARD GLENN                3805 KIMBLE RD-BALTIMORE MD 21218
46- 76  MOSS, JOHN LESTER                 420 TULLIS AVE - LONGWOOD FL 32750
26- 59  MOSS, RAYMOND EARL                3734 KINGS RD - CHATTANOOGA TN 37416
54- 72  MOSSI, DONALD LOUIS               1340 SANFORD RANCH RD - UKIAH CA 95482
51- 69  MOSSOR, EARL DALTON               652 MARIETTA - CINCINNATI OH 45245
18- 52  MOSTIL, JOHN ANTHONY              D. DECEMBER 10, 1970 MIDLOTHIAN, ILL.
62- 94  MOTA, MANUEL RAFAEL               27 DE FABRERO,#89 PROL-SANTO DOMINGO DOM REP
81- 87  MOTLEY, DARRYL DEWAYNE            2717 NE 12TH - PORTLAND OR 97208
45- 72  MOTT, ELISHA MATTHEW              806 EAST EMMA ST - TAMPA FL 33603
67- 76  MOTTON, CURTELL HOWARD            1522 25TH AVE - OAKLAND CA 94601
46- 77  MOULDER, GLEN HUBERT              2946 LAVISTA CT - DECATUR GA 30083
11-124  MOULTON, ALBERT THEODORE          D. JULY 10, 1968 PEABODY, MASS.
13-130  MOWE, RAYMOND BENJAMIN            D. AUGUST 14, 1968 SARASOTA, FLA.
33- 44  MOWRY, JOSEPH ALOYSIUS            6321 BANCROFT - ST LOUIS MO 63109
10-109  MOYER, CHARLES EDWARD             D. NOVEMBER 18, 1962 JACKSONVILLE, FLA.
54- 73  MROZINSKI, RONALD FRANK           1972 ADD: 1326 S MAIN ST - PHILLIPSBURG NJ
63- 83  MUDROCK, PHILIP RAY               2548 EAST 6600 SOUTH-SALT LAKE CITY UT 84121
```

20- 88	MUELLER, CLARENCE FRANCIS	D. JANUARY 23, 1975 DESOTO, MO.
48- 74	MUELLER, DONALD FREDERICK	11224 MUELLER LN - HAZELWOOD MO 63043
38- 68	MUELLER, EMMETT JEROME	OLD ADD: 1851 UNION RD - ST. LOUIS, MO
50- 70	MUELLER, JOSEPH GORDON	1404 CHESAPEAKE AVE - MIDDLE RIVER MD 21220
41- 76	MUELLER, LESLIE CLYDE	RR 2 BOX 294 - MILLSTADT IL 62260
35- 76	MUELLER, RAY COLEMAN	4231A KING GEORGE DR - HARRISBURG PA 17109
22-101	MUELLER, WALTER JOHN	D. AUGUST 16, 1971 ST. LOUIS, MO.
78- 87	MUELLER, WILLARD LAWRENCE	1246 WALLACE LAKE - WEST BEND WI 53095
42- 71	MUELLER, WILLIAM LAWRENCE	161 CROSS KEYS - FLORISSANT MO 63033
57- 59	MUFFETT, BILLY ARNOLD	706 BAYOU SHORES DR - MONROE LA 71205
24- 83	MUICH, IGNATIUS ANDREW	9244 LODGE POLE LN - ST LOUIS MO 63126
51- 70	MUIR, JOSEPH ALLEN	D. JUNE 25, 1980 BALTIMORE, MD.
35- 77	MULCAHY, HUGH NOYES	175 WAYNE ST - BEAVER PA 15009
30- 56	MULLEAVY, GREGORY THOMAS	D. FEBRUARY 1, 1980 ARCADIA, CALIF.
10-110	MULLEN, CHARLES GEORGE	D. JUNE 6, 1963 SEATTLE, WASH.
44- 95	MULLEN, FORD PARKER	7127 MULLEN RD SE - OLYMPIA WA 98503
20- 89	MULLEN, WILLIAM JOHN	D. MAY 4, 1971 ST. LOUIS, MO.
33- 45	MULLER, FREDERICK WILLIAM	D. OCTOBER 20, 1976 DAVIS, CALIF.
15-111	MULLIGAN, EDWARD JOSEPH	21 PEPPER WAY - SAN RAFAEL CA 94901
34- 77	MULLIGAN, JOSEPH IGNATIUS	441 W ROXBURY PARKWAY - BOSTON MA 02132
41- 77	MULLIGAN, RICHARD CHARLES	1205 E WALNUT AVE - VICTORIA TX 77901
40- 65	MULLIN, PATRICK JOSEPH	320 CHURCH ST - BROWNSVILLE PA 15417
77- 99	MULLINIKS, STEVEN RANCE	707 TEPIC - EL PASO TX 79932
80- 94	MULLINS, FRANCIS JOSEPH	6180 BROADWAY TER - OAKLAND CA 94618
21- 71	MULRENAN, DOMINICK JOSEPH	D. JULY 27, 1964 MELROSE, MASS.
30- 57	MULRONEY, FRANCIS JOSEPH	205 W 8TH - ABERDEEN WA 98520
74- 92	MUMPHREY, JERRY WAYNE	RR 3 BOX 539 - TYLER TX 75705
18- 53	MUNCH, JACOB FERDINAND	D. JUNE 8, 1966 LANSDOWNE, PA.
37- 81	MUNCRIEF, ROBERT CLEVELAND	731 RIDGE CREST - DUNCANVILLE TX 75116
13-131	MUNDY, WILLIAM EDWARD	D. SEPTEMBER 23, 1958 KALAMAZOO, MICH.
43- 96	MUNGER, GEORGE DAVID	8163 BARKLEY DR - HOUSTON TX 77017
31- 61	MUNGO, VAN LINGLE	108 N PINE ST - PAGELAND SC 29728
71- 73	MUNIZ, MANUEL	CALLE 23-R-12 VILLA NUEVA - CAGUAS PR 00626
80- 95	MUNNINGHOFF, SCOTT ANDREW	3743 ANDREW AVE - CINCINNATI OH 45209
34- 78	MUNNS, LESLIE ERNEST	236 E 5TH - WAHOO NE 68066
25- 76	MUNSON, JOSEPH MARTIN NAPOLEON	7274 LAMPORT RD - UPPER DARBY PA 19082
69-120	MUNSON, THURMAN LEE	D. AUGUST 2, 1979 AKRON-CANTON AIRPORT, O.
78- 88	MURA, STEPHEN ANDREW	1300 GIUFFRIAS AVE - METAIRIE LA 70001
64- 76	MURAKAMI, MASANORI	#4-32-20 - SETAGAYA TOKYO JAPAN
65- 80	MURCER, BOBBY RAY	OLD ADD: 3244 WHIPPOORWILL - OKLAHOMA CITY OK
17- 53	MURCHISON, THOMAS MALCOM	D. OCTOBER 20, 1962 LIBERTY, N. C.
56- 62	MURFF, JOHN ROBERT "RED"	1005 LAWNDALE - BRENHAM TX 77833
76- 67	MURPHY, DALE BRIAN	841 MAXIE LN - LAWRENCEVILLE GA 30245
60- 73	MURPHY, DANIEL FRANCIS	11 EISENHOWER RD - BEVERLY MA 01915
78- 89	MURPHY, DWAYNE KEITH	1132 "W" AVE #H-6 - LANCASTER CA 93534
42- 72	MURPHY, EDWARD JOSEPH	1317 JEFFERSON ST-JOLIET IL 60435
14-160	MURPHY, HERBERT COURTLAND	D. AUGUST 10, 1962 TALLAHASSEE, FLA.
12-136	MURPHY, JOHN EDWARD	D. FEBRUARY 20, 1969 DUNMORE, PA.
32- 57	MURPHY, JOHN JOSEPH	D. JANUARY 14, 1970 NEW YORK, N. Y.

15-112	MURPHY, LEO JOSEPH	D. AUGUST 12, 1960 RACINE, WIS.
12-137	MURPHY, MICHAEL JEROME	D. OCTOBER 26, 1952 JOHNSON CITY, N.Y.
54- 74	MURPHY, RICHARD LEE	MIAMI HILLS DR - CINCINNATI OH 45243
18- 54	MURPHY, ROBERT R.	D. MAY 11, 1938 DENVER, COLO.
68- 70	MURPHY, THOMAS ANDREW	996 TIAJUANA ST - LAGUNA BEACH CA 92651
31- 62	MURPHY, WALTER JOSEPH	1971 ADD: 2000 PARSONS #55-COSTA MESA CA
66- 66	MURPHY, WILL9A4 5D7EE5	10214 88TH AVE SW - TACOMA WA 98498
23- 97	MURRAY , ROBERT HAYES	D. JANUARY 4, 1979 NASHUA, N. H.
36- 63	MURRAY, AMBROSE JOSEPH	8297 SE COCONUT ST - HOBO SAND FL 33455
23- 96	MURRAY, ANTHONY JOHN	D. MARCH 19, 1974 CHICAGO, ILL.
74- 93	MURRAY, DALE ALBERT	202 E CLEVELAND - CUERO TX 77954
77-100	MURRAY, EDDIE CLARENCE	327 RINGOLD VALLEY CIR-COCKEYSVILLE MD 21030
17- 54	MURRAY, EDWARD FRANCIS	D. NOVEMBER 8, 1970 CHEYENNE, WYO.
22-102	MURRAY, GEORGE KING	D. OCTOBER 18, 1955 MEMPHIS, TENN.
22-103	MURRAY, JAMES FRANCIS	D. JULY 15, 1973 NEW YORK, N. Y.
50- 71	MURRAY, JOSEPH AMBROSE	2719 VIA SANTA TOMAS - SAN CLEMEMTE CA 92672
74- 94	MURRAY, LARRY	3544 S CALUMET AVE - CHICAGO IL 60653
19- 58	MURRAY, PATRICK JOSEPH	%BISSELL,5757 MAIN ST-WILLIAMSVILLE NY 14221
48- 75	MURRAY, RAYMOND LEE	BOX 453 - KENNEDALE TX 76060
80- 96	MURRAY, RICHARD DALE	435 E 108TH ST - LOS ANGELES CA 90061
17- 55	MURRAY, WILLIAM ALLENWOOD	D. SEPTEMBER 14, 1943 BOSTON, MASS.
63- 84	MURRELL, IVAN AUGUSTUS	4840 ZION ST - SAN DIEGO CA 92120
41- 78	MURTAUGH, DANIEL EDWARD	D. DECEMBER 2, 1976 CHESTER PA.
69-121	MUSER, ANTHONY JOSEPH	11222 MARYHA ANN DR - LOS ALAMITOS CA 90720

```
65- 81  MUSGRAVES, DENNIS EUGENE        RR FOUR - CENTRALLIA MO 65240
41- 79  MUSIAL, STANLEY FRANK           85 TRENT DR - LADUE MO 63124
12-138  MUSSER, PAUL                    D. JULY 7, 1973 STATE COLLEGE, PA.
32- 58  MUSSER, WILLIAM DANIEL          1062 HOMEWOOD CT - DECATUR GA 30033
44- 96  MUSSILL, BERNARD JAMES          912 MOORLAND DR -GROSSE POINTE WOODS MI 48236
40- 66  MUSTAIKIS, ALEXANDER DOMINICK D. JANUARY 17, 1970 SCRANTON, PA.
38- 69  MYATT, GEORGE EDWARD            1623 CANTON AVE ORLANDO FL 32803
20- 90  MYATT, GLENN CALVIN             D. AUGUST 9, 1969 HOUSTON, TEX.
25- 77  MYER, CHARLES SOLOMON           D. OCTOBER 31, 1974 BATON ROUGE, LA.
15-113  MYERS, ELMER GLENN              D. JULY 29, 1976 COLLINGSWOOD, N. J.
38- 70  MYERS, LINWOOD LINCOLN          1001 ULMERTON RD #345 - LARGO FL 3354/
10-111  MYERS, RALPH EDWARD             D. JUNE 30, 1967 SAN FRANCISCO, CALIF.
56- 63  MYERS, RICHARD                  5400 SAMPSON BLVD - SACRAMENTO CA 95820
35- 78  MYERS, WILLIAM HARRISON         204 SALT RD ENOLA PA 17025
76- 68  MYRICK, ROBERT HOWARD           1923 ADELINE ST - HATTIESBURG MS 39401
15-114  NABORS, HERMAN JOHN             D. OCTOBER 29, 1923 WILTON, ALA.
39- 79  NAGEL, WILLIAM TAYLOR           4025 CAMELOT LN - MEMPHIS TN 38118
12-139  NAGELSON, LOUIS MARCELLUS       D. OCTOBER 22, 1965 FORT WAYNE, IND.
68- 71  NAGELSON, RUSSELL CHARLES       %S.NAGELSON,10920 AIRLINE-BATON ROUGE LA70816
11-125  NAGLE, WALTER HAROLD            D. MAY 27, 1971 SANTA ROSA, CALIF.
69-122  NAGY, MICHAEL TIMOTHY           315 REVERE AVE - BRONX NY 10465
47- 64  NAGY, STEPHEN                   OLD ADD: 5441 37TH AVE SW - SEATTLE WA
38- 71  NAHEM, SAMUEL RALPH             624 VINCENTE - BERKELEY CA 94704
76- 69  NAHORODNY, WILLIAM GERARD       204 S COMET - CLEARWATER FL 33515
36- 64  NAKTENIS, PETER ERNEST          125 ADELAIDE RD MANCHESTER CO 06041
24- 84  NALEWAY, FRANK                  D. JANUARY 28, 1949 CHICAGO, ILL.
12-140  NAPIER, SKELTON LEROY           D. MARCH 29, 1968 DALLAS, TEX.
49- 57  NAPLES, ALOYSIUS FRANCIS        52 RODGER CT - WYCKOFF NJ 07481
65- 82  NAPOLEON, DANIEL                116 OLIVE AVE - TRENTON NJ 08618
51- 71  NARAGON, HAROLD RICHARD         1521 HAGEY DR - BARBERTON OH 44203
56- 64  NARANJO, LAZARO RAMON GONZALO D #270, 10 Y 11 - LAWTON, HAVANA CUBA
54- 75  NARLESKI, RAYMOND EDMOND        1183 CHEWS LANDING RD-LAUREL SPRINGS NJ 08021
29- 77  NARLESKI, WILLIAM EDWARD        D. JULY 22, 1964 LAUREL SPRINGS, N. J.
79- 76  NARRON, JERRY AUSTIN            232 HILLCREST DR - GOLDSBORO NC 27530
35- 79  NARRON, SAMUEL                  RR 1 MIDDLESEX NC 27557
63- 85  NARUM, LESLIE FERDINAND         324 S GLENWOOD AVE - CLEARWATER FL 33515
67- 77  NASH, CHARLES FRANCIS           600 SUMMERSHADE CIR - LEXINGTON KY 40502
66- 67  NASH, JAMES EDWIN               405 REGINA DR - MARIETTA GA 30060
12-141  NASH, KENNETH LELAND            D. FEBRUARY 16, 1977 EPSOM, N. H.
78- 90  NASTU, PHILIP                   119 AUSTIN ST - BRIDGEPORT CT 06604
53- 62  NATON, PETER ALPHONSUS          4136 SPLIT ROCK RD - CAMILLUS NY 13031
62- 95  NAVARRO, JULIO VENTURA          LUBRIEL STADIUM - BAYAMON PR 00619
42- 73  NAYLOR, EARL EUGENE             616 IDAHO AVE E-ST PAUL MN 55117
17- 56  NAYLOR, ROLEINE CECIL           D. JUNE 18, 1966 FORT WORTH, TEX.
39- 80  NAYMICK, MICHAEL JOHN           OLD ADD: 8334 BERWICK WAY - STOCKTON CA
56- 65  NEAL, CHARLES LENARD            9931 BOWMAN BLVD - DALLAS TX 75220
```

```
16- 64  NEALE, ALFRED EARLE             D. NOVEMBER 2, 1973 LAKE WORTH, FL.
52- 78  NECCIAI, RONALD ANDREW          201 ROSEWOOD DR - MONONGAHELA PA 15063
57- 60  NEEMAN, CALVIN AMANDUS          808 ESTHER ST - CAHOKIA IL 62206
14-161  NEFF, DOUGLAS WILLIAM           D. MAY 23, 1932 CAPE CHARLES, VA.
52- 79  NEGRAY, RONALD ALVIN            587 WEST NIMISLIA RD - AKRON OH 44319
12-142  NEHER, JAMES GILMORE            D. NOVEMBER 11, 1951 BUFFALO, N.Y.
15-115  NEHF, ARTHUR NEUKOM             D. DECEMBER 18, 1960 PHOENIX, ARIZ.
69-123  NEIBAUER, GARY WAYNE            714 W 25TH - SCOTTSBLUFF NE 69361
60- 74  NEIGER, ALVIN EDWARD            213 PINEHURST RD - WILMINTON DE 19803
39- 81  NEIGHBORS, ROBERT OTIS          D. AUGUST 8, 1952 NORTH KOREA
46- 78  NEILL, THOMAS WHITE             OLD ADD: 8951 BRAESMONT DR - HOUSTON TX
20- 91  NEIS, BERNARD EDMUND            D. NOVEMBER 29, 1972 INVERNESS, FLA.
29- 78  NEKOLA, FRANCIS JOSEPH          13 DEVONSHIRE DR - NEW HYDE PARK NY 11044
19- 59  NELSON, LUTHER MARTIN           BOX 14 - MATHERVILLE ILL 61263
10-112  NELSON, ALBERT FRANCIS          D. OCTOBER 26, 1956 ST PETERSBURG, FLA.
68- 72  NELSON, DAVID EARL              8801 GREENHAVEN DR - FORT WORTH TX 76135
35- 80  NELSON, GEORGE EMMETT           D. AUGUST 25, 1967 SIOUX FALLS, S. D.
49- 58  NELSON, GLENN RICHARD           BOX 35 - PORTSMOUTH OH 45662
70-100  NELSON, JAMES LORIN             1515 PLANETA WAY - FLOSOM CA 95630
30- 58  NELSON, LYNN BERNARD            D. FEBRUARY 15, 1955 KANSAS CITY, MO.
60- 75  NELSON, MELVIN FREDERICK        27420 FISHER ST - HIGHLAND CA 92346
55- 85  NELSON, ROBERT SIDNEY           6614 WOFFARD - DALLAS TX 75227
67- 78  NELSON, ROGER EUGENE            OLD ADD: 533 WINDSOR - ARCADIA CA 91006
45- 73  NELSON, TOM COUSINEAU           D. SEPTEMBER 24, 1973 SAN DIEGO, CAL.
81- 88  NELSON, WAYLAND EUGENE          BOX 458 - LACOOCHIE FL 33537
63- 86  NEN, RICHARD LEROY              4233 BANYAN - SEAL BEACH CA 90740
```

11-126 NESS, JOHN CHARLES
67- 79 NETTLES, GRAIG
70-101 NETTLES, JAMES WILLIAM
74- 95 NETTLES, MORRIS
17- 58 NEU, OTTO ADAM
25- 78 NEUBAUER, HAROLD CHARLES
72- 78 NEUMEIER, DANIEL GEORGE
25- 79 NEUN, JOHN HENRY
50- 72 NEVEL, ERNIE WYRE
26- 60 NEVERS, ERNEST ALONZO
49- 59 NEWCOMBE, DONALD

D. DECEMBER 3, 1957 DELAND, FLA.
11 CARTER ST - NORWOOD NJ 07648
4632 DARIEN DR - TACOMA WA 98407
551 1/2 SAN JUAN - VENICE CA 90291
D. SEPTEMBER 19, 1932 KENTON, O.
D. SEPTEMBER 9, 1949 PROVIDENCE, R. I.
RR 3 BOX 438E - LODI WI 53555
3501 ST PAUL ST #718 - BALTIMORE MD 21218
615 MADDUX ST - BRANSON MO 65616
D. MAY 3, 1976 SAN RAFAEL, CALIF.
20507 PEALE DR - WOODLAND HILLS CA 91364

72- 79 NEWHAUSER, DONALD LOUIS
39- 82 NEWHOUSER, HAROLD
34- 79 NEWKIRK, FLOYD ELMO
19- 60 NEWKIRK, JOEL IVAN
40- 67 NEWLIN, MAURICE MILTON
62- 96 NEWMAN, FREDERICK WILLIAM
76- 70 NEWMAN, JEFFREY LYNN
71- 74 NEWMAN, RAYMOND FRANCIS
10-113 NEWNAM, PATRICK HENRY
29- 79 NEWSOM, NORMAN LOUIS
41- 80 NEWSOME, HEBER HAMPTON
35- 81 NEWSOME, LAMAR ASHBY
46- 79 NIARHOS, CONSTANTINE GREGORY
52- 80 NICHOLAS, DONALD LEIGH
26- 61 NICHOLS, CHESTER RAYMOND SR
51- 72 NICHOLS, CHESTER RAYMOND JR
58- 67 NICHOLS, DOLAN LEVON
44- 97 NICHOLS, ROY
80- 97 NICHOLS, THOMAS REID
60- 76 NICHOLSON, DAVID LAWRENCE
12-143 NICHOLSON, FRANK COLLINS

1295 NW 147TH DR - MIAMI FL 33167
2584 MARCY-BLOOMFIELD HILLS MI 48013
D. APRIL 15, 1976 CLAYTON, MO.
D. JANUARY 22, 1966 ELDORADO, ILL.
D. AUGUST 14, 1978 HOUSTON, TEXAS
17 ELDA RD - FRAMINGHAM MA 01704
1027 ORANGE - FORT WORTH TX 76110
1361 HOWARD - MUSKEGON MI 49442
D. JUNE 20, 1938 SAN ANTONIO, TEX.
D. DECEMBER 7, 1962 ORLANDO, FLA.
D. DECEMBER 15, 1965 AHOSKIE, N. C.
1626 17TH AVE COLUMBUS GA 31901
OLD ADD: 347 FIRST AVE - PHOENIXVILLE PA
12311 CHASE - GARDEN GROVE CA 92645
3 LINCOLN AVE - LINCOLN RI 02865
18 COLONIAL DR - LINCOLN RI 02865
OLD ADD: 1351 OLD HICKORY RD - MEMPHIS TN
104 ARIAS WAY - HOT SPRINGS VILLAGE AR 71901
OLD ADD: 640 WILLOW BEND LN - BESSEMER AL
527 SPRINGSGUTH - ROSELLE IL 60172
D. NOVEMBER 11, 1972 JERSEY SHORE, PA.

17- 57 NICHOLSON, FREDERICK   RR2 BOX 14B - KILGORE TEX 75662
12-144 NICHOLSON, OVID EDWARD   D. MARCH 24, 1968 SALEM, IND.
36- 65 NICHOLSON, WILLIAM BECK   RR 3 - CHESTERTOWN MD 21620
78- 91 NICOSIA, STEVEN RICHARD   11822 SW 44TH ST - DAVIE FL 33330
21- 73 NIEBERGALL, CHARLES ARTHUR   45-10 28TH AVE - LONG ISLAND CITY NY 11103
81- 89 NIEDENFUER, THOMAS EDWARD   12833 NE 90TH - KIRKLAND WA 98033
25- 80 NIEHAUS, ALBERT BERNARD   D. OCTOBER 14, 1931 CINCINNATI, O.
13-132 NIEHAUS, RICHARD J.   D. MARCH 12, 1957 ATLANTA, GA.
13-133 NIEHOFF, JOHN ALBERT   D. DECEMBER 8, 1974 INGLEWOOD, CALIF.
67- 80 NIEKRO, JOSEPH FRANKLIN   214 ASH LN - LAKELAND FL 33801
64- 77 NIEKRO, PHILIP HENRY   4781 CASTLEWOOD DR - LILBURN GA 30247
49- 60 NIELSON, MILTON ROBERT   824 MCGILL - ST PETER MN 56082
43- 97 NIEMAN, ELMER LEROY   1324 BOSWELL AVE-TOPEKA KS 66604
51- 73 NIEMAN, ROBERT CHARLES   1400 S SUNKIST #95 - ANAHEIM CA 92806
79- 77 NIEMANN, RANDY HAROLD   233 VALLEY AVE - FORTUNA CA 95540
43- 98 NIEMES, JACOB LELAND   D. MARCH 4, 1966 HAMILTON, O.
34- 80 NIEMIEC, ALFRED JOSEPH   BOX 467 - KIRKLAND WA 98033
64- 78 NIESON, CHARLES BASSETT   3209 W HIGHLAND DR - BRUNSVILLE MN 55374
21- 72 NIETZKE, ERNEST FREDRICH   D. APRIL 27, 1977 SYLVANIA, O.
38- 72 NIGGELING, JOHN ARNOLD   D. SEPTEMBER 16, 1963 LEMARS, IA.
62- 97 NIPPERT, MERLIN LEE   1015 N MICHIGAN ST - MANGUM OK 73554
61- 78 NISCHWITZ, RONALD LEE   6790 GARBER RD - DAYTON OH 45415
45- 74 NITCHOLAS, OTHO JAMES   1500 ERWIN - MCKINNEY TX 75069
15-116 NIXON, ALBERT RICHARD   D. NOVEMBER 9, 1960 OPELOUSAS, LA.
57- 61 NIXON, RUSSELL EUGENE   BOX 557 - WILLIAMSBURG OH 45176
50- 73 NIXON, WILLARD LEE   335 REECEBURG SE - SILVER CREEK GA 30173
51- 74 NOBLE, RAFAEL MIGUEL   698 CHAUNCEY ST - BROOKLYN NY 11207
67- 81 NOLAN, GARY LYNN   OLD ADD: 188 RIVERVIEW DR - OROVILLE CA
72- 80 NOLAN, JOSEPH WILLIAM   9515 ALIX DR - MEHLVILLE MO 63123
67- 82 NOLD, RICHARD LOUIS   121 PARK PLAZA DR #6 - DALY CITY CA 94015
79- 78 NOLES, DICKIE RAY   OLD ADD: 1109 OPAL ST - CHARLOTTE NC
33- 46 NONNENKAMP, LEO WILLIAM   1 OAKWOOD RD - LITTLE ROCK AR 72202
74- 96 NORDBROOK, TIMOTHY CHARLES   2906 BAYONNE AVE - BALTIMORE MD 21214
76- 71 NORDHAGEN, WAYNE OREN   23954 SARDAD - VALENCIA CA 91355
50- 74 NOREN, IRVING ARNOLD   55 N GOLDEN WEST AVE - ARCADIA CA 91006
69-124 NORIEGA, JOHN ALAN   2 EAST 900 SOUTH - KAYSVILLE UT 84037
77-101 NORMAN, DANIEL EDMUND   1336 MESA DR - BARSTOW CA 92311
62- 98 NORMAN, FREDIE ROBERT   10558 SWANSON CT - CINCINNATI OH 45242
31- 63 NORMAN, HENRY WILLIS PATRICK   D. APRIL 21, 1962 MILWAUKEE, WIS.
78- 92 NORMAN, NELSON AUGUSTO   ING CONSUELO CALLE D5 SAN PEDRO DEMACORIS DR
77-102 NORRIS, JAMES FRANCIS   2131 LEDGE RD - HINCKLEY OH 44233
36- 66 NORRIS, LEO JOHN   ZACHARY HOME, DRAWER C - ZACHARY LA 70791
75- 85 NORRIS, MICHAEL KELVIN   193 CAINE ST - SAN FRANCISCO CA 94112
13-134 NORTH, LOUIS ALEXANDER   D. MAY 16, 1974 SHELTON, CONN.
71- 75 NORTH, WILLIAM ALEX   3303 E MADISON - SEATTLE WA 98102
10-114 NORTHEN, HUBBARD ELWIN   D. OCTOBER 1, 1947 SHREVEPORT, LA.
42- 74 NORTHEY, RONALD JAMES   D. APRIL 16, 1971 PITTSBURGH, PA.
69-125 NORTHEY, SCOTT RICHARD   OLD ADD: 481 RIVIERA BLVD W - NAPLES FL
18- 55 NORTHROP, GEORGE HOWARD   D. NOVEMBER 16, 1945 MONROETON, PA.
64- 79 NORTHRUP, JAMES THOMAS   7250 OLD MILL RD - BIRMINGHAM MI 48010
72- 81 NORTON, THOMAS JOHN   4900 SOUTHWOOD - SHEFFIELD LAKES OH 44054
77-103 NORWOOD, WILLIE   2250 FASHION AVE - LONG BEACH CA 90810
64- 80 NOSSEK, JOSEPH RUDOLPH   437 TERRA LN - AMHERST OH 44001
60- 77 NOTTEBART, DONALD EDWARD   5442 LYMBAR - HOUSTON TX 77035
41- 81 NOVIKOFF, LOUIE ALEXANDER   D. SEPTEMBER 30, 1970 SOUTH GATE, CAL.
49- 61 NOVOTNEY, RALPH JOSEPH   2311 W 165TH ST - TORRANCE CA 90504
13-135 NOYES, WINFIELD CHARLES   D. APRIL 8, 1969 CASHMERE, WASH.
11-127 NUNAMAKER, LESLIE GRANT   D. NOVEMBER 14, 1938 HASTINGS, NEB.
59- 60 NUNN, HOWARD RALPH   RR1 - WESTFIELD NC 27053
19- 61 NUTTER, EVERETT CLARENCE   D. JULY 25, 1958 BATTLE CREEK, MICH.
44- 98 NUXHALL, JOSEPH HENRY   5706 LINDENWOOD LN - FAIRFIELD OH 45014

66- 68 NYE, RICHARD RAYMOND   5110 N MONITOR - CHICAGO IL 60630
68- 73 NYMAN, GERALD SMITH   2627 N 16TH E - LOGAN UTAH 84321
74- 97 NYMAN, NYLS WALLACE REX   ATH DEPT, S ILL. UNIV. -CARBONDALE IL 62901
34- 81 OANA, HENRY KAUHANE   D. JUNE 19, 1976 AUSTIN, TEX.
70-102 OATES, JOHNNY LANE   COLONIAL HEIGHTS VA 23834
77-104 OBERKFELL, KENNETH RAY   305 S DONK ST - MARYVILLE IL 62062
79- 79 OBERRY, PRESTON MICHAEL   1100 DEARING DOWNS DR - HELENA AL 35017
78- 93 OBRADOVICH, JAMES THOMAS   2714 VISTAVIEW DR - TACOMA WA 98407
78- 94 OBRIEN, DANIEL JOGUES   2656 MCKELVEY RD - MARYLAND HEIGHTS MO 63043
53- 63 OBRIEN, EDWARD JOSEPH   3414 108TH PL NE #1 - BELLEVUE WA 98004

```
23- 98  OBRIEN, FRANK ALOYSIUS          D. NOVEMBER 4, 1971 MONTEREY PARK, CAL.
15-117  OBRIEN, GEORGE JOSEPH           D. MARCH 24, 1966 COLUMBUS, O.
53- 64  OBRIEN, JOHN THOMAS             938 21ST ST E - SEATTLE WA 98112
16- 65  OBRIEN, RAYMOND JOSEPH          D. MARCH 31, 1942 ST. LOUIS, MO.
71- 76  OBRIEN, ROBERT ALLEN            3628 N SHIRLEY - FRESNO CA 93727
69-126  OBRIEN, SYDNEY LLOYD            OLD ADD: 5452 EBELL ST - LONG BEACH CA 90808
43- 99  OBRIEN, THOMAS EDWARD           D. NOVEMBER 5, 1978 ANNISTON, ALA.
11-128  OBRIEN, THOMAS JOSEPH           D. JULY 25, 1959 DORCHESTER, MASS.
35- 82  OCK, HAROLD DAVID               D. MARCH 18, 1975 MOUNT KISCO, N. Y.
44- 99  OCKEY, WALTER ANDREW            D. DECEMBER 4, 1971 STATEN ISLAND, N.Y.
50- 75  OCONNELL, DANIEL FRANCIS        D. OCTOBER 2, 1969 CLIFTON, N. J.
23- 99  OCONNELL, JAMES JOSEPH          D. NOVEMBER 11, 1976 BAKERSFIELD, CALIF.
28- 72  OCONNELL, JOHN CHARLES          1611 19TH ST - NORTHEAST CANTON OH 47714
81- 90  OCONNOR, JACK WILLIAM           BOX 430 - YUCCA VALLEY CA 92284
16- 66  OCONNOR, JOHN J.                ATTENDED UNIV OF ILLINOIS
35- 83  ODEA, JAMES KENNETH             MAIN ST LIMA NY 14485
44-100  ODEA, PAUL                      D. DECEMBER 11, 1978 CLEVELAND, O.
54- 76  ODELL, WILLIAM OLIVER           RR 1 BOX 60 - NEWBERRY SC 29108
21- 74  ODENWALD, THEODORE JOSEPH       D. OCTOBER 23, 1965 SHAKOPEE, MINN.
43-100  ODOM, DAVID EVERETT             303 72ND AVE N #3 - MYRTLE BEACH SC 29577
25- 81  ODOM, HERMAN BOYD               D. AUGUST 31, 1970 RUSK, TEXAS
64- 81  ODOM, JOHNNY LEE                10225C LAHACIENDA - FOUNTAIN VALLEY CA 92708
54- 77  ODONNELL, GEORGE DANA           WINCHESTER IL 62694
27- 67  ODONNELL, HARRY HERMAN          D. JANUARY 31, 1958 PHILADELPHIA, PA.
63- 87  ODONOGHUE, JOHN EUGENE          500 S CEDAR - INDEPENDENCE MO 64053
19- 62  ODOUL, FRANCIS JOSEPH           D. DECEMBER 7, 1969 SAN FRANCISCO, CAL.
12-145  ODOWD (JOHN LEO DOWD)           D. JANUARY 31, 1981 FORT LAUDERDALE, FLA.
58- 68  OERTEL, CHARLES FRANK           BOX 90 - PONTIAC MI 48055
14-162  OESCHGER, JOSEPH CARL           OESCHGER LN - FERNDALE CA 95536
78- 95  OESTER, RONALD JOHN             3971 HAMBLER DR - CINCINNATI OH 45230
15-118  OFARRELL, ROBERT ARTHUR         27 SOUTH&65BT   WIUKEGAN ILL 60085
72- 82  OFFICE, ROWLAND JOHNIE          3212 HARBOR VIEW CT - DECATUR GA 30034
18- 56  OGDEN, JOHN MAHLON              D. NOVEMBER 9, 1977 PHILADELPHIA, PA.
22-104  OGDEN, WARREN HARVEY            D. AUGUST 6, 1964 CHESTER, PA.
36- 67  OGLESBY, JAMES DORN             D. SEPTEMBER 1, 1955 TULSA, OKLA.
71- 77  OGLIVIE, BENJAMIN AMBROSIO      115-02 209TH ST - CAMBRIA HEIGHTS NY 11411
36- 68  OGRODOWSKI, AMBROSE FRANCIS     D. MARCH 5, 1956 SAN FRANCISCO, CAL.
25- 82  OGRODOWSKI, JOSEPH ANTHONY      D. JUNE 24, 1959 ELMIRA, N. Y.
80- 98  OJEDA, ROBERT MICHAEL           14884 ROAD 312 - VISALIA CA 93277
20- 92  OKRIE, FRANK ANTHONY            D. OCTOBER 16, 1959 DETROIT, MICH.
48- 76  OKRIE, LEONARD JOSEPH           OLD ADD: 4501 ALE CT - FAYETTEVILLE NC
14-163  OLDHAM, JOHN CYRUS              D. JANUARY 28,1961 COSTA MESA, CALIF.
56- 66  OLDHAM, JOHN HARDIN             1845 ANNE WAY - SAN JOSE CA 95124
53- 65  OLDIS, ROBERT CARL             306 VIRGINIA DR - IOWA CITY IA 52240
62- 99  OLIVA, PEDRO                    212 SPRING VALLEY DR - BLOOMINGTON MN 55420
60- 78  OLIVARES, EDWARD BALZAC         CARRO 330 KIH2 BUZON 427-SAN GERMAN PR 00750
68- 74  OLIVER, ALBERT                  %J.OLIVER.1219 WALLER - PORTSMOUTH OH 45662
77-105  OLIVER, DAVID JACOB             1830 FUNSTON AVE - STOCKTON CA 95205
59- 61  OLIVER, EUGENE GEORGE           2805 35TH ST - ROCK ISLAND IL 61201
63- 88  OLIVER, NATHANIEL               1320 104TH AVE - OAKLAND CA 94603
65- 83  OLIVER, ROBERT LEE              2772 ROWLAND CIR - ANAHEIM CA 92804
30- 59  OLIVER, THOMAS NOBLE            BOX 1701 - MONTGOMERY AL 36104
60- 79  OLIVO, CIOMEDES ANTONIO         D. FEBRUARY 15, 1977 SANTO DOMINGO, DOM. REP.
61- 79  OLIVO, FEDERICO EMILIO          D. FEBRUARY 3, 1977 GUAYUBIN, DOMINICAN REP.
66- 69  OLLOM, JAMES DONALD             OLD ADD: 6221 BROADWAY - EVERETT WA
43-101  OLMO, LUIS FRANCISCO RODRIGUEZ  BOX 9172-SANTURCE PR 00908
80- 99  OLMSTED, ALAN RAY               13061 LAKERIDGE DR - SAINT LOUIS MO 63138
43-102  OLSEN, ALBERT WILLIAM           5032 FABOR WAY-SANDIEGO CA 92115
22-105  OLSEN, ARTHUR                   D. SEPTEMBER 12, 1980 NORWALK, CONN.
41- 82  OLSEN, BERNARD CHARLES          D. MARCH 30, 1977 EVERETT, MASS.
39- 83  OLSEN, VERN JARL                1916 BRISTOL AVE-WESTCHESTER IL 60153
11-129  OLSON, IVAN MASSIE              D. SEPTEMBER 1, 1965 INGLEWOOD, CALIF.
51- 75  OLSON, KARL ARTHUR              1046 KERRY LN - GARDNERVILLE NV 89410
31- 64  OLSON, MARVIN CLEMENT           BOX 95 - GAYVILLE SD 57031
36- 69  OLSON, THEODORE OTTO            D. DECEMBER 9, 1980 WEYMOUTH, MASS.
12-146  OMARA, OLIVER EDWARD            1550 S MARCH AVE - RENO NV 89502
25- 83  ONEAL, CRAN HERBERT             BOX 187 - REPUBLIC MO 65738
19- 63  ONEIL, GEORGE MICHAEL           D. APRIL 8, 1964 ST. LOUIS, MO.
46- 80  ONEIL, JOHN FRANCIS             18 CROSS ST - JAMESTOWN NY 14701
39- 84  ONEILL, HARRY MINK              D. MARCH 8, 1945 IWO JIMA, MARIANAS IS.
20- 93  ONEILL, JAMES LEO               D. SEPTEMBER 5, 1976 CHAMBERSBURG, PA.
22-106  ONEILL, JOSEPH HENRY            D. SEPTEMBER 5, 1969 RIDGETOWN, ONT.
43-103  ONEILL, ROBERT EMMETT           748 RANCHO VISTA - SPARKS NV 89431
11-130  ONEILL, STEPHEN FRANCIS         D. JANUARY 26, 1962 CLEVELAND, O.
```

```
35- 84  ONIS, MANUEL DOMINGUEZ           1515 RIVER LA TAMPA FL 33603
12-148  ONSLOW, JOHN JAMES               D. DECEMBER 22, 1960 WEST ACTON, MASS.
12-147  ONSLOW,EDWARD JOSEPH             D. MAY 8, 1981 DENNISON, O.
73- 89  ONTIVERCS, STEVEN ROBERT         20 LIGGET - BAKERSFIELD CA 93307
55- 86  ORAVETZ, ERNEST EUGENE           4417 PAUL AVE - TAMPA FL 33611
43-104  ORDENANA, ANTONIO RODRIGUEZ      NAZARENO 157 - GUANABACOA, HAVANA CUBA
39- 85  ORENGO, JOSEPH CHARLES           866 FAXON AVE-SAN FRANCISCO CA 94112
69-127  ORILEY, DONALD LEE               117 E TWELFTH ST - KANSAS CITY MO 64106
20- 94  ORME, GEORGE WILLIAM             D. MARCH 16, 1962 INDIANAPOLIS, IND.
79- 80  OROSCO, JESSE                    1654 CALLE NUEVE - LOMPOC CA 93436
12-149  OROURKE, FRANCIS JAMES           589 RIVERSIDE DR - ELIZABETH NJ 07205
59- 62  OROURKE, JAMES PATRICK           2316 E 61ST AVE - SPOKANE WA 99203
29- 80  OROURKE, JOSEPH LEO              3151 ARAMINGO AVE - PHILADELPHIA PA 19134
13-136  ORR, WILLIAM JOHN                D. MARCH 10, 1967 ST. HELENA, CALIF.
43-105  ORRELL, FORREST GORDON           420 PARKWAY - CHULA VISTA CA 92010
27- 68  ORSATTI, ERNEST RALPH            D. SEPTEMBER 4, 1968 CANOGA PARK, CAL.
51- 80  ORSINO, JOHN JOSEPH              OLD ADD: 241 BROAD AVE - FAIRVIEW NJ 07022
72- 83  ORTA, JORGE                      SAL CREEL 165,LOS MARGARITAS-TORREON COA MEX
50- 80  ORTEGA, FILOMENO CORONADO        1973 ADD: 4242 SPRING ST - LA MESA CA 92041
73- 90  ORTENZIO, FRANK JOSEPH           723 W GETTYSBURG - FRESNO CA 93705
59-128  ORTIZ, JOSE LUIS                 CLE 14 HH5(,VLA D'CARMEN-PLAYA PONCE PR 00731
44-101  ORTIZ, OLIVRIO NUNEZ             CENTRAL SENADO - CAMAGUEY CUBA
41- 83  ORTIZ, ROBERTO GONZALO NUNEZ     D. SEPTEMBER 15, 1971 MIAMI, FLA.
28- 73  ORWOLL, OSWALD CHRISTIAN         D. MAY 8, 1967 DECORAH, IA.
75- 86  OSBORN, DANNY LEON               7620 KNOX CT - WESTMINSTER CO 80030
25- 84  OSBORN, ROBERT                   D. APRIL 19, 1960 PARIS, ARK.
22-107  OSBORNE, ERNEST PRESTON          D. JANUARY 5, 1969 ATLANTA, GA.
57- 62  OSBORNE, LAWRENCE SIDNEY         1969 SEABOARD PLACE NW - ATLANTA GA 30318
35- 85  OSBORNE, WAYNE HAROLD            820 WASHINGTON BLVD OAK PARK IL 60302
74- 98  OSBURN, LARRY PAT                RR 2 BOX 308 - BRADENTON FL 33508
44-102  OSGOOD, CHARLES BENJAMIN         11 HARGRAVES CT - SAUGUS MA 01906
62-100  OSINSKI, DANIEL                  OLD ADD: SQUIRES INN - OAK FOREST IL
57- 63  OSTEEN, CLAUDE WILSON            RR 3 BOX 453 - ANNVILLE PA 17003
65- 83  OSTEEN, MILTON DARRELL           OLD ADD: 281 S SPAULDING #H-BEVERLY HILLS CA
14-164  OSTENDORF, FREDERICK             D. MARCH 9, 1965 HAMPTON, VA.
54- 78  OSTER, WILLIAM CHARLES           9 HARBOR HEIGHTS - CENTERPORT NY 11721
21- 75  OSTERGARD, ROBERT LUND           OLD ADD: 2636 JULIET ST - LOS ANGELES CA
34- 82  OSTERMUELLER, FREDERICK RAYMOND  D. DECEMBER 17, 1957 QUINCY, ILL.
73- 91  OSTROSSER, BRIAN LEONARD         21 LAKE  AVE S - STONEY CREEK ONT
43-106  OSTROWSKI, JOHN THADDEUS         4943 S KOMENSKY AVE-CHICAGO IL 60632
48- 77  OSTROWSKI, JOSEPH PAUL           441 TRIPP ST - WEST WYOMING PA 18644
45- 75  OTERO, REGINO JOSEPH GOMEZ       4675 W 8TH AVE - HIALEAH FL 33010
67- 83  OTIS, AMOS JOSEPH                1116 MT VERNON AVE - PORTSMOUTH VA 23705
```

```
12-150  OTIS, PAUL FRANKLIN              2310 E THIRD ST - DULUTH MN 55817
69-129  OTOOLE, DENNIS JOSEPH            3453 RIDGEWOOD DR - ERLANGER KY 41018
58- 69  OTOOLE, JAMES JEROME             1010 LANETTE DR - CINCINNATI OH 45230
26- 62  OTT, MELVIN THOMAS               D. NOVEMBER 21, 1958 NEW ORLEANS, LA.
74- 99  OTT, NATHAN EDWARD               909 FLEXER AVE - ALLENTOWN PA 18103
62-101  OTT, WILLIAM JOSEPH              OLD ADD: 25 DONGAN PL - NEW YORK NY 10040
74-100  OTTEN, JAMES EDWARD              BOX 242 - KALISPELL MT 59901
33- 47  OULLIBER, JOHN ANDREW            D. DECEMBER 26, 1980 NEW ORLEANS, LA.
33- 48  OUTEN, WILLIAM AUSTIN            D. SEPTEMBER 11, 1961 DURHAM, N. C.
37- 82  OUTLAW, JAMES PAULUS             118 JAMES ST - JACKSON AL 36545
43-107  OVERMIRE, FRANK                  D. MARCH 3, 1977 LAKELAND, FLA.
76- 72  OVERY, HARRY MICHAEL             101 FAIRVIEW PL - CLINTON IL 61727
11-131  OVITZ, ERNEST GAYHART            D. SEPTEMBER 11, 1980 GREEN BAY, WISC.
76- 73  OWCHINKO, ROBERT DENNIS          11317 SARASOTA - REDFORD TWP. MI 48239
37- 83  OWEN, ARNOLD MALCOM              GREENE CO SHERIFF SPRINGFIELD MO 65802
81- 91  OWEN, LAWRENCE THOMAS            804 WHITE PINE ST - NEW CARLISLE OH 45344
31- 65  OWEN, MARVIN JAMES               42 HAWTHORNE WAY - SAN JOSE CA 95110
35- 86  OWENS, FURMAN LEE                D. NOVEMBER 14, 1958 GREENVILLE, S. C.
55- 87  OWENS, JAMES PHILIP              1761 CROTON DR - VENICE FL 33595
72- 84  OWENS, PAUL FRANCIS              BOX 7575 - PHILADELPHIA PA 19101
65- 85  OYLER, RAYMOND FRANCIS           D. JANUARY 26, 1981 REDMOND, WASH.
73- 92  OZARK, DANIEL LEONARD            2737 OCEAN DR #25 - VERO BEACH FL 32960
23-100  OZMER, HORACE ROBERT             D. DECEMBER 28, 1970 ATLANTA, GA.
77-106  PACELLA, JOHN LEWIS              72 YALE AVE - OAKDALE NY 11769
63- 89  PACIOREK, JOHN FRANCIS           8400 HUNTINGTON DR - SAN GABRIEL CA 91775
70-103  PACIOREK, THOMAS MARIAN          2389 BROAD CREEK DR - STONE MOUNTAIN GA 30089
49- 62  PACK, FRANKIE                    1316 OAKLAND ST - HENDERSONVILLE NC 28739
12-151  PACKARD, EUGENE MILO             D. MAY 19, 1959 RIVERSIDE, CALIF.
75- 87  PACTWA, JOSEPH MARTIN            232 154TH PL - CALUMET CITY IL 60409
32- 59  PADDEN, THOMAS FRANCIS           D. JUNE 11, 1973 MANCHESTER, N. H.
12-152  PADDOCK, DELMAR HAROLD           D. FEBRUARY 6, 1952 REMER, MINN.
37- 84  PADGETT, DON WILSON              D. DECEMBER 9, 1980 HIGH POINT, N. C.
23-101  PADGETT, ERNEST KITCHEN          D. APRIL 15, 1957 EAST ORANGE, N. J.
69-130  PAEPKE, DENNIS RAY               DRAWER #CE - CRESTLINE CA 92325
```

108

```
43-108  PAFKO, ANDREW                      1420 BLACKHAWK DR - MOUNT PROSPECT IL 60056
73- 93  PAGAN, DAVID PERCY                 BOX 1819 - NIPAWIN SASKATECHEWAN SOE 1EO
59- 63  PAGAN, JOSE ANTONIO                CALLE JASPE #15 - CAGUAS PR 00625
44-103  PAGE, JOSEPH FRANCIS               D. APRIL 21, 1980 LATROBE, PA.
68- 75  PAGE, MICHAEL RANDY                136 BRISTOW LN - SPARTANBURG SC 29301
77-107  PAGE, MITCHELL OTIS                125 E 93RD ST - LOS ANGELES CA 90003
39- 86  PAGE, SAMUEL WALTER                BOX 204-WOODRUFF SC 29388
38- 73  PAGE, VANCE LINWOOD                D. JULY 14, 1951 WILSON, N. C.
28- 74  PAGE,PHILIP RAUSAC                 D. JUNE 26, 1958 SPRINGFIELD, MASS.
78- 96  PAGEL, KARL DOUGLAS                6241 NORTH SIXTEENTH AVE - PHOENIX AZ 85015
55- 88  PAGLIARONI, JAMES VINCENT          10388 PARTRIDGE DR - GRASS VALLEY CA 95945
11-132  PAIGE, GEORGE LYNN                 D. JUNE 8, 1939 BERLIN, WIS.
48- 78  PAIGE, LEROY                       2626 EAST 28TH ST - KANSAS CITY MO 64128
51- 76  PAINE, PHILLIPS STEERE             D. FEBRUARY 19, 1978 LEBANON, PA.
39- 87  PALAGYI, MICHAEL RAYMOND           167 14TH ST-CONNEAUT OH 44030
45- 76  PALICA, ERVIN MARTIN               9592 INDIAN WELLS - HUNTINGTON BEACH CA 92646
48- 79  PALM, RICHARD PAUL                 63 NICHOLS RD - COHASSET MA 02025
78- 97  PALMER, DAVID WILLIAM              61 SHERMAN AVE - GLENS FALLS NY 12801
17- 59  PALMER, EDWIN HENRY                BOX 225 - MARLOW OK 73055
65- 86  PALMER, JAMES ALVIN                BOX 145 - BROOKLANDVILLE MD 21022
69-131  PALMER, LOWELL RAYMOND             1857 50TH ST - SACRAMENTO CA 95814
15-119  PALMERO, EMILIO ANTONIO            D. JULY 15, 1970 TOLEDO, O.
31- 66  PALMISANO, JOSEPH                  D. NOVEMBER 5, 1971 ALBUQUERQUE, N. M.
60- 81  PALMQUIST, EDWIN LEE               2810 EXPOSITION PL - LOS ANGELES CA 90018
53- 66  PALYS, STANLEY FRANCIS             RR ONE - MOSCOW PA 18444
71- 78  PANTHER, JAMES EDWARD              1125 SHARI LN - LIBERTYVILLE IL 60048
61- 81  PAPA, JOHN PAUL                    29 PHILLIPS DR - SHELTON CT 06484
48- 80  PAPAI, ALFRED THOMAS               2553 S 7TH ST - SPRINGFIELD IL 62703
76- 74  PAPE, KENNETH WAYNE                2529 NACOGDOCHES RD - SAN ANTONIO TX 78217
74-101  PAPI, STANLEY GERARD               1111 WEST SIERRA MADRE - FRESNO CA 93705
45- 77  PAPISH, FRANK RICHARD              D. AUGUST 30, 1965 PUEBLO, COLO.
57- 64  PAPPAS, MILTON STEPHEN             205 THOMPSON DR - WHEATON ILL 60187
```

```
43-109  PARISSE, LOUIS PETER               D. JUNE 2, 1956 PHILADELPHIA, PA.
15-120  PARK, JAMES                        D. DECEMBER 17, 1970 LEXINGTON, KY.
37- 85  PARKER, CLARENCE MCKAY             210 SNEAD'S FAIRWAY PORTSMOUTH VA 23701
15-121  PARKER, CLARENCE PERKINS           D. MARCH 21, 1967 CLAREMONT, N.H.
73- 94  PARKER, DAVID GENE                 4221 MIDDLE RD - ALLISON PARK PA 15101
23-102  PARKER, DOUGLAS WOOLLEY            D. MAY 15, 1972 GREEN POND, ALA.
36- 70  PARKER, FRANCIS JAMES              8003 MEADOWBRIAR - HOUSTON TX 77042
70-104  PARKER, HARRY WILLIAM              RR 1 BOX 123 - BEGGS OK 74421
64- 82  PARKER, MAURICE WESLEY             2140 COLORADO AVE - SANTA MONICA CA 90404
19- 64  PARKER, ROY W.                     B. 1897
71- 79  PARKER, WILLIAM DAVID              1975 EL PARQUE DR - TEMPE AZ 85282
21- 76  PARKINSON, FRANK JOSEPH            D. JULY 4, 1960 TRENTON, N.J.
37- 86  PARKS, ARTIE WILLIAM               127 S HARVEY GREENVILLE MS 38701
21- 77  PARKS, VERNON HENRY                OLD ADD: 1811 W 14 MOLE RD- ROYAL OAK MI
29- 81  PARMELEE, LEROY EARL               D. AUGUST 31, 1981 MONROE, MICH.
47- 65  PARNELL, MELVIN LLOYD              700 TURQUOISE ST - NEW ORLEANS LA 70124
```

16- 67	PARNHAM, JAMES ARTHUR	D. NOVEMBER 25, 1963 MCKEESPORT, PA.
70-105	PARRILLA, SAMUEL	33 WYCKOFF ST - BROOKLYN NY 11201
77-108	PARRISH, LANCE MICHAEL	2400 SUNBRIGHT DR - DIAMOND BAR CA 91765
74-102	PARRISH, LARRY ALTON	4989 E STATE RD #544 - HAINES CITY FL 33844
77-109	PARROTT, MICHAEL EVERETT	ARCH 2784 MAGNOLIA ST - CAMARILLO CA 93010
10-115	PARSON, WILLIAM EDWIN	D. MAY 19, 1967 INGLEWOOD, CALIF.
81- 92	PARSONS, CASEY ROBERT	10613 E 8TH - SPOKANE WA 99206
39- 88	PARSONS, EDWARD DIXON	4723 W MARSHALL ST - LONGVIEW TX 75601
63- 90	PARSONS, THOMAS ANTHONY	LINCOLN CITY RD - LAKEVILLE CT
71- 80	PARSONS, WILLIAM RAYMOND	2725 S AZALEA - TEMPE AZ 85281
43-110	PARTEE, ROY ROBERT	DRAWER AJ - TRINIDAD CA 95570
13-137	PARTENHEIMER, HAROLD PHILIP	D. JUNE 16, 1971 MANSFIELD, O.
44-104	PARTENHEIMER, STANWOOD WENDELL	117 BEAVER RD - SEWICKLEY PA 15143
27- 69	PARTRIDGE, JAMES BAGG	D. JANUARY 4, 1974 NASHVILLE, TENN.
15-122	PASCHAL, BENJAMIN EDWIN	D. NOVEMBER 10, 1974 CHARLOTTE, N. C.
78- 98	PASCHALL, WILLIAM HERBERT	4557 PRINCESS ANNE RD-VIRGINIA BEACH VA 23462
54- 79	PASCUAL, CAMILO ALBERTO	7741 SW 32ND - MIAMI FL 33155
50- 76	PASCUAL, CARLOS LUIS	2540 SW 92ND CT - MIAMI FL 33165
33- 49	PASEK, JOHN PAUL	D. MARCH 13, 1976 NIAGARA FALLS, N. Y.
74-103	PASLEY, KEVIN PATRICK	22 HAYPATH RD - BETHPAGE NY 11714
19- 65	PASQUELLA, MICHAEL JOHN	D. APRIL 5, 1965 BRIDGEPORT, CONN.
35- 87	PASSEAU, CLAUDE WILLIAM	113 LONDON ST - LUCEDALE MS 39452
79- 81	PASTORE, FRANK ENRICO	1542 N FRAMIS WAY - UPLAND CA 91786
26- 63	PATE, JOSEPH WILLIAM	D. DECEMBER 26, 1948 FORT WORTH, TEX.
80-100	PATE, ROBERT WAYNE	17509 NAUSET CT - CARSON CA 90746
68- 76	PATEK, FREDERICK JOSEPH	4110 EVERGREEN LN - KANSAS CITY MO 64015
41- 84	PATRICK, ROBERT LEE	107 N 18TH-FORT SMITH AR 72901
68- 77	PATTERSON, DARYL ALAN	TOLLHOUSE CA 93667
79- 82	PATTERSON, DAVID GLENN	15669 VELOUR DR - CHINO CA 91710
77-110	PATTERSON, GILBERT THOMAS	8185 NW 8 MANOR - PLANT FL 33324
32- 60	PATTERSON, HENRY JOSEPH	D. SEPTEMBER 30, 1970 PANORAMA CITY, CAL.
81- 93	PATTERSON, MICHAEL LEE	2419 RIDGELEY DR #9 - LOS ANGELES CA 90016
81- 94	PATTERSON, REGINALD ALLEN	2900 ARLINGTON AVE - BESSEMER AL 35020
21- 78	PATTERSON, WILLIAM JENNINGS	BRYAN D. OCTOBER 1, 1977 ST. LOUIS, MO.
68- 78	PATTIN, MARTIN WILLIAM	1520 ALVAMAR DR - LAWRENCE KS 66044
29- 82	PATTISON, JAMES WELLS	RR 2 SPRING LAKE RD - RED HOOK NY 12571
44-105	PATTON, GENE TUNNEY	60 S 17TH AVE - COATESVILLE PA 19320
35- 88	PATTON, GEORGE WILLIAM	1604 CHERRY LN FLOURTOWN PA 19031
10-116	PATTON, HARRY C.	B. DAVENPORT, IA.
57- 65	PATTON, THOMAS ALLEN	RR 2 BOX 220-B - HONEY BROOK PA 19344
68- 79	PAUL, MICHAEL GEORGE	4441 CAMINO DEL REY - TUCSON AZ 85718
54- 80	PAULA, CARLOS CONNIL	1972 ADD: 1274 NW 6TH #3 - MIAMI FL
11-133	PAULETTE, EUGENE EDWARD	D. FEBRUARY 8, 1966 LITTLE ROCK, ARK.
25- 85	PAULSEN, GUILFORD PAUL HANS	2022 8TH ST NE - PUYALLUP WA 98371
57- 66	PAVLETICH, DONALD STEPHEN	11934 W HAYES AVE - WEST ALLIS WI 53227
46- 81	PAWELEK, THEODORE JOHN	D. FEBRUARY 12, 1964 CHICAGO HEIGHTS, ILL.
55- 89	PAWLOSKI, STANLEY WALTER	1013 GORMAN ST - PHILADELPHIA PA 19116
77-111	PAXTON, MICHAEL DEWAYNE	OLD ADD: 345 LINCOLN #10 - BOSTON MA 02111
20- 95	PAYNE, GEORGE WASHINGTON	D. JANUARY 24, 1959 LONG BEACH, CAL.
75- 88	PAZIK, MICHAEL JOSEPH	1889 BUCCANEER CT - SARASOTA FL 33581
37- 87	PEACOCK, JOHN GASTON	D. OCTOBER 17, 1981 WILSON, N. C.
33- 50	PEARCE, FRANKLIN THOMAS	D. SEPTEMBER 3, 1950 VAN BUREN, N. Y.
12-153	PEARCE, GEORGE THOMAS	D. OCTOBER 11, 1935 JOLIET, ILL.
17- 60	PEARCE, HARRY JAMES	D. JANUARY 8, 1942 PHILADELPHIA, PA.
49- 63	PEARCE, JAMES MADISON	RR2 - ZEBULON NC 27597
58- 70	PEARSON, ALBERT GREGORY	1834 RANCHERO - WEST COVINA CA 91790
39- 89	PEARSON, ISAAC OVERTON	970 BLANCHARD - MEMPHIS TN 38116
32- 61	PEARSON, MONTGOMERY MARCELLUD.	JANUARY 27, 1978 FRESNO, CALIF.
10-117	PEASLEY, MARVIN WARREN	D. DECEMBER 27, 1948 SAN FRANCISCO, CALIF.
15-123	PECHOUS, CHARLES EDWARD	D. SEPTEMBER 13, 1980 KENOSHA, WIS.
43-111	PECK, HAROLD ARTHUR	RR 2 BOX 334 - FORT ATKINSON WI 53185
10-118	PECKINPAUGH, ROGER THORPE	D. NOVEMBER 17, 1977 CLEVELAND, O.

53- 67	PEDEN, LESLIE EARL	BOX 426 - BRADFORD FL 32008
41- 85	PEEK, STEPHEN GEORGE	204 W HAMILTON AVE-SHERRILL NY 13461
27- 70	PEEL, HOMER HEFNER	3757 GREENWAY - SHREVEPORT LA 71105
35- 89	PEERSON, JACK CHILES	D. OCTOBER 23, 1966 FT. WALTON BEACH, FLA.
27- 71	PEERY, GEORGE A	144 W UTAH AVE - PAYSON UT 84651
56- 67	PEETE, CHARLES	D. NOVEMBER 27, 1956 CARACAS, VENEZ.
46- 82	PELLAGRINI, EDWARD CHARLES	103 WEBB ST - WEYMOUTH MA 02188
74-104	PEMBERTON, BROCK	1012 S FLORENCE - TULSA OK 74104
81- 95	PENA, ADALBERTO	19-2-0-5, BAIROA MIRABEL-CAGUAS PR 00625
81- 96	PENA, ALEJANDRO	SANTIAGO CALLE 19 #6-PEKIN, SANTO DOMINGO D R

80-101	PENA, ANTONIO FRANCISCO	COMP HAB 30 DEMARZO,MAN #1 ED 14-SANTIAGO DR
69-132	PENA, JOSE	OLD ADD: ANDES L DE GARCIA 560-CD JUAREZ MEX
58- 71	PENA, ORLANDO GREGORY	8650 NW 30TH RD - MIAMI FL 33117
65- 87	PENA, ROBERTO CESAR	F-28,URBAN.,LAS COLISHA - SANTIAGO DOM REP
22-108	PENCE, ELMER CLAIR	D. SEPTEMBER 17, 1968 SAN FRANCISCO, CAL.
21- 79	PENCE, RUSSELL WILLIAM	D. AUGUST 11, 1971 HOT SPRINGS, ARK.
53- 68	PENDLETON, JAMES EDWARD	4558 REDBUD AVE - ST. LOUIS MO 63115
16- 68	PENNER, KENNETH WILLIAM	D. MAY 28, 1959 SACRAMENTO, CAL.
17- 61	PENNINGTON, GEORGE LOUIS	D. MAY 5, 1953 NEWARK, N. J.
12-154	PENNOCK, HERBERT JEFFERIS	D. JANUARY 30, 1948 NEW YORK, N.Y.
54- 81	PENSON, PAUL EUGENE	4316 DIXIE COURT - KANSAS CITY KS 66106
75- 89	PENTZ, EUGENE DAVID	1203 HEENEY AVE - JOHNSTOWN PA 15904
62-102	PEPITONE, JOSEPH ANTHONY	667 E 79TH ST - BROOKLYN NY 11236
29- 83	PEPLOSKI, HENRY STEPHEN	23-B COLUMBUS BLVD - WHITING NJ 08759
13-139	PEPLOSKI, JOSEPH ANTHONY	D. 1946 OR 1947
66- 70	PEPPER, DONALD HOYTE	RR2 - GANSEVOORT NY 12831
54- 82	PEPPER, HUGH MCLAURIN	123 HOLCOMB BLVD - OCEAN SPRINGS MS 39564
32- 62	PEPPER, RAYMOND WATSON	#40 - MOORESVILLE AL 35649
15-124	PEPPER, ROBERT ERNEST	D. APRIL 8, 1968 FORD CLIFF, PA.
69-133	PERAZA, LUIS	CALLE 6 C.F. 13 RES. BAIROA-CAGUAS PR 00625
80-102	PERCONTE, JOHN PATRICK	1016 JOHN ST - JOLIET IL 60435
11-134	PERDUE, HERBERT RODNEY	D. OCTOBER 31, 1968 GALLATIN, TENN.
64- 83	PEREZ, ATANASIO RIGAL	LOS FLORES 113 - SANTURCE PR 00911
58- 72	PEREZ, GEORGE THOMAS	39646 87TH ST W - LEONA VALLEY CA 93550
69-134	PEREZ, MARTIN ROMAN	30 WILLOWICK DR - DECATUR GA 30034
80-103	PEREZ, PASCUAL (GROSS)	SALVADOR, CUCURULO #105-SANTIAGO DOMINICAN RE
78- 99	PERKINS, BRODERICK PHILLIP	3317 IMPERIAL AVE - SAN DIEGO CA 92102
67- 84	PERKINS, CECIL BOYCE	RR 1 BOX 100-P - MARTINSBURG WV 25401
30- 60	PERKINS, CHARLES SULLIVAN	OLD ADD: 249 MURRAY AVE - RIDGEWOOD NJ
15-125	PERKINS, RALPH FOSTER	D. OCTOBER 2, 1963 PHILADELPHIA, PA.
50- 77	PERKOVICH, JOHN JOSEPH	3003 S AVERS - CHICAGO IL 60623
47- 66	PERKOWSKI, HAROLD WALTER	211 MCGINNIS - BECKLEY WV 25801
77-112	PERLOZZO, SAMUEL BENEDICT	532 WASHINGTON ST - CUMBERLAND MD 21502
42- 75	PERME, LEONARD JOSEPH	3350 D ST - HAYWARD CA 94541
10-119	PERNOLL, HENRY HUBBARD	D. FEBRUARY 18, 1944 GRANTS PASS, ORE.
61- 82	PERRANOSKI, RONALD PETER	1000 ELYSIAN PARK AVE - LOS ANGELES CA 90012
21- 80	PERRIN, JOHN STEPHENSON	D. JUNE 24, 1969 DETROIT, MICH.
34- 83	PERRIN, WILLIAM JOSEPH	D. JUNE 30, 1974 NEW ORLEANS, LA.
12-155	PERRITT, WILLIAM DAYTON	D. OCTOBER 15, 1947 SHREVEPORT, LA.
41- 86	PERRY, BOYD GLENN	RR 1 - SNOW CAMP NC 27349
62-103	PERRY, GAYLORD JACKSON	RR 3 BOX 565 - WILLIAMSTON NC 27892
15-126	PERRY, HERBERT SCOTT	D. OCTOBER 27, 1959 KANSAS CITY, MO.
59- 64	PERRY, JAMES EVAN	6516 NAVOHO TR - EDINA MN 55435
63- 91	PERRY, MELVIN GAY "BOB"	621 HOLIDAY CITY - NEW BERN NC 28562
12-156	PERRY, WILLIAM HENRY	D. JULY 18, 1956 PONTIAC, MICH.
15-127	PERRYMAN, EMMETT KEY	D. SEPTEMBER 12, 1966 STARKE, FLA.
18- 57	PERTICA, WILLIAM ANDREW	D. DECEMBER 28, 1967 LOS ANGELES, CAL.
71- 81	FERZANOWSKI, STANLEY	3250 173RD ST - HAMMOND IN 46323
42- 76	PESKY, JOHN MICHAEL	25 PARSONS DR-SWAMPSCOTT MA 01907
42- 77	PETERMAN, WILLIAM DAVID	9823 WISTERIA ST - PHILADELPHIA PA 19115
59- 65	PETERS, GARY CHARLES	2626 ESPANOLA AVE - SARASOTA FL 33580
15-128	PETERS, JOHN WILLIAM	D. FEBRUARY 21, 1932 KANSAS CITY, MO.
12-157	PETERS, OSCAR C	B. MARCH 15, 1886 GRAND FORK, ILL.
70-106	PETERS, RAYMOND JAMES	1512 E FORGE AVE - MESA AZ 85204
79- 83	PETERS, RICHARD DEVIN	12601 HALO DRIVE - COMPTON CA 90221
36- 71	PETERS, RUSSELL DIXON	BOX 751 - BEDFORD VA 24523
55- 90	PETERSON, CARL FRANCIS	8665 FLORIN RD #101 - SACRAMENTO CA 95828
62-104	PETERSON, CHARLES ANDREW	D. MAY 16, 1980 TACOMA WA
66- 71	PETERSON, FRED INGELS "FRITZ"	3515 W TOUHY - LINCOLNVILLE IL 60645
55- 91	PETERSON, HARDING WILLIAM	348 ORCHARD DR - PITTSBURGH PA 15228
31- 67	PETERSON, JAMES NIELS	D. APRIL 8, 1975 PALM BEACH, FLA.
44-106	PETERSON, KENT FRANKLIN	1533 S 240TH EAST - OREM UT 84057
43-112	PETERSON, SIDNEY HERBERT	G-28 E ARROWHEAD DR.STAR RT-HENRIETTA TX76365
34- 84	PETOSKY, FRED LEE	RR 2 - HOPKINS SC 29061
63- 92	PETROCELLI, AMERICO PETER	19 TOWNSEND RD - LYNNFIELD MA 01940
79- 84	PETRY, DANIEL JOSEPH	1808 CARTLEN DRIVE - PLACENTIA CA 92670
14-165	PETTIGREW, JIM NED	D. AUGUST 20, 1952 DUNCAN, OKLA.
80-104	PETTINI, JOSEPH PAUL	BOX 37 - WINDSOR HEIGHTS WV 26075
51- 77	PETTIT, GEORGE WILLIAM PAUL	WOODWARD ST - LOMITA CA 90717
35- 90	PETTIT, LEON ARTHUR	D. NOVEMBER 21, 1974 COLUMBIA, TENN.
21- 81	PETTY, JESSE LEE	D. OCTOBER 23, 1971 ST. PAUL, MINN.
14-166	PEZOLD, LORENZ JOHANNES	D. OCTOBER 22, 1957 BATON ROUGE, LA.
35- 91	PEZZULLO, JOHN	3127 W LEDBETTER DALLAS TX 75233
11-135	PFEFFER, EDWARD JOSEPH	D. AUGUST 15, 1972 CHICAGO, ILL.
13-138	PFEFFER, MONTE	D. SEPTEMBER 27, 1941 NEW YORK, N. Y.
69-135	PFEIL, ROBERT RAYMOND	840 BENJAMIN HALT DR - STOCKTON CA 95207
61- 83	PFISTER, DANIEL ALBIN	3600 NW 91ST AVE - WEST HOLLYWOOD FL 33024
41- 87	PFISTER, GEORGE EDWARD	215 JOHN ST - BOUND BROOK NJ 08805
45- 78	PFUND, LEROY HERBERT	1028 HARVARD ST - WHEATON IL 60188
36- 72	PHEBUS, RAYMOND WILLIAM	930 LAKEVIEW AVE BARTOW FL 33830
10-120	PHELAN, ARTHUR THOMAS	D. DECEMBER 27, 1964 FORT WORTH, TEX.
31- 68	PHELPS, ERNEST GORDON	1417 HALE ST - ODENTON MD 21113
80-105	PHELPS, KENNETH ALLEN	7531 E TURQUOISE AVE - SCOTTSDALE AZ 85258
30- 61	PHELPS, RAYMOND CLIFFORD	D. JULY 7, 1971 FT. PIERCE, FLA.
41- 88	PHILLEY, DAVID EARL	1336 E POLK ST-PARIS TX 75460
64- 84	PHILLIPS, ADOLFO EMILIO	APARTADO 6109 - CHORILLA PANAMA
30- 62	PHILLIPS, ALBERT ABERNATHY	D. NOVEMBER 6, 1964 BALTIMORE, MD.
34- 85	PHILLIPS, CLARENCE LEMUEL	2111 S ESTELLE - WICHITA KS 67211
42- 78	PHILLIPS, DAMON ROSWELL	BOX 805 HENDERSON, TX 75652
24- 85	PHILLIPS, EDWARD DAVID	D. JANUARY 26, 1968 BUFFALO, N.Y.
69-136	PHILLIPS, HAROLD ROSS	D. JUNE 12, 1972 FULLERTON, CAL.
53- 69	PHILLIPS, HOWARD EDWARD	WEST ELY - HANNIBAL MO 63401
47- 67	PHILLIPS, JACK DORN	MAY RD #2 - POTSDAM NY 13676
45- 79	PHILLIPS, JOHN	D. JUNE 16, 1958 ST. LOUIS, MO.
55- 92	PHILLIPS, JOHN MELVIN	2704 MIMOSA LN - HATTIESBURG MS 39401
73- 95	PHILLIPS, MICHAEL DWAINE	3222 RIDGEFIELD - IRVING TX 75060
70-107	PHILLIPS, NORMAN EDWIN	93 PLEASANT AVE - PORTLAND ME 04103

```
62-105  PHILLIPS, RICHARD EUGENE      217 PAKOHANA - HONOLULU HI 96813
15-129  PHILLIPS, THOMAS GERALD       D. APRIL 12, 1929 PHILIPSBURG, PA.
56- 68  PHILLIPS, WILLIAM TAYLOR       BOX 13 - AUSTELL GA 30001
66- 72  PHOEBUS, THOMAS HAROLD         207 46TH ST NW - BRADENTON FL 33505
77-113  PICCIOLO, ROBERT MICHAEL       6421 FIREBRAND ST - LOS ANGELES CA 90045
45- 80  PICCIUTO, NICHOLAS THOMAS      OLD ADD: 60 WYNNEWOOD RD - LIVINGSTON NJ
60- 82  PICHE, RONALD JACQUES          26 LOUVIGNY BOX 953 - LORRAINE QUEBEC
16- 69  PICINICH, VALENTINE JOHN       D. DECEMBER 5, 1942 NOBLEBORO, ME.
14-167  PICK, CHARLES THOMAS           D. JUNE 26, 1954 LYNCHBURG, VA.
23-103  PICK, EDGAR EVERETT            D. MAY 13, 1967 WEST LOS ANGELES, CAL.
31- 69  PICKERING, URBANE HENRY        D. MAY 13, 1970 MODESTO, CALIF.
10-121  PICKETT, CHARLES A             B. COLUMBUS, O.
33- 51  PICKREL, CLARENCE DOUGLAS      RR3 - ROCKY MOUNT VA 24151
18- 58  PICKUP, CLARENCE WILLIAM       D. AUGUST 2, 1974 PHILADELPHIA, PA.
47- 68  PICONE, MARIO PETER            8876 BAY 16 - BROOKLYN NY 11214
40- 68  PIECHOTA, ALOYSIUS EDWARD      1656 N MAYFIELD AVE-CHICAGO IL 60639
13-140  PIEH, EDWIN JOHN               D. SEPTEMBER 12, 1945 JACKSONVILLE, FLA.
73- 96  PIERCE, LAVERN JACK            454 N 9TH ST - SAN JOSE CA 95112
24- 86  PIERCE, RAYMOND LESTER         D. MAY 4, 1963 DENVER, COLO.
67- 85  PIERCE, TONY MICHAEL           500 2 WILLOW CROOK - COLUMBUS GA 31904
45- 81  PIERCE, WALTER WILLIAM         9000 SOUTH FRANCISCO - EVERGREEN PARK IL60642
17- 62  PIERCY, WILLIAM BENTON         D. AUGUST 28, 1951 LONG BEACH, CAL.
45- 82  PIERETTI, MARINO PAUL          D. JANUARY 30, 1981 SAN FRANCISCO, CALIF.
20- 96  PIEROTTI, ALBERT FELIX         D. FEBRUARY 12, 1964 REVERE, MASS.
50- 78  PIERRO, WILLIAM LEONARD        1751 74TH ST - BROOKLYN NY 11204
50- 79  PIERSALL, JAMES ANTHONY        WMAQ RADIO - CHICAGO IL 60601
18- 59  PIERSON, WILLIAM MORRIS        D. FEBRUARY 20, 1959 ATLANTIC CITY, N. J.
31- 70  PIET, ANTHONY FRANCIS          D. DECEMBER 1, 1981 HINSDALE, ILL.
```

```
14-168  PIEZ, CHARLES WILLIAM          D. DECEMBER 29, 1930 ATLANTIC CITY, N.J.
57- 67  PIGNATANO, JOSEPH BENJAMIN     150 78TH ST - BROOKLYN NY 11209
46- 83  PIKE, JESSE WILLARD            601 BLACKSHAW LN - SANYSIDRO CA 92073
56- 69  PIKTUZIS, GEORGE RICHARD       OLD ADD: 7230 HARRISON - DOWNEY CA 90240
56- 70  PILARCIK, ALFRED JAMES         BOX 185 - ST JOHN IN 46373
49- 64  PILLETTE, DUANE XAVIER         165 BLOSSOM HILL RD #404 - SAN JOSE CA 95123
17- 63  PILLETTE, HERMAN POLYCARP      D. APRIL 30, 1960 SACRAMENTO, CAL.
15-130  PILLION, CECIL RANDOLPH        D. SEPTEMBER 30, 1962 PITTSBURGH, PA.
36- 73  PILNEY, ANDREW JAMES           3309 RIDGEWAY DR METAIRIE LA 70002
68- 69  PINA, HORACIO GARCIA           OLD ADD: VENUSTIANA CARRANZA 207-COAHUILA MEX
18- 60  PINELLI, RALPH ARTHUR          BOX 845 - BOYES HOT SPRINGS CA 95416
64- 85  PINIELLA, LOUIS VICTOR         6617 GLENCOE DR - TAMPA FL 33617
58- 73  PINSON, VADA EDWARD            710 31ST ST - OAKLAND CA 94609
22-109  PINTO, WILLIAM LERTON          424 WEST IRIS - OXNARD CA 93030
32- 63  PIPGRAS, EDWARD JOHN           D. APRIL 13, 1964 CURRIE, MINN.
23-104  PIPGRAS, GEORGE WILLIS         BOX 192 - INVERNESS FL 32650
13-141  PIPP, WALTER CHARLES           D. JANUARY 11, 1965 GRAND RAPIDS, MICH.
36- 74  PIPPEN, HENRY HAROLD           206 JAYST-COLUSA 95932
78-100  PIRTLE, GERALD EUGENE          OLD ADD: 8725 E 46TH PL - TULSA OK 74145
53- 72  PISONI, JAMES PETE             10832 MUELLER RD - ST LOUIS MO 63123
38- 74  PITKC, ALEXANDER               936 ELM EMPORIA KS 66801
17- 64  PITLER, JACOB ALBERT           D. FEBRUARY 3, 1968 BINGHAMTON, N. Y.
70-108  PITLOCK, LEE PATRICK THOMAS    11335 S HOOPER AVE - LOS ANGELES CA 90059
21- 82  PITTENGER, CLARKE ALONZO       D. NOVEMBER 4, 1977 FT LAUDERDALE, FLA.
81- 97  PITTMAN, JOSEPH WAYNE          1007 FLEMING AVENUE - COLUMBUS GA 31906
74-105  PITTS, GAYLEN RICHARD          BOX 318 - MOUNTAIN HOME AR 72653
57- 68  PITULA, STANLEY                D. AUGUST 16, 1965 HACKENSACK, N. J.
57- 69  PIZARRO, JUAN CORDOVA          278 DEL RIO - SANTURCE PR 00912
79- 85  PLADSON, GORDON CECIL          14756 69TH AVE - SURREY BC
31- 71  PLANETA, EMIL JOSEPH           D. FEBRUARY 2, 1963 ROCKY HILL, CONN.
78-101  PLANK, EDWARD ARTHUR           1468 W JUANITA - MESA AZ 85202
55- 93  PLARSKI, DONALD JOSEPH         D. DECEMBER 29, 1981 ST. LOUIS, MO.
62-106  PLASKETT, ELMO ALEXANDER       BOX 1764 - FREDERIKSTED VI 00840
42- 79  PLATT, MIZELL GEORGE           D. JULY 27, 1970 WEST PALM BEACH, FLA.
13-142  PLATTE, ALFRED FREDERICK JOSEPH  D. AUGUST 29, 1976 GRAND RAPIDS, MICH.
61- 84  PLEIS, WILLIAM                 5 MARNE DR - LAKE SAINT LOUIS MO 63367
56- 71  PLESS, RANCE                   RR4 - GREENEVILLE TN 37743
56- 72  PLEWS, HERBERT EUGENE          1460 NORTHWESTERN RD - LONGMONT CO 80501.
18- 61  PLITT, NORMAN WILLIAM          D. FEBRUARY 1, 1954 NEW YORK, N. Y.
72- 85  PLODINEC, TIMOTHY ALFRED       899 ROOSEVELT AVE - ALIQUIPPA PA 15001
68- 81  PLUMMER, WILLIAM FRANCIS       2170 RHONDA RD - COTTONWOOD CA 96022
42- 80  POAT, RAYMOND WILLIAM          4833 W 109TH ST - OAK LAWN IL 60453
```

```
5- 90  POCOROBA, BIFF BENEDICT          1328 HIDDEN HILLS PKWY-STONE MOUNTAIN GA30087
9- 65  PODBIELAN, CLARENCE ANTHONY      207 KIMBERLY DR W - SYRACUSE NY 13219
0- 69  PODGAJNY, JOHN SIGMUND            D. MARCH 2, 1971 CHESTER, PA.
3- 71  PODRES, JOHN JOSEPH              192 LAMOS PLACE - WITHERBEE NY 12998
5- 91  POEPPING, MICHAEL HAROLD         RR 2 - PIERZ MN 56364
6- 64  POETZ, JOSEPH FRANK              D. FEBRUARY 7, 1942 ST. LOUIS, MO.
0- 70  POFAHL, JAMES WILLARD            823 HARRIET-OWATONNA MN 55060
9- 86  POFF, JOHN WILLIAM               401 BROOKBEND RD - FAIRFIELD CT 06430
7- 88  POFFENBERGER, CLETUS ELWOOD      13 1/2 N CONOCOCHEAGUE-WILLIAMSPORT MD 21795
0- 80  POHOLSKY, THOMAS GEORGE           177 HORSESHOE DR - KIRKWOOD MO 63122
6- 75  POINDEXTER, CHESTER JENNINGS      620 W MCCLURE - PAULS VALLEY OK 73075
3- 93  POINTER, AARON ELTON             4406 ARBORDALE AVE W - TACOMA WA 98466
3-113  POLAND, HUGH REID                GUTHRIE KY 42234
3- 97  POLE, RICHARD HENRY              21069 BROOKLAWN DR - DEARBORN HEIGHTS MI48217
7- 69  POLIVKA, KENNETH LYLE            1532 BROOKBROOK DR - NAPERVILLE IL 60540
1- 89  POLLET, HOWARD JOSEPH            D. AUGUST 8, 1974 HOUSTON, TEX.
2- 64  POLLI, LOUIS AMERICO             #45 - GRANITEVILLE VT 05654
7- 89  POLLY, NICHOLAS JOSEPH           2331 N LEAVITT AVE CHICAGO IL 60647
7-114  POLONI, JOHN PAUL                3205 ELLIS - CHANDLER AZ 85224
4- 86  POMORSKI, JOHN LEON              D. DECEMBER 6, 1977 BRAMPTON, ONTARIO
0-122  POND, RALPH BENJAMIN             D. SEPTEMBER 8, 1947 CLEVELAND, O.
7- 65  PONDER, CHARLES ELMER            D. APRIL 20, 1974 ALBUQUERQUE, N. M.
4- 87  POOL, HARLIN WELTY               D. FEBRUARY 15, 1963 RODEO, CAL.
5- 86  POOLE, JAMES RALPH               D. JANUARY 2, 1975 HICKORY, N. C.
1- 90  POOLE, RAYMOND HERMAN             RR 10 BOX 655-SALISBURY NC 28144
2- 81  POPE, DAVID                      9020 PARMELEE AVE - CLEVELAND OH 44108
4- 86  POPOVICH, PAUL EDWARD            2501 PARTRIDGE - NORTHBROOK IL 60062
9-137  POPOWSKI, EDWARD JOSEPH          BOX 5 CRESTVIEW APTS - SAYREVILLE NJ 08872
3- 98  POQUETTE, THOMAS ARTHUR          3404 RIDGEWAY RD - EAU CLAIRE WI 54701
4-169  PORRAY, EDMUND JOSEPH            D. JULY 13, 1954 LACKAWAXEN, PA.
1- 98  PORTER, CHARLES WILLIAM          9321 SNYDER LN - PERRY HALL MD 21128
1- 78  PORTER, DANIEL EDWARD            7360 COWLES MT BLVD - SAN DIEGO CA 92119
1- 82  PORTER, DARRELL RAY              337 SE 52ND ST - OKLAHOMA CITY OK 73109
4-170  PORTER, IRVING MARBLE            D. FEBRUARY 20, 1971 LYNN, MASS.
2- 82  PORTER, J. W.                    9677 HEATHER CIR W-PALM BCH GARDENS FL 33410
6- 65  PORTER, NED SWINDELL             D. JUNE 30, 1968 GAINESVILLE, FLA.
9- 84  PORTER, RICHARD TWILLEY          D. SEPTEMBER 24, 1974 PHILADELPHIA, PA.
1- 99  PORTER, ROBERT LEE               OLD ADD: 930 ELNORA CT - NAPA C A
8- 81  PORTERFIELD, ERWIN COOLIDGE      D. APRIL 28, 1980 CHARLOTTE, N. C.
8- 82  PORIC, ALFRED                    3250 SPANISH RAVINE - PLACERVILLE CA 95667
4- 83  PORTOCARRERO, ARNOLD MARIO       7810 CHARLES - SHAWNEE MISSION KS 66216
0- 83  POSADA, LEOPOLDO JESUS           385 NW 77TH AVE - MIAMI FL 33126
8- 75  POSEDEL, WILLIAM JOHN            179 HAUS AVE - SAN LEANDRO CA 94577
2- 65  POSER, JOHN FALK                 551 W SCHOOL - COLUMBUS WI 53925
6- 84  POSSEHL, LOUIS THOMAS            1509 SMITH RD #2-203 - PALATINE IL 60067
2-110  POST, SAMUEL GILBERT             D. MARCH 31, 1971 PORTSMOUTH, VA.
9- 66  POST, WALTER CHARLES             D. JANUARY 6, 1982 SAINT HENRY, O.
2-111  POTT, NELSON ADOLPH              D. DECEMBER 3, 1963 MACK,O.
8- 76  POTTER, MARYLAND DYKES           RR 5 BOX 476 - ASHLAND KY 41101
6- 75  POTTER, MICHAEL GARY            21582 ARCHER CIR - HUNTINGTON BEACH CA 92646
6- 76  POTTER, NELSON THOMAS            RR 1 MT MORRIS IL 61054
```

```
23-105  POTTER, SQUIRE                  3131 WINCHESTER AV #662 - ASHLAND KY 41101
14-171  POTTS, JOHN FREDERICK           D. SEPTEMBER 5, 1962 CLEVELAND, O.
67- 86  POULSEN, KEN STERLING           684 E WEAVER - SIMI VALLEY CA 93065
30- 63  POWELL, ALVIN JACOB             D. NOVEMBER 4, 1948 WASHINGTON, D. C.
63- 94  POWELL, GROVER DAVID            %EVA POWELL, RR CNE - MILAN PA 18831
78-102  POWELL, HOSKEN                  115 MEMORY LANE - PENSACOLA FL 32503
61- 85  POWELL, JOHN WESLEY             810 N MYERS - ELOY AZ 85231
71- 83  POWELL, PAUL RAY                U. S. ANGLERS MARINE - KEY WEST FL 33040
13-143  POWELL, RAYMOND REATH           D. OCTOBER 16, 1962 CHILLICOTHE, O .
55- 94  POWELL, ROBERT LEROY            5366 STAMPA ST - LAS VEGAS NV 89102
13-144  POWELL, SAMUEL
81-100  POWER, TED HENRY                10310 NW 18TH PL - PEMBROKE FL 33026
54- 84  POWER, VICTOR PELLOT            CONDOMINEO TORRE,MOLINOS 703-GUAYNABO PR00657
32- 66  POWERS, ELLIS FOREE             1012 ELLINGSWORTH - MIDDLETOWN KY 40043
55- 95  POWERS, JOHN CALVIN             6727 FIRST AVE S - BIRMINGHAM AL 35206
27- 72  POWERS, JOHN LLOYD              D. DECEMBER 22, 1968 HANCOCK, MD.
38- 77  POWERS, LESLIE EDWIN            OLD ADD: 11928 DARLINGTON #106 - LOS ANGELES
57- 70  POWIS, CARL EDGAR               OLD ADDD BOX 392 - BAYTOWN TX 77520
75- 92  PRALL, WILFRED ANTHONY          351 TERHUNE AVE - PASSAIC NJ 07055
49- 67  PRAMESA, JOHN STEVEN            4324 SUNBURST LN - CINCINNATI OH 45238
12-158  PRATT, DERRILL BURNHAM          D. SEPTEMBER 30, 1977 TEXAS CITY, TEX.
21- 83  PRATT, FRANCIS BRUCE            D. APRIL 8, 1974 CENTREVILLE, ALA.
```

```
14-172  PRATT, LESTER JOHN              D. JANUARY 8, 1969 PEORIA, ILL.
63- 95  PREGENZER, JOHN ARTHUR          OLD ADD: 5128 N 40TH - TACOMA WA
40- 71  PREIBISCH, MELVIN ADOLPHUS      D. APRIL 12, 1980 SEALY, TEXAS
48- 83  PRENDERGAST, JAMES BARTHOLOMEW  330 FAIRFIELD AVE - BUFFALO NY 14223
14-173  PRENDERGAST, MICHAEL THOMAS     D. NOVEMBER 18, 1967 OMAHA, NEB.
61- 86  PRESCOTT, GEORGE BERTRAND       ESTAFETA PARQUE LEFVRE-PANAMA 10 PANAMA
51- 79  PRESKO, JOSEPH EDWARD           1024 NE 42ND TERRACE - KANSAS CITY MO 64116
38- 78  PRESSNELL, FOREST CHARLES       329 E LIMA ST FINDLAY OH 45840
67- 87  PRICE, JIMMIE WILLIAM           3365 BUCKINGHAM TR - WEST BLOOMFIELD MI 4803
46- 85  PRICE, JOHN THOMAS REID         D. OCTOBER 2, 1967 SAN FRANCISCO, CAL.
28- 75  PRICE, JOSEPH PRESTON           D. JANUARY 15, 1961 WASHINGTON, D. C.
80-106  PRICE, JOSEPH WALTER            10726 VISTA CAMINO - LAKESIDE CA 92040
39- 90  PRICHARD, ROBERT ALEXANDER      BOX 1205-STAMFORD TX 79553
41- 91  PRIDDY, GERALD EDWARD           D. MARCH 3, 1980 NORTH HOLLYWOOD, CALIF.
62-107  PRIDDY, ROBERT SIMPSON          10134 PARKWOOD RD #1 - CUPERTINO CA 95014
11-136  PRIEST, JOHN GOODING            D. NOVEMBER 4, 1979 WASHINGTON, D. C.
33- 52  PRIM, RAYMOND LEE               11553 E BEVERLY BLVD - WHITTIER CA 90601
62-108  PRINCE, DONALD MARK             OLD ADD: 26 ROBERT E LEE DR - WILMINGTON NC
57- 71  PRITCHARD, HAROLD WILLIAM       507 E SUNNY HILL RD - FULLERTON CA 92635
59- 66  PROCTOR, JAMES ARTHUR           609 COUNT FLEET CT - NAPERVILLE IL 60540
```

```
23-106  PROCTOR, NOAH RICHARD           D. DECEMBER 17, 1954 RICHMOND, VA.
76- 76  PROLY, MICHAEL JAMES            4400 E 15TH ST - TULSA OK 74112
23-107  PROFST, WILLIAM JACOB           D. FEBRUARY 24, 1967 COLUMBUS, MISS.
20- 97  PROTHRO, JAMES THOMPSON         D. OCTOBER 14, 1971 MEMPHIS, TENN.
12-160  PROUGH, HERSCHEL CLINTON        D. NOVEMBER 29, 1936 RICHMOND, IND.
29- 85  PRUDHOMME, JOHN OLGUS           3025 WALLACE DR - SHREVEPORT LA 71109
20- 98  PRUESS, EARL HENRY              D. AUGUST 28, 1979 BRANSON, MO.
22-112  PRUETT, HUBERT SHELBY           D. JANUARY 28, 1982 LADUE, MO.
44-107  PRUETT, JAMES CALVIN            1906 MADERA ST - WAUKESHA WI 53186
75- 93  PRUITT, RONALD RALPH            1510 SKYLAND DR - HINCKLEY OH 44223
76- 77  PRYOR, GREGORY RUSSELL          6315 AMBASSADOR DR - ORLANDO FL 32808
30- 64  PUCCINELLI, GEORGE LAWRENCE     D. APRIL 16, 1956 SAN FRANCISCO, CAL.
11-137  PUCKETT, TROY LEVI              D. APRIL 13, 1971 WINCHESTER, IND.
70-109  PUENTE, MIGUEL ANTONIO          COBRE 106,COL MORALES-SAN LUIS POTOSI SLP ME.
77-115  PUHL, TERRANCE STEPHEN          BOX 8 - MELVILLE SASKATCHEWAN
74-106  PUIG, RICHARD GERALD            1714 DEMPSEY AVE - TAMPA FL 33603
77-116  PUJOLS, LUIS BIENVENIDO         NICOLAS HEREDIA 29 - BANI DOMINICAN REPUBLIC
81-101  PULEO, CHARLES MICHAEL          44 EDISON ST - BLOOMFIELD NJ 07003
25- 87  PUMPELLY, SPENCER ARMSTRONG     D. DECEMBER 5, 1973 SAYRE, PA.
64- 87  PURDIN, JOHN NOLAN              637 LIME AVE - SARASOTA FL 33577
26- 66  PURDY, EVERETT VIRGIL           D. JANUARY 16, 1951 BEATRICE, NEB.
54- 85  PURKEY, ROBERT THOMAS           5767 KING SCHOOL RD - BETHEL PARK PA 15102
76- 78  PUTNAM, EDDY WILLIAM            1161 W QUEENSIDE DR - COVINA CA 91722
77-117  PUTNAM, PATRICK EDWARD          2311 CARRELL RD - FORT MYERS FL 33901
55- 96  PYBURN, JAMES EDWARD            ATH DEPT UNIV OG GEORGE - ATHENS GA 30602
54- 86  PYECHA, JOHN NICHOLAS           407 KNOB CT - CHAPEL HILL NC 27514
28- 76  PYLE, HARLAN ALBERT             BOX 307 - LIBERTY NE 68381
39- 91  PYLE, HERBERT EWALD             538 HALLIDAY AVE-DUQUOIN IL 62832
32- 67  PYTLAK, FRANK ANTHONY           D. MAY 8, 1977 BUFFALO, N. Y.
69-138  QUALLS, JAMES ROBERT            OLD ADD: 7074 AVE 248 - TULARE CA 93274
53- 72  QUALTERS, THOMAS FRANCIS        RR 2 BOX 39 - SOMERSET PA 15501
64- 88  QUEEN, MELVIN DOUGLAS           BOX 1025 - MORRO BAY CA 93442
42- 81  QUEEN, MELVIN JOSEPH            OLD ADD: 10553 SEMORA - BELLFLOWER CA 90704
54- 87  QUEEN, WILLIAM EDDLEMAN         1616 E PERCY ST - GASTONIA NC 28052
31- 72  QUELLICH, GEORGE WILLIAM        D. AUGUST 31, 1958 JOHNSVILLE, CALIF.
39- 92  QUICK, JAMES HAROLD             OLD ADD: 1526 BATTLEFIELD DR - NASHVILLE TN
65- 88  QUILICI, FRANK RALPH            BOX 3017 - NORTHBROOK IL 60062
13-145  QUINLAN, THOMAS ALOYSIUS        D. FEBRUARY 17, 1966 SCRANTON, PA.
49- 68  QUINN, FRANK WILLIAM            3390 FOXCROFT RD #C309 - MIRAMAR FL 33025
11-138  QUINN, JOHN EDWARD PICK         D. APRIL 9, 1956 MARLBORO, MASS.
41- 92  QUINN, WELLINGTON HUNT          D. SEPTEMBER 1, 1954 LOS ANGELES, CAL.
74-107  QUINTANA, LUIS JOAQUIN          CASCRIO CATONI ED 12 #57 - VEGA BAJA PR 0076
62-109  QUIRK, ARTHUR LINCOLN           27 PIPPIN DR - GLASTONBURY CT 06033
75- 94  QUIRK, JAMES PATRICK            16263 E SKAGWAY ST - WHITTIER CA 90603
79- 87  QUISENBERRY, DANIEL RAYMOND     811 ARNO RD - KANSAS CITY MO 64113
22-113  RABBITT, JOSEPH PATRICK         D. DECEMBER 5, 1969 NORWALK, CONN.
57- 72  RABE, CHARLES HENRY             7725 LINDEN AVE - DARIEN IL 60559
40- 72  RACHUNOK, STEPHEN STEPANOVICH   2660 W BALL RD #1 - ANAHEIM CA 92805
47- 70  RACKLEY, MARVIN EUGENE          3314 COVINGTON DR - DECATUR GA 30030
62-110  RADATZ, RICHARD RAYMOND         2413 E JOLLY RD #8 - LANSING MI 48910
34- 88  RADCLIFF, RAYMOND ALLEN         D. MAY 23, 1962 ENID, OKLA.
11-139  RADEBAUGH, ROY                  D. JANUARY 17, 1945 CEDAR RAPIDS, IA.
```

```
71- 84  RADER, DAVID MARTIN              14644 POWAY MESA DR - POWAY CA 92064
43-146  RADER, DONALD RUSSELL            817 N MAIN ST #D-7 - WALLA WALLA WA 99362
57- 88  RADER, DOUGLAS LEE               2000 E OCEAN BLVD #112-7 - STUART FL 33494
21- 84  RADER, DREW LEON                 D. JUNE 5, 1975 CATSKILL, N. Y.
36- 77  RADTKE, JACK WILLIAM             289 S LOCUST - TWIN FALLS ID 83301
54- 88  RAETHER, HAROLD HERMAN           5920 MEROLD DR - EDINA MN 55424
39- 93  RAFFENSBERGER, KENNETH DAVID     669 CHESTNUT ST-YORK PA 17403
59-139  RAFFO, ALBERT MARTIN             BOX 866 - JASPER TN 37347
32- 68  RAGLAND, FRANK ROLAND            D. JULY 28, 1959 PARIS, MISS.
71- 85  RAGLAND, THOMAS                  20201 GREENLAWN ST - DETROIT MI 48224
75- 95  RAICH, ERIC JAMES                OLD ADD: 4200 HARTLE AVE #F - CUDAHY CA
57- 73  RAINES, LAWRENCE GLENN HOPE      810 WISCONSIN - LANSING MI 48915
79- 88  RAINES, TIMOTHY                  2316 AIRPORT BLVD - SANFORD FL 32771
79- 89  RAINEY, CHARLES DAVID            4153 DONNA AVE - SAN DIEGO CA 92115
78-108  RAJSICH, DAVID CHRISTOPHER       5324 NORTH SIXTH ST - PHOENIX AZ 85012
60- 84  RAKOW, EDWARD CHARLES            1970 ADD: RR 6 BOX 184 - MORGANTON NC 28655
10-123  RALSTON, SAMUEL BERYL            D. AUGUST 29, 1950 LANCASTER, PA.
46- 86  RAMAZOTTI, ROBERT LOUIS          1111 SOUTH 26TH ST - ALTOONA PA 16602
39- 94  RAMBERT, ELMER DONALD            1974 ADD: BOX 1711 - STUART FL 29483
26- 67  RAMBO, WARREN DAWSON             CROWN POINT RD - THOROFARE NJ 08086
60-107  RAMIREZ, MATIO (TORRES)          RR 2 BOX 7 - YAUCO PR 00768
70-110  RAMIREZ, MILTON                  7 TULIO LARRINAGA ST - MAYAGUEZ PR 00708
74-108  RAMIREZ, ORLANDO                 SOCORRO MONZANA #9 G-1 - CARTAGENA COLOMBIA
80-108  RAMIREZ, RAFAEL EMILIO           GAZETT #8 ENS PRIMAVERA-SAN PEDRO MACORIS DR
55- 97  RAMOS , PEDRO                    3222 NW 7TH ST - MIAMI FL 33125
78-104  RAMOS, DOMINGO ANTONIO           CARR DUARTE KM 8 1/2 LICEYALMEDIO SANTIAGO DR
44-108  RAMOS, JESUS MANUEL GARCIA       AVE SANTADER, LAPINTA #4 - EL PARAISO VENEZ
78-105  RAMOS, ROBERTO                   45 W 22ND ST #8 - HIALEAH FL 33010
47- 71  RAMSDELL, JAMES WILLARD,         D. OCTOBER 8, 1969 WICHITA, KAN.
78-106  RAMSEY, MICHAEL JEFFREY          2900 CEDAR KNOLL DR - ROSWELL GA 30076
45- 83  RAMSEY, WILLIAM THRACE           769 ROSEBANK RD - MEMPHIS TN 38116
53- 73  RAND, RICHARD HILTON             414 E 55TH ST - LONG BEACH CA 90805
76- 79  RANDALL, ROBERT LEE              308 OPAL CIR - AMES IA 50010
71- 86  RANDLE, LEONARD SHENOFF          4415 14TH AVE NE - BELLEVUE WA 98004
75- 96  RANDOLPH, WILLIE LARRY           86 LILLIAN ST - PARK RIDGE NJ 07656
62-111  RANEW, MERRITT THOMAS            RR THREE - LEESBURG GA 31763
49- 69  RANEY, FRANK ROBERT              11242 CHARLES DR - WARREN MI 48093
81-102  RANSOM, JEFFERY DEAN             2131 CURTIS ST - BERKELEY CA 94702
49- 70  RAPP, EARL WELLINGTON            126 EAST AVE - SWEDESBORO NJ 08085
21- 85  RAPP, JOSEPH ALOYSIUS            D. JULY 1, 1966 LAMESA, CALIF.
77-118  RAPP, VERNON FREDERICK           9454 W 75TH WAY - ARVADA CO 80003
46- 87  RASCHI, VICTOR JOHN ANGELO       1255 W WESTLAKE RD - CONESUS NY 14435
55- 97  RASMUSSEN, ERIC RALPH            6070 RANCHO MISSION RD - SAN DIEGO CA 92101
15-131  RASMUSSEN, HENRY                 D. JANUARY 1, 1949 CHICAGO, ILL.
68- 82  RATH, FRED HELSHER               200 N MIDLAND - LITTLE ROCK AR 72202
65- 89  RATLIFF, KELLY EUGENE            3403 MILLERFIELD RD - MACON GA 31201
63- 96  RATLIFF, PAUL HAWTHORNE          31717 1/2 SEACLIFF - SOUTH LAGUNA CA 92677
80-109  RATZER, STEVEN WAYNE             %C.EILERT.5310 HOLDER AVE-BALTIMORE MD 21214
72- 86  RAU, DOUGLAS JAMES               RR 1 BOX 154-A - COLUMBUS TX 78934
72- 87  RAUCH, ROBERT JOHN               236 N CLIFFORD - RIALTO CA 92376
66- 73  RAUDMAN, ROBERT JOYCE            BOX 905 - CAMBRIA CA 93428
77-119  RAUTZHAN, CLARENCE GEORGE        RR 4 BOX 4454 - POTTSVILLE PA 17901
78-107  RAWLEY, SHANE WILLIAM            5615 ALBURG AVE - RACINE WI 53406
14-174  RAWLINGS, JOHN WILLIAM           D. OCTOBER 16, 1972 INGLEWOOD, CALIF.
15-132  RAY, CARL GRADY                  D. APRIL 3, 1970 WALNUT COVE, N.C.
65- 90  RAY, JAMES FRANCIS               OLD ADD:1911 FOUNTAIN VIEW #1-HOUSTON TX
81-103  RAY, JOHN CORNELIAS              RR 1 BOX 64 - CHAUTEAU OK 74337
10-124  RAY, ROBERT HENRY                D. MARCH 11, 1963 ELECTRA, TEX.
58- 74  RAYDON, CURTIS LOWELL            1112 BEECHWOOD AVE - BLOOMINGTON IL 61701
80-110  RAYFORD, FLOYD KINNARD           OLD ADD: 1252 W 38TH ST - LOS ANGELES CA
59- 67  RAYMOND, JOSEPH CLAUDE           580 MAISONNE AVE - ST JEAN QUE
19- 66  RAYMOND, LOUIS ANTHONY           D. MAY 2, 1979 ROCHESTER, N. Y.
73- 99  RAZIANO, BARRY JOHN              1315 4TH ST - KENNER LA 70062
69-140  REAMS, LEROY                     1807 73RD AVE - OAKLAND CA 94621
79- 90  REARDON, JEFFREY JAMES           5067 KIRKLAND AVE - SPRINGHILL FL 33526
38- 79  REBEL, ARTHUR ANTHONY            1726 W FORE DR TAMPA FL 33610
68- 83  REBERGER, FRANK BEALL            OLD ADD: 1604 FILLMORE ST - CALDWELL ID 83605
12-161  REDDING, PHILIP HAYDEN           D. MARCH 30, 1929 GREENWOOD, MISS.
32- 69  REDER, JOHN ANTHONY              BOX 1892 - FALL RIVER MA 02722
28- 77  REDFERN, GEORGE HOWARD           D. SEPTEMBER 8, 1964 ASHEVILLE, N. C.
76- 80  REDFERN, PETER IRVINE            15131 PADDOCK - SYLMAR CA 91342
74-109  REDMON, GLENN VINCENT            19431 UNIVERSITY - ALLEN PARK MI 48101
65- 91  REDMOND, HOWARD WAYNE            OLD ADD: 24514 WILLOUGHBY - EAST DETROIT MI
35- 92  REDMOND, JACKSON MCKITTRICK      D. JULY 28, 1968 GARLAND, TEX.
78-108  REECE, ROBERT SCOTT              3589 S NUCLA ST - AURORA CO 80013
58- 75  REED, HOWARD DEAN                BOX 837 - MATHIS TX 78368
81-104  REED, JERRY MAXWELL              21 GRANDVIEW RD - ASHEVILLE NC 28806
61- 87  REED, JOHN BURWELL               BOX 97 - SILVER CITY MS 39166
11-140  REED, MILTON D.                  D. JULY 27, 1938 ATLANTA, GA.
15-133  REED, RALPH EDWIN                D. FEBRUARY 16, 1959 BEAVER, PA.
69-141  REED, ROBERT EDWARD             OLD ADD: 6224 KING ARTHUR-SCHWARTZ CREEK MI
66- 74  REED, RONALD LEE                 2613 CLIFFVIEW DR - WESLACO TX 78596
52- 83  REED, WILLIAM JOSEPH            2306 EAGLE ROCK - HOUSTON TX 77080
49- 71  REEDER, WILLIAM EDGAR            605 HELM LN - SULPHUR SPRING TX 75482
18- 62  REES, STANLEY MILTON            D. AUGUST 29, 1937 LEXINGTON, KY.
27- 73  REESE, ANDREW JACKSON           D. JANUARY 10, 1966 TUPELO, MISS.
40- 73  REESE, HAROLD HENRY             3211 BEALS BRANCH RD-LOUISVILLE KY 40206
```

```
30- 65  REESE, JAMES HERMAN            10797 ASHTON AVE - LOS ANGELES CA 90024
64- 89  REESE, RICHARD BENJAMIN        4210 DEVONSHIRE CT - NORTBROOK IL 60062
26- 68  REEVES, ROBERT EDWIN           702 BELVOIR AVE - CHATTANOOGA TN 37412
54- 89  REGALADC, RUDOLPH VALENTINO    5122 LOS ALTOS COURT - SAN DIEGO CA 92109
17- 66  REGAN, MICHAEL JOHN            D. MAY 23, 1961 ALBANY, N. Y.
60- 85  REGAN, PHILIP RAYMOND          1375 108TH ST - BYRON CENTER MI 49315
26- 69  REGAN, WILLIAM WRIGHT          D. JUNE 11, 1968 PITTSBURGH, PA.
24- 87  REGO, ANTONE                   D. JANUARY 6, 1978 TULSA, OKLA.
12-162  REHG, WALTER PHILLIP           D. AUGUST 5, 1946 BURBANK, CALIF.
33- 53  REIBER, FRANK BERNARD          BOX 6284 - SARASOTA FL 33578
49- 72  REICH, HERMAN CHARLES          3779 PALA MESA DR - FALLBROOK CA 92028
64- 90  REICHARDT, FREDERIC CARL       1653 NW 19TH CIR - GAINESVILLE FL 32605
22-114  REICHLE, RICHARD WENDELL       D. JUNE 13, 1967 ST. LOUIS, MO.
46- 88  REID, EARL PERCY               1120 15TH ST SW - BIRMINGHAM AL 35211
69-142  REID, SCOTT DONALD             5112 TONIKO DR - PHOENIX AZ 85044
17- 67  REILLY, ARCHER EDWIN           D. NOVEMBER 29, 1963 COLUMBUS, O.
19- 67  REILLY, HAROLD J.
74-110  REINBACH, MICHAEL WAYNE        % CREAMER, 9459 SLOPE ST - SANTEE CA 92071
19- 68  REINHART, ARTHUR CONRAD        D. NOVEMBER 11, 1946 HOUSTON, TEX.
28- 78  REINHOLZ, ARTHUR AUGUST        D. DECEMBER 29, 1980 NEWPORT RICHEY, FLA.
15-134  REINICKER, WALTER JOSEPH       D. APRIL 18, 1957 PITTSBURGH, PA.
11-141  REIS, HARRIE CRANE             D. JULY 20, 1939 CINCINNATI, O.
31- 73  REIS, ROBERT JOSEPH THOMAS     D. MAY 1, 1973 ST. PAUL, MINN.
38- 80  REIS, THOMAS EDWARD            41 HOLLY LN - FORT THOMAS KY 41075
40- 74  REISER, HAROLD PATRICK         D. OCTOBER 25, 1981 PALM SPRINGS, CALIF.
11-142  REISIGL, JACOB                 D. FEBRUARY 24, 1957 AMSTERDAM, N.Y.
32- 70  REISS, ALBERT ALLEN            RR 1 BOX 474 - ODESSA FL 33556
72- 88  REITZ, KENNETH JOHN            BOX 427 - CHESTERFIELD MO 63017
79- 91  REMMERSWAAL, WILHELMUS ABR     DOKTOR VAN PRAAG ST 16 - WASSENAAR HOLLAND
12-163  REMNEAS, ALEXANDER NORMAN      D. AUGUST 27, 1975
75- 98  REMY, GERALD PETER             5 DENNIS DR - WESTPORT MA 02790
13-147  RENFER, ERWIN ARTHUR           D. OCTOBER 26, 1957 SYCAMORE, ILL.
59- 68  RENFROE, MARSHALL DALTON       D. DECEMBER 10, 1970 PENSACOLA, FLA.
68- 84  RENKER, WARREN RICHARD         RR4 - LONDON OH 43140
61- 88  RENIFF, HAROLD EUGENE          424 STAFFORD - SCRANTON PA 18505
38- 81  RENINGER, JAMES DAVID          RR 1 S-18 - LEES SUMMIT MO 64063
69-143  RENKO, STEVEN                  10347 ALHAMBRA - OVERLAND PARK KS 66207
53- 74  RENNA, WILLIAM BENEDITTO       1476 LESHER CT - SAN JOSE CA 95125
30- 66  RENSA, TONY GEORGE             O'KARMA TERRACE #515-WILKES-BARRE PA 18702
39- 95  REPASS, ROBERT WILLIS          169 BRIMFIELD RD-WETHERSFIELD CT 06109
78- 86  REPLOGLE, ANDREW DAVID         1115 YELLOWWOOD CIR - NOBLESVILLE IN 46060
64- 91  REPOZ, ROGER ALLEN             1106 IRVING ST - BELLINGHAM WA 98225
53- 75  REPULSKI, ELDON JOHN           1541 8TH AVE N - ST CLOUD MN 56301
43-114  RESCIGNO, XAVIER FREDERICK     OLD ADD: BOX 276 - ELMHURST "A" NY 11380
49- 73  RESTELLI, DINO PAUL            1860 SAN CARLOS AVE - SAN CARLOS CA 94070
68- 85  RETTENMUND, MERVIN WELDON      16670 ESPOLA RD - POWAY CA 92064
22-115  RETTIG, ADOLPH JOHN            D. JUNE 16, 1977 STUART, FLA.
61- 89  RETZER, KENNETH LEO            1554 PLANTATION WAY - EL CAJON CA 92020
75- 99  REUSCHEL, PAUL RICHARD         RR 1 BOX 76 - CAMP POINT IL 62320
72- 89  REUSCHEL, RICKEY EUGENE        1031 N WILSHIRE - ARLINGTON HEIGHTS IL 60004
69-144  REUSS, JERRY                   795 S GOLDFINCH - ANAHEIM CA 92807
78-110  REVERING, DAVID ALVIN          OLD ADD: 2847 SAN LEANDRO BLVD-SAN LEANDRO CA
43-115  REYES, NAPOLEON AGUILERA       OLD ADD: CLE 24 #3622 ST ROSA-BAYAMON PR
42- 82  REYNOLDS, ALLIE PIERCE         2709 CASHION PL-OKLAHOMA CITY OK 73112
68- 86  REYNOLDS, ARCHIE EDWARD        1828 PINECREST - TYLER TX 75701
27- 74  REYNOLDS, CARL NETTLES         D. MAY 29, 1978 HOUSTON, TEX.
45- 84  REYNOLDS, DANIEL VANCE         BOX 55 - SCOTTS NC 28576
78-111  REYNOLDS, DONALD EDWARD        2605 SOUTHEAST RYAN - CORVALLIS OR 97330
75-100  REYNOLDS, GORDON CRAIG         4607 FOUNTAINHEAD - HOUSTON TX 77066
70-111  REYNOLDS, KENNETH LEE          53 CUMMONWEALTH AVE - MARLBORO MA 01752
69-145  REYNOLDS, ROBERT ALLEN         2138 N 112TH #309 - SEATTLE WA 98133
14-175  REYNOLDS, ROSS ERNEST          D. JUNE 23, 1970 ADA, OKLA.
63- 97  REYNOLDS, THOMAS D             1577 SAN ALTOS - LEMON GROVE CA 92045
13-148  REYNOLDS, WILLIAM DEE          D. JUNE 5, 1924 CARNEGIE, OKLA.
47- 72  RHAWN, ROBERT JOHN             208 OAK ST - DANVILLE PA 17821
14-176  RHEAM, KENNETH JOHNSTON        D. OCTOBER 23, 1947 PITTSBURGH, PA.
24- 88  RHEM, CHARLES FLINT            D. JULY 30, 1969 COLUMBIA, S. C.
29- 86  RHIEL, WILLIAM JOSEPH          D. AUGUST 16, 1946 YOUNGSTOWN, O.
74-111  RHODEN, RICHARD ALAN           1 STAGECOACH PL - CANOGA PARK CA 91307
52- 84  RHODES, JAMES LAMAR "DUSTY"    245 DIXON AVE - STATEN ISLAND NY 10303
29- 87  RHODES, JOHN GORDON            D. MARCH 22, 1960 LONG BEACH, CAL.
26- 70  RHYNE, HAROLD J.               D. JANUARY 7, 1971 ORANGEVALE, CAL.
64- 92  RIBANT, DENNIS JOSEPH          1615 POINT CHARLES PL - NEWPORT BEACH CA92660
76- 81  RICCELLI, FRANK JOSEPH         311 SCHAEFFER AVE - SYRACUSE NY 13206
45- 85  RICE, DELBERT W                2910 TRENTON AVE - ORANGE CA 92667
15-135  RICE, EDGAR CHARLES            D. OCTOBER 13, 1974 ROSSMOR, MD.
48- 84  RICE, HAROLD HOUSTEN           720 HAINES AVE - MUNCIE IN 47303
23-108  RICE, HARRY FRANCIS            D. JANUARY 1, 1971 PORTLAND, ORE.
```

```
74-112 RICE, JAMES EDWARD              RR 8 BOX 686 - ANDERSON SC 29621
44-109 RICE, LEONARD OLIVER           BOX 54 - ARNOLD CA 95223
26- 71 RICE, ROBERT TURNBULL          127-B N RIDGE DR - ASHEVILLE NC 28804
39- 96 RICH, WOODROW EARL             RR 6 BOX 178 - MORGANTON NC 28655
71- 87 RICHARD, JAMES RODNEY          10235 SAGEDALE - HOUSTON TX 77089
71- 88 RICHARD, LEE EDWARD            1621 E 14TH ST - PORT ARTHUR TX 77640
60- 86 RICHARDS, DUANE LEE            BOX 54 - PALESTINE OH 45352
77-120 RICHARDS, EUGENE               RR 2 BOX 105 - BLAIR SC 29015
51- 80 RICHARDS, FRED CHARLES         1760 DODGE NW - WARREN OH 44485
32- 71 RICHARDS, PAUL RAPIER          BOX 545 - WAXAHACHIE TX 75165
29- 88 RICHARDSON, CLIFFORD NOLEN     D. SEPTEMBER 25, 1951 ATHENS, GA.
64- 93 RICHARDSON, GORDON CLARK       RR 3 BOX 217 - COLQUITT GA 31737
15-136 RICHARDSON, JOHN WILLIAM       D. JANUARY 18, 1970 MARION, ILL.
42- 83 RICHARDSON, KENNETH FRANKLIN   3456 CENTINELA #24 - LOS ANGELES CA 90066
55- 98 RICHARDSON, ROBERT CLINTON     47 ADAMS - SUMTER SC 29150
17- 68 RICHARDSON, THOMAS MITCHELL    D. NOVEMBER 15, 1939 ONAWA, IA.
80-111 RICHARDT, MICHAEL ANTHONY      1177 E SAN BRUNO AVE - FRESNO CA 93710
21- 86 RICHBOURG, LANCELOT CLAYTON    D. SEPTEMBER 10, 1975 CRESTVIEW, FLA.
62-112 RICHERT, PETER GERARD          5932 PARADISE PLAZA- PALM SPRINGS CA 92264
53- 54 RICHMOND, BERYL JUSTICE        RR3 - CAMERON WV 26033
41- 93 RICHMOND, DONALD LESTER        D. MAY 24, 1981 ELMIRA, N. Y.
20- 99 RICHMOND, RAYMOND SINCLAIR     D. OCTOBER 21, 1969 DESOTO, MO.
51- 81 RICHTER, ALLEN GORDON          3810 ATLANTIC AVE - NORFOLK VA 23510
11-143 RICHTER, EMIL HENRY            D. AUGUST 3, 1934 CHICAGO, ILL.
42- 84 RICKERT, MARVIN AUGUST         D. JUNE 3, 1978 OAKVILLE, WASH.
63- 98 RICKETTS, DAVID WILLIAM        717 SEWARD ST - ROCHESTER NY 14611
69-146 RICKETTS, RICHARD JAMES        2S706 DEVONSHIRE LN - GLEN ELLYN IL 60137
69-146 RICO, ALFREDO CRUZ             5207 TEESDALE - NORTH HOLLYWOOD CA 91607
16- 70 RICO, ARTHUR RAYMOND           D. JANUARY 3, 1919 BOSTON, MASS.
23-109 RICONDA, HARRY PAUL            D. NOVEMBER 15, 1958 MAHOPAC, N. Y.
39- 97 RIDDLE, ELMER RAY              1518 30TH ST-COLUMBUS GA 31904
30- 67 RIDDLE, JOHN LUDY              5600 AVENUE J - ENSLEY AL 35208
70-112 RIDDLEBERGER, DENNIS MICHAEL   OLD ADD: 5613 SPRINGWOOD AVE - NORFOLK VA
14-177 RIDGWAY, JACOB A               D. FEBRUARY 23, 1928 PHILADELPHIA, PA.
50- 81 RIDZIK, STEPHEN GEORGE         4825 PONDEROSA DR - ANNANDALE VA 22003
42- 85 RIEBE, HARVEY DONALD           28031 LAKE SHORE BLVD-CLEVELAND OH 44132
10-125 RIEGER, ELMER JAY              D. OCTOBER 21, 1959 LOS ANGELES, CALIF.
11-144 RIGGERT, JOSEPH ALOYSIUS       D. DECEMBER 10, 1973 KANSAS CITY, MO.
34- 89 RIGGS, LEWIS SIDNEY            D. AUGUST 12, 1975 DURHAM, N. C.
79- 92 RIGHETTI, DAVID ALLAN          1574 KOCH LN - SAN JOSE CA 95125
22-116 RIGNEY, EMORY ELMO             D. JUNE 6, 1972 SAN ANTONIO, TEX.
37- 90 RIGNEY, JOHN DUNGAN            410 ASHLAND AVE - RIVER FOREST IL 60305
46- 89 RIGNEY, WILLIAM JOSEPH         3136 ROUND HILL RD - ALAMO CA 94507
41- 94 RIKARD, CULLEY                 50 HWY 304 - OLIVE BRANCH MS 38654
79- 93 RILEY, GEORGE MICHAEL          2737 S. SHERIDAN ST - PHILADELPHIA PA 19148
10-126 RILEY, JAMES JOSEPH            D. MARCH 25, 1949 BUFFALO, N.Y.
21- 87 RILEY, JAMES NORMAN            D. MAY 25, 1969 SEGUIN, TEXAS
44-110 RILEY, LEON FRANCIS            D. SEPTEMBER 13, 1970 SCHENECTADY, N. Y.
80-112 RINCON, ANDREW JOHN            5425 LOS TOROS - PICO RIVERA CA 90660
79- 94 RINEER, JEFFREY ALAN           3608C ORKNEY RD - MOUNTVILLE PA 17554
17- 69 RING, JAMES JOSEPH             D. JULY 2, 1965 NEW YORK, N. Y.
50- 82 RINKER, ROBERT JOHN            10 NORTH MADISON - MCADOO PA 18237
69-147 RIOS, JUAN                     OLD ADD: PASO TABLA 9-SAN SEBASTIAN PR
81-105 RIPKEN, CALVIN EDWIN JR.       410 CLOVER ST - ABERDEEN MD 21001
78-112 RIPLEY, ALLEN STEVENS          55 WEST ST - NORTH ATTLEBORO MA 02760
35- 93 RIPLEY, WALTER FRANKLIN        55 WEST ST - NORTH ATTLEBORO MA 02760
62-113 RIPPELMEYER, RAYMOND ROY       BOX 28 - VALMEYER IL 62295
44-111 RIPPLE, CHARLES DAWSON         D. MAY 6, 1979 WILMINGTON, N. C.
36- 78 RIPPLE, JAMES ALBERT           D. JULY 16, 1959 GREENSBURG, PA.
17- 70 RISBERG, CHARLES AUGUST        D. OCTOBER 13, 1975 RED BLUFF, CAL.
44- 94 RISLEY, JAY SEAY               1108 TERRACE DR - SALISBURY NC 28144
12-164 RITTER, WILLIAM HERBERT        D. SEPTEMBER 3, 1964 AKRON, O.
70-113 RITTWAGE, JAMES MICHAEL        23931 COLUMBUS RD - BEDFORD HEIGHTS OH 44146
75-101 RIVERA, JESUS MANUEL           G#2 AMALIA MARIN - PONCE PR 00732
52- 85 RIVERA, MANUEL JOSEPH          RR 5 BOX 90 - ANGOLA IN 46703
70-114 RIVERS, JOHN MILTON            350 NW 48TH ST - MIAMI FL 33142
21- 88 RIVIERE, ARTHUR BERNARD        D. SEPTEMBER 27, 1965 LIBERTY, TEX.
12-165 RIXEY, EPPA                    D. FEBRUARY 28, 1963 TERRACE PARK, O.
38- 82 RIZZO, JOHN COSTA              D. DECEMBER 4, 1977 HOUSTON, TEX.
41- 95 RIZZUTO, PHILIP FRANCIS        912 WESTMINSTER AVE-HILLSIDE NJ 07205
53- 76 ROACH, MELVIN EARL             106 W 30TH ST - RICHMOND VA 23225
```

10-127	ROACH, WILBUR CHARLES	D. DECEMBER 26, 1947 BAY CITY, MICH.
61- 90	ROARKE, MICHAEL THOMAS	11 ROSEVIEW DR - CRANSTON RI 02910
79- 95	ROBBINS, BURCE DUANE	RR ONE - DUNKIRK IN 47336
33- 55	ROBELLO, THOMAS VARDASCO	3504 WESLEY AV - FT WORTH TX 76111
79- 96	ROBERGE, BERTRAND ROLAND	184 BROAD ST - AUBURN ME 04210
41- 96	ROBERGE, JOSEPH ALBERT ARMAND	173 CRAWFORD-LOWELL MA 01854
43-116	ROBERTS, CHARLES EMORY	RR2 #109 - CARROLLTON GA 30117
13-149	ROBERTS, CLARENCE ASHLEY	D. DECEMBER 24, 1963 LONG BEACH, CALIF.
54- 90	ROBERTS, CURTIS BENJAMIN	D. NOVEMBER 14, 1969 OAKLAND, CALIF.
67- 89	ROBERTS, DALE	206 BERRY AVE - VERSAILLES KY 40383
69-148	ROBERTS, DAVID ARTHUR	OLD ADD: 1930 JERVIS RD - COLUMBUS OH
62-114	ROBERTS, DAVID LEONARD	17510 MAYALL ST - NORTHRIDGE CA 91324
72- 90	ROBERTS, DAVID WAYNE	16513 CALLE ANA - POWAY CA 92064
24- 89	ROBERTS, JAMES NEWSOM	616 3RD ST S - COLUMBUS MISS 39701
74-113	ROBERTS, LEON KAUFFMAN	3200 TRANQUILITY - ARLINGTON TX 76016
19- 69	ROBERTS, RAYMOND	D. JANUARY 30, 1962 CRUGER, MISS.
48- 85	ROBERTS, ROBIN EVAN	504 TERRACE HILL RD - TEMPLE TERRACE FL 33617
54- 91	ROBERTSON, ALFRED JAMES	828 W INVERNESS - PEORIA IL 61614
81-106	ROBERTSON, ANDRE LEVETT	2229 CROSS LN ST - ORANGE TX 77360
19- 70	ROBERTSON, CHARLES CULBERTSON	1006 UNIVERSITY PLACE - FT WORTH TX 76107
62-115	ROBERTSON, DARYL BERDINE	755 PRINCTON DR - MIDVALE UT 84047
12-166	ROBERTSON, DAVIS AYDELOTRE	D. NOVEMBER 5, 1970 VIRGINIA BEACH, VA.
54- 92	ROBERTSON, DONALD ALEXANDER	3724 E SAHUARO DR - PHOENIX AZ 85028
19- 99	ROBERTSON, EUGENE EDWARD	D. OCTOBER 21, 1981 FALLON, NEV.
69-149	ROBERTSON, JERRY LEE	3620 MULVANE - TOPEKA KS 66611
13-150	ROBERTSON, PRESTON	D. OCTOBER 2, 1944 NEW ORLEANS, LA.
66- 75	ROBERTSON, RICHARD PAUL	10330 STOKES - CUPERTINO CA 95014
67- 90	ROBERTSON, ROBERT EUGENE	RR 1 SHINNAMON DR - LAVALE MD 21502
40- 75	ROBERTSON, SHERRARD ALEXANDER	D. OCTOBER 23, 1970 HOUGHTON, S. D.
43-117	ROBINSON, AARON ANDREW	D. MARCH 9, 1966 LANCASTER,O.
55- 99	ROBINSON, BROOKS CALBERT	1506 SHERBROOK RD - LUTHERVILLE MD 21093
78-113	ROBINSON, BRUCE PHILLIP	1310 DELLCREST LANE - LAJOLLA CA 92037
72- 91	ROBINSON, CRAIG GEORGE	39 N TRAYMORE AVE - IVYLAND PA 18974
70-115	ROBINSON, DAVID TANNER	6140 CAMINO DEL RINSON - SAN DIEGO CA 92120
79- 97	ROBINSON, DEWEY EVERETT	1733 W ARTHUR AVE - CHICAGO IL 60626
78-114	ROBINSON, DON ALLEN	2012 POPLAR ST - KENOVA WV 25530
58- 76	ROBINSON, EARL JOHN	LANEY COLLEGE,900 PATTON ST-OAKLAND CA 94609
60- 87	ROBINSON, FLOYD ANDREW	5837 MARKET - SAN DIEGO CA 92114
56- 73	ROBINSON, FRANK	15557 AQUA VERDE DR - BEL AIR CA 90024
55-100	ROBINSON, HUMBERTO VALENTINO	OLD ADD: 2020 DOMINGO OBALDIA - COLON PANAMA
47- 73	ROBINSON, JACK ROOSEVELT	D. OCTOBER 24, 1972 STAMFORD, CONN.
49- 74	ROBINSON, JOHN EDWARD	11 WINDING WAY - CEDAR GROVE NJ 07009
11-145	ROBINSON, JOHN HENRY	D. JULY 3, 1965 NORTH LITTLE ROCK, ARK.
42- 86	ROBINSON, WILLIAM EDWARD	BOX 1111 - ARLINGTON TX 76010
66- 76	ROBINSON, WILLIAM HENRY	1137 SAVEY AVE - DUQUESNE PA 15110
69-150	ROBLES, RAFAEL RADAMES	INGENIO QUISQUEYA-SAN PEDRO DE MARCORIS DOM R
72- 92	ROBLES, SERGIO	ESCOBEDO #402 - MAGDALENA SONORA MEXICO
74-114	ROBSON, THOMAS JAMES	4449 E WOOD - PHOENIX AZ 85040
43-118	ROCCO, MICHAEL DOMINICK	868 WEST IOWA AVE - ST PAUL MN 55117
45- 86	ROCHE, ARMANDO BAEZ	OLD ADD: AVE LOS PINOS - HAVANA CUBA
14-178	ROCHE, JOHN JOSEPH	1065 SW 206TH AVE - ALOHA OR 97005
14-179	ROCHEFORT, BENNETT HAROLD	D. APRIL 2, 1981 RED BANK, N. J.
44-112	ROCHELLI, LOUIS JOSEPH	3306 GREENWOOD DR - VICTORIA TX 77901
36- 79	ROCK, LESTER HENRY	OLD ADD: 1027 OLIVE DR - DAVIS CA
76- 82	ROCKETT, PATRICK EDWARD	1335 VIEWRIDGE - SAN ANTONIO TX 78213
57- 74	RODGERS, KENNETH ANDRE IAN	P. O. BOX 4581 - NASSAU BAHAMAS
61- 91	RODGERS, ROBERT LEROY	5181 WEST KNOLL DR - YORBA LINDA CA 92686
15-137	RODGERS, WILBUR KINCAID	D. DECEMBER 24, 1978 GOLIAD, TEX.
44-113	RODGERS, WILLIAM SHERMAN	1433 NAUDAIN - HARRISBURG PA 17104
54- 93	RODIN, ERIC CHAPMAN	OLD ADD: RR 5 - FLEMINGTON NJ
52- 86	RODRIGUEZ, ANTONIO HECTOR	SAN JOSE 218 - LAYANO, HAVANA CUBA
67- 91	RODRIGUEZ, AURELIO HUARTE	ROSENDO 6 CASTRO #112 - LOS MOCHIS SONORA MEX
73-100	RODRIGUEZ, EDUARDO	URB CATALINA CALLE 4E-34-BARCELONETA PR 00617
68- 87	RODRIGUEZ, ELISEO C	BOX 188 - BAYAMON PR 00619
58- 77	RODRIGUEZ, FERNANDO PEDRO	OLD ADD: 555 MAYIA RODRIGUEZ - HAVANA CUBA
16- 71	RODRIGUEZ, JOSE	D. MARCH 23, 1948 HAVANA, CUBA
67- 92	RODRIGUEZ, ROBERTO MUNOZ	CORTIJITO DESARRIAS-8 CJN RECOBE30-CARACAS VZ
38- 83	ROE, ELWIN CHARLES	936 NICHOLAS DR - WEST PLAINS MO 65775
23-110	ROE, JAMES CLAY	D. APRIL 3, 1956 CLEVELAND, MISS.
55-101	ROEBUCK, EDWARD JACK	3434 WARWOOD RD - LAKEWOOD CA 90712
76- 83	ROENICKE, GARY STEVEN	1017 W SERVICE AVE - WEST COVINA CA 91790
81-107	ROENICKE, RONALD JON	1017 W SERVICE - WEST COVINA CA 91790
23-111	ROETTGER, OSCAR FREDERICK LOUIS	11566 POGEMOELLER LN - ST LOUIS MO 63108
27- 75	ROETTGER, WALTER HENRY	D. SEPTEMBER 14, 1951 CHAMPAIGN, ILL.
29- 89	ROETZ, EDWARD BERNARD	D. MARCH 16, 1965 PHILADELPHIA, PA.
38- 84	ROGALSKI, JOSEPH ANTHONY	D. NOVEMBER 20, 1951 ASHLAND, WIS.
25- 88	ROGELL, WILLIAM GEORGE	17214 GLASTON BURY RD - DETROIT MI 48219

```
4-180  ROGERS, JAY LOUIS            D. JULY 18 1964 CARLISLE, PA.
8- 85  ROGERS, LEE OTIS             4920 HAWTHORNE RD LITTLE ROCK AR 72207
5- 94  ROGERS, ORLIN WOODROW        RR ONE BOX 222  - BLAIRS VA 24527
8- 86  ROGERS, STANLEY FRANK        964 WALNUT ST ELMIRA NY 14901
3-101  ROGERS, STEPHEN DOUGLAS      2335 E BERKELEY - SPRINGFIELD MO 65804
7- 71  ROGERS, THOMAS ANDREW        D. MARCH 7, 1936 NASHVILLE, TENN.
5-138  ROGGE, FRANCIS CLINTON       D. JANUARY 6, 1969 MOUNT CLEMENS, MICH.
3- 99  ROGGENBURK, GARRY EARL       3482 W 150TH ST - CLEVELAND OH 44111
3-102  ROGODZINSKI, MICHAEL GEORGE  7 TICONDEROGA - LAUREL SPRINGS NJ 08021
9- 75  ROGOVIN, SAUL WALTER         420 W 24TH DR - NEW YORK NY 10011
7- 93  ROHR, LESLIE NORVIN          1340 WICKS LN - BILLINGS MT 89105
7- 94  ROHR, WILLIAM JOSEPH         429 HELIOTROPE - NEWPORT BEACH CA 92661
1- 89  ROHWER, RAY                  BOX 331 - DIXON CA 95620
3- 77  ROIG, ANTON AMBROSE          23310 INLET DR #12 - LIBERTY LAKE WA 99019
6- 77  ROJAS, MINERVINO ALEJANDRO LANDIN 7101A PLASKA-HUNTINGTON PARK CA 90255
2-116  ROJAS, OCTAVIO               15245 MELROSE DR - STANLEY KS 66221
2- 87  ROJEK, STANLEY ANDREW        288 STENZIL ST - NORTH TONAWANDA NY 14120
2-117  ROLAND, JAMES IVAN           %I.ROLAND,8420 STUFF DR - ORLANDO FL 32809
1- 74  ROLFE, ROBERT ABIAL          D. JULY 8, 1969 GILFORD, N. H.
2-167  ROLLINGS, RAYMOND COPELAND   D. AUGUST 25, 1966 ST.PAUL, MINN.
7- 76  ROLLINGS, WILLIAM RUSSELL    D. DECEMBER 31, 1964 MOBILE, ALA.
1- 92  ROLLINS, RICHARD JOHN        2751 E WALLINGS RD - BROADVIEW HGTS OH 44147
4- 95  ROMAN, WILLIAM ANTHONY       4318 FAWN CT - CROSS PLAINS WI 53528
0- 83  ROMANO, JAMES KING           233 BURLINGTON AVE - DEER PARK NY 11729
8- 78  ROMANO, JOHN ANTHONY         7 TANGLEWOOD HOLLOW-UPPER SADDLE RIVERNJ07458
4- 94  ROMBERGER, ALLEN IRVING      KLINGERSTOWN PA 17941
7-121  ROMERO, EDGARDO RALPH        CALLE 6 BLOQUE 2 #6 - CAROLINA PR 00630
0-100  ROMMEL, EDWIN AMERICUS       D. AUGUST 26, 1970 BALTIMORE, MD.
7-122  ROMO, ENRIQUE                AVENIDA S N CARLOS #923-TORREON COAHULIA MEX
8- 88  ROMO, VICENTE                CALLE 32 AVENIDA 17 #45 - GUAYAMAS, SONORA MX
3- 78  ROMONOSKY, JOHN              1078 INNIS AVE - COLUMBUS OH 43207
3-151  RONDEAU, HENRI JOSEPH        D. MAY 28 1943 WOONSOCKET , R.I.
6- 84  RONDON, GILBERT              1836 WATSON AVE #3E - BRONX NY 10472
1-108  ROOF, EUGENE LAWRENCE        RR 10 BOX 223 - PADUCAH KY 42001
1- 93  ROOF, PHILLIP ANTHONY        RR 1 BOX 402 - BOAZ KY 42027
8- 89  ROOKER, JAMES PHILIP         1684 CITATION DR - LIBRARY PA 15129
4-181  ROONEY, FRANK                D. APRIL 6, 1977 BESSEMER, MICH.
1-109  ROONEY, PATRICK EUGENE       925 S WALNUT - ARLINGTON HEIGHTS IL 60005
3-112  ROOT, CHARLES HENRY          D. NOVEMBER 5, 1970 HOLLISTER, CAL.
0-116  ROQUE, JORGE                 BO SAN ANTON #135 - PONCE PR 00731
7-123  ROSADO, LUIS (ROBLES)        CALLE 26 BLQ 13 LOT 12-CAROLINA PR 00630
9- 98  ROSAR, WARREN VINCENT        733 EGGERT RD-BUFFALO NY 14215
1- 89  ROSARIO, ANGEL RAMON         CALLE 1 #421 HERNANDES DAVILA-BAYAMON PR00619
5- 92  ROSARIO, SANTIAGO            1972 ADD: VILLA GRILLASCA D.5B - PONCE PR
```

```
1- 90  ROSE, DONALD GARY            1272 PASEO DORADO - SAN DIMAS CA 91773
3-100  ROSE, PETER EDWARD           5946 COUNTRY HILLS - CINCINNATI OH 45238
7- 75  ROSEBORO, JOHN JUNIOR        1703 VIRGINIA RD - LOS ANGELES CA 90019
5-102  ROSELLI, ROBERT EDWARD       1548 HEMLOCK AVE - SAN MATEO CA 94401
2- 93  ROSELLO, DAVID               PAZ 160 - BO PARIS - MAYAGUEZ PR 00708
7- 74  ROSEN, ALBERT LEONARD        BOX 288 - HOUSTON TX 77001
7- 91  ROSEN, GOODWIN GEORGE        120 SHELBURNE AVE #1205 TORONTO ONT
0- 68  ROSENBERG, HARRY             23 MEADOWBROOK DR - SAN FRANCISCO CA 94127
3-113  ROSENBERG, LOUIS C           320 ALEMANY BLVD - SAN FRANCISCO CA 94110
1- 75  ROSENFELD, MAX               D. MARCH 10, 1969 MIAMI, FLA.
6- 80  ROSENTHAL, LAWRENCE JOHN     1335 WHITE BEAR AVE - ST. PAUL MN 55106
5- 89  ROSENTHAL, SIMON             D. APRIL 7, 1969 BOSTON, MASS.
```

44-114 ROSER, EMERSON COREY	1714 BURRSTONE RD - NEW HARTFORD NY 13413
22-118 ROSER, JOHN JOSEPH	D. MAY 6, 1979 ROCKY HILL, CONN.
24- 90 ROSS, CHESTER FRANKLIN	822 W LEE ST - MAYFIELD KY 42066
39- 99 ROSS, CHESTER JAMES	2454 SENECA ST - BUFFALO NY 14220
54- 95 ROSS, CLIFFORD DAVID	2581 ROSEWOOD - ROSLYN PA 19001
38- 87 ROSS, DONALD RAYMOND	416 S OLD RANCH RD ARCADIA CA 91006
50- 84 ROSS, FLOYD ROBERT	2245 E VERMONT - ANAHEIM CA 92806
68- 90 ROSS, GARY DOUGLAS	7985 LA BRUSCA WAY - CARLSBAD NM 92008
18- 63 ROSS, GEORGE SIDNEY	D. APRIL 22, 1935 AMITYVILLE, N. Y.
36- 81 ROSS, LEE RAVON	RR 2 ALBEMARLE NC 28001
52- 87 ROSSI, JOSEPH ANTHONY	934 STANNAGE AVE - ALBANY CA 97406
44-115 ROSSO, FRANCIS JAMES	65 BROZ TERRACE - FEEDING HILLS MA 61030
48- 86 ROTBLATT, MARVIN JOSEPH	180 N LASALLE ST - CHICAGO IL 60601
14-182 ROTH, ROBERT FRANK	D. SEPTEMBER 11, 1936 CHICAGO, ILL.
45- 87 ROTHEL, ROBERT BURTON	40259 BUTTERNUT RIDGE DR - ELYRIA OH 44035
25- 90 ROTHROCK JOHN HOUSTON	D. FEBRUARY 2, 1980 SAN BERNARDINO, CALIF.
81-110 ROTHSCHILD, LAWRENCE LEE	1136 BREABURN ST - FLOSSMOR IL 60422
70-117 ROUNSAVILLE, VIRL GENE	2901 LONE TREE WAY - ANTIOCH CA 94509
13-152 ROUSH, EDD J.	122 S MAIN ST - OAKLAND CITY IN 47560
11-146 ROWAN, DAVID	D. JULY 30, 1955 TORONTO, ONT.
63-101 ROWE, DONALD HOWARD	19791 SCENIC BAY LN-HUNTINGTON BEACH CA 9264
16- 72 ROWE, HARLAND STIMSON	D. MAY 26, 1969 SPRINGVALE, ME.
63-102 ROWE, KENNETH DARRELL	2244 E PEACH FORD RD - CHAMBLEE GA 30341
33- 56 ROWE, LYNWOOD THOMAS	D. JANUARY 8, 1961 EL DORADO, ARK.
39-100 ROWELL, CARVEL WILLIAM	CITRONELLE ALABAMA 36522
23-114 ROWLAND, CHARLIE LELAND	HIGHWAY 64 RR 2 - WENDELL NC 27591
15-139 ROWLAND, CLARENCE HENRY	D. MAY 17, 1969 CHICAGO, ILL.
80-113 ROWLAND, MICHAEL EVAN	6425 EAST VIRGINIA - SCOTTSDALE AZ 85257
33- 57 ROY, EMILE ARTHUR	OLD ADD: RR 1 BOX 57 - CRYSTAL RIVER FL
46- 90 ROY, JEAN PIERRE	BOX 500, STATION R - MONTREAL 326, QUEBEC
24- 91 ROY, LUTHER FRANKLIN	D. JULY 24, 1963 GRAND RAPIDS, MICH.
50- 85 ROY, NORMAN BROOKS	BOX 116 - BEDFORD MA 01730
73-103 ROYSTER, JERON KENNIS	2933 PANTHERSVILLE RD NT-22-DECATUR GA 30034
81-111 ROYSTER, WILLIE ARTHUR	229 55TH ST NE - WASHINGTON DC 20019
50- 86 ROZEK, RICHARD LOUIS	BOX 249 - CEDAR RAPIDS IA 52406
77-124 ROZEMA, DAVID SCOTT	2609 52ND ST - WYOMING MI 49509
64- 96 ROZNOVSKY, VICTOR JOSEPH	1686 W BULLARD - FRESNO CA 93711
40- 76 RUBELING, ALNERT WILLIAM	3054 OAK FOREST DR-BALTIMORE MD 21234
69-151 RUBERTO, JOHN EDWARD	3264 ACACIA DR - INDIANAPOLIS IN 46224
66- 78 RUBIO, JORGE JESUS	1001 LERDO AVE - MEXICALI BAJA CA
27- 77 RUBLE, WILLIAM ARTHUR	709 NEFF ST - MARYVILLE TN 37801
81-112 RUCKER, DAVID MICHAEL	130 E RANDALL - RIALTO CA 92376
40- 77 RUCKER, JOHN JOEL	RED PEBBLE FARM-MOULTRIE GA 31768
67- 95 RUDI, JOSEPH ODEN	BOX 98 - LAGUNA BEACH CA 92652
45- 88 RUDOLPH, ERNEST WILLIAM	RR 2 BOX 14A - BLACK RIVER FALLS WI 54615
57- 76 RUDOLPH, FREDERICK DONALD	D. SEPTEMBER 12, 1968 ENCINO, CAL.
69-152 RUDOLPH, KENNETH VICTOR	OLD ADD: 11815 KINGSFORT PL #1-FLORISSANT MO
10-128 RUDOLPH, RICHARD	D. OCTOBER 20, 1949 BRONX, N.Y.
15-140 RUEL, HEROLD DOMINIC	D. NOVEMBER 13, 1963 PALO ALTO, CALIF.
17- 72 RUETHER, WALTER HENRY	D. MAY 16, 1970 PHOENIX, ARIZ.
49- 76 RUFER, RUDOLPH JOSEPH	649 CORNWELL AVE - MALVERNE NY 11565
24- 92 RUFFING, CHARLES HERBERT	25382 CONCORD DRIVE - CLEVELAND O 44122
74-115 RUHLE, VERNON GERALD	34637 WOOD DR - LIVONIA MI 48154
64- 97 RUIZ, HIRALDO SABLON	D. FEBRUARY 9, 1972 SAN DIEGO, CALIF.
78-115 RUIZ, MANUEL	TAPIA 267 - SANTUCE PR 00912
43-119 RULLO, JOSEPH VINCENT	D. OCTOBER 28, 1969 PHILADELPHIA, PA.
14-183 RUMLER, WILLIAM GEORGE	D. MAY 26, 1966 LINCOLN, NEB.
81-113 RUNGE, PAUL WILLIAM	646 DELAWARE AVE - KINGSTON NY 12401
51- 82 RUNNELS, JAMES EDWARD	1106 WILMA-LOIS ST - PASADENA TX 77502
25- 91 RUSH, JESS HOWARD	D. MARCH 16, 1969 FRESNO, CAL.
48- 87 RUSH, ROBERT RANSOM	1358 E 1ST PLACE - MESA AZ 85201
15-141 RUSSELL, ALLAN E.	D. OCTOBER 20, 1972 BALTIMORE, MD.
10-129 RUSSELL, CLARENCE DICKSON	D. JANUARY 22, 1962 BALTIMORE, MD.
13-153 RUSSELL, EWELL ALBERT	D. SEPTEMBER 30, 1973 INDIANAPOLIS, IND.
39-101 RUSSELL, GLEN DAVID	D. SEPTEMBER 26, 1976 LOS ANGELES CAL.

aNSTON

14-184 RUSSELL, HARVEY HOLMES	D. JANUARY 8, 1980 ALEXANDRIA, VA.
26- 72 RUSSELL, JACK ERWIN	BOX 748 - CLEARWATER FL 33515
42- 88 RUSSELL, JAMES WILLIAM	OLD ADD: RR ONE - BELLE VERNON PA
17- 73 RUSSELL, JOHN ALBERT	D. NOVEMBER 19, 1930 ELY, NEV.
38- 88 RUSSELL, LOYD OPAL	D. MAY 24, 1968 WACO, TEX.
69-153 RUSSELL, WILLIAM ELLIS	6081 SADDLETREE LN - YORBA LINDA CA 92686
39-102 RUSSO, MARIUS UGO	27 NORFOLK DR-ELMONT NY 11714
66- 79 RUSTECK, RICHARD FRANK	6315 SW PEYTON RD - PORTLAND OR 97219

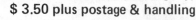

HIGHLY AUTOGRAPHABLE CARD SETS
NONE MARRED BY OBVERSE PRINTING

NEW SET!! slightly larger than postcards
BEAUTIFUL COLOR
18 HALL OF FAMERS
LIVING AS OF PRINTING DATE OF THIS BOOK
$ 3.50 plus postage & handling

POSTCARD SET
20-card set

ORDER FROM:
DEN'S COLLECTORS DEN
P.O. BOX 606
LAUREL, MD 20707

Postage & Handling
.01 to $ 20.00 add $ 2.00
$20.01 to $ 30.00 add $ 2.50
$ 30.01 or more add $ 3.00

U. S. FUNDS ONLY

ADD Postage & Handling to all orders

THE 1960's—Series No. 2
89 CARDS IN FULL COLOR

More of the great stars and many
the obscure players from the
decade of the 60's

COMPLETE 2nd SERIES
89 Cards

$ 10.00
per set
plus postage
handling

1ST SERIES
STILL AVAILABLE
293 CARDS
$ 15.00

SEE PAGE 149 for ADDITIONAL SET

121

RUSZOWSKI   SANCHEZ

```
44-116  RUSZKOWSKI, HENRY ALEXANDER   8815 HARVARD AVE - CLEVELAND OH 44105
14-185  RUTH, GEORGE HERMAN           D. AUGUST 16, 1948 NEW YORK, N.Y.
10-130  RUTHERFORD, JAMES HOLLIS      D. SEPTEMBER 18, 1956 LAKEWOOD, O.
52- 88  RUTHERFORD, JOHN WILLIAM      16100 WOODLAND DR - DEARBORN MI 48120
73-104  RUTHVEN, RICHARD DAVID        2940 BRIDLEWOOD DR - PALM HARBOR FL 33563
47- 75  RUTNER, MILTON MICKEY         14 SHOTGUN LN - LEVITTOWN NY 11756
42- 89  RYAN, CORNELIUS JOSEPH        626 BEAU CHENE N - MANDERVILLE LA 70448
12-168  RYAN, JOHN BUDD               D. JULY 9, 1956 SACRAMENTO, CALIF.
30- 69  RYAN, JOHN COLLINS            D. NOVEMBER 28, 1959 SWAMPSCOTT, MASS.
29- 90  RYAN, JOHN FRANCIS            D. SEPTEMBER 2, 1967 ROCHESTER, MINN.
66- 80  RYAN, LYNN NOLAN              BOX 409 - ALVIN TX 77511
64- 98  RYAN, MICHAEL JAMES           RR 2 BOX 534 - PLAISTOW NH 03865
19- 71  RYAN, WILFRED PATRICK DOLAN   D. DECEMBER 10, 1980 PHOENIX, ARIZ.
35- 95  RYBA, DOMINIC JOSEPH          D. DECEMBER 13, 1971 SPRINGFIELD, MO.
```

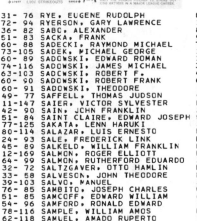

```
31- 76  RYE, EUGENE RUDOLPH            OLD ADD: 8213 N CRIOLE - NILES IL 60649
72- 94  RYERSON, GARY LAWRENCE        1059 TERRACE CT - EL CAJON CA 92040
36- 82  SABO, ALEXANDER               816 ANCHOR DR - FORKED DRIVE NJ 08731
51- 83  SACKA, FRANK                  968 SYCAMORE ST - WYANDOTTE MI 48192
60- 88  SADECKI, RAYMOND MICHAEL      7710 EVERETT - KANSAS CITY KS 66112
73-105  SADEK, MICHAEL GEORGE         1030 ROSSI WAY - SAN MATEO CA 94403
60- 89  SADOWSKI, EDWARD ROMAN        11181 CLARISSA ST - GARDEN GROVE CA 92640
74-116  SADOWSKI, JAMES MICHAEL       3909 LIBERTY AVE - PITTSBURGH PA 15224
63-103  SADOWSKI, ROBERT F.           4053 ASHENTREE DR - CHAMBLEE GA 30341
60- 90  SADOWSKI, ROBERT FRANK        632 DENNISON DR - BALLWIN MO 63011
60- 91  SADOWSKI, THEODORE            196 ALMA ST - PITTSBURGH 15223 PA
49- 77  SAFFELL, THOMAS JUDSON        420 GOLDEN GATE POINT #11 - SARASOTA FL 335
11-147  SAIER, VICTOR SYLVESTER       D. MAY 14, 1967 EAST LANSING, MICH.
42- 90  SAIN, JOHN FRANKLIN           25707 AVE LATOUR - OAKBROOK IL 60521
51- 84  SAINT CLAIRE, EDWARD JOSEPH   52 CHAMPLAIN AVE - WHITEHALL NY 12887
77-125  SAKATA, LENN HARUKI           3060 MARIE CT - MERCED CA 95340
80-114  SALAZAR, LUIS ERNESTO         PRINC. DE HUACARAPA 34-HUARENAS MIRANDA VENE
24- 93  SALE, FREDERICK LINK          D. MAY 27, 1956 HERMOSA BEACH, CAL.
45- 89  SALKELD, WILLIAM FRANKLIN     D. APRIL 22, 1967 LOS ANGELES, CAL.
12-169  SALMON, ROGER ELLIOTT         D. JUNE 17, 1974 BELFAST, ME.
64- 99  SALMON, RUTHERFORD EDUARDO    3422 SYLVANHURST RD - CLEVELAND OH 44112
32- 72  SALTZGAVER, OTTO HAMLIN       D. FEBRUARY 2, 1978 KEOKUK, IA.
33- 58  SALVESON, JOHN THEODORE       D. DECEMBER 28, 1974 NORWALK, CALIF.
39-103  SALVO, MANUEL                 3541 WOODBROOK DR - NAPA CA 94558
76- 85  SAMBITO, JOSEPH CHARLES       ONE KEY CAPRI #501E - TREASURE ISLAND FL3370
51- 85  SAMCOFF, EDWARD WILLIAM       6514 S HERITAGE PL E - ENGLEWOOD CO 80111
54- 96  SAMFORD, RONALD EDWARD        1325 W CANTERBURY CT - DALLAS TX 75208
78-116  SAMPLE, WILLIAM AMOS          BOX 225 - SALEM VA 24153
62-118  SAMUEL, AMADO RUPERTO         1931 YALE DR - LOUISVILLE KY 40205
30- 70  SAMUELS, JOSEPH JONES         9 HOWELL - BATH NY 14810
23-115  SANBERG, GUSTAVE E.           D. FEBRUARY 3, 1930 LOS ANGELES, CAL.
72- 95  SANCHEZ, CELERINO             AV. COYOCAN 351 - COL DEL VALLE MEXICO 12 DF
81-114  SANCHEZ, LUIS MERCEDES        CALLE SAN FELIPE 11-CARIACO.EST. SUCRE VENE
```

(SEE PAGE 149)

Sincerely
Babe Ruth

122

```
81-115  SANCHEZ, ORLANDO              BOX SAN ISODRO P-52 - CANOVANAS PR 00629
52- 89  SANCHEZ, RAUL GUADALUPE       17821 NW 56TH AVE - CORAL CITY FL 33054
23-116  SAND, JOHN HENRY              D. NOVEMBER 3, 1958 SAN FRANCISCO, CAL.
81-116  SANDBERG, RYNE DEE            723 W AUGUSTA AVE - SPOKANE WA 99205
45- 90  SANDERS, DEE WILMA            1312 COUNTRY CLUB RD - MCALESTER OK 74501
65- 93  SANDERS, JOHN FRANK           2310 CAMELOT CT - LINCOLN NE 68512
64-100  SANDERS, KENNETH GEORGE       12141 PARKVIEW LN - HALES CORNERS WI 53130
42- 91  SANDERS, RAYMOND FLOYD        3120A PROVIDENCE PL - ST LOUIS MO 63111
74-117  SANDERS, REGINALD JEROME      5281 NEWPORT - DETROIT MI 48213
17- 74  SANDERS, ROY GARVIN           D. JANUARY 17, 1950 KANSAS CITY, MO.
18- 64  SANDERS, ROY L.               OLD ADD: 525 S THIRD ST - LOUISVILLE KY 40202
78-117  SANDERSON, SCOTT DOUGLAS      1271 WENDY DR - NORTHBROOK IL 60062
42- 92  SANDLOCK, MICHAEL JOSEPH      18 ROCK LAND PL-OLD GREENWICH CT 06870
67- 96  SANDS, CHARLES DUANE          BOX 6656 - CHARLOTTESVILLE VA 22906
75-102  SANDT, THOMAS JAMES           3661 GLACIER CT - PLEASANTON CA 94566
40- 78  SANFORD, JOHN DOWARD          1001 KINON ST-WILSON NC 27893
43-120  SANFORD, JOHN FREDERICK       1046 WEST 600 NORTH - SALT LAKE CITY UT 84116
56- 74  SANFORD, JOHN STANLEY         GENERAL DELIVERY - MARSHFIELD HILLS MA 02051
67- 97  SANGUILLEN, MANUEL DE JESUS   OLD ADD: 351 S RIDGE DR-UPPER ST CLAIR PA
49- 78  SANICKI, EDWARD ROBERT        12 BARTON RD - OLD BRIDGE NJ 08857
29- 91  SANKEY, BENJAMIN TURNER       BOX 661 - BREWTON AL 36426
54- 97  SANTIAGO, JOSE GUILLERMO      56-SE-NO. 1167 - RIO PIEDRAS PR 00921
63-104  SANTIAGO, JOSE RAFAEL         BOX 211 - JUANA DIAZ PR 00665
79- 98  SANTO DOMINGO, RAFAEL         BOX 277--OROCOVIS PR 00720
60- 92  SANTO, RONALD EDWARD          2000 VALLEY LA - GLENVIEW IL 60025
68- 91  SANTORINI, ALAN JOEL          2279 STECHER AVE - UNION NJ 07083
21- 90  SARGENT, JOSEPH ALEXANDER     D. JULY 5, 1950 ROCHESTER, N. Y.
76- 86  SARMIENTO, MANUEL EDUARDO     AVE DIAZ MORENO #90-13-VALENCIA CARABOBO VENE
51- 86  SARNI, WILLIAM F              11726 LINDEMERE DR - KIRKWOOD MO 63131
61- 94  SATRIANO, THOMAS VICTOR       4816 LOS FELIZ BLVD - LOS ANGELES CA 90027
51- 87  SAUCIER, FRANCIS FIELD        1408 BLUEBONNET LN - BORGER TX 79007
78-118  SAUCIER, KEVIN ANDREW         202 ADA WILSON AVE - PENSACOLA FL 32507
43-121  SAUER, EDWARD                 8625 FENWICK #21 - SUNLAND CA 91040
41- 97  SAUER, HENRY JOHN             207 VALLEJO CT - MILLBRAE CA 94030
70-118  SAUNDERS, DENNIS JAMES        OLD ADD: 18520 RIO SECO C - ROWLAND HGTS CA
27- 78  SAUNDERS, RUSSELL COLLIER     D. NOVEMBER 24, 1967 DOVER TWP.,OCEAN CO,N.J.
44-117  SAVAGE, DONALD ANTHONY        D. DECEMBER 25, 1961 MONTCLAIR, N. J.
12-170  SAVAGE, JAMES HAROLD          D. JUNE 26, 1940 NEW CASTLE, PA.
42- 93  SAVAGE, JOHN ROBERT           296 HOWARD ST - BERLIN NH 03570
62-119  SAVAGE, THEODORE EPHESIAN     4311 DRYDEN CT - ST LOUIS MO 63115
59- 70  SAVERINE, ROBERT PAUL         228 SLICE DR - STAMFORD CT 06907
29- 92  SAVIDGE, DONALD SNYDER        OLD ADD: 7979 W NORTON AVE #4 - LOS ANGELES
54- 98  SAVRANSKY, MORRIS             2178 CEDARVIEW DR - CLEVELAND OH 44121
48- 88  SAWATSKI, CARL ERNEST         1501 N UNIVERSITY #412 - LITTLE ROCK AR 72207
15-142  SAWYER, CARL EVERETT          D. JANUARY 17, 1957 LOS ANGELES, CALIF.
48- 89  SAWYER, EDWIN MILBY           BOX 296 - VALLEY FORGE PA 19481
74-118  SAWYER, RICHARD CLYDE         3219 KAIBAB - BAKERSFIELD CA 93306
28- 79  SAX, ERIK LOUIS               23 SHEPHERD PLACE - ARLINTON NJ 07032
81-117  SAX, STEPHEN LOUIS            RR 1 BOX 5120 HART AVE-WEST SACRAMENTOCA.KL.U
39-104  SAYLES, WILLIAM NISBETH       2830 NE LAKE DR - LINCOLN CITY OR 97367
48- 90  SCALA, GERARD DANIEL          19 BERNADOTTE CT - PERRY HALL MD 21128
39-105  SCALZI, FRANK JOSEPH          ZANE KNOLL - MARTINS FERRY OH 43935
31- 77  SCALZI, JOHN ANTHONY          D. SEPTEMBER 27, 1962 PORT CHESTER, N. Y.
74-119  SCANLON, JAMES PATRICK        7400 PORTLAND AVE S - RICHFIELD MN 55423
56- 75  SCANTLEBURY, PATRICIO ATHELSTAN  47 WOODLAND AVE - MONTCLAIR NJ 07042
79- 99  SCARBERY, RANDY JAMES         5010 EAST LEWIS - FRESNO CA 93727
42- 94  SCARBOROUGH, RAY WILSON       BOX 448-MOUNT OLIVE NC 28365
```

Gus Sandberg

```
72- 96  SCARCE, GUERRANT MCCURDY      1708 BROADMOOR DR - RICHMOND VA 23221
29- 93  SCARRITT, RUSSELL MALLORY     429 POU STATION RD - PENSACOLA FL 32507
35- 96  SCARSELLA, LESLIE GEORGE      D. DECEMBER 16, 1958 SAN FRANCISCO, CAL.
64-101  SCHAAL, PAUL                  416 N IRONWOOD DR - MESA AZ 85201
11- 72  SCHACHT, ALEXANDER            397B HERITAGE VILLAGE - SOUTHBURY CONN 06488
50- 87  SCHACHT, SIDNEY               783 NW 30TH AVE - DELRAY BEACH FL 33445
45- 91  SCHACKER, HAROLD              4609 NORTH MATANZAS AVE - TAMPA FL 33614
52- 90  SCHAEFFER, HARRY EDWARD       412 WHEATLAND AVE - SHILLINGTON PA 19607
72- 97  SCHAEFFER, MARK PHILIP        12220 KRISTOPHER PL - NORTHRIDGE CA 91321
61- 95  SCHAFFER, JIMMIE RONALD       655 BIRCH TER - COOPERSBURG PA 18036
59- 71  SCHAFFERNOTH, JOSEPH ARTHUR   20 MARIAN AVE - BERKLEY HEIGHTS NJ 07922
58- 79  SCHAIVE, JOHN EDWARD          37 GROTON DR - SPRINGFIELD IL 62704
32- 73  SCHALK, LEROY JOHN            RR 3 BROADWAY MANOR - GAINESVILLE TX 76240
12-171  SCHALK, RAYMOND WILLIAM       D. MAY 19, 1970 CHICAGO, ILL.
11-148  SCHALLER, WALTER              D. OCTOBER 9, 1939 EMERYVILLE, CALIF.
51- 88  SCHALLOCK, ARTHUR LAWRENCE    155 CREST RD - NOVATO CA 94947
14-186  SCHANG, ROBERT MARTIN         D. AUGUST 29, 1966 SACRAMENTO, CALIF.
```

13-154	SCHANG, WALTER HENRY	D. MARCH 6, 1965 ST. LOUIS, MO.
44-118	SCHANZ, CHARLEY MURRELL	2217 MEER WAY - SACRAMENTO CA 95822
11-149	SCHARDT, WILBURT	D. JULY 20, 1964 VERMILION, O.
32- 74	SCHAREIN, ARTHUR OTTO	D. JULY 3, 1969 SAN ANTONIO, TEX.
37- 92	SCHAREIN, GEORGE ALBERT	1826 E DECATUR ST - DECATUR IL 62521
81-118	SCHATTINGER, JEFFERY CHAS.	1322 W SAN MADELE - FRESNO CA 93711
77-126	SCHATZEDER, DANIEL ERNEST	33 E MADISON ST - VILLA PARK IL 60181
13-155	SCHAUER, ALEXANDER JOHN	D. APRIL 15, 1957 MINNEAPOLIS, MINN#
13-156	SCHEER, ALLAN G.	D. MAY 6, 1959 LOGANSPORT, IND.
22-119	SCHEER, HENRY	D. MARCH 21, 1976 NEW HAVEN, CONN.
14-187	SCHEEREN, FREDERICK	D. JUNE 17, 1973 OIL CITY, PA.
43-122	SCHEETZ, OWEN FRANKLIN	275 ROBIN LN - REYNOLDSBURG OH 43068
41- 98	SCHEFFING, ROBERT BODEN	6117 E EXETER BLVD - SCOTTSDALE AZ 85251
12-172	SCHEGG, (GILBERT EUGENE PRICE)	D. FEBRUARY 27, 1963 NILES, O.
43-123	SCHEIB, CARL ALVIN	2922 OLD RANCH RD - SAN ANTONIO TX 78217
65- 94	SCHEINBLUM, RICHARD ALAN	10141 OLD RANCH CIR - VILLA PARK CA 92667
54- 99	SCHELL, CLYDE DANIEL	D. MAY 11, 1972 MAYVILLE, MICH.
39-106	SCHELLE, GERARD ANTHONY	7501 FAR HILLS DR - BALTIMORE MD 21204
23-117	SCHEMANSKE, FREDERICK GEORGE	D. FEBRUARY 18, 1960 DETROIT, MICH.
45- 92	SCHEMER, MICHAEL	7825 BAYSHORE CT #503 - MIAMI FL 33138
13-157	SCHENEBERG, JOHN BLUFORD	D. SEPTEMBER 7, 1950 HUNTINGTON, W. VA.
46- 91	SCHENZ, HENRY LEONARD	4055 LANSDOWNE AVE - CINCINNATI OH 45236
19- 73	SCHEPNER, JOSEPH MARTIN	D. JULY 25, 1959 MOBILE, ALA.
50- 88	SCHERBARTH, ROBERT ELMER	4858 N 61ST ST - MILWAUKEE WI 53218
69-164	SCHERMAN, FREDERICK JOHN	11546 STECK RD RT#1 - BROOKVILLE OH 45309
31- 78	SCHESLER, CHARLES	D. NOVEMBER 19, 1953 HARRISBURG, PA.
10-131	SCHETTLER, LOUIS MARTIN	D. MAY 1, 1960 YOUNGSTOWN, O.
17- 75	SCHICK, MAURICE FRANCIS	D. OCTOBER 25, 1979 HAZEL CREST, ILL.
61- 96	SCHILLING, CHARLES THOMAS	8 VILLAGE WAY - SMITHTOWN NY 11787
22-120	SCHILLING, ELBERT ISAIAH	D. JANUARY 7, 1954 OKLAHOMA CITY, OKLA.
20-101	SCHINDLER, WILLIAM GIBBONS	D. FEBRUARY 6, 1979 PERRYVILLE, MO.
14-188	SCHIRICK, HARRY ERNEST	D. NOVEMBER 12, 1968 KINGSTON, N.Y.
65- 95	SCHLESINGER, WILLIAM CORDES	5708 ABELIA COURT - CINCINNATI OH 45213
23-118	SCHLIEBNER, FREDERICK PAUL	D. APRIL 15, 1975 TOLEDO, O.
71- 91	SCHLUETER, JAYD	20 CANDLEWOOD - WALNUT CREEK CA 94595
38- 89	SCHLUETER, NORMAN JOHN	4205 ATLANTIC #F-4-NEW SMYRNA BEACH FL 32069
15-143	SCHMANDT, RAYMOND HENRY·	D. FEBRUARY 1, 1969 ST. LOUIS, MO.
52- 91	SCHMEES, GEORGE EDWARD	2803 MONTE CRESTA WAY - SAN JOSE CA 95132
67- 98	SCHMELZ, ALAN GEORGE	9670 LANNETT AVE - WHITTIER CA 90605
81-119	SCHMIDT, DAVID FREDERICK	26636 PORTALES - MISSION VIEJO CA 92675
81-120	SCHMIDT, DAVID JOSEPH	9511 CAMEDO AVE - NORTHRIDGE CA 91324
44-119	SCHMIDT, FREDERICK ALBERT	WINFIELD ST - EMMAUS PA 18049
13-158	SCHMIDT, HERMAN	B. ST. LOUIS, MO.
72- 98	SCHMIDT, MICHAEL JACK	24 LAKEWOOD DR - MEDIA PA 19063
58- 80	SCHMIDT, ROBERT BENJAMIN	9 HARDWOOD ST - ST CHARLES MO 63301
16- 73	SCHMIDT, WALTER JOSEPH	D. JULY 4, 1973 CERES, CALIF.
52- 92	SCHMIDT, WILLARD RAYMOND	902 CAREY DR - NORMAN OK 73069
41- 99	SCHMITZ, JOHN ALBERT	526 E UNION AVE-WAUSAU WI 54401
43-124	SCHMULBACH, HENRY ALRIVES	29 DALE ALLEN DR - BELLEVILLE IL 62223
14-189	SCHMUTZ, CHARLES OTTO	D. JUNE 27, 1962 SEATTLE, WASH.
72- 99	SCHNECK, DAVID LEE	RR 1 BOX 395 - NORTHAMPTON PA 18067
10-132	SCHNEIBERG, FRANK FREDERICK	D. MAY 18, 1948 MILWAUKEE, WIS.
63-105	SCHNEIDER, DANIEL LOUIS	MUELLER & ASOC., BOX 12648 - TUCSON AZ 85732
81-121	SCHNEIDER, JEFFERY THEODORE	2340 41ST - ROCK ISLAND IL 61201
14-190	SCHNEIDER, PETER JOSEPH	D. JUNE 1, 1957 LOS ANGELES, CALIF.
22-121	SCHNELL, KARL OTTO	130 MELVILLE AVE - PALO ALTO CA 94301
68- 92	SCHOEN, GERALD THOMAS	OLD ADD: 8588 DE INDIAN SCHOOL-SCOTTSDALE AZ
45- 93	SCHOENDIENST, ALBERT FRED	331 LADUE WOODS CT - CREVE COEUR MO 63141
53- 79	SCHOFIELD, JOHN RICHARD	138 CIRCLE DR - SPRINGFIELD IL 62703
55-103	SCHOONMAKER, JERALD LEE	13 CAMBRIDGE CT - LEBANON MO 6553L
15-144	SCHORR, EDWARD WALTER	D. SEPTEMBER 12, 1969 ATLANTIC CITY, N.J.
35- 97	SCHOTT, ARTHUR EUGENE	13902 NEBRASKA AVE TAMPA FL 33612
53- 80	SCHRAMKA, PAUL EDWARD	4155 N 40TH - MILWAUKEE WI 53218
11-150	SCHREIBER, DAVID HENRY	D. OCTOBER 6, 1964 CHILLICOTHE, O.
14-191	SCHREIBER, HENRY WALTER	D. FEBRUARY 23, 1968 INDIANAPOLIS, IND.
22-122	SCHREIBER, PAUL FREDERICK	D. JANUARY 28, 1982 SARASOTA, FLA.
63-106	SCHREIBER, THEODORE HERMAN	144 JEROME RD - STATEN ISLAND NY 10305
65- 96	SCHRODER, ROBERT JAMES	4 DELOND PL - HATTIESBURG MS 39401
58- 81	SCHROLL, ALBERT BRINGHURST	3031 ASBER - ALEXANDRIA LA 71301
80-115	SCHROM, KENNETH MARVIN	425 "G" IRONDALE - EL PASO TX 79912
27- 79	SCHUBLE, HENRY GEORGE	1802 FLORIDA ST - BAYTOWN TX 77520
72-100	SCHUELER, RONALD RICHARD	5737 E COLBY RD - MESA AZ 85205
79-100	SCHULER, DAVID PAUL	4575 SUNSTONE RD - MURRAY UT 84107

```
31- 79  SCHULMERICH, EDWARD WESLEY    135 PICARDY LANE - ALBANY OR 97321
53- 81  SCHULT, ARTHUR WILLIAM        510 WEST LAKE DR - VALHALLA NY 10595
27- 80  SCHULTE, FRED WILLIAM         336 W BOONE ST - BELVIDERE ILL 61008
40- 79  SCHULTE, HERMAN JOSEPH        1655 S RIVER RD-SAINT CHARLES MO 63301
23-119  SCHULTE, JOHN CLEMENT         D. JUNE 28, 1978 ST. LOUIS, MO.
44-120  SCHULTE, LEONARD WILLIAM      5517 BARTON DRIVE - ORLANDO FL 32807
75-103  SCHULTZ, CHARLES BUDD         8410 E JENAN DR - SCOTTSDALE AZ 85253
55-104  SCHULTZ, GEORGE WARREN        790 WOODLANE RD - BEVERLY NJ 08010
43-125  SCHULTZ, HOWARD HENRY         741 N LEXINGTON - ST PAUL MN 55104
12-173  SCHULTZ, JOSEPH CHARLES SR    D. APRIL 13, 1941 COLUMBIA, S.C.
39-107  SCHULTZ, JOSEPH CHARLES       838 COALPORT - ST LOUIS MO 63141
51- 89  SCHULTZ, ROBERT DUFFY         D. MARCH 31, 1979 NASHVILLE, TENN.
24- 94  SCHULTZ, WEBB CARL            BOX 331 - DELAVAN WI 53115
47- 76  SCHULTZ, WILLIAM MICHAEL      502 ROBY AVE - EAST SYRACUSE NY 13057
12-174  SCHULZ, ALBERT CHRISTOPHER    D. DECEMBER 13, 1931 TOLEDO, O.
20-102  SCHLLZ, WALTER FREDERICK      D. FEBRUARY 27, 1928 PRESCOTT, ARIZ.
31- 80  SCHUMACHER, HAROLD HENRY      90 S MAIN ST - DOLGEVILLE NY 13329
13-159  SCHUPP, FERDINAND MAURICE     D. DECEMBER 16, 1971 LOS ANGELES, CALIF.
64-102  SCHURR, WAYNE ALLEN           RR ONE - HUDSON IN 46747
37- 93  SCHUSTER, WILLIAM CHARLES     12700 ELLIOTT AVE #224 - EL MONTE CA 91732
61- 97  SCHWALL, DONALD BERNARD       1770 FERGUSON RD - ALLISON PARK PA 15101
48- 91  SCHWAMB, RALPH RICHARD        1974 ADD: 1348 PINE AVE - LONG BEACH CA 90813
65- 97  SCHWARTZ, DOUGLAS RANDALL     757 EL RANCHO DR - EL CAJON CA 92021
14-192  SCHWARZ, WILLIAM DWIGHT       D. JUNE 24, 1949 JACKSONVILLE BEACH, FLA.
13-160  SCHWENK, HAROLD EDWARD        D. SEPTEMBER 3, 1955 KANSAS CITY, MO.
14-193  SCHWERT, PIUS LOUIS           D. MARCH 11, 1941 WASHINGTON, D.C.
12-175  SCHWIND, ARTHUR EDWIN         D. JANUARY 13, 1968 SULLIVAN ,ILL.
55-105  SCHYPINSKI, GERALD ALBERT     10830 BALFOR AVE - DETROIT MI 48224
80-116  SCIOSCIA, MICHAEL LORRI       36 PROVIDENCE RD - MORTON PA 19070
36- 83  SCOFFIC, LOUIS                600 W 5TH ST JOHNSTON CITY IL 62951
13-161  SCOGGINS, JAMES LYNN          D. AUGUST 16, 1923 COLUMBIA, S.C.
81-122  SCONIERS, DARYL ANTHONY       OLD ADD: 11687 MILLER AVE - FONTANA CA
55-106  SCORE, HERBERT JUDE           RAKIO STATION WWWE - CLEVELAND OH 44101
73-106  SCOTT, ANTHONY                1526 DIXMONT AVE - CINCINNATI OH 45207
26- 73  SCOTT, FLOYD JOHN             D. MAY 3, 1953 DALY CITY, CAL.
66- 81  SCOTT, GEORGE CHARLES         9 KETTLE HOLE RD - FALMOUTH MA 02540
20-103  SCOTT, GEORGE WILLIAM         OLD ADD: CORSICANA TX 75110
14-194  SCOTT, JAMES WALTER           D. MAY 12, 1972 SOUTH PASADENA, FLA.
74-120  SCOTT, JOHN HENRY             1766 E 111TH PLACE - LOS ANGELES CA 90059
16- 74  SCOTT, JOHN WILLIAM           D. NOVEMBER 30 1959 DURHAM, N. C.
39-108  SCOTT, LEGRANT EDWARD         OLD ADD: LAY LAKE - COLUMBIANA AL 35051
14-195  SCOTT, LEWIS EVERETT          D. NOVEMBER 2, 1960 FORT WAYNE, IND.
45- 94  SCOTT, MARSHALL               D. MARCH 3, 1964 HOUSTON, TEX.
72-101  SCOTT, MICHAEL WARREN         5417 WEST 134TH PLACE - HAWTHORNE CA 90250
72-101  SCOTT, RALPH ROBERT           1134 VESTAL AVE - BINGHAMTON NY 13903
63-107  SCOTT, RICHARD LEWIS          124 SHORTLEAF PL - THOMASVILLE GA 31792
75-104  SCOTT, RODNEY DARRELL         9215 SINGING QUAIL DR - AUSTIN TX 78758
75-105  SCRIVENER, WAYNE ALLISON      20925 LAHSER RD #613 - SOUTHFIELD MI 48075
80-117  SCURRY, RODNEY GRANT          130 PRATER WAY - SPARKS NV 89431
64-103  SEALE, JOHNNIE RAY            1941 COUNTY RD 207 - DURANGO CO 81301
79-102  SEAMAN, KIM MICHAEL           4212 KREOLE AVE - MOSS POINT MS 39563
81-123  SEARAGE, RAYMOND MARK         19 FLORIDA ST - DEER PARK NY 11729
43-126  SEARS, KENNETH EUGENE         D. JULY 17, 1968 BRIDGEPORT, TEX.
12-176  SEATON, THOMAS GORDON         D. APRIL 10, 1940 ELPASO, TEX.
40- 80  SEATS, THOMAS EDWARD          2655 45TH AVE-SAN FRANCISCO CA 94116
67- 99  SEAVER, GEORGE THOMAS         LARKSPUR LN - GREENWICH CT 06830
```

```
40- 81  SECORY, FRANK EDWARD          3026 MILITARY ST - PORT HURON MI 48060
69-155  SECRIST, DONALD LAVERN        104 N LEONARD - DUQUOIN IL 62832
21- 91  SEDGWICK, HENRY KENNETH       1425 LOGAN BLVD - ALTOONA PA 16602
19- 74  SEE, CHARLES HENRY            D. JULY 19, 1948 BRIDGEPORT, CONN.
30- 71  SEEDS, ROBERT IRA             STAR RT BOX 152-A - GRAFORD TX 76045
71- 92  SEELBACH, CHARLES FREDERICK   20715 BEACHCLIFF BLVD - ROCKY RIVER OH 44116
43-127  SEEREY, JAMES PATRICK         9256 LEAMONT - ST LOUIS MO 63136
52- 93  SEGRIST, KAL HILL             3813 55TH ST - LUBBOCK TX 79413
62-120  SEGUI, CIEGO PABLO            OLD ADD: 10422 PARALLEL ST - KANSAS CITY KS
79-103  SEIBERT, KURT ELLIOTT         2608 BOEING DR - MIDLAND TX 79701
15-145  SEIBOLD, HARRY                D. SEPTEMBER 21, 1965 PHILADELPHIA, PA.
80-118  SEILHEIMER, RICKY ALLEN       1203 L J STREET - BRENHAM TX 77833
34- 90  SELKIRK, GEORGE ALEXANDER     405 N OCEAN BLVD - POMPANO BEACH FL 33062
22-123  SELL, ELWOOD LESTER           D. FEBRUARY 20, 1961 READING, PA.
10-133  SELLERS, OLIVER               D. JANUARY 14, 1952 PITTSBURGH, PA.
72-102  SELLS, DAVID WAYNE            143 BROWN ST - VACAVILLE CA 95688
65- 98  SELMA, RICHARD JAY            1493 DELMAR AVE - FRESNO CA 93728
```

29- 94	SELPH, CAREY ISOM	D. FEBRUARY 24, 1976 HOUSTON, TEX.
77-128	SEMBER, MICHAEL DAVID	17511 BERNADINE ST - LANSING IL 60438
65- 99	SEMBERA, CARROLL WILLIAM	BOX 654 - SHINER TX 77984
43-128	SEMINICK, ANDREW WASIL	1920 S PARK AVE - MELBOURNE FL 32901
58- 82	SEMPROCH, ROMAN ANTHONY	4220 BUECHNER AVE - CLEVELAND OH 44109
52- 94	SENERCHIA, EMANUEL ROBERT	4 JUDITH CT - OCEAN NJ 07712
77-127	SEOANE, MANUEL MODESTO	4703 N ROME AVE - TAMPA FL 33603
42- 95	SEPKOWSKI, THEODORE WALTER	128 INVERNESS RD - SEVERNA PARK MD 21146
49- 79	SERENA, WILLIAM ROBERT	26777 CALAROGA AVE - HAYWARD CA 94541
81-124	SERNA, PAUL DAVID	1375 CAMINO VERDE - HOLTVILLE CA 92250
77-129	SERUM, GARY WAYNE	710 DOUGLAS - ALEXANDRIA MN 56308
41-100	SESSI, WALTER ANTHONY	351 WEST ST - MOBILE AL 36604
28- 80	SETTLEMIRE, EDGAR MERLE	603 IROQUOIS - BELLEFONTAINE OH 43311
65-100	SEVCIK, JOHN JOSEPH	5321 GOLDEN VLY RD - GOLDEN VALLEY MN 55422
11-151	SEVERAID, HENRY LEVAI	D. DECEMBER 17, 1968 SAN ANTONIO, TEX.
69-156	SEVERINSEN, ALBERT HENRY	1032 ARCHER PL - BALDWIN NY 11510
70-119	SEVERSON, RICHARD ALLEN	15218 LINCOLN CIR - OMAHA NE 68131
43-129	SEWARD, FRANK MARTIN	117 LARCHMONT RD - ELMIRA NY 14905
21- 92	SEWELL, JAMES LUTHER	722 SUNNYSIDE AV - AKRON OH 44303
20-104	SEWELL, JOSEPH WHEELER	1618 DEARING PLACE - TUSCALOOSA ALA 35401
27- 81	SEWELL, THOMAS WESLEY	D. JULY 30, 1956 MONTGOMERY, ALA.
32- 75	SEWELL, TRUETT BANKS	827 RUSSELL DR - PLANT CITY FL 33566
48- 92	SEXAUER, ELMER GEORGE	109 RICHWOOD DR - DANVILLE IN 46122
77-130	SEXTON, JIMMY DALE	RR 2 BOX 187-B - WILMER AL 36587
63-108	SEYFRIED, GORDON CLAY	832 STANLEY AVE - LONG BEACH CA 90804
14-196	SHAFER, RALPH NEWTON	D. FEBRUARY 5, 1950 AKRON, O.
65-101	SHAMSKY, ARTHUR LEWIS	209 DECHERT DR - GULPH ,ILLS PA 19406
73-107	SHANAHAN, PAUL GREGORY	240 W HAWTHORNE ST - EUREKA CA 95501
23-120	SHANER, WALTER DEDAKER	370 E WINDMILL - LAS VEGAS NV 89119
70-120	SHANK, HARVEY TILLMAN	5420 E LAUREL LN - SCOTTSDALE AZ 85254
12-177	SHANKS, HOWARD SAMUEL	D. JULY 30, 1941 MONACA, PA.
12-178	SHANLEY, HENRY ROOT	D. DECEMBER 14, 1934 ST. PETERSBURG, FLA.
20-105	SHANNER, WILFRED WILLIAM	4316 PENNINGTON AVE - EVANSVILLE IN 47712
15-146	SHANNON, JOSEPH ALOYSIUS	D. JULY 28, 1955 JERSEY CITY, N.J.
15-147	SHANNON, MAURICE JOSEPH	D. APRIL 12, 1970 JERSEY CITY, N.J.
62-121	SHANNON, THOMAS MICHAEL	2028 ELKINS DR - ST LOUIS MO 63136
59- 72	SHANNON, WALTER CHARLES	416 TWIN CREEK RD - CREVE COEUR MO 63141
49- 80	SHANTZ, ROBERT CLAYTON	152 MOUNT PLEASANT AVE - AMBLER PA 19002
54-100	SHANTZ, WILMER EBERT	3430 NW 40TH CT - FT LAUDERDALE FL 33309
17- 76	SHARMAN, RALPH EDWARD	D. MAY 24, 1918 CAMP SHERIDAN, ALA.
73-108	SHARON, RICHARD LOUIS	208 EMMA ST - COEUR D'ALENE ID 83414
73-109	SHARP, WILLIAM HOWARD	1523 OAKLAND PKWY - LIMA OH 45805
22-124	SHAUTE, JOSEPH BENJAMIN	D. FEBRUARY 21, 1970 SCRANTON, PA.
17- 77	SHAW, BENJAMIN NATHANIEL	D. MARCH 16, 1959 AURORA, O.
67-100	SHAW, DONALD WELLINGTON	1439 COVE LN - ST LOUIS MO 63138
13-162	SHAW, JAMES ALOYSIUS	D. JANUARY 27, 1962 WASHINGTON, D.C.
57- 77	SHAW, ROBERT JOHN	31 SADDLE BACK RD - JUPITER FL 33458
13-163	SHAWKEY, JAMES ROBERT	D. DECEMBER 31, 1980 SYRACUSE, N. Y.

16- 75	SHAY, ARTHUR JOSEPH	D. FEBRUARY 20, 1951 WORCESTER, MASS.
47- 77	SHEA, FRANCIS JOSEPH	72 JOHNSON - NAUGATUCK CT 06770
28- 81	SHEA, JOHN MICHAEL JOSEPH	D. NOVEMBER 30, 1956 MALDEN, MASS.
27- 82	SHEA, MERVYN DAVID JOHN	D. JANUARY 27, 1953 SACRAMENTO, CAL.
18- 65	SHEA, PATRICK HENRY	115 BURNS AVE - SPRINGFIELD MA 01103
68- 93	SHEA, STEVEN FRANCIS	OLD ADD: RR 1, JUNIPER DR - AMHERST NH
28- 82	SHEALY, ALBERT BERLEY	D. MARCH 7, 1967 HAGERSTOWN, MD.
57- 78	SHEARER, RAY SOLOMON	D. FEBRUARY 21, 1982 YORK, PA.
12-179	SHEARS, GEORGE PENFIELD	D. NOVEMBER 12, 1978 LOVELAND, COLO.
36- 84	SHEEHAN, JAMES THOMAS	107 ROBERT DR - EAST HAVEN CT 06512
20-106	SHEEHAN, JOHN THOMAS	360 PALMETTO ST - WEST PALM BEACH FL 33405
15-148	SHEEHAN, THOMAS CLANCY	OLD ADD: 24 BAYTREE WAY - SAN MATEO CA
21- 93	SHEELY, EARL HOMER	D. SEPTEMBER 16, 1952 SEATTLE, WASH.
51- 90	SHEELY, HOLLIS KIMBALL	OLD ADD: - 6400 HAVENSIDE - SACRAMENTO CA
36- 85	SHEERIN, CHARLES JOSEPH	158 FAIRFIELD ST - VALLEY STREAM NY 11581
81-125	SHELBY, JOHN T	711 HEADLEY AVE - LEXINGTON KY 40508
74-121	SHELDON, BOB MITCHELL	1521 TEMPLE HEIGHTS DR - OCEANSIDE CA 92054
61- 98	SHELDON, ROLAND FRANK	614 CORONADO - LEES SUMMIT MO 64063
18- 66	SHELLENBACK, FRANK VICTOR	D. AUGUST 17, 1969 NEWTON, MASS.
66- 82	SHELLENBACK, JAMES PHILIP	BOX 614 - BAKER OR 97814
35- 98	SHELLEY, HUBERT LENEIRRE	D. JUNE 16, 1978 BEAUMONT, TEX.
15-149	SHELTON, ANDREW KEMPER	D. JANUARY 9, 1954 HUNTINGTON, W. VA.
44-121	SHEMO, STEVEN MICHAEL	1313 WOODSIDE DR - GREENSBORO NC 27405
53- 82	SHEPARD, JACK LEROY	53 MCCORMICK LN - ATHERTON CA 94025
68- 94	SHEPARD, LAWRENCE WILLIAM	1716 PINEDALE - LINCOLN NE 68520

```
45- 95  SHEPARD, ROBERT EARL          8014 BANGOR AVE - HESPERIA CA 92345
24- 95  SHEPHARDSON, RAYMOND FRANCISD. NOVEMBER 8, 1975 LITTLE FALLS, N. Y.
18- 67  SHERDEL, WILLIAM HENRY        D. NOVEMBER 14, 1968 MCSHERRYSTOWN, PA.
29- 95  SHERID, ROYDAN RICHARD        WOODLAND AVE - OAKS PA 19456
18- 68  SHERIDAN, EUGENE ANTHONY      D. NOVEMBER 25, 1975 QUEENS VILLAGE, N. Y.
48- 93  SHERIDAN, NEILL RAWLINS       150 CHAUCER DR - PLEASANT HILL CA 94523
81-126  SHERIDAN, PATRICK ARTHUR      31654 TAFT - WAYNE MI 48184
24- 96  SHERLING, EDWARD CREECH       D. NOVEMBER 16, 1965 ENTERPRISE, ALA.
30- 72  SHERLOCK, JOHN CLINTON        299 MCKINLEY AVE - KENMORE NY 14217
35- 99  SHERLOCK, VINCENT THOMAS      237 SUMMIT AVE BUFFALO NY 14214
14-197  SHERMAN, DANIEL L.            OLD ADD: 1146 LEEDS ST - UTICA NY 13501
15-150  SHERMAN, JOEL POWERS          5318 MALALUKA CT - CAPE CORAL FL 33904
78-119  SHERRILL, DENNIS LEE          240 SOUTHWEST 63RD CT - MIAMI FL 33144
11-152  SHERRY, FRED PETER            D. JULY 27, 1975 HONESDALE, PA.
58- 83  SHERRY, LAWRENCE              27181 ARENA LN - MISSION VIEJO CA 92675
59- 73  SHERRY, NORMAN BURT           24181 TORENA CIR - MISSION VIEJO CA 92675
59- 74  SHETRONE, BARRY STEVAN        1208 WILSON RD - GLEN BURNIE MD 21061
30- 73  SHEVLIN, JAMES CORNELIUS      D. OCTOBER 30, 1974 FORT LAUDERDALE, FLA.
24- 97  SHIELDS, BENJAMIN COWAN       RR 1 BOX 466A - WOODRUFF SC 29389
15-151  SHIELDS, FRANCIS LEROY        D. FEBRUARY 11, 1961 JACKSON, MISS.
24- 98  SHIELDS, VINCENT WILLIAM      D. NOVEMBER 24, 1952 PLASTER ROCK, NEB.
57- 79  SHIFFLETT, GARLAND JESSIE     1095 CODY - LAKEWOOD CO 80215
33-109  SHILLING, JAMES ROBERT        OLD ADD: 1849 N INDIANAPOLIS - TULSA OK
21- 94  SHINAULT, ENOCH ERSKINE       D. DECEMBER 29, 1930 DENVER, COLO.
22-125  SHINNERS, RALPH PETER         D. JULY 23, 1962 MILWAUKEE, WIS.
58- 84  SHIPLEY, JOSEPH CLARK         29 HONEY LOCUST LN #7 - ST CHARLES MO 63301
28- 83  SHIRES, CHARLES ARTHUR        D. JULY 13, 1967 ITALY, TEX.
20-107  SHIREY, CLAIR LEE             D. SEPTEMBER 1, 1962 HAGERSTOWN, MD.
41-101  SHIRLEY, ALVIS NEWMAN         BOX 64 - MAYPEARL TX 77064
64-104  SHIRLEY, BARTON ARVIN         9621 SW 79TH ST - MIAMI FL 33143
24- 99  SHIRLEY, ERNEST RAEFORD       D. AUGUST 3, 1955 GOLDSBORO, N. C.
77-131  SHIRLEY, ROBERT CHARLES       3456 CAMINO DEL RIO #200 - SAN DIEGO CA 92108
31- 81  SHIVER, IVEY MERWIN           D. AUGUST 31, 1972 SAVANNAH, GA.
16- 76  SHOCKER, URBAN JAMES          D. SEPTEMBER 9, 1928 DENVER, COLO.
64-105  SHOCKLEY, JOHN COSTEN         405 WALTER ST - GEORGETOWN DE 19947
61- 99  SHOEMAKER, CHARLES LANDIS     2310 FAIRVIEW AVE - MOUNT PENN PA 19606
29- 96  SHOFFNER, MILBURN JAMES       D. JANUARY 19, 1978 MADISON, O.
47- 78  SHOFNER, FRANK STRICKLAND     620 HEWITT DT #34 - HEWITT TX 76643
41-102  SHOKES, EDWARD CHRISTOPHER    381 MILLWOOD AVE-WINCHESTER VA 22601
16- 77  SHOOK, RAYMAND CURTIS         D. SEPTEMBER 16, 1970 SOUTH BEND, IND.
59- 75  SHOOP, RONALD LEE             BOX 92 - RURAL VALLEY PA 16249
67-101  SHOPAY, THOMAS MICHAEL        8501 SW 179TH ST - MIAMI FL 33152
12-180  SHORE, ERNEST GRADY           D. SEPTEMBER 24, 1980 WINSTON-SALEM, N.C.
46- 92  SHORE, RAYMOND EVERETT        675 SILVER LEDGE LN - CINCINNATI OH 45231
28- 84  SHORES, WILLIAM DAVID         BOX 546 - LEXINGTON OK 73051
59- 76  SHORT, CHRISTOPHER JOSEPH     BOX 31 - WILMINGTON DE 19899
40- 82  SHORT, DAVID ORVIS            435 SANDEFUR ST - SHREVEPORT LA 71105
60- 93  SHORT, WILLIAM ROSS           2975 57TH ST - SARASOTA FL 33580
15-152  SHORTEN, CHARLES HENRY        D. OCTOBER 23, 1965 SCRANTON, PA.
35-100  SHOUN, CLYDE MITCHELL         D. MARCH 20, 1968 MOUNTAIN HOME, TENN.
11-153  SHOVLIN, JOHN JOSEPH          D. FEBRUARY 16, 1976 BETHESDA, MD.
81-127  SHOW, ERIC VAUGHN             4615 FELTON #1 - SAN DIEGO CA 92116
22-126  SHRIVER, HARRY GRAYDON        D. JANUARY 21, 1970 MORGANTOWN, W. VA.
48- 94  SHUBA GEORGE THOMAS           3421 BENT WILLOW LN - YOUNGSTOWN OH 44511
11-154  SHULTZ, WALLACE LUTHER        D. JANUARY 30, 1959 MCKEESPORT, PA.
42- 96  SHUMAN, HARRY                 7402 MALVERN AVE - PHILADELPHIA PA 19151
45- 96  SHUPE, VINCENT WILLIAM        D. APRIL 5, 1962 CANTON, O.
16- 78  SICKING, EDWARD JOSEPH        D. AUGUST 30, 1978 CINCINNATI, O.
56- 76  SIEBERN, NORMAN LEROY         3612 S FOREST ST - INDEPENDENCE MO 64052
74-122  SIEBERT, PAUL EDWARD          6608 SOUTHDALE RD - EDINA MN 55435
32- 76  SIEBERT, RICHARD WALTHER      D. DECEMBER 9, 1978 MINNEAPOLIS, MINN.
```

```
64-106  SIEBERT, WILFRED CHARLES      2583 BRUSH CREEK - ST LOUIS MO 63129
63-109  SIEBLER, DWIGHT LEROY         12755 DEANVILLE DR - OMAHA NE 68137
25- 92  SIEMER, OSCAR SYLVESTER       D. DECEMBER 5, 1959 ST. LOUIS, MO.
49- 81  SIEVERS, ROY EDWARD           11505 BELLEFONTAINE RD - ST LOUIS MO 63138
26- 74  SIGAFOOS, FRANCIS LEONARD     D. APRIL 12, 1968 INDIANAPOLIS, IND.
14-198  SIGLIN, WESLEY PETER          D. AUGUST 5, 1956 OAKLAND, CALIF.
29- 97  SIGMAN, WESLEY TRIPLETT       D. MARCH 8, 1971 AUGUSTA, GA.
43-130  SIGNER, WALTER DONALD ALOYSIUS D. JULY 23, 1974 GREENWICH, CONN.
37- 94  SILBER, EDWARD JAMES          D. OCTOBER 26, 1976 DUNEDIN, FLA.
19- 75  SILVA, DANIEL JAMES           D. APRIL 4, 1974 HYANNIS, MASS.
55-107  SILVERA, AARON ALBERT         723 N SIERRA DR - BEVERLY HILLS CA 90210
```

```
48- 95  SILVERA, CHARLES ANTHONY RYAN  1240 MANZANITA DR - MILLBRAE CA 94030
78-120  SILVERIC, LUIS PASCUAL          CALLE NUMA SILVERIO#7 VIL GONZALEZ SAN DOM
70-121  SILVERIO, TOMAS ROBERTO         CALLE 9#14 COLINAS - SANTO DOMINGO DOM REP
39-110  SILVESTRI, KENNETH JOSEPH       3328 W LAKE SHORE DR - TALLAHASEE FL 32303
50- 89  SIMA, ALBERT                    BOX 28 - BRANDON FL 33511
24-100  SIMMONS, ALOYSIUS HARRY         D. MAY 26, 1956 MILWAUKEE, WIS.
47- 79  SIMMONS, CURTIS THOMAS          200 PARK RD - PROSPECTVILLE PA 19002
10-134  SIMMONS, GEORGE WASHINGTON      D. APRIL 26, 1942 ARVERNE, N.Y.
49- 82  SIMMONS, JOHN EARL              9 LEE DR - FARMINGDALE NY 11735
68- 95  SIMMONS, TED LYLE               BOX 26 - CHESTERFIELD MO 63017
28- 85  SIMMONS, PATRICK CLEMENT        D. JULY 3, 1968 ALBANY, N. Y.
23-121  SIMON, SYLVESTER ADAM           D. FEBRUARY 28, 1973 CHANDLER, IND.
31- 82  SIMONS, MELBERN ELLIS           D. OCTOBER 11, 1974 PADUCAH, KY.
51- 91  SIMPSON, HARRY LEON             D. APRIL 3, 1979 AKRON, O.
75-106  SIMPSON, JOE ALLEN              603 JEAN MARIE DR - NORMAN OK 73069
62-122  SIMPSON, RICHARD CHARLES        696 SAN JUAN AVE - VENICE CA 90291
72-103  SIMPSON, STEVEN EDWARD          5031 SW 26TH TER - TOPEKA KS 66614
53- 83  SIMPSON, THOMAS LEO             4701 SAN FELICIANO - WOODLAND HILLS CA 91364
70-122  SIMPSON, WAYNE KIRBY            330 COLLAMER DR - CARSON CA 90744
15-153  SIMS, CLARENCE                  D. DECEMBER 2, 1968 DALLAS, TEX.
64-107  SIMS, DUANE B                   BOX 714 - BINGHAMTON NY 13902
66- 83  SIMS, GREGORY EMMETT            5345 CROWN CT - CASTRO VALLEY CA 94546
81-128  SINATRO, MATTHEW STEPHEN        10 LONG VIEW RD - WEST HARTFORD CT 06107
64-108  SINGER, WILLIAM ROBERT          311 WILLAPALL - DIAMOND BAR CA 91766
45- 97  SINGLETON, BERT ELMER           2489 NORTH 4425 WEST - OGDEN UT 84404
22-127  SINGLETON, JOHN EDWARD          D. OCTOBER 23, 1937 DAYTON, O.
70-123  SINGLETON, KENNETH WAYNE        409 SENECA AVE - MOUNT VERNON NY 10553
34- 91  SINGTON, FREDERIC WILLIAM       2017 5TH AVE N - BIRMINGHAM AL 35203
45- 98  SIPEK, RICHARD FRANCIS          1611 JACKSON ST - QUINCY IL 62301
69-157  SIPIN, JOHN WHITE               328 HERMAN AVE - WATSONVILLE CA 95076
62-123  SISK, TOMMIE WAYNE              3292 MOHAWK CIR - PROVO UT 84601
56- 77  SISLER, DAVID MICHAEL           11 HACIENDA DR - ST LOUIS MO 63124
15-154  SISLER, GEORGE HAROLD           D. MARCH 26, 1973 ST. LOUIS, MO.
46- 93  SISLER, RICHARD ALLEN           2315 ABBOTT MARTIN RD - NASHVILLE TN 37212
39-111  SISTI, SEBASTIAN DANIEL         39 CLIFFORD HEIGHTS - AMHERST NY 14226
36- 86  SIVESS, PETER                   RR 1 BOX 124E - ST MICHAELS MD 21663
69-158  SIZEMORE, THEODORE CRAWFORD     989 W OAKCRST - BREA CA 92621
35-101  SKAFF, FRANCIS MICHAEL          2449 SPRINGLAKE DR - TIMONIUM MD 21093
```

```
77-132  SKAGGS, DAVID LINDSEY           OLD ADD: 2121 W 161ST - GARDENA CA 90247
57- 80  SKAUGSTAD, DAVID WENDELL        1511 N DURANT - SANTA ANA CA 92706
10-135  SKEELS, DAVID                   D. DECEMBER 2, 1926 SPOKANE, WASH.
42- 97  SKETCHLEY, HARRY CLEMENT        D. DECEMBER 19, 1979 LOS ANGELES, CALIF.
70-124  SKIDMORE, ROBERT ROE            815 S STONE - DECATUR IL 62521
21- 95  SKIFF, WILLIAM FRANKLIN         D. DECEMBER 25, 1976 BRONXVILLE, N. Y.
22-128  SKINNER, ELISHA HARRISON CAMP   D. AUGUST 4, 1944 DOUGLASVILLE, GA.
54-101  SKINNER, ROBERT RALPH           1576 DIAMOND ST - SAN DIEGO CA 92109
56- 78  SKIZAS, LOUIS PETER             2101 W WHITE - CHAMPAIGN IL 61821
73-110  SKOK, CRAIG RICHARD             37 POWDERSVILLE RD, RR 7 - EASLEY SC 29640
54-102  SKOWRON, WILLIAM JOSEPH         1118 BEACHCOMBER DR - SCHAUMBURG IL 60193
30- 74  SLADE, GORDON LEIGH             D. JANUARY 2, 1974 LONG BEACH, CALIF.
79-104  SLAGLE, ROGER LEE               536 W THIRD ST - LARNED KS 67550
10-136  SLAGLE, WALTER JENNINGS         D. JUNE 17, 1974 SAN GABRIEL, CALIF.
11-155  SLAPNICKA, CYRIL CHARLES        D. OCTOBER 20, 1979 CEDAR RAPIDS. IA.
20-108  SLAPPEY, JOHN HENRY             D. JUNE 10, 1957 MARIETTA, GA.
71- 93  SLATON, JAMES MICHAEL           43515 28TH ST W - LANCASTER CA 93534
15-155  SLATTERY, PHILIP RYAN           D. MARCH 2, 1968 LONG BEACH, CAL9F.
10-137  SLAUGHTER, BYRON ATKINS         D. MAY 17, 1961 PHILADELPHIA PA.
38- 90  SLAUGHTER, ENOS BRADSHER        RR 2 ROXBORO NC 27573
64-109  SLAUGHTER, STERLING FEORE       OLD ADD: 2128 E HUNTINGTON - TEMPE AZ
26- 75  SLAYBACK, ELBERT                DECATUR ST - AURORA IN 47001
72-104  SLAYBACK, WILLIAM GROVER        4918 CECILVILLE - LACRESCENTA CA 91214
28- 86  SLAYTON, FOSTER HERBERT         TROW HILL - BARRE VT 05641
50- 90  SLEATER, LOUIS MORTIMER         515 BROOK RD - TOWSON MD 21204
44-122  SLOAN, BRUCE ADAMS              D. SEPTEMBER 24, 1973 OKLAHOMA CITY, OKLA.
13-164  SLOAN, YALE YEASTMAN            D. SEPTEMBER 12, 1956 AKRON, O.
48- 96  SLOAT, DWAIN CLIFFORD           2101 E 5TH ST - ST PAUL MN 55119
69-159  SLOCUM, RONALD REECE            RR 1 BOX 281 - OLEY PA 19547
30- 75  SMALL, CHARLES ALBERT           D. JANUARY 14, 1953 LEWISTON, ME.
78-121  SMALL, GEORGE HENRY             4475 EAST CONWAY DR - ATLANTA GA 30312
55-108  SMALL, JAMES ARTHUR             RR 1 - STANWOOD MI 49346
75-107  SMALLEY, ROY FREDERICK III      221A 6TH ST - MANHATTAN BEACH CA 90266
48- 97  SMALLEY, ROY FREDERICK JR       534 W ARBOR VITAE - INGLEWOOD CA 90301
```

```
17- 78  SMALLWOOD, WALTER CLAYTON    D. APRIL 29, 1967
46- 94  SMAZA, JOSEPH PAUL           D. MAY 30, 1979 ROYAL OAK, MICH.
34- 92  SMITH, ALFRED JOHN           D. APRIL 28, 1977 BROWNSVILLE, TEX.
26- 76  SMITH, ALFRED KENDRICKS      23928 GREEN HAVEN - RAMONA CA 92065
53- 84  SMITH, ALPHONSE EUGENE       9009 E 25TH ST - TUCSON AZ 85710
12-182  SMITH, ARMSTRONG FREDERICK   D. NOVEMBER 15, 1959 SPRINGFIELD, MASS.
32- 77  SMITH, ARTHUR LAIRD          21 OLD NURSERY DR - WILTON CT 06897
75-108  SMITH, BILLY EDWARD          5439 TIMBER POST - SAN ANTONIO TX 78250
81-129  SMITH, BILLY LAVERN          2121 N COUNTRY CLUB #4 - TUCSON AZ 85716
57- 81  SMITH, BOBBY GENE            BOX 604 - HOOD RIVER OR 97031
81-130  SMITH, BRYN NELSON           812 E FELSER - SANTA MARIA CA 93454
70-125  SMITH, CALVIN BERNARD        BOX 513 - LUTCHER LA 70071
66- 84  SMITH, CARL REGINALD         20321 TAU PL - CHATSWORTH CA 91311
23-122  SMITH, CARR E                731 SHIRLEY AV - NORFOLK VA 23517
60- 94  SMITH, CHARLES WILLIAM       3060 SPROUT WAY - SPARKS NV 89431
81-131  SMITH, CHRISTOPHER WILLIAM   27117 MESABA DR - RANCHO PALOS VERDES CA90274
13-165  SMITH, CLARENCE OSSIE        D. FEBRUARY 16, 1924 SWEETWATER, TEX.
38- 91  SMITH, CLAY JAMIESON         CAMBRIDGE KS 67023
38- 92  SMITH, DAVID MERWIN          BOX 671 WHITEVILLE NC 28472
80-119  SMITH, DAVID STANLEY         325 S SIERRA #8 - SOLONA BEACH CA 92075
12-181  SMITH, DOUGLASS WELDON       D. SEPTEMBER 18, 1973 GREENFIELD, MASS.
55-109  SMITH, EARL CALVIN           2764 N LEONARD - FRESNO CA 93727
16- 79  SMITH, EARL LEONARD          D. MARCH 14, 1943 PORTSMOUTH, O.
19- 76  SMITH, EARL SUTTON           D. JUNE 9, 1963 LITTLE ROCK, ARK.
36- 87  SMITH, EDGAR                 RT 130 KINKOVER - BORDENTOWN NJ 08505
45- 99  SMITH, EDWARD MAYO           D. NOVEMBER 24, 1977 BOYNTON BEACH, FLA.
14-199  SMITH, ELMER JOHN            DILLON ST - COLUMBIA KY 42748
26- 77  SMITH, ELWOOD HOPE           1432 CHESAPEAKE AVE - SOUTH NORFOLK VA 23506
30- 76  SMITH, ERNEST HENRY          D. APRIL 6, 1973 BROOKLYN, N. Y.
50- 91  SMITH, FRANK THOMAS          1968 ADD: 5627 4TH ST N - ST PETERSBURG FL
13-166  SMITH, FREDERICK VINCENT     D. MAY 28, 1961 CLEVELAND, O.
16- 80  SMITH, GEORGE ALLEN          D. JANUARY 7, 1965 GREENWICH, CONN.
63-110  SMITH, GEORGE CORNELIUS      2728 LAKEVIEW AVE - ST PETERSBURG FL 33712
26- 78  SMITH, GEORGE SELBY          D. MAY 26, 1981 RICHMOND, VA.
32- 78  SMITH, HAROLD LAVERN         5200 N OCEAN BLVD - FT LAUDERDALE FL 33308
56- 79  SMITH, HAROLD RAYMOND        6602 WINKLEMAN - HOUSTON TX 77083
55-110  SMITH, HAROLD WAYNE          %PERKINS, 2314 RIDGEMONT-MISSOURI CTY TX77459
12-183  SMITH, HARRISON M            D. JULY 26, 1964 DUNBAR, NEB.
10-138  SMITH, HENRY JOSEPH          D. FEBRUARY 26, 1961 SAN JOSE, CALIF.
62-124  SMITH, JACK HATFIELD         621 TAHOE CIR - STONE MOUNTAIN GA 30083
11-156  SMITH, JACOB G               B. DUBOIS, PA.
11-157  SMITH, JAMES CARLISLE        D. OCTOBER 11, 1966 ATLANTA, GA.
14-200  SMITH, JAMES HARRY           D. APRIL 1, 1922 CHARLOTTE, N.C.
14-201  SMITH, JAMES LAWRENCE        D. JANUARY 1, 1974 PITTSBURGH, PA.
15-156  SMITH, JOHN                  D. MAY 2, 1972 WESTCHESTER, ILL.
31- 83  SMITH, JOHN MARSHALL         OLD ADD: COCKEYSVILLE MD 21030
13-167  SMITH, JOHN WILLIAM          D. OCTOBER 11, 1935 DAYTON, KY.
77-133  SMITH, KEITH LAVARNE         522 11TH ST DR N - PALMETTO FL 33561
81-132  SMITH, KENNETH EARL          100 LANDSDOWNE BLVD - YOUNGSTOWN OH 44506
20-109  SMITH, LAWRENCE PATRICK      2738 N MILITARY TRAIL #109-W PLM BCH FL 33409
80-120  SMITH, LEE ARTHUR            RR 2 BOX 266A - JAMESTOWN LA 71045
78-122  SMITH, LONNIE                1209 WEST PIRU - COMPTON CA 90222
25- 93  SMITH, MARVIN HAROLD         D. FEBRUARY 19, 1961 LOS ANGELES, CAL.
55-111  SMITH, MILTON                497A FARR RD - COLUMBUS GA 31907
62-125  SMITH, NATHANIEL BEVERLY     1233 BLAND - HOUSTON TX 77018
78-123  SMITH, OSBORNE EARL          8004 HILLANDALE - SAN DIEGO CA 92120
53- 85  SMITH, PAUL LESLIE           27 RAVENSWORTH RD - CONROE TX 77301
16- 81  SMITH, PAUL STONER           D. JULY 3, 1958 DECATUR, ILL.
62-126  SMITH, PETER LUKE            13 YALE DR - NEW CITY NY 10956
81-133  SMITH, RAYMOND EDWARD        1063 OAK DR - VISTA CA 92083
63-111  SMITH, RICHARD ARTHUR        1196 SW OXFORD DR - LAKE OSWEGO OR 97034
51- 92  SMITH, RICHARD HARRISON      1926 NORWOOD LN - STATE COLLEGE PA 16801
69-160  SMITH, RICHARD KELLY         RR 7 BOX 200 - LINCOLNTON NC
27- 83  SMITH, RICHARD PAUL          D. MARCH 8, 1978 TOLEDO, O.
13-169  SMITH, ROBERT ASHLEY         1914 ADD: HARDWICK VT
23-123  SMITH, ROBERT ELDRIDGE       OLD ADD: 1653 JOHNSON RD NE - ATLANTA GA
55-112  SMITH, ROBERT GILCHRIST      7613 NE 69TH ST - VANCOUVER WA 98662
```

```
58- 85  SMITH, ROBERT WALKUP         CLARENCE MO 63437
27- 84  SMITH, RUFUS FRAZIER         BOX 473 - NEW ELLENTON SC 29809
13-168  SMITH, SALVATORE GIUSEPPE    D. JANUARY 12, 1974 YONKERS, N. Y.
11-158  SMITH, SHEROD MALONE         D. SEPTEMBER 12, 1949 REIDSVILLE, GA.
73-111  SMITH, TOMMIE ALEXANDER      1299 E CANNON AVE - ALBEMARLE NC 28001
41-103  SMITH, VINCENT AMBROSE       D. DECEMBER 14, 1979 VIRGINIA BEACH, VA.
```

11-159 SMITH, WALLACE H.	D. JUNE 10, 1930 FLORENCE, ARIZ.
17- 79 SMITH, WILLARD JEHU	D. JULY 17, 1972 NOBLESVILLE, IND
58- 86 SMITH, WILLIAM GARLAND	1970 ADD: 109 POTTER - JAMESTOWN NC 27282
63-112 SMITH, WILLIE	607 BRADFORD ST - HOBSON CITY AL 36201
40- 83 SMOLL, CLYDE HETRICK	157 S 3RD ST-QUAKERTOWN PA 18951
12-184 SMOYER, HENRY NEITZ	D. FEBRUARY 28, 1958 DUBOIS, PA.
16- 82 SMYKAL, FRANK JOHN	D. AUGUST 11, 1950 CHICAGO, ILL.
44-123 SMYRES, CLARENCE MELVIN	11470 ORCAS AVE - SAN FERNANDO CA 91342
15-157 SMYTH, JAMES DANIEL	D. APRIL 14, 1958 INGLEWOOD, CALIF.
29- 98 SMYTHE, WILLIAM HENRY	D. AUGUST 28, 1980 AUGUSTA, GA.
12-185 SNELL, CHARLES ANTHONY	1033 AMITY ST - READING PA 19604
13-170 SNELL, WALTER HENRY	D. JULY 23, 1980 PROVIDENCE, R. I.
47- 80 SNIDER, EDWIN DONALD	3037 LAKEMONT DR - FALLBROOK CA 92028
23-124 SNIPES, WYATT EURE	D. MAY 1, 1941 FAYETTEVILLE, N. C.
73-112 SNOOK, FRANK WALTER	RR 2 BOX 460 - WHITEHOUSE STATION NJ 08822
19- 77 SNOVER, COLONEL LESTER	D. APRIL 30, 1969 ROCHESTER, N. Y.
35-102 SNYDER, BERNARD AUSTIN	2415 WAVERLY - PHILADELPHIA PA 19146
59- 77 SNYDER, EUGENE WALTER	1960 N SHERMAN ST - YORK PA 17402
12-186 SNYDER, FRANK ELTON	D. JANUARY 5, 1962 SAN ANTONIO, TEX.
52- 95 SNYDER, GERALD GEORGE	OLD ADD: 2420 GOLFCREST BLVD - HOUSTON TX
61-100 SNYDER, JAMES ROBERT	BOX 145 - DEARBORN HEIGHTS MI 48127
14-202 SNYDER, JOHN WILLIAM	D. DECEMBER 13, 1981 BROWNSVILLE, PA.
59- 78 SNYDER, RUSSELL HENRY	BOX 114 - NELSON NE 68961
19- 78 SNYDER, WILLIAM NICHOLAS	D. OCTOBER 8, 1934 VICKSBURG, MICH.
37- 95 SODD, WILLIAM	3845 DIAMON LOCK W - FT WORTH TX 76118
71- 94 SODERHOLM, ERIC THANE	10S360 HAMPSHIRE LN W - HINSDALE IL 60521
79-105 SOFIELD, RICHARD MICHAEL	4 WATNONG DRIVE - MORRIS PLAINS NJ 07950
68- 96 SOLAITA, TOLIA	317 ALTA VISTA DR-SOUTH SAN FRANCISCO CA9408
58- 87 SOLIS, MARCELINO	1972 ADD: CALLE VIDREA 8370 - MONTEREY MEXIC
73-113 SOLOMON, EDDIE	309 UTAH - WARNER ROBINS GA 31093
23-125 SOLOMON, MOSES H.	D. JUNE 25, 1966 MIAMI, FLA.
34- 93 SOLTERS, JULIUS JOSEPH	D. SEPTEMBER 28, 1975 PITTSBURGH, PA.
10-139 SOMERLOTT, JOHN WESLEY	D. APRIL 21, 1965 BUTLER, IND.
12-187 SOMMERS, RUDOLPH	D. MARCH 18, 1949 LOUISVILLE, KY.
50- 92 SOMMERS, WILLIAM DUNN	44 POLO RD - MASSAPEQUA NY 11758
24-101 SONGER, DON	D. OCTOBER 3, 1962 KANSAS CITY, MO.
77-134 SORENSON, LARY ALAN	23610 MYRTLE DR - MOUNT CLEMENS MI 48043
28- 87 SORRELL, VICTOR GARLAND	D. MAY 4, 1972 RALEIGH, N. C.
65-102 SORRELL, WILLIAM	%S.G.SORRELL,1683 WINGATE-YPSILANTI MI 48197
22-129 SORRELLS, RAYMOND EDWIN	RR 1 - ROYSE CITY TX 75089
72-105 SOSA, ELIAS	8658 E IRISH HUNTER TR - SCOTTSDALE AZ 85158
75-109 SOSA, JOSE YNOCENCIO	HAINA KM12 CARRETERA SANCHEZ-STO DOMINGO DOM
26- 79 SOTHERN, DENNIS ELWOOD	BOX 624 - RICHLANDS NC 28574
14-203 SOTHORON, ALLEN SUTTON	D. JUNE 17, 1939 ST. LOUIS, MO
77-135 SOTO, MARIO MELVIN	JOACHS-LACHAUSTEGUI #42 SUR-BANI DOMINICAN R
46- 95 SOUCHOCK, STEPHEN	441 SW 55TH TER - FORT LAUDERDALE FL 33314
11-160 SOUTHWICK, CLYDE AUBRA	D. OCTOBER 14, 1961 FREEPORT, ILL.
64-110 SOUTHWORTH, WILLIAM FREDERICK	320 DOBBEN RD - WEBSTER GROVES MO 63119
13-171 SOUTHWORTH, WILLIAM HARRISON	D. NOVEMBER 15, 1969 COLUMBUS, O.
80-121 SOUZA, KENNETH MARK	2519 DEKOVEN - BELMONT CA 94002
42- 98 SPAHN, WARREN EDWARD	RR 2 - HARTSHORNE OK 74547
27- 85 SPALDING, CHARLES HARRY	D. FEBRUARY 3, 1950 PHILADELPHA, PA.
59- 79 SPANGLER, ALBERT DONALD	27202 AFTON WAY - HUFFMAN TX 77336
64-111 SPANSWICK, WILLIAM HENRY	10 ST THOMAS STREET - ENFIELD CT 06082
64-112 SPARMA, JOSEPH BLASE	767 1/2 11TH ST SE -MASSILLON OH 44646
55-113 SPEAKE, ROBERT CHARLES	4742 SW URISH RD - TOPEKA KS 66604
24-102 SPEECE, BYRON FRANKLIN	D. SEPTEMBER 29, 1974 ELGIN, ORE.
75-110 SPEED, HORACE ARTHUR III	1301 BANKERS DR - CARSON CA 90744
43-131 SPEER, VERNIE FLOYD	D. MARCH 22, 1969 LITTLE ROCK, ARK.
71- 95 SPEIER, CHRIS EDWARD	BOX 849 - ST ADELE QUEBEC
69-161 SPENCE, JOHN ROBERT	2521 SAN MARCOS - SAN DIEGO CA 92104
40- 84 SPENCE, STANLEY ORVILLE	1505 CAREY RD-KINSTON NC 28501
52- 96 SPENCER, DARYL DEAN	2740 LARKIN DRIVE - WICHITA KS 67216
12-188 SPENCER, FRED CALVIN	D. FEBRUARY 5, 1969 ST. ANTHONY, MINN.
50- 93 SPENCER, GEORGE ELWELL	8160 HICKORY AVE - GALENA OH 43021
28- 88 SPENCER, GLENN EDWARD	D. DECEMBER 30, 1958 BINGHAMTON, N. Y.
78-124 SPENCER, HUBERT THOMAS	132 PINE ST - GALLIOPOLIS OH 45631
68- 97 SPENCER, JAMES LLOYD	725A OLD BANFIELD RD - SEVERNA PARK MD 21146
13-172 SPENCER, LLOYD BENJAMIN	D. SEPTEMBER 1, 1970 FINKSBURG, MD.
25- 94 SPENCER, ROY HAMPTON	D. FEBRUARY 8, 1973 PORT CHARLETTE, FLA.

(SEE PAGE 149)

20-110	SPENCER, VERNON MURRAY	D. JUNE 3, 1971 WIXOM, MICH.
20-111	SPERAW, PAUL BACHMAN	D. FEBRUARY 22, 1962 CEDAR RAPIDS, IA.
24-103	SPERBER, EDWIN GEORGE	D. JANUARY 5, 1976 CINCINNATI, O.
74-123	SPERRING, ROBERT WALTER	2606 HUGHES - MIDLAND TX 79701
36- 88	SPERRY, STANLEY KENNETH	D. SEPTEMBER 27, 1962 EVANSVILLE,WIS.
55-114	SPICER, ROBERT OBERTON	423 MCPHEE DR - FAYETTEVILLE NC 28305
64-113	SPIEZIO, EDWARD WAYNE	601 ELSIE AVE - JOLIET IL 60435
72-106	SPIKES, LESLIE CHARLES	10921 KINNEIL RD - NEW ORLEANS LA 70127
74-124	SPILLNER, DANIEL RAY	111 SW 307TH - FEDERAL WAY WA 98002
78-125	SPILMAN, WILLIAM HARRY	RURAL ROUTE 4 BOX 36 - DAWSON GA 31742
39-112	SPINDEL, HAROLD STEWART	12816 EL MORO AVE-LA MIRADA CA 90638
69-162	SPINKS, SCIPIO RONALD	34 NE 66TH - OKLAHOMA CITY OK 73105
70-126	SPLITTORFF, PAUL WILLIAM	4204 HICKORY LN - BLUE SPRING MO 64015
32- 79	SPOGNARDI, ANDREA ETTORE	4394 WASHINGTON ST - ROSLINDALE MA 02131
28- 89	SPOHRER, ALFRED RAY	D. JULY 21, 1972 CARMEL, N. Y.
54-103	SPOONER, KARL BENJAMIN	104 SW 20TH PLACE - VERO BEACH FL 32960
30- 77	SPOTTS, JAMES RUSSELL	D. JUNE 15, 1964 MEDFORD, N. J.
47- 81	SPRAGINS, HOMER FRANK	BOX 113 - MINTER CITY MS 38944
68- 98	SPRAGUE, EDWARD NELSON	5152 OAKDALE CT - PLEASANTON CA 94566
11-161	SPRATT, HENRY LEE	D. JULY 3, 1969 WASHINGTON, PA.
65-103	SPRIGGS, GEORGE HERMAN	282 W BAY FRONT RD - LOTHIAN MD 20820
55-115	SPRING, JACK RUSSELL	8506 EAST DALTON - SPOKANE WA 99206
25- 95	SPRINGER, BRADFORD LOUIS	D. JANUARY 4, 1970 BIRMINGHAM, MICH.
30- 78	SPRINZ, JOSEPH CONRAD	1359 33RD AVE - SAN FRANCISCO CA 94122
45-100	SPROULL, CHARLES WILLIAM	D. JANUARY 13, 1980 ROCKFORD, ILL.
61-101	SPROLT, ROBERT SAMUEL	2858 FLEETWOOD DR - LANCASTER PA 17601
78-126	SPROWL, ROBERT JOHN	114 E 144TH AVE - TAMPA FL 33612
24-104	SPURGEON, FRED	D. NOVEMBER 5, 1970 KALAMAZOO, MICH.
75-111	SQUIRES, MICHAEL LYNN	2815 RANDOM RD - KALAMAZOO MI 49004
80-122	STABLEIN, GEORGE CHARLES	OLD ADD: 4104 52ND ST #12 - SAN DIEGO CA
10-140	STACK, WILLIAM EDWARD	D. AUGUST 28, 1958 CHICAGO, ILL.
64-114	STAEHLE, MARVIN GUSTAVE	570 CHECKER DR - BUFFALO GROVE IL 60090
60- 95	STAFFORD, BILL CHARLES	6108 COURTLAND - PLYMOUTH MI 48170
16- 83	STAFFORD, HENRY ALEXANDER	D. JANUARY 29, 1972 LAKE WORTH, FLA.
77-136	STAGGS, STEPHEN ROBERT	6850 S ZEPHYR CT - LITTLETON CO 80123
64-115	STAHL, LARRY FLOYD	RR1 - FREEBURG IL 62243
75-112	STAIGER, ROY JOSEPH	5789 E 26TH ST - TULSA OK 74115
34- 94	STAINBACK, GEORGE TUCKER	1000 ELYSIAN AVE - LOS ANGELES CA 90012
25- 96	STALEY, GEORGE GAYLORD	1935 GOLDEN RAIN RD - WALNUT CREEK CA 94529
47- 82	STALEY, GERALD LEE	2600 NE 99TH ST - VANCOUVER WA 98665
60- 96	STALLARD, EVAN TRACY	HERALD VA 24230
47- 83	STALLCUF, THOMAS VIRGIL	RR 6 - GREENVILLE SC 29601
43-132	STALLER, GEORGE WALBORN	321 N 67TH ST - HARRISBURG PA 17111
41-104	STANCEU, CHARLES	D. APRIL 3, 1969 CANTON, O.
25- 97	STANDAEART, JEROME JOHN	D. AUGUST 4, 1964 CHICAGO, ILL.
11-162	STANDRIDGE, ALFRED PETER	D. AUGUST 2, 1963 SAN FRANCISCO, CALIF.
63-113	STANEK, AL	96 ALLYN ST - HOLYOKE MA 01070
79-106	STANFIELD, KEVIN BRUCE	7565 NEWCOMB ST - SAN BERNARDINO CA 92410
61-102	STANGE, ALBERT LEE	9365 BUTTERCUP AVE - FOUNTAIN VALLEY CS 92708
72-107	STANHOUSE, DONALD JOSEPH	OLD ADD: 418 N POPE - DUQUOIN IL
59- 80	STANKA, JOE DONALD	874 YORKCHESTER - HOUSTON TX 77024
43-133	STANKY, EDWARD RAYMOND	2100 SPRING HILL RD - MOBILE AL 36607
69-163	STANLEY, FREDRICK BLAIR	BOX 6181 SCOTTSDALE AZ 85255
14-204	STANLEY, JAMES F.	B. 1889
11-163	STANLEY, JOHN LEONARD	D. AUGUST 13, 1940 NORFOLK, VA.
64-116	STANLEY, MITCHELL JACK	OLD ADD: 5533 NORTHCOTE LN-W BLOOMFIELD MI
77-137	STANLEY, ROBERT WILLIAM	21 DEVON ST - KEARNY NJ 07032
18- 69	STANSBURY, JOHN JAMES	D. DECEMBER 26, 1970 EASTON, PA.
31- 84	STANTON, GEORGE WASHINGTON	401 WINDING WAY DR - SAN ANTONIO TX 78232
70-127	STANTON, LEROY BOBBY	1751 NORWOOD LN - FLORENCE SC 29501
75-113	STANTON, MICHAEL THOMAS	1751 NORWOOD LN - FLORENCE SC 29501
80-123	STAPLETON, DAVID LESLIE	RR 1 BOX 600 - LOXLEY AL 36551
62-127	STARGELL, WILVER DORNEL	126 CONOVER RD - PITTSBURGH PA 15208

32- 80	STARR, RAYMOND FRANCIS	D. FEBRUARY 9, 1963 BAYLISS, ILL.
47- 84	STARR, RICHARD EUGENE	613 N CRESCENT DR - KITTANNING PA 19201
35-103	STARR, WILLIAM	666 UPAS ST #1801 - SAN DIEGO CA 92103
63-114	STARRETTE, HERMAN PAUL	208 HERMITAGE RD - STATESVILLE NC 28677
72-108	STATON, JOSEPH	1433 33 D AVE - SEATTLE WA 98122
19- 79	STATZ, ARNOLD JOHN	2011-B VIA MARIPOSA - LAGUNA HILLS CA 92653
63-115	STAUB, DANIEL JOSEPH	1271 3RD AVE - NEW YORK NY 10021
23-126	STAUFFER, CHARLES EDWARD	D. JULY 2, 1979 ST PETERSBURG, FLA.
74-125	STEARNS, JOHN HARDIN	2649 S PEORIA - AURORA CO 80232
16- 84	STEELE, ROBERT WESLEY	D. JANUARY 27, 1962 OCALA, FLA.
10-141	STEELE, WILLIAM MITCHELL	D. OCTOBER 19, 1949 OVERLAND, MO.
12-189	STEEN, WILLIAM JOHN	D. MARCH 13, 1979 SIGNAL HILL, CALIF.
24-105	STEENGRAFE, MILTON HENRY	D. JUNE 2, 1977 OKLAHOMA CITY, OKLA.
62-128	STEEVENS, MORRIS DALE	527 GENERAL KRUEGER - SAN ANTONIO TX 78213
78-127	STEGMAN, DAVID WILLIAM	316 EAST OAK - LOMPOC CA 93436
32- 81	STEIN, IRVIN MICHAEL	BOX 184 - MADISONVILLE LA 70447
38- 93	STEIN, JUSTIN MARION	1915 GRAPE AVE - ST LOUIS MO 63136
72-109	STEIN, WILLIAM ALLEN	2433 LEGAY ST - COCOA FL 32922
78-128	STEIN, WILLIAM RANDOLPH	1540 PALMER ST - POMONA CA 91766
37- 96	STEINBACHER, HENRY JOHN	D. APRIL 3, 1977 SACRAMENTO, CALIF.
12-190	STEINBRENNER, WILLIAM GASS	D. APRIL 25, 1970 PITTSBURGH, PA.
31- 85	STEINECKE, WILLIAM ROBERT	311 ST GEORGE ST - ST AUGUSTINE FL 32084
23-127	STEINEDER, RAYMOND J	220 PLUM ST - VINELAND NJ 08360
45-101	STEINER, BENJAMIN SAUNDERS	402 S 2ND AVE - HIGHLAND PARK NJ 08904
45-102	STEINER, JAMES HARRY	17700 S WESTERN AVE - GARDENA CA 90248
16- 85	STELLBAUER, WILLIAM JENNINGS	D. FEBRUARY 16, 1974 HOUSTON, TEX.
71- 96	STELMASZEK, RICHARD FRANCIS	2734 E 97TH ST - CHICAGO IL 60617
80-124	STEMBER, JEFFREY ALAN	330 W JERSEY ST - ELIZABETH NJ 07202
12-191	STENGEL, CHARLES DILLON	D. SEPTEMBER 29, 1975 GLENDALE, CAL.
62-129	STENHOUSE, DAVID ROTCHFORD	70 WOODBURY RD - CRANSTON RI 02905
71- 97	STENNETT, RENALDO ANTONIO	5704 PENN AVE - PITTSBURGH PA 15206
68- 99	STEPHEN, LOUIS ROBERTS	308 N PARKVIEW - PORTERVILLE CA 93257
47- 85	STEPHENS, BRYAN MARIS	10222 WESLEY CIR - HUNTINGTON BEACH CA 92646
52- 97	STEPHENS, GLEN EUGENE	5804 N BILLEN ST - OKLAHOMA CITY OK 73112
41-105	STEPHENS, VERNON DECATUR	D. NOVEMBER 4, 1968 LONG BEACH, CAL.
71- 98	STEPHENSON, CHESTER EARL	711 MCCULLOCH ST - RALEIGH NC 27603
21- 96	STEPHENSON, JACKSON RIGGS	917 INDIAN HILLS DR - TUSCALOOSA AL 35401
63-116	STEPHENSON, JERRY JOSEPH	1425 MARELEN DR - FULLERTON CA 92635
64-117	STEPHENSON, JOHN HERMAN	400 CRESTMOND AVE - HATTIESBURG MS 39401
43-134	STEPHENSON, JOSEPH CHESTER	822 JADE WAY - ANAHEIM CA 92805
55-116	STEPHENSON, ROBERT LOYD	1518 BROOKHAVEN BLVD - NORMAN OK 73069
35-104	STEPHENSON, WALTER MCQUEEN	3160 REISOR RD SHREVEPORT LA 71108
74-126	STERLING, RANDALL WAYNE	2516 LINDA AVE - KEY WEST FL 33040
12-192	STERRETT, CHARLES HURLBUT	D. DECEMBER 9, 1965 BALTIMORE, MD.
41-106	STEVENS, CHARLES AUGUSTUS	12062 VALLEY VIEW #211-GARDEN GROVE CA 92645
45-103	STEVENS, EDWARD LEE	5610 BRAESVALLEY - HOUSTON TX 77035
14-205	STEVENS, JAMES ARTHUR	D. DECEMBER 25, 1966 BALTIMORE, MD.
58- 88	STEVENS, R. C.	1405 MOUND ST - DAVENPORT IA 52803
31- 86	STEVENS, ROBERT JORDAN	803 ROXBORO RD - ROCKVILLE MD 20850
13-173	STEWART, CHARLES EUGENE	D. NOVEMBER 18, 1934 CHICAGO, ILL.
78-129	STEWART, DAVID KEITH	2512 HAVENSCOURT BLVD - OAKLAND CA 94605
41-107	STEWART, EDWARD PERRY	5501 W 119TH ST-INGLEWOOD CA 90304
27- 86	STEWART, FRANK	RR 1 STILLWATER MINN 55082
40- 85	STEWART, GLEN WELDON	60 S ALICIA-MEMPHIS TN 38112
63-117	STEWART, JAMES FRANKLIN	RR 1 - LAFAYETTE AL 36862
16- 86	STEWART, JOHN FRANKLIN	D. DECEMBER 30, 1980 LAKE CITY, FLA.
13-174	STEWART, MARK	D. JANUARY 17, 1942 MEMPHIS, TENN.
78-130	STEWART, SAMUEL LEE	107 SCENIC VIEW DR - SWANNANOA NC 28778
52- 98	STEWART, VESTON GOFF	RAY MCCOTTER REALTY CO - NEW BERN NC28560
21- 97	STEWART, WALTER CLEVELAND	D. SEPTEMBER 26, 1974 KNOXVILLE, TENN.

"Jigger" Statz

40- 86	STEWART, WALTER NESBITT	RR 2 - LONDON OH 43140
44-124	STEWART, WILLIAM MACKLIN	D. MARCH 21, 1960 MACON, GA.
55-117	STEWART, WILLIAM WAYNE	2484 PONTIAC DR - SYLVAN LAKE MI 48053
79-107	STIEB, DAVID ANDREW	16740 CERRO VISTA DR - MORGAN HILL CA 95037
29- 99	STIELY, FREDERICK WARREN	D. JANUARY 6, 1981 VALLEY VIEW, PA.
60- 97	STIGMAN, RICHARD LEWIS	12914 5TH AVE S - BURNSVILLE MN 55337
30- 79	STILES, ROLLAND MAYS	OLD ADD: 10020 JEFFLEIGH LN - ST LOUIS MO
75-114	STILLMAN, ROYLE ELDON	5201 HARTFORD WAY - WESTMINSTER CA 92683
61-103	STILLWELL, RONALD ROY	1417 DOVER - THOUSAND OAKS CA 91360
80-125	STIMAC, CRAIG STEVEN	OLD ADD: 10856 CARAVELLE PL - SAN DIEGO CA
23-128	STIMSON, CARL REMUS	D. NOVEMBER 9, 1936 OMAHA, NEB.
34- 95	STINE, LEE ELBERT	1939 CALLE PASITO - HEMET CA 92343
69-164	STINSON, GORRELL ROBERT	OLD ADD: BOX 241 - BOONEVILLE NC

132

```
43-135  STIRNWEISS, GEORGE HENRY        D. SEPTEMBER 15, 1958 NEWARK, N. J.
47- 86  STOBBS, CHARLES KLEIN           OLD ADD: 5251 ASHTON RD - SARASOTA FL
13-175  STOCK, MILTON JOSEPH            D. JULY 16, 1977 MONTROSE, ALA.
59- 81  STOCK, WESLEY GAY               5917 FRANCES AVE NE - TACOMA WA 98422
81-134  STODDARD, ROBERT LYLE           15760 SUNNYSIDE AVE - MORGAN HILL CA 95037
75-115  STODDARD, TIMOTHY PAUL          3928 E BUTTERNUT ST - EAST CHICAGO IN 46312
25- 98  STOKES, ALBERT JOHN             55 CAVALRY HILL RD - WILTON CT 06897
25- 99  STOKES, ARTHUR MELTON           D. JUNE 3, 1962 TITUSVILLE, PA.
45-104  STONE, CHARLES RICHARD          D. FEBRUARY 18, 1980 OKLAHOMA CITY, OKLA.
63- 86  STONE, DARRAH DEAN              1221 7TH AVE CT - SILVIS IL 61282
13-176  STONE, DWIGHT ELY               D. JULY 3, 1976 GLENDALE, CALIF.
23-129  STONE, EDWIN ARNOLD             D. JULY 29, 1948 HUDSON FALLS  N. Y.
69-165  STONE, EUGENE DANIEL            367 F AVENUE - CORONADO CA 92118
67-102  STONE, GEORGE HEARD             BOX 260 AVON AVE - RUSTON LA 71270
66- 85  STONE, HARRY RONALD             3870 FERRY ST - EUGENE OR 97405
28- 90  STONE, JOHN THOMAS              D. NOVEMBER 30, 1955 SHELBYVILLE, TENN.
43-136  STONE, JOHN VERNON              9462 BEVAN - WESTMINSTER CA 92685
71- 99  STONE, STEVEN MICHAEL           10 COLDWATER CT - TOWSON MD 21204
23-130  STONE, WILLIAM ARTHUR           D. JANUARY 1, 1960 JACKSONVILLE, FLA.
33- 59  STONEHAM, JOHN ANDREW           7201 OAK HILL DR - HOUSTON TX 77017
67-103  STONEMAN, WILLIAM HAMBLY        ROUTE 3 - GEORGETOWN ONTARIO LFG 455
22-130  STONER, ULYSSES SIMPSON GRANT   D. JUNE 26, 1966 ENID, OKLA.
31- 87  STORIE, HOWARD EDWARD           D. JULY 2, 1968 PITTSFIELD, MASS.
30- 80  STORTI, LINDO IVAN              9915 RAMONA AVE -NLA MONTCLAIR CA 91763
64-118  STOTTLEMYRE, MELVIN LEON        5804 W CHESTNUT - YAKIMA WA 98908
31- 88  STOUT, ALLYN MCCLELLAND         D. DECEMBER 22, 1974 SIKESTON, MO.
38- 94  STOVIAK, RAYMOND THOMAS         2501 S OCEAN BLVD #208 - BACON RATON FL 33432
60- 98  STOWE, HAROLD RUDOLPH           RR 3 BOX 281 - GASTONIA NC 28006
70-128  STRAHLER, MICHAEL WAYNE         2746 WENDY PL - PORT HUENEME CA 93041
54-104  STRAHS, RICHARD BERNARD         1334 TOUHY - CHICAGO IL 60626
79-108  STRAIN, JOSEPH ALLAN            1781 SOUTH FOREST - DENVER CO 80222
72-110  STRAMPE, ROBERT EDWIN           603 MILTON AVE - JANESVILLE WI 53545
13-177  STRAND, PAUL EDWARD             D. JULY 2, 1974 SALT LAKE CITY, UT.
15-158  STRANDS, JOHN LAWRENCE          D. JANUARY 19, 1957 FOREST PARK, ILL.
15-159  STRANDS, LEWIS
34- 96  STRANGE, ALAN COCHRANE          8239 41ST AVE NE - SEATTLE WA 98115
34- 97  STRATTON, MONTY FRANKLIN PIERCE RR 2 BOX 97 - GREENVILLE TX 75401
```

```
28- 91  STRELECKI, EDWARD HAROLD               D. JANUARY 9, 1968 NEWARK, N. J.
54-105  STREULI, WALTER HERBERT                1107 WESTMINSTER - GREENSBORO NC 27410
50- 94  STRICKLAND, GEORGE BEVAN               6328 CONSTANCE ST - NEW ORLEANS LA 70118
71-100  STRICKLAND, JAMES MICHAEL              796 CATHEDRAL DR - APTOS CA 95003
37- 97  STRICKLAND, WILLIAM GOSS               1335 EDGEWATER BEACH DR - LAKELAND FL 33801
59- 82  STRIKER, WILBUR SCOTT                  120 SCHELL AVE - BUCYRUS OH 44820
40- 87  STRINCEVICH, NICHOLAS MIHAILOVICH      3667 JACKSON ST - GARY IN 46408
41-108  STRINGER, LOUIS BERNARD                207 CALLE FELICIDAD - SAN CLEMENTE CA 92672
28- 92  STRIPP, JOSEPH VALENTINE               1001 W NEW HAMPSHIRE - ORLANDO FL 32802
70-129  STROHMAYER, JOHN EMERY                 3532 PARK ST - CENTRAL VALLEY CA 96019
72-111  STROM, BRENT TERRY                     1628 WHITSETT DR - EL CAJON CA 92020
39-113  STROMME, FLOYD MARVIN                  BOX 84 - NORTH BEND OR 97459
29-100  STRONER, JAMES M.                      D. NOVEMBER 16, 1971 CHICAGO, ILL.
66- 86  STROUD, EDWIN MARVIN                   264 E MARKET ST - WARREN OH 44481
10-142  STROUD, RALPH VIVIAN                   D. APRIL 11, 1970 STOCKTON, CALIF.
34- 98  STRUSS, CLARENCE HERBERT               1060 DEVON RD #11 - PLAINWELL MI 49080
24-106  STRYKER, STERLING ALPA                 D. NOVEMBER 5, 1964 RED BANK, N. J.
22-131  STUART, JOHN DAVIS                     D. MAY 13, 1970 CHARLESTON, W. VA.
21- 98  STUART, LUTHER LANE                    D. JUNE 15, 1947 WINSTON-SALEM, N. C.
49- 83  STUART, MARLIN HENRY                   RR 1 BOX 133 - PARAGOULD AR 72450
58- 89  STUART, RICHARD LEE                    %T.GEORGE,202 E MAIN ST - HUNTINGTON NY 11743
67-104  STUBING, LAWRENCE GEORGE               10627 QUEZADA - EL PASO TX 79935
21- 99  STUELAND, GEORGE ANTON                 D. SEPTEMBER 9, 1964 ONAWA, IA.
50- 95  STUFFEL, PAUL HARRINGTON               11000 JULIE NE - ALLIANCE OH 44601
57- 82  STUMP, JAMES GILBERT                   939 WESTON - LANSING MI 48906
31- 89  STUMPF, GEORGE FREDERICK               222 STAFFORD AV - NEW ORLEANS LA 70124
12-193  STUMPF, WILLIAM FREDRICK               D. FEBRUARY 14, 1966 CROWNSVILLE, MD.
55-118  STURDIVANT, THOMAS VIRGIL              OLD ADD: 4005 NW 18TH - OKLAHOMA CITY OK
27- 87  STURDY, GUY R.                         D. MAY 4, 1965 MARSHALL, TEX.
40- 88  STURGEON, ROBERT HARWOOD               3903 LEWIS AVE-LONG BEACH CA 90807
14-206  STURGIS, DEAN DONNELL                  D. JUNE 4, 1950 UNIONTOWN, PA.
41-109  STURM, JOHN PETER JOSEPH               3840 FRENCH CT-ST LOUIS MO 63116
26- 80  STUTZ, GEORGE                          D. DECEMBER 29, 1930 PHILADELPHIA, PA.
19- 80  STYLES, WILLIAM GRAVES                 D. MARCH 14, 1956 HUNTSVILLE, ALA.
66- 87  SUAREZ, KENNETH RAYMOND                1810 PARK HILL DR - ARLINGTON TX 76010
```

```
44-125  SUAREZ, LUIS ABELARDO          OLD ADD: AGUILA #4 - HAVANA CUBA
70-130  SUCH, RICHARD STANLEY          3110 HICKORY HILL DR - SANFORD NC 27330
38- 95  SUCHE, CHARLES MORRIS          1215 VIEWRIDGE DR - SAN ANTONIO TX 78213
50- 96  SUCHECKI, JAMES JOSEPH         OLD ADD: 1745 FAGERNESSE POINT RD-WAYZATA MN
68-100  SUDAKIS, WILLIAM PAUL          21295 SEASPRITE - HUNTINGTON BEACH CA 92646
41-110  SUDER, PETER                   903 ROOSEVELT AVE - ALIQUIPPA PA 15001
30- 81  SUHR, AUGUST RICHARD           341 HAZEL AVE - MILLBRAE CA 94030
26- 81  SUKEFORTH, CLYDE LEROY         RR 3 - WALDOBORO ME 04572
64-119  SUKLA, EDWARD ANTHONY          926 HYDE CT - COSTA MESA CA 92626
80-126  SULARZ, GUY PATRICK            6225-108 SHOUP AVE - WOODLAND HILLS CA 91364
36- 89  SULIK, ERNEST RICHARD          D. MAY 31, 1963 OAKLAND, CAL.
44-126  SULLIVAN, CARL MANUEL          OLD ADD: 4901 43RD ST - LUBBOCK TX
28- 93  SULLIVAN, CHARLES EDWARD       D. MAY 28, 1935 MAIDEN, N. C.
53- 87  SULLIVAN, FRANKLIN LEAL        BOX 1873 - LIHUE HI 96766
55-119  SULLIVAN, HAYWOOD COOPER       FENWAY PARK - BOSTON MA 02215
21-100  SULLIVAN, JAMES RICHARD        D. FEBRUARY 12, 1972 BURTONSVILLE, MD.
35-105  SULLIVAN, JOE                  BOX 1497 - SEQUIM WA 98382
19- 81  SULLIVAN, JOHN JEREMIAH        D. JULY 7, 1958 CHICAGO, ILL.
20-112  SULLIVAN, JOHN LAWRENCE        D. APRIL 1, 1966 UNION CO., PA.
42- 99  SULLIVAN, JOHN PATRICK         9539 PRAIRIE AVE - HIGHLAND IN 46322
63-118  SULLIVAN, JOHN PETER           19 CLAY ST - DANSVILLE NY 14437
39-114  SULLIVAN, PAUL THOMAS          6602 N 82ND WAY - SCOTTSDALE AZ 85253
51- 93  SULLIVAN, RUSSELL GUY H        1701 HILL-N-DALE DR - FREDERICKSBURG VA 22401
22-132  SULLIVAN, THOMAS AUGUSTIN      D. SEPTEMBER 23, 1962 WEST ROXBURY, MASS.
25-100  SULLIVAN, THOMAS BRANDON       D. AUGUST 16, 1944 SEATTLE, WASH.
31- 90  SULLIVAN, WILLIAM JOSEPH JR    BOX 2505 - SARASOTA FL 33578
20-113  SUMMA, HOMER WAYNE             D. JANUARY 29, 1966 LOS ANGELES, CAL.
74-127  SUMMERS, JOHN JUNIOR           1511 E WINDJAMMER WAY - TEMPE AZ 85251
28- 94  SUMNER, CARL RINGDAHL          18 WINTERSET DR - CHATHAM MA 02633
74-128  SUNDBERG, JAMES HOWARD         4610 RIVERFOREST DR - ARLINGTON TX 76017
56- 80  SUNDIN, GORDON VINCENT         5916 FAIRWOOD DR - MINNETONKA MN 55343
36- 90  SUNDRA, STEPHEN RICHARD        D. MARCH 23, 1952 CLEVELAND, O.
37- 98  SUNKEL, THOMAS JACOB           RR 6 PARIS IL 61944
49- 84  SURKONT, MATTHEW CONSTANTINE   94 BROOKDALE BLVD - PAWTUCKET RI 02861
29-101  SUSCE, GEORGE CYRIL METHODIUS SR 7803 BROUGHTON - SARASOTA FL 33580
55-120  SUSCE, GEORGE DANIEL JR        12 JARVIS CIRCLE - NEEDHAM MA 02192
34- 99  SUSKO, PETER JONATHAN          D. MAY 22, 1978 JACKSONVILLE, FLA.
38- 96  SUTCLIFFE, CHARLES INIGO       33 MALVEY ST FALL RIVER MA 02720
76- 87  SUTCLIFFE, RICHARD LEE         9914 E 38TH TER - KANSAS CITY MO 64133
64-120  SUTHERLAND, DARRELL WAYNE      3445 LAS PALMAS AVE - GLENDALE CA 91208
66- 88  SUTHERLAND, GARY LYNN          338 N OAK CLIFF - MONROVIA CA 91016
21-101  SUTHERLAND, HARVEY SCOTT       D. MAY 11, 1972 PORTLAND, ORE.
49- 85  SUTHERLAND, HOWARD ALVIN       D. AUGUST 26, 1979 WASHINGTON, D. C.
80-127  SUTHERLAND, LEONARDO CANTIN    12172 PEARCE AVE - GARDEN GROVE CA 92643
76- 88  SUTTER, HOWARD BRUCE           12009 TINDALL DR - TOWN & COUNTRY MO 63131
66- 89  SUTTON, DONALD HOWARD          4367 N PARK VICENTE - CALABASAS PARK CA 91302
```

```
77-138  SUTTON, JOHNNY IKE             RR 1 BOX 857 - DESOTO TX 75115
73-114  SWAN, CRAIG STEVEN             72 ROCKWOOD LN - GREENWICH CT 06830
14-207  SWANN, HENRY                   B. 1892
55-121  SWANSON, ARTHUR LEONARD        565 SEYBURN ST - BATON ROUGE LA 70808
29-102  SWANSON, ERNEST EVAR           D. JULY 17, 1973 GALESBURG, ILL.
28- 95  SWANSON, KARL EDWARD           212 HILLCREST DR - AVON PARK FL 33825
71-101  SWANSON, STANLEY LAWRENCE      2305 JAMES HOWE RD - DALLAS OR 97338
14-208  SWANSON, WILLIAM ANDREW        D. OCTOBER 14, 1954 NEW YORK, N.Y.
47- 87  SWARTZ, SHERWIN MERLE          1937 N BEVERLY DR - BEVERLY HILLS CA 90210
20-114  SWARTZ, VERNON MONROE          D. JANUARY 13, 1980 GERMANTOWN, O.
14-209  SWEENEY, CHARLES FRANCIS       D. MARCH 13, 1955 PITTSBURGH, PA.
44-127  SWEENEY, HENRY LEON            D. MAY 6, 1980 COLUMBIA, TENN.
28- 96  SWEENEY, WILLIAM JOSEPH        D. APRIL 18, 1957 SAN DIEGO, CAL.
78-131  SWEET, RICHARD JOE             OLD ADD: 1120 OCEAN BEACH HWY - LONGVIEW WA
27- 88  SWEETLAND, LESTER LEO          D. MARCH 4, 1974 MELBOURNE, FL.
22-133  SWENTOR, AUGUST WILLIAM        D. NOVEMBER 10, 1969 WATERBURY, CONN.
29-103  SWETONIC, STEPHEN ALBERT       D. APRIL 22, 1974 CANONSBURG, PA.
40- 89  SWIFT, ROBERT VIRGIL           D. OCTOBER 17, 1966 DETROIT, MICH.
```

32- 82 SWIFT, WILLIAM VINCENT   D. FEBRUARY 23, 1969 BARTOW, FLA.
39-115 SWIGART, OADIS VAUGHN   ARCHIE MO 64725
17- 80 SWIGLER, ADAM WILLIAM   D. FEBRUARY 58 1975 PHILADELPHIA, PA.
11-164 SWINDELL, JOSHUA ERNEST   D. MARCH 19, 1969 FRUITA, COLO.
74-129 SWISHER, STEVEN EUGENE   2503 DIVISION ST EXT - PARKERSBURG WV 26101
65-104 SWOBODA, RONALD ALAN   2504 LAKEVIEW AVE - BALTIMORE MD 21219
77-139 SYKES, ROBERT JOSEPH   603 SIXTH AVE - BELMAR NJ 07719
53- 88 SZEKELY, JOSEPH   3260 ALLEN - PARIS TX 75460
70-131 SZOTKIEWICZ, KENNETH JOHN   1709 BEECH ST - WILMINGTON DE 19805
76- 89 TABB, JERRY LYNN   2414 FIR - PAMPA TX 79065
26- 82 TABER, EDWARD TIMOTHY   3240 S 31ST ST - LINCOLN NE 68502
81-135 TABLER, PATRICK SEAN   1023 NIMITZ LN - CINCINNATI OH 45230
38- 97 TABOR, JAMES REUBIN   D. AUGUST 22, 1953 SACRAMENTO, CAL.
13-178 TAFF, JOHN GALLATIN   D. MAY 15, 1961 HOUSTON, TEX.
28- 97 TAITT, DOUGLAS JOHN   D. DECEMBER 12, 1970 PORTLAND, ORE.
63-119 TALBOT, FREDERICK LEALAND   770 LUNSEFORD LN - FALLS CHURCH VA 22043
53- 89 TALBOT, ROBERT DALE   608 W KAWEAH - VISALIA CA 93277
43-137 TALCOTT, LEROY EVERETT   5060 SW 82ND AVE - MIAMI BEACH FL 33143
66- 90 TALTON, MARION LEE   RR2 BOX 156A - PIKEVILLE NC 27863
76- 90 TAMARGO, JOHN FELIX   1425 E PARIS - TAMPA FL 33604
34-100 TAMULIS, VITAUTIS CASIMIRUS   D. MAY 5, 1974 NASHVILLE, TENN.
73-115 TANANA, FRANK DARYL   23666 LAGARTO - MISSION VIEJO CA 92691
25-101 TANKERSLEY, LAWRENCE WILLIAM   830 GRIFFITH AVE - TERRELL TX 75160
55-122 TANNER, CHARLES WILLIAM   34 MAITLAND LN E - NEW CASTLE PA 16101
54-106 TAPPE, ELVIN WALTER   2424 SPRING ST - QUINCY IL 62301
50- 97 TAPPE, THEODORE NASH   203 MARR - WENATCHEE WA 98801
14-221 TAPPEN, WALTER VAN DORN   D. DECEMBER 19, 1967 LYNWOOD, CALIF.
27- 89 TARBERT, WILBER ARLINGTON   D. NOVEMBER 27, 1946 CLEVELAND, O.
62-130 TARTABULL, JOSE   4105 NW 185TH ST - MIAMI FL 33164
58- 90 TASBY, WILLIE   1486 12TH ST - OAKLAND CA 94607
46- 96 TATE, ALVIN WALTER   739 WEST 3400 S - BOUNTIFUL UT 84010
24-107 TATE, HENRY BENNETT   D. OCTOBER 27, 1973 FRANKFORT, ILL.

58- 91 TATE, LEE WILLIE   6905 PRATT - OMAHA ND 68131
75-116 TATE, RANDALL LEE   RR 1 BOX 284 - KILLEN AL 35645
68-101 TATUM, JARVIS   1213 E 57TH ST - LOS ANGELES CA 90011
69-166 TATUM, KENNETH RAY   340 WOODWARD RD - BIRMINGHAM AL 35228
41-111 TATUM, THOMAS VEE TEE   4929 PATE AVE-OKLAHOMA CITY OK 73112
35-106 TAUBY, FRED JOSEPH   D. NOVEMBER 23, 1955 CONCORDIA, CAL.
28- 98 TAUSCHER, WALTER EDWARD   2600 WESTERN PARKWAY - ORLANDO FL 32803
58- 92 TAUSSIG, DONALD FRANKLIN   OLD ADD: RR 3 - KATONAH NY 10536
21-102 TAVENER, JOHN ADAM   D. SEPTEMBER 14, 1969 FT. WORTH, TEX.
76- 91 TAVERAS, ALEJANDRO ANTONIO   A. MONSANTO 8 TAMBORIL-SANTIAGO DOMINICAN REP
71-102 TAVERAS, FRANKLIN CRISOSTOMO   CALLE 31-#16-LOS COLINOS,SANTIAGO DOM REP
58- 93 TAYLOR, ANTONIO   7 ROBIN RD - YEADON PA 19051
21-103 TAYLOR, ARLOS   OLD ADD: HAMMOND IN
12-194 TAYLOR, BENJAMIN HARRISON   D. NOVEMBER 3, 1946 MARTIN COUNTY, IND.
77-140 TAYLOR, BRUCE BELL   8 HIGHLAND PARK RD - RUTLAND MA 01543
25-102 TAYLOR, C. L.   D. JULY 7, 1980 TEMPLE, TEXAS
68-102 TAYLOR, CARL MEANS   530 S VENICE BY-PASS #11-B - VENICE FL 33595
69-167 TAYLOR, CHARLES GILBERT   1619 GEORGETOWN LN - MURFREESBORO TN 37130
26- 83 TAYLOR, DANIEL TURNEY   D. OCTOBER 11, 1972 LATROBE, PA.
26- 84 TAYLOR, EDWARD JAMES   500 5TH AVE W #23 - SEATTLE WA 98119
51- 94 TAYLOR, EUGENE BENJAMIN   12677 COULSON - HOUSTON TX 77015
50- 98 TAYLOR, FREDERICK RANKIN   3144 DRRBY RD - COLUMBUS OH 43221
69-168 TAYLOR, GARY WILLIAM   28991 GRANDVIEW - INKSTER MI 48141
57- 83 TAYLOR, HARRY EVANS   2125 COOKS LN - FORT WORTH TX 76112
32- 83 TAYLOR, HARRY WARREN   D. APRIL 27, 1969 TOLEDO, O.
46- 97 TAYLOR, JAMES HARRY   RR 13 BOX 3 - WEST TERRE HAUTE IN 47885
20-115 TAYLOR, JAMES WREN   D. SEPTEMBER 19, 1974 ORLANDO, FLA.
54-107 TAYLOR, JOE CEPHUS   705 WATT LN - PITTSBURGH PA 15219
23-131 TAYLOR, LEO THOMAS   11520 GREENWOOD #102 - SEATTLE WA 98133
11-165 TAYLOR, PHILIP WILEY   D. JULY 9, 1954 TOPEKA, KAN.
57- 84 TAYLOR, ROBERT DALE   RR 5 BOX 1028 - MURRAY KY 40271
70-132 TAYLOR, ROBERT LEE   27 SUNNYBROOK RD - SPRINGFIELD MA 01109
62-131 TAYLOR, RONALD WESLEY   75 BANFF RD - TORONTO ONT
58- 94 TAYLOR, SAMUEL DOUGLAS   RR 13, HERON CIR / SPARTANBURG SC 29301
24-108 TAYLOR, THOMAS LIVINGSTONE   CARLTON D. APRIL 5, 1956 GREENVILLE, MISS.
52- 99 TAYLOR, VERNON CHARLES   823 CEDARCROFT DR - MILLERSVILLE MD 21108
54-108 TAYLOR, WILLIAM MICHAEL   BOX 146 - ACTON CA 93510
30- 82 TEACHOUT, ARTHUR JOHN   31388 FLYING CLOUD - LAGUNA NIGUEL CA 92677
36- 91 TEBBETTS, GEORGE ROBERT   229 OAK AVE ANNA MARIA FL 33501
14-211 TEDROW, ALLEN SEYMOUR   D. JANUARY 23, 1958 WESTERVILLE, O.
53- 90 TEED, RICHARD LEROY   128 CUSTER DR - WINDSOR CT 06095

74-130	TEKULVE, KENTON CHARLES	1531 SEQUOIA - PITTSBURGH PA 15241
79-109	TELLMANN, THOMAS JOHN	271 YANKEE BUSH RD - STARBRICK PA 16365
52-100	TEMPLE, JOHN ELLIS	BOX 1047 - BALLANTINE SC 29002
55-123	TEMPLETON, CHARLES SHERMAN	BOX 457 - WYOMING MN 55092
76- 92	TEMPLETON, GARRY LEWIS	18052 MARK CIR - VILLA PARK CA 92667
69-169	TENACE, FURY GENE	15368 MARKER RD - POWAY CA 92064
29-104	TENNANT, JAMES MCDONNELL	95 DAVIS ST - HAUPPAUGE NY 11787
12-195	TENNANT, THOMAS FRANCIS	D. FEBRUARY 16, 1955 SAN CARLOS, CALIF.
67-105	TEPEDINO, FRANK RONALD	95 DAVIS ST - HAUPPAUGE NY 11787
46- 98	TEPSIC, JOSEPH JOHN	RR3 BOX 164 - TYRONE PA 16686
72-112	TERLECKI, ROBERT JOSEPH	760 NORWAY AVE - TRENTON NJ 08629
75-117	TERLECKY, GREGORY JOHN	1042 E GROVECENTER ST - WEST COVINA CA 91790
74-131	TERPKO, JEFFREY MICHAEL	RR 1 BOX 156 - SAYRE PA 18840
73-116	TERRELL, JERRY WAYNE	7524 DARBY - RESEDA CA 91335
40- 90	TERRY, LANCELOT YANK	D. NOVEMBER 4, 1979 BLOOMINGTON, IND.
56- 81	TERRY, RALPH WILLARD	801 PARK - LARNED KS 67550
23-132	TERRY, WILLIAM HAROLD	BOX 2177 - JACKSONVILLE FL 32203
16- 87	TERRY, ZEBULON ALEXANDER	300 S HIGHLAND AVE - LOS ANGELES CA 90036
32- 84	TERWILLIGER, RICHARD MARTIN	D. JANUARY 21, 1969 GREENVILLE, MICH.
49- 86	TERWILLIGER, WILLARD WAYNE	7617 NOREAST DR - FORT WORTH TX 76118
15-160	TESCH, ALBERT JOHN	D. AUGUST 3, 1947 JERSEY CITY, N.J.
12-196	TESREAU, CHARLES MONROE	D. SEPTEMBER 24, 1946 HANOVER, N.H.
58- 95	TESTA, NICHOLAS	2544 LURTING AVE - BRONX NY 10469
55-124	TETTELBACH, RICHARD MORLEY	OLD ADD: 295 PRESTON RD - CHESHIRE CT 06410
14-212	TEXTOR, GEORGE	D. MARCH 11, 1954 MASSILLON, O.
58- 96	THACKER, MORRIS BENTON	10206 BLUFFSPRINGS TRACE - LOUISVILLE KY40201
78-132	THAYER, GREGORY ALLEN	1000 3RD ST N - SAUK RAPIDS MN 56379
20-116	THEIS, JOHN LOUIS	D. JULY 6, 1941 GEORGETOWN, O.
77-141	THEISS, DUANE CHARLES	5 COLUMBUS ST - SOMERSET OH 43703
71-103	THEOBALD, RONALD MERRILL	9 FLEUTI - MORAGA CA 94556
73-117	THEODORE, GEORGE BASIL	3254 ELGIN DR - SALT LAKE CITY UT 84109
44-128	THESENGA, ARNOLD JOSEPH	3907 COUNTRYSIDE PLAZA - WICHITA KS 67218
24-109	THEVENOW, THOMAS JOSEPH	D. JULY 28, 1957 MADISON, IND.
52-101	THIEL, MAYNARD BERT	RR2 - MARION WI 54950
63-120	THIES, DAVID ROBERT	6140 ARCTIC WAY - MINNEAPOLIS MN 55436
54-109	THIES, VERNON ARTHUR	4 CORNFLOWER COURT - FLORISSANT MO 63033
67-106	THOENEN, RICHARD CRISPIN	51 N PEACH ST - MEDFORD OR 97501
26- 85	THOMAS, ALPHONSE	RR 1 - DALLASTOWN PA 17313
11-166	THOMAS, BLAINE M.	D. AUGUST 21, 1915 GLOBE, ARIZ.
60- 99	THOMAS, CARL LESLIE	5850 E ORANGE BLOSSOM LN - PHOENIX AZ 85018
12-197	THOMAS, CHESTER DAVID	D. DECEMBER 24, 1953 MODESTO, CALIF.
25-103	THOMAS, CLARENCE FLETCHER	D. MARCH 21, 1952 CHARLOTTESVILLE, VA.
16- 88	THOMAS, CLAUDE ALFRED	D. MARCH 6, 1946 SULPHUR, OKLA.
76- 93	THOMAS, DANNY LEE	D. JUNE 12, 1980 MOBILE ALA.
71-104	THOMAS, DERREL OSBON	3340 OLIPHANT ST - SAN DIEGO CA 92106
27- 90	THOMAS, FAY WESLEY	10526 ANDORA AV - CHATSWORTH CA 913114
51- 95	THOMAS, FRANK JOSEPH	118 DORAY DR - PITTSBURGH PA 15237
18- 70	THOMAS, FRED HARVEY	RR 1 BOX 183 - BIRCHWOOD WI 54817
57- 85	THOMAS, GEORGE EDWARD	12733 PORTLAND AVE S - BURNSVILLE MN 55337
24-110	THOMAS, HERBERT MARK	818 W PRATT ST - STARKE FL 32071
73-118	THOMAS, JAMES GORMAN	759 TALLWOOD RD - CHARLESTON SC 29412
61-104	THOMAS, JAMES LEROY	50 E CARDIGAN - ST LOUIS MO 63135
51- 96	THOMAS, JOHN TILLMAN	2607 STEVENSON ST - SEDALIA MO 65301
52-102	THOMAS, KEITH MARSHALL	12F CYPRESS GROVE APTS - WILMINGTON NC 28401
50- 99	THOMAS, LEO RAYMOND	2024 SANDCREEK WAY - ALAMEDA CA 94501
32- 85	THOMAS, LUTHER BAXTER	RR 1 BOX 400 - NORTH GARDEN VA 22959
26- 86	THOMAS, MYLES LEWIS	D. DECEMBER 12, 1963 TOLEDO, O.
38- 98	THOMAS, RAYMOND JOSEPH	607 W VANCE ST - WILSON NC 27893
21-104	THOMAS, ROBERT WILLIAM	D. MARCH 29, 1962 FREMONT, O.
77-142	THOMAS, ROY JUSTIN	134 SATINWOOD - SAINT CHARLES MO 63301
74-132	THOMAS, STANLEY BROWN	23 MIDDLE AVE - MEXICO ME 04257
57- 86	THOMAS, VALMY	BOX 9184 - SANTURCE PR 00908
10-143	THOMASEN, ARTHUR WILSON	D. MAY 2, 1944 KANSAS CITY, MO.
74-133	THOMASON, MELVIN ERSKINE	405 S BROAD ST - CLINTON SC 29325
72-113	THOMASSON, GARY LEAH	4515 E ONYX ST - PHOENIX AZ 85028
78-133	THOMPSON, BOBBY LARUE	3106 CAPITOL DR #2 - CHARLOTTE NC 28208
54-110	THOMPSON, CHARLES LEMOINE	536 SUMMIT DR - LEWISTOWN PA 17044
70-133	THOMPSON, DANNY LEON	D. DECEMBER 10, 1976 ROCHESTER, MINN.
48- 98	THOMPSON, DAVID FORREST	D. FEBRUARY 26, 1979 CHARLOTTE, N. C.
49- 87	THOMPSON, DONALD NEWLIN	87 E EUCLID PKWY - ASHEVILLE NC 28804
39-116	THOMPSON, EUGENE EARL	8731 E CAMELBACK RD-SCOTTSDALE AZ 85252
20-117	THOMPSON, FRANK E.	D. JUNE 27, 1940 MINERAL TWP., MO.
11-167	THOMPSON, FULLER WEIDNER	D. FEBRUARY 19, 1972 LOS ANGELES, CALIF.

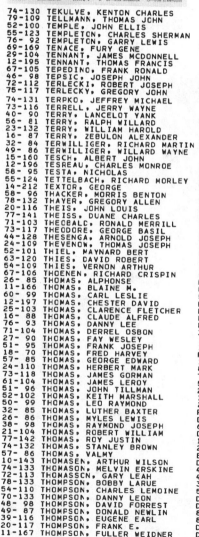

19- 82 THOMPSON, HAROLD   D. FEBRUARY 14, 1951 RENO, NEV.
47- 88 THOMPSON, HENRY CURTIS   D. SEPTEMBER 30, 1969 FRESNO, CAL.
14-213 THOMPSON, JAMES ALFRED   101 SECOND ST - BLACK MOUNTAIN NC 28711
76- 94 THOMPSON, JASON DOLPH   26026 VIA REMOLINO - MISSION VIEJO CA 92691
21-105 THOMPSON, JOHN DUDLEY   D. FEBRUARY 17, 1965 SANTA BARBARA, CAL.
48- 99 THOMPSON, JOHN SAMUEL   10 BEL PRE CT - ROCKVILLE MD 20853
25-104 THOMPSON, LAFAYETTE FRESCO   D. NOVEMBER 20, 1968 FULLERTON, CAL.
71-105 THOMPSON, MICHAEL WAYNE   7565 TURNER DR - DENVER CO 80221
33- 60 THOMPSON, RUPERT LUCKHART   D. MAY 24, 1971 AUBURN, CAL.
12-198 THOMPSON, THOMAS CARL   D. JANUARY 16, 1963 LAJOLLA, CALIF.
12-199 THOMPSON, THOMAS HOMER   D. SEPTEMBER 19, 1957 ATLANTA, GA.
78-134 THOMPSON, VERNON SCOT   110 BEACON RD - RENFREW PA 16053
46- 99 THOMSON, ROBERT BROWN   122 SUNLIT DR - WATCHUNG NJ 07060
79-110 THON, RICHARD WILLIAM   HB-12 LOMBARDIA ST - RIO PIEDRAS CA 00924
17- 81 THORMAHLEN, HERBERT EHLER   D. FEBRUARY 6, 1955 LOS ANGELES, CALIF.
77-143 THORMODSGARD, PAUL GAYTON   884 N 4TH - BANNING CA 92220
73-119 THORNTON, ANDRE   17222 E VIEW DR - CHAGRIN FALLS OH 44022
73-120 THORNTON, OTIS BENJAMIN   BOX 164 - DOCENA AL 35060
51- 97 THORPE, BENJAMIN ROBERT   BOX 46 - WAVELAND MS 39576
13-179 THORPE, JAMES FRANCIS   D. MARCH 28, 1953 LOMITA, CALIF.
55-125 THORPE, ROBERT JOSEPH   D. MARCH 17, 1960 SAN DIEGO, CAL.
16- 89 THRASHER, FRANK EDWARD   D. JUNE 12, 1938 CLEVELAND, TENN.
55-126 THRONEBERRY, MARVIN EUGENE   12102 MACON RD - COLLIERVILLE TN 38017
52-103 THRONEBERRY, MAYNARD FAYE   12016 MACON RD - COLLIERVILLE TN 38017
75-118 THROOP, GEORGE LYNFORD   672 W HIGHLAND AVE - SIERRA MADRE CA 91024
39-117 THUMAN, LOUIS CHARLES FRANK   6117 EDLYNNE RD-BALTIMORE MA 21212
55-127 THURMAN, ROBERT BURNS   2820 VASSAR - WICHITA KS 67220
23-133 THURSTON, HOLLIS JOHN   D. SEPTEMBER 14, 1973 LOS ANGELES, CAL.
64-121 TIANT, LUIS CLEMENTE   BOX 298 - SUDBURY MA 01776
72-114 TIDROW, RICHARD WILLIAM   404 JACKSON - KANSAS CITY MO 64123
52-104 TIEFENAUER, BOBBY GENE   300 S LINCOLN - DESLOGE MO 63603
62-132 TIEFENTHALER, VERLE MATHEW   1852 QUINT AVE - CARROLL IA 51401
20-118 TIERNEY, JAMES ARTHUR   D. APRIL 18, 1953 KANSAS CITY, MO.
33- 61 TIETJE, LESLIE WILLIAM   RR 2 BOX 107 - KASSON MN 55944
57- 87 TIGHE, JOHN THOMAS   14159 CLEVELAND - SPRING LAKE MI 49456
15-161 TILLMAN, JOHN LAWRENCE   D. APRIL 7, 1964 HARRISBURG, PA.
62-133 TILLMAN, JOHN ROBERT   403 WADERBROOK DR - GALLATIN TN 37066
67-107 TILLOTSON, THADDEUS ASA   870 DONNA DR - MERCED CA 95340
69-170 TIMBERLAKE, GARY DALE   LACONIA IN 47135
69-171 TIMMERMAN, THOMAS HENRY   720 N WALNUT - BREESE IL 62230
14-214 TINCUP, AUSTIN BEN   D. JULY 5, 1980 CLAREMORE, OK.
32- 86 TINNING, LYLE FORREST   D. JANUARY 17, 1961 EVANSVILLE, IND.
15-162 TIPPLE, DANIEL E   D. MARCH 26, 1960 OMAHA, NEB.
39-118 TIPTON, ERIC GORDON   125 NINA LN - WILLIAMSBURG VA 23185
48-100 TIPTON, JOSEPH JOHN   1129 2ND AVE - PLEASANT GROVE AL 35127
69-172 TISCHINSKI, THOMAS ARTHUR   815 N CHESTNUT - KANSAS CITY MO 64120
36- 92 TISING, JOHNNIE JOSEPH   D. SEPTEMBER 5, 1967 LEADVILLE, COLO.
78-135 TOBIK, DAVID VANCE   1243 CROYDEN RD - CLEVELAND OH 44124
37- 99 TOBIN, JAMES ANTHONY   D. MAY 19, 1969 OAKLAND, CAL.

32- 87 TOBIN, JOHN MARTIN   2 WESTCHESTER AV - WHITE PLAINS NY 106021
45-105 TOBIN, JOHN PATRICK   D. JANUARY 18, 1982 OAKLAND, CALIF.
14-215 TOBIN, JOHN THOMAS   D. DECEMBER 10, 1969 ST. LOUIS, MO.
41-112 TOBIN, MARION BROOKS   D. JANUARY 21, 1975 SHREVEPORT, LA.
32- 88 TODD, ALFRED CHESTER   931 GRAND CENTRAL AV - HORSEHEADS NY 14845
77-144 TODD, JACKSON A   4527 E 25TH PL - TULSA OK 74114
74-134 TODD, JAMES RICHARD JR.   8630 E PAWNEE DR - PARKER CO 80134
24-111 TOOT, PHILIP JULIUS   D. NOVEMBER 15, 1973 ST. LOUIS, MO.
47- 89 TOENES, WILLIAM HARRELL   5119 BRANCH AVE - TAMPA FL 33603
65-105 TOLAN, ROBERT   529 RANCHO BAUER - HOUSTON TX 77079
81-136 TOLLESON, JIMMY WAYNE   RR 10 PEACH VALLEY DR-SPARTANBURG SC 29303
81-137 TOLMAN, TIMOTHY LEE   121 HART AVE - SANTA MONICA CA 90405
25-105 TOLSON, CHESTER JULIUS   D. APRIL 16, 1965 WASHINGTON, D. C.
53- 91 TOMANEK, RICHARD CARL   165 DUFF DR - AVON LAKE OH 44012
49- 88 TOMASIC, ANDREW JOHN   230 7TH ST - WHITEHALL PA 18052
13-180 TOMER, GEORGE CLARENCE   1905 WARFORD - PERRY IA 50220
72-115 TOMLIN, DAVID ALLEN   RR 1 - MANCHESTER OH 45144
12-200 TOMPKINS, CHARLES HERBERT   D. SEPTEMBER 20, 1975 PRESCOTT, ARK.
65-106 TOMPKINS, RONALD EVERETT   188 E "J" ST - CHULA VISTA CA 92010
75-119 TOMS, THOMAS HOWARD   1707 ROXBURY DR - WILSON NC 27893
11-168 TONEY, FRED ALEXANDRA   D. MARCH 11, 1953 NASHVILLE, TENN.

11-169 TONNEMAN, CHARLES RICHARD   D. AUGUST 7, 1951 PRESCOTT, ARIZ.
11-170 TOOLEY, ALBERT   D. AUGUST 17, 1976 MARSHALL, MICH.
21-106 TOPORCER, GEORGE   30 TEED ST - HUNTINGDON STATION NY 11747
62-134 TOPPIN, RUPERTO   OLD ADD: 601 CROWN ST - BROOKLYN NY 11213
64-122 TORBORG, JEFFREY ALLEN   1375 CHAPEL HILL - MOUNTAINSIDE NJ 07092
47- 90 TORGESON, CLIFFORD EARL   2121 RUCKER - EVERETT WA 98201
17- 82 TORKELSON, CHESTER LEROY   D. SEPTEMBER 22, 1964 CHICAGO, ILL.
20-119 TORPHY, WALTER ANTHONY   D. FEBRUARY 11, 1980 FALL RIVER, MASS.
56- 82 TORRE, FRANK JOSEPH   %RAWLINGS,2300 DELMAR BLVD-ST LOUIS MO 63166
60-100 TORRE, JOSEPH PAUL   114 ANDERSON AVE - DEMAREST NJ 07627
75-120 TORREALBA, PABLO ARNOLDO   AVE PTE.MEDINA,MARIO 50,PISO 19-CARACAS VENEZ
77-145 TORRES, ANGEL RAFAEL   AZUA APARTADO #197 - AZUA DOMINICAN REPUBLIC
40- 91 TORRES, DON GILBERTO NUNEZ CESPEDES 17-REGLA HAVANA CUBA
62-135 TORRES, FELIX   RR 3 BOX 105 - SANTA ISABEL PR 00757
68-103 TORRES, HECTOR EPITACIO   11416 MENKAR PL - SAN DIEGO CA 92101
20-120 TORRES, RICARDO J.   D. HAVANA, CUBA
71-106 TORRES, ROSENDO   151-34 136TH AVE - JAMAICA NY 11434
67-108 TORREZ, MICHAEL AUGUSTINE   208 N LAKE ST - TOPEKA KS 66616
42-100 TOST, LOUIS EUGENE   D. FEBRUARY 22,1967 SANTA CLARA, CAL.
62-136 TOTH, PAUL LOUIS   6538 SUDER - ERIE MI 48133
28- 99 TOUCHSTONE, CLAYLAND MAFFITT D. APRIL 28, 1949 BEAUMONT, TEX.
65-107 TOVAR, CESAR LEONARDO   CALLE REAL PRADO MARIA #58 - CARACAS VENEZ
20-121 TOWNSEND, IRA DANCE   D. JULY 21, 1965 SCHULENBERG, TEX.
20-122 TOWNSEND, LEO ALPHONSE   D. DECEMBER 3, 1976 MOBILE, ALA.
62-137 TRACEWSKI, RICHARD JOHN   5 FLORA DR - PECKVILLE PA 18452
80-128 TRACY, JAMES EDWIN   4785 CELADON AVE - FAIRFIELD OH 45014
13-181 TRAGESSER, WALTER JOSEPH   D. DECEMBER 14, 1970 LAFAYETTE, IND.
40- 92 TRAMBACK, STEPHEN JOSEPH   D. DECEMBER 28, 1979 BUFFALO, N. Y.
77-146 TRAMMELL, ALAN STUART   BOX 17091 - SAN DIEGO CA 92117
15-163 TRAUTMAN, FREDERICK ORLANDO D. FEBRUARY 15, 1964 BUCYRUS, O.
12-201 TRAVERS, ALOYSIUS JOSEPH   D. APRIL 21, 1968 PHILADELPHIA, PA.
74-135 TRAVERS, WILLIAM EDWARD   49 CLAIR DR - STOUGHTON MA 02072
33- 62 TRAVIS, CECIL HOWELL   2260 HWY 138 - RIVERDALE GA 30274
20-123 TRAYNOR, HAROLD JOSEPH   D. MARCH 16, 1972 PITTSBURGH, PA.
30- 83 TREADAWAY, EDGAR RAYMOND   D. OCTOBER 12, 1935 CHATTANOOGA, TENN.
44-129 TREADWAY, THADFORD LEON   750 DALRYMPLE RD NW #D-3 - ATLANTA GA 30328
37-100 TRECHOCK, FRANK ADAM   4600 29TH AVE S - MINNEAPOLIS MINN 55406
13-182 TREKELL, HARRY ROY   D. NOVEMBER 4, 1963 SPOKANE, WASH.
34-101 TREMARK, NICHOLAS JOSEPH   1906 LAUREL DR - HARLINGEN TX 78550
54-111 TREMEL, WILLIAM LEONARD   315 E 23RD AVE - ALTOONA PA 16601
27- 91 TREMPER, CARLTON OVERTON   15777 BOLESTA RD #143 - CLEARWATER FL 33520
38- 99 TRESH, MICHAEL   D. OCTOBER 1, 1966 DETROIT, MICH.
61-105 TRESH, THOMAS MICHAEL   4206 E WING RD, RR 6-MOUNT PLEASANT MI 48858
78-136 TREVINO, ALEJANDRO   ALONDRA #103,CUAUHTEMOC-MONTERREY N.L. MEXICO
68-104 TREVINO, CARLOS CASTRO   ALONDRA #102 COLONIA CUANHTEMON-MONTERREY MEX
53- 92 TRIANDOS, CONSTANDIN GUS   1207 WOODLAWN AVE - SAN JOSE CA 95128
53- 93 TRICE, ROBERT LEE   RR 1 BOX 25 - WEIRTON WV 26062
73-121 TRILLO, JESUS MANUEL   RIO MANAPIRE #1B-PRADOS DEL ESTE CARACAS VEN
55-128 TRIMBLE, JOSEPH GERARD   71 ARBOR DR - PROVIDENCE RI 02903
43-138 TRINKLE, KENNETH WAYNE   404 W WATER ST - PAOLI IN 47454
38-100 TRIPLETT, HERMAN COAKER   RR 1 BOX 72-C - BOONE NC 28607
73-122 TROEDSON, RICHARD LAMONTE   505 CHURCHILL PARK DR - SAN JOSE CA 95136
58- 97 TROSKY, HAROLD ARTHUR JR   1919 HAMILTON ST SW - CEDAR RAPIDS IA 52404
33- 63 TROSKY, HAROLD ARTHUR SR   D. JUNE 18, 1979 CEDAR RAPIDS, IOWA
37-101 TROTTER, WILLIAM FELIX   1107 W DELAWARE ST FAIRFIELD IL 62837
52-105 TROUPE, QUINCY THOMAS   1115 3RD AVE - LOS ANGELES CA 90019
39-119 TROUT, PAUL HOWARD   D. FEBRUARY 28, 1972 HARVEY, ILL.
78-137 TROUT, STEVEN RUSSELL   719 RIVERVIEW DR - SOUTH HOLLAND IL 60473
56- 83 TROWBRIDGE, ROBERT   D. APRIL 3, 1980 HUDSON, N. Y.
12-202 TROY, ROBERT   D. OCTOBER 7, 1918 MEUSE, FRANCE
41-113 TRUCKS, VIRGIL OLIVER   2028 BUENA VISTA DR - BIRMINGHAM AL 35216
10-144 TRUESDALE, FRANK DAY   D. AUGUST 27, 1943 ALBUQUERQUE, N. M.
57- 88 TSITOURIS, JOHN PHILIP   RR 5 BOX 714 - MONROE NC 28110
27- 92 TUCKER, OSCAR DINWIDDIE   D. JULY 13, 1940 RADIANT, VA.
42-101 TUCKER, THURMAN LOWELL   OLD ADD: GORDON TX
79-111 TUDOR, JOHN THOMAS   14 FOREST ST - PEABODY MA 09160
18- 71 TUERO, OSCAR MONZON   D. OCTOBER 21, 1960 HOUSTON, TEXAS
81-138 TUFTS, ROBERT MALCOLM   27 WING RD - LYNNFIELD MA 01940
35-107 TURBEVILLE, GEORGE ELKINS   VETERANS ADMIN HOSP SALISBURY NC 28144
43-139 TURCHIN, EDWARD LAWRENCE   1 KNOB HILL DR - SMITHTOWN NY 11787
23-134 TURGEON, EUGENE JOSEPH   D. JANUARY 24, 1977 WICHITA FALLS, TEX.
22-134 TURK, LUCAS NEWTON   BOX 166 HOMER GA 30547
51- 98 TURLEY, ROBERT LEE   5629 BALL MILL RD - DUNWOODY GA 30338
48-101 TURNER, EARL EDWIN   332 FIRST - PITTSFIELD MA 01201
37-102 TURNER, JAMES RILEY   1004 WOODMONT BLVD NASHVILLE TN 37204
74-136 TURNER, JOHN WEBBER   807 CALIFORNIA - VENICE CA 90291
67-109 TURNER, KENNETH CHARLES   OLD ADD: 10041 VISTA LA CUESTA - SAN DIEGO CA
77-162 TURNER, ROBERT EDWARD   1018 PEACHTREE ST NW - ATLANTA GA 30309
20-124 TURNER, THEODORE HOLTOP   D. FEBRUARY 4, 1958 LEXINGTON, KY.
15-164 TURNER, THOMAS LOVATT   D. FEBRUARY 25, 1962 PHILADELPHIA, PA.
40- 93 TURNER, THOMAS RICHARD   4541 E OWENS #3 - LAS VEGAS NV 89110
52-106 TUTTLE, WILLIAM ROBERT   1119 E WILLCOX - PEORIA IL 61603
11-171 TUTWEILER, GUY ISBELL   D. AUGUST 15, 1930 ANNISTON, ALA.
28-100 TUTWILER, ELMER STRANGE   D. MAY 3, 1976 PENSACOLA, FLA.
16- 90 TWINING, HOWARD EARLE   D. JUNE 14, 1973 LANSDALE, PA.
70-134 TWITCHELL, WAYNE LEE   9050 SW 38TH ST - PORTLAND OR 97219
80-129 TWITTY, JEFFREY DEAN   1734 C AVENUE - NORTH COLUMBIA SC 29169
20-125 TWOMBLY, CLARENCE EDWARD   D. NOVEMBER 23, 1974 SAN CLEMENTE, CALIF.
21-107 TWOMBLY, EDWIN PARKER   D. DECEMBER 3, 1974 SAVANNAH, GA.
14-216 TWOMBLY, GEORGE FREDERICK   D. FEBRUARY 17, 1975 LEXINGTON, MASS.
43-140 TYACK, JAMES FRED   2901 MANOR AVE - BAKERSFIELD CA 93308
14-217 TYLER, FREDERICK FRANKLIN   D. OCTOBER 14, 1945 DERRY, N.H.
10-145 TYLER, GEORGE ALBERT   D. SEPTEMBER 29, 1953 LOWELL, MASS.
34-102 TYLER, JOHN ANTHONY   D. JULY 11, 1972 MOUNT PLEASANT, PA.
14-218 TYREE, EARL CARLTON   D. MAY 17, 1954 RUSHVILLE, ILL.
62-138 TYRIVER, DAVID BURTON   600 MERRITT AVE - OSHKOSH WI 54901
72-116 TYRONE, JAMES VERNON   107 ENCINAL ST - ALICE TX 78332

76- 95 TYRONE, OSCAR WAYNE   2301 NW 10TH AVE - MIAMI FL 33127
26- 87 TYSON, ALBERT THOMAS   D. AUGUST 16, 1953 BUFFALO, N. Y.
44-130 TYSON, CECIL WASHINGTON   RR 1 BOX 202, TYSON LN - ELM CITY NC 27822
72-117 TYSON, MICHAEL RAY   479 THUNDERHEAD CANYON DR-BALDWIN MO 63011
26- 88 UCHRINSKO, JAMES EMERSON   204 WATER ST - WEST NEWTON PA 15089
62-139 UECKER, ROBERT GEORGE   NORTH 60 WEST 15734-MENOMONEE FALLS WI 53051
34-103 UHALT, BERNARD BARTHOLOMEW   231 CROSS RD - OAKLAND CA 94618

A.C. Dazzy "Vance

THE SPORT AMERICANA PRICE GUIDE TO THE NON-SPORTS CARDS IS THE BEST SOURCE FOR INFORMATION AND PRICES FOR NON-SPORTS CARDS. SEE THE INSIDE BACK COVER FOR DETAILS.

65-108 UHLAENDER, THEODORE OTTO   BOX 1355 - MCALLEN TX 78502
19- 83 UHLE, GEORGE ERNEST   29925 WOLF RD - BAY VILLAGE OH 44140
38-101 UHLE, ROBERT ELLWOOD   OLD ADD: 534 MERAMAR AVE - SAN FRANCISCO CA
14-219 UHLER, MAURICE W.   D. MAY 4, 1918 BALTIMORE, MD.
34-104 UHLIR, CHARLES   OLD ADD: 11 S LASALLE - CHICAGO IL
80-130 UJDUR, GERALD RAYMOND   3312 BERKELEY RD - DULUTH MN 55811
45-106 ULISNEY, MICHAEL EDWARD   1405 NW 4TH AVE - FT LAUDERDALE FL 33311
44-131 ULLRICH, CARLOS SANTIAGO CASTELLO 3671 NW 15TH ST - MIAMI FL 33125
25-106 ULRICH, FRANK W.   D. FEBRUARY 11, 1929 BALTIMORE, MD.
64-123 UMBACH, ARNOLD WILLIAM   655 SOUTH DEAN RD - AUBURN AL 36830
75-121 UMBARGER, JAMES HAROLD   23788 VIA KANNELA - VALENCIA CA 91355
59- 83 UMBRICHT, JAMES   D. APRIL 8, 1964 HOUSTON, TEX.
53- 94 UMPHLETT, THOMAS MULLEN   RR 2 BOX 17C - AHOSKIE NC 27910
27- 93 UNDERHILL, WILLIE VERN   D. OCTOBER 26, 1970 BAY CITY, TEXAS
79-112 UNDERWOOD, PATRICK JOHN   420 N BERKLEY RD - KOKOMO IN 46901
74-137 UNDERWOOD, THOMAS GERALD   420 NORTH BERKLEY RD - KOKOMO IN 46901
42-102 UNSER, ALBERT BERNARD   2096 N UNION-DECATUR IL 62526
68-105 UNSER, DELBERT BERNARD   495 FERNWOOD DR - MORAGO CA 94556
35-108 UPCHURCH, JEFFERSON WOODROW   D. OCTOBER 23, 1971 BUIES CREEK, N. C.
67-110 UPHAM, JOHN LESLIE   1502 PIERRE AVE - WINDSOR ONTARIO
15-165 UPHAM, WILLIAM LAWRENCE   D. SEPTEMBER 14, 1959 NEWARK, N.J.
53- 95 UPRIGHT, ROY T.   1105 BIRCH ST - KANNAPOLIS NC 28081
66- 91 UPSHAW, CECIL LEE   3371 LUXEMBOURG CIR - DECATUR GA 30034
78-138 UPSHAW, WILLIE CLAY   BOX 395 - BLANCO TX 78606
50-100 UPTON, THOMAS HERBERT   7803 LUXOR - DOWNEY CA 90241
54-112 UPTON, WILLIAM RAY   7400 PARKWAY DR #81 - LAMESA CA 92041
57- 89 URBAN, JACK ELMER   8607 FOWLER - OMAHA NE 68134
27- 94 URBAN, LOUIS JOHN   D. DECEMBER 7, 1980 SOMERSET, MASS.
31- 91 URBANSKI, WILLIAM MICHAEL   D. JULY 12, 1973 PERTH AMBOY, N. J.
77-147 URREA, JOHN GODBY   12540 YOSEMITE - CERRITOS CA 90701
46-100 USHER, ROBERT ROYCE   9515 GREGORY ST - LAMESA CA 92041
25-107 USSAT, WILLIAM AUGUST   D. MAY 29, 1959 DAYTON, O.
25-108 VACHE, ERNEST LEWIS   D. JUNE 11, 1953 LOS ANGELES, CALIF.
75-122 VAIL, MICHAEL LEWIS   737 CASCADE DR - SAN JOSE CA 95129
44-132 VALDES, ARMANDO VIERA   OLD ADD: AS 1E, DES 16 - CARDENAS CUBA
57- 90 VALDES, RENE GUTIERREZ   AVENIDA 7A,14511 ALTURAS-MANANA,HAVANA CUBA
65-109 VALDESPINO, HILARIO BORRATO 17920 NW 43RD AVE - CAROL CITY FL 33054
80-131 VALDEZ, JULIO JULIAN CASTILLO MAXIMO GAHEZ #4-NIZAO BANI DOMINICAN REPUB
55-129 VALDIVIELSO, JOSE LOPEZ   14 RITA DR - MOUNT SINAI NY 11766
75-123 VALENTINE, ELLIS CLARENCE   OLD ADD: 1646 W 54TH ST - LOS ANGELES CA
59- 84 VALENTINE, FRED LEE   4838 BLAGDEN AVE NW - WASHINGTON DC 20011
54-113 VALENTINE, HAROLD LEWIS   RR 1, OLD BIRMINGHAM RD - CANTON GA 30114
69-173 VALENTINE, ROBERT JOHN   640 BIENVENEDA - PACIFIC PALISADES CA 90272
54-114 VALENTINETTI, VITO JOHN   271 SUMMIT AVE - MOUNT VERNON NY 10552
58- 98 VALENZUELA, BENJAMIN BELTRAN 267 CALLEJON GUASAVE - LOS MOCHIS SIN MEXICO
80-132 VALENZUELA, FERNANDO   TOL Y DOBLADO,711 SUR NAVOJOA-SONORA MEXICO
65-110 VALLE, HECTOR JOSE   URB. CATONI #7 - VEGA BAJA PR 00763
40- 94 VALO, ELMER WILLIAM   571 COLUMBIA AVE-PALMERTON PA 18071
27- 95 VANALSTYNE, CLAYTON EMERY   D. JANUARY 5, 1960 HUDSON, N. Y.
33- 64 VANATTA, RUSSELL   BOX 201 - LAFAYETTE NJ 07848
54-115 VANBRABANT, CAMILLE OSCAR   2322 N WASHINGTON - ROYAL OAK MI 48073
28-101 VANCAMP, ALBERT JOSEPH   D. FEBRUARY 2, 1981 DAVENPORT, IOWA
15-166 VANCE, CLARENCE ARTHUR   D. FEBRUARY 16, 1961 HOMOSASSA SPRINGS, FLA.
70-135 VANCE, GENE COVINGTON   858 1/2 SILVER FIR RD - WALNUT CA 91789
35-109 VANCE, JOSEPH ALBERT   D. JULY 4, 1978 DEVINE, TEXAS
50-101 VANCUYK, CHRISTIAN GERALD   4002 SEVILLA ST - TAMPA FL 33609
47- 91 VANCUYK, JOHN HENRY   OLD ADD: 1443 E CALUMET AVE - APPLETON WI
14-220 VANDAGRIFT, CARL WILLIAM   D. OCTOBER 9, 1920 FORT WAYNE, IND.
35-110 VANDENBURG, HAROLD HARRIS   10143 THIRD AVE S - MINNEAPOLIS MN 55420
37-103 VANDERMEER, JOHN SAMUEL   4005 LEONA AVE TAMPA FL 33606
55-130 VANDUSEN, FREDERICK WILLIAM 826 ROCKRIMMON RD - STAMFORD CT 06903
19- 84 VANGILDER, ELAM RUSSELL   D. APRIL 30, 1977 CAPE GIRARDEAU, MO.
13-183 VANN, JOHN SILAS   D. JUNE 10, 1958 SHREVEPORT, LA.
51- 99 VANNOY, JAY LOWELL   1092 NORTH 1700 EAST - LOGAN UT 84321
39-120 VANROBAYS, MAURICE RENE   D. MARCH 1, 1965 DETROIT, MICH.
50-102 VARGA, ANDREW WILLIAM   1964 ADD: 2429 M - BELLVILLE KS 66935

see page 149

76- 97	WAGNER, MARK DUANE	1346 ELEANOR DR - ASHTABULA OH 44004
13-184	WAGNER, WILLIAM GEORGE	D. OCTOBER 2, 1967 MUSKEGON, MICH.
14-223	WAGNER, WILLIAM JOSEPH	D. JANUARY 11, 1951 WATERLOO, IA.
44-137	WAHL, KERMIT EMERSON	5001 E SPEEDWAY - TUCSON AZ 85712
41-114	WAITKUS, EDWARD STEPHEN	D. SEPTEMBER 15, 1972 BOSTON, MASS.
73-127	WAITS, MICHAEL RICHARD	4750 N CAMINO CATO - TUCSON AZ 85718
41-115	WAKEFIELD, RICHARD CUMMINGS	23790 W WARREN - DEARBORN HEIGHTS MI 48127
64-125	WAKEFIELD, WILLIAM SUMNER	327 KEARNY ST - SAN FRANCISCO CA 94108
23-137	WALBERG, GEORGE ELVIN	D. OCTOBER 27, 1978 TEMPE, ARIZ.
45-108	WALCZAK, EDWIN JOSEPH	544 NEW LONDON - NORWICH CT 06360
17- 85	WALDBAUER, ALBERT CHARLES	D. JULY 16, 1969 YAKIMA, WASH.
12-207	WALDEN, THOMAS FRED	D. SEPTEMBER 27, 1955 JEFFERSON BARRACKS, MO.
80-136	WALK, ROBERT VERNON	%C.SHIELDS,BOX 954 - FRAZIER PARK CA 93225
48-104	WALKER, ALBERT BLUFORD	967 CLOPPER RD - GAITHERSBURG MD 20760
17- 86	WALKER, CHARLES FRANKLIN	D. SEPTEMBER 16, 1974 BRISTOL, TENN.
11-172	WALKER, CLARENCE WILLIAM	D. SEPTEMBER 21, 1959 UNICOI, TENN.
80-137	WALKER, CLEOTHA	B. NOVEMBER 25, 1957 JACKSON, MISS.
13-185	WALKER, ERNEST ROBERT	D. APRIL 1, 1965 PELL CITY, ALA.
31- 94	WALKER, FRED	4145 OLD LEEDS LN - BIRMINGHAM AL 35213
10-146	WALKER, FREDERICK MITCHELL	D. FEBRUARY 1, 1958 OAK PARK, ILL.
31- 95	WALKER, GERALD HOLMES	D. MARCH 20, 1981 WHITFIELD, MISS.

SPORT AMERICANA HOBBY REFERENCE MATERIAL
IS THE RECOGNIZED STANDARD FOR INFORMATION
AND CURRENT MARKET PRICES OF SPORTS RELATED
COLLECTIBLES. SEE DETAILS ON THE INSIDE COVERS.

40- 96	WALKER, HARRY WILLIAM	RR1 BOX 145-LEEDS AL 35094
31- 96	WALKER, HARVEY WILLOS	OLD ADD: 2130 PARK AVE - SAN JOSE CA
65-114	WALKER, JAMES LUKE	610 CANNON - NEW BOSTON TX 75570
12-208	WALKER, JAMES ROY	D. FEBRUARY 10, 1962 NEW ORLEANS, LA.
57- 91	WALKER, JERRY ALLEN	2015 COLLINS BLVD - ADA OK 74820
19- 85	WALKER, JOHN MILES	D. AUGUST 19, 1976 HOLLYWOOD, FLA.
23-138	WALKER, JOSEPH RICHARD	D. JUNE 20, 1959 WEST MIFFLIN, PA.
28-102	WALKER, MARTIN VAN BUREN	D. APRIL 24, 1978 PHILADELPHIA, PA.
72-118	WALKER, ROBERT THOMAS	985 HOME AVE - PITTSBURGH PA 15237
19- 86	WALKER, WILLIAM CURTIS	D. DECEMBER 9, 1955 BEEVILLE, TEX.
27- 96	WALKER, WILLIAM HENRY	D. JUNE 14, 1966 EAST ST. LOUIS, ILL.
34-106	WALKUP, JAMES ELTON	HAVANA AR 72842
27- 97	WALKUP, JAMES HUEY	1111 GRAND - DUNCAN OK 73533
50-103	WALL, MURRAY WESLEY	D. OCTOBER 8, 1971 LONE OAK, TEXAS
75-125	WALL, STANLEY ARTHUR	9907 E. 80TH ST - RAYTOWN MO 64138
15-169	WALLACE, CLARENCE EUGENE	D. OCTOBER 15, 1960 WINNFIELD, LA.
73-128	WALLACE, DAVID WILLIAM	4 OAKLAND AVE - WATERBURY CT 06710
67-111	WALLACE, DONALD ALLEN	23 KRIS LN - MANITOU SPRINGS CO 80829
19- 87	WALLACE, FREDERICK RENSHAW	D. DECEMBER 31, 1964 HAVERFORD TWP, PA.
12-209	WALLACE, HARRY CLINTON	D. JULY 9, 1951 CLEVELAND, O.
42-105	WALLACE, JAMES HAROLD	1504 OLYMPIC CT - EVANSVILLE IN 47715
73-129	WALLACE, MICHAEL SHERMAN	1670 PARKCREST CIR #300 - RESTON VA 22090
80-138	WALLACH, TIMOTHY CHARLES	14742 FEATHERHILL RD - TUSTIN CA 92680
40- 97	WALLAESA, JOHN	30 MACYWOOD LN - EASTON PA 18042
45-109	WALLEN, NORMAN EDWARD	3429 NORTH WEIL - MILWAUKEE WI 53212
80-139	WALLER, ELLIOTT TYRONE	5146 LAPAZ DR - SAN DIEGO CA 92114
75-126	WALLING, DENNIS MARTIN	RR 1, CASINO DR - FARMINGDALE NJ 07727
75-127	WALLIS, HAROLD JOSEPH	2135 BARCELONA - FLORISSANT MO 63033
52-108	WALLS, RAYMOND LEE	1129 W COLUMBINE - SANTA ANA CA 92707
27- 98	WALSH, AUGUST	2004 5TH AVE - SAN RAFAEL CA 94901
14-224	WALSH, AUSTIN	B. 1892
28-103	WALSH, EDWARD ARTHUR	D. OCTOBER 31, 1937 MERIDEN, CONN.
12-210	WALSH, JAMES CHARLES	D. JULY 3, 1962 SYRACUSE, N.Y.
46-101	WALSH, JAMES GERALD	RR 1, LAYTON RD - OLYPHANT PA 18447
21-108	WALSH, JAMES THOMAS	D. MAY 13, 1967 BOSTON, MASS.
10-147	WALSH, JOSEPH FRANCIS	D. JANUARY 6, 1967 BUFFALO, N.Y.
38-103	WALSH, JOSEPH PATRICK	12 SURREY ST - BRIGHTON MA 02135
13-186	WALSH, LEO THOMAS	D. JULY 14, 1971 ST. LOUIS, MO.
10-148	WALSH, MICHAEL TIMOTHY	D. JANUARY 21, 1947 BALTIMORE, MD.
20-127	WALSH, WALTER WILLIAM	D. JANUARY 15, 1966 NEPTUNE, N. J.
30- 85	WALTER, JAMES BERNARD	BOX 121 - DOVER TN 37058
15-170	WALTERS, ALFRED JOHN	D. JUNE 3, 1956 ALAMEDA, CALIF.
69-175	WALTERS, CHARLES LEONARD	3234 HAYES ST NE - MINNEAPOLIS MN 55418
45-110	WALTERS, JAMES FREDERICK	BOX 474 - LAUREL MS 39441
60-101	WALTERS, KENNETH ROGERS	9545 BELLE MEADE DR - SAN RAMON CA 94583
31- 97	WALTERS, WILLIAM HENRY	515 FOX RD - GLENSIDE PA 19038
68-106	WALTON, DANIEL JAMES	BOX 291 - CEDAR CREST NM 87008
80-140	WALTON, REGINALD SHERARD	1151 MASSERIN AVE #4 - LOS ANGELES CA 90019
14-225	WAMBSGANSS, WILLIAM ADOLFH	1176 ELBUR AVE - LAKEWOOD OH 44107
27- 99	WANER, LLOYD JAMES	252 EDGEMERE COURT - OKLAHOMA CITY OK 73118
26- 90	WANER, PAUL GLEE	D. AUGUST 29, 1965 SARASOTA, FLA.
25-110	WANNINGER, PAUL LOUIS	D. MAY 7, 1981 NORTH AUGUSTA, S. C.

WANTZ

WEBB

```
65-115  WANTZ, RICHARD CARTER       D. MAY 13, 1965 INGLEWOOD, CAL.
17- 87  WARD, AARON LEE             D. JANUARY 30, 1961 NEW ORLEANS, LA.
17- 88  WARD, CHARLES WILLIAM       D. APRIL 4, 1969 ST. PETERSBURG, FLA.
72-119  WARD, CHRIS GILBERT         17469 VIA LA JOLLA - SAN LORENZO CA 94580
12-211  WARD, E. "HAP"
79-116  WARD, GARY LAMELL           318 W RAYMOND ST - COMPTON CA 90220
63-122  WARD, JOHN FRANCIS          RR 3 BOX 112 - MOUNTAIN GROVE MO 65711
62-141  WARD, PETER THOMAS          5757 "G" AVE - LAKE OSWEGO OR 97034
48-105  WARD, PRESTON MEYER         4371 DESILVA PL - LAS VEGAS NV 89101
34-107  WARD, RICHARD OLE           D. JUNE 1, 1966 FREELAND, WASH.
68-107  WARDEN, JONATHAN EDGAR      770 QUAILWOODS DR - LOVELAND OH 45140
13-187  WARES, CLYDE ELLSWORTH      D. MAY 26, 1964 SOUTH BEND, IND.
16- 91  WARMOTH, WALLACE WALTER     D. JUNE 20, 1957 MOUNT CARMEL, ILL.
30- 86  WARNEKE, LONNIE             D. JUNE 23, 1976 HOT SPRINGS, ARK.
12-212  WARNER, EDWARD EMORY        D. FEBRUARY 2, 1954 FITCHBURG, MASS.
16- 92  WARNER, HOKE HAYDEN         D. FEBRUARY 19, 1947 SAN FRANCISCO, CAL.
62-142  WARNER, JACK DYER           1307 E OREGON - PHOENIX AZ 85014
66- 96  WARNER, JOHN JOSEPH         512 E LEADORA - GLENDORA CA 91740
25-111  WARNER, JOHN RALPH          831 AUSTIN AVE #2 - INGLEWOOD CA 90302
35-112  WARNOCK, HAROLD CHARLES     907 VALLEY NATL BANK BUILDING TUCSON AZ 85701
39-123  WARREN, BENNIE LOUIS        3708 NW 18TH ST-OKLAHOMA CITY OK 73107
44-138  WARREN, THOMAS GENTRY       D. JANUARY 2, 1968 TULSA, OKLA.
14-226  WARREN, WILLIAM HACKNEY     D. JANUARY 28, 1960 WHITEVILLE, TENN.
30- 87  WARSTLER, HAROLD BURTON     D. MAY 31, 1964 NORTH CANTON,O.
75-128  WARTHEN, DANIEL DEAN        6336 N 38TH ST - OMAHA NE 68111
61-106  WARWICK, CARL WAYNE         6115 BERMUDA DUNES - HOUSTON TX 77040
```

```
21-109  WARWICK, FIRMAN NEWTON      RR 10 BOX 14 - NEW BRAUNFELS TX 78130
37-105  WASDELL, JAMES CHARLES      3114 HAMILTON LN - HOLIDAY FL 33589
37-106  WASEM, LINCOLN WILLIAM      D. MARCH 6, 1979 SOUTH LAGUNA, CALIF.
41-115  WASHBURN, GEORGE EDWARD     D. JANUARY 5, 1979 BATON ROUGE, LA.
69-176  WASHBURN, GREGORY JAMES     STELLON & DEWEY, RR 1 - COAL CITY IL 60416
61-107  WASHBURN, RAY CLARK         19309 JUANITA WOODVILLE WY NE-BOTHELL WA98011
74-138  WASHINGTON, CLAUDELL        2326 SPAULDING AVE - BERKELEY CA 94703
74-139  WASHINGTON, HERBERT         642 E AUSTIN ST - FLINT MI 48505
78-139  WASHINGTON, LARUE           709 WEST PLUM ST - COMPTON CA 90222
77-148  WASHINGTON, RONALD          1133 N PRIEUR ST - NEW ORLEANS LA 70125
35-113  WASHINGTON, SLOANE VERNON   RR 2 - LINDEN TX 75563
77-149  WASHINGTON, U. L.           BOX 164 - STRINGTOWN OK 74569
67-112  WASLEWSKI, GARY LEE         MCKENZIE DR - SOUTHINGTON CT 06489
76- 98  WATERBURY, STEVEN CRAIG     1306 N STATE - MARION IL 62958
55-134  WATERS, FRED WARREN         1350 EAST AVERY - PENSACOLA FL 32503
76- 99  WATHAN, JOHN DAVID          1401 DEER RUN TRAIL - BLUE SPRINGS MO 64015
69-177  WATKINS, DAVID ROGER        1502 ROOSEVELT RD - OWENSBORO KY 42301
30- 88  WATKINS, GEORGE ARCHIBALD   D. JUNE 1, 1970 HOUSTON, TEX.
69-178  WATKINS, ROBERT CECIL       1205 S ACACIA - COMPTON CA 90220
53- 97  WATLINGTON, JULIUS NEAL     BOX 418 - YANCEYVILLE NC 27379
14-227  WATSON, ARTHUR STANHOPE     D. MAY 9, 1950 BUFFALO, N. Y.
13-188  WATSON, CHARLES JOHN        D. DECEMBER 30, 1949 SAN DIEGO, CALIF.
18- 72  WATSON, JOHN REEVES         D. AUGUST 25, 1949 SHREVEPORT, LA.
30- 89  WATSON, JOHN THOMAS         D. APRIL 29, 1965 HUNTINGTON, W. V.
16- 93  WATSON, MILTON W.           1917 ADD: PARIS TX 75460
66- 97  WATSON, ROBERT JOSE         552 WINTHROP RD - TEANECK NJ 07666
20-128  WATT, ALBERT BAILEY         D. MARCH 15, 1968 NORFOLK, VA.
66- 98  WATT, EDDIE DEAN            BOX 7 - NORTH BEND NE 68649
31- 98  WATT, FRANK MARION          D. AUGUST 31, 1956 GLEN COVE, MD.
29-106  WATWOOD, JOHN CLIFFORD      D. MARCH 1, 1980 GOODWATER, ALA.
52-109  WAUGH, JAMES ELDEN          501 N COLUMBIA - UNION CITY IN 47390
27-100  WAY, ROBERT CLINTON         D. JUNE 20, 1974 PITTSBURGH, PA.
24-114  WAYENBERG, FRANK            D. APRIL 16, 1975 ZANESVILLE, O.
36- 94  WEAFER, KENNETH ALBERT      66 RYCKMAN AVE - ALBANY NY 12208
36- 95  WEATHERLY, CYRIL ROY        2495 PECOS - BEAUMONT TX 77702
62-143  WEAVER, DAVID FLOYD         BOX 31 - POWDERLY TX 75473
68-108  WEAVER, EARL SIDNEY         19016 W LAKE DR - HIALEAH FL 33015
12-213  WEAVER, GEORGE DANIEL       D. JANUARY 31, 1956 CHICAGO, ILL.
15-171  WEAVER, HARRY A.            375 HIGHLAND AVE - ROCHESTER NY 14620
67-113  WEAVER, JAMES BRIAN         459 PARKWYNN RD - LANCASTER PA 17601
28-104  WEAVER, JAMES DEMENT        817 FOUNTAINVIEW LAKE - LAKELAND FL 33801
31- 99  WEAVER, MONTGOMERY MORTON   826 S LAKE ADAIR BLVD - ORLANDO FL 32804
10-149  WEAVER, ORLIE FOREST        D. NOVEMBER 28, 1970 NEW ORLEANS, LA.
80-141  WEAVER, ROGER EDWARD        BOX 15 - SAINT JOHNSVILLE NY 13452
10-150  WEBB, CLEON EARL            D. JANUARY 12, 1958 CIRCLEVILLE, O.
72-120  WEBB, HENRY GAYLON          38 HARBOR OAKS CIR - SAFETY HARBOR FL 33572
32- 90  WEBB, JAMES LEVERNE         4118 POPLAR SPRING DR - MERIDIAN MS 39303
```

```
48-106  WEBB, SAMUEL HENRY                5609 35TH PLACE - HYATTSVILLE MD 20781
25-112  WEBB, WILLIAM EARL                D. MAY 22, 1965 JAMESTOWN, TENN.
43-141  WEBB, WILLIAM FREDERICK           3758 SHARON DR - POWDER SPRINGS GA 30073
17- 89  WEBB, WILLIAM JOSEPH              D. JANUARY 12, 1943 CHICAGO, ILL.
42-106  WEBBER, LESTER ELMER              1645 S MCCLELLAND - SANTA MARIA CA 93454
67-114  WEBSTER, RAMON ALBERTO            BOX 1340 - COLON REP PANAMA
59- 86  WEBSTER, RAYMOND GEORGE           BOX 1437 - YUBA CITY CA 95991
11-173  WEEDEN, CHARLES ALBERT            D. JANUARY 7, 1939 NORTHWOOD, N.H.
62-144  WEEKLY, JOHN                      D. NOVEMBER 24, 1974 WALNUT CREEK, CAL.
69-179  WEGENER, MICHAEL DENIS            3650 S FEDERAL #191 - ENGLEWOOD CO 80110
30- 90  WEHDE, WILBUR                     D. SEPTEMBER 21, 1970 SIOUX FALLS,S.D.
45-111  WEHMEIER, HERMAN RALPH            D. MAY 21, 1973 DALLAS, TEX.
76-100  WEHRMEISTER, DAVID THOMAS         4216 DUBBE CT - CONCORD CA 94521
46-102  WEIGEL, RALPH RICHARD             1404 WHEATON RD - MEMPHIS TN 38117
48-107  WEIK, RICHARD HENRY               17532 70TH CT - TINLEY PARK IL 60477
40- 98  WEILAND, EDWIN NICHOLAS           D. JULY 12, 1972 CHICAGO, ILL.
28-105  WEILAND, ROBERT GEORGE            5518 W MELROSE - CHICAGO ILL 60641
12-214  WEILMAN, CARL WOOLWORTH           D. MAY 25, 1924 HAMILTON, O.
19- 88  WEINERT, PHILLIP WALTER           D. APRIL 17, 1973 ROCKLEDGE, FLA.
45-112  WEINGARTNER, ELMER WILLIAM        13604 LORAIN - CLEVELAND OH 74111
33- 65  WEINTRAUB, PHILIP                 2091 CALIENTE - PALM SPRINGS CA 92262
36- 96  WEIR, WILLIAM FRANKLIN            1521 W CRIS PLACE - ANAHEIM CA 92802
62-145  WEIS, ALBERT JOHN                 902 SOUTH POPLAR - ELMHURST IL 60126
22-136  WEIS, ARTHUR JOHN                 209 KINGSVILLE CT - WEBSTER GROVES MO 63119
15-172  WEISER, HARRY BUDSON              D. JULY 31, 1961 SHAMOKIN, PA.
80-142  WEISS, GARY LEE                   RR 1 BOX 80 - BRENHAM TX 77833
15-173  WEISS, JOSEPH HAROLD              D. JULY 7, 1967 CEDAR RAPIDS, IA.
39-124  WELAJ, JOHN LUDWIG                1519 COLLEGE ST #103 - ARLINGTON TX 76010
19- 89  WELCH, FRANK TIGUER               D. JULY 25, 1957 BIRMINGHAM, ALA.
25-113  WELCH, HERBERT M.                 D. APRIL 13, 1967 MEMPHIS, TENN.
26- 91  WELCH, JOHN VERNON                D. SEPTEMBER 2, 1940 ST. LOUIS, MO.
45-113  WELCH, MILTON EDWARD             4049 WILSHIRE DR - ABILENE TX 79603
78-140  WELCH, ROBERT LYNN               2114 LEITCH - FERNDALE MI 48220
14-228  WELCH, THEODORE                  B. 1893
11-174  WELCHONCE, HARRY MONROE          D. FEBRUARY 26, 1977 ARCADIA, CALIF.
16- 94  WELF, OLIVER HENRY               D. JUNE 25, 1967 CLEVELAND, O.
48-108  WELLMAN, ROBERT JOSEPH           2321 ADAMS AVE - NORWOOD OH 75212
23-139  WELLS, EDWIN LEE                 2085 MYRTLEWOOD DR - MONTGOMERY ALA 36111
```

```
81-139  WELLS, GREGORY DEWAYNE           MCINTOSH AL 36553
44-139  WELLS, JOHN FREDERICK            404 ALDER #1 - OLEAN NY 14760
42-107  WELLS, LEO DONALD                1755 HIGHLAND PKWY - ST PAUL MN 55116
81-140  WELSH, CHRISTOPHER CHARLES       8760 APPLEKNOLL LN - CINCINNATI OH 45236
25-114  WELSH, JAMES DANIEL              D. OCTOBER 30, 1970 OAKLAND, CAL.
48-109  WELTEROTH, RICHARD JOHN          122 ELDRED ST - WILLIAMSPORT PA 17702
26- 92  WELZER, ANTON FRANK             D. MARCH 18, 1971 MILWAUKEE, WIS.
15-174  WENDELL, LEWIS CHARLES          D. JULY 11, 1953 BRONX, N.Y.
43-142  WENSLOFF, CHARLES WILLIAM       8 RYAN AVE - MILL VALLEY CA 94941
45-114  WENTZEL, STANLEY AARON          2900 OLEY TURNPIKE RD - READING PA 19606
68-109  WENZ, FREDERICK CHARLES         1 CIRCLE DR - SOMERVILLE NJ 08876
27-101  WERA, JULIAN VALENTINE          D. DECEMBER 12, 1975 ROCHESTER, MINN.
30- 91  WERBER, WILLIAM MURRAY          350 NEPTUNES BIGHT - NAPLES FL 33940
64-126  WERHAS, JOHN CHARLES            5851 FURNACE CREEK - YORBA LINDA CA 92686
49- 89  WERLE, WILLIAM GEORGE           833 W 28TH AVE - SAN MATEO CA 94403
56- 85  WERLEY, GEORGE WILLIAM          16429 HORSESHOE RIDGE - CHESTERFIELD MO 63017
75-129  WERNER, DONALD PAUL             19 FAIRWAY CT - APPLETON WI 54911
63-123  WERT, DONALD RALPH              RR 1 BOX 288 - NEW PROVIDENCE PA 17560
79-117  WERTH, DENNIS DEAN              BOX 8 - MOUNT PULASKI IL 62548
14-229  WERTZ, DWIGHT LEWIS             B. 1891
26- 93  WERTZ, HENRY LEVI               1704 NANCE ST - NEWBERRY SC 29108
47- 92  WERTZ, VICTOR WOODROW           BOX 804 - MOUNT CLEMONS MI 48043
79-118  WESSINGER, JAMES MICHAEL        504 KINGSTON RD - UTICA NY 13502
38-104  WEST, MAX EDWARD                507 SIERRA KEYS DR SIERRA MADRE CA 91024
38-105  WEST, RICHARD THOMAS            RR ONE, WILDWOOD ISLE - LEESBURG IN 46538
27-102  WEST, SAMUEL FILMORE            3808 23RD - LUBBOCK TX 79410
28-106  WEST, WALTER MAXWELL            D. APRIL 25, 1971 HOUSTON, TEX.
44-140  WEST, WELDON EDISON             D. JULY 23, 1979 HENDERSONVILLE, N.C.
55-135  WESTLAKE, JAMES PATRICK         909 SEAMAS AVE - SACRAMENTO CA 95801
47- 93  WESTLAKE, WALDON THOMAS         3800 61ST - SACRAMENTO CA 95820
29-107  WESTON, ALFRED JOHN             1 ALPINE TER - NEEDHAM MA 02192
47- 94  WESTRUM, WESLEY NOREEN          BOX 3001 - MESA AZ 85205
27-103  WETZEL, CHARLES EDWARD          D. MARCH 7, 1941 GLOBE, ARIZ.
20-129  WETZEL, FRANKLIN BURTON         D. MARCH 5, 1942 BURBANK, CAL.
23-140  WHALEY, WILLIAM CARL            D. MARCH 3, 1943 INDIANAPOLIS, IND.
```

13-189	WHALING, ALBERT JAMES	D. JANUARY 21, 1965 LOS ANGELES, CALIF.
54-116	WHEAT, LEROY WILLIAM	6125 PINE TER - FT LAUDERDALE FL 33317
15-175	WHEAT, MCKINLEY DAVIS	D. AUGUST 14, 1979 LOS BANOS, CALIF.
12-215	WHEATLEY, CHARLES	2909 E 29TH - TULSA OK 74114
43-143	WHEATON, ELWOOD PIERCE	%H.R.WHEATON;1135 WABANK-LANCASTER PA 17603
49- 90	WHEELER, DONALD WESLEY	8127 COLFAX AVE S - MINNEAPOLIS MN 55420
45-115	WHEELER, EDWARD RAYMOND	OLD ADD: 135 N EUCALYPTUS ST - INGLEWOOD CA
21-110	WHEELER, FLOYD CLARK	D. SEPTEMBER 18, 1968 MARION, KY.
10-151	WHEELER, GEORGE HARRISON	D. JUNE 14, 1918 CLINTON, IND.
18- 73	WHEELER, RICHARD	D. FEBRUARY 12, 1962 LEXINGTON, MASS.
76-101	WHEELOCK, GARY RICHARD	18856 VIA SERENO - YORBA LINDA CA 92686
13-190	WHELAN, JAMES FRANCIS	D. NOVEMBER 29, 1929 DAYTON, O.
20-130	WHELAN, THOMAS JOSEPH	D. JUNE 26, 1957 BOSTON, MASS.
71-107	WHILLOCK, JACK FRANKLIN	2007 EDGEBROOK CT - ARLINGTON TX 76015
52-110	WHISENANT, THOMAS PETER	218 W GRACE ST - PUNTA GORDA FL 33950
77-150	WHISENTON, LARRY	2507 SLATTERY ST - ST LOUIS MO 63106
77-151	WHITAKER, LOUIS RODMAN	803 PIPE - MARTINSVILLE VA 24112
66- 99	WHITAKER, STEVE EDWARD	5505 S FAWCETT - TACOMA WA 98408
64-127	WHITBY, WILLIAM EDWARD	RR 1 BOX 491-D - HUNTERSVILLE NC 28078
45-116	WHITCHER, ROBERT ARTHUR	156 GRAHAM RD - CUYAHOGA FALLS OH 44223
37-107	WHITE, ADEL	2040 DOVER HILL PL NE - ATLANTA GA 30345
40- 99	WHITE, ALBERT EUGENE	BOX 578-BRANSON MO 65616
54-117	WHITE, CHARLES	8167 HUDSON ST - VANCOUVER BC V6P 4M2
48-110	WHITE, DONALD WILLIAM	OLD ADD: % DONGOS - KIHEI HI
55-136	WHITE, EDWARD PERRY	309 AZALEA ST - LAKELAND FL 33803

62-146	WHITE, ELDER LAFAYETTE	919 COLONY AVE - AHOSKIE NC 27910
40-100	WHITE, ERNEST DANIEL	D. MAY 22, 1974 AUGUSTA, GA.
73-130	WHITE, FRANK	8925 LAMBERT DR - LEES SUMMIT MO 64063
41-117	WHITE, HAROLD GEORGE	238 BRIDGE ST - CORNING NY 14830
74-140	WHITE, JEROME CARDELL	1255 ALICANTE DR - PACFICA CA 94044
27-104	WHITE, JOHN PETER	D. JUNE 19, 1971 FLUSHING, N. Y.
32- 91	WHITE, JOYNER CLIFFORD	40 THUNDERBIRD WAY SW #M8 - TACOMA WA 98498
63-124	WHITE, JOYNER MICHAEL	1820 284TH EAST - ROY WA 98580
78-141	WHITE, MYRON ALAN	3201 SOUTH DEEGAN DR - SANTA ANA CA 92704
65-116	WHITE, ROY HILTON	30 ASPEN WAY - UPPER SADDLE RIVER NJ 07458
19- 90	WHITE, SAMUEL	B. 1895
51-101	WHITE, SAMUEL CHARLES	BOX 121 - HANALEI HI 96714
12-216	WHITE, STEPHEN VINCENT	D. JANUARY 29, 1975 BRAINTREE, MASS.
45-117	WHITE, WILLIAM BARNEY	3721 DARRELL LN - TYLER TX 75701
56- 86	WHITE, WILLIAM DEKOVA	71 CALLOWHILL RD - CHALFONT PA 18914
33- 66	WHITEHEAD, BURGESS URQUHART	206 KING ST - WINDSOR NC 27983
35-114	WHITEHEAD, JOHN HENDERSON	D. OCTOBER 20, 1964 BONHAM, TEX.
23-141	WHITEHILL, EARL OLIVER	D. OCTOBER 22, 1954 OMAHA, NEB.
14-231	WHITEHOUSE, CHARLES EVIS	D. JULY 19, 1960 INDIANAPOLIS, IND.
12-217	WHITEHOUSE, GILBERT ARTHUR	D. FEBRUARY 14, 1926 BREWER, ME.
81-141	WHITEHOUSE, LEONARD JOSEPH	1874 NORTH AVE - BURLINGTON VT 05401
62-147	WHITFIELD, FRED DWIGHT	RR 1 BOX 19 1/2 B - STERRETT AL 35147
74-141	WHITFIELD, TERRY BERTLAND	849 CLEARFIELD - MILLBRAE CA 94030
46-103	WHITMAN, DICK CORWIN	184 PETER DR - CAMPBELL CA 95008
46-104	WHITMAN, WALTER FRANKLIN	2100 VANDALIA AVE - COLLINSVILLE IL 62234
80-143	WHITMER, DANIEL CHARLES	823 ROBINHOOD LN - REDLANDS CA 92373
28-107	WHITNEY, ARTHUR CARTER	518 W KINGS HWY - SAN ANTONIO TX 78212
77-152	WHITSON, EDDIE LEE	127 YELTON ST - ERWIN TN 37650
76-102	WHITT, ERNEST LEO	18330 13 MILE RD - ROSEVILLE MI 48066
16- 95	WHITTAKER, WALTER ELTON	D. AUGUST 7, 1965 PEMBROKE, MASS.
12-218	WHITTED, GEORGE BOSTIC	D. OCTOBER 16, 1962 WILMINGTON, N.C.
68-110	WICKER, FLOYD EULISS	RR2 - SNOW CAMP NC 27349
36- 97	WICKER, KEMP CASWELL	D. JUNE 11, 1973 KERNERSVILLE, N. C.
60-102	WICKERSHAM, DAVID CLIFFORD	9118 W 104TH TER - OVERLAND PARK KS 66204
13-191	WICKLAND, ALBERT	D. MARCH 14, 1980 PORT WASHINGTON, WISC.
47- 95	WIDMAR, ALBERT JOSEPH	3919 SOUTH OSWEGO AV - TULSA OK 74135
58-101	WIEAND, FRANKLIN DELANO ROOSEVELT	216 WALNUT ST - SLATINGTON PA 18080
34-108	WIEDEMEYER, CHARLES JOHN	1935 ADD: 4103 CRYSTAL ST - CHICAGO IL
79-119	WIEDENBAUER, THOMAS JOHN	618 N KEEN PL - TUCSON AZ 85710
81-142	WIEGHAUS, THOMAS ROBERT	RR 1 BOX 169 - GRANT PARK IL 60940
21-111	WIENEKE, JOHN	D. MARCH 16, 1933 PLEASANT RIDGE, MICH.
51-102	WIESLER, ROBERT GEORGE	2325 INDIAN CUP DR - FLORISSANT MO 63031
39-125	WIETELMANN, WILLIAM FREDERICK	3564 MISSION BLVD-SAN DIEGO CA 92109
81-143	WIGGINS, ALAN ANTHONY	1009 N RAYMOND #17 - PASADENA CA 91103
46-105	WIGHT, WILLIAM ROBERT	6247 MEADOW VISTA DR - CARMICHAEL CA 95608
23-142	WIGINGTON, FREDERICK THOMAS	D. MAY 8, 1980 MESA, ARIZ.
79-120	WIHTOL, ALEXANDER AMES	891 ROBLE AVE - SUNNYVALE CA 94086
46-106	WILBER, DELBERT QUENTIN	513 WOODLEAF CT - KIRKWOOD MO 63122

0-101	WILBORN, CLAUDE EDWARD	RR 1-ROXBORO NC 27573
79-121	WILBORN, THADDEAUS IGLEHART	6429 SURFSIDE WAY - SACRAMENTO CA 95831
70-137	WILCOX, MILTON EDWARD	6405 RAINTREE DR - CANTON MI 48187
77-153	WILES, RANDALL E	136 CARTERS GROVE - CONROE TX 77301
75-130	WILEY, MARK EUGENE	4444 71ST ST - LAMESA CA 92041
77-154	WILFONG, ROBERT DONALD	16246 BENBOW - COVINA CA 91722
53-98	WILHELM, CHARLES ERNEST	2721 ALDEN RD - BALTIMORE MD 21234
52-111	WILHELM, JAMES HOYT	BOX 2217 - SARASOTA FL 33578
78-142	WILHELM, JAMES WEBSTER	BOX 99 - BELVEDERE CA 94920
16-96	WILHOIT, JOSEPH WILLIAM	D. SEPTEMBER 25, 1930 SANTA BARBARA, CALIF.
11-175	WILIE, DENNEY EARNEST	D. JUNE 20, 1966 HAYWARD, CALIF.
27-105	WILKE, HENRY JOSEPH	1002 HARMON AV - HAMILTON OH 45011
41-118	WILKIE, ALDON JAY	PO BOX 362 902 W 1ST ST-NEWBERG OR 97132
79-122	WILKINS, ERIC LAMOINE	2233 E MILLER - SEATTLE WA 98112
44-141	WILKINS, ROBERT LINWOOD	CADDO PARISH COURT HOUSE-SHREVEPORT LA 71101
11-176	WILKINSON, EDWARD E.	OLD ADD: 1019 CHESTNUT ST - OAKLAND CA 94607
18-74	WILKINSON, ROY HAMILTON	D. JULY 2, 1956 LOUISVILLE, KY.
44-142	WILKS, TEDDY	5531 MCCORMICK - HOUSTON TX 77023
57-92	WILL, ROBERT LEE	410 N MICHIGAN AVE - CHICAGO IL 60611
58-102	WILLEY, CARLTON FRANCIS	PO BOX 64 - CHERRYFIELD MAINE 04622
63-125	WILLHITE, JON NICHOLAS	701 E ORCHARD RD - LITTLETON CO 80120
80-144	WILLIAMS, ALBERT HAMILTON	PEARL LAGOON,DEPOT ZELOYA-NICARAGUA,C.A. NIC
37-108	WILLIAMS, ALMON EDWARD	D. JULY 19, 1969 GROVES, TEX.
11-177	WILLIAMS, ALVA MITCHEL	D. JULY 23, 1933 KEOKUK, IA.
11-178	WILLIAMS, AUGUST JOSEPH	D. APRIL 16, 1964 STERLING, ILL.
70-138	WILLIAMS, BERNARD	861 47TH ST - OAKLAND CA 94608
59-87	WILLIAMS, BILLY LEO	586 PRINCE EDWARD RD - GLEN ELLYN IL 60137
71-108	WILLIAMS, CHARLES PROSEK	259-04 KENSINGTON PL - GREAT NECK NY 11021
13-192	WILLIAMS, CLAUD PRESTON	NOVEMBER 4, 1959 LAGUNA BEACH, CALIF.
81-144	WILLIAMS, DALLAS MCKINLEY	11 EDGEWOOD AVE - ROCHESTER NY 14618
49-91	WILLIAMS, DAVID CARLOUS	4645 COUNTRY CREEK #1101 - DALLAS TX 75236
13-193	WILLIAMS, DAVID CARTER	D. MARCH 30, 1962 FAYETTEVILLE, ARK.
44-143	WILLIAMS, DEWEY EDGAR	720 THIRTEENTH - WILLISTON ND 58801
58-103	WILLIAMS, DONALD FRED	11405 ROKEBY AVE - GARRETT PARK MD 20766
63-126	WILLIAMS, DONALD REID	5546 CHATEAU DR - SAN DIEGO CA 92117
28-108	WILLIAMS, EARL BAXTER	D. MARCH 10, 1958 KNOXVILLE, TENN.
70-139	WILLIAMS, EARL CRAIG	OLD ADD: 2900 CAMP CREEK PKWY - COLLEGE PK GA
30-92	WILLIAMS, EDWIN DIBRELL	BOX 43 - GREENBRIER AR 72058
21-112	WILLIAMS, EVON DANIEL	D. MARCH 24, 1929 LOS ANGELES CO., CAL.
45-118	WILLIAMS, FRED	1120 46-A AVE - MERIDIAN MS 39304
12-219	WILLIAMS, FREDERICK	D. APRIL 23, 1974 EAGLE RIVER, WIS.
61-108	WILLIAMS, GEORGE	4267 TYLER ST - DETROIT MI 48238
13-194	WILLIAMS, HARRY PETER	D. DECEMBER 20, 1963 HAYWOOD, CALIF.
69-180	WILLIAMS, JAMES ALFRED	OLD ADD: 2000 CRYSTAL SPRINGS RD-SAN BRUNO CA
66-100	WILLIAMS, JAMES FRANCIS	4238 S DERBYSHIRE - SALT LAKE CITY UT 84107
14-232	WILLIAMS, JOHN BRODIE	D. SEPTEMBER 8, 1963 LONG BEACH, CALIF.
15-176	WILLIAMS, KENNETH ROY	D. JANUARY 29, 1959 GRANTS PASS, ORE.
26-94	WILLIAMS, LEON THEO	626 OLD IVY RD NE - ATLANTA GA 30305
77-155	WILLIAMS, MARK WESTLY	15 CLINTON ST - CORNWALL NY 12518
16-97	WILLIAMS, MARSHALL MCDIARMID	D. FEBRUARY 22, 1935 TUCSON, ARIZ.
14-233	WILLIAMS, REES GEPHARDT	D. JUNE 29, 1979 DEER RIVER, MINN.
78-143	WILLIAMS, RICHARD ALLEN	1516 NORTH D STREET - MADERA CA 93637
51-103	WILLIAMS, RICHARD HIRSCHFIELD	16407 AVELA BLVD - TAMPA FL 33616
14-234	WILLIAMS, RINALDO LEWIS	D. APRIL 24, 1966 COTTONWOOD, ARIZ.
11-179	WILLIAMS, ROBERT ELIAS	D. AUGUST 6, 1962 NELSONVILLE, O.
40-102	WILLIAMS, ROBERT FULTON	OLD ADD: CROSS ST - MARSHFIELD MA 02050
58-104	WILLIAMS, STANLEY WILSON	4702 HAYTER AVE - LAKEWOOD CA 90712
39-126	WILLIAMS, THEODORE SAMUEL	BOX 481 - ISLAMORADA FL 33036
64-128	WILLIAMS, WALTER ALLEN	1113 CROTHERS ST - BROWNWOOD TX 76801
69-181	WILLIAMS, WILLIAM	3227 RANDOLPH AVE - OAKLAND CA 94602
38-106	WILLIAMS, WOODROW WILSON	PAMPLIN VA 23958
28-109	WILLIAMSON, NATHANIEL HOWARD	OLD ADD: 322 S ADAMS - FORT WORTH TX
28-110	WILLIAMSON, SILAS ALBERT	D. NOVEMBER 29, 1978 HOT SPRINGS, ARK.
30-93	WILLINGHAM, THOMAS HUGH	412 S MACOMB ST - EL RENO OK 73036

Williams (signature)

25-115	WILLIS, CHARLES WILLIAM	D. MAY 10, 1962 BETHESDA, MD.
63-127	WILLIS, DALE JEROME	1110 ESTATEWOOD DR - BRANDON FL 33511
53-99	WILLIS, JAMES GLADDEN	BOX 35 - BOYCE LA 71409
11-180	WILLIS, JOSEPH DENK	D. DECEMBER 3, 1966 IRONTON, O.
47-96	WILLIS, LESTER EVANS	D. JANUARY 22, 1982
77-156	WILLIS, MICHAEL HENRY	479 ROCHELLE DR - NASHVILLE TN 37220
66-101	WILLIS, RONALD EARL	D. NOVEMBER 21, 1977 MEMPHIS, TENN.
25-116	WILLOUGHBY, CLAUDE WILLIAM	D. AUGUST 14, 1973 MCPHERSON, KAN.
71-109	WILLOUGHBY, JAMES ARTHUR	205 BONITA AVE - MODESTO CA 95351

WILLS

WITEK

77-157	WILLS, ELLIOTT TAYLOR	6008 LAKE HURST DR - ARLINGTON TX 76012
59- 88	WILLS, MAURICE MORNING	245 FOWLING - PLAYA DEL REY CA 90291
59- 89	WILLS, THEODORE CARL	RR 1 N CAMPBELL RD - OTIS ORCHARDS WA 99027
18- 75	WILLSON, FRANK HOXIE	D. APRIL 17, 1964 UNION GAP, WASH.
34-109	WILSHERE, VERNON SPRAGUE	78 CHESTNUT ST - COOPERSTOWN NY 13326
73-131	WILSHUSEN, TERRY WAYNE	1839 W 255TH ST - LOMITA CA 90717
51-104	WILSON, ARCHIE CLIFTON	1620 WOODLAND ST SE - DECATUR AL 35601
51-105	WILSON, ARTHUR LEE	2226 NE 10TH AVE - PORTLAND OR 97212
31-100	WILSON, CHARLES WOODROW	D. DECEMBER 19, 1970 ROCHESTER, N. Y.
66-102	WILSON, DONALD EDWARD	D. JANUARY 5, 1975 HOUSTON, TEX.
58-105	WILSON, DUANE LEWIS	501 BUTLER - VALLEY CENTER KS 67147
59- 90	WILSON, EARL LAWRENCE	BOX 661 - PONCHATOULA LA 70454
36- 98	WILSON, EDWARD FRANCIS	D. APRIL 11, 1979 HAMDEN, CONN.
14-235	WILSON, FINIS ELBERT	D. MARCH 9, 1959 CORAL GABLES, FLA.
24-115	WILSON, FRANCIS EDWARD	D. NOVEMBER 25, 1974 LEICESTER, MASS.
79-123	WILSON, GARY STEVEN	RURAL ROUTE 2 BOX 644 - CAMDEN AR 71701
11-181	WILSON, GEORGE FRANCIS	D. MARCH 26, 1967 WINTHROP, ME.
34-110	WILSON, GEORGE PEACOCK	D. OCTOBER 13, 1973 MORAGA, CAL.
52-112	WILSON, GEORGE WASHINGTON	D. OCTOBER 29, 1974 GASTONIA, N.C.
24-116	WILSON, GOMER RUSSELL	D. SEPTEMBER 15, 1946 SULPHUR SPRINGS, TEX.
48-111	WILSON, GRADY HERBERT	3601 RIVER RD - COLUMBUS GA 31904
23-143	WILSON, JAMES	D. JUNE 1, 1947 PALMETTO, FLA.
45-119	WILSON, JAMES ALGER	2701 VISTA UMBROSA - NEWPORT BEACH CA 92660
34-111	WILSON, JOHN FRANCIS	4111 164TH AVE SW #62 - LYNNWOOD WA 98036

13-195	WILSON, JOHN NICODEMUS	D. SEPTEMBER 23, 1954 ANNAPOLIS, MD.
27-106	WILSON, JOHN SAMUEL	D. AUGUST 27, 1980 CHATTANOOGA, TENN.
11-182	WILSON, LESTER WILBUR	D. APRIL 4, 1969 EDMONDS, WASH.
23-144	WILSON, LEWIS ROBERT	D. NOVEMBER 23, 1948 BALTIMORE, MD.
40-103	WILSON, MAX	D. JANUARY 2, 1977 GREENSBORO, N. C.
58-106	WILSON, ROBERT	627 COVE HOLLOW DR - DALLAS TX 75224
51-106	WILSON, ROBERT JAMES	806 CABOT LN - MADISON WI 53711
28-111	WILSON, ROY EDWARD	D. DECEMBER 3, 1969 CLARION, IA.
60-103	WILSON, SAMMY O'NEIL	RR1 BOX 285 - LEXINGTON TN 38351
21-113	WILSON, SAMUEL MARSHALL	D. MAY 16, 1978 BOYNTON BEACH, FLA.
14-236	WILSON, THOMAS C.	1911 ADD: HARTFORD, ARK.
45-120	WILSON, WALTER WOOD	RR 3 BOX 345 - LAGRANGE GA 30240
20-131	WILSON, WILLIAM CLARENCE	D. AUGUST 31, 1962 WILDWOOD, FLA.
50-104	WILSON, WILLIAM DONALD	11121 AGNES PL - CERRITOS CA 90701
69-182	WILSON, WILLIAM HARLAN	OLD ADD: 3321 ASH CT - BROKEN ARROW OK
80-145	WILSON, WILLIAM HAYWOOD	15-1 FOUNTAIN DR - LAKEWOOD NJ 08701
76-103	WILSON, WILLIE JAMES	OLD ADD: 5 GLENWOOD PL - SUMMIT NJ
26- 95	WILTSE, HAROLD JAMES	701 WALNUT ST - BUNKIE LA 71322
56- 87	WINCENIAK, EDWARD JOSEPH	10828 S AVE "O" - CHICAGO IL 60617
59- 91	WINDHORN, GORDON RAY	3220 WESTOVER DR - DANVILLE VA 24543
28-112	WINDLE, WILLIS BREWER	D. DECEMBER 8, 1981 CORPUS CHRISTI TX.
60-104	WINE, ROBERT PAUL	2612 WOODLAND AVE - NORRISTOWN PA 19401
29-108	WINEAPPLE, EDWARD	960 PARK AVE - NEW YORK NY 10028
30- 94	WINEGARNER, RALPH LEE	245 WICHITA ST - BENTON KS 67017
73-132	WINFIELD, DAVID MARK	1600 PARKER AVE #29H - FORT LEE NJ 07824
32- 92	WINFORD, JAMES HEAD	D. DECEMBER 16, 1970 MIAMI, OKLA.
24-117	WINGARD, ERNEST JAMES	D. JANUARY 17, 1977 PRATTVILLE, ALA.
23-145	WINGFIELD, FREDERICK DAVIS	D. JULY 18, 1975 JOHNSON CITY, TENN.
19- 91	WINGO, ABSALOM HOLBROOK	D. OCTOBER 9, 1954 DETROIT, MICH.
20-132	WINGO, EDMOND ARMAND	D. DECEMBER 5, 1964 LACHINE, QUE.
11-183	WINGO, IVEY BROWN	D. MARCH 1, 1941 NORCROSS, GA.
73-133	WINKLES, BOBBY BROOKS	1608 E ELM - ANAHEIM CA 92805
19- 92	WINN, GEORGE BENJAMIN	D. NOVEMBER 1, 1969 ROBERTA, GA.
30- 95	WINSETT, JOHN THOMAS	3320 HIGHLAND PARK - MEMPHIS TN 68111
33- 67	WINSTON, HENRY RUDOLPH	D. FEBRUARY 7, 1974 JACKSONVILLE, FLA.
24-118	WINTERS, CLARENCE JOHN	D. JUNE 29, 1945 DETROIT, MICH.
19- 93	WINTERS, JESSE FRANKLIN	2142 S 10TH ST - ABILENE TEX 79605
78-144	WIRTH, ALAN LEE	1012 WEST MOUNTAIN VIEW - MESA AZ 85201
21-114	WIRTS, ELWOOD VERNON	D. JULY 12, 1968 SACRAMENTO, CAL.
32- 93	WISE, ARCHIBALD EDWIN	D. FEBRUARY 2, 1978 WAXAHACHIE, TEX.
30- 96	WISE, HUGH EDWARD	8931 N NEW RIVER CANAL #1-F-PLANTATIONFL33324
57- 93	WISE, KENDALL COLE	1818 HURRICANE DR - NAPLES FL 33940
64-129	WISE, RICHARD CHARLES	RR 2 BOX 317 - HILLSBORO OR 97123
44-144	WISE, ROY OGDEN	11841 MELODY LN DR - GARDEN GROVE CA 92640
19- 94	WISNER, JOHN HENRY	2521 NORWOOD RD - JACKSON MI 49203
64-130	WISSMAN, DAVID ALVIN	20 WELLINGTON ST - SHELBURNE FALLS MA 01370
34-112	WISTERT, FRANCIS MICHAEL	3822 W CENTRAL #931-43601 - TOLEDO OH 43606
14-230	WISTERZIL, GEORGE J.	D. JUNE 27, 1964 SAN ANTONIO, TEX.
40-104	WITEK, NICHOLAS JOSEPH	RR 5 BOX 341 - SHAVERTOWN PA 18708

20-133 WITHROW, FRANK BLAINE
53-128 WITHROW, RAYMOND WALLACE
57- 94 WITT, GEORGE ADRIAN
46- 98 WITT, LAWTON WALTER
31-145 WITT, MICHAEL ATWATER
46-107 WITTE, JEROME CHARLES
38-107 WITTIG, JOHN CARL
74-142 WOCKENFUSS, JOHN BILTON
23-146 WOEHR, ANDREW EMIL
72-121 WOHLFORD, JAMES EUGENE
62-148 WOJCIK, JOHN JOSEPH
54-118 WOJEY, PETER PAUL
12-220 WOLF, ERNEST A
27-107 WOLF, RAYMOND BERNARD
69-183 WOLF, WALTER BECK
21-115 WOLF, WALTER FRANCIS
23-147 WOLFE, CHARLES HENRY
52-113 WOLFE, EDWARD ANTHONY
17- 90 WOLFE, HAROLD
77-158 WOLFE, LAURENCE MARCY
12-221 WOLFE, ROY CHAMBERLAIN
41-119 WOLFF, ROGER FRANCIS
14-237 WOLFGANG, MELDON JOHN
66-103 WOMACK, HORACE GUY
26- 96 WOMACK, SIDNEY KIRK
30- 97 WOOD, CHARLES ASHER
23-148 WOOD, CHARLES SPENCER
61-109 WOOD, JACOB
44-145 WOOD, JOE FRANK
43-144 WOOD, JOSEPH PERRY
48-112 WOOD, KENNETH LANIER
13-196 WOOD, ROY WINTON
61-110 WOOD, WILBUR FORRESTER
20-134 WOODALL, CHARLES LAWRENCE
78-145 WOODARD, DARRELL LEE
11-184 WOODBURN, EUGENE STEWART
44-146 WOODEND, GEORGE ANTHONY
56- 88 WOODESHICK, HAROLD JOSEPH
43-145 WOODLING, EUGENE RICHARD
14-239 WOODMAN, DANIEL COURTENAY
77-159 WOODS, ALVIS
14-238 WOODS, CLARENCE COFIELD
76-104 WOODS, GARY LEE
43-146 WOODS, GEORGE ROWLAND
57- 95 WOODS, JAMES JEROME

D. SEPTEMBER 5, 1966 OMAHA, NEB.
1730 QUEENSWAY CT - OWENSBORO KY 42301
TUSTIN H. S. - TUSTIN CA 92680
RR 1 BOX 522 - WOODSTOWN NJ 08098
8042 SAN LEON CIR DR - BUENA PARK CA 90620
7515 OAK VISTA - HOUSTON TX 77017
163 STAFFORD STREET - BALTIMORE MD 21227
2107 BARR RD - WILMINGTON DE 19808
211 W WILDWOOD AV - FT WAYNE IN 46807
13895 EL CAMINO REAL - ATASCADERO CA 93422
33 HAMILTON ST - BUFFALO NY 14207
2359 S BUENA DR - MOBILE AL 36605
D. MAY 23, 1964 ATLANTIC HIGHLANDS, N.J.
D. OCTOBER 6, 1979 FORT WORTH, TEXAS
17711 TRAIL VIEW - YORBA LINDA CA 92686
D. SEPTEMBER 25, 1971 NEW ORLEANS, LA.
D. NOVEMBER 27, 1957 SCHELLSBURG, PA.
OLD ADD: 41 HAVEN PL - SAN RAMON CA
D. JULY 28, 1971 FORT WAYNE, IND.
2616 SARDA WAY - RANCHO CORDOVA CA 95670
D. NOVEMBER 21, 1938 MORRIS, ILL.
1307 KNOTT-CHESTER IL 62233
D. JUNE 30, 1947 ALBANY, N.Y.
119 CENTURY DR - COLUMBIA SC 29210
D. AUGUST 8, 1958 JACKSON, MISS.
3901 E ELM - WICHITA KS 67208
D. NOVEMBER 3, 1974 NEW ORLEANS, LA.
1289 MARCELLA DR - UNION NJ 07083
#53 EGYPT LANE - CLINTON CT 06413
OLD ADD: GENERAL DELIVERY - WIMBERLEY TX
6337 TERESA AVE - CHARLOTTE NC 28214
D. APRIL 6, 1974 FAYETTEVILLE, ARK.
8 WACHUSETT DR - LEXINGTON MA 02173
D. MAY 6, 1963 NEWTON, MASS.
1227 EAST 69TH ST - LOS ANGELES CA 90001
D. JANUARY 18, 1961 SANDUSKY, O.
D. FEBRUARY 6, 1980 HARTFORD, CONN.
803 WYCLIFFE - HOUSTON TX 77024
926 REMSEN RD - MEDINA OH 44256
D. DECEMBER 14, 1962 TOPSFIELD, MASS.
2518 60TH AVE - OAKLAND CA 94605
D. JULY 2, 1969 RISING SUN, IND.
945 WARD DR #28 - SANTA BARBARA CA 93111
248 S OCCIDENTAL #12 - LOS ANGELES CA 90057
151 ROSS WAY - SAN BRUNO CA 94066

24-119 WOODS, JOHN FULTON
69-184 WOODS, RONALD LAWRENCE
69-185 WOODSON, RICHARD LEE
18- 76 WOODWARD, FRANK RUSSELL
63-129 WOODWARD, WILLIAM FREDERICK
55-137 WOOLDRIDGE, FLOYD LEWIS
47- 97 WOOTEN, EARL HAZELL
14-240 WORDEN, FRED B
38-108 WORKMAN, CHARLES THOMAS
24-120 WORKMAN, HARRY HALL
50-105 WORKMAN, HENRY KILGARIFF
78-146 WORTHAM, RICHARD COOPER
53-100 WORTHINGTON, ALLAN FULTON
31-101 WORTHINGTON, ROBERT LEE
16- 99 WORTMAN, WILLIAM LEWIS
33- 68 WRIGHT, ALBERT EDGAR
35-115 WRIGHT, ALBERT OWEN
16-100 WRIGHT, CEYLON
66-104 WRIGHT, CLYDE
24-121 WRIGHT, FORREST GLENN
45-121 WRIGHT, HENDERSON EDWARD
27-108 WRIGHT, JAMES
78-147 WRIGHT, JAMES CLIFTON
81-146 WRIGHT, JAMES LEON
70-140 WRIGHT, KENNETH WARREN
54-119 WRIGHT, MELVIN JAMES
15-177 WRIGHT, ROBERT CASSIUS
56- 89 WRIGHT, ROY EARL

D. OCTOBER 4, 1946 NORFOLK, VA.
413 PLYMOUTH ST - INGLEWOOD CA 90302
9840 SHADOW RD - LAMESA CA 92041
D. JUNE 11, 1961 NEW HAVEN, CONN.
5499 ELMCREST LN - CINCINNATI OH 45242
BOX 74 - GREENFIELD MO 65661
702 WILLIAMS ST - WILLIAMSTON SC 29697
D. NOVEMBER 9, 1941 ST. LOUIS, MO.
D. JANUARY 3, 1953 KANSAS CITY, MO.
D. MAY 20, 1972 FORT MYERS, FLA.
307 19TH ST - SANTA MONICA CA 90402
1408 NORTH KELLY - ODESSA TX 79760
LYNCHBURG BAPTIST COL - LYNCHBURG VA 24504
D. DECEMBER 8, 1963 LOS ANGELES, CAL.
D. AUGUST 19, 1977 LAS VEGAS, NEV.
156 JOHN ST - OAKLAND CA 94611
407 S PAYNE ST - STILLWATER OK 74074
D. NOVEMBER 7, 1947 HINES, ILL.
528 JEANINE AVE - ANAHEIM CA 92806
2706 W ASHLAN #38 - FRESNO CA 93705
116 N MAIN ST - DYERSBURG TN 38024
D. APRIL 12, 1963 OAKLAND, CAL.
439 HARRISON ST - COOPERSVILLE MI 49404
2727 RENICK ST - ST JOSEPH MO 64503
1416 WISTERIA AVE - PENSACOLA FL 32507
ONE HOGAN COVE - MAUMELLE AR 72118
2724 ELVYRA WA #19 - SACRAMENTO CA 95821
331 PINEHURST CIR - CHICKAMAUGA GA 30707

38-109	WRIGHT, TAFT SHEDRON	D. OCTOBER 22, 1981 ORLANDO, FLA.
48-113	WRIGHT, THOMAS EVERETT	RR 2 BOX 45 - SHELBY NC 28150
17- 91	WRIGHT, WAYNE BROMLEY	D. JUNE 12, 1948 COLUMBUS, O.
15-178	WRIGHT, WILLIAM JAMES	D. JANUARY 24, 1952 BETHLEHEM, PA.
20-135	WRIGHTSTONE, RUSSELL GUY	D. MARCH 1, 1969 HARRISBURG, PA.
29-109	WUESTLING, GEORGE	D. APRIL 26, 1970 ST. LOUIS, MO.
44-147	WURM, FRANK JAMES	7 CLINTON ST - GLENS FALLS NY 12801
61-111	WYATT, JOHN THOMAS	2517 BENTON - KANSAS CITY MO 64127
29-110	WYATT, JOHN WHITLOW	BUCHANAN GA 30113
24-122	WYATT, LORAL JOHN	D. DECEMBER 5, 1970 OBLONG, ILL.
13-197	WYCKOFF, JOHN WELDON	D. MAY 8, 1961 SHEBOYGAN FALLS, WIS.
76-105	WYNEGAR, HAROLD DELANO	RR 3 BOX 259 - YORK PA 17402
39-127	WYNN, EARLY	525 BAYVIEW PKWY - NOKOMIS FL 33555
63-130	WYNN, JAMES SHERMAN	OLD ADD: 1440 VETERAN - LOS ANGELES CA
67-115	WYNNE, WILLIAM VERNON	4642 MORRIS RD - JACKSONVILLE FL 32225
42-108	WYROSTEK, JOHN BARNEY	2749 N 44TH ST-E ST LOUIS IL 62201
42-109	WYSE, HENRY WASHINGTON	1133 SE 14TH ST- PRYOR OK 74361
30- 98	WYSONG, HARLIN	D. AUGUST 8, 1951 XENIA, O.
72-122	YANCY, HUGH	BOX 9064 - SARASOTA FL 33578
42-110	YANKOWSKI, GEORGE EDWARD	164 CHAPMAN ST-WATERTOWN MA 02172
12-222	YANTZ, GEORGE WEBB	D. FEBRUARY 26, 1967 LOUISVILLE, KY.
26- 97	YARNALL, WALDO WARD	18 MOORE RD - NABNASSET MA 01860
22-137	YARRISON, BYRON WARDSWORTH	D. APRIL 22, 1977 WILLIAMSPORT, PA.
21-116	YARYAN, CLARENCE EVERETT	D. NOVEMBER 16, 1964 BIRMINGHAM, ALA.
61-112	YASTRZEMSKI, CARL MICHAEL	HIGHLAND BEACH FL 33444
71-110	YATES, ALBERT ARTHUR	OLD ADD: 11613 W YUMA CT - NEW BERLIN WI
24-123	YDE, EMIL OGDEN	D. DECEMBER 4, 1968 LEESBURG, FLA.
19- 95	YEABSLEY, ROBERT WATKINS	D. FEBRUARY 8, 1961 PHILADELPHIA, PA.
72-123	YEAGER, STEPHEN WAYNE	23501 PARK SORRENTO - CALABASAS CA 91302
22-138	YEARGIN, JAMES ALMOND	D. MAY 8, 1937 GREENVILLE, S. C.
17- 92	YELLE, ARCHIE JOSEPH	906 2ND ST - WOODLAND CA 95695
63-131	YELLEN, LAWRENCE ALAN	OLD ADD: 1611 E 5TH ST - BROOKLYN NY
21-117	YELLOWHORSE, MOSES J.	D. APRIL 10, 1964 PAWNEE, OKLA.
27-109	YERKES, CHARLES CARROLL	D. DECEMBER 20, 1950 OAKLAND, CAL.
57- 96	YEWCIC, THOMAS	31 CHEORKEE RD - ARLINTON MA 02174
11-185	YINGLING, EARL HERSHEY	D. OCTOBER 2, 1962 COLUMBUS, O.
51-107	YOCHIM, LEONARD JOSEPH	316 NELSON DR - NEW ORLEANS LA 70123
48-114	YOCHIM, RAYMOND AUSTIN ALOYSIUS	3728 45TH ST - METAIRIE LA 70001
19- 96	YORK, JAMES E.	D. APRIL 9, 1961 YORK, PA.
70-141	YORK, JAMES HARLAN	10957 E HOLBECK AVE - NORWALK CA 90650
34-113	YORK, RUDOLPH PRESTON	D. FEBRUARY 5, 1970 ROME, GA.
44-148	YORK, TONY BATTEN	D. APRIL 18, 1970 HILLSBORO, TEXAS
80-146	YOST, EDGAR FREDERICK	23 CASTLEWOOD DR - PLEASANTON CA 94566
44-149	YOST, EDWARD FRED JOSEPH	74 EAGLE LN - HAUPPAUGE NY 11788
21-118	YOTER, ELMER ELLSWORTH	D. JULY 26, 1966 CAMP HILL, PA.
15-179	YOUNG, CHARLES	D. MAY 12, 1952 RIVERSIDE, N. J.
37-109	YOUNG, DELMER EDWARD	D. DECEMBER 8, 1979 SAN FR ANCISCO, CALIF.
65-117	YOUNG, DONALD WAYNE	OLD ADD: 1350 TRENTON ST - DENVER CO 80220
13-198	YOUNG, GEORGE JOSEPH	D. MARCH 13, 1950 BRIGHTWATERS, N.Y.
11-186	YOUNG, HERMAN JOHN	D. DECEMBER 13, 1966 IPSWICH, MASS.
71-111	YOUNG, JOHN THOMAS	124 W 57TH ST - LOS ANGELES CA 90037
78-148	YOUNG, KIP LANE	RR 2 BOX 113-C - WINCHESTER OH 45697
33- 69	YOUNG, LEMUEL FLOYD	D. JANUARY 14, 1962 JAMESTOWN, N. C.
36- 99	YOUNG, NORMAN ROBERT	SEYMOUR VILLAGE N 3 - EAST GRANBY CT 06026
13-199	YOUNG, RALPH STUART	D. JANUARY 24, 1965 PHILADELPHIA, PA.
51-108	YOUNG, RICHARD ENNIS	2200 192ND PL SW - ALDERWOOD MANOR WA 98036
48-115	YOUNG, ROBERT GEORGE	3627 FLORIDA AVE - BALTIMORE MD 21207
31-102	YOUNG, RUSSELL CHARLES	OLD ADD: 916 LEWIS ST - ROSEVILLE CA
22-139	YOUNGBLOOD, ARTHUR CLYDE	D. JULY 6, 1968 AMARILLO, TEX.
76-106	YOUNGBLOOD, JOEL RANDOLPH	4309 HARBY ST - HOUSTON TX 77023
17- 93	YOUNGS, ROSS MIDDLEBROOK	D. OCTOBER 22, 1927 SAN ANTONIO, TEX.
37-110	YOUNT, FLOYD EDWIN	D. OCTOBER 26, 1973 NEWTON, N. C.
14-241	YOUNT, HERBERT MACON	D. MAY 9, 1970 WINSTON-SALEM, N. C.
71-112	YOUNT, LAWRENCE KING	4304 N HUNT CLUB LN - WESTLAKE VLG CA 91360
74-143	YOUNT, ROBIN R	4196 MINNECOTA - THOUSAND OAKS CA 91360
24-124	YOWELL, CARL COLUMBUS	BOX 147 - RUSK TX 75785
52-114	YUHAS, JOHN EDWARD	1855-G FRANCISCAN TER-WINSTON-SALEM NC 27107
78-149	YURAK, JEFFREY LYNN	2810 JOERS WAY SOUTH #8 - SEATTLE WA 98188
47- 98	YVARS, SALVADOR ANTHONY	54 ALLEN ST - VALHALLA NY 10595
45-122	ZABALA, ADRIAN RODRIGUEZ	11243 ANDREA DR - JACKSONVILLE FL 32218
13-200	ZABEL, GEORGE WASHINGTON	D. MAY 31, 1970 BELOIT, WIS.
44-150	ZACHARY, ALBERT MYRON	OLD ADD: 252-04 82ND DR - BELLEROSE NY 11426
18- 77	ZACHARY, JONATHAN THOMPSON WALTON	D. JANUARY 24, 1969 GRAHAM, N. C.

ZACHARY   ZUVERINK

63-132	ZACHARY, WILLIAM CHRIS	6825 COCHISE DR - HALLS CROSS ROADS TN 37918
10-152	ZACHER, ELMER HENRY	D. DECEMBER 20, 1944 BUFFALO, N.Y.
76-107	ZACHRY, PATRICK PAUL	1112 N 60TH ST - WACO TX 76710
11-187	ZACKERT, GEORGE CARL	D. FEBRUARY 18, 1977 BURLINGTON, IA.
73-134	ZAHN, GEOFFREY CLAYTON	7141 E MOCKINGBIRD WAY - ANAHEIM CA 92807
23-149	ZAHNISER, PAUL VERNON	D. SEPTEMBER 26, 1964 KLAMATH FALLS, ORE.
44-151	ZAK, FRANK THOMAS	D. FEBRUARY 6, 1972 PASSAIC, N.J.
13-201	ZAMLOCH, CARL EUGENE	D. AUGUST 19, 1963 SANTA BARBARA, CALIF.
74-144	ZAMORA, OSCAR JOSE	17505 NORTH BAY RD #526 - MIAMI FL 33160
58-107	ZANNI, DOMINICK THOMAS	7 SUSSEX AVE N - MASSAPEQUA NY 11758
33- 70	ZAPUSTAS, JOSEPH JOHN	16 VESEY RD - RANDOLPH MA 02368
45-123	ZARDON, JOSE ANTONIO SANCHEZ	11990 BIRD DR - MIAMI FL 33175
43-147	ZARILLA, ALLEN LEE	431 NAHUA ST #705 - HONOLULU HI 96815
51-109	ZAUCHIN, NORBERT HENRY	818 N MONTEZ DR - THOMAS ACRES AL 35020
77-160	ZDEB, JOSEPH EDWARD	6802 ACUFF - SHAWNEE KS 66215
77-161	ZEBER, GEORGE WILLIAM	307 S WRIGHTWOOD - ORANGE CA 92669
10-153	ZEIDER, ROLLIE HUBERT	D. SEPTEMBER 12, 1967 AUBURN, IND.
14-242	ZEISER, MATTHEW J.	D. JUNE 10, 1942 NORWOOD PARK, ILL.
70-142	ZELLER, BARTON WALLACE	5112 IMPERIAL DR - RICHTON PARK IL 60471
69-186	ZEPP, WILLIAM CLINTON	35430 BROOKVIEW DR - LIVONIA MI 48152
49- 92	ZERNIAL, GUS EDWARD	361 W INDIANAPOLIS - CLOVIS CA 93612
54-120	ZICK, ROBERT GEORGE	#7 AVE L'ETOILE POLAIRE-1410 WATERLOO BELGIUM
41-120	ZIENTARA, BENEDICT JOSEPH	10723 AVE G-CHICAGO IL 60617
54-121	ZIMMER, DONALD WILLIAM	10124 YACHT CLUB DR - ST PETERSBURG FL 33706
61-113	ZIMMERMAN, GERALD ROBERT	13650 FERNRIDGE - MILWAUKIE OR 97222
45-124	ZIMMERMAN, ROY FRANKLIN	24 NORTH ST - TREMONT PA 17981
15-180	ZIMMERMAN, WILLIAM H.	D. OCTOBER 4, 1952 NEWARK, N.J.
21-119	ZINK, WALTER NOBLE	D. JUNE 12, 1964 QUINCY, MASS.
11-188	ZINN, GUY	D. OCTOBER 6, 1949 CLARKSBURG, W. VA.
19- 97	ZINN, JAMES EDWARD	5614 APPLEWOOD DR - NORTH LITTLE ROCK AR72118
44-152	ZINSER, WILLIAM FREDERICK	OLD ADD: 177 CALDWEL #1-J - CINCINNATI OH
61-114	ZIPFEL, MARION SYLVESTER	57 WHITESIDE DR - BELLEVILLE IL 62221
71-113	ZISK, RICHARD WALTER	1990 N FEDERAL HWY - POMPANO BEACH FL 33062
19- 98	ZITZMANN, WILLIAM ARTHUR	44 EVELYN PLACE - NUTLEY NJ 07110
10-154	ZMICH, EDWARD ALBERT	D. AUGUST 20, 1950 CLEVELAND, O.
44-153	ZOLDAK, SAMUEL WALTER	D. AUGUST 25, 1966 MINEOLA, N. Y.
36-100	ZUBER, WILLIAM HENRY	HOMESTEAD IA 52236
57- 97	ZUPO, FRANK JOSEPH	2824 MARIPOSA DR - BURLINGAME CA 94010
51-110	ZUVERINK, GEORGE	1721 E ELLIS DR - TEMPE AZ 85281

UMPIRES DEBUTING FROM 1910 TO 1981

```
UMP-14  ANDERSON, OLIVER O              D. JULY 7, 1945 LOS ANGELES, CALIF.
UMP-70  ANTHONY, GEORGE MERLYN          1520 HOLLY TREE DR - YUBA CITY CA 95991
UMP-66  ASHFORD, EMMETT LITTLETON       4139 VIA MARINA #808-8-MARINA DEL REY CA9029
UMP-69  AVANTS, NICK R                  5805 WOODLAWN - LITTLE ROCK AR 72205
UMP-36  BALLANFANT, EDWARD LEE          7018 CASA LOMA - DALLAS TX 75214
UMP-40  BARLICK, ALBERT JOSEPH          RR 1 - RIVERTON IL 62561
UMP-68  BARNETT, LAWRENCE ROBERT        6464 HUGHES RD PROSPECT OH 43342
UMP-31  BARR, GEORGE MCKINLEY           D. JULY 26, 1974 SULPHUR, OKLA.
UMP-28  BARRY, DANIEL                   OLD ADD: 173 METROPOLITAN AVE-ROSLINDALE MA
UMP-36  BASIL, STEPHEN JOHN             D. JUNE 24, 1962 GILCHRIST, TEX.
UMP-42  BERRY, CHARLES FRANCIS          PLAYER DEBUT 1925
UMP-76  BETCHER, RALPH                  153 PARKFEL AVE - PITTSBURGH PA 15237
UMP-70  BLANDFORD, FRED                 1123 CHARLES ST - ELMIRA NY 14904
UMP-44  BOGGESS, LYNTON ROSS            D. JULY 8, 1968 DALLAS, TEX.
UMP-44  BOYER, JAMES MURRY              D. JULY 25, 1959 FINKSBURG, MD.
UMP-17  BRANSFIELD, WILLIAM EDWARD      PLAYER DEBUT 1898
UMP-74  BREMIGAN, NICHOLAS GREGORY      1610 N ARGULE #102 - ARCADIA CA 91006
UMP-15  BREWER,
UMP-73  BRINKMAN, JOSEPH NORBERT        1223 13TH ST N - ST PETERSBURG FL 33705
UMP-79  BROCKLANDER, FRED               123-40 83RD AVE #7C - KEW GARDENS NY 11415
UMP-57  BURKHART, WILLIAM KENNETH       PLAYER DEBUT 1945
UMP-11  BUSH, GARNET C.                 D. DECOMBER 30, 1919 ST. LOUIS, MO.
UMP-13  BYRON, WILLIAM J                D. DECEMBER 27, 1955 YPSILANTI, MICH.
UMP-28  CAMPBELL, WILLIAM M             1938 ADD: 676 S BELVEDERE - MEMPHIS TN
UMP-61  CARRIGAN, HERVE SAMUEL          651 MCKINSTRY AVE - CHICOPEE FALLS MA 01020
UMP-14  CHILL, CLIVER P                 1926 ADD: MAJESTIC HOTEL - KANSAS CITY MO
UMP-54  CHYLAK, NESTOR                  D. FEBRUARY 17, 1982 DUNMORE, PA.
UMP-76  CLARK, ALAN MARSHALL            16 INDEPENDENCE PL - NEWTOWN PA 18940
UMP-30  CLARKE, ROBERT M
UMP-15  COCKILL, GEORGE W
UMP-76  COHEN, ALFRED                   1026 N HIGHLAND AVE - PITTSBURGH PA 15206
UMP-10  COLLIFLOWER, JAMES HARRY        PLAYER DEBUT 1899
UMP-68  COLOSI, NICHOLAS                68-17 54TH AVE - MASPETH NY 11378
UMP-41  CONLAN, JOHN BERTRAND           PLAYER DEBUT 1934
UMP-75  COONEY, TERRENCE JOSEPH         6814 EAST LANE - FRESNO CA 93727
UMP-14  CORCORAN, THOMAS WILLIAM        PLAYER DEBUT 1890
UMP-79  COUSINS, DERRYL                 605 VIRGINIA ST - EL SEGUNDO CA 90245
UMP-76  CRAWFORD, GERALD JOSEPH         1 PINZON AVE - HAVERTOWN PA 19083
UMP-56  CRAWFORD, HENRY CHARLES         1530 VIRGINIA AVE - HAVERTOWN PA 19083
UMP-14  CROSS, MONTFORD MONTGOMERY      PLAYER DEBUT 1892
UMP-71  DALE, JERRY PARKER              428 W HUNTINGTON DR #4 - ARCADIA CA 9100L
UMP-48  DASCOLI, FRANK                  25 L'HOMME CT - DANIELSON CT 06239
UMP-69  DAVIDSON, DAVID LEONARD         6950 STATE RT 142 SE-WEST JEFFERSON OH 43162
UMP-70  DEEGAN, WILLIAM EDWARD JOHN     2745 SURREY LN - ESCONDIDO CA 92025
UMP-56  DELMORE, VICTOR                 D. JUNE 10, 1960 SCRANTON, PA.
UMP-69  DENKINGER, DONALD ANTON         132 WOODSTOCK RD - WATERLOO IA 50701
UMP-66  DEZELAN, FRANK JOHN             1314 WOOD ST - PITTSBURGH PA 15221
UMP-63  DIMURO, LOUIS JOHN              3740 N CALLE CANCION - TUCSON AZ 85718
UMP-53  DIXON, HAL HAYWORTH             D. JULY 28, 1966 CHURNEE, S.C.
UMP-50  DONATELLI, AUGUST JOSEPH        OLD ADD: 611 BELMONT AVE - EBENSBURG PA 1593X
UMP-31  DONNELLY, CHARLES H             D. DECEMBER 13, 1968 LAKE WORTH, FLA.
UMP-30  DONOHUE, MICHAEL R              D. AUGUST 7, 1968 ST. LOUIS, MO.
UMP-11  DOYLE, JOHN JOSEPH              PLAYER DEBUT 1889
UMP-63  DOYLE, WALTER JAMES             OLD ADD: 3314 HENDERSON BLVD - TAMPA FL 33609
UMP-60  DRUMMOND, CALVIN TROY           D. MAY 2, 1970 DES MOINES, IOWA
UMP-51  DUFFY, JAMES FRANCIS            165 2ND ST - PAWTUCKET RI 02861
UMP-39  DUNN, THOMAS PATRICK            D. JANUARY 20, 1976 PRINCE GEORGES CO., MD.
UMP-14  ELDRIDGE, CLARENCE E
UMP-65  ENGEL, ROBERT ALLEN            3500 HARMONY LN - BAKERSFILED CA 93306
UMP-52  ENGELN, WILLIAM RAYMOND         D. APRIL 17, 1968 PALO ALTO, CALIF.
UMP-72  EVANS, JAMES BREMOND            8504 DOROTHA CT - AUSTIN TX 78759
UMP-13  FERGUSON, CHARLES AUGUSTUS      PLAYER DEBUT 1901
UMP-79  FIELDS, STEVE                   216 E GLENDALE #2 - ALEXANDRIA VA 22301
UMP-11  FINNERAN, WILLIAM F             D. JULY 30, 1961 ERIE, PA.
UMP-79  FITZPATRICK, MICHAEL            1319 CHEROKEE - KALAMAZOO MI 49007
UMP-53  FLAHERTY, JOHN FRANCIS          9 FOWLER LN - FALMOUTH MA 02540
UMP-75  FORD, ROBERT DALE               RR 7 BOX 88 - JONESBORO TN 37659
UMP-61  FORMAN, ALLEN SANFORD           479 NEW JERSEY AVE - LAKE HOPATCONG NJ 07849
UMP-69  FRANTZ, ARTHUR FRANK            276 LYCEUM ST - ROCHESTER NY 14609
UMP-11  FRARY, RALPH                    D. NOVEMBER 10, 1925 ABERDEEN, WASH.
UMP-20  FRIEL, WILLIAM EDWARD           PLAYER DEBUT 1901
UMP-71  FROEMMING, BRUCE NEAL           5045 ELK CT - MILWAUKEE WI 53223
UMP-52  FROESE, GROVER A                24 BARRISTER RD - LEVITTOWN NY 11756
UMP-15  FYFE, LOUIS
UMP-75  GARCIA, RICHARD RAUL            2633 FIRESTONE DR - CLEARWATER FL 33519
UMP-25  GEISEL, HARRY CHRISTIAN         D. FEBRUARY 20, 1966 INDIANAPOLIS, IND.
UMP-14  GOECKEL, E
UMP-36  GOETZ, LAWRENCE JOHN            D. OCTOBER 31, 1962 CINCINNATI, O.
UMP-68  GOETZ, RUSSELL LOUIS            1010 VERMONT ST - GLASSPORT PA 15045
UMP-46  GORE, ARTHUR JOSEPH             BOX 154 - MIRROR LAKE NH 03853
UMP-51  GORMAN, THOMAS DAVID            PLAYER DEBUT 1939
UMP-77  GREGG, ERIC VANAN DALE          3901 CONSHOHOCKEN #163-PHILADELPHIA PA 19131
UMP-38  GRIEVE, WILLIAM TURNER          D. AUGUST 17, 1979 YONKERS, N. Y.
UMP-70  GRIMSLEY, JOHN WILLIAM          204 RAVENWOOD DR - GREENVILLE NC 27834
UMP-14  GROOM, ROBERT                   PLAYER DEBUT 1909
UMP-70  GRYGIEL, GEORGE                 OLD ADD: BOX 401 - SOUTH BEND IN
UMP-76  GUCKERT, ELMER                  590 CRANE AVE - PITTSBURGH PA 15216
UMP-52  GUGLIELMO, ANGELO AUGIE         183 JERSEY ST - WATERBURY CT 06706
UMP-13  GUTHRIE, WILLIAM J              D. MARCH 6, 1950 CHICAGO, ILL
UMP-61  HALLER, WILLIAM EDWARD          1231 THISTLE DR - VANDALIA IL 62471
UMP-79  HARRIS, LANNY                   3313 COLLEGE CORNER RD - RICHMOND IN 47374
UMP-16  HARRISON, PETER A               D. MARCH 9, 1921 SARANAC LAKE, N. Y.
UMP-12  HART, EUGENE F                  D. MAY 10, 1937 LOWELL MASS.
UMP-62  HARVEY, HARVEY DOUGLAS          10231 VERA CRUZ CT - SAN DIEGO CA 82124
UMP-77  HENDRY, EUGENE                  203 JEFFERSON ST - OREGON CITY OR 97045
UMP-45  HENLINE, WALTER JOHN            PLAYER DEBUT 1921
UMP-12  HILDEBRAND, GEORGE ALBERT       PLAYER DEBUT 1902
```

```
UMP-23  HOLMES, HOWARD ELBERT          PLAYER DEBUT 1906
UMP-49  HONOCHICK, GEORGE JAMES        10 S OTT ST - ALLENTOWN PA 18104
UMP-15  HOWELL, HARRY                  PLAYER DEBUT 1898
UMP-36  HUBBARD, ROBERT CAL            D. OCTOBER 16, 1977 ST PETERSBURG, FLA.
UMP-47  HURLEY, EDWIN HENRY            D. NOVEMBER 12, 1969 BOSTON, MASS.
UMP-12  HYATT, ROBERT HAMILTON         PLAYER DEBUT 1909
UMP-52  JACKOWSKI, WILLIAM ANTHONY     64 CHURCH ST - NORTH WALPOLE NH 03608
UMP-14  JOHNSON, HARRY S               D. FEBRUARY 20, 1951 MEMPHIS, TENN.
UMP-25  JOHNSTON, CHARLES EDWARD       D.
UMP-44  JONES, NICHOLAS ITTNER         2837 PIERCE ST #15 - HOLLYWOOD FL 33020
UMP-27  JORDA, LOUIS DE LAROND         D. MAY 27, 1964 LARGO, FL
UMP-77  KAISER, KENNETH JOHN           10 PARKWAY - ROCHESTER NY 14608
UMP-13  KECHER, W. H.
UMP-63  KIBLER, JOHN WILLIAM           3046 SONJA CT - OCEANSIDE CA 92054
UMP-10  KINNAMON, WILLIAM ERVIN        1013 BERKSHIRE RD - DAYTONA BEACH FL 32017
UMP-33  KOLLS, LOUIS CHARLES           D. FEBRUARY 23, 1941 HOOPPOLE, ILL.
UMP-76  KOSC, GREGORY JOHN             NORMANDY PARK #C176 - MEDINA OH 44256
UMP-76  KUNKEL, WILLIAM GUSTAVE JAMES  PLAYER DEBUT 1961
UMP-55  LANDES, STANLEY ALBERT         BOX 9608 - PHOENIX AZ 85020
UMP-15  LANGEVIN, JOSEPH               D. MARCH 18, 1953 BINGHAMTON, N. Y.
UMP-08  LANIGAN, CHARLES               D. OCTOBER 19, 1918 PROVIDENCE, R. I.
UMP-79  LAWSON, WILLIAM                7228 E EASTVIEW DR - TUCSON AZ 85710
UMP-14  LINCOLN, FREDERICK H
UMP-61  LINSALATA, JOSEPH N            4017 WASHINGTON ST - HOLLYWOOD FL 33021
UMP-69  LUCIANO, RONALD MICHAEL        105 BADGER AVE - ENDICOTT NY 13760
UMP-28  MAGEE, SHERWOOD ROBERT         PLAYER DEBUT 1904
UMP-70  MAGERKURTH, GEORGE LEVI        D. OCTOBER 7, 1966 ROCK ISLAND, ILL.
UMP-70  MALONEY, GEORGE PATRICK        3745 NE 171ST ST #60 - NORTH MIAMI FL 33160
UMP-35  MARBERRY, FRED                 PLAYER DEBUT 1923
UMP-14  MAXWELL, JAMES ALBERT          PLAYER DEBUT 1906
UMP-14  MCCORMICK, WILLIAM J           PLAYER DEBUT 1895
UMP-10  MCCOY, LARRY SANDERS           RR1 GREENWAY AR 72430
UMP-25  MCGINNIS,
UMP-25  MCGOWAN, WILLIAM ALOYSIUS      D. DECEMBER 9, 1954 SILVER SPRING, MD.
UMP-12  MCGREEVY, EDWARD
UMP-30  MCGREW, HARRY HANCOCK          D. JUNE 29, 1969 BEDFORD, VA
UMP-74  MCKEAN, JAMES GILBERT          6505 COTE ST LUC RD #101 - MONTREAL QUEBEC
UMP-46  MCKINLEY, WILLIAM FRANCIS      D. AUGUST 1, 1980 MOUNT PLEASANT, PA.
UMP-29  MCLAUGHLIN, EDWARD J           D. NOVEMBER 28, 1965 PHILADELPHIA, PA.
UMP-24  MCLAUGHLIN, PETER J            1926 ADD: 99 POPLAR ST - WATERTOWN MA
UMP-71  MCSHERRY, JOHN PATRICK         BOX 361 - BRONX NY 10468
UMP-77  MERRILL, EDWIN DURWOOD         BOX 115 - HOOKS TX 75561
UMP-76  MONTAGUE, EDWARD MICHAEL       2047 KINGS LN - SAN MATEO CA 94402
UMP-17  MORAN, CHARLES BARTHEL         PLAYER DEBUT 1903
UMP-76  MORGENWECK, HENRY CHARLES      33 BOGERT ST - TEANECK NJ 07666
UMP-17  MORIARTY, GEORGE JEROME        PLAYER DEBUT 1903
UMP-15  MULLANEY, DOMINIC J            D. AUGUST 21, 1964 JACKSONVILLE, FLA.
UMP-14  MURRAY, J. A.                  1919 ADD: 95 MALCOLM ST - MINNEAPOLIS MN
UMP-15  NALLIN, RICHARD F              D. SEPTEMBER 7, 1956 FREDERICK, MD.
UMP-51  NAPP, LARRY ALBERT             200 NW BEL AIR DR - FT LAUDERDALE FL 33314
UMP-79  NELSON, RICHARD                250 SOUTH 557 EAST - CLEARFIELD UT 84015
UMP-66  NEUDECKER, JEROME A            125 VALENCIA-FORT WALTON BEACH FL 32548
UMP-12  O'BRIEN, JOSEPH                D. NOVEMBER 5, 1925
UMP-14  O'CONNOR, ARTHUR
UMP-68  ODOM, JAMES CECIL              304 KING ST - BENNETTSVILLE SC 29512
UMP-68  O'DONNELL, JAMES MICHAEL       OLD ADD: 204 N DIAMOND ST - CLIFTON HEIGHTS P
UMP-15  O'HARA,
UMP-68  OLSEN, ANDREW HOLGER           451 93RD AVE N - ST PETERSBURG FL 33702
UMP-23  ORMSBY, EMMETT T               D. OCTOBER 11, 1962 CHICAGO, ILL.
UMP-22  O'SULLIVAN, JOHN J
UMP-77  PALERMO, STEPHEN MICHAEL       138 NATCHAUG DR - MERIDIAN  CT 06450
UMP-79  PALLONE, DAVID                 5 DELORES AVE #5 - WALTHAM MA 02154
UMP-46  PAPARELLA, JOSEPH JAMES        RR 1 CRYSTAL LAKE - CARBONDALE PA 18407
UMP-36  PARKER, GEORGE LAMBACH         OLD ADD: 18320 NE 20TH PL-N MIAMI BCH FL
UMP-11  PARKER, HARLEY P
UMP-79  PARKS, DALLAS                  1902 E ORANGESIDE RD - PALM HARBOR FL 33563
UMP-41  PASSARELLA, ARTHUR MATTHEW     D. OCTOBER 12, 1981 HEMET, CALIF.
UMP-65  PELEKOUDAS, CHRIS G            1452 LACROSSE DR - SUNNYVALE CA 94087
UMP-22  PFIRMAN, CHARLES H             D. MAY 16, 1937 NEW ORLEANS, LA.
UMP-12  PHELPS, EDWARD JOSEPH          PLAYER DEBUT 1902
UMP-71  PHILLIPS, DAVID ROBERT         5 CHALON CT - LAKE ST LOUIS MO 63376
UMP-35  PINELLI, RALPH ARTHUR          PLAYER DEBUT 1918
UMP-38  PIPGRAS, GEORGE WILLIAM        PLAYER DEBUT 1923
UMP-23  POWELL, CORNELIUS JOSEPH       D. JULY 25, 1971 LYNWOOD, CALIF.
UMP-61  PRYOR, JOHN PAUL               1088 45TH AVE NE - ST PETERSBURG FL 33703
UMP-72  PULLI, FRANK VICTOR            20 ALPINE DR - EASTON PA 18042
UMP-76  PUSKARIC, JOSEPH               429 35TH AVE - MCKEESPORT PA 15132
UMP-76  QUICK, JAMES EDWARD            1729 CALARO CT - CARLSBAD CA 92008
UMP-35  QUINN, JOHN ALOYSIUS           D. JULY 4, 1968 PHILADELPHIA, PA.
UMP-14  QUISSER, ARTHUR
UMP-26  REARDON, JOHN EDWARD           2721 E OCEAN BLVD - LONG BEACH CA 90802
UMP-77  REILLY, MICHAEL                140 INDIAN RD - BATTLE CREEK MI 49017
UMP-73  RENNERT, LAURENCE HENRY        306 N LARK ST - OSHKOSH WI 54901
UMP-55  RICE, JOHN LA CLAIRE           2666 E 73RD ST #A12W - CHICAGO IL 60649
UMP-14  ROBB, DOUGLAS W.               D. APRIL 10, 1969 MONTCLAIR, N.J.
UMP-53  ROBERTS, LEONARD WYATT         5505 SPRUCE VIEW - DALLAS TX 75232
UMP-74  RODRIGUEZ, ARMANDO HUMBERTO    INDEPENCIA 1375 - VERACRUZ VERACRUZ MEXICO
UMP-38  ROMMEL, EDWIN AMERICUS         PLAYER DEBUT 1920
UMP-38  ROWLAND, CLARENCE HENRY        MANAGERIAL DEBUT 1915
UMP-38  RUE, JOSEPH WILLIAM            5518 PASEO DEL LASO E-LAGUNA HILLS CA 92653
UMP-72  RUNGE, EDWARD PAUL             4949 CRESITA DR - SAN DIEGO CA 92115
UMP-72  RUNGE, PAUL EDWARD             649 CALLE DE LA SIERRA - EL CAJON CA 92021
UMP-46  RYAN, WALTER                   708 NE 21ST DR - WILTON MANORS FL 33305
UMP-62  SALERNO, ALEX JOSEPH           1913 TILDEN AVE - NEW HARTFORD NY 13413
UMP-70  SATCHELL, DAROLD L             OLD ADD: 1613 N DUKE ST - DURHAM NC 27701
UMP-60  SCHWARTS, HARRY CLARK          D. FEBRUARY 22, 1963 CLEVELAND, O.
UMP-30  SCOTT, JAMES                   PLAYER DEBUT 1909
```

UMP-34	SEARS, JOHN WILLIAM	D. DECEMBER 16, 1956 HOUSTON, TEX.
UMP-52	SECORY, FRANK EDWARD	PLAYER DEBUT 1940
UMP-14	SHANNON, WILLIAM PORTER	PLAYER DEBUT 1904
UMP-79	SHULOCK, JOHN	3175 62ND AVE - VERO BEACH FL 32960
UMP-75	SMITH, VINCENT AMBROSE	PLAYER DEBUT 1941
UMP-60	SMITH, WILLIAM ALARIC	609 DELHI ST - BOSSIER CITY LA 71111
UMP-50	SOAR, ALBERT HENRY	60 CONCH RD - NARRAGANSETT RI 02882
UMP-77	SPENN, FREDERICK CHARLES	6905 11TH AVE NW - BRADENTON FL 33505
UMP-66	SPRINGSTEAD, MARTIN JOHN	5 BRUCE CT - SUFFERN NY 10901
UMP-28	STARK, ALBERT D	D. AUGUST 24, 1968 NEW YORK, N.Y.
UMP-61	STEINER, MELVIN JAMES	1701 HARBOR WAY - SEAL BEACH CA 90740
UMP-68	STELLO, RICHARD JACK	10800 US HWY 19 #111 - PINELLAS PARK FL 335
UMP-48	STEVENS, JOHN WILLIAM	D. SEPTEMBER 9, 1981 PHILADELPHIA PA.
UMP-41	STEWART, ERNEST DRAPER	%ELVIS STEWART 505 5PRINGS - DEL RIO TX 788
UMP-59	STEWART, ROBERT WILLIAM	52 OWEN DR - CUMBERLAND RI 02864
UMP-33	STEWART, WILLIAM JOSEPH	D. FEBRUARY 18, 1964 JAMAICA PLAIN, MASS.
UMP-15	STOCKDALE, M. J.	1919 ADD: 314 W 42ND ST - NEW YORK NY
UMP-57	SUDOL, EDWARD LAWRENCE	415 REVILO BLVD - DAYTONA BEACH FL 32014
UMP-33	SUMMERS, WILLIAM REED	D. SEPTEMBER 12, 1966 UPTON, MASS.
UMP-24	SWEENEY, JAMES M	D. JANUARY 29, 1950 TYLER, TEX.
UMP-56	TABACCHI, FRANK TULE	304 WILSON AVE - FAIRVIEW NJ 07022
UMP-73	TATA, TERRY ANTHONY	8 PROMONTORY DR - CHESHIRE CT 06410
UMP-70	TREMBLAY, RICHARD HENRY	1974 ADD: 9 CRESTVIEW DR - GREENVILLE RI
UMP-54	UMONT, FRANK WILLIAM	OLD ADD: 13 CHURCH ST-PISCATAWAY NJ 08854
UMP-63	VALENTINE, WILLIAM TERRY	BOX 5599 - LITTLE ROCK AR 72215
UMP-27	VAN GRAFLAN, ROY	D. SEPTEMBER 4, 1953 ROCHESTER, N. Y.
UMP-14	VAN SICKLE, CHARLES F	D. 1950
UMP-60	VARGO, EDWARD PAUL	101 FREEDOM RD - BUTLER PA 16001
UMP-57	VENZON, ANTHONY	D. SEPTEMBER 20, 1971 PITTSBURGH PA
UMP-77	VOLTAGGIO, VITO HENRY	646 BRENTWOOD DR - VINELAND NJ 08360
UMP-22	WALSH, EDWARD AUGUSTIN	PLAYER DEBUT 1904
UMP-61	WALSH, FRANK D	619 NW LOOP 410 #205 - SAN ANTONIO TX 78216
UMP-49	WARNEKE, LONNIE	PLAYER DEBUT 1930
UMP-43	WEAFER, HAROLD LEON	1113 GROVE AVE - RICHMOND VA 23220
UMP-66	WENDELSTEDT, HARRY HUNTER	88 S ST ANDREWS - ORMOND BEACH FL 32074
UMP-76	WEST, JOSEPH HENRY	BOX 298 - BATH NC 27808
UMP-11	WESTERVELT, FREDERICK E	D. MAY 4, 1955 DREXEL HILL, PA.
UMP-61	WEYER, LEE HOWARD	1727 1/2 SYCAMORE AVE - HOLLYWOOD CA 90028
UMP-72	WILLIAMS, ARTHUR	D. FEBRUARY 8, 1979 BAKERSFIELD, CALIF.
UMP-78	WILLIAMS, CHARLES H.	OLD ADD: 440 S CENTRAL #D-13 - COMPTON CA
UMP-63	WILLIAMS WILLIAM GEORGE	RR 2 BOX 822 #0-29 - POMPANO BEACH FL 33067
UMP-21	WILSON, FRANK	D. JUNE, 1928 BROOKLYN, N. Y.

COACHES WITH NO MAJOR LEAGUE PLAYER OR MANAGERIAL EXPERIENCE DEBUTING 1910 TO 1981

COA-67	BERINGER, CARROLL JAMES	4917 GRANITE SHOALS - FORT WORTH TX 76103
COA-64	BLACKBURN, WAYNE CLARK	1414 OFFNERE ST - PORTSMOUTH OH 45662
COA-74	BLOOMFIELD, GORDON LEIGH	1310 IRIS - MCALLEN TX 78501
COA-77	BRAGAN, JAMES ALTON	1059 MARTINWOOD LN - BIRMINGHAM AL 35235
COA-69	CAMACHO, JOSEPH GOMES	48 MASSASOIT AVE - FAIRHAVEN MA 02719
COA-70	CARNEVALE, DANIEL JOSEPH	161 DORCHESTER RD - BUFFALO NY 14213
COA-59	CARTER, RICHARD JOSEPH	D. SEPTEMBER 11, 1969 PHILADELPHIA, PA.
COA-77	CLEAR, ELWOOD ROBERT	120 E 234TH ST - CARSON CA 90745
COA-79	CLUCK, ROBERT	4344 CORINTH DR - SAN DIEGO CA 92115
COA-77	CRESSE, MARK EMERY	1000 ELYSIAN PAEK AVE - LOS ANGELES CA 90012
COA-79	DEWS, ROBERT W	2233 SHARON AVE #1 - ALBANY GA 31707
COA-61	DOUGLAS, OTIS W	HAGUE VA 22469
COA-69	DUNLOP, HARRY ALEXANDER	7470 29TH ST - SACRAMENTO CA 95820
COA-47	FITZGERALD, JOSEPH PATRICK	D. AUGUST 29, 1967 ORLANDO, FLA.
COA-53	FITZPATRICK, JOHN ARTHUR	1728 E COMMONWEALTH #102-FULLERTON CA 92631
COA-70	FREY, JAMES GOTTFRIED	1805 REUTER RD - TIMONIUM MD 21093
COA-48	HOLT, GOLDEN DESMOND	4937 STERN AVE - SHERMAN OAKS CA 91423
COA-68	HOSCHEIT, VERNARD ARTHUR	BOX 36 - PLAINVIEW NE 68769
COA-55	KAHN, LOUIS	916 TIFT ST - ALBANY GA 61701
COA-30	KELLY, BERNARD FRANCIS	D. OCTOBER 23, 1968 INDIANAPOLIS, IND.
COA-69	KISSELL, GEORGE MARSHALL	658 MT DALE DR NE - ST PETERSBURG FL 33702
COA-71	KITTLE, HUBERT MILTON	RR 6 BOX 255E - YAKIMA WA 98902
COA-70	KOENIG, FRED CARL	6721 E 51ST ST - TULSA OK 74145
COA-77	KROL, JOHN THOMAS	3012 FLEET ST - WINSTON-SALEM NC 27107
COA-57	LEVY, LEONARD HOWARD	%J.SNELSON,324 COLTART ST-PITTSBURGH PA 1521
COA-51	LOBE, WILLIAM CHARLES	D. JANUARY 7, 1969 CLEVELAND, O.
COA-72	LOWE, Q. V.	RED LEVEL AL 36474
COA-51	MCDONNELL, ROBERT	7423 REVERE ST - PHILADELPHIA PA 19152
COA-78	MILLER, RAYMOND ROGER	BOX 41 - NEW ATHENS OH 43981
COA-77	MOZZALI, MAURICE JOSEPH	5802 STONE BLUFF RD - LOUISVILLE KY 40291
COA-62	O'NEIL, JOHN B	3049 E 32ND ST - KANSAS CITY MO 64128
COA-58	OCEAK, FRANK JOHN	208 FREEMAN DR - JOHNSTOWN PA 15904
COA-63	OSBORN, DONALD EDWIN	D. MARCH 23, 1979 TORRANCE, CALIF.
COA-74	PACHECO, ANTONIO ARISTIDES	401 NW 56TH AVE - MIAMI FL 33126
COA-61	PAEPKE, JACK	DRWAER CE - CRESTLINE CA 92325
COA-69	PLAZA, RONALD EDWARD	2050 68TH AVE S - ST PETERSBURG FL 33712
COA-66	RESINGER, GROVER S	RR2 - EOLIA MO 63344
COA-81	REYES, BENJAMIN	MATAMOROS Y CACATECAS - HERMOSILLO SONORA ME
COA-76	RIPKEN, CALVIN EDWIN	410 CLOVER ST - ABERDEEN MD 21001
COA-66	ROBINSON, WARREN GRANT	OLD ADD: 305 OAKLEY ST - CAMBRIDGE MD
COA-73	ROSENBAUM, GLEN OTIS	BOX 1 - UNION MILLS IN 46382
COA-72	ROWE, RALPH EMANUEL	14800 GULF BLVD #602 - MADEIRA BEACH FL 3370
COA-76	SAUL, JAMES ALLEN	2405 OSBORNE ST - BRISTOL VA 23201
COA-70	SCHERGER, GEORGE RICHARD	701 ST JULIEN - CHARLOTTE NC 28205
COA-77	SOMMERS, DENNIS JAMES	210 W BATH - HORTONVILLE WI 54944
COA-79	SPARKS, JOSEPH EVERETT	3915 E CHOLLA ST - PHOENIX AZ 85028
COA-22	THOMAS, RAY	
COA-81	VAN ORNUM, JOHN CLAYTON	6624 N HAZEL ST - FRESNO CA 93711
COA-43	VINCENT, ALBERT LINDER	260 MANOR AVE - BEAUMONT TX 77706
COA-61	WALKER, VERLON LEE	D. MARCH 24, 1971 CHICAGO, ILL.
COA-73	WALTON, JAMES ROBERT	BOX 787 - SHATTUCK OK 73858
COA-77	WARNER, HARRY CLINTON	106 BELFAIR - REEDERS PA 18352
COA-77	WILLIAMS, DONALD ELLIS	RR 2 BOX 127 - PARAGOULD AR 72450
COA-81	WILLIAMS, JAMES BERNARD	61 PURDUE ST - PUEBLO CO 81005
COA-32	WOLGAMOT, CLIFTON EARL	D. APRIL 25, 1970 INDEPENDENCE, IA.

LATE ADDITIONS, CORRECTIONS & DEATHS

THESE MAILING ADDRESS CHANGES
SUPERCEDE ALL MAILING ADDRESSES
WITHIN THE TEXT OF THIS BOOK

77 – 2	ADAMS, ROBERT MELVIN	5700 WHITSETT AVE – NORTH HOLLYWOOD CA 91607
73 – 3	ALEXANDER, MATTHEW	6802 OAK BRANCH – SHREVEPORT LA 71109
20 – 2	ALTEN, ERNEST MATTHIAS	D. SEPTEMBER 9, 1981 NAPA, CA
54 – 5	AMALFITANO, JOHN JOSEPH	6101 N SHERIDAN RD – CHICAGO IL 60660
31 – 4	ANDRUS, WILLIAM MORGAN	D. MARCH 12, 1982 WASHINGTON, D. C.
UMP –70	ANTHONY, GEORGE MERLYN	920 SOUTH LAND DR – YUBA CITY CA 95991
73 – 8	ASHBY, ALAN DEAN	12118 HUNTINGTON VENTURE DR – HOUSTON TX 77099
70 – 3	AUSTIN, RICK GERALD	1804 COMMERCIAL – STEILACOOM WA 98388
76 – 10	BAIR, CHARLES DOUGLAS	6401 PHEASANT RD – LOVELAND OH 45140
74 – 4	BALAZ, JOHN LARRY	2819 WORDEN ST – SAN DIEGO CA 92110
60 – 4	BARBER, STEPHEN DAVID	OLD ADD : 8324 E LEWIS AVE – SCOTTSDALE AZ
UMP –40	BARLICK, ALBERT JOSEPH	RR 2 – RIVERTON IL 62561
74 – 7	BARRIOS, FRANCISCO XAVIER	D. APRIL 9, 1982 HERMOSILLO SONORA MEXICO
63 – 9	BEAUCHAMP, JAMES EDWARD	BOX 788 – GROVE OK 74344
76 – 15	BELL, KEVIN ROBERT	OLD ADD: ALGONQUIN – ROLLING MEADOWS IL
UMP – 74	BREMIGAN, NICHOLAS GREGORY	1602 SOLWAY – LEWISVILLE TX 75067
44 – 14	BREWER, JOHN HERNDON	OLD ADD: 605 N DEL NORTE – ONTARIO CA
75 – 19	BRIGGS, DANIEL LEE	231 FRANCE ST – SONOMA CA 95476
79 – 12	BRIZZOLARA, ANTHONY JOHN	910 SW 69TH TER – PLANTATION FL 33317
72 – 14	BROHAMER, JOHN ANTHONY	1551 W SEMINOLE ST – SAN MATEO CA 92069
73 – 15	BURRIS, BERTRAM RAY	2304 WOODSONG TR – ARLINGTON TX 76016
50 – 16	BUSBY, JAMES FRANKLIN	806 – F NOB HILL DR – BIRMINGHAM AL 35209
71 – 18	BUSSE, RAYMOND EDWARD	OLD ADD: 501 MYRTLE LN SOUTH – DAYTONA BEACH FL
72 – 17	CABELL, ENOS MILTON	7011 COUNTRY CLUB LN – ANAHEIM CA 92807
23 – 19	CASTNER, PAUL HENRY	OLD ADD: 1999 DE SOTA – ST PAUL MN
73 – 21	CHALK, DAVID LEE	6126 SUMMER CREEK CIR – DALLAS TX 75231
76 – 26	CLAREY, DOUGLAS WILLIAM	OLD ADD: 2280 EARL ST – LOS ANGELES CA
55 – 28	COLAVITO, ROCCO DOMENICO	30 SCENIC DR, RR 3 – BERNVILLE PA 19506
14 – 38	COLLINS, JOHN EDGAR	6258 N KENSINGTON AVE – MCLEAN VA 21101
59 – 16	COTTIER, CHARLES KEITH	11715 CORTE TEMPLANZA – SAN DIEGO CA 92128
UMP – 79	COUSINS, DERRYL	702 4th ST – HERMOSA BEACH CA 90254
78 – 33	DARWIN, DANNY WAYNE	2218 FALL RIVER DR – ARLINGTON TX 76011
60 – 28	DAVIS, WILLIAM HENRY	7250 FRANKLIN No. 1010 – LOS ANGELES CA 90038
69 – 44	DECKER, GEORGE HENRY "JOE"	OLD ADD: 2606 W VAN BUREN – PHOENIX AZ
74 – 25	DEMOLA, DONALD JOHN	OLD ADD: 460 VILLAGE DR – HAUPPAUGE NY
COA – 79	DEWS, ROBERT W	423 AUDUBON – ALBANY GA 31707
23 – 28	DICKERMAN, LEO LOUIS	D. APRIL 30, 1982 ATKINS, ARK.
69 – 46	DIDIER, ROBERT DANIEL	1311 RUE DESIRE – BATON ROUGE LA 70805
UMP – 63	DIMURO, LOUIS JOHN	D. JUNE 7, 1982 ARLINGTON, TEX.
79 – 28	DONOHUE, THOMAS JAMES	29 RUGBY RD – WESTBURY NY 11590
79 – 29	DOTSON, RICHARD ELLIOTT	813 ALBATROSS DR – NOVATO CA 94947
57 – 17	DOTTERER, HENRY JOHN JR.	1920 SHERRY LN No. 53 – SANTA ANA CA 92701
29 – 30	DUDLEY, ELISE CLISE	BOX 143 – LAKE CITY SC 25960
64 – 28	DUNCAN, DAVID EDWIN	8850 CAMINO DE LA RERRA – TUCSON AZ 85741
71 – 29	ELLIS, ROBERT WALTER	13210 LAKEWOOD DR NE – AURORA OR 97002
46 – 27	ENDICOTT, WILLIAM FRANKLIN	BOX 48, 5 MILE LANDING – TOPOCK AZ 86436
54 – 24	ESCALERA, SATURNINO CUADRADOCOND	LAGUNA GARDEN 4 No. 1E – ISLA VERDE PR 00913
19 – 22	FAIRCLOTH, JAMES LAMAR	D. OCTOBER 5, 1953 TUCSON, ARIZ.
54 – 25	FANNING, WILLIAM JAMES	4000 DE MAISONNEUVE W No. 2608 – MONTREAL H3Z 1J9
44 – 38	FAUSETT, ROBERT SHAW	3104 AVE P 1/2 – GALVESTON TX 77550
56 – 34	FISCHER, WILLIAM CHARLES	6122 NIVARRE PL – CINCINNATI OH 45227
51 – 29	FISHER, HARRY DEVEREAUX	D. SEPTEMBER 20, 1981 WATERLOO, ONT.
28 – 35	FOLEY, RAYMOND KIRWIN	D. MARCH 22, 1980
78 – 44	FORD, DAVID ALAN	3585 W 49TH ST – CLEVELAND OH 44102
UMP – 75	FORD, ROBERT DALE	RR 7 BOX 114 – JONESBORO TN 37659
64 – 33	FOSNOW, GERALD EUGENE	13 BROWN AVE – PARKERSBURG WV 26101
69 – 64	GARVEY, STEVEN PATRICK	27124 MALIBU COVE COLONY RD – MALIBU CA 90265
69 – 65	GASPAR, RODNEY EARL	1150 CASTLE HOLLOW RD – MIDLOTHIAN VA 23113
47 – 38	GEBRIAN, PETER	103 RIVER RD No. E–4 – NUTLEY NJ 07110
50 – 30	GENOVESE, GEORGE MICHAEL	11474 ERWIN ST – HOLLYWOOD CA 91606
51 – 36	HAIRSTON, SAMUEL	3800 CENTERPLACE WEST – BIRMINGHAM AL 35207
UMP – 61	HALLER, WILLIAM EDWARD	RR 3 – VANDALIA IL 62471
18 – 25	HANNAH, JAMES HARRISON	D. APRIL 27, 1982 FOUNTAIN VALLEY, CALIF.
58 – 42	HANSEN, RONALD LAVERN	13602 ALLISTON DR – BALDWIN MD 21013
74 – 47	HARDY, HOWARD LAWRENCE	2402 DRAWBRIDGE RD – ARLINGTON TX 76012
50 – 33	HATFIELD, FRED JAMES	STAR ROUTE 519-0 – TALLAHASSEE FL 32304
66 – 43	HEPLER, WILLIAM LEWIS	10271 BLOSSOM LAKE DR – SEMINOLE FL 33542
23 – 64	HERMANN, ALBERT BARTEL	D. AUGUST 20, 1980 LEWES, DEL.
56 – 44	HERZOG, DORREL HORMAN ELVERT	3613 S FOREST – INDEPENDENCE MO 64052
40 – 36	HOERST, FRANK JOSEPH	2841 GILHAM ST – PHILADELPHIA PA 19149
34 – 47	HOGG, WILBERT GEORGE	D. 1973
46 – 48	HOPPER, JAMES MCDANIEL	D. JANUARY 23, 1982 CHARLOTTE, N. C.
29 – 52	HORNE, BERLYN DALE	422 MISSION LN – FRANKLIN OH 45005
22 – 59	HULIHAN, HARRY JOSEPH	D. SEPTEMBER, 1980
23 – 67	HULVEY, JAMES HENSEL	D. APRIL 9, 1982 MOUNT SIDNEY, VA.
66 – 47	HUTTON, THOMAS GEORGE	2940 BRIDLEWOOD DR – PALM HARBOR FL 33563
29 – 54	JAMES, ROBERT BYRNE	OLD ADD: LOOKOUT RD – SAN ANTONIO TX
52 – 57	JOHNSON, DARRELL DEAN	308 E REPUBLICAN – SEATTLE WA 98102
68 – 45	JOHNSON, JERRY MICHAEL	1515 MCCALL – ODESSA TX 79761
44 – 67	JURISICH, ALVIN JOSEPH	D. NOVEMBER 3, 1981 NEW ORLEANS, LA.
UMP – 77	KAISER, KENNETH JOHN	123 NORTHWOOD DR – ROCHESTER NY 14616
14 – 106	KANTLEHNER, ERVINE LESLIE	66-2 BARRANCE AVE – SANTA BARBARA CA 93109
65 – 56	KEKICH, MICHAEL DENNIS	BOX 1072 – ARTESIA CA 90701
14 – 113	KELLY, EDWARD LEO	D. NOVEMBER 4, 1928 RED LODGE, MONT.
56 – 47	KEOUGH, RICHARD MARTIN	BOX 12– COTO – TRABUCO CANYON CA 92678
69 – 93	KIRBY, CLAYTON LAWS	1602 E MISSION AVE – ESCONDIDO CA 92027
71 – 59	KISON, BRUCE EUGENE	801 BLUEBIRD – ANAHEIM HILLS CA 92807
76 – 49	KNEPPER, ROBERT WESLEY	8617 E THOROUGHBRED TR – SCOTTSDALE AZ 85258
23 – 75	KNODE, ROBERT TROXELL	D. APRIL 12, 1982
64 – 61	KNOOP, ROBERT FRANK	1218 IRVINE AVE – NEWPORT BEACH CA 92660
49 – 43	KRSNICH, ROCCO PETER	OLD ADD: 5420 E HARRY – WICHITA KS
46 – 62	LAMBERT, CLAYTON PATRICK	D. APRIL 3, 1981 OGDEN, UTAH
63 – 66	LARUSSA, ANTHONY	2620 OAK GROVE CIR – SARASOTA FL 33580
67 – 62	LAUZERIQUE, GEORGE ALBERT	3471 CUMBERLAND GAP CT – PLEASANTO CA 94566
65 – 62	LEFEBVRE, JAMES KENNETH	8225 MANITOBA ST – MARINA DEL REY CA 90291
24 – 66	LEFLER, WADE HAMPTON	D. MARCH 6, 1981 HICKORY, N. C.
50 – 51	LENHARDT, DONALD EUGENE	13317 WOODLAKE VILLAGE CT – ST LOUIS MO 63141
58 – 56	LINDSTROM, CHARLES WILLIAM	218 KEOKUK – LINCOLN IL 62656
22 – 78	MACK, FRANK GEORGE	D. JULY 2, 1971 CLEARWATER, FLA.
72 – 65	MADDOX, GARRY LEE	219 SOUTH HARBOR – SAN PEDRO CA 90731
12 – 111	MAHARG, WILLIAM JOSEPH	D. NOVEMBER 20, 1953 PHILADELPHIA, PA
74 – 80	MARTINEZ, FELIX ANTHONY	1524 DELLSWAY ROAD – TOWSON MD 21204
69 – 112	MAXIE, LARRY HANS	BOX 814 – UPLAND CA 91786
39 – 75	MAY, MERRILL GLEND	116 52ND STREET – HOLMES BEACH FL 33510
70 – 87	MAY, MILTON SCOTT	2424 MANATEE AVE WEST – BRADENTON FL 33505
59 – 55	MCBRIDE, KENNETH FAYE	2138 DAVENPORT AVE – CLEVELAND OH 44114
39 – 77	MCCRABB, LESTER WILLIAM	412 SOUTH CHURCH STREET – QUARRYVILLE PA 17566
44 – 85	MCGHEE, WILLIAM MAC	910 K STREET – GULF BREEZE FL 32561
22 – 86	MCGOWAN, FRANK BERNARD	D. MAY 6, 1982 HAMDEN, CT
UMP – 74	MCKEAN, JAMES GILBERT	4601 DOVER STREET NORTHEAST – ST. PETERSBURG FL 33703
72 – 71	MCKEE, JAMES MARION	OLD ADD: RR, LITHOPOLIS RD – GROVEPORT OH
12 – 224	MERCER, JOHN LOCKE	FOUNTAIN TOWERS APTS – SHREVEPORT LA 71106
66 – 60	MILLAN, FELIX BERNARDO	CALLE FLORIDA No. 420 – RIO PIEDRAS PR 00928
71 – 70	MILLER, RICHARD ALAN	130 DRAPER RD – WAYLAND MA 01778
37 – 77	MILLER, WILLIAM FRANCIS	D. FEBRUARY 26, 1982
58 – 63	MONBOUQUETTE, WILLIAM CHARLES	271 CLARK HILL RD – NEW BOSTON NH 03070
76 – 64	MONROE, LAWRENCE JAMES	VILLA VERDE DR No. 213 – BUFFALO GROVE IL 60090
62 – 94	MOTA, MANUEL RAFAEL	27 DE FABRERO, No. 445 – SANTO DOMINGO DOM REP
15 – 111	MULLIGAN, EDWARD JOSEPH	D. MARCH 15, 1982 SAN RAFAEL, CALIF.
60 – 73	MURPHY, DANIEL FRANCIS	8 CROSS ST – BEVERLY MA 01915
39 – 79	NAGEL, WILLIAM TAYLOR	1030 SALEM – MEMPHIS TN 38122
68 – 71	NAGELSON, RUSSELL CHARLES	ONE POWDERDHORN CT – LITTLE ROCK AR 72212
UMP – 66	NEUDECKER, JEROME A	700 BRIAN CIR – MARY ESTHER FL 32569
77 – 102	NORRIS, JAMES FRANCIS	5524 MANSFIELD RD – ARLINGTON TX 76017
74 – 97	NYMAN, NYLS WALLACE REX	ATH DEPT, S ILL. UNIV-EDWARDSVILLE IL 62026
70 – 102	OATES, JOHNNY LANE	3718 PERTSCIRE LN – COLONIAL HEIGHTS VA 23834
15 – 115	OFARRELL, ROBERT ARTHUR	27 SOUTH WEST – WAUKEGAN ILL 60085
25 – 83	ONEAL, ORAN HERBERT	D. JUNE 2,1981 SPRINGFIELD, MO
21 – 75	OSTERGARD, ROY LUND	D. JANUARY 13, 1977 HEMET, CA
48 – 78	PAIGE, LEROY "SATCHEL"	D. JUNE 8, 1982 KANSAS CITY, MO.
45 – 76	PALICA, ERVIN MARTIN	D. MAY 29, 1982
76 – 74	PAPE, KENNETH WAYNE	OLD ADD: 2529 NACOGDOCHES RD – SAN ANTONIO TX
73 – 94	PARKER, DAVID GENE	4200 GULFSANDS DR No. 203 – HOLMES BEACH FL 33510
68 – 76	PATEK, FREDERICK JOSPEH	965 E WEINERT ST – SEQUIN TX 78155
29 – 82	PATTISON, JAMES WELLS	11 S SAXON AVE – BAYSHORE NY 11706
58 – 71	PENA, ORLANDO GREGORY	1750 W 46TH – HIALEAH FL 33012
54 – 81	PENSON, PAUL EUGENE	3408 METROPOLITAN – KANSAS CITY KS 66106
61 – 82	PERRANOSKI, RONALD PETER	5614 ROCK CREEK RD – AGOURA CA 91301
66 – 71	PETERSON, FRED INGELS "FRITZ"	BOX 601 – CRYSTAL LAKE IL 60014
74 – 105	PITTS, GAYLEN RICHARD	5901 JFK BLVD – NORTH LITTLE ROCK AR 72116
43 – 113	POLAND, HUGH REID	BOX 175 – GUTHRIE KY 42234
46 – 84	POSSEHL, LOUIS THOMAS	3536 N NEW ENGLAND – CHICAGO IL 60634
57 – 70	POWIS, CARL EDGAR	5501 W WASHINGTON ST No. 211 – GROVES TX 77619
63 – 95	PREGENZER, JOHN ARTHUR	6314 104TH ST E – PUYALLUP WA 98373
48 – 83	PRENDERGAST, JAMES BARTHOLOMEW	D. MAY, 1982 BUFFALO, N.Y.
42 – 81	QUEEN, MELVIN JOSEPH	D. APRIL 4, 1982 FORT SMITH, ARK.
67 – 88	RADER, DOUGLAS LEE	2441 SE GOLFWOOD DR – STUART FL 33494
74 – 108	RAMIREZ, ORLANDO	TORICES PASO ABADIO No. 1325 – CARTAGENA COLOMBIA
36 – 79	ROCK, LESTER HENRY	1027 OLIVE DR No. 5 – DAVIS CA 95616
57 74	RODGERS, KENNETH ANDRE IAN	BOX N386 – NASSAU BAHAMAS
UMP – 80	ROE, JOHN "ROCKY"	2644 ST JOSEPH – WEST BLOOMFIELD MI 48033
62 – 117	ROLAND, JAMES IVAN	OLD ADD: 236 COMPTON DR – GREENVILLE SC 29607
63 – 100	ROSE, PETER EDWARD	1203 NEEB RD – CINCINNATI OH 45238
24 – 90	ROSS, CHESTER FRANKLIN	D. APRIL 24, 1982 MAYFIELD, KY .
42 – 88	RUSSELL, JAMES WILLIAM	RR TWO – BELLE VERNON PA 15012
28 – 79	SAX, ERIK OLIVER	D. MARCH 21, 1982 NEWARK, N. J.
45 – 92	SCHEMER, MICHAEL	OLD ADD: 7825 BAYSHORE CT No. 503 – MIAMI FL
13 – 158	SCHMIDT, HERMAN FREDERICK	D. NOVEMBER 11, 1973 PEMBROKE, ONT.
72 – 100	SCHUELER, RONALD RICHARD	106 KING HENRY CT – PALATINE IL 60007
79 – 100	SCHULER, DAVID PAUL	4575 SUNSTONE RD No. 119 – MURRAY UT 84017
57 – 77	SHAW, ROBERT JOHN	698 SALVADOR DR – WESTERVILLE OH 43081
24 – 97	SHIELDS, BENJAMIN COWAN	D. JANUARY 24, 1982 WOODRUFF, S. C.
64 – 104	SHIRLEY, BARTON ARVIN	1038 DRIFTWOOD DR – CORPUS CHRISTI TX 78411
77 – 131	SHIRLEY, ROBERT CHARLES	3838 CAMINO DEL RIO N No. 252 – SAN DIEGO CA 92108
77 – 132	SKAGGS, DAVID LINDSEY	4349 MAHOGANY CIR – YORBA LINDA CA 92686
26 – 75	SLAYBACK, ELBERT	D. NOVEMBER 30, 1979 CINCINNATI, O.
50 – 91	SMITH, FRANK THOMAS	120 89TH AVE – ST PETERSBURG FL 33702
14 – 202	SNYDER, JOHN WILLIAM	D. DECEMBER 13, 1981 REDSTONE TWP., PA
26 – 79	SOTHERN, DENNIS ELWOOD	D. DECEMBER 7, 1977 DURHAM, N. C.
61 – 102	STANGE, ALBERT LEE	9065 BUTTERCUP AVE – FOUNTAIN VALLEY CS 92708
UMP – 59	STEWART, ROBERT WILLIAM	D. 1982 WOONSOCKET RI
47 – 86	STOBBS, CHARLES LEIN	5158 HONORE AVE – SARASOTA FL 33583
66 – 87	SUAREZ KENNETH RAYMOND	1301 FINDLAY DR – ARLINGTON TX 76012
74 – 127	SUMMERS, JOHN JUNIOR	1834 E BASELINE DR No. 201 – TEMPE AZ 85283
25 – 101	TANKERSLEY, LAWRENCE WILLIAM	D. SEPTEMBER 18, 1980 DALLAS, TEXAS
21 – 103	TAYLOR, ARLAS WALTER	D. SEPTEMBER 10, 1958 DADE CITY, FLA.
23 – 131	TAYLOR, LEO THOMAS	D. MAY 20, 1982 SEATTLE, WASH.
49 – 86	TERWILLIGER, WILLARD WAYNE	2208 PRESIDENTS CORNER No. 301 – FT WORTH TX 76118
11 – 166	THOMAS, BLAINE M.	D. AUGUST 21, 1915 PAYSON, ARIZ.
41 – 113	TRUCKS, VIRGIL OLIVER	RR 3 No. 5 GREEN VALLEY – LEEDS AL 35094
46 – 100	USHER, ROBERT ROYCE	1022 N FIFTH ST – SAN JOSE CA 95112
73 – 125	VELEZ, OTONIEL FRONCESCHI	LOS CAOBOS CALLE No. 35 T–2 – PONCE PR 00731
75 – 124	VUCKOVICH, PETER DENNIS	6080 S 118TH ST – HALES CORNER WI 53130
70 – 136	VUKOVICH, JOHN CHRISTOPHER	11 SHERI WAY – PINE HILL NJ 08021
31 – 94	WALKER, FRED "DIXIE"	D. MAY 17, 1982 BIRMINGHAM, ALA.
73 – 128	WALLACE , DAVID WILLIAM	20 STOCKADE CIR – ATTLEBORO MA 02703
12 – 211	WARD, JOSEPH NICHOLAS	D. SEPTEMBER 13, 1979 ELMER, N. J.
16 – 93	WATSON, MILTON WILSON	D. APRIL 10, 1962 PINE BLUFF, ARK
UMP – 76	WEST, JOSPEH HENRY	118 CORONATION– HOUSTON TX 77034
76 – 101	WHEELOCK, GARY RICHARD	15446 SE 20TH PL – BELLEVUE WA 98007
52 – 110	WHISENANT, THOMAS PETER	7720 DUNCAN RD – PUNTA GORDA FL 33950
54 – 117	WHITE, CHARLES	OLD ADD: 8167 HUDSON ST – VANCOUVER BC
47· 96	WILLIS, LESTER EVANS	D. JANUARY 22, 1982 JASPER, TEXAS
UMP – 78	WILLIAMS, CHARLES H.	16 LAFFERTY – PITTSBURGH PA 15210
14 – 230	WISTERZIL, GEORGE JOHN	D. JUNE 27, 1964 SAN ANTONIO, TEX.
74 – 143	YOUNT, ROBIN R	4304 HUNTCLUB LN – WESTLAKE VILLAGE CA 91361

THESE MAILING ADDRESS CHANGES
SUPERCEDE ALL MAILING ADDRESSES
WITHIN THE TEXT OF THIS BOOK

GLOSSARY

The definitions presented in this glossary are definitions as they are interpreted by autograph collectors. For example, PHOTO refers to an autographed photo and HOFer refers to the autograph of a HOFer. Some of the definitions may appear self-explanatory and hence unnecessary; however, they are included for completeness.

ALL STAR BALL—A ball autographed by most or all members of a particular baseball all star game.

AUTOPEN—A mechanical device used to affix a signature on a document, letter or other paper medium. Autopen autographs are not considered collectible.

BALL POINT—A type of pen through which the ink is delivered by means of a revolving ball tip.

BASEBALL COMMEMORATIVE ENVELOPE—A stamped envelope postmarked on the date of a significant event in baseball history. The envelope contains some graphic or illustrative identification of the event. These envelopes autographed by a participant of the event are quite attractive and popular with autograph collectors. These envelopes should not be confused with first day covers popular with stamp collectors, although a hybrid first day cover/baseball commemorative envelope does exist. (This envelope contains the 1969 commemorative stamp of baseball's first hundred years and is cacheted with many different baseball superstars.)

CARD—A card autographed by the player portrayed on the card. Cards are normally autographed on the front; however, cards autographed on the back still qualify under this definition.

CHECK—A cancelled check or bank note containing the autograph of a ball player. Checks are quite often obtained from the estate of deceased ball players. Official ball club checks in many cases contain more than one autograph.

CLUB ISSUED POSTCARDS—Postcard size pictures of ball players, the older ones normally being in black and white with modern postcards being predominantly in color. They are usually blank backed, sold at ballparks and make excellent autograph media. Many players send autographed copies of these postcards to fans requesting autographs.

CONTRACT—A legal document, for any purpose, including agreements concerning players and management, equipment or other product manufacturers, or personal agreements signed by the sports personality.

CUT—An autograph that has been "cut" from a larger piece of paper, photo, letter or other written or printed matter.

DATED—An autograph which contains both the signature and the date when the signature was written.

DEBUT YEAR—The year in which a player first appeared in a game in the big leagues. For a manager or coach with no player experience the debut year refers to the year he first appeared as a manager or coach.

DEBUT YEAR NUMBER—Within a particular debut year the number for a player obtained by placing in alphabetical order all players who debuted that particular year and placing a number on each, from 1 to "the total number of players debuting that year," based on this alphabetical order.

FACSIMILE—A copy of an original signature. Facsimile autographs are not considered collectible.

FELT TIP—A type of pen which has a felt tip and which provides a smooth unbroken signature.

HOFer—The autograph of a member of baseball's Hall of Fame.

LETTER—A typed or handwritten communication with a heading listing to whom the letter is written and a closing autographed by a sports personality.

ORIGINAL ART—A unique drawing, painting or other piece of artwork portraying a personality or an event and bearing the signature of a partici-pant of the event or the personality portrayed.

PENCIL—A signature in pencil by a sports personality. Pencil signatures predominated during the early parts of this century and are sometimes the only types of signatures available of certain sports personalities. Care should be taken with pencil signatures as they smear quite easily.

PLACQUE—Postcard pictures of the bronzed placques of Hall of Fame base-ball players in the Baseball Hall of Fame in Cooperstown, NY. Through the years there have been several different color placques issued by the Hall of Fame, including black and white types.

PERSONALIZED—An autograph which contains a reference to the person for whom the autograph was written.

PHOTO—A glossy picture, normally 5" X 7" or 8" X l0," which contains an autograph of the player portrayed on the photo.

SASE—Self-addressed stamped envelope. When requesting autographs, SASE's should be sent to insure that returned autographs will be sent to the proper place and to provide the autograph giver a convenient means of returning autographed material.

SHARPIE—A brand of ink pen very popular with autograph collectors because of its broad stroke and its rapid drying characteristics on almost any surface.

STAMP—A signature affixed by means of a rubber or wooden device which contains a facsimile of the sports personality's autograph. Stamped signatures are not considered collectible.

TEAM BALL—A ball autographed by most or all members of a particular team.

TEAM SHEET—A single sheet of paper containing the autographs of most or all members of a particular team during a particular year. Many team sheets are on club stationery.

3 X 5—An index card, either lined or unlined, which many collectors use for obtaining autographs. The 3 X 5 refers to the approximate dimensions of the card. 3 X 5's usually contain only one signature.

AUTOGRAPHS
1982 BASEBALL CARDS

HALL of FAME 3x5 AUTOGRAPHS

30 different Living Hall of Famers - $14.00 ppd.

20 different Deceased Hall of Famers - $30.00 ppd.
All are my choice.

LIVING PLAYER 3x5 AUTOGRAPHS

1908 to 1930 debut - 100 different - $25.00 ppd.
1931 to 1950 debut - 100 different - $19.00 ppd.
1951 to 1981 debut - 100 different - $13.00 ppd.
1908 to 1950 debut - 600 different - $100.00 ppd.
1908 to 1981 debut - 2000 different - $250.00 ppd.
All are my choice. Larger quantities of the first three groups are available.

HALL OF FAME PLAQUES

15 different yellow and brown Hall of Fame plaques, signed by living players are $20.00 postpaid. All plaques are my choice and signed on the front.

DECEASED PLAYER 3x5 AUTOGRAPHS

25 different - $13.00 ppd.
50 different - $32.50 ppd.
100 different - $70.00 ppd.
200 different - $165.00 ppd.
350 different - $365.00 ppd.
500 different - $608.00 ppd.
700 different - $979.00 ppd.
All are my choice.

INDESTRUCTO BOXES

Size #7 (Holds 730 cards)
10 for $5.75 ppd.
25 for $11.00 ppd.
50 for $19.50 ppd.
100 for $35.00 ppd.

Size #BL (Holds 800 cards)
10 for $6.00 ppd.
25 for $11.75 ppd.
50 for $21.00 ppd.
100 for $40.00 ppd.

AUTOGRAPH and SPORTS CARD SALE LIST

My latest sale list is available. Send 20¢ in stamps.

1982 TOPPS BASEBALL

The 792 card 1982 Topps Baseball card set, in MINT condition, is $14.00 plus $1.50 UPS charges. Total postpaid cost is $15.50.

1982 FLEER BASEBALL

The 660 card 1982 Fleer Baseball card set, in MINT condition is $12.00 plus $1.50 UPS charges. Total postpaid cost is $13.50.

1982 DONRUSS BASEBALL

The 660 card 1982 Donruss Baseball card set, in MINT condition is $11.00 plus $1.50 UPS charges. Included will be the puzzle set that Donruss is enclosing with their packages. Total postpaid cost is $12.50.

ALL THREE SETS

A package deal of all three sets costs $36.00 plus $3.00 UPS charges. Total cost is $39.00 including UPS charges. All three sets will be shipped together. Shipped separately, add another $1.50.

INVESTMENT LOT of 1982 SETS

You may purchase 10 sets of 1982 sets as follows: 1982 Topps - 10 sets for $130.00; 1982 Fleer - 10 sets for $110.00; 1982 Donruss - 10 sets for $100.00. Add $8 shipping for each lot of ten.

SPECIAL PLASTIC SHEET OFFER

You may purchase plastic sheets (Size #9) in lots of 50 or more when you buy any 1981 or 1982 Fleer, Donruss or Topps sets. For each set you purchase, you may buy a lot of 50 #9 plastic sheets. The additional cost is $8.50 per lot of 50. There is no additional shipping charge. All sheets and sets will be shipped together.

PRICES QUOTED HERE

All prices in this ad are subject to change without notice.

1981 TOPPS TRADED SET

The 1981 Topps Traded set (#'s 727 to 858) is still available for $14.00 plus $1.00 shipping. Total cost is $15.00 postpaid.

1981 SETS AVAILABLE

The following prices are in effect for 1981 sets. 1981 Topps $14.50, with the Traded set $28.00; 1981 Fleer $13.50; 1981 Donruss $18.00. Add $1.50 shipping to each set ordered. If you order all three sets w/o the Traded set the cost is $44.00 plus $3.00 shipping or $47.00. All three sets with the Traded set is $58.00 plus $3.00 shipping or $61.00 postpaid.

BASEBALL CARD SHOW

There will be baseball card shows at the Quality Inn, Ames, Iowa on June 5, December 4 in 1982. Shows are also scheduled for the first Saturday in June 1983 and December 1983. Admission is free.

1982 FLEER LOGO STICKERS

A complete set of 104 Fleer Logo Stickers is $7.00 plus $1.00 shipping.

CANADIAN ORDERS

Please add $3.00 per set for all Canadian orders.

1982 TOPPS UPDATE SET

Topps will issue an update baseball card set in September, 1982. This set will be 132 cards. It will include all traded players in their new uniforms. The cost is $9.00 plus $1.50 shipping. Available in late Sept.

R.J. "Jack" Smalling
2308 Van Buren Avenue
Ames, Iowa 50010